Nigerian Income Tax Law and Pr

M. A. HARTE

Nigerian Income Tax Law and Practice

Incorporating Income Tax Laws relating to Personal
Income Tax Law, Partnership Tax Law, Companies Income
Tax Law, Petroleum Profits Tax Law, Capital Gains Tax Law,
Capital Transfer Tax Law and Guidelines to a Tax System
under the Presidential System of Government with
Accountancy and Decided Cases Illustrations
and a **Supplement** (1985)

C.S. OLA, JP; LL M (Lond); Ph D (Lond); FCA; FCIS;
BL; AMNIM; FIBA

Barrister-at-law; Notary Public and practising Chartered Accountant
(England and Wales and Nigeria); Associate Lecturer in Law and in Postgraduate
Studies, University of Ibadan; formerly Professor of Income Tax Law
and Accountancy, University of Ife

MACMILLAN
PUBLISHERS

First published 1985

Published by *Macmillan Publishers Ltd*
London and Basingstoke
Associated companies and representatives in Accra,
Auckland, Delhi, Dublin, Gaborone, Hamburg, Harare,
Hong Kong, Kuala Lumpur, Lagos, Manzini, Melbourne,
Mexico City, Nairobi, New York, Singapore, Tokyo

ISBN 0-333-40007-0

British Library Cataloguing in Publication Data
Ola, Christopher S.
  Nigerian income tax law and practice: incorporating
  income tax laws relating to personal income tax law,
  partnership tax law, companies income tax law,
  petroleum profits tax law, capital gains tax law,
  capital transfer tax law and guidelines to tax
  system under the presidential system of government
  with accountancy and decided cases illustrations.
1. Income tax – Nigeria – Law
I. Title
346.69035'2   [LAW]

ISBN 0-333-40007-0

Dedication

To my parents and family, my *alma mater*, the University College, London and my former Law and Accountancy students at Ife and Ibadan Universities.

Contents

Abbreviations

FRC   Judgement of the Federal Revenue Courts, now Federal High Court

HC   Judgements of the High Court

APP/COMM   Judgements of the Federal Body of Appeal Commissioners

NMLR   Nigerian Monthly Law Reports

ALR   African Law Reports

NCLR   Nigerian Commercial Law Reports

LRN   Law Reports of Nigeria

FBIR   Federal Board of Inland Revenue

CITA   Companies Income Tax Act

ITMA   Income Tax Management Act

LLR   Report of the Judgement of the High Court of Lagos

FSC/SC   Selected Judgements of the Federal Supreme Court

Table of Statutes

Table of Cases

Bentleys, Stokes & Lowless *v* Beeson
Berry *v* Farrow
T. Beynor & Co. Ltd *v* Ogg
Bidwell *v* Gardiner
Birmingham and District Cattle By-Products Co. Ltd *v* CIR
Board of Inland Revenue *v* Razcallah
Boarland *v* Kramat Pulai Ltd
Bobo *v* Anthony
Brokers Agricultural Holding Ltd *v* FBIR
Boyce *v* Whitwick Colliery Co.
Bristow *v* Dickinson Ltd
British Commonwealth International Newsfilm Agency *v* Mahany
British Dyestuffs Corporation (Blackley) Ltd *v* IRC
British Insulated and Helsby Cable Ltd *v* Atherton (Inspector of Taxes)
Brown *v* Bullock
Burmah SS Co. *v* IRC
Bush, Beach & Gent Ltd *v* Road

Caledonian Ry *v* Banks
Calders Ltd *v* IRC
California Copper Syndicate *v* Harris
Calvert *v* Wainwright (1947)
Cape Brandy Syndicate *v* IRC (1921)
Carpenter & Anor *v* Bello
Carlisle and Siloth Golf Club *v* Smith (1913)
Cayzer, Irvine & Co. Ltd *v* IRC
Cenlon Finance Co. Ltd *v* Ellwood
Chairman of the Board of Inland Revenue *v* Joseph Razcallah and Sons
    Ltd
Chapman *v* CFAO
Charles Brown & Co. *v* IRC
Chibbet *v* Joseph Robinson & Sons Ltd
Chua Chee Chor *v* Chuai Kiai Yen and Ors
Chime and Ors *v* Elikwu and Ors
Coleshill *v* Manchester Corporation
Colquhon *v* Brooks
Coman *v* Rotunda Hospital, Dublin
Commercial Structures Ltd *v* Briggs
Commissioner of Customs and Excise *v* Cure and Deeley
Commissioner of Income Tax *v* Hanover Agencies Ltd
Commissioner of Income Tax *v* Rewane
Commissioner of Income Tax *v* Shaw Wallace Co.
Commissioner of Taxation *v* Kirk (1900)
Commissioner of Taxation *v* Mooney
Commissioners of Income Tax *v* Pemsel (1891)
Commissioners of Inland Revenue *v* Cornish Mutual Assurance Co. Ltd
Commissioners of Inland Revenue *v* Fraser
Commissioners of Inland Revenue *v* Helson

Evans Medical Supplies *v* Moriarty
Ezenwa *v* Mazelli

Fairlakes Hotel Ltd *v* Registrar of Companies and 2 Ors
Fairrie *v* Hall
Federal Board of Inland Revenue *v* Alluminium Industries Aktien
  Gesellschaft
Federal Board of Inland Revenue *v* R.A.S. Babaoye
Federal Board of Inland Revenue *v* Joseph Rezcallah & Sons Ltd
Federal Board of Inland Revenue *v* Manila Industrial Security Services Ltd
Federal Board of Inland Revenue *v* Max Optiom Products (Nigeria) Ltd
Federal Board of Inland Revenue *v* NASR
Federal Board of Inland Revenue *v* Nigeria and Overseas Ventures Ltd
Federal Board of Inland Revenue *v* Nigerian Construction, Designing and
  Planning Group Ltd
Federal Board of Inland Revenue *v* Nigerian General Insurance Co. Ltd
Federal Board of Inland Revenue *v* Nigerian Insurance Co. Ltd
Federal Board of Inland Revenue *v* K.A. Shittu
Federal Board of Inland Revenue *v* Sylvester Mayaki
Federal Commissioner of Taxation *v* Clarke
Federal Minister of Internal Affairs and 3 Ors *v* Shuguba Abdurrahaman
  Darman
Ferrostall A.G. *v* FBIR
Fitzgerald *v* IRC
Frasers (Glasgow) Bank Ltd *v* IRC
Foulds *v* Clayton
Fullwood Foundry Co. Ltd *v* CIR

Hagart and Burn-Murdoch *v* IRC
Geo. Humphries and Co. *v* Cook
G.L. Baker Ltd *v* Medway Building and Supplies Ltd
G.N. Everitt *v* FBIR
Gleaner Co. Ltd *v* Assessment Committee
Golden Horse Shoe (New) Ltd *v* Thurgood
Golder *v* Great Boulder Proprietary Gold Mines Ltd
Graham *v* Greene (1925)
Graham *v* Greene
Grainger & Son *v* Gough (Surveyor of Taxes)
Granite Supply Association *v* Kitton
Gramophone and Typewriter Ltd *v* Stanley
Granville Building Co. Ltd *v* Oxby
Gray *v* Lord Penrhyn
Gray and Gillitt *v* Tiley
Green *v* Glisbten & Son Ltd
Gresham Life Assurance Society *v* Style
Griffiths *v* J.P. Harrison (Watford) Ltd
Grove *v* YMCA (1903)

Potts Executors *v* IRC (1951)
Pretoria-Pietersburg Ry Co. Ltd *v* Elwood
Pritchard *v* Arundale
Psalms and Hymns Trustees *v* Whitwell (1890)

Rand *v* The Alberni Land Co. Ltd (1920)
Ratcliffe *v* Evans
Reed *v* Seymour (1927)
Regional Tax Administrator (W. State) *v* African Press Ltd
Reid's Brewery Co. Ltd *v* Male
Reiss & Co. (Nigeria) Ltd *v* FBIR
Religious Tract and Book Society *v* Forbes (1896)
Rellion Ltd *v* Vise
Rev. M.F. Shodipo, Mr T.R.B. Macaulay (Trustees of the Methodist
    Church Mission), Development Trust (Nigeria) Ltd *v* FBIR
Renfrew Town Council *v* IRC
Reynolds Construction Co (Nigeria) Ltd *v* FBIR
Reynold's Executors *v* Bennett
Rex *v* Newmarket Income Tax Commissioners ex parte Huxley (1916)
Rhodesia Railways Ltd *v* Bechuanaland Income Tax Collector
Riches *v* Westminster Bank Ltd
Ricketts *v* Colquhoun
Roebank Printing Co. Ltd *v* IRC
Rotunda Hospital, Dublin (Governors) *v* Coman
Royal Agricultural Society *v* Wilson (1924)
Royal Insurance Co. *v* Stephen
Runka *v* Katsina NA
Rushden Heal Co. Ltd *v* Keene
Russell *v* Town and Country Bank
Rutledge *v* CIR (1929)
Rutter *v* Tregent
Ryhope Coal Co. Ltd *v* Foyer

SA Authority *v* Regional Tax Board
St Aubyn Estates Ltd *v* Strick
Salomon *v* Salomon and Co.
Scales *v* Geo. Thompson & Co. Ltd
Scottish Investment Trust Co. *v* Forbes
Scottish Union and National Insurance Co. *v* Smiles
Seaham Harbour Dock Co. *v* Crook
Seaward Bros *v* Varty
S.E. Ola *v* FBIR
Seymour *v* Reed
Senior Inspector of Taxes (W. Nigeria) *v* J.O. Adigun
Service Press Ltd *v* Nnamdi Azikiwe
Severne *v* Dadswell
Sharkey *v* Wernher
Sharpless *v* Rees

Shaw v Kay
Shell-BP Petroleum Development Co. (Nigeria) Ltd v FBIR
Shindler v Northern Raincoat Co.
Short Bros Ltd v IRC
Simmonds v League Against Cruel Sports
Smith v Incorporated Council of Law Reporting
Smith v Lion Brewery
Smith v Westinghouse Brake Co.
Smith & Co. v Greenwood
Smith Barry v Cordy
Smith, Stone and Knight v Birmingham Corporation
Smith's Potato Estates Ltd v Bolland
Sommerfelds Ltd v Freeman
Southern v A.B. Ltd
Spofforth and Prince v Colder
Steward Dry Goods Co. v Lewis
Strong and Co. v Woodifield
Sulley v AG
Summer v Brown
Sun Insurance Office v Clark

Tarrif Re-insurance Ltd v Commissioner of Taxes
Tawiah III v Edwuzi
Tebrau (Johore) Rubber Syndicate Ltd v Farmer
Teru v Scalan
Thomas Wilson (Keighley) Ltd v Emmerson
Thompson v Magnesium Elektron Ltd
Thompson v Trust and War Loan Co. of Canada
Thorp v Holdsworth
Tiddesley v Harper
Timitimi v Amabebe
Tin and Associated Minerals Ltd v FBIR
Toufic Karam v CIT
Trustees of Psalms and Hymns v Whitwell (1890)

Union Cold Storage Co. Ltd v Adamson
Union Cold Storage Co. Ltd v Jones
US v Butler (1936)
United Steel Companies Ltd v Cullington
Usher's Wiltshire Brewery Co. Ltd v Bruce

Van Den Berghs Ltd v Clarke (1935)

Walter W. Saunders Ltd v Dixon
Ward and Co. v Commissioner of Taxes
Warner Bros v Sampson
Watson v Samson Bros
West v Phillips

Preface

Tax law is not different from other laws such as the law of contract, the law of torts, the law of trusts or even the law of property because, as lawyers and law students realise, law cannot be studied in a piecemeal fashion. The basic principles have to be understood and appreciated after which much of the details will follow.

Whilst most Nigerian lawyers are not tax lawyers, they will spend endless time groping for solutions to problems, unless they have sufficient knowledge to diagnose a tax problem and where to look for solutions.

Some accountants and law and accountancy students find Income Tax a difficult subject. This textbook and work of reference provides accountancy problems and solutions of the type that they will meet with in practice and in their examinations. One of my reasons for writing this book is to make the subject interesting and to provide a regular supply of a suitable text to law and accountancy students because experience has shown that existing similar books on the subject, even by the same author, can run out of stock for years, to the detriment of the student and the practitioner. The book contains illustrations on the change to calendar year, and looks after students taking overseas accountancy examinations. Students of economics, especially those studying public finance, will find it useful, as well law and accountancy students, economists, Master of Business Administration students, accountants, lawyers, bankers, stockbrokers and insurance staff. Anyone undertaking serious research for other Higher Degrees on this subject should have, as his companion to this book, *A Guide to Accountancy and Taxation Law* (University Press), *Nigerian Taxation*, *Questions and Answers on Nigerian Taxation* (Graham Burn Publishers, 122 Derwent Road, Linslade, Leighton Buzzard, Beds, UK), *Case Law and Notes on Nigerian Taxation*, *Income Tax Law for Corporate and Unincorporated Bodies in Nigeria* (Heinemann), and *Tax Planning and Auditing* (University Press).

Administrative measures[1] should not conflict with the law. For example, deduction of tax at source of every contract awarded by governments, Tax Clearance Certificates (to be obtained even by a student without income), etc., has its legal implications. Money retained by awarders of contracts must be for poorly executed and/or incompleted work and cannot be retained for payment of income tax on account, since income does not emerge until after the completion of the contract and audited accounts show profits. This practice would offend against fundamental human rights since there cannot be income tax until there is an income to tax. Thanks are now due to the Government for the insertion of a new section 33 in the Income Tax Management Act 1961, as amended in S.13 of the 1985 Decree to legalise the illegality.

The Government should be able to amend the Income Tax law to reduce unemployment, misemployment and under-employment by rewarding progressive companies that not only upgrade their employees' value and financially assist universities to maintain academic excellence and relevant research but also contribute substantially to national productivity.

Because the Third Schedule of the 1961 tax law is still in force, it is possible for civil servants to be exempted from the taxation of their gratuities, to the obvious disadvantage of those in the private sector. Specifically, the relevant clause in that statute provides that 'gratuities payable to a public officer by the Government of the Federation of a Region (now State) in respect of services rendered by him under a contract of service with such Government and described as gratuities' will be exempted from taxation. This privilege has been extended to *bona fide* technical assistance personnel. It is therefore necessary to amend the Income Tax Acts with a view to removing the payment of tax on the gratuities of employees in the private sector. It is unfair to have employees in the public sector enjoying tax-free gratuities when workers in the private sector are made to give up as much as 50 per cent of their gratuities to the taxmen.

Tax can be a means of cutting the cost of children's education if the law is suitably amended. Where governments are able to finance education in a period of economic depression, the burden of school fees can be eased if our tax laws are amended to permit use of deeds of covenant. Under this suggestion, parents and anyone other than the parents can help with the cost of school fees and general maintenance of the child under 18. A deed of covenant is a legal agreement between two people whereby the donor agrees to pay the recipient a sum of money by regular instalments over seven years. The attraction is that the giver gets tax relief at the basic rate on the payments and the recipient – provided he or she is a non-taxpayer – is able to reclaim the tax deducted at source by the giver. This means that every ₦100 handed over by a parent or grandparent to a child costs the giver ₦55 after tax relief but is worth ₦100 in the hands of the child.

There is the need to index taxes to inflation. As consumer prices rise, so do the deduction, the personal exemption and both ends of each tax bracket. The United States has already tied social security and various other forms of government benefits to the rate of inflation. And at least fifteen other countries and nine states index their tax systems in some way. The concept has been given momentum now by the continuing high rate of inflation. As it pushes wages up, it continually thrusts people into higher and higher tax brackets, even though their real incomes have not risen once inflation is taken into account. If Nigeria had a flat tax rate (only one bracket) for all individuals, rather than a progressive system requiring people with higher incomes to pay higher rates of taxes, indexing would not be an issue. Inflation has seriously affected the Nigerian economy since the mid-1960s. Indexing would end unlegislated increases in both taxes and revenues and would automatically limit Government spending.

The country ought not to depend on the availability of inflation-induced revenues. Whatever equity is built into the tax code would remain there under indexing. Without indexing, people on lower incomes tend to be hit hardest by the tax bracket creep that results as wages go up. A 13.3 per cent inflation rate in 1980, by lifting taxpayers into higher brackets, would have meant an average 17 per cent tax increase for individuals with income of ₦5000 or less, an 11 per cent increase for people with incomes between ₦5000 and ₦10 000, a 9 per cent increase for individuals in the ₦30 000–50 000 range and a 1 per cent increase for people with incomes over ₦200 000. Indexing, however, would reduce the government's flexibility in setting budget policy. It could also lead to bigger budget deficits if spending is not held in check. Cushioning the impact of inflation would weaken the nation's determination to battle inflation. Again, if we are ever going to lick inflation in this nation, it is absolutely essential that everyone should feel the pain. The pain must be spread around so that the pressure is constantly on every one to defeat inflation, to eliminate those evils that produce inflation. But who has pain? If there are to be tax cuts, they must be targeted in a particular direction. Higher tax rates can act as a brake on an inflationary economy that becomes overheated because of too much spending on goods without enough productive capacity. However, the automatic stabilising effect is negligible and whatever impact there is, tends to occur with a substantial lag. Indexing is based on the Consumer Price Index rather than some other measure of inflation. The adjustments that would be made effective on 1 January 1985, for example, would reflect the increase in the index in the fiscal year 1984 as compared with the index a year before that. The Consumer Price Index may not measure the real real impact of inflation well enough. Whether indexing will become law depends largely on the political manoeuvring in the Senate. Indexing is politically seductive; a vote against indexing looks like a vote against protecting Mr and Mrs Hardlife against inflation.

Inland Revenue Divisions resemble a declawed, toothless pussycat if they are not independent, like the Audit Department. They should constitute an independent Department of their own to avoid political interference.

Partial Africanisation of our tax law to increase our tax yield from the very rich and to remove the alien character of Nigeria's Income Tax laws, which have increased the rate of tax evasion in our acquisitive society, is desirable. It is time Nigeria's Income Tax law had regard for our own social milieu. At present, the law is modelled mainly on a foreign pattern and we find ourselves poor seconds. The law should be uniquely suited to our environment if we are to lead in response to the changing needs of African society.

Tax can be used to start a social welfare and social security scheme, including unemployment benefits, in Nigeria. Taxpayers should receive some benefits in cash for taxes previously or currently paid, even if there is an end to pot-holes on the road, erratic water and electricity supplies and silent boxes called telephones for which payment is made. Child benefit may serve as an example. The taxes of the rich and the childless would then be financing the child benefits of the rest. It may be argued that this proposal is to make a clean break with the past and redefine child benefit as welfare for the poor. To align child benefit to poverty relief would effect great money savings and immense simplification to social security; but it would also imply that society, through the state, had lost interest in the size of families, the participation of women in the labour market, the quality of motherhood – in the mechanisms of its continuation, in fact. Why, the reformers and economists may ask, should the state waste taxpayers' money by giving such as the rich businessman – or any working family of means – child benefit?

But have we yet gone as far as a recent, cogent school of benefit reformers, the Institute of Fiscal Studies, in believing that procreation is a matter only of 'personal pleasure' for parents, giving them no claim on the rest of society? The state's proxy for successor generations requires it to prosecute that claim, which it does by the provision, for example, of public education. The state might well take a view on the influence on the domestic environment of the number of women of child-bearing years who enter the labour force. Such state intervention is no less justifiable – and no less fraught with hazard – than making special provision for the children of poor parents, which most recent recipes for benefit reform accept without question.

Since Lloyd George introduced a child tax allowance – 'a bounty for the maintenance of children' – the fiscal system has recognised some public interest in the finances of families with young dependants.

The question to be settled before technical issues of implementation are broached is whether in the demographic and social circumstances of the 1980s that interest remains. The value of the benefit tax allowance has been much whittled away since the Second World War. The strongest arguments against it is not its profligacy but that it often fails, on its own terms, as an incentive towards the better care of children.

That it might be commuted into a two-tier benefit and credit (for the majority of parent-taxpayers) is an interesting if far from straightforward suggestion. Child benefit, appositely, is a mother's aid, paid to women; it is a close fiscal kin of the extra tax allowance paid to married men. Both deserve the reformers' attention, but not until there has been a more thorough exposition of the state's latter-day disengagement from the business of child rearing.

With a few ups and downs the birthrate has been declining for twenty years for inflationary reasons, and for over eleven years has been consistently below the long-term replacement level. If the current fertility rate stopped falling and stabilised at the present level there would be, in due course, a fall in the population of about 18 per cent per generation, disregarding any effect of immigration.

Many people welcome this prospect of a falling population, and the task of restabilising population at a lower level may well be left to a future generation. There is, however, surely no demographic argument at the present time for depriving that minority of couples who produce most of the next generation of any 'bounty for the maintenance of children.'

The prospects of employment are declining permanently for young persons without marketable knowledge or skills. It is not possible for Nigeria to enjoy the full fruits of modern industry, agriculture or services without a large investment in the upbringing, education and training of the coming generation.

The greater part of the cost of this investment will, in any event, fall upon parents. More competent and trained young persons will take longer to educate and be dependent longer upon their parents. A tax system which makes little distinction between a married couple with and without dependent children reduces the resources available for investment in the next generation and so too does any reduction in any fiscal payment for children – child benefit will replace the child tax allowance for taxpayers and give the same benefit to parents who pay no tax but are on the tax nominal roll. Alfred Marshall once said that regard for the future was both a chief product and a chief cause of civilisation – regard for the future points to children as the crucial resource.

To deny child benefit to taxpayers would mean that thousands of low income families would not in fact receive any benefit. To ignore child benefit entirely, in exchange for general tax cuts, would redistribute income from those with to those without children. Yet the tax positions of families with children has already worsened relative to the childless, and tax cuts, unlike increases in child benefit, give more help to the better-off.

Child benefit reaches all those who need it; gives many women their only independent income; and operates as a tax allowance for families with children. Those who will claim child benefit, it is suggested, should produce evidence of either tax-payment or being on tax nominal roll even if they are not liable to pay tax.

The needs of children should not be met from the wage system but from the nation in the form of family allowance payments. The higher statutory minimum wage has the disadvantage that it will increase employer's costs and if implemented without compensatory measures, will lead to unemployment, inflation and anti-social behaviour such as murder and burglary. A minimum wage accompanied by child benefits will abolish child poverty and bring about a major transfer of income to all women. Income Tax Law can revolutionalise the country's economic system.

Note

1   See 'Personal taxation' in *Questions and Answers on Nigerian Taxation* (Graham Burns Publishers); and *The Historical Development of the Tax System in the Western State of Nigeria 1957–8 to 1973–4* (Ministry & Finance, Ibadan, 1974), p.63.

1 Legal History and Legal Interpretation of Income Tax Laws

(i) Introduction

The legal history of the Nigerian tax system can be traced to Nigerian native customs and traditions, which, in spite of the denial of the name of law to customary law by John Austin[1] – form the basis of Nigerian Customary Law. Duguit of the Sociological School equates customary law to law and Goodheart extends his definition of law to include law even in a primitive society by proving that primitive law is in truth the totality of the customs of the tribe[2], and one of the sources of Nigerian law is customary law. Under native customs and traditions, Nigerians cheerfully paid their taxes in kind by rendering free services to the community in which they lived; the few tax defaulters were punished by erecting community buildings such as the Manor House at Iseyin etc., or by slaughtering their fattest cattle for the benefit of the community.

Customary law is based on only those traditions and customs of the people which can be enforced by the local community or by the *Oba*. It is to be distinguished from common law, which is judge-made law, and the common law itself grew as a result of Court decisions. A decision reached by the Supreme Court of Nigeria is the law of the land until changed by the Legislative assemblies. Judicial precedents or court decisions exclusive of equity constitute another source of Nigerian Income Tax Law and judicial precedents bring stability and certainty into the Income Tax law. Some of these precedents come from English Law; law textbooks and law reports are also sources of Nigerian Income Tax Law.

Taxation may be defined as the demand made by the government of a country for a compulsory payment of money by the citizens of the country. Taxation has two main objectives:

(i) Primarily, to raise revenue to finance government expenditure.

(ii) Secondly, to influence activity in the economy as a whole.

1

Tax policy provides a mechanism for influencing consumer demand and for providing incentives for production, investment and savings. It is therefore a key factor for promoting the government's overall economic and social objectives.

For example, taxation is used to:

(a) achieve economic growth
(b) fight depression, inflation and deflation
(c) achieve equitable distribution of income and wealth
(d) allocate resources in a socially desirable manner
(e) discourage the consumption of certain goods
(f) encourage and protect new industries within the country
(g) ensure that the balance of payments of the country is in a healthy position.

The principal Act, ITMA 1961, which contains the main provisions of the Act, deals with fundamental income tax principles applicable to the whole country and these are:

1 Determination of residence
2 Chargeable income
3 Treatment of dividends
4 Taxation of partnerships
5 Basis of computing income
6 Capital allowances on income-earning assets
7 Double taxation arrangements
8 Exemptions
9 Provision for a Joint Tax Board.

The Income Tax year runs from 1 January to 31 December. The liability to Income Tax extends, in general to:

(a) all persons resident in Nigeria, whether Nigerians or not, as long as income is derived from Nigeria,
(b) all persons not resident, whether Nigerians or not in so far as they derive income from property, trade, profession, vocation or employment in Nigeria.

Taxes Acts include Personal Income Tax Act, Companies Income Tax Act, Capital Gains Tax Act, Petroleum Profits Tax and Capital Transfer Tax Acts.

Direct taxes are:

(i) Personal Income Tax which applies to employees, sole traders, partnerships, and pensioners.
(ii) Capital Gains Tax which affects companies throughout the Federation, individuals and non-corporate bodies.
(iii) Companies Income Tax which applies to limited-liability companies.
(iv) Capital Transfer Tax which applies to assets transferred by

one individual to another whether *inter vivos* or at death. The first ₦100 000 of such transfer is free from tax; the next 150 000 at 10%; others at graduated rates.

(v) Petroleum Profits Tax which is payable by entities that engage in prospecting for, or the extraction of and transportation of petroleum oil or natural gas. This does not include petroleum service companies which are treated under Companies Income Tax.

Indirect Taxes are:
   (i) Stamp Duties
  (ii) Custom Duties
 (iii) Excise Duties
 (iv) Entertainment, Pool and Casino Taxes
  (v) Industrial Training Fund.

The history of personal income taxation law in Nigeria is based mainly on statute. The statutory provisions have, however, been construed and interpreted by the Appeal Commissioners and the Law Courts. The statutory Law is traceable to the Raisman Commission of 1957. The accepted recommendations of the Commission are embodied in Section 70 of the 1960 Nigerian Constitution. Under this Section, the Federal Government has the exclusive powers to levy tax on the income of all limited-liability companies whilst the Federal Government and the State Governments have concurrent powers in respect of personal Income Tax. In exercise of these powers, the Federal Government enacted the Income Tax Management Act 1961, now referred to as ITMA.

As a result of the operation of the Income Tax Management Act, 1961, regional Income Tax laws which were in existence before 1961 were amended by their respective regional legislatures to bring them into conformity with the 1961 Act. The Western Region Income Tax Law, Cap. 48 of 1959, was amended by the Income Tax (Amendment) Law, 1961, to bring that law into conformity with ITMA. Similarly, the Eastern Region repealed its Finance Law of 1956 and enacted the Finance Law, 1962, whilst the Northern Region, which prior to 1961 had no Income Tax Law of its own, enacted the Personal Tax Law, 1962. The Personal Tax Law of 1962 repeated the Direct Taxation Ordinance, Cap. 54 of 1940, as amended and the Income Tax Ordinance, Cap. 92 of 1948, then in operation in the Northern Region, and at the same time brought the 1962 Act into comformity with ITMA.

Under the 1963 Republican Constitution, all the Regions, including Mid-Western Region (now Bendel State) created in 1963, assumed jurisdiction over income tax of persons other than limited-liability companies.

Under the 1979 Presidential Constitution of Nigeria, Income Tax of persons other than companies income tax is under the Government List – in Part II of the Constitution. Thus, although the National Assembly has the powers to impose any tax on capital gains and profits of persons other than companies, the State Government may do so subject to such conditions as the National Assembly may prescribe.

The National Assembly[3] has the exclusive right to legislate on taxation of incomes, profits and capital gains whilst collection of taxes at state level is on the Concurrent List[4].

In amending or making the Acts of the legislatures, it should be borne in mind that, under section 4 (8)[5] of the 1979 Presidential constitution, no legislature (neither the National Assembly nor each State House Assembly), can enact a tax law which has the tendency to oust or usurp, or purport to oust the functions of the law courts or of any judicial tribunal established by law.

Under the Militocracy, Section 2, subsection (1) of the Constitution (Suspension and Modification) Decree No. 1 1984 states: 'The Federal Military Government shall have power to make laws for the peace, order and good government of Nigeria or any part thereof in respect to any matter whatsoever.' The Exclusive list to the 1979 Constitution which it amends contains, *inter alia*, taxation of incomes, profits and capital gains, and the Federal Government may legislate on the imposition of Capital Gains Tax, personal Income Tax, sales tax, purchase tax, Companies Income Tax, Petroleum Profits Tax, export duties, import duties, excise duties, custom duties and stamp duties. Item D, paragraphs 7 and 8, dealing with concurrent legislation, empowers the Federal Government to delegate to the State government the exercise of an executive function: the collection of taxes specified i.e. Capital Gains Tax, personal Income Tax and stamp duties. Item D does not, of course, envisage the delegation of concurrent legislative functions of state governments. As stated in *Attorney General of Bendel State v AG of the Federation and 22 Others (1982)* 3 NLLR (1), *AG of Ogun State v AG of the Federation (1982)* 3 NLLR 166 and *Federal Minister of Internal Affairs and 3 Others v Shugaba Abdurrahaman Darman* (1982) 3 NLLR, 918, where the constitutional provisions are clear, caution must be exercised in importing foreign cases.

Subject to subsection (2) of Decree No. 1 of 1984 and the 1979 partially-suspended Constitution, the Governor of a State has power to make laws for the people, order and good government of that State. State governments can therefore legislate on any subject matter of tax

4

not specifically allocated to the Federal Government, i.e. the residual tax powers and matters specified under the concurrent legislative list. Item D of the concurrent legislative list, in conjunction with 5.2(1) of Decree No. 1 of 1984, states these to be tax, fee or rate on building, land, market stalls or petty trading, entertainment, motor vehicle licences, any community and any such matter or thing as it may determine, for the administration of the law or Edict providing for such collection by a local government council but that in so doing, the state government should regulate the liability of persons to the tax, fee or rate in such manner as to ensure that such tax, fee or rate is not levied on the same person in respect of the same liability by more than one local government.

The taxing powers of the Federal and State governments are currently determined by the partially suspended 1979 Constitution as amended by the Constitution (Suspension and Modification) Decree 1984, otherwise known as Decree No. 1.

Chief Justice Latham of the Australian Supreme Court said in *Mathews v Chicory Marketing Board* (Vict) (1938) 60 CLR 263 at p.276 that 'a tax is a compulsory exaction of money by a Public authority for public purpose .... taxation is raising money for the purposes of government by means of contributions from individual persons', whilst Justice Roberts of the USA said in *US v Butler*, 297 US 1 (1936) at p.61 'a tax ... signifies an exaction for the support of government' and the US Supreme Court said of tax in *Nichols v Ames* 173 US 509 (1899) at p.515, 'the one power upon which the whole national fabric is based. It is necessary to the existence and prosperity of a nation and is in the air he breathes for the natural man. It is not only the power to destroy, it is also the power to keep alive'.

Three major tax laws were passed in the country in 1961 immediately after independence. These were the Federal Income Tax Act (FITA), Income Tax Management Act (ITMA) and the Companies Income Tax Act (CITA).

FITA was applicable to Lagos Federal territory residents. It was later adopted by Lagos state as the basis of its own tax laws when the state was created.

ITMA served as the model for the various regions. Each of the regions adopted about 95 per cent of ITMA. They later became states and adopted the modified ITMA.

During this time, the states had the legal basis to impose and collect taxes in their areas of jurisdiction until 1979, when the Federal Government amended the CITA. The imposition of tax is in the exclusive legislative list of the Federal Government while the collection of tax is in the concurrent legislative list.

The Federal Government reserves the exclusive right to impose tax on both persons and companies. However, states are allowed to collect the tax in the way they deem appropriate.

The construction and application of Income Tax laws

In *IRC v Westminster*,[6] Lord Tomlin said, 'Every man is entitled ... to order his affairs so that the tax attached under the appropriate Acts is less than it otherwise would be ...' but documents such as deeds of covenant, etc., can only be disregarded if they are not *bona fide* or are used as a cloak to conceal a different transaction.

In *Pott's Executors v IRC*,[7] it was held that the court was not entitled to treat the actual transaction as 'machinery' and that the substance or equivalent financial results are the relevent consideration.

In *Howard de Walden v IRC*[8], Lord Green, MR said, 'It scarcely lies in the mouth of the taxpayer who plays with fire to complain of burnt fingers'.

Income Tax Law is to be interpreted in *stricto senso*; there is no equity in tax law. The taxpayer must be brought within the letter of the law and rigid adherence is the rule. Nothing is to be read in; nothing is to be implied.[9] The onus of bringing a taxpayer into the tax net is on the Revenue.

If a later Act amends the meaning of an earlier Act, then the meaning expressed in the later Act prevails. Where the earlier Act says one thing and the later Act another, and by inference this shows that its framers misapprehended the law as it then stood, then the earlier Act must be construed without reference to the later Act unless a provision in the earlier Act is so ambiguous that it is open to two perfectly clear and plain constructions,[10] or contains a phrase fairly and equally open to diverse meanings.[11] Where the Local Act is not in *pari materia* with the English statute, reasoning from it to the other is of no advantage.[12]

Imposition of tax

Income tax is imposed on the individuals, partnerships, trustees, executors of settlements and family income under section 3 of the Federal Government Income Tax Management Act, 1961, as amended, and known as ITMA for short, and each State Income Tax Law. Limited liability companies are assessed under Companies Income Tax Act, 1979, or CITA for short.

Also refer to Supplement (1985)

(ii) Determination of residence

(a) The relevant tax authority for an individual or corporation sole or body of individuals for a year of assessment, is the tax authority of the state in which the individual or corporation sole or body of individuals is deemed to be resident for that year;

(b) for an executor, it is the tax authority of the state in which the deceased individual was last deemed to be resident or would have been deemed to be resident if the provisions of ITMA had been in force prior to the date of his death;

(c) for a trustee of any trust or settlement, it is the tax authority of the state in which is situated the seat of administration of the trust or settlement on 1 April 1961, or if the trust or settlement is created after that date, the place from which it is first administered.

(d) for an itinerant worker, that is, a worker, other than a member of the Nigerian Army or Nigerian Navy, for a daily wage who earns his livelihood in more than one place in Nigeria and whose total income does not exceed ₦600 a year is taxed in the state in which he is found during the year [section 3(3) of ITMA]. Surely the word 'place' can mean a village or a state or a town. The law is not clear on whether the word 'place' means 'state or territory' as defined by section 2 of ITMA and this provision does not cover bandleaders and contractors who earn more than ₦600 per annum.

(e) for partnership for a year of assessment, the relevant tax authority is the tax authority of the state in which the principal office or place of business of the partnership in Nigeria is situated on the first day of that year or is first established during that year. A partnership as a business unit is not taxed under section 2(4) of ITMA. It is submitted that section 6(4) of ITMA must be complied with and the state of registration should supply the state of residence of all partners. The profits of partnership are distributed among partners under section 6 of ITMA.

Tax Authority[13]. The person or body of persons responsible under a law of a territory imposing Income Tax for the administration of that law is the tax authority, usually the Inland Revenue Section of the Ministry of Finance.

Territory[14]. A state or the Federal Territory.

Earned Income[15]. Income derived from the exercise of carrying on a trade, business, profession, vocation or employment, and income derived from a pension in respect of any previous employment. For

7

the earned income, other than a pension, liable to tax in Nigeria, the place of residence is the one nearest to the taxpayer's usual place of work.

Rules of Determination

There are six rules to follow. Where an individual has only one source of income, residence is determined by reference to the appropriate rule. For an individual who has more than one source of income, residence is determined by reference to the first of the rules applicable to his circumstances.

1 An employment where the duties are wholly performed outside Nigeria except during a temporary visit of the employee to Nigeria is foreign employment.[16]

    (a) An individual, holding a foreign employment on the first day of the year of assessment, is resident for that year where the principal office of his employer is situated on the same day.

    (b) An individual, who first becomes liable to Income Tax in Nigeria for a year of assessment because he enters a foreign employment during a year of assessment, is resident for that year where the principal office of his employer is situated on the day his foreign employment starts.

2 An employment, other than a foreign employment, where the duties are wholly or partly performed in Nigeria is known as Nigerian employment under the first schedule of ITMA.[17]

    (a) An individual, holding a Nigerian employment on the first day of the year of assessment, is resident for that year where he has a place or principal place of residence on the same day.

    (b) An individual, who first becomes liable to Income Tax in Nigeria because he enters a Nigerian employment during a year of assessment, is resident for that year where he has a place or principal place of residence on the day he takes up the full duties of the employment in Nigeria.

    (c) An individual, who is on leave from a Nigerian employment on the first day of the year of assessment, is resident for that year where he had a place or principal place of residence immediately before his leave began.

    (d) Exceptions to rule 2(a), (b), and (c) are the people who are in whole-time employment in a combatant, non-combatant or civilian capacity in the armed forces. These people are resident in the Federal Territory, if they are so employed on the first day of the year of assessment, or first become liable to Income Tax in Nigeria for a year of assessment because of taking up such employment during that year.

3 An employee whose remuneration is subject to Income Tax in Nigeria for a year of assessment, but whose residence cannot be determined under rule 2 is deemed to hold a foreign employment. If his residence cannot then be determined under rule 1, he is deemed to be resident in Lagos.

4 (a) An individual, whose only earned income arising in Nigeria on the first day of a year of assessment is a pension, is resident where he has a place or principal place or residence on that day.

  (b) An individual whose only earned income arising in Nigeria on the first day of a year of assessment is a pension, but who has no place of residence on that day, is resident:

   (i) if the pension is a Nigerian pension wholly payable by the Lagos State Government.

   (ii) if the pension is a Nigerian pension wholly payable by the government of another territory in that territory;

   (iii) if the pension is a Nigerian pension payable by more than one government in the federal territory;

   (iv) if the pension is not a Nigerian pension at the place of the principal office in Nigeria of the pension fund or other person authorising payment of the pension; or

   (v) if there are two or more pensions arising in different territories to the individual on the first day of the year of assessment in the federal territory.

5 (a) An individual, who has earned income in Nigeria (other than from an employment or pension) for a year of assessment, is resident for that year where he has a place or principal place of residence on the first day of that year.

  (b) If the source of such earned income in Nigeria (other than an employment or pension) is first acquired by the individual during the year of assessment *and* he has no place of residence on the first day of that year, he is resident for that year where he first establishes a place of residence during the year.

Nigerian pension[18]. A pension for past services under, and payable by, a government or governments in Nigeria.

Place of residence[19]. A place available for domestic use in Nigeria. (It does not include any place of temporary lodging where a more permanent place is available for domestic use.)

6 An individual whose only income in Nigeria is unearned income such as dividends and whose main place of residence is in Nigeria on 1 January of the year of assessment. In the case of limited-liability companies, they are deemed to be resident in the Federal Capital of

Nigeria wherever they are located and their profits are assessed for tax by the Federal Board of Inland Revenue.

(iii) Disputes as to residence determination

There is provision for objections and disputes to be submitted to the Joint Tax Board with the right of appeal to the State High Court and thence to Federal Revenue Court, Federal Court of Appeal and finally to the Supreme Court.

If personal taxation is to contribute substantially to rapid industrialisation, the codification of Tax Laws should ensure that all State Income Tax Boards have similar provisions as ITMA. The present system where taxpayers in some states such as Lagos State can transfer their real property to their children who are minors to avoid declaration of income accruing from the landed property is open to criticism.

Notes

1   Austin also excludes Constitutional Law and International Law as law. He regarded them as law by analogy. Austin's definition of law is generally regarded as narrow. Kelsen and the Scandinavian jurists dislike the term 'command' as a feature of law. Austin presents principles and definitions but fails to give evidence for how he gets these or how he works the principles out.
2   J. Hartland, *Primitive Law* (London, 1924)
3   See item 56, part I, of the Exclusive Legislative List, Second Schedule to the 1979 Constitution.
4   Item 7 part II, of the 1979 Constitution.
5   Under sub-section 9, no Legislature has the power, in relation to any law with restrospective power.
6   (1936) AC I; 19 TC 490.
7   (1951) 32 TC 211 at p.230.
8   (1942) IKB 389 at p.397.
9   *Cape Brandy Syndicate v IRC* (1921) IKB 64 at p.71 cited with approval by Viscount Simon, LC, in *Canadian Eagle Oil Co. Ltd v R* (1946) AC 119 at p.140; 27 TC 205 at p.248.
10 *Ormond Investment Co. Ltd v Betts* (1928) AC 143 at p.154.
11 *Ormond Investment Co. Ltd v Betts* (1928) *supra* at p.156.
12 *CIT v Shaw Wallace Co.* (1931) LR Ind. p.206.
13 ITMA, s.2.
14 ITMA, s.2.
15 ITMA, First Schedule.
16 ITMA, s.3.
17 ITMA, First Schedule, paras 2–8.
18 ITMA, First Schedule.
19 ITMA, First Schedule.

2 Administration of Personal Income Tax

(i) Introduction

The administrative authority is the Director of Internal Revenue. He is assisted by a Deputy Director and such other officials as may be necessary. He is also the Chairman of the State Tax Board, consisting of other officials from other ministries.

The duties of the Director of Internal Revenue are to assess, collect, and account for the tax imposed by the law. He has various other powers including power to:

  (a) authorise the communication of tax records;
  (b) compound an offence arising from the making or delivery of a false return, statement or record;
  (c) appoint a person to be the agent of other persons;
  (d) appoint a person or body of persons for the purpose of assessing the total income of taxpayers;
  (e) impose or remit a penalty for breach of any rule which is a continuing offence under the Income Tax (Deduction At Source) Rules;
  (f) vary assessments, estimates, and computations;
  (g) direct PAYE tax-collecting agents to make deductions from employment income and appoint 'direct assessment' tax collectors;
  (h) direct taxpayers to keep accounts;
  (i) require a bank to supply information about its customers in respect of interest paid or credited to those customers exceeding ₦30 in any period of twelve months;
  (j) make refunds of excess tax paid.

Some of these are often delegated to officials of the Internal Revenue Divisions such as the Deputy Director, Chief Inspectors of Taxes, Inspectors of Taxes, Principal, Senior, Higher and Executive Officers.

The State Tax Board consists usually of the Chief Statistician, an officer not below the rank of Principal Assistant Secretaries (Revenue) in the Ministries of Finance and Economic Development, and Local Government and Information. The function of the Board is advisory. The Board receives up-to-date information on the position of revenue and it acts as an adviser to local governments on revenue matters.

Sections 6(7) and 28 of the Income Tax Management Act give powers to the Director, as a tax authority, to procure information. These powers are not unlimited. For example:

(a) banks are under no obligation to supply information where interest credited to a customer in any period of 12 months does not exceed ₦30;

(b) persons who are under statutory obligation to observe secrecy cannot disclose such information which they are statutorily prohibited from divulging.

The power of the Director in this section is further eroded by section 29(2) of the Act which deals also with collection of tax by one authority for another. Banks are now obliged to supply information if the request is written, and authorised or signed by the director of the FIRD.

Section 28(1) (ITMA) does not extend to the transfer of information relating to a company, partnership, trustee, executor, family or community because the sub-section deals with the 'individual'. The limitation of the powers conferred by section 29(2) should also be noted. A tax authority may operate the law of another tax authority at the request of that other authority but only for the purposes of:

(a) obtaining information;

(b) collecting or enforcing payment of tax due.

A tax authority cannot make an assessment on behalf of another authority, however, desirable it may be.

The distinction between the provisions of sections 28(1) and 29(2) must be carefully noted. The former relates to the transfer of information in respect of *individuals* whereas the latter deals with *persons* in relation to obtaining information, collecting or enforcing payment of tax due.

Secrecy is important to tax administration, as its absence will not have salutary effect on tax assessment and collection. Information may be difficult to obtain and taxpayers are naturally unwilling to make a full disclosure of their name, hence ITMA, adopted by all the State Governments, stipulates that a person employed in, or having an official duty connected with administration of income tax law shall regard and deal with as secret and confidential, all *information*, documents, returns, records or copies of those records relating to any person by whom the taxes imposed are payable. In the Eastern States, for example, this provision is re-enacted in section 4 of the Finance Law, 1962, as amended. The implications of the section should be particularly noted. It covers the following category of persons:

(a) Internal Revenue staff;
(b) The staff of the Government Audit duly authorised by the Director of Audit;
(c) Tax Collectors, Tax Collecting Agents, and members of Assessment Committees;
(d) Appeal Commissioners, Court judges, registrars, and bailiffs.

All the people are either employed or have official duties connected with the administration of the finance law. Appeals before the Board of Commissioners or the High Court are to be heard *in camera*.

It is important to remember that information which is normally secret becomes confidential in the Revenue Office as soon as it is received therein. For example, a firm may pay a commission of ₦672 to its customer. This fact may be known to the firm's employees and they may be under obligation to keep it confidential. If the payment of ₦672 is communicated by the firm to the Revenue it takes the cloak of secrecy as between the firm, the taxpayer, and Revenue.

There are circumstances under which secrecy need not be maintained. These include:

(a) specific authorisation by the commissioner;
(b) matters relating specifically to a prosecution for an offence under the law;
(c) execution of the provisions of the law (e.g. recovery action);
(d) audit duties by the Director of Audit and his staff;
(e) disclosure of information between Tax Authorities [s.28(1) – ITMA];
(f) double Taxation arrangements [s.24(1) ITMA].

In *Shaw v Kay* (5 TC 74), the Court refused production of tax documents in court on grounds of secrecy and public interest. This decision is embodied in Section 4(3) of the law; except for the purposes already noted the Court cannot compel the production of tax records or information obtained in the course of tax duties. A creditor, for example, cannot successfully subpoena a tax official to produce records to show that his debtor is worth more than the debtor has stated before the Court. Provided no names are mentioned, knowledge gained from examination of papers of other taxpayers (e.g. profit ratios) may be used by an Assessment Authority in dealing with a taxpayer. A penalty of two years' imprisonment and a fine of ₦400 attach to infringement of secrecy provisions.

Persons chargeable to tax are:

(a) individuals who have taxable incomes;
(b) itinerant workers;

(c) a body of individuals and partnerships;

(d) an indigenous community;

(e) an indigenous family;

(f) a trustee or an executor.

An individual includes a corporation sole and any body of individuals but not a company, a partnership, a community, a trustee or an executor or a body of trustees or executors. An intinerant worker is an individual (other than members of the armed forces) who works for a daily wage and whose total income does not exceed ₦600 during a year of assessment, or one who normally earns his living in more than one place in Nigeria and whose total income does not exceed ₦600 during a year of assessment.

Indigenous community is defined in the law as a body of indigenous Nigerian citizens residing in a town, village, or settlement. 'Indigenous family' is not defined either in the law or in the Act, but may be taken as a body of indigenous Nigerian citizens 'recognised under any law or custom in Nigeria' as a family.

A trustee is not defined and therefore carries the normal meaning attached to it by general usage. An 'executor' according to the Act includes any person who administers the estate of a deceased person.

(ii) Family and community

In the case of a body of individuals or a community, an assessment is made on the body in the name of a member who manages its activities. In regard to a family, the taxpayer is the member of the family who customarily receives the family income from its source. In view of the varied customs in each locality, the Assessment Authority has to decide after a thorough investigation in whose name an assessment on a family has to be made.

One interesting feature of an assessment on a body of individuals, a community, or a family is that any part of the total income of such a body, which is ascertainable as the separate income of an individual, who is a member of the group, is not taxable on the group.

The ITMA is 'indeterminate or uncertain' (see section 3(5) of ITMA). Is 'ascertainment' a matter of the custom of the people irrespective of the disposition of the income? It is submitted that 'ascertainment' refers to the state of the income at the time it is received by the member who customarily receives it, and not to its disposal after it has been so received. Put in another way, a sum is 'subject' of 'ascertainment' if, looking at the income at the time of receipt, one can point a finger at it and say very definitely 'this portion belongs to ...'. Where this is not so, but the income is received and later shared among the members of the family in mutually agreed proportions, it is the group and not the individual that is liable.

It is a settled principle of income tax law that the destination of taxable income is immaterial for the purpose of assessment action [e.g. *Psalms & Hymns Trustees v Whitwell* (1890), 3 TC 7]. Where a community or family in receipt of taxable income, decided to give the whole income or a portion of it out to charity the amount liable to assessment is not affected. The names of members of the village who customarily received ₦500 from the tenants will be valid and the tax is legally recoverable.

Body of individuals

Where a body of individuals makes a profit on transactions with members only, the profit is not subject to tax. However, when part of the profit relates to transactions with non-members, the proportion of such profit is liable to tax. (*Carslisle and Siloth Golf Club v Smith* (1913), 6 TC 198).

Charitable organisations are not exempted from income tax. Paragraph (k) of the third schedule to the Act, however, exempts the income of a charity where such income is not derived from a trade or business carried on by the organisation. In *Commissioners of Income Tax v Pemsel* [(1891), 3 TC 53,96], a charity is defined as a body established for the relief of poverty, the advancement of education, the advancement of religion, and for other purposes beneficial to the community. Where a charity carries on a trade or business the profit from such a trade is liable to tax [*Grove v YMCA* (1903), 4 TC 613].

Incapacitated taxpayers

Assessment on income derived by an incapacitated individual (e.g., an infant or a lunatic) may be made in the name of his agent, guardian, or some other person acting on his behalf. If an infant, for example, has no guardian or trustee, an assessment may properly be made in his own name. (*Rex v Newmarket Income Tax Commissioners ex parte Huxley* 1916, 7 TC 49). Where possible, the Commissioner may appoint an Agent under section 29(1) of the Act.

(iii) Persons outside Nigeria

A person outside Nigeria who carries on a trade or business in Nigeria is liable to tax on the profits, arising from such a trade or business. The proportion of the profit attributable to the business in Nigeria is subject to tax. Where such an individual is taxable in a state by virtue of his being deemed to be resident therein, an assessment may be made on him in the name of his agent. The amount of tax payable will be such as the non-resident would have paid, had he been physically resident.

In respect of a deceased person, the income which arose before his death (if not already assessed before his death) is assessed in the name of his executor. Full allowances are given as if the deceased had not died but had ceased to carry on trade, etc., or to derive income from any source. The tax due is payable out of the estate. In respect of income arising after his death, assessment will be made on the executor as a single person.

(iv) Income chargeable

Section 4 of the ITMA deals with 'gains or profits' from various sources and of 'income' derived from, accruing in, brought into, or received in Nigeria. Nowhere in the Act or in the law are the terms 'income', 'gain' or 'profit' defined.

Lord MacNaghten in *London County Council v A.G.* (ATC 265) said, 'Income tax, if I may be pardoned for saying so, is a tax on income. It is not meant to be a tax on anything else'. The impression from 'income' does not necessarily imply a receipt of money but rather a gain or profit in the nature of income. There is in principle no line of demarcation between a gain and a profit. Each connotes an excess, in appropriate cases, of revenue over expenditure.

The classical distinction between capital and revenue is just like the relation between a tree and its fruits. The tree represents capital (the source) and the fruits represent the income. Receipts may be grouped broadly into three types:

(a) revenue receipts;
(b) capital receipts;
(c) windfall revenue receipts.

In *Van Den Berghs Ltd v Clark* (19 TC 390), Lord Macmillan said, 'Circulating capital is the capital which is turned over, and in the process of being turned over yields profit or loss. Fixed capital is not

16

involved directly in that process, and remains unaffected by it ...'
While the income on revenue account is liable to tax in normal circumstances, income on capital account and windfall receipts are not, unless there are specific provisions for them to be taxed. There is no comprehensive definition of the word 'income' in the taxing statutes. It is, however, clear that gross receipts do not necessarily constitute income. It is important to take account of the expenditure incurred before the receipts are due. Put simply, income liable to tax in normal circumstances represents the difference, on revenue account, of gross receipts over total expenditure (i.e. profit or gain).

In many cases, it is easy to identify income (e.g. salary, interest, rent, profits from a trade or profession, etc.). In some cases, however, the identification is not so obvious and the Courts are called in to adjudicate. The dividing line in many cases is so thin that great care is necessary in treating them.

No hard and fast rule can be laid down for determining the borderline cases; what is taxable income and what is not. Every case depends on its special circumstances. Examples are provided by the cases decided by the Courts, but it must be remembered that these cases were decided on particular facts. In general, however, attention must be paid to the following:

(a) What is the intention of the taxpayer?
(b) Is the property an ordinary trading article or one capable of being held as an investment?
(c) For what period of time is it held as an investment?
(d) Was a trading organisation set up?
(e) How is the transaction financed?
(f) Is the transaction repeated and if so, how soon and how often?
(g) Is the taxpayer engaged in a trade, etc., involving such property or articles?

The aim of these questions is to ascertain whether each receipt is one of capital or revenue. The intention of the taxpayer can thus be gathered from the surrounding circumstances.

In regard to receipts from the disposal of 'know-how' (i.e. technical skill or secret processes), the guiding principle is whether the trader by the disposal 'effectively gives up his business in a particular area'; that is, whether it strikes at the root of the business undertaking and disorganises it even partially. When this is the case, the receipt is one of capital. Where, however, there is no sale in reality but a mere service – the product of the taxpayer being manufactured by another company in the particular area – the receipt is one of revenue.

Generally, the principle of revenue compensation is based on a revenue receipt compensation which arises from the contract of

employment. Borderline cases are decided on consideration including the following:
(a) Whether it is compensation paid for services rendered or to be rendered
(b) Whether it relates to the cessation of taxable income (i.e. the final liquidation of the taxpayer's source of income)
(c) Whether it arises from the terms of employment and is enforceable in law
(d) Whether it is in cancellation of a right during, or before taking up an employment (e.g. loss of amateur status).

Where an agent is involved in compensation payment, two principles are necessary on which a decision may be based. If the compensation is paid for loss of an agency (the agent still holding other agencies) the receipt is one of revenue. On the other hand, the compensation is for the loss of the taxpayer's only source, if it is one of capital. The Act lays down in Section 4(1) what income is liable to income tax. The income liable is that accruing in, derived from, brought into, or received in Nigeria. It then proceeds to name specifically five types of income which are covered and then adds a sixth (which takes care of any omissions). These are:

1 *Trade, Business, etc.* Gains or profits from any trade, business, profession, or vocation for whatever period of time the trade is carried on are recorded. It is possible to assess the profit where a trade, etc., is carried on for only a part of a year. It is not certain whether the word 'business' covers undertakings which are only a side-line or those conducted once in a while and those which are merely adventures in the nature of a trade. Howbeit, it is thought that the sweeping clause of section 4(1)(f) takes care of any gaps.

2 *Isolated transaction.* There are as yet no decided cases in Nigeria, dealing with borderline transactions which may be regarded as 'adventures in the nature of a trade'. From decisions reached in United Kingdom cases, some guidance is available in knowing where any particular adventure partakes of the nature of a trade. For example:
(a) Was there an intention to re-sell the property or article?
(b) Was any trading organisation set up?
(c) What is the nature of the property?
    (i) Is it capable of being held as an investment?
    (ii) For what period of time was it held as an investment?
    (iii) Was it more than would normally suffice for personal (self, friends and family) use?
(d) Was the property held as plant and machinery for the purposes of a trade already in existence?

18

(e) Where the transaction is indulged in more than once, what is the length of time between the first and subsequent transactions?

(f) Does the second transaction derive from the success of the first?

(g) Has anything been done to alter the character of the article? Was the action taken no more than what the owner of property could normally do?

(h) How was the transaction financed?

(i) Is the taxpayer engaged in trade involving such articles? If so, was the article held (or set aside) as an investment?

(j) Was the sale made in lots over a period of time?

What points to consider depends on the type of transaction in question and the nature of the article or property involved. No hard and fast rule can, therefore, be given and court decisions so far have shown very thin lines of division.[1]

3 *Illegal transactions.* Liability of income to income tax is not affected by the illegality of the transactions which give rise to the profits. Where a person carries on an illegal trade (e.g. involving fraud on the Customs) the gains from such a trade are liable to assessment (*Lindsay and Others v CIR*, 1932, 18 TC 43). A transporter who regularly cheats the traffic regulations is taxable on the profits of his business. Any gains from criminal undertakings (e.g. the 'profits' of a robbery) are, however, not subject to tax. This principle is supported by the decision in *Southern v AB Ltd*, 1933, 18 TC 59.

4 *Employment.* The Income Tax Management Act 1961 defines 'employment' as including 'any appointment of office whether public or otherwise for which remuneration is payable'. By this definition, Natural Rulers, Ministers, etc., who hold offices of state of one kind or another for which remuneration is payable are therefore employees. A director of a company is deemed to be an employed person.

Income tax on employment income is charged on 'any salary, wages, fees, allowances or other gains or profits from an employment which are paid or payable in money by the employer to the employee'. Gains or profits from an employment include such items as bonus, commission, rent allowance, gratuity, holiday pay, lump-sum payments, etc., except to the extent that they are specifically exempted by any provisions of the laws [e.g. paragraph (p) of the Third Schedule to the Income Tax Management Act]. Allowances are not subject to tax to the extent that the Commissioner accepts that:

(a) they 'represent reimbursement to the employee of expenses incurred by him in the performance of his duties';

(b) the employee does not make any profit or gain from them.

It is important to remember that taxability depends also on whether:

(c) the payment is made by the employer to the employee; and

(d) the salary, etc., is paid or payable in money. If the payment is made to a third person by the employer and the transaction is neither 'artificial' nor 'fictitious' it is not assessable on the employee even though he may be the beneficiary. Payments in kind, e.g. rent-free quarters, supply of cooks and stewards by employer, are taxable.

Assessment of employment income is based on the earnings of the year of assessment, not on the earnings of a preceding year. If, however, the income is in the nature of a bonus, commission, or allowance payable on one occasion only or at intervals exceeding one month, the material date is the date of payment and not the period during which the income was earned.

For the purpose of determining derivation of gains or profits from an employment, two cases have to be considered:

(a) When the duties of the employment are wholly or partly performed in Nigeria, and gains or profits are deemed to be derived from Nigeria, except where:

    (i) the duties are performed on behalf of an employer who is in a country other than Nigeria; and

    (ii) the employee is not in Nigeria for 183 days or more in a year of assessment; and

    (iii) the remuneration of the employee is liable to tax in that other country.

(b) Where the employer is in Nigeria and any gain or profit is derived in Nigeria. It is, however, also subject to the exception that the duties of the employment are wholly performed and remuneration paid outside Nigeria; then the income is not regarded as being derived from Nigeria. This exception is not affected by any temporary visit to or leave in Nigeria by the employee and does not apply to government employees in certain circumstances to be noted later. The exemption here relates to income from employment. The other sources of income of the taxpayer will be brought into the assessment. Relief will be given, where appropriate, if the income from the other sources is also taxed outside Nigeria.

Example 1

(a) Olufunmilayo is employed by Hollyoake Ltd, Akure. She was sent on 15.10.64 to carry out contract work in Nigeria on behalf of her employer. She completed the contract and left the country on 31.8.65. Tax was paid on her emoluments in the United Kingdom.

Exemption applies and no tax is payable in Nigeria on the emoluments [15.10.64 to 31.3.65 (1964–65)] and 1.4.65 to 31.8.65 (1965–66) since the periods are less than 183 days each).

(b) Oluseyi is employed by Bara-Hart Ltd at their office in Ghana where his remuneration is paid. During 1965–66 he spent three months in Nigeria on vacation and spent ₦120 which he remitted to the country in 1964–65.

No tax is payable [see also paragraph (x) of the Third Schedule to the Act].

It is immaterial, when employment is exercised in Nigeria, that the gains or profits from such employment are received outside Nigeria. Liability is fixed irrespective of whether payment to the employee is made outside Nigeria, and whether or not it is remitted to the country. Where an employee exercises his employment wholly or mainly in this country, the income earned by him during any period of leave or temporary absence on duty is liable to tax. If the employee is a government officer and performs his duties outside Nigeria, tax is recoverable on his emoluments, even when the country in which his duties are performed exempts the employee from tax on those emoluments either as a result of an agreement or in consequence of a diplomatic usage. The place of payment is irrelevant.

Example 2

(a) Akinkunmi is employed by Dolman & Sons Ltd and works at Port Harcourt. His salary of ₦800 p.a. is paid by his contract of service, in the UK and is not remitted to Nigeria. He lives on his net rental income of ₦740 p.a. from property situated in Ibadan and Efon-Alaye.

Tax is payable on his income of ₦1540 (i.e. ₦800 + 740).

(b) Olayinka is the Manager of Hillman Brothers Ltd, situated in Lagos. During 1965–66 he spent three months' leave and received his salary during those months in the UK (i.e. ₦1800 in Nigeria and ₦600 in the UK).

Tax attaches to his total emoluments of ₦2400.

(c) Ayodele is a secretary at the Nigeria High Commission in Togo. His salary of ₦1368 is paid in Togo.

Tax on ₦1368 is eligible.

If an employee receives a net salary after deduction of an amount for board and lodging, the gross salary is taxable (*Machon v McLoughlin*, 1926, 11 TC 83). Tips for services rendered (e.g. in hotels) are liable to tax (*Calvert v Wainwright*, 1947-27, TC 475).

The remuneration derived by a professor or teacher who is ordinarily resident in the United Kingdom for teaching during a period of temporary residence not exceeding two years, at a university, college, school or other educational institution in a state in Nigeria, is exempted from income tax. The same exemption but without the limit, extends to the income of nationals of the United States of America from employment by the ICA.

5 *Lump-sum payment*. The liability to tax of lump-sum payments made to an employee depends on the nature of the payments, that is, the circumstances under which the payments are made. If the payment is made in lieu of notice on termination of the employee's service, no tax is eligible. Where the lump-sum compensation arises from the contract of employment, it is liable to tax.

In other cases, liability depends on a full examination of the facts and consideration of the following questions:

(a) Does the compensation arise from a cancellation of a right to which the employee is entitled? If the answer is in the affirmative, then it is not liable to tax.

(b) Is the compensation paid for services rendered or to be rendered? An affirmative answer supports taxability.

(c) Does the lump-sum relate to the final liquidation of the taxpayer's source of income which is not covered by the terms of his employment? If such is the case, then no liability to tax attaches.

(d) If the lump-sum paid arises from the terms of employment and is enforceable at law by the employee, then it is liable to tax.[2]

Lord Atkin in *Reed v Seymour*, 1927, 11 TC 625 stated:

It seems to me that a sum of money paid to obtain a release from a contingent liability under a contract of employment cannot be said to be received 'under' the contract of employment; it is not remuneration for services rendered or to be rendered under the contract of employment, and is not received 'from' the contract of employment.

In *Weston v Hearn*, 1943, 25 TC 425, it was held that an employee was liable on a payment made to him on his completing 25 years' service (not retirement). Although the company was under no legal obligation to make the payment it was proved that it was customary in the company to make similar payments.

Gratuities paid to employees out of a fund not approved by the Joint Tax Board, have been held liable to tax.

Reliefs granted against employment income are done on the basis provided by law, that is, either on current year or on preceding year basis. Reliefs of this nature cover such items as life assurance, provident fund, pension fund, and reliefs for married persons and children. When an employee is not covered under the PAYE scheme, although his income is assessed on a current year basis, his reliefs in relation to wife and children are calculated on a preceding year basis.

6 *Rent and premium.* Section 4(1) (c) of the Income Tax Management Act charges to Income Tax 'gains or profits including any premium arising from a right granted to any other person for the use or occupation of any property.' It should be noted that only 'gains or profits' are liable to the tax. It is not the gross receipts that are taxable but the net receipt, that is, after allowing for all expenses or any part thereof wholly, necessarily, reasonably and exclusively incurred by the individual in the production of the income. It is important also to remember that the rental income must arise from 'property'. Since the word 'property' is not defined in the Act, the ordinary dictionary meaning is applicable. Consequently, it includes land, buildings, plant and machinery of any nature (e.g. block moulding machines).

Returns of income

These are required to be completed, dated and signed by the taxpayer withing twenty-one days of its service on him. The return must be made in accordance with the provisions of the Income Tax Management Act (Uniform Taxation Provisions, etc.) Tax is levied on a taxpayer's world or global income. The onus is on the tax authority to show that tax is levied on the individual and no tax can be levied unless the law says so.[3]

Service of notice of assessment

Service of notice of assessment can be effected by registered post or personally or through an agent such as a solicitor or an accountant. In *Senior Inspector of Taxes (former Western Nigeria) v J.O. Adigun,*[4] compliance with section 48 of the former Western State Income Tax Law, 1957, which provides that notices of assessment should be served on the taxpayer either personally or by registered post was dealt with.

It was the view of the court that strict compliance with this provision of the law is a condition precedent to the right of Government to demand tax – personal service in law means service on the very person of the person intended to be served, and not on a proxy, and registered post means a free-paid registered post through the post office.

The question for decision was whether the statute required notice of assessment and demand to be served on the person charged, before action could be instituted to recover the assessed amount.

What the court had to decide was whether, at the time the notice of assessment was delivered, the address was the usual or last known place of abode of the plaintiff. It is clear that the object of notice is to

23

give the person charged an opportunity of challenging the correctness of the assessment by appealing against it.

The judge considered the question of either dismissing the suit or not-suiting it. The defendant had at all times submitted returns, the accuracy of which the plaintiff never challenged. A claim for the sum of ₦6087.30, being arrears of tax owed by the defendant for the period 1963–64 to 1970–71, was made by the Revenue.

The evidence was that the defendant, who at the material time was a Minister in the former Western region, had paid income tax under the PAYE system on his official income during the period in issue. He had also duly, punctually, rendered the returns of his income from rents accruing from his landed properties during the relevant period, but was not assessed thereon. It was in respect of these latter incomes during the period that plaintiff made additional assessments and for which a claim was made in this suit.

The short point for decision was whether the claim was maintainable in the absence of proof that he was served with the assessment notice in accordance with the provision of section 48(2) of the Income Tax Law, cap. 48 of the Laws of the former Western Region of Nigeria.

Section 48(2) reads:

Where any person has been assessed at a total income of more than the assumed minimum income for any year of assessment the area assessment committee shall cause to be served personally or sent by registered post to such person a notice of assessment stating the amount of his chargeable income, the tax payable by him, and the place at which or the person to whom such payment is to be made.

The plaintiff's evidence was that the assessment was delivered to someone who signed for it, and who must have been a relation of the defendant (the receipt of service was Exhibit A). There was no doubt that it was never served on him personally, nor was it sent by registered post as required by law. There was, however, evidence that reminders were sent to him, but the defendant never acknowledged receipt of same.

Penalty Demand Notes (Exhibits E-E4) were later sent. There was evidence also that an accountant wrote to the plaintiff on his behalf in respect of these additional assessments and requesting time for him to submit returns. There was also evidence that he paid some sums thereafter.

However, the only defence was that the claim was not maintainable in that he was never personally served with the assessment notice and in consequence he had been denied the right to appeal against them.

The question therefore was: is service of the assessment notice condition precedent to recovery under the law, even if the defendant had notice of the assessments and perhaps paid part thereof? The case of *Berry v Farrow* (1914) 1 KB 632 was a case under section 16(c) of the Taxes Management Act 1880, which provided that 'all notices or forms required or allowed to be served on any person may be either delivered to such person or left at the usual or last known place of abode of such person'.

The plaintiff brought the action and it was contended on his behalf that no valid assessment had been made upon him for the year in question and consequently that no proceedings to recover the assessed amount claimed could be lawfully taken.

The court held finally that as no valid assessment was made upon the defendant for the year in question, the proceedings taken to recover the amount assessed were unlawful.

The judge held, therefore, that proper service of the notice of assessment was a condition precedent to instituting legal proceedings to recover the amount on the assessments. As no proper or lawful service of the said assessments notice was effected on the defendant, the judge held that the actor therefore failed.

The judge, with regret, decided in the circumstances to dismiss the suit with costs which he fixed at ₦55.

Effect on assessment where return is not specifically requested

It is the practice of the Revenue to begin each year's work by requesting taxpayers whose total income exceeds a specified limit to make a return of income for the previous and current year. An assessment could properly be made if the Revenue did not call for a return of income from a taxpayer. Although the Director of Internal Revenue should in his own interest as well as that of the taxpayer call for a return of income from the taxpayer, he has nevertheless not infringed or failed to comply with any requirement of the law if he did not do so. An assessment authority is not bound to require a taxpayer to deliver a statement of income but it is wise to do so, especially where there is not sufficient material available in the office on which a reasonable assessment may be based. In fact, it stands the Revenue in good stead where a return of income is called for and is not forthcoming and an appeal is made against a best of judgement assessment, arising from a failure on the part of the taxpayer to file the statement of income.

Effect on assessment made before receipt of return is specially called for

A return of income is called for and the time for filling the return has not expired, it is improper to make an assessment. The taxpayer once given an opportunity to state his case must be allowed to do so. Whether the statement he submits falls a short of reality is immaterial. Such an assessment would be irregular. If the authority called on the appellant for a return of his income and there was no evidence that he unduly delayed his return, the court could not sustain an assessment made without waiting for the taxpayer's return, if such a return has been called for and the time for making the return had not expired. To make an assessment without waiting for the return is no better than to make an assessment without considering a return actually made.

Reassessments and assessments accompanied by notice of refusal to amend

The court has held that assessments accompanied by notice to amend is *ultra vires* and void. In *Okupe v Federal Board of Inland Revenue*,[5] it was said that it is *ultra vires* and illegal to accompany an assessment to income tax with a refusal to amend the assessment; in breach of the provisions of the Personal Income Tax (Lagos) Act, 1961, it denies the taxpayer his right of objecting to the assessment and shows that any objection he may attempt to make is refused in advance, and *certiorari* to quash the assessment, and prohibition to bar any fresh assessment for the same tax period, will lie.

The principle that justice must not only be done but must manifestly be seen to be done may require that an *ultra vires* decision should be reversed finally, and no retrial ordered, where the tribunal which gave the decision has shown a clear intention not to alter it, and is the only tribunal which could retry the matter.

A lack of jurisdiction in the proceedings of an inferior tribunal makes the decision a nullity and calls for the exercise of the supervisory jurisdiction of the superior court; and though want of jurisdiction is not shown merely because the inferior tribunal has decided contrary to the facts or without evidence to justify its findings, an error of law appearing on the face of the record is ground for *certiorari*, and excess of jurisdiction arises in other ways as well: there may be an absence of those formalities or things which are conditions precedent to the tribunal having any jurisdiction to embark on an inquiry, or at the end of a proper inquiry the tribunal may make an order that it has no jurisdiction to make, or while engaged on the inquiry it may ask itself the wrong questions or take into account matters which it was not directed to take into account, or it may depart from the rules of natural justice; and excess of jurisdiction is manifested where there is a complete disregard of the fundamental conditions of the administration of justice, and where there has been shown a real likelihood of bias or prejudice in the tribunal, it is a case of excess of jurisdiction.

The appellant applied to the High Court of the Lagos State of Nigeria for *certiorari* and prohibition in respect of assessments to income tax made on the appellant by the respondents.

The respondents sent the appellant notices of additional assessments to income tax accompanied by notices of refusal to amend the assessments bearing the same date as the notices of assessment. The appellant instituted the present proceedings to quash the assessments and prohibit any proceedings to enforce payment. The High Court (Adedipe, J.) dismissed the applications on the ground, among others, that *certiorari* and prohibition were not appropriate remedies.

On appeal, the appellant contended that (a) notice of refusal to amend an assessment could only be issued when the respondents refused to accede to an objection to an assessment; and (b) the service of the notices of refusal to amend along with the notices of assessment was an intimation to the appellant that he might not object to the assessments, because any objection would be, and had been, refused.

The respondents conceded that the issue and service of the notices of refusal were wrong, and that this would be ground for an order of *certiorari* were it not for the provisions of s.35 of the Personal Income Tax (Lagos) Act, 1961, but contended that (a) the issue and service of the notices of refusal were a mistake for which s.35 provided a complete answer; and (b) the notices of assessment were valid.

The court held that s.35 did not apply, and that the assessments were contrary to the provisions of the Act. The court allowed the appeal, and granted an order of *certiorari* to quash the assessments and an order of prohibition against any fresh assessments for the same tax periods.

Jurisdiction of Federal Board of Inland Revenue on Personal Income Tax cases

State Internal Revenue Departments deal with personal taxation unless as in *Federal Board of Inland Revenue v Sylvester Mayaki*[6] and *F.A. Adesina and Others v Federal Board of Inland Revenue*[7] where the revenue concerned is a Federal Government one, the Federal Inland Revenue deals with it. Furthermore, Act No. 51 of 1972 authorised the Federal Board to impose income tax on armed forces personnel and certain other classes of individuals. Those subject to the Act are classified as follows:

(a) persons employed in the Nigerian Army, the Nigerian Navy or the Nigerian Air Forces, other than in a civilian capacity;

(b) officers of the Nigerian Foreign Service;

(c) persons in receipt of Nigerian pensions where such pensions are payable overseas; and

(d) persons resident outside Nigeria who are shareholders of Nigerian companies.

Before the Act, civilian employees in the Nigerian Army, Nigerian Navy and the Nigerian Air Force were under the tax jurisdiction of the states in which they were resident. These are now included in the category of persons who are subject to the personal income tax by the Federal Board of Inland Revenue. The salaries and allowances of members of the 'other ranks' in the Nigerian armed forces would be specifically exempted as established by convention in the past, which in effect means that only 'commissioned officers in the Nigerian Armed Forces, the Nigerian Navy and the Nigerian Air Forces' would be subject to the Act apart from those mentioned above. It is to be emphasised that the exemption of the salaries and allowances of members of the 'other ranks' in the Nigerian Armed Forces should not preclude the taxation of any other income, for example, rent, bank interest, etc. in their hands in the normal way and it is obligatory for them to inform the Federal Board of Inland Revenue of these other incomes.

Time within which tax is payable

Tax assessed is payable within two months after the date of service of the notice of assessment, one half of the tax charged may be paid within two months of the date of service of the notice of assessment and the balance paid not later than the end of the financial year. If payment is not made, a penalty of 10 per cent of the tax payable will be added and any right of payment will be lost. Failure to pay income tax without lawful excuse now results in a fine of ₦500, or six months' imprisonment or both, on conviction. Payment of the tax may be paid in cash, money order, postal order or cheque drawn on a recognised bank in Nigeria, crossed 'A/C Payee Only' and should be endorsed 'Commission to Drawer's A/C'. Tax is due when the tax has been made final and conclusive. Tax is, however, not due during the year in which assessment is made if there is objection or appeal. In *Azikiwe v Federal Electoral Commission*,[8] the court held that if an objection to tax was pending, the assessment could not be made final and conclusive. The court further held that it was within the powers of tax authorities to extend the time of delivery of returns of income.

The case deals with Income Tax-liability, time when liability arises and becomes final, statutory obligation on assessment authority to serve taxpayer with written notices demanding returns and stating amount of assessed income under Anambra State Finance Law, ss.20(3), 28(1). If an objection is pending, the assessment cannot be final or conclusive.

This case also deals with the meaning of 'current' and 'late' assessments. It is within the powers of tax authorities to extend the time of delivery of returns. The case also deals with interpretation of statutes.

Chief Nnamdi Azikiwe sought a declaration in the High Court of Anambra State (suit E/138/79) against the Federal Electoral Commission and the Attorney-General that he had fully paid his income tax for the financial years 1976–77, 1977–78 and 1978–79 as it became due and that he had satisfied the provisions of s.72(1) and (2) of the Electoral Law 1977.

The taxpayer, who is a former President of the Federal Republic of Nigeria, was the presidential candidate of the Nigerian People's Party (NPP) at the 1979 Federal elections.

It is true that the Board of Internal Revenue or the Director normally publishes a notice in the Gazette under s.15(1) of the Finance Law calling on everyone liable to pay income tax to prepare and deliver not later than 30 days after the publication of the notice to the assessment authority a statement of his anticipated income. Such notices are published in the Gazette: exhibits 0 and 01 were the publications made in the Gazette in respect of the 1976–77 and 1977–78 financial years. But s.15(2) provides that:

An assessment authority may, at any time and at such additional times as may be necessary, by notice in writting require any taxpayer for any year of assessment, to prepare and deliver not later than 30 days after the date of service of the notice, to the assessment authority at the place specified in that notice, a return in the form incorporating that notice; but the assessment authority may – (a) extend the period specified for delivery of the return as may be reasonable in the circumstances; or (b) by notice in writing reduce the period if he has reason to anticipate any undue delay in completing the assessment.

The position, therefore, is that whilst the Board or the Director of Internal Revenue publishes the notice under s.15(1) of the Finance Law, the assessment authority is required under s.15(2) to serve on the taxpayer notice to prepare and deliver his returns. This is also in line with *Federal Board of Inland Revenue v Joseph Rezcallah & Sons Ltd* (1962) 1 All NLR 1, cited by both counsel for the taxpayer and counsel for the defendants. In that case the Supreme court clearly held that an income tax assessment made without any request by the assessment authority for a return of income is made without jurisdiction and is null and void and must remain null and void.

It therefore follows that whilst the Board or Director of Internal Revenue makes a general publication in the Gazette or newspapers calling on the general public to prepare and deliver a true and correct statement of its income, the assessment authority is enjoined by law to call on each taxpayer by notice in writing to deliver a return of his income for the purpose of carrying out due assessment. It must also be borne in mind that whilst the assessment authority may 'at such additional time as may be necessary', issue the notice in writing calling for the returns, he still has the right under s.15(2)(a) to extend the period specified in the notice for the delivery of the return.

An assessment authority shall serve upon every taxpayer a notice in writing specifying the amount of assessed income, the amount of tax payable by him, and the time within which the payment should be made.

It is true that s.20(3) of the Finance Law provides that a 'taxpayer shall for any year of assessment take such steps as are necessary to ascertain the amount of tax payable by him and the place at which, and the time within which payment should be made', nevertheless no tax is payable by any taxpayer unless he has been served with the notice of assessment stating the amount of assessed income, the amount of tax payable by him and the time within which the payment should be made. It is immaterial whether the taxpayer had taken steps to ascertain from the assessment authority the amount of tax payable by him and the time within which the payment should be made. What is important in all cases is that the notice of assessment must be delivered or served on each taxpayer.

In any event, the assessment authority has power again under s.20(5)(a) of the Finance Law to extend the period specified in the assessment notice for payment of the tax as may be reasonable in the circumstances. Therefore, no fault is attributable to any taxpayer if the assessment authority has extended the period specified in the assessment notice for the payment of the tax.

The combined effect of ss.15, 19, 20 and 23 of the Finance Law is, that tax is due and payable only when a notice in writing has been issued and served on the taxpayer calling for his return under s.15(2) of the Finance Law and when the assessment authority has also served a notice of assessment on the taxpayer specifying the amount of tax payable by him under s.20(1) and no extension of time for making the payment had been granted to the taxpayer under s.20(5) and no objection has been made by the taxpayer to the assessment under s.23(1). This is completely in accord with the evidence of Mr Nweri to the effect that:

'a tax is due and payable when an assessment has been made and the notice served on the taxpayer and no appeal or objection is made against the said assessment and no extension of time is granted by the assessment authority for the payment of the tax.'

It may also be necessary to mention in this regard that s.28(1) of the Finance Law provides that, where no valid objection or appeal has been made within time, the assessment is final and conclusive. Therefore, if an appeal or objection is pending, no assessment can ever be final and conclusive. The assessment becomes final and conclusive only after the determination of the appeal or objection and the tax then becomes due and payable.

From the above it can be seen that it is not in all cases that tax is due and payable during the year to which the assessment in question relates. The tax for one financial year, for example, may be due and payable in a subsequent year.

This is so because, on the determination of the objection against an assessment, the assessment authority pursuant to s.23(3) of the Finance Law shall serve a notice in writing upon the taxpayer in accordance with subsection (1) of section 20. Section 20(1), it will be remembered, requires the assessment authority to:

serve upon every taxpayer a notice in writing specifying the amount of assessed income, the amount of tax payable by him, and the time within which the payment should be made.

It is certainly only after the expiration of the period given to a taxpayer in the assessment notice to pay his tax that the tax becomes in arrears.

It may also be necessary to consider in this light s.21 of the Finance Law, which gives the assessment authority power to make an additional assessment. Section 21 reads as follows:

If an assessment authority or assessment committee has reason to believe, by reference to the omission or failure of any taxpayer to deliver a statement or return under s.15, or by reference to any information available, that any taxpayer has not been charged tax or has been charged at a lesser amount than he ought to have been charged for any year of assessment, the assessment authority or assessment committee shall, at any time and at such additional times as may be necessary, within that year or within six years after the expiration of that year, assess or additionally assess the total income of that person and determine the amount or additional amount of tax which ought to have been payable by him, and all the provisions of this part relating to assessment, notification of assessment, appeal, collection of tax and other proceedings apply to such an assessment or additional assessment and to the amount of tax determined as payable.

It follows therefore that the assessment authority can additionally assess any taxpayer within a period of six years after the first year of assessment and determine the additional tax to be paid by the taxpayer. Such additional assessment can never by any stretch of the imagination be taken as payment in arrears or instalmental payment. An additional assessment can be due to the fault of the taxpayer in omitting to deliver to the assessment authority a true statement of his accounts or return, or it may be due to the fault of the assessment authority in assessing the taxpayer inadequately. The error might even be detected from the auditor's report.

There is therefore no question whatsoever of this payment being made in arrears. It was paid on the day the assessment was raised. In short, it was paid on the very same day that it become due and payable. A payment is said to be in arrears only when there is a fixed time for payment and that time has elapsed. 'Arrears presupposes a time fixed for payment of a sum of money and the lapse of time thereafter without payment,' *per* Mann CJ in *Paice v Ayton* (1941) VIR 63 at 68, quoted in Stroud's *Judicial Dictionary* (3rd Edn) 189.

It is pertinent to note also that in the income tax receipt forms issued to taxpayers there is a column for stating the type of tax paid, i.e. whether current, late, additional, or arrears. The receipt issued to the taxpayer for the payment made on 25 January 1978 is clearly marked 'late tax.' The receipt issued after the additional assessment is clearly marked 'addition'.

Objection. Objection to assessment should be given in writing to the tax office within thirty days from the date of service of the notice of assessment stating the grounds of the objection. In *Azikiwe v The Federal Electoral Commission*,[9] The court said:

There is again in the Finance Law appropriate provision for the making of objections against assessments considered by a taxpayer to be exorbitant. Section 23 of the Finance Law deals with objections to assessments and it reads:

(1) Subject to this part, where a taxpayer is aggrieved by an assessment of his income tax he may make objection and apply in person or in writing to the assessment authority of the specified area in which the assessment was made, to review and revise the assessment.

(2) Such an application shall state precisely the grounds of objection and shall be made not later than 21 days after the date of service of the notice of assessment; but the assessment authority may extend the period specified for making application as may be reasonable in the circumstances.

(3) Upon receipt of such an application the assessment authority shall make such enquiry as he deems necessary, and determine the objection to the best of his judgement and give notice to the taxpayer of his decision; but where the assessment authority revises the assessment and reduces or enhances the amount of tax payable, he shall issue a notice in writing upon the taxpayer in accordance with subsection (1) of section 20.

Appeal, etc. An appeal may be made to the tax board, then to Magistrates' Courts, the High Courts, Federal or State, Federal Appeal Court[10] and finally to the Supreme Court. In *Federal Board of Inland Revenue v R.A.S. Babaoye*[11] (Anyaegbunam, J) held that leave to appeal is not automatic as it is within the discretion of the court to grant it and sufficient grounds must be furnished to the court before the court can exercise its discretion.

Separate assessments. A married male taxpayer with a wife in employment is separately assessed to tax from his wife.

Additional assessments

The Board has power to make retrospective assessments within six years of the end of the year of assessment without any rancour or scepticism if a discovery has been made. This word discovery is not, in fact, defined in the present Tax Acts in Nigeria but it can be regarded to mean a mere change of opinion by the inspector of taxes on a point of law; or an opinion based on inconclusive information, or mere suspicion.

In *S.E. Ola v Federal Board of Inland Revenue*,[12] the defendant taxpayer appealed against the decision of Board of Appeal Commissioners' dismissal of his appeal against the refusal of the Board of Inland Revenue to consider the objection raised by the taxpayer to additional assessment made against him in respect of the tax years 1962–1968 inclusive. The appellant, an employee-cum-agent of the UAC Ltd, on a commission and salary basis, had other sources of income which he did not disclose to the respondents. The appellant paid income rates on his salary and commission which were deducted at source under the PAYE system. Consequent upon the discoveries that the appellant was the owner of two houses at Ebute-Metta and some lorries which were used in transport business, the respondent after interviewing the appellant, made additional assessments covering the period 1962–1968 on the appellant on the best of judgement because the appellant or his agent did not promptly respond to notices of assessment sent to him.

In the High Court, Counsel for the appellant sought for and obtained leave to file and additional grounds of appeal. The respondent was also granted leave to file a reply to documents filed by the appellant. In his argument Counsel for the appellant contended that once an assessment is final and conclusive on a set of facts, it cannot be reopened on those facts. He submitted therefore that the respondent was wrong in law in making additional assessment in respect of the same year. It is concealed that additional assessments can be made if the reasons are not reopened.

It was further contended that the additional assessments were bad in law because they did not contain the particulars on which the assessments were made. It was also argued that it was an error in law for the Board of Appeal Commissioners to confirm the assessment made, without making any capital allowance in favour of the appellant. It was also a misdirection on the part of the Appeal Commissioners when there was sufficient evidence before them to the contrary, to hold that the appellant only paid income rate for 1964–65. He submitted that income tax was raised against the appellant for all the years of assessment and were paid.

Counsel for the respondent replied to all the submissions. He submitted that the appellant submitted early declarations as to his salaries and commissions and never submitted any other accounts in respect of earlier years. The Board had power to make additional assessments in the circumstances. He submitted that the accounts submitted by the appellant were found to be untrue and unhelpful, and that the Appeal Commissioners were right in rejecting them and accepting the assessments made on the best of judgement basis. Counsel submitted that there was insufficient evidence before the Appeal Commissioners to consider granting of capital allowance claimed by the appellant. Finally, Counsel submitted that the additional assessments did not necessitate reopening of earlier assessments. They were based on new discoveries of the appellant's sources of income, hitherto undisclosed by the appellant. These are allowed under s.31(1) of the Personal Income Tax (Lagos) Act, 1961, which held that:

(a) Where the Board of Inland Revenue, after making an assessment, discovers some source of income not included in the earlier assessment, they are entitled and under a duty under s.31(1) of the Personal Income Tax (Lagos) Act, 1961, to raise additional tax assessments, after service of the relevant notices on the taxpayer.

(b) Assessment notices which do not contain, in substance and effect, the particulars on which the assessments were made, are not in compliance with the proviso to section 35 of the Personal Income Tax (Lagos) Act, 1961, and are therefore null and void. This is a point of law which can be raised before the Appeal Commissioners. The six notices of additional assessment are discharged.

(c) Where the law allows capital allowances, to a taxpayer, it is the duty of the Board to show on the assessment notices, that such allowances have in fact been granted. This is especially so where the taxpayer has expressly claimed. The Appeal Commissioners therefore in this case erred by confirming the assessments made by the Board when the Board gave no capital allowances to the taxpayer in any of the assessment notices in accordance with Section 20 of the Personal Income Tax (Lagos) Act, 1961.

(d) The procedure adopted by the Appeal Commissioners when hearing the appeal was wrong as they were acting judicially. When hearing appeals which come before them, and taking evidence from parties to the dispute, they should call upon such parties respectively to testify before it and where a party refuses or chooses not to testify, the refusal or choice should be placed on record. All parties should be given the opportunity to cross-examine all persons who come to testify in such matters.

(e) The Appeal Commissioners misdirected themselves in the appraisal of the facts of the case. Where a misdirection even if regarded as minor, forms part of a chain of events in the same case, the totality of which was likely to cause a miscarriage of justice to the applicant, the appeal will be allowed and the decision arrived at from appraisal of the facts set aside.

(f) The Court would not allow officials of the Board to use their powers of taxation oppressively or as a punitive measure. Where it appeared on the facts and circumstances of the case that notices of additional assessment of tax were arbitrary, excessive and vindictive, such assessment would be discharged by the Court in the interest of justice. The appeal was allowed.

In *Lagos State Internal Revenue Board v Odusami*[13], the Internal Revenue Board claimed under s. 51 of the Personal Income Tax Law for the recovery of tax in accordance with additional assessments properly made by the Board and against which the taxpayer had raised no objection and had not appealed; the court held that it did not have jurisdiction to alter or review the amount claimed except in so far as it considered that the Board's assessment was not reasonable.

Repayment of tax

No claim for repayment of tax shall be entertained by the Board unless it is made in writing within six years next after the end of the year of assessment to which it relates.

(v) Death of Taxpayer

Where the taxpayer dies during the year of assessment the whole of the allowances and relief to which he was entitled for the fiscal year may be deducted from the statutory income for the period from the commencement of the fiscal year to the date of death. The income for the remainder of the year will be assessed in the hands of the trustees or beneficiaries according to circumstances, and in the latter case, the whole of such allowances as are applicable may be deducted.

In the case of a business carried on by a sole trader, his death brings about a discontinuance of this business for Income Tax purposes, and an adjustment of the assessment for the year in which death occurred becomes necessary, while the Board has the right to increase the assessment of the penultimate year to the actual profits of that year.

(vi) Income exempted

There shall be exempt from tax in Nigeria:
  (a) the official emoluments of the President and Commander-in-Chief of the Federation of Nigeria, and of the Governor of any State, and of any person performing the functions of the said Governor-General and Commander-in-Chief or Governor received by such person in his capacity as such;
  (b) all consular fees received on behalf of a foreign trade, or by a consular officer or employee of such a state for his own account, and all income of such an officer or employee other than income in respect of any trade, business, profession, or vocation carried on by such an officer or employee, or in respect of any other employment exercised by him, within Nigeria, provided that this exemption shall not apply where such an employee ordinarily resides in Nigeria and is not also a national of such foreign state;
  (c) official emoluments of Deputy Governors of the Federation (Income Tax [Exemption of Certain Office Holders] Notice, 1983, *Federal Gazette* no. 54, vol. 70, 13.10.83, which amends the Third Schedule of the Income Tax Management Act, 1961). Also see Appendix 2.

Notes
1 *Martin v Lowry*, 1926, II TC 297.
   Rutledge v CIR, 1929, 14 TC 490.
   Edwards v Bairstow & Harrison, 1955, 36 TC 207.
   CIR v Livingstone & Others, 1926, II TC 538.
   Rand v The Alberni Land Co. Ltd, 1920, 7 TC 629.
   CIR v Nelson, 1939, 22 TC 716.
2 *Henry v Foster*, 1931, 16 TC 605; and *Hunter v Dewhurst, 1931, 16 TC 605.*
3 See *Ayrshire Employers Mutual Insurance Association Limited v IRC* (1974), 27 TC 331.
4 Suit No. 1/169/71 in the High Court of Justice, Ibadan before D.O. Coker, J.
5 (1974) NCLR before (Coker, Udoma and Fatayi-Williams, JJ SC).
6 FRC/2/24/75 in the Federal Revenue Court before Belgore, J.
7 FRC/L/2A/74.
8 (1979) 3 LRN at p.286 in the High Court of Anambra State before Araka CJ on 28 May 1979. See also *Federal Board of Inland Revenue v Joseph Rezcallah & Sons Ltd* (1962) 1 All NLR 1, SC, *Ibebeweka v Egbuna* (1964) 1 WLR 249, *Onasile (Emmanuel) v Daniel Sami* (1962) 1 All NLR 272.
9 (1979) 3 LRN at p.286 in the High Court of Anambra State before Araka CJ on 28 May 1979; See also *Federal Board of Inland Revenue v Joseph Rezcallah & Sons Ltd* (1962) 1 All NLR 1, SC, *Ibebeweka v Egbuna* (1964) 1 WLR 219, *Onasile (Emmanuel) v Daniel Sami* (1962) 1 All NLR 272.

10   Appeal used to be made to the Federal Revenue Court now abolished and in its place the Federal High Court: Section 230(2) of the 1979 Constitution. Both the Federal High Court and State High Courts are courts of coordinate jurisdiction.
11   (1974) (1) NMLR.
12   1 FRCR (1974) at p.73; Suit No. FRC/L/IA/73.
13   1979 3 LRN published by Butterworth & Co. (Nigeria) Ltd, 119–25 before Omotoso J.

3 The Law Relating to Personal Taxation Assessments[1]

(i) Introduction

Section 20(1) of ITMA provides that, for all source of income, the basis of assessment for any year is the income of the immediately preceding year ended on the 31 December. The advantage of this to the department handling tax is obvious; the measure of any assessment is a definite ascertained figure and, in consequence, an interval of time is secured in the year of assessment to obtain that figure from the taxpayer and to set the machinery of assessments and collection in motion.

There are two important exceptions to the general rule, namely, where the sources are an employment or pension and a trade, business, profession or vocation. Before dealing with these exceptions, however, the importance and the significance of certain other words in section 20(1) of ITMA have to be noted:

shall be ... the income ... from each source, notwithstanding that he ... (the individual ... may have ceased to possess any such source or that any such source may have ceased to produce income.)

From these words – and it should be noted that they do *not* appear in CITA – if monies can be shown to have originated from an individual's income source one, two, five, ten or even more years ago, whether or not temporarily invested during the intervening period, they are assessable to tax on the preceding year basis. The important thing is the absence of a time-limit for all monies except those brought into or received in Nigeria in a year preceding one of non-residence or residence of less than 183 days. (See [x] Third Schedule, ITMA.)

Employment and pension income (Section 20(5) of ITMA)

Since 1 April 1961, employment and pension income has been assessed on the actual basis in accordance with the principles of Pay As You Earn (PAYE) scheme. Income from employment is deemed to arise from day to day except to the extent that it comes from any bonus, commission and allowance payable once and once only or at intervals exceeding one month. In such cases the bonus, commission or allowance is deemed to be income either of the day of payment or, if that day is after the employment has ceased, of the last day of the employment to include terminal leave.

Example 1

The remuneration received in the year ended 31 December 1981 by the manager of a Nigerian trading company was made up of the following:

(i)	monthly salary payments for January to December 1981 inclusive	₦10 000.00
(ii)	bonus for trading year ended 18 November 1980 – paid on 28 November 1981	5 000.00
(iii)	bonus for trading year ended 28.11.81 – paid on 15 December 1981	4 000.00
		₦19 000.00

The assessable income for the year 1981 is ₦19 000.00. The bonus was payable at intervals (exceeding one month) so the whole is regarded as the income of the year 1981.

Example 2

The assistant manager of a Nigerian trading company terminated his employment on 28 November 1981 after terminal leave for the months of September, October and November. The remuneration paid for the year 1981 was as follows:

(i)	monthly salary paid in each of the months January to August 1981	₦8 000.00
(ii)	monthly salary for September, October and November paid on 2 January 1981	3 000.00
		N11 000.00

The assessable income for the year 1981 is ₦11 000.00. The salary was payable monthly so the date of payment has no significance.

Instead the payment on 2 April 1979 is related to the period in which it arose, i.e. the months of September, October and November.

Example 3

The sub-manager of a Nigerian trading company was promoted to manager on 1 December 1980. As sub-manager he had a monthly salary of ₦800 per month: as manager his monthly salary was ₦1000 per month, but his salary was not altered until January 1981 when he received backpay of ₦200 for the month of December 1980. An annual bonus of ₦4000 for the year ended 30 November 1979 was paid on 20 December 1980. An annual bonus of ₦5500 for the year ended 30 November 1981 was paid on 2 January 1982.

The assessable income for the year 1980 is:

11 months ₦800 =	₦8 800
1 month at ₦1000 =	1 000
Annual bonus paid on 25 December 1980	5 000
	₦14 800

The assessable income for the year 1981 is:

12 months at ₦1000 =	₦12 000

The annual bonus paid on 2 January 1982 is income of the year 1982.

Example 4

The Marina manager of a Nigerian trading company terminated his employment on 30 November 1980 after terminal leave for the months of September, October and November. The total remuneration paid was made up of:

(i) monthly salary paid in each of the months January to August 1980	₦8000
(ii) Salary due for the months of September, October and November paid on 31 August 1980	₦3000
(iii) annual bonus for year ended 30 November 1979 paid on 1 January 1980	₦4000
(iv) annual bonus for year ended 30 November 1980 paid on 1 January 1981	₦8500

The assessable income of the year 1980 is ₦23 500. The salary was payable monthly so the dates of payment mean nothing – the payments are related to the period in which the income arose. As regards the annual bonuses, however, that for the year ended 30

November 1980 is taken as income of the date of payment (i.e. of 1980) while that for the year ended 30 November 1980 is taken as income of the last day of employment including terminal leave – 30 November 1980 (i.e. of 1980 also.)

In *Commissioner of Internal Revenue (former Western State) v J.A.O. Aworeni*[2], the case concerned failure to pay tax deducted to the Government Treasury. In this case, Mr Aworeni was sued in respect of the PAYE tax deduction from the salaries of various employees of his school, Adesola High School, which he did not pay to the Government Treasury.

On 13 March 1973, both plaintiff and defendant presented their case on the question of penalty. The case was then adjourned *sine die* for judgement. On 30 March 1973 judgement was given and the defendant was found liable to pay the sum of ₦1179.67 as penalty with ₦80.00 costs.

A motion for instalment payment was brought by the defendant. The motion was heard by Justice Odumosu on 21 May 1973. Before the case was heard in court, Mr Aworeni paid the sum of ₦832.70 but refused to pay the penalty on the ground that he was not liable to penalty. The defendant/applicant was ordered to pay ₦100.00 immediately and the rest by ₦60 monthly instalments until the total amount was liquidated. A sum of ₦20 was awarded as costs against him. The court also stated that if any instalment was not paid at the end of any month the whole debt should become recoverable.

Later, Mr Asola, a Higher Executive Office (Tax) stated that, after making the immediate payment of ₦100 on 23 May 1973, and the first monthly instalment of ₦60 on 6 July 1973, Mr Aworeni had made no further payment.

The Revenue had the right under section 4(2) of the Sheriff and Civil Process Law, cap. 116, Laws of former Western State by issuing writ of execution for the enforcement of the remaining amount. In *Regional Tax Administrator (former Western State of Nigeria) (Plaintiff) v African Press Limited, Ibadan (Defendant)*[3], the appeal concerned failure by the employer to pay tax collected into Government Treasury. Such tax due must be paid, at that time, on penalty of ₦600 fine and/or three years imprisonment.

Judgement had first been given in this suit on 23 June 1964, but in consequence of an appeal filed by the plaintiff, on 7 February 1967 the case was sent back by the Supreme Court for rehearing *de novo*.

In his writ of summons, the plaintiff was claiming the sum of ₦1603, this being the amount of tax collected by the defendant for the years 1961–62 and 1962–63 on behalf of the Regional Tax Board from the staff of the African Press Ltd at Ibadan. By paragraphs 5 and 6 of the Statement of Claim, the amount claimed was made up as follows:

(a) *Balance of tax collected in 1961–62*   ₦585.70
(b) *Balance of tax collected in 1962–63*
    (April–October 1962)   1017.30
                                                  ₦1603.00

In its amended statement of defence, the defendant pleaded as follows:

The defendant denies that any tax is due from it as alleged in the statement of claim and writ of summons originally or as amended, nor has it deducted nor received any tax from any employees which it did not pay to them regularly.

The defendant avers that it had paid to the Treasury what was collected on emoluments paid to its employees.

The defendant further avers that in 1962–63, as a result of financial hardship, it was unable to pay its staff emoluments shown on the wage sheets as due to them and the employees did not in fact receive such emoluments.

The judge said:

I have given due consideration to all the evidence led and after hearing both counsel, I am satisfied that the defendant is liable, as admitted by its counsel, in the sum of ₦585.70, being tax due from the defendant under the PAYE scheme for the period 1961–62. Apart from the evidence of the first principal witness, which I believe, the deduction cards, Exhibit 1, and the defendant's letter, Exhibit 3, clearly establish the Company's liability for the sum claimed.

With regard to the tax due for the year 1962/63, the defendant has not in my view put forward any serious defence to the claim. It is alleged that because of some grave financial difficulty the Company was unable to pay its employees for part of that year, and consequently it did not deduct any tax under the PAYE Scheme.

This may well have been so, but all the evidence produced by the defendant was that of a secretary-typist who was not in charge of staff matters; this witness did not work in the accounts department, nor did he have any access to any accounting papers or record. During the period in question, Mr Ladejobi was said to be the Company's accountant (he now resides in Lagos), whilst Mr Jakande was the Company's secretary. Neither of these persons was called to testify, not did the defendant call any of the five Company directors listed at the foot of their letter, Exhibit 3. Surely these are the persons who could have spoken with authority, not only about the financial condition of the Company, but about the employment, discharge and payment of its staff.

The defendant's witness said that most of the employees left when they were not paid any salaries. Now under Rule 17(1) of the Income Tax (Emoluments) Rules 1961, an employer to whom a tax deduction card has been issued, shall 'forthwith' inform the Inspector of Taxes on a prescribed form whenever he ceases to employ an employee. There is no evidence before me that the defendant took any step to inform the plaintiff when his workers left. Furthermore, by Rule 28(1) of the same Rules, the defendant is bound, at the end of each financial year, to submit to the Inspector of Taxes an account of the tax deducted from its employees. There is evidence that the defendant did not render this account at the end of 1962/63 year. If it is true that the employees did not receive any salaries for any part of that year, it should have been quite easy to make a 'nil' return for that part of the year.

In the result, I remained unconvinced that the defendant was unable to pay its employees' wages for the period April to October 1962, and hold that the defendant has failed to prove the averments contained in paragraph 5 of its Statement of Defence.

I accept the evidence of Mr Osinowo, the second plaintiff's witness, that he called at the defendant's office in July 1963, that he inspected the wage sheets, and that the accountants, Mr Ladejobi, informed him that the wages on those sheets had been paid. Out of a total sum of ₦1487.20 collected by the defendant, it paid ₦467.90 into the Treasury in August 1962, leaving a balance ... for which the Company is liable.

Judgement was accordingly given in favour of the former Western State Internal Revenue.

Probably the only employment income cases that give rise to difficulty are those of directors of 'small' private companies who have current, loan and/or deposit accounts with those companies. Salaries, bonuses, commissions and perhaps even allowances are credited to one or more of these accounts, but tax is not immediately deducted under PAYE and paid over to the department in charge of tax.

The directors, who are invariably the principal shareholders, want the best of both worlds: minimal company tax by deduction of the remuneration in arriving at the assessable profits and no PAYE tax on that remuneration, which is being allowed to rest wholly or partly as an interest-free loan with the company. The argument advanced is that mere credit of remuneration to the individual director's accounts with their companies is not payment within the meaning of the PAYE regulations, and thus there can be no paying over of any PAYE tax until such time as the directors are actually seen to have drawn the money and used it for their own private purposes. This argument goes too far and is not to be accepted as it stands.

In a tax case involving interest, *Dowar v IR Commissioners* 19 TC 516 the judge implied that if the appellant had done something which showed that he lawfully held the dominion over the amount of interest he would have been treated as having received the amount. This is essentially the same as lawful right to the enjoyment of the use of the money; so it follows that if the directors (or their representatives) confirm, on enquiry, that they have the right to draw on their accounts – whether or not they exercise that right is immaterial – then there has been a payment of remuneration and the PAYE tax must be paid over.

Self-employment

The total income of any individual for any year of assessment or statutory total income is:

(a) the amount of his total assessable income of global or world income from all sources for that year, *plus*

(b) any balancing charges for that year, *minus*

(c) any loss relief for that year, *minus*

(d) any capital allowances for that year.

43

From the total assessable income are deducted reliefs. The net is *chargeable* income upon which tax is leviable at progressive rates.

Housing

The applicable tax incentives are granted to the individual, the owner-occupier of a building, and are only relevant to residents in the Mainland District of Lagos. Interest payable on the loan used for erecting a building is deductible from any income accruing to the owner and the expenditure incurred in erecting the building is eligible for capital allowances up to a ceiling of ₦100 000. Only one house per person is allowed and the house must be owner-occupied. The allowable interest on loan may be more than ₦100 000, but the capital alowance should not be an amount which exceeds ₦100 000, the amount that only salaried income earners can claim.

Cases on chargeable income

In *Owen v Burden*[4] the taxpayer's expenses in travelling to conference on his own initiative whether wholly, exclusively and necessarily incurred, were not deductible from taxable income. The taxpayer attended the World Road Congress at Tokyo in 1967 substantially at his own expense and claimed a deduction of £485 from his taxable income in respect of the air fare. At the conference he obtained an opinion on a scheme for a breach which was involved in his work. The expenses incurred were not reimbursed by his employer. The Court of Appeal upheld the decision of Plowman, J. who, in turn, had affirmed that of the General Commissioners, holding that as the taxpayer was not necessarily obliged to attend the conference as part of the duties of his office but had undertaken the trip on his own initiative the deduction claimed was not allowable. The expenses incurred were not laid out wholly, exclusively and necessarily in the performance of his duties.

In *Pritchard v Arundale*[5] the taxpayer, who had been a chartered accountant, gave up the practice of his profession to become a full-time company director upon terms that the principal shareholder and managing director would transfer to him 4000 shares, worth £7000, in the company 'in consideration of (the taxpayer) undertaking to serve the company'. The taxpayer was assessed under Schedule E on the value of the shares as a receipt of an emolument of an office or employment. The Special Commissioners decided that the value of the shares did not represent a reward for future services. Megarry, J. has affirmed that decision, holding that the onus of proof that the transfer fell within the charge to tax was upon the Crown and that it had not been discharged, and that there was not an emolument 'from' any office or employment nor one which was in the nature of a reward for services. Ultimately, '... it is the realities of the payments that matter and not any disguises or labels with which they may be provided.

In Ball v *Johnson*[6] the taxpayer, a bank employee, received rewards of £30 and £100 from his employer for passing examinations held by the Institution of Bankers. He was assessed to tax on this amount as additional remuneration. The General Commissioners found, in the taxpayer's favour, that the rewards were not made to the taxpayer for being an employee of the bank, that he had no legal entitlement to them, that they were discretionary payments, and that they were paid not for performing his duties as an employee but for his personal success in passing the examinations. Plowman, J. has affirmed the Commissioner's decision.

(ii) Income chargeable: income from trade, business, profession, and vocation

Two simple points should always be kept in mind. They are:
  (a) Income Tax is a tax on 'income',
  (b) The sources from which income arises are defined for tax purposes in the Income Tax Management Act.

The meaning given to 'income' by the Act does not entirely coincide with the popular conception of income. Examples will be seen of items commonly regarded as incomings but excluded from the scope of taxation and, on the other hand, items being brought within the tax field even though the man in the street would consider no income arose therefrom. Income is the fruit whilst capital is the tree. Thus rent (income) is the fruit from property (capital). Fares (income) are the fruits from vehicles (capital). Income means world income or global income or income from all sources.

In *Chief F.R.A. Williams v Regional Tax Board*,[7] The judge said that, in section 8 of the Income Tax Law of the former Western Region (now Oyo, Ondo, and Ogun States) provision is made for the definition of 'income' as follows: 'For the purpose of sub-section (1) of this section "income" shall mean income in respect of (a) gains or profits from any trade, business, profession or vocation ...' What then is gain or profit in the context of this provision? *The Concise Oxford Dictionary* defines profit as 'excess of returns over outlay' and gain as 'profit'. In section 13(1) of the Income Tax Law, this passage occurs:

For the purpose of ascertaining the income of any period from any source chargeable with tax there shall be deducted all outgoings and expenses wholly and exclusively incurred during that period by such person in the production of income...

At page 201 of Simon's *Income Tax*, the following is stated:

The general rule is that an item of expenses can be deducted in computing the profit of a trade if its deduction would be justified on business or accounting principles, but that, if a particular kind of deduction is statutorily prohibited, the deduction cannot be made even though it would be proper to make it from the point of view of commercial accountancy.

In *Lothian Chemical Co. Ltd v Inland Revenue Commissioners*[8] Lord Clyde said as follows:

... it has been said times without number – it has been said repeatedly in this Court – that in considering what is the true balance of profits or gains in the Income Tax Acts ... you deal in the main with ordinary principles of commercial accountancy. They do expressly exclude a number of deductions and allowances, some of which according to ordinary principles of commercial accounting might be allowable. But where these principles are not invaded by Statute they must be allowed to prevail.

The same principle as stated above was also followed in *Usher's Wiltshire Brewery Ltd v Bruce*[9] by Lord Sumner and there is no doubt that it has found favour with eminent English judges who were called upon to deal with tax problems from time to time. So that as far as those distinguished jurists were concerned, the general principles of commercial accounting will prevail unless prohibited by statute. In the Russell case cited by appellant, the point that fell to be decided by their lordships was whether or not the bank in the case was entitled to deduct from their profits before returning them for assessment under Schedule D the annual value of the whole bank premises, including the part occupied by the manager, and without hesitation they held that it was the proper thing to do. Lord Herschell in his lucid judgement said: 'The duty is to be charged upon a sum not less than the full amount of the balance of the profits or gains of the trade, manufacture, adventure or concern; and it appears to the Nigerian court that that language implies that for the purpose of arriving at the balance of profits all that expenditure which is necessary for the purpose of earning the receipts must be deducted, otherwise you do not arrive at the balance of profits, indeed, you do not ascertain and cannot ascertain, whether there is such a thing as profit or not. The profit of a trade or business,' continued Lord Herschell, 'is the surplus by which the receipts from the trade or business exceed the expenditure necessary for the purpose of earning those profits.' He went on, 'Unless and until you have ascertained that there is such a balance, nothing exists to which the word "profits" can properly be applied.' In another passage, the noble and learned lord said:

Now it is not disputed that the annual value of the premises exclusively used for business purposes is properly to be deducted in arriving at the balance of profits and gain.... It is quite true that, strictly speaking, the annual value where premises are owned and not rented, is not money laid out or expended for the purpose of the trade, but it is admitted, and must, I think, have been admitted, that in either the one way or the other that deduction is to be made, because inasmuch as it is clear that even in the case of a dwelling house a part of which is used for purposes wholly unconnected with the trade, the annual value of the portion which is used for the purpose of the trade is to be deducted.... It is to be deducted either by taking it as an element before arriving at the balance of profits and gains, or as included in a very broad construction of the provision relating to disbursement and expenses.

The Nigerian court holds that if the appellant does not own the portion of his house used exclusively for the purpose of earning his income, he would have had to hire one, since it is not disputed that the use of such premises is essential or necessary for carrying on his profession – indeed he cannot carry it on without such a place. Therefore, when section 8 of the Income Tax Law speaks of gains or profits and section 13 speaks of outgoings or expenses the Nigerian court applied[10] the same principles applied by Lords Herschell, Sumner and Clyde to several of their tax cases in arriving at gains or profits taxable, to this case. In the result the court came to the conclusion that in computing the chargeable income of the appellant the sum of £300 which he claimed as the annual rent of the apartment he used exclusively for the earning of his income was rightly deducted as coming within the spirit and intendment of the words 'outgoings and expenses' used in section 13 of the Income Tax Law and should be allowed to him as being necessary for the carrying-on of his profession.

Income Tax is strictly a tax on income. Lord Macmillan in *Van den Berghs Ltd v Clarke*[11] stated:

The Income Tax Acts nowhere define 'income' any more than they define 'capital'; they describe sources of income and prescribe methods of computing income, but what constitutes income they discreetly refrain from saying.... Consequently, it is to the decided cases that one must go in search of light.

The decided cases merely show that there are mainly three categories of income, namely:

1 income from personal services rendered by one person[12] to another;
2 income from property rights;
3 income from the profits of a trade, profession, or vocation.

'Income' must be money or something capable of being turned into money but not a mere privilege, even though valuable, except benefits in kind received by employees from their employers. Unless the use or occupation of land produces income, it is not regarded as income. Income is not capital and unless capital is taxable under Capital Gains Tax Act, it escapes tax altogether as it is not income. Similarly, an accretion to capital is not income as was decided in *Jones v Leaming* (1930), AC 415; *Kneen v Martin*[13] (1935), IKB 409, 19 TC 45; and *IRC v British Salmson Aero Engines Ltd* (1938), 2 KB 482, because it is used to increase or re-coup capital. The best definition of income for property comes from the Supreme Court of the United States:[14]

Here we have the essential matter; not a gain accruing to capital, not a profit, something of exchangeable value proceeding from the property, severed from the capital, however, invested or employed, and coming in, being derived, that is, received or drawn by the recipient (the taxpayer) for his separate use, benefit, and disposal; that is, income derived from property. Nothing else answers the description.

Emoluments which have been earned are not taxable until they are paid but when they are paid they are related back to the year for which they were paid as decided in *Heasman v Jordan* 1954 3 AER 101.

Trade, profession and vocation

The words 'trade, profession, and vocation' are not precise words and no law has laid down where 'trade' begins and ends. One has to study a large body of case law to determine what is 'trade'. Whether a transaction is a 'trade' depends on facts[15] and the word must be given its ordinary dictionary meaning[16]. Land managed on a commercial basis with a view to realising profits[17] constitutes trading. Buying and selling of food and services are generally regarded as trade. Where a finding of no trade is reversed, the Court must decide that the facts must constitute trading.[18] Where a finding of trade is affirmed, the Court must decide that there is an evidence to support the findings. The test of trading is objective and not subjective. What is important is the method used by the taxpayer not his motives.[19]

Thus if a taxpayer adopts commercial methods, his motive of non-profit-making may be immaterial even though profit motive is a factor in arriving at a trade. Presence of profit motive is not a conclusive test. Thus a man who invests his money in some asset in the hope that it will rise in value and that he will thereby make a profit has been held not to be a trader in *Jones v Leaming* (1930) AC 415. In *Religious Tract and Book Society v Forbes*,[20] the business of selling hymn books has been held to be a trade although the profits were distributed among widows and orphans of ministers and missionaries;[21] so was that of a restaurant whose proceeds went to support an institution for religions and social improvement.[22] A society for the advancement of agriculture has been held to be trading by an annual show.[23] The six 'badges' of trade are:

(1) the subject matter of the realisation;
(2) the length of the period of ownership;
(3) the frequency of the transaction;
(4) supplementary work on the property;
(5) the circumstances responsible for the transaction; and
(6) motive.[24]

Profits from the contracts before dissolution of a partnership or before the death of a trader have been held taxable in *Hillerns and Fowler v Murray* (1932) 17 TC 77.

A limited company cannot exercise a profession even if it employs professional men. The company carries on a trade.[25] A person who makes his living by successfully backing horses or playing cards is neither carrying on a profession nor a vocation.[26] An employee who writes plays in his spare time and gets one accepted is carrying on the profession of a dramatist,[27] and this goes for writers of books, who carry on the profession of a writer. Whilst trade includes an adventure or concern in the nature of trade there is no such extension of 'profession'.

The terms 'Profession and vocation' are well known. The provisions of the Regulated and other Professions (Miscellaneous Provisions) Act No. 5 of 1978,[28] the Institute of Chartered Accountants' Act No. 15 of 1965, the Medical Practitioners' Act, the Legal Practitioners' Act, etc., are guides to what is a 'profession' in Nigeria.

Income Tax is payable in respect of the gains or profits from any trade, business, profession, or vocation for whatever period of time that trade, business, profession or vacation may have been carried on, or exercised, inside or outside Nigeria.

(iii) Trade or business partly carried on in Nigeria[29]

If a trade or business is carried on partly inside and partly outside Nigeria by a taxable person *who is not himself in Nigeria*, the profits derived from Nigeria are deemed to be the profits attributable to that part of the operations carried on in Nigeria. In certain circumstances a person in Nigeria may carry on business with an individual, corporation sole, body of individuals, executor, or trustee outside Nigeria in such a way that less profits than normal accrue to the person in Nigeria. If such is the case then the person outside Nigeria is assessed to tax in the name of the person in Nigeria.

Where it is difficult to compute the true profits of the individuals, corporation sole, body of individuals, trustee or executor outside Nigeria but assessed in the name of a person in Nigeria, those profits may be estimated on a fair and reasonable percentage of the turnover of the business done through or with the person in Nigeria.

If the trade or business carried on by the individual, corporation sole, body of individuals, executor or trustee is outside Nigeria, but assessed in the name of a person in Nigeria, as the sale of goods or produce manufactured or produced outside Nigeria, then the person in Nigeria may apply to have the assessment based on the probable profits of a merchant or retailer dealing in the goods or produce directly. No such application can be made if the assessment is final and conclusive.

(iv) Computation of liability

Basis period

The main difficulties in devising a simple basis for the assessment of a trade, etc., are the fluctuations in profits and the taxpayer's right (whether he is an individual or a company) to make up his accounts to any date in the year that he considers most convenient to him and then to change that date whenever he wishes. First, let us consider the treatment of a well-established business, then the treatment of commencing and ceasing businesses and, finally, the treatment where there is a change of accounting date.

(A) *Normal basis period* (established businesses). The profits to be assessed are those of the preceding year ended 31 December [section 20(1) of ITMA and section 30(1) of CITA] but where the relevant tax authority – the Federal Board – is satisfied that the taxpayer (i.e. an individual or company) makes or intends to make up the accounts of his trade, etc., to some day other than 31 December it shall direct that the assessment from the trade, etc., source is to be the profits of the year ended on that day in the year preceding the year of assessment.

It should be noted that if the Board is satisfied (enquiry is, therefore, necessary about the permanent accounting date) the Board shall direct. This is the mandatory 'shall' and not the permissive 'may'; so, on the face of it, once satisfied, the Board must do what the Acts say, and it has no option to do otherwise.

(B) *New business* [section 20(3)(a)(b) & (c) of ITMA]. Note in this connection:

(i) that a foreign company, no matter how long or well established, is treated as setting up a new business in Nigeria when it first comes here to trade;

(ii) that, if a company engages in a trade or business *with any other person in Nigeria*, that trade or business is to be treated as a *separate* source of income and the profits of such company, subject to the proviso of section 30(8) CITA as regards capital allowances, shall be determined under the provision of section 6 of Income Tax Management Act in the same way as the assessable income of an individual partner in a partnership. As a separate source of income, the commencing and ceasing provisions will apply, subject only to section 20(8) of ITMA;

(iii) that, if it is necessary to split an account as submitted by a taxpayer to arrive at the profit of any trade, etc., for any specific period or periods, the allocation, apportionment or aggregation shall be made in proportion to the number of days in the respective periods, unless the Board directs otherwise having regard to any specific circumstances.

(a) *First year of Assessment, etc.* [section 20(3)(a) ITMA]. The basis of assessment for the year in which the trade is commenced is the actual profits of the period of trading from the date of commencement to the succeeding 31 December.

(b) *Second year of Assessment, etc.* [section 20(3)(b) ITMA]. The normal basis of assessment is the actual profits of the first year of trading from the date of commencement.

(c) *Third year of Assessment, etc.* [section 20(3)(c) ITMA]. The normal basis of assessment is the profits of the preceding year ended 31 December, but, where the Board is satisfied [see (A) above], the profits taken are those of the year to the permanent accounting date ended within that preceding year.

Example 5

A trade is commenced on 1 February 1980 and the accounts show the following profits:

Year ended 31 January 1981	₦6 000
Year ended 31 January 1982	₦9 000

The assessments are as follows:

1980 (first year of assessment)
Profits of period 1.2.80 to 31.12.80
$\frac{11}{12} \times$ ₦6000   ₦5 500
1981 (second year of assessment)
Profits of first twelve months to 31.1.81   ₦6 000
1982 (third year of assessment)
Profits of preceding year
(i.e. profits of accounting year to 31.1.81)   ₦6 000
1983
Profits of preceding trading year
(i.e. 31.1.82)   ₦9 000

Example 6

A trade is commenced on 1.11.80 and the accounts show the following profits:

8 months to 30.6.81	₦16 000
12 months to 30.6.82	₦30 000
12 months to 30.6.82	₦48 000

The assessments are as follows:

1980 (first year of assessment)
Profits of period 1.11.80 to 31.12.80
$\frac{1}{4} \times$ ₦16 000   ₦4 000
1981 (second year of assessment)
Profits of first 12 months to 31.10.81
₦16 000 + ($\frac{1}{2} \times$ ₦30 000   ₦31 000
1982 (third year of assessment)
As no 12 months' accounts ending in previous
year, profit of year to 31.12.81
($\frac{3}{4} \times$ ₦16 000) + ($\frac{1}{2} \times$ ₦30 000)   ₦27 000
1983
Profits of preceding trading year (Y/E 30.6.82)   ₦30 000
1984
Profits of preceding trading year (Y/E 30.6.83)   ₦48 000

Relief available for second and third year of trading

The taxpayer (i.e. any individual or company) is entitled to claim that the assessments for both the second and the third years of assessments (not either separately) shall be adjusted to the profits actually made in those years ended on 31 December. And to avoid delay in claiming the relief, it is provided that he may claim the benefit for the second year as soon as the figures are available with the right to revoke that claim if the results of the next year's trading, etc., show that there is no ultimate advantage to him. The relief is subject to time limits. The claim must be made within two years of the end of the second year of assessment and the revocation of any claim within twelve months of the end of the third. In short, the last date for making any claim is the same as for revoking one already made.

It is important to remember that the claims are in respect of the second and third years during which the trade, etc., is carried on, even though no assessment might have been made for the first year of trading on the grounds that the period of such trading was too short to justify an assessment in practice. Hence, the suspicion with which an inspector should view any statement that a trade, etc., was commenced on 1 April or a few days afterwards. The statements might be correct, but enquiry should be made to ensure that the date of commencement was not 31 December or a few days, or a week or a month before.

Example 7

A trade is commenced in Nigeria on 1.10.80 and the accounts shows the following profits:

1.10.81 to 31.12.81 (three months)	₦6 000
Year ending 31.12.82	8 000
Year ending 31.12.83	9 000
Year ending 31.12.84	16 000

If election for relief for the second and third years is not made, the assessments are as follows:

1981 (first year of assessment)
Profits of period 1.10.81 to 31.12.81
i.e. profit 1.10.81 to 31.12.81   ₦6 000
1982 (second year of assessment)
Profits of first twelve months 1.10.81 to 30.9.82
i.e. profit 1.10.81 to 31.12.81   ₦6 000
+ profit 1.1.82 to 30.9.82 ($\frac{3}{4} \times$ ₦8000)   ₦6 000
                                        ₦12 000

1983	8 000
1984	9 000
1985	16 000

If an election is made, the assessments for 1982 and 1983 become:

1982
Actual profits to 31.12.82
= (1.1.82 to 31.12.82)
= ₦8000 as compared with ₦12 000 originally assessed.
1983

Actual profits of year ended 31.12.83 (i.e. 1.1.83 to 31.12.83) equal ₦9000 as compared with ₦8000 originally assessed.

Revised assessment on actual basis		*Original assessment on normal basis*
1982	₦8 000	₦12 000
1983	₦9 000	₦ 8 000
Total for years 2 & 3	₦17 000	₦20 000

The assessments for 1984 and 1985, however, remain unaltered. Regard will be paid by an individual to changes in personal deductions and rates of tax in making up his mind to make a claim; and by a company to changes in the rates of tax and capital allowances, even to any title it has to small companies relief, and exemption from tax on first ₦6000 profits, where applicable.

(v) Cessation[30]

When a taxpayer (an individual or a company) permanently ceases to carry on or to exercise a trade, etc., (and this includes a non-Nigerian company ceasing to carry on or to exercise a trade, etc., in Nigeria) both the assessments of the year of cessation and the year immediately preceding that year (i.e. the penultimate year) have to be reviewed. The assessment for the year of cessation is adjusted to the actual profits from the preceding 1 January to the date of cessation. The assessment for the penultimate year remains unaltered, unless the amount of actual profits earned in that year is more than the amount already assessed on the normal preceding year basis, in which case an additional assessment is made to increase the final assessment up to those actual profits. 'Provided that where the income of the year of assessment preceding that in which cessation occurs is for a period of nine months from 1st April to 31st December 1980, the income shall be grossed up as if it was the income of twelve months'.

As is not the case with income from other sources, where the liability to tax continues whether the source has ceased or not, the adjustments on cessation of a trade, etc., (but only of a trade , etc.)

are final. Liability ceases immediately the source itself ceases. See ITMA 20(10) and CITA 30(7) for authority to treat income or expenses received or incurred after cessation of trade as having been received or paid on the last day of business.

The case of *Mansen v Wesley* 16 TC 654 provides authority, if authority is required, to split accounts in order to arrive at the actual profits. It enables the profits of the taxpayer's accounting year to end within the year of assessment.

Example 8

An individual permanently ceased to carry on his trade in Nigeria on 30.9.82. His accounts have shown the following profits:

year ended 31.12.80	₦10 000
year ended 31.12.81	₦12 000
1.1.82 to 30.9.82	6 000

The original assessments were:

1981 – year ended 31.12.80	₦10 000
1982 – year ended 31.12.81	12 000

On cessation of the trade:

(a) the assessment for the penultimate year 1981 is reviewed; the actual profit of the year (i.e. 1.1.81–31.12.81)

₦12 000

₦12 000

is compared with the amount assessed, ₦10 000 and the assessment is increased to the larger of the two figures and *never* reduced to the smaller of the two;

(b) the assessment for the year of cessation, 1982, is reduced from the amount assessed, ₦12 000, to the actual profits of the period (i.e. 1.1.82–30.9.82), ₦6000;

(c) there is no assessment for the year 1983.

Example 9

A company permanently ceased to carry on its trade in Nigeria on 30.6.82. Its accounts have shown the following profits:

year to 30.6.80	₦10 000
year to 30.6.81	8 000
year to 30.6.82 (date of cessation)	16 000

If there was *no* cessation the assessment would be based on

1981	₦10 000
1982	8 000
1983	16 000

But because of the cessation, there is no assessment for 1983. The profit for 1982 is increased to ₦16 000 and the profit for 1981 is reduced from ₦10 000 to ₦8000 the actual profits of the penultimate year.

Example 10 (commencing and ceasing business)

A company began to trade on 1.7.81 and ceased on 30.9.87 with the following results:

12 months to 30.6.82 profit	₦30 000
12 months to 30.6.83 profit	6 000
12 months to 30.6.84 profit	12 000
12 months to 30.6.85 profit	10 000
12 months to 30.6.86 profit	40 000
12 months to 30.9.86 profit	3 000

The assessments are calculated as follows:

1981: 6 months to 31.12.81 $\frac{6}{12} \times$ ₦30 000 = ₦15 000
1982: 12 months to 30.6.82   ₦30 000 (first year basis)
1983: 12 months to 30.6.82   ₦30 000 (preceding year basis)

Review of 1983 and 1984

1981: 1.1.82 to 30.6.82	$\frac{1}{2} \times$ ₦30 000	=	₦15 000	
1.7.82 to 31.12.82	$\frac{1}{2} \times$ ₦6000	=	3 000	
Actual profits of the year			₦18 000	₦18 000

1982: 1.1.83 to 30.6.83	$\frac{1}{2} \times$ ₦6000	=	₦3000	
1.7.83 to 31.12.83	$\frac{1}{2} \times$ ₦12 000	=	6000	
			₦9000	9 000

Combined revised profits	₦27 000
Combined assessments ₦30 000 + ₦30 000	₦60 000

This ₦60 000 is clearly in excess of ₦27 000 so reduce 1982 to ₦18 000, and 1983 to ₦9000. This is not always a fool-proof test.

1984 assessment on preceding year basis to 30.6.83 =	₦6 000
1985 assessment on preceding year basis to 30.6.84 =	₦12 000

But, as 1984 is the penultimate year of the trade, review as under:

56

1.1.85 to 30.6.85	$\frac{1}{2} \times$ ₦10 000 =	₦5 000
1.7.85 to 31.12.85	$\frac{1}{2} \times$ ₦40 000 =	20 000
		₦25 000

The actual profits of ₦25 000 exceed ₦12 000 as increase 1985 to ₦25 000. (This adjustment to actual profits *must* be made by the Department whether or not any additional liability in terms of tax arises from the adjustment.)

1986 final year, based on actual profits, thus:

1.4.86 to 30.6.86	$\frac{1}{2} \times$ ₦40 000 =	₦20 000
1.7.86 to 30.9.86	=	3 000
		₦23 000

Example 11

Mr Spaghetti, an Italian, was the Managing Director of Efon-Alaye Trading Company Ltd, until 30 September 1988 when as a result of Nigerianisation he found himself redundant. Mr Spaghetti was on a salary of ₦24 000 per annum and enjoyed the following benefits from his employment:

(i) He lived in a house rented by his employers at a rent of ₦30 000 per annum. The annual value of the house for local rates was ₦3000.

(ii) Furnishings cost ₦50 000 and were paid for by the Efon-Alaye Trading Co. Ltd.

(iii) Mr Spaghetti had an entertainment allowance of ₦300 a month and was not required to provide details of his expenses in this connection and he never did.

(iv) Security at his residence cost ₦10 000 a year and Efon-Alaye Trading Co. Ltd, paid for his steward which cost 3₦600 a year.

(v) Company cars for his sole use cost ₦20 000.

As compensation for loss of office, his employment contract provided for three times his terminal annual salary. Mr Spaghetti was a bachelor but maintained his aged father and mother and paid ₦1500 as life assurance premium. He left Nigeria as an expatriate on 1 October 1988. Compute Mr Spaghetti's tax liabilities assuming his effective income tax rate was 35 per cent. Also state the relevant year of assessment.

Solution

Mr Spaghetti: *Income Tax Computation for the 1988 year of assessment*

Salary (Note 1)		₦18 000.00
Compensation for loss of office (Note 2)		72 000.00

Add: *Benefits in kind:*

House occupied (Note 3)	₦2 250.00	
Furnishings (Note 4)	1 875.00	
Entertainment allowance (Note 5)	2 700.00	
Steward (Note 6)	2 700.00	
Company car (Note 7)	750.00	
		10 275.00
Assessable Income		100 275.00

Less: *Reliefs:*

Personal allowance (Note 8)	13 734.00	
Dependent relative	400.00	
Life Insurance	1 500.00	15 634.00
Chargeable Income		₦84 641.00
Tax Payable at 35%		₦33 856.00

Note 1

This is in respect of salary earned by him for nine months between 1 January 1988 and 30 September 1988. He did not complete the 1988 fiscal year before he became redundant; i.e. $\frac{9}{12} \times$ ₦24 000 = ₦18 000.

Note 2

His Contract of Employment provided for three times his terminal annual salary as compensation for loss of office, i.e. 3 × ₦24 000 = ₦72 000.

Note 3

Where any premises in Nigeria are made available to an employee, the benefit in kind shall be deemed to be the rateable value. In practice 20 per cent of the rent paid by the employer is assessed where the rateable value is unknown. However the relevant period, as stated in Note 1, is $\frac{9}{12}$ ₦3000 = ₦2250 (s.4A ITMA 1961).

Note 4

Where any asset which continues to belong to an employer is used by the employee (in this case furniture) the benefit in kind shall be deemed to be 5 per cent of the cost or market value if cost cannot be ascertained, i.e. 5% × 50 000 = 2500 but because he enjoyed it for only nine months during the tax year $\frac{9}{12} \times$ 2500 = ₦1875 will be added to his income.

Note 5

Entertainment allowance of (₦300 × 9) = ₦2700 is assessable in the hand of Mr Spaghetti because he was not required to provide details of his expenses. This means that he may not even spend any part of the money on entertainment!

Note 6
Cost of maintaining a steward for him is also assessable. This is the salary paid to the steward for nine months, i.e. $\frac{9}{12} \times$ ₦3600 = ₦2700.

Note 7
These cars are assets belonging to the employer and the benefit in kind from their use by the employee is 5 per cent of their cost by virtue of sec. 4A of the 1961 Act. Thus 5% $\times$ 20000 = ₦1000, but he used it for only nine months; it will be $\frac{9}{12} \times 1000$ = ₦750.

Note 8
Personal allowance for Mr Spaghetti is ₦1200 plus $12\frac{1}{2}$% of ₦100275 = ₦13734: section 8 of the 1985 Decree.

Receipts and payments after cessation

Sums may be received or paid after an individual's trade has ceased. If those sums would have been treated as trading receipts or expenses while the trade continued, and they were received or paid by the individual (or after his death by his personal representatives) then they are deemed to have been received or paid on the last day on which the individual carried on his trade.

Change of residence

If the state in which an individual carrying on a trade is deemed to be resident is changed from one year to another then the individual is not treated as having commenced or ceased to trade for that reason alone. The assessments on his trading profits continue on the normal basis.

Partnerships

If an individual carrying on a trade becomes a partner in a partnership which then carries on the same trade, continuity of assessment applies and the cessation and commencement provisions are not imposed.

Similarly, if an individual carries on the same trade, previously carried on by a partnership of which he was a partner, continuity of assessment applies.

If a former employee enters into partnership with his former employer, the employee's remuneration in the basis period is not to be added back in computing the partnership profits.

(vi) The discriminatory aspect of Income Tax law

Apart from the law exempting from tax the official emoluments of Head of State, State Governors, and the non-official salary of others, Income Tax law also appears to encourage sex discrimination. There is a growing consensus that the present system of personal taxation is in need of reform so as to promote greater equality between men and women in terms of treatment, benefits and allowances. The main point here is to stimulate a wide-ranging discussion of the feasible options for reform.

Taxation is not only a method of raising revenue; it is also an instrument of social policy. Governments customarily use changes in taxation as a way of encouraging or discouraging a very wide range of social behaviour. Private decisions to invest in industrial development in regions where such development would not otherwise have taken place; individual decisions to buy foreign products in preference to domestic products; the general trend towards an increase in tobacco or alcohol consumption – all these trends can be encouraged or discouraged by the government's taxation policy. The same is true in the field of personal taxation. Here too, the structure of personal taxation can, either deliberately or, more often, unwittingly, contribute to, or hinder progress towards equal opportunities for men and women.

Any system of taxation on personal income is bound not only to be complex, but also to reveal inconsistencies from time to time, simply because the system changes as a result of the economic policies of successive governments, and as a result of the introduction of new forms of tax liabilities and new forms of benefits and allowances, the consequences of which cannot be completely foreseen at once. In this way a structure of personal taxation can evolve piecemeal over time which works to the disadvantage of one group compared to another.

It follows from this traditional pattern of piecemeal evolution that for many people the way in which the tax system works is likely to remain an impenetrable mystery. This difficulty is one shared by men and women alike, although the Inland Revenue's reluctance to advertise certain benefits which might be advantageous to many women (such as separate assessment) can arguably contribute to a greater degree of ignorance as well as disadvantage among women than among men.

It should be noted that the complaints come exclusively from women. Naturally, women form the larger group of persons who have written to complain about the humiliation involved in the assumption, at all stages of their dealings with the Inland Revenue, that joint income is the property of the husband, as well as about the anomalies involved (e.g. where a working woman whose husband is unemployed is not usually given the reliefs to which she is entitled without considerable correspondence and delay).

Secondly, women are earning more and their contribution to the total family income is increasing, and more of their income is now coming within the tax threshold. The central question which must underlie any discussion of reform is: what is to be the basic tax unit? If it is to be the family as a whole, how can a system which treats the family as its basic unit be amended so as not to discriminate against either husbands or wives? If it is to be the individual, what implications will this have for the family as a social unit? But total disaggregation is not the only way in which the tax system can recognise the individual existence of partners in a marriage. Nor does treating partners in a marriage as individuals in their own right involve a disregard for the importance of marriage as an institution or of the family as a social unit.

The present practices of the Inland Revenue could be held to involve a substantial amount of interference in the internal affairs of a married couple: Can a woman have a little cash to call her own without upsetting a marriage and causing a lot of misery? How much information about each other should the partners in a marriage choose to reveal to each other? What many people, men as well as women, find distressing is not only that the Inland Revenue's practices involve an invasion of this privacy, but also that the information is divulged only in one direction – it is always the wife's financial affairs which are required to be disclosed to the husband, never *vice versa*. A taxation system for the future which is based on the proposition that the partners in a marriage are entitled to be treated as individuals in their own right is not likely therefore to weaken or damage the unity of the family. On the contrary, it will prevent a good deal of the unnecessary humiliation and distress caused by the present arrangements. It is also much more likely to be in tune with emerging social trends.

The more prosperous a Nigerian is, the more so his dependent relatives. Nigerian culture and the Nigerian Constitution recognise plurality of wives and children. It is an open secret that Nigerian working married women employ house-helps in the discharge of their marital duties whilst at the same time, they contribute their quota in their places of employment without enjoying the same reliefs as their husbands. A wife's earned income relief of ₦1000 or one-tenth of earned income is suggested to be given to all married women in employment.

The maximum income tax rate of 70 per cent, which encourages tax evasion, should be reduced to 45 per cent, as this is the maximum that limited liability companies pay. Children's allowance should be for six and not for four children. Taxpayers' fraudulent practices in the manipulation of personal reliefs are partly due to ineffective tax administration and to the low degree of technical knowledge by some state tax officials. Experience in 1980, when the country's fiscal year was changed to January–December, showed, for example, that allowable expenses were disallowed and personal reliefs were proportionately reduced because the 1980 financial year was a nine-month period. The Tax authorities do not see themselves as umpires between government and the taxpayers. Instead, some of them deny the taxpayers their statutory rights. Voluntary compliance by the taxpayers is hardly possible under a condition in which the public have no confidence in the revenue officials. Funding the Treasuries at the expense of the taxpayers' statutory rights can only increase the rate of tax evasion and expensive and ineffective compulsory compliance.

Discouragement by the tax officials of audited accounts of taxpayers raises another question of lack of confidence between the practising accountants and the Revenue; and the use of best of judgement assessments by the Revenue as a basis of issue of tax clearance certificates is annoying to the law-abiding educated elites.

The law which is so expensively administered that it collects more revenue from employees than from the self-employed in spite of its old age and the number of taxpayers is obviously discriminatory. A civilian government should be able to accord any Internal Revenue Division a parastatal status with a statistics section, finding out from institutional sources (banks, ministries, firms, etc.) taxpayers' sources of income locally and overseas and employ Tax Messengers whose duties should be confined to combing of every area and collecting names and addresses from every street, vehicles, markets, etc. This country also urgently needs to issue National Identity Cards to all taxable citizens. This will not only increase the number of taxpayers but will also lead to pre-determined scientific incomes for almost every person rather than the present best of judgement assessments which 'manufacture' figures of income of taxpayers which are usually lower than their actual income. More, and decent, tax offices should also be opened to bring tax offices nearer to the people. The pattern of the future is clear. So is the case for change. The next step forward will be to decide what form this change should take.

(vii) The Pay-As-You-Earn system of tax

The PAYE method of deducting Income Tax from salaries and wages is applied, on the direction of the relevant tax authority under the

Income Tax Management Act, 1961 and the Personal Tax Act, 1981 to income from employments, appointments, and offices for which remuneration is payable and to pensions. Thus PAYE applies not only to weekly or monthly salaries, wages and pensions but also to annual salaries, bonuses, commissions, directors' fees, etc.; it is a method by which an employee pays the Income Tax on his earnings from employment and other sources in twelve monthly instalments over the year. It is not a tax separate or different from Income Tax.

This method of deducting income tax applies to all employees resident in all States of the Federation and to all income from employment exercised in Nigeria by such residents, even if the employee is temporarily outside Nigeria (on leave or otherwise), or receives his pay outside Nigeria.

Residence revisited for PAYE tax purposes

Not all employees are automatically subject to a State Income Tax. It is only when such employees are deemed to be resident in a State that they are liable to PAYE.

There is no difficulty with the majority of employees: those who live and work constantly in a State are normally within the scope of the State PAYE scheme.

An employee may be deemed to be resident in a different State in Nigeria from year to year if he changes the place of his home, employment, etc. At the same time, an employee can only be deemed to be resident in one State for any one Income Tax year: once the State of residence has been determined it may not be changed until the following 1 January at the earliest.

In the case of **Nigerian Employment** i.e. an employment the duties of which are wholly or partly performed in Nigeria: if an individual is in Nigerian employment on 1 January starting an Income Tax year, he is deemed to be resident for that Income Tax year where his home is situated on that 1 January.

If his home is in a State on 1 January the employee is deemed to be resident in that State for that Income Tax year.

'Home' means a place available for the individual's domestic use in Nigeria: it does not include any hotel, rest-house, etc. at which he is lodging temporarily unless there is no more permanent place available for his use.

If an individual has more than one home in different territories on the same day, the home to be taken for residence purposes is:

(a) for a pensioner with no income from employment, trade, business, profession or vocation, the place where he usually resides;

(b) for an employee, the place nearest to his usual place of work.

(c) for an individual on leave from Nigerian employment on 1 January starting an Income Tax year, where his employment is exercised on 1 January of that year.

If his home was in a particular State just before his leave began, the employee is deemed to be resident in that State for that Income Tax year.

If an individual first becomes liable to any Nigerian Income Tax year by entering Nigerian employment in that year, he is deemed to be resident for that Income Tax year where his home is situated on the day the full duties of the employment start.

If his home is in a particular State on the day the full duties of the employment start the employee is deemed to be resident in that State for that Income Tax year.

In the case of a **foreign employment,** i.e. an employment the duties of which are wholly performed outside Nigeria except during any temporary visit of the employee to Nigeria:

(a) if an individual is in foreign employment on 1 January starting an Income Tax year, he is deemed to be resident for that Income Tax year where his employer's principal office is situated on that 1 January.

If the employer's principal office is in a particular State on 1 January the employee is deemed to be resident in that State for that Income Tax year.

(b) If an individual first becomes liable to any Nigerian Income Tax for an Income Tax year by entering foreign employment during that year, he is deemed to be resident for that Income Tax year where his employer's principal office is situated on the day his foreign employment starts.

If the employer's principal office is in a particular State on the day his employment starts, the employee is deemed to be resident in that State for that Income Tax year.

In the case of **other employment:**

(a) An employee whose remuneration is subject to any Nigerian Income Tax for an Income Tax year but who cannot be deemed to be resident in a State for that year under the provisions headed 'Nigerian employment' is to be treated as an individual in 'Foreign employment'. If he has no territory of residence under those provisions then he is deemed to be resident in Lagos.

(b) A full-time employee in any capacity in the armed forces of Nigeria on 1 January starting an Income Tax year, or who first becomes liable to Nigerian Income Tax for an Income Tax year by entering such employment during that year, is deemed to be resident in Lagos for that Income Tax year.

As for **pensioners who are still in employment,** the rules applicable to employment will determine whether or not the individual is deemed to be resident in any one State.

Any other pensioner who has a home in Nigeria on 1 January starting an Income Tax year, and has no income from employment, trade, business, profession or vocation on that day, is deemed to be resident for that Income Tax year where his home is situated on that 1 January.

If his home is in a particular State on 1 January the pensioner is deemed to be resident in that State for that Income Tax year.

A pensioner who has no home in Nigeria on 1 January starting an Income Tax year, and has no income from employment, trade, business or vocation on that day, is deemed to be resident for that Income Tax year as follows:

(a) If the pension is not a government pension wholly payable by the government of one territory, the pensioner is deemed to be resident in that territory.

If the pension is wholly payable by a State government the pensioner is deemed to be resident in that State for that year.

(b) If the pension is not a government pension, the pensioner is deemed to be where the principal office in Nigeria of the person authorising payment is situated.

If the payer's principal office is in a particular State government the pensioner is deemed to be resident in that State for that year.

(c) If the pension is a government pension payable by more than one government in Nigeria or there are two or more pensions arising in different territories on 1 January the pensioner is deemed to be resident in Lagos.

Meaning of earnings liable to PAYE tax or total pay

The sum of all items of 'pay' to the employee during any remuneration period is called 'total pay'.

The 'total pay' of any week, fortnight, half-month or month may include one or more of the following items.

(a) All incomes including salary/fees, commissions, bonus and allowances and all expenses paid and incurred by the company on behalf of the director which are not wholly, exclusively, necessarily, and reasonably for the purpose of the business are regarded as taxable income of the director. All incomes from sources other than the company are also liable to tax.

(b) Any salary, wages, fees, allowances or other gains or profits from an employment which are paid or payable in money by the employer to the employee:

bonus	lodging and ration allowance
commission	language gratuities
pension	responsibility allowance
overtime pay	allowance in lieu of overtime allowance
sick pay	acting pay or allowance
dirty pay	cost of Living pay or allowance
danger pay	employee's share of profits
holiday pay	family, child etc, allowance
leave pay	pay paid to an employee after he has left
deferred pay	payments in lieu of benefits in kind, e.g.
trade pay	board wages
duty and staff pay	

(c) Gratuities paid out by the employer, e.g. from a service charge other than:
  (i) so much of any such sums as may be admitted by the Relevant Tax Authority to represent reimbursement to the employee of expenses incurred by him in the performance of his duties and from which it is not intended that the employee should make any profit or gain;
  (ii) in respect of medical or dental expenses incurred by the employee; or
  (iii) in respect of the cost of any passage to or from Nigeria incurred by the employee.

The list above is not exhaustive and if an employer is in doubt as to whether any payment is to be included in 'total pay' he should consult the Relevant Tax Authority, giving full details of the circumstances in which payment is being made. Other payments are described below.

Lump sum payments, gifts and voluntary allowances

A sum paid by an employer to his employee under this heading should be included in 'total pay' unless it can clearly be established that the payment was not for services in that employment.

In the case of non-subordinate employees, e.g. directors, managers, etc., and in other cases not covered by the following paragraph the full facts behind such a payment should be reported to the Relevant Tax

Authority for a decision as to whether the payment is to be included in 'total pay':

    (a) salary or wages in lieu of notice;

    (b) *ex gratia* payments such as redundancy payments, severance pay, leaving-gratuities, etc. made, when their jobs end, to classes of workers who become redundant for reasons beyond their control and this treatment may apply even when:

        (i) payment is calculated by length of service;

        (ii) payment may be conditional upon continued service by the employee for a short period consistent with the reasonable requirements of the employer's business; or

        (iii) payment is covered by an agreement with a trade union;

    (c) voluntary payments casually given by an employer to an employee primarily as token of personal esteem or as a contribution for a specific private purpose (e.g. as a wedding gift, but not as a Christmas present).

Accommodation provided by employer

The value of living accommodation provided directly by the employer for the use of an employee is not to be taken into account in arriving at 'total pay'.

Any rent payable by the employee is not to be deducted from 'total pay' for PAYE purposes.

Pecuniary responsibilities

If the employee is, under his contract of service, personally and pecuniarily liable to his employer in respect of any loss incurred in the performance of his duties the remuneration to be shown on the Tax Deduction Card as 'total pay' should be the net amount after the deduction by the employer of any sum making good such deficiency.

Loans to employees

A loan made by an employer to his employee is not 'pay'. If the loan repayments are made by deduction from the employee's remuneration those repayments are not to be taken into account for PAYE purposes, i.e. the 'total pay' to be shown on the Tax Deduction Card should be the remuneration before deduction of loan repayments.

Payments in advance or on account of remuneration are not loans.

Expenses payments

Payments for medical or dental expenses
The employer is to exclude from 'total pay' any sum paid by him to the employee in respect of *bona fide* medical or dental expenses which have been incurred by the employee.

Payments for passages
The employer is to exclude from 'total pay' any sum paid by him to the employee in respect of the cost of any passage to or from Nigeria incurred by the employee.

The amount of any payment made by the employer to the employee in respect of the cost of leave transport inside Nigeria is to be excluded from 'total pay' but the amount of the payment during the year should be noted in the blank space on the back of the Tax Deduction Card.

Payment for expenses incurred by the employee in performing his duties
The employer is not to exclude from 'total pay' any sum intended to reimburse the employee for expenses incurred by the employee in performing his duties unless written authority to exclude such sum from 'total pay' has been received from the Relevant Tax Authority. That written authority is called a dispensation.

If the Revenue officials do not give specific direction as to the treatment of any expenses payment and a dispensation has not been given, the employer must include the expenses in 'total pay'. If the employer wishes, he may apply for dispensation by furnishing the Relevant Tax Authority with a full statement in writing of the cases and the circumstances in which the expenses payment is made.

Otherwise, the employee himself is entitled to claim relief for any allowable portion of an expenses payment which the employer has included in 'total pay'.

Guest Allowance
Any allowance paid to the employee as reimbursement of expenses incurred in accommodating a guest of the employer may be excluded from 'total' provided that such allowance does not exceed ₦2 per day per guest.

Entertainment Allowance
Any entertainment allowance, other than Guest allowances paid to the employee is to be included in 'total pay' unless written dispensation

authorising exclusion has been obtained by the employer from the relevant tax authority.

Motor Mileage Allowance
Any motor mileage allowance paid to the employee is to be included in 'total pay' unless written dispensation authorising exclusion has been obtained by the employer from the Relevant Tax Authority.

Motor Basic Allowance
Any motor basic allowance paid to the employee is to be included in 'total pay' unless:
- (a) written dispensation authorising exclusion has been obtained by the employer from the Relevant Tax Authority;
- (b) the allowance
  - (i) is not greater than the Government basic allowance;
  - (ii) is primarily intended to assist the employee to own a vehicle available for use in the employment; and
  - (iii) is payable only in respect of a vehicle which is owned or is being acquired under a hire purchase agreement by the employee.

If any basic allowance is excluded from 'total pay' under (b) above, the amount of the payment during the year should be noted in the blank space on the back of the Tax Deduction Card.

Bicycle Allowance
Any allowance paid to the employee and calculated to do no more than reimburse the employee for providing a bicycle for use in his employment may be excluded from 'total pay'.

Other travelling and allied allowances
Any other travelling or allied allowance paid to the employee is to be included in 'total pay' unless written dispensation authorising exclusion has been obtained by the employer from the Relevant Tax Authority.

Tools, etc. Allowance
Any allowance paid to the employee and calculated to do no more than reimburse the employee for providing a uniform or protective clothing for wear in his employment may be excluded from 'total pay'.

Clothing Allowance
Any allowance paid to the employee and calculated to do no more

than reimburse the employee for providing a uniform or protective clothing for wear in his employment may be excluded from 'total pay'.

Allowances to student employees

If an employee or former employee is attending any educational or training establishment, all payments in respect of allowances or educational endowment made to him by the employer are to be included in 'total pay' unless written dispensation authorising exclusion has been obtained by the employer from the Relevant Tax Authority.

Dispensation may be granted on concessionary basis within the following annual limits:

₦800 per annum if full-time instruction is received in West Africa in preparation for a degree in medicine.

₦600 per annum if other full-time instruction is received in West Africa, or

₦1100 per annum if full-time instruction is received elsewhere than in West Africa.

In arriving at the amount of the dispensation in any case, there will be deducted from the annual limit above any payments made for the benefit of the employee but not paid directly to him.

Payments in advance or on account

Payments in advance or on account (including drawings in advance or on account of directors, remuneration) should be entered in the 'total pay' column in the month in which the advance or payment was made. Income Tax is to be deducted by reference to Tax Tables for the month in which the payment was made.

A salary advance to an employee paid weekly should not, however be entered in the 'total pay' column when it is paid. Care must be taken so that Income Tax is deducted from the full amount and so that the advance is properly included in the 'total pay'.

Payments credited to an account of a director or other employee

Crediting pay to a director's or other employee's bank account constitutes 'payment' in the same way as payment in cash. Tax should be deducted or refunded, and the Tax Deduction Card completed, accordingly.

This applies also to remuneration voted to a director and credited to an account with the Company on which he is free to draw, or applied to the reduction of a debt due from him to the Company (unless the debt arose from a payment in advance or on account of remuneration from which Income Tax was earlier deducted).

Meal Vouchers

Where an employer has an arrangement under which meal vouchers are issued to his employees, the value of the vouchers issued to an employee is not regarded as part of his taxable income provided the following conditions are satisfied:

(a) the vouchers are non-transferable and used for meals only;

(b) where any restriction is placed on their issue to employees they are available to the lower-paid staff;

(c) the value of vouchers issued to an employee does not exceed 15k each full working day.

The value of vouchers not satisfying conditions (a) and (b) is chargeable to tax; at the end of the year the employer will be required to make a return of their value. When condition (c) alone is not satisfied only the value in excess of 15k a day is regarded as taxable income and is to be shown in a return at the end of the year.

Cash payments to employees for meals should be included in pay for tax deduction purposes of the employees concerned except where the payments are for extra living expenses incurred by employees working temporarily away from their normal place of work.

If the employer is doubtful whether a voucher arrangement complies with the conditions set out above or whether a cash payment should be treated as pay for tax deduction purposes he should consult the Relevant Tax Authority.

Doubtful 'payment'

Should 'pay' be credited to a director or other employee in some special way which makes it doubtful whether the 'pay' has actually been 'paid', the full facts should be reported to the Relevant Tax Authority for advice.

Income exempted under PAYE

Certain income from employments and pensions which would otherwise be chargeable to Income Tax is exempted by the Taxing Acts.

Under the Adaptation of Laws (Miscellaneous Provisions) Order, 1965, certain modifications were made to the Income Exemption Provisions of the Income Tax Management Act, 1961.

1 The official emoluments of the Governor, and of any person performing the functions of the Governor, received by such person in his capacity as such.

2 The establishment allowance of a chief.

3 Allowances paid to any member of the Executive Council or the

Legislative Houses of a State or of the Council of Minister or Parliament for attendance at meetings of any such body or of any committee thereof.

4   The remuneration of any consular officer or employee of a foreign state except where:
- (a) the employee is engaged on domestic duties or
- (b) the employee ordinarily resides in Nigeria and is not also a national of that foreign State.

5   The emoluments payable from United Kingdom funds to an individual in the permanent service of the United Kingdom government in Nigeria in respect of his office under the United Kingdom government except where:
- (a) the employee is a citizen of Nigeria; or
- (b) the employee ordinarily resides in Nigeria.

6   The remuneration of any employee, other than a citizen of Nigeria, of any government, organisation or agency between which and the Government of the Federation or of a State there exists an arrangement for technical assistance, in so far as and to the extent only that the employment is solely in pursuit of such technical assistance arrangement.

7   The income of any national of the United States of America from employment by the Internal Cooperation Administration, being an Administration or Agency formed and directed by the Government of that country.

8   The income of any national of the United States of America from employment by the International Development Services as agents for the International Cooperation Administration.

9   The income of any individual from employment by the Ohio University of Athens, Ohio, as agent for the International Cooperation Administration, in connection with any scheme for the training of teachers in Nigeria.

10   Wound and disability pensions granted to members of the armed forces or of any recognised national defence organisation or to persons injured as a result of enemy action.

11   Pensions granted to any person under the provisions of Widow's and Orphans' Pensions Ordinance.

12   Gratuities payable to a public officer by the Government of the Federation or of a State in respect of services rendered by him under a contract of service with such Government and described as gratuities either in such contract or some other document issued by or on behalf of such Government in connection with such contract.

Where, however,
- (a) the period of service (if continuous) does not amount to five years; or

(b) the aggregate period of service in any 63 consecutive months (if gratuities exceed a sum calculated at the rate of ₦1000 per annum for such period or aggregate period, the amount of any such excess shall be exempt but shall be deemed to be income of the last day of the employment including any terminal leave arising from the employment.

13   Gratuities payable to a member or former member of the staff of the Nigerian College of Arts, Science and Technology by the College in respect of service with the college and described as gratuities either in such contract or in some other document issued by or on behalf of the College in connection with such contract. 'Member of the staff' means here an individual appointed to an office specified in the Second Schedule to the Nigeria College of Arts, Science and Technology Ordinance.

Where, however,

(a) the period of service (if continuous) does not amount to five years; or

(b) the aggregate period of service in any 63 consecutive months (if service is not continuous) does not amount to five years, and the total gratuities exceed a sum calculated at the rate of ₦1000 per annum for such period or aggregate period, the amount of any such excess shall be exempt but shall be deemed to be income of the last day of the employment including any terminal leave arising from the employment.

14   Gratuities payable to an employee or former employee under a contract of service with a body established by any of the following:

West African Institute for Trypanosomiasis Research Ordinance,
West African Institute for Oil Palm Research Ordinance,
West African Council for Medical Research Ordinance, being a gratuity so described either in his contract of service with such body or in some other document issued by or on behalf of such body in connection with that contract, subject to the following conditions:

(a) Where the service of an employee with any such body terminates then if the gratuity or aggregate gratuities paid or payable in respect of that service exceed one-quarter of the whole income arising to him from that employment including such gratuity or aggregate gratuities, that excess shall not be exempt but shall be deemed to be income of the employee of the last day of his employment including any terminal leave arising from that employment;

(b) where the service of an employee with any such body (or the aggregate service under two or more contracts within any period of 63 months) does not amount to five years, then upon the employee permanently ceasing such service with the body, if the gratuity or aggregate of the gratuities paid or payable in respect of that service exceeds a sum calculated at ₦1000 per annum for the period or day of such service in Nigeria or, if he is entitled to terminal leave following such service in Nigeria, of the last day of such leave.

(c) If any part of a gratuity paid or payable to an employee fails to be deemed to be his income under both conditons (a) and (b) then such part shall be deducted in ascertaining the excess under condition (b).

15   Any sums received by way of death gratuities or as consolidated compensation for death or injuries.

16   Any sum withdrawn or received by an employee from a pension, provident or other retirement benefits scheme established under the provisions of any Act for employees throughout Nigeria.

17   Any income from an employment or pension which is not derived or not deemed to be derived, from Nigeria and chargeable to tax solely by reason of its being brought into or received in Nigeria during any year preceding a year of assessment if the employee or pensioner is not in Nigeria for a period or any time during that year of assessment, or is not in Nigeria for a period or periods amounting to 183 days or more during that year of assessment.

18   Sums deducted from the employee's remuneration in respect of his contributions other than a penalty, to the National Provident Fund are to be excluded from 'pay'. The amount so excluded during the Income Tax year is to be recorded at the bottom of the Tax Deduction Card before the card is returned to the Relevant Tax Authority.

19   Sums deducted from the employee's remuneration in respect of his contributions to pension, provident or other retirement benefits fund, society or scheme approved by the Joint Tax Board are to be excluded from 'pay'. The amount so excluded during the year is, however, to be recorded at the bottom of the Tax Deduction Card before the card is returned to the Relevant Tax Authority.

Rights of an employee under the PAYE scheme

An employee who is ordinarily resident in Nigeria would normally be entitled to the following Personal Reliefs and other reliefs to which he is entitled.

It should be noted that apart from Personal Allowance which is automatic, others are based on the circumstances of the taxpayer during the previous year. The taxpayer has also the following rights:

(i) right to be given a tax receipt at the end of the year by his employer;

(ii) right of objection to the relevant Tax Authority, for reliefs not properly granted;

(iii) right of objection to the relevant Tax Authority for any over-deduction;

(iv) right of refund from the relevant Tax Authority for excess tax paid; and

(v) right to be given Tax Clearance Certificate by his relevant Tax Authority if he so requests, after tax has been fully paid.

Duties of an employee under the PAYE scheme

1 For an employee to get all reliefs due to him, he has a duty to ask for Return of Income Form at the beginning of the year to complete and return to the relevant Tax Authority.

2 Whenever an employee is on transfer or changes employment he has to obtain from his present employer, leaving/transfer certificate for his new employer.

Duty of directed employer to deduct Income Tax

It is the duty of the employer, when directed by the Relevant Tax Authority, to deduct Income Tax, in accordance with the direction, from the pay of his employees who are subject to Nigerian Income Taxation and who are resident for tax purposes in the State of the Relevant Tax Authority.

How PAYE is worked

Under the PAYE scheme the amount of tax which the employer has to deduct on any pay day depends on:

(a) the employee's total pay since the beginning of the Income Tax year which starts on 1 January;

(b) the employee's Income Tax allowances and any income from outside sources, for the same period; and

(c) the total tax deducted on previous pay days.

On each pay day, the employer first works out the pay due to the employee and then adds to that pay the total of all previous payments made to the employee from 1 January up to date. He deducts any Income Tax allowance or adds any outside income, if he has been so instructed by the Relevant Tax Authority, to arrive at the taxable pay to date.

He looks up the resulting figure in a special ready-reckoner, called a Tax Table, which shows the total tax due to date. From the figure of total tax shown in the Tax Table, the employer subtracts the figure of total tax already deducted; the remainder is the amount to be deducted from the employee's pay on the day in question.

Sometimes the figure of total tax shown by the Tax Table may be less than the tax already deducted. In that case the employer must refund the difference to the employee instead of making any deduction.

The employer must keep records of the figure of pay and tax at each pay day, and each month the employer totals the tax deducted in the month and the tax refunded in the month and remits the net amount to the Relevant Tax Authority.

Employers within the PAYE scheme

Only those employers who have been specifically directed by the Relevant Tax Authority to do so may deduct Income Tax from the remuneration of their employees under the PAYE deduction scheme. Such employers include Government, Local Governments and many commercial, industrial and other concerns.

Special arrangements with certain directed employers

Special arrangements have been made with Governments, Local Governments and certain other directed employers.

Employers who have not been directed

An employer who has not received a notice of direction has no authority to operate the PAYE deduction scheme. If any employer wishes to extend the benefits of this scheme to his employees, he may apply to the Relevant Tax Authority for notice of direction.

Meaning of the word 'employer'

For PAYE purposes the term 'employer' is to be taken, when necessary, to include:
  (a) any person having control of payment of remuneration;
  (b) any agent, manager or other representative in Nigeria of any employer who is outside Nigeria;
  (c) any agent, manager or other representative in a State of any employer in Nigeria; and
  (d) any paying officer of Government or any Local Government.

Employers within the PAYE scheme

Meaning of the word 'employee'

The word 'employee' is used in the taxing acts and pamphlets issued by the Relevant Tax Authority. This word is defined as inclusive of any holder of an appointment or office, whether public or otherwise, for which remuneration is payable. 'Employee' should be read as including, for example, Minister, Chief, Local Government Councillor, any public servant, Company Director, Secretary, pensioner, etc. in addition to those more commonly known as employees.

Employees within the PAYE scheme

All directed employers are to operate the PAYE scheme in respect of their employees and pensioners who:
   (a) are deemed to be resident in a State for the Income Tax year (see Appendix A for the meaning of 'deemed to be resident') and
   (b) are not before retirement casual workers, seasonal workers, or attributers or contract workers in the mines.

Meaning of 'casual worker' and 'seasonal worker'

Casual worker: a worker so defined for National Provident Fund purposes, i.e. any worker engaged on a daily contract of service who has not been employed by one employer for a continuous period of three months, the continuity of which is not construed as interrupted if broken by not more than 14 days during the period of three months. *Seasonal worker*: a worker engaged for less than six months in any year in connection with seasonal work, e.g. produce clearance, groundnut loading, etc.

Supply of Tax Tables and Tax Deduction Cards

Copies of the official Tax Tables and Tax Deduction Cards are supplied to the employer free of charge in quantities sufficient to meet his reasonable requirements. A copy should be made available by the employer for reference by any employee wishing to check the tax deductions made from his remuneration.

Use of Tax Deduction Card

The Tax Deduction Card provides for a record to be kept by the employer of remuneration paid and of tax deducted or refunded during the Income Year in respect of an employee within the PAYE scheme. At the end of the Income Tax Year, the Tax Deduction Card is sent to the Relevant Tax Authority by the employer as part of his annual return.

Employer wishing to use his own Tax Deduction Cards

If an employer wishes to print and use cards in substitution for the official Tax Deduction Cards, he may do so, provided that:
- (a) he bears the whole cost;
- (b) the card gives the information regarding Income Tax required by the official card;
- (c) the proposed design is approved by the Relevant Tax Authority before it is printed; and
- (d) the employer guarantees to operate as necessary from any special Tax Deduction Cards and to return, at the end of the year, such cards with his annual return and his own Tax Deduction Cards.

Retention of Tax Deduction Cards by employer

The Tax Deduction Cards should be returned to the Relevant Tax Authority at the end of the Income Tax year.

If, however, an employer with a large number of employees wishes to retain the Tax Deduction Cards he may do so, provided that:
- (a) he undertakes to supply the Relevant Tax Authority with a separate document for each employee giving the information required by paragraph 24; and
- (b) the proposed design of such document is approved by the Relevant Tax Authority before it is printed.

The employer will be required to undertake to keep the Tax Deduction Cards intact for at least six years after the end of the Income Tax year.

Employee's right to see his Tax Deduction Card

An employee may see and examine his own Tax Deduction Card during the year it is in operation by his employer. He has no right to take the card away and must not be permitted to do so.

Notes

1 From time immemorial, personal income tax has been the main source of revenue to kingdoms and governments, all over the world. Personal income tax was in fact the main source of revenue in biblical Caesar's ancient realm. In

78

Nigeria it accounts rather sadly for a little over 10 per cent of states governments' revenue whilst companies tax plus petroleum profits tax account for 80 per cent of Federal Government's revenue.

Personal income tax was in existence in Nigeria before the advent of the British. There were various tributes and personal services rendered to the *Obas, Obis* and *Emirs* in various parts of the country. The first personal income tax to be enacted in this country was the Northern Nigeria Land Revenue Proclamation Law of 1904. There were no such laws in the southern part of Nigeria until after the amalgamation of the Northern Provinces with the Colony and Protectorate of Nigeria in 1914 when the Native Revenue Ordinance of 1917 was enacted to cover the areas of the former Western Region of Nigeria. It was in 1927 that the first personal tax law was introduced into the former Eastern Region of the country. This led to riots, including the Aba Tax riots of 1930.

2   Suit No. 1/404/72 in the High Court of former Western Nigeria.

3   Suit No. 1/373 (63: 1/85/67) before Mr Justice E.B. Craig at the Western State High Court on 11 November 1968.

4   1971 115 SJ 951; *The Times*, 21.10.71.

5   1971 3WLR 877; 115 SJ 658; 1971 3All ER1011.

6   1971 TR 147. It is my view that this case shows that to tax our labours and excise our brains is not given to Inland Revenue.

7   In the High Court of Justice, former Western State of Nigeria before the Hon. Mr Justice Olujide Somolu on 22 April 1963. Suit No. 1/ITA/62 of 22 April 1963.

8   (1926) 11 TC 508, 520, 521.

9   (1915) AC 433, 468.

10   Apparently because of absence of local decisions.

11   (1935) AC 431 at page 438; 19 TC 390 at pp.428, 429.

12   'Person' includes a corporation; where corporations are meant to be excluded, 'individual' is used.

13   *Hudson's Bay Company Ltd v Stevens* (1900) 5 TC 424.

14   *Per* Pitney, J. in *Eisner v Macomber* 252 US 189 (1919) at pp.206 and 207 cited with approval by Sankey, J. in *Pool v Guardian Investment Ltd* (1921) 8 TC 167.

15   *Balgownie Land Trust Ltd v IRC* (1920).

16   *Smith Barry v Cordy* (1946) 28 TC 250 at p.258.

17   ITA 1952 s.82.

18   *Edwards v Bairstow & Harrison* 1956 AC 14; 36 TC 207.

19   *J. & R. O'Kane & Co. v IRC* (1922) 12 TC 308 at p.347.

20   (1896) 3 TC 415. The tax assessment of traders and self-employed persons as well as partnerships are under the jurisdiction of the States Tax Boards. These groups of taxpayers are required to submit annually Returns of Income at the end of three months in the relevant year of assessment. The return of income is to include each taxpayer's world or global income.

     A uniform Taxation Bill to ensure uniformity of practice in the States is before the National Assembly.

21   *Trustees of Psalms and Hymns v Whitwell* (1890) 3 TC 7.

22   *Grove v Young Men's Christian Association* (1903).

23   *Royal Agricultural Society v Wilson* (1924) 9 TC 62.

24   See the final Report of the 1954 Royal Commission Cmd 9474, para. 116.

25   *William Esplen v IRC* (1919) 2KB 731.

26   *Graham v Greene* (1925) 2KB37; 9 TC 309.

27   *Patridge v Mallamdaine* (1886) 15QB 276.

28 Act No. 5 of 1978.
29 ITMA, s.5.
30 The rules of commencing and cessation are archaic, and actual basis is less cumbersome and fairer.

4 Income From Property Rights

Introduction[1]

Income Tax is payable upon income:
- (i) accruing in Nigeria,
- (ii) derived from Nigeria,
- (iii) brought into Nigeria,

or (iv) received in Nigeria,

in respect of gains or profits including any premiums arising from a right granted to any other person for the use or occupation of any property. Expenses which are allowed or deductible from the rent must be wholly, exclusively, necessarily and reasonably incurred in the earning of the income.

Expenditure not allowed

Examples are:
1. Capital expenditure is not allowed, for the obvious reason. A capital expenditure is one usually made once and for all with a view to bringing an asset into being or substantially improving it: capital allowance may be claimed on it. The term 'once and for all' is not conclusive.
2. Appropriations of profit are not allowed. Drawings out of rent should be disallowed because it is the profit that should be taxed and not what is left out of profit after setting aside some of it. Income Tax paid/payable is not allowed as a deduction on similar grounds.
3. Expenditure not connected with the earning of the income is not allowed. Expenses that are allowed must be incidental to the trade.
4. Depreciation of the building is not allowed since capital allowance will be given in lieu if formally claimed.

Example

Mr Omotoso is a landlord as well as the director of a limited liability company from where he draws director's fees of ₦6000 per annum. He is married and has four children, one of whom is a medical practitioner at the University of Ife hospital, Ife. During the year ended 31.12.80 he contributed ₦500 towards the maintenance of his aged mother while his younger sister contributed ₦300. He took out a Life Assurance Policy on his life for the sum ₦10 000. The premium is ₦720 per annum and was paid for seven months on preceding-year basis. The director's fees were paid in 1981. Mr Omotoso has four houses, the total value of which was ₦130 300 as at 31.12.80. The amount includes the value of a house he lives at Ring Road whose rent on 31.12.80 was ₦20 750. The sum of ₦4300 included under repairs and renovation is expended in constructing a garage and boys' quarters to house A – one of the houses let out. ₦500 of the expenses relate to house B where Mr Omotoso lives.

You are required to compute:
(a) his adjusted income, clearly stating the relevant year of assessment;
(b) capital allowances for the relevant year of assessment;
(c) the chargeable income; and
(d) the tax payable.
(1985 reliefs are inapplicable.)

Solution

Net income per accounts	₦15 295
Add back	
Repairs and renovation	₦4 800
Depreciation	10 562
	15 362
	30 657
Deduct	
Capital allowance, 10% of ₦114 050	11 405
Adjusted income	19 252

1981 Income Tax Computation

Assessable Income		₦19 252
Less Reliefs		
Personal	₦600	
Wife	300	
Children (3)	750	
Life Assurance	420	
Dependent Relative	250	2 320
Chargeable income		₦16 932

82

Tax payable		
₦2 000 @ 10%	₦200	
2 000 " 15%	300	
2 000 " 20%	400	
2 000 " 25%	500	
2 000 " 30%	600	
5 000 " 35%	1 750	
1 932 " 40%	772.80	
	₦4 522.80	

Notes

(a) Relief is granted in respect of only three children as the fourth one is in employment. All reliefs are on preceding-year basis. The year of assessment is 1981.

(b) Dependent relative allowance has been restricted to ₦$\frac{500}{800}$ × 400) i.e. ₦250, as contributions of ₦800 towards the maintenance of their mother had been made.

(c) Life Assurance premium is only allowed for seven months, i.e. 31 May 1981 to 31 December 1981 (₦60 × 7).

(d) The sum of ₦4300 expended on garage and boys quarters of house A is not a revenue expenditure and so this amount is capitalised.

Expenses on house B where Mr Omotoso lives are not allowed as it is private and yields no rental income.

Capital allowance is calculated on:

Total value of houses	₦130 500
Less:	
Value of house B	20 750
	₦109 750
Add:	
Amount expended on house A	4 300
	₦114 050

(e) Repairs added back:

Repairs of residence	₦500
Construction of garage and boys' quarters (capitalized)	4 300
	4 800

(f) $\frac{1}{10}$ths of ₦19 252 is inapplicable as ₦6000 is the only earned income, hence the personal allowance is not ₦1925 but ₦600. If ₦19 252 is earned income, personal allowance will be ₦1925.

(ii) Income Tax (Rents) Act, 1963

In recognition of the contractor finance scheme used by Nigerians to finance housing development in certain areas of Lagos such as Victoria Island, South West Ikoyi and other growing areas, the Federal Government in 1965 enacted the Income Tax Rent Act to afford tax relief to the property-owners. The principle involved was that since the contractor who built such houses for lease for a number of years without actually paying over any rents to the owners (rents being used to satisfy the financing of construction expended by the contractor) for the number of years required to recover his money, it was considered inequitable to ask such property-owners to pay tax on rents on the deemed income not actually collected.

The Act accordingly allows the owner the option not to pay tax in respect of assumed rent until the cost of the building or ₦100 000 whichever is less, is recouped. Where the option is exercised, no capital allowance will be claimable on the property after the end of the relevant period of relief. In the short run, that is, during the relief period, the Internal Revenue Division will not collect tax on such properties but at the expiry of the relief period, the Internal Revenue Division will collect substantial tax, as capital allowance will not be granted on whatever rent is collected and charged to tax when the rental income on the property would likely have increased.

(iii) Payments in advance[2]

Where rent is paid in advance under a lease or assignment of a lease, that payment is treated as accruing to the recipient from day to day over the period for which it has been paid. If, however, that period is greater than five years, the advance payment is treated as accruing evenly over the first five years of the period.

Under the proviso to Section 4(2)(c) of the Income Tax Management Act 1961, where rent paid in advance is for a period exceeding five years, the whole of the rent so paid shall be treated as accruing evenly from day to day over the five years commencing on the first day of that said period.

Example 1

Miss Charming who had been trading for several years, was paid a rent advance of ₦20 000 for twenty years on 11.9.81. Show the necessary Income Tax computation ignoring reliefs and capital allowances.

1982 $3\frac{2}{3}$ of a month from
1.9.81 to 31.12.81 at 14 000 per annum ₦1 222
1983 12 months from 1.1.82–31.12.82 at ₦4000 p.a. 4 000
1984 12 months from 1.1.83–31.12.83 at ₦4000 p.a. 4 000
1985 12 months from 1.1.84–31.12.84 at ₦4000 p.a. 4 000
1986 12 months from 1.1.85–31.12.85 at ₦4000 p.a. 4 000
1987 $8\frac{1}{3}$ months from 1.1.86–10.9.86
5 years at ₦4000 p.a. 2 778
₦20 000

Lessors

The most common type of 'right granted' is that granted by a landlord to his tenant for the occupation of houses, buildings or lands. It should not be overlooked, however, that the provision extends also to the right granted by a superior lessor to an inferior lessor who might in his turn sub-lease the property to a tenant.

For example:

A leases the whole of a property to B
B sub-leases part to C and part to D
C occupies his part himself
D further leases his part to E who occupies that part.

A, B, and D all fall within the scope of the charging provision and their respective profits are assessable.

Property

Income from property is not limited to income from real property, that is, buildings or land. Income chargeable may arise from other property, for example, plant and machinery hired out at a profit.

Computation of liability

The income of an individual, from the grant of property rights, for a year of assessment is the income of the preceding year.[3]

In the case of a property outside of Nigeria, the phrase 'income of the preceding year' means 'income brought into, or received in, Nigeria in the preceding year' and is subject to the Double Taxation Relief provisions contained in ITMA Part VI.[4]

(iv) Practical assessment procedures under the Rent Act

The Rent Act is designed to meet a specific contingency arising from the tax burden imposed by the provision of section 4(c) of Income Tax management Act 1961 as amended.

There are three main steps of action in the administration of the Rent Act. These are:

(i) Election and approval under the law;

(ii) Creation of charge on the eligible property; and

(iii) Release of the charge.

Step (i)

When a taxpayer incurs a qualifying expenditure and gives an indication to have the Rent Act applied to him, he is sent the instrument of election by the internal revenue. On receipt of the instrument of election duly completed the Revenue scrutinises it to see that it is in order. In addition to the particulars to be filled on the form the originals and copies of Contract and Tenancy Agreements are to accompany the completed instrument of election. Where the taxpayer omits to attach these, the Revenue will call for them.

With the submission of the Tenancy and the Contract Agreements the application is processed by the Internal Revenue. The Director of Internal Revenue will thereafter recommend the approval of election to the Hon. Commissioner for Finance. When the election is finally approved by the Commissioner for Finance, the Internal Revenue will write the taxpayer stating:

(a) the cost of construction;

(b) amount of rent received;

(c) amount to relief approved;

(d) period for which rent was received. The originals of Tenancy and Contract Agreements will be returned to the taxpayer.

A copy of the letter is endorsed to the appropriate tax office along with a copy of instrument of election. Where there is excess rent the appropriate tax office assesses the excess.

Step (ii): Creation of charge

Almost immediately after approval of election the tax-payer is asked to submit the deed of conveyance in respect of the property on which a charge is to be created. Three copies of the instrument of charge are attached to the letter for completion and return with the deed by the taxpayer.

The instrument of charge and the deed are then sent to the land registry in the High Court for registration. When the charge is created a copy of the instrument of charge and the receipt for the deposited deed are sent to the taxpayer for safe keeping.

Step (iii): Release of charge
On full discharge of the taxpayer's liability on the property under the charge he (usually) sends in a letter of request for release of the charge. The Secretary writes to the appropriate tax district to confirm whether the taxpayer has been declaring income on the same property since expiration of the election period. When this is confirmed the Secretary then submits minutes to the Commissioner of Internal Revenue recommending the issue of a release charge. (Reference is usually made to the official receipt for the Land Certificate or deed of conveyance and the charge certificate in the minute.) Then, the release of charge is executed with the land registry.

On release of the deed of conveyance the taxpayer is written to call personally to collect the deed. Acknowledgement receipt is obtained.

Notes on records and forms
The following forms and records are in use:
   (1) There are three statutory forms: Instrument of Election, Instrument of charge and Release of charge.
   (2) All the statutory forms are to be stamped in the stamp duty.
   (3) Disposal of copies of each of the statutory forms are as indicated on the form.
   (4) Register of Elections, a specimen of which is as set out below.
The Act of 1965 was repealed in 1968 by the Federal Government but not by the Lagos State Government which instead made the provisions of the Act as affecting individuals to be applicable in the State through the Income Tax (Rents) Regulations 1973 (Lagos State Legal Notice No. 17 of 1973) with retrospective effect from 1 May 1968. The result was that those liable to Lagos State tax could take advantage of the law whereas others who paid their personal income tax to the Federal Government (such as members of the Armed Forces and Foreign Service Officers) could not, even though the property from which the rent was derived might be in the Lagos State.

In his 1975–76 Budget, the former Head of the Federal Military Government and Commander-in-Chief of the Armed Forces of the Federal Republic of Nigeria directed that in order to encourage further investments in housing development, the benefits of the Income Tax (Rents) Act, 1965 formerly repealed by the Income Tax (Rents) Repeal Act, 1969, which was then enjoyed only in Lagos State and Federal Capital as from 1.4.75 was extended in its application to the whole of the Federation, and that the limit on the value of eligible property should be raised from the 1975 level of ₦50 000 to ₦100 000 to accord with present-day price levels. In pursuance of this directive, the State Governments, excepting Lagos State Government which is already enjoying the benefits of the Income Tax Rent Act, 1965, promulgated edicts to adopt the provisions of the Income Tax Rent Act, 1965 in their areas of jurisdiction.

Taxpayers who build houses with borrowed monies, for example, contractor-finance buildings under an agreement that the lender of the contractor should let the property and receive the rental income of the property until the cost of the buildings is fully paid, would appear to benefit from the Act.

Cost of construction (a) shall be the lower of (1) the cost of construction and (2) the cost to the person or company making election or acquiring that property, i.e. the consideration given for it; (b) the cost of construction shall exclude (1) ground rent, (2) cost of land, (3) rate levied, (4) cost of furnishing, (5) cost of repairs to the eligible property, (6) legal fees.

Disqualification for making election follows if (1) rents from eligible property are not disclosed in the Income Tax Return or false disclosure of such rent is made, (2) the owner fails to make a return of such rent when asked to do so by the Inland Revenue.

Example

Mr Olusegun acquired a piece of land on Ikeja GRA on 10.6.79 for ₦8000. He came to an arrangement with a firm of building contractors under which the builders were to develop the property, find a suitable tenant, deduct the contract sum from the rent received, and hand over the balance to Mr Olusegun. The building contractors commenced the construction of the foundation on 1.4.80. They erected a block of four flats on the land, and during the year ended 31.12.81, let the flats to an oil company who paid seven years' rent in advance, amounting to ₦235 200.

The contractors gave account to Mr Olusegun as follows:

Rent received	₦235 200
Less our costs	160 000
Balance representing cheque enclosed	75 000

You are informed that costs included

Cost of land	8 000
Ground rent 2 years to 31.12.88	1 600
Rates at ₦200 per annum	4 000
Legal fees – registration of titles, etc.	10 400
	₦24 000

88

Mr Olusegun made an election under the Rents Act, 1965 in respect of the rent he received from this property on 1 November 1989.

Assume:
 (i) Mr Olusegun's other income is his salary.
 (ii) Capital allowance rate is initial allowance of 10 per cent.
 (iii) Annual allowance of 2 per cent.
 (iv) Insurance of property by Mr Olusegun ₦2000 per annum.

Compute:
(a) the amount which will be included in Mr Olusegun's assessment in respect of the above rent;
(b) what difference it would make if he had made his election on May 1988?

Solution:

Mr Olusegun's 1989 Assessment: Salary 1.1.89–31.12.89
Rent   1.1.88–31.12.88

Rent was received in the 1988 year of assessment: election must therefore be made between 1.1.89 and 31.5.89: so for part (a) of the question the election is null and void. Section 4(2)(c) of the 1961 Act must therefore be invoked.

$$\text{Gross Rent} = \frac{235\,200}{5} = 47\,040 \text{ per annum}$$

(a) *Gross Rent*   ₦47 040

Less		
Insurance	₦2 000	
Ground Rent 1.1.88–31.12.88	800	
Rates 1.1.88–31.12.88	2 000	4 800
		42 240
Less capital allowances		
Cost of building	160 000	
Less cost of land, etc.	24 000	
(NB no initial allowance)	136 000	
Annual allowance thereon @ 2%	2 720	2 720
Balance c/f	133 280	
Rent to be included in Tax Return		39 520

	Cost of building	Rent
(b) *Total*		
Less disallowable items	₦160 000	₦235 200
Cost of land	24 000	
	136 000	
Maximum relief under Rent Act, 1965 as amended by Act No. 65 of 1966	50 000	50 000
Amount not subject to Rent Relief	86 000	185 200
Net not relieved as above		185 200
Deduct expenses		
Insurances	2 000	
Ground rent (one year)	800	
Rates (one year)	2 000	4 800
Capital allowances: 2% of (annual allowance)	₦2 720	₦2 720
		7 520
		₦177 680

Rates of capital allowances are assumed.

Amount chargeable along with salary, etc.
Buildings of up to ₦100 000 now qualify under the Act.[5]

Notes

1 ITMA, s.4(1)(c).
2 ITMA, s.4(2)(c).
3 ITMA, s.20(1).
4 ITMA, s.10.
5 There is now a tendency for landlords to recover tax deducted at source from the rents they receive through notice of ejection, which they ought not to do.

5 Income from Dividends, Interest or Discounts and Pensions, Annuities, Miscellaneous Sources and Income Exempted

(i) Introduction[1]

Income Tax is payable upon income:
- (a) accruing in Nigeria,
- (b) derived from Nigeria,
- (c) brought into Nigeria,

or (d) received in Nigeria

in respect of dividends, interest or discounts, pensions, charges or annuities, miscellaneous sources and income of a trade, business, profession or vocation.

The income of an individual, from dividends, interest or discounts, charge or annuity for a year of assessment is the income of the preceding year[2].

In the case of dividends paid by a company other than a 'Nigerian company' and interest or discounts from a source outside Nigeria, the phrase 'income of the preceding year' means 'income brought into, or received in, Nigeria in the preceding year' and is subject to the Double Taxation Relief provisions contained in ITMA Part VI.[3]

Income from abroad

The income, as defined in ITMA s.4(1), of a chargeable person is subject to Income Tax whether it arises in Nigeria or abroad.

Only that part of the income from a source outside of Nigeria which is brought into or received in Nigeria is assessable, but no deductions are allowed from that amount. If, however, that income arose in a country to which the Double Taxation Relief arrangements apply, the amount of the income to be taken for assessment is adjusted in accordance with those arrangements.[4]

In the case of an individual, corporation sole or body of individuals chargeable of tax only because of foreign income brought into or received in Nigeria during the year preceding the year of assessment, exemption is granted to that income if the individual, corporation sole or body of individuals was not in Nigeria for *more than 182 days during the year of assessment*. This time limit may be made up of several periods during which visits to Nigeria were made.[5]

(ii) Dividends

A dividend is the sum of money set aside out of profits of a company for distribution amongst the shareholders. (The term is sometimes also applied to interest payable out of public funds.)

The word 'company' means any company or corporation (other than a corporation sole) established by law either in Nigeria or elsewhere. A 'Nigerian company' is any company the control and management of whose business are exercised in Nigeria.[6]

Nigerian dividends

The income from a dividend distributed by a *Nigerian company* is:
 (a) income derived from Nigeria, and
 (b) income arising on the day payment becomes due.[7]

The amount of income is the gross dividend before deduction of tax by the company. The recipient is provided by the company with a certificate showing the gross dividend and if tax has been deducted, the net dividend.[8]

Certain Nigerian dividends are specifically exempted from tax. These are dividends distributed by a Nigerian company:
 (a) out of exempted profits of the company (e.g. profits exempted under the Pioneer Industries provisions);
 (b) out of certain profits of the company chargeable to Petroleum Profits Tax.

Dividends paid to State Government

The promulgation of Enterprises Promotion Act No. 4, 1972, threw a great challenge to Nigerian businessmen, and forced many companies to put on market for sale, part or all of the shares held by non-Nigerians in their respective companies. Unfortunately, some

Nigerian businessmen could not afford to buy any appreciable number of the shares of these companies and as a result, State Governments had to come to the rescue of these Nigerian businessmen in buying some shares in trust with the hope of re-selling them to State indigenous businessmen in due course.

The shares referred to above were bought through each 'State Ministry of Finance Incorporated'. The institution was established in order to handle government investments, not to participate as a trading concern.

Each year, a State Government receives some dividends for its various investments made in some of these Nigerian companies but these companies deducted tax at 50% when making payments of these dividends to each State Government. The total tax deducted so far and paid to the Federal Board of Inland Revenue amounts in respect of each State Government to about ₦475 000. Each State Director of Internal Revenue already submitted his claim for refund by the Federal Board of Inland Revenue in accordance with section 26(3) of the Nigeria Income Tax Management Act of 1961.

The Federal Board of Inland Revenue did not refund the amount claimed by each State Director of Internal Revenue because:
  (a) the dividends were paid out from the Nigerian companies' profits derived from their trade or business;
  (b) the companies' profits from which these dividends were paid do not fall under 'Profit Exempted' under the provision of section 26 of the Companies Income Tax Act;
  (c) under the provision of section 26(3) of the Income Tax Management Act, reimbursement to a State Tax Authority can only be made if the tax claimed had been refunded or off-set by the State Tax Authority making the claim; and
  (d) no tax was refunded or off-set by each State Director of Internal Revenue since each State Ministry of Finance Incorporated's income is exempted from tax under paragraph (j) of the 3rd Schedule to the Income Tax Management Act.

Under the provision of paragraph (j) of the 3rd Schedule to the Income Tax Management Act, 1961, the income of any State Government Institution is exempted from tax no matter whether the income includes profits from its investments or not. Through whatever source any State Government derived income, whether through taxation or investments income, this could not be regarded as gains or profits in the real sense, especially when compared to gains or profits of individuals and private companies within the context of the Income Tax Management Act.

The Federal Government too has similar investments in some companies, for example, insurance companies, banks, etc., and would suffer the same 45 per cent tax deductions at source whenever dividends are paid to the Federal Government. But because the Federal Government both collects and retains such revenue from companies, the tax deducted at source on the Federal Government investments is paid back to the Federal Government through the Federal Board of Inland Revenue, unlike any State Government which is not empowered to collect tax from companies.

The Joint Tax Board has always agreed that the case is purely a subject for the Commissioners for Finance Conference which could, if agreed, recommend to the Federal Government to amend section 26(3) of the Income Tax Management Act, 1961 to include reimbursement to a State Government for tax deducted on State Government's dividends received from its investments. So far, section 26(3) remains unamended.

Tax deduction from dividends

See Supplement (1985).

(iii) Interest and royalties

Interest has been defined as 'money paid for the use of money' or as 'compensation or rent paid by a borrower for a loan of money'. Interest on money deposited in a bank is the most common example of income coming within the scope of ITMA, s.4(1)(d).

Interest paid or credited to any person by the Nigerian Post Office Savings Bank or in respect of any Nigerian Savings Certificates is exempted from Income Tax.[9] Interest accruing to non-residents on certain official and semi-official loans as specified in ITMA, 3rd Schedule (e) is also exempted.

Refer also to Supplement (1985).

Discounts

The word 'discounts' covers only those profits arising from discounting transactions in the ordinary financial sense.

The discount on a bill is the interest deducted from the principal sum when an advance is made before the bill becomes payable; it is calculated by the time the bill still has to run. In this context, 'discounts' does *not* include ordinary trade discounts on commercial purchases.

Annuities

An 'annuity' is a fixed sum payable at stated intervals for so many years or for life. It may be provided for by the terms of a trust or by a life insurance policy, or by a separate deed or covenant. Sometimes the income from a particular source is earmarked to provide the annuity.

An annuity may be purchased by the payment of a lump sum which is not returnable when the period for which the annuity is to be paid has expired.

(iv) Withholding tax

Refer to Supplement (1985).

Pensions

Certain payments which are commonly known as 'pensions' are not necessarily income. For example, a 'pension' awarded by a charitable society to a person in need of assistance may be, in substance, a series of annual gifts and is assessable only if the pensioner was previously employed by the society.

Charges

A 'charge' is a sum which a person is under a legal obligation to pay. The term has a wide meaning including such payments as loan interest, mortgage interest, and annuities. A more specific instance is alimony received by a divorced or separated wife from the former husband. Another is the payment to a beneficiary out of the income of a trust, settlement or estate.

(v) Income exempted by statute

Legislation
Statutory exemption in respect of certain classes of income is provided by ITMA s.16 and Third Schedule as amended by:

(i) the Income Tax Management (Technical Assistance Personnel) (Exemption) Notice, 1963;

(ii) the Income Tax Management (interest on Loans Granted to the Nigerian Sugar Company Limited) (Exemption) Notice, 1962;

(iii) the Adaptation of Laws (Miscellaneous Provisions) Order, 1965.

Income exempted by Double Taxation Agreements[11]

Certain classes of income are exempted under the provisions of Double Taxation Agreements made with those foreign countries listed in ITMA, Sixth Schedule. Reference should be made to the Agreements specified.

Notes

1 ITMA, s.4(1)(d).
2 ITMA, s.20(1).
3 ITMA, s.9, s.10, s.11.
4 ITMA, s.10, s.17(2), s.23, s.24, s.25, s.26.
5 ITMA, Third Schedule.
6 ITMA, s.2.
7 ITMA, s.9(1).
8 CITA, 1979, ss.15–16.
9 ITMA, Third Schedule.
10 These Acts were formerly known as Decrees.
11 ITMA, s.24(6).

6   Loss Relief

(i) Introduction[1]

In these instructions the word 'individual' includes any partner and any corporation sole or body of individuals.

The general scheme of the Income Tax Management Act is to charge tax on income which arises. If it happens that an activity, which would normally be regarded as a source of income, results in a loss, no income arises and the assessment in respect of that source of income is nil.

There are, however, special relieving provisions which enable an individual who has sustained a loss in certain specified circumstances to set off that loss against his income.

The general relieving provision, in section 21(1) of the Income Tax Management Act, directs that when loss relief is due it is to be deducted in computing the total income of an individual. Such relief is to be so deducted before relief for Capital Allowances.

(ii) Methods of relieving losses

Under ITMA, s.21(1), relief for losses is to be deducted from the total assessable income in arriving at the total income of an individual for a year of assessment. The relief so given may be in respect of:
  (a) a loss incurred during the year of assessment itself, when the relief is called 'current year relief;[2]
  (b) a loss incurred during any year preceding the year of assessment, when the relief is called 'carry forward relief';[3]
  (c) a combination of (a) and (b).

Current year relief

Current year loss relief can only be given in respect of a loss incurred *in a trade, business, profession or vocation*. The relief does not extend to any other source of income such as the letting of property.

Deduction of losses
The provisions of section 21(2)(a) and (b) of the Income Tax Management Act, 1961, set out the procedure to be followed in the treatment of loss. Attention is particularly drawn to proviso (iii) to sub-section 2(b) because it lays down that a *deficit* on Property Rental Income Account (where the allowable expenses exceed the income) is to be regarded as though it were a *loss in trade or business*. Accordingly, *LOSS* can arise not only in trade or business, but on Property Income Account as well, and must be allowed like a trading loss.

It is to be noted that Capital Allowances are not part of allowable expenses under section 17, and therefore they do not come into the computation of loss whether on Business Income Account or Property Income Account. The Capital Allowances which are unabsorbed by profit must be carried forward.

Section 21(2)(a) of our Law lays down that the relevant loss is the loss incurred *during the year of assessment*. This is the loss which is to be deducted in computing total income under section 21(1). Clearly, this loss is to be deducted from incomes of all other sources which make up the total income. Note the difference, however, in the fact that while the incomes of the other sources (excluding employment income) will be incomes arising during the previous year, the loss is *the loss during the assessment year*. If at any time within twelve months after the end of the year of assessment 1976–77, i.e., not later than 31 March 1978, a taxpayer shows that he incurred a loss during the year of assessment 1976–77, the 1976–77 assessment should be reopened to give effect to this loss, provided the taxpayer makes a claim in writing. It would be totally wrong to treat his claim as though it related to the assessment year 1977–78. The loss was incurred during 1976–77 and it must be dealt with for purposes of the 1976–77 assessment.

It is essential to get the provisions of section 21(2)(a) clear because the provisions of section 21(2)(b) only operate where the former have not been applied in the absence of a claim in writing. For the purposes of good public relations, the taxpayer should always be informed about his rights under section 21(2)(a).

In applying section 21(2)(b) the great difference from section 21(2)(a) is that the loss in any particular trade or business (or on Property Income Account) cannot be set-off against other income. If a loss was incurred during 1976–77 and no claim is made during

98

1977–78, then the 1977–78 assessment will regard the income from the particular source as nil. The loss will not be set-off against any other income relevant for the 1976–77 assessment, but will be carried forward to the 1978–79 assessment and deducted from the income (if any) from the particular source, arising during 1977–78.

It should be noted that the position of an employed taxpayer is slightly different, where he suffers a *loss* on Property Income Account. For example, suppose the loss was incurred during the assessment year 1976–77. Normally, the amount of loss will only be determined after 31 March 1977. If he claims it in writing not later than 31 March 1978, the amount must be deducted from the employment income of the year ending 31 March 1977. Since PAYE tax would have been deducted from that employment income, a repayment of tax will have to be made. It would not be correct to set-off the loss against employment income of the year 1977–78.

Losses cannot be carried forward for more than four years now, but losses on agricultural projects trades are not so restricted.

Computation of relief [4]
Current year loss relief is to be computed by reference to the amount of loss incurred during the year of assessment. In considering whether a loss has been incurred and, if so, the amount of the loss, the net profit or net loss shown by the accounts of the trade, etc., must be adjusted in the same way as it would be for the purposes of determining the amount of the assessment.

In all cases where ITMA, s.20(2) is applicable, that is, continuing trades, etc., where accounts are made up to some date other than 31 March, the phrase 'loss incurred during the year of assessment' is defined by section 21(3) of the Income Tax Management Act to mean the loss of the twelve months, ending in that year of assessment, which would have been adopted as the basis year in computing the assessable income of the following year of assessment under ITMA, s.20(2) had a profit arisen.

In all other cases, for example, where no accounts are rendered, where accounts are made up to 31 March, or where the commencing and ceasing provisions apply, the phrase 'loss incurred during the year of assessment' means the loss of the year of assessment itself.

When there has been a change of accounting date in an established trade, business, profession or vocation carried on by an individual, the case is to be submitted to Head Office so that the Commissioner may compute, as he thinks fit, the assessable income for:

(a) the year of assessment in which the individual fails to make up his accounts to the accounting date used in earlier years; and

(b) the next two years of assessment.

99

Unless the Director of Internal Revenue directs the amount of any loss relief to be given in respect of losses incurred at any time during the basis periods of those three years of assessment, any claim for current year loss relief for such losses is to be referred to Head Office with a full statement of all relevant facts and the taxpayer's file. Losses on property rental can only be relieved by carry forward and not against current year profits.

Claims for relief[5]

Current year loss relief may only be allowed if a written claim is made before the end of the year of assessment following the year of assessment for which relief is claimed.

Any written notice of claim dated up to 31 March following the year of claim, but not received in the centre of office until April because of postal delays, is to be accepted.

It is not necessary for the written notice of claim to be accompanied by a computation of the loss relief claimed; but if the relief due cannot immediately be ascertained because of delay by the taxpayer in submitting any necessary information, any tax assessed for the year of claim should be collected and the relief dealt with by way of repayment.

Method of giving relief[6]

Current year loss relief is to be given by deducting, as far as possible, the amount of the loss incurred during the year of assessment from the total of assessable income from all sources for that year and any balancing charges for that year.

Any balance of unused loss is available for carry forward loss relief in later years of assessment subject to the limitations mentioned later on.

As relief for losses takes priority over relief for Capital Allowances, it may be that part or the whole of the Capital Allowances for the year of assessment are displaced.

It should be noted particularly that current year loss relief extends to the total assessable income and balancing charges for the year of assessment. This is quite different from carry forward loss relief which can be allowed in any year only up to the amount of assessable income (excluding any Balancing Charge) from the trade, etc., in which the loss was incurred.[7]

Example 1

Ekaner commenced business on 1 September 1981 and the profit and loss as adjusted for tax purposes were as follows:

Year ended 31.8.82 – Loss   ₦2400
Year ended 31.8.83 – Profit   ₦4000

You are required to show the necessary computations.

Year of Assessment	Basis of Assessment	Amount of Assessable Income
1981	$\frac{4}{12}$ × loss ₦2400 = ₦800 loss (4 months' trading from date of Commencement to following 31 December actual)	NIL
1982	12 months' trading: loss ₦2400	NIL
1983	8 months to 31.8.82, loss ₦1600 4 months to 31.12.82 profit ₦1334, leaving ₦266 loss	NIL

The total amount of loss will be carried forward to the 1984 year of assessment. Aggregate deduction from assessable income in respect of any loss should, in any case, not exceed the amount of such loss.

Example 2

Yinka Green Revolution Ltd, which runs a large farm in Plateau State has the following adjusted profits record:

Year to 31 December	1977	Loss	₦59 000
Year to 31 December	1978	Profit	21 000
Year to 31 December	1979	Loss	20 000
Year to 31 December	1980	Profit	33 000
Year to 31 December	1981	Profit	1 000

The Revenue, showing the examination of the computations, established that Yinka Green Revolution Ltd engaged in rice distribution and that the results incorporated in the above figures were as follows:

Year to 31 December	1977	Loss	₦45 000
Year to 31 December	1978	Profit	14 000
Year to 31 December	1979	Loss	3 000

Year to 31 December 1980 Profit 7 000
Year to 31 December 1981 Profit 4 000

No capital allowances were available as fixed assets used by the company were rented.

Compute the losses if any, available to be carried forward each year of assessment, with a brief explanation.

Solution

Yinka Green Revolution Ltd
Normal computation of loss to be carried forward

	1978–79	1979–80	1980	1981	1982
Profit (*loss*) for the year	(59 000)	–	(20 000)	–	–
Loss brought forward	–	38 000	38 000	25 000	24 000
	59 000	38 000	58 000	25 000	24 000
Less current year relief	21 000	–	33 000	1 000	–
Loss carried forward	38 000	38 000	25 000	24 000	24 000

Note
Section 26(3) of the Companies Income Tax Act, 1979 states:

(3) The amount of loss incurred by a Company engaged in an agricultural trade or business for the year of assessment in which it commenced to carry on such trade or business shall be deducted as far as possible from the assessable profits of the first year of assessment after that in which the loss was incurred and so far as it cannot be so made, then from such amount of such assessable profits of the next year of assessment, and so on (without limit as to time) until the loss has been completely set off against the Company's subsequent assessable profits.

However s.9(8) of the Companies Income Tax Act, 1979 defines an agricultural trade or business as:

(a) the establishment or management of plantations for the production of rubber, oil, palm, cocoa, coffee, tea and similar crops;
(b) the cultivation or production of cereal crops, tubers, fruits of all kinds, cotton, beans, groundnuts, sheanuts, beniseed, vegetables, pineapples, bananas and plantains; and
(c) animal husbandry, that is to say, poultry, piggery, cattle rearing and the like and fish farming.

Consequently the computation will be:

Yinka Green Revolution Ltd
Computation of loss to be carried forward.

	1978–79	1979–80	1980	1981	1982
Profit (*loss*) for the year	₦(45 000)	₦ –	₦(3 000)	₦ –	₦ –
Loss brought forward	–	31 000	(31 000)	27 000	3 000*
	45 000	31 000	34 000	27 000	3 000
Less current year relief	14 000	–	7 000	4 000	–
Loss carried forward	31 000	31 000	27 000	23 000	3 000

*Although at the end of 1981 there is a total loss of ₦23 000 available for carry forward the maximum period a loss can be carried forward is four years. Therefore only ₦3000 loss incurred in 1979 can be carried forward to 1982.

(iii) Carry-forward loss relief

A loss arising on the letting of land or buildings can only be relieved under the carry forward provisions. In no circumstances can relief be given against other income of the year of assessment in which the loss was incurred (current year relief).

In any case taken over from the Federal or other States' authorities, relief for losses brought forward may only be allowed to the extent that those losses have been agreed by those authorities and remain unused. No carry-forward loss relief is to be allowed in respect of losses incurred prior to 1961–62 in any case not dealt with by the tax authorities of the Federal Territory of Lagos or other States prior to take over by the States from the Federal Tax Authority.[8]

There is no provision for the allowance of loss relief in any year of assessment after the cessation of the trade, etc., or letting of property, in which the loss was incurred.

Losses can only be carried forward only up to a maximum period of four years except in the case of companies and individuals engaged in agricultural production in which case losses can be carried forward indefinitely and allowed for set off against future profits in the same line of business.

Computation of relief[9]
Carry-forward loss relief is to be computed by reference to the amount of the loss incurred during any year preceding the year of assessment

which has not been allowed against the individual's assessable income of a preceding year.

Claims for relief
No formal claim to carry-forward loss relief within any specified period is necessary. The deduction for unused losses brought forward is to be made without request by the taxpayer.

Method of giving relief[10]
Carry-forward loss relief is to be given by deducting the unused loss brought forward so far as is possible from the assessable income from the trade, etc., in which the loss was incurred.

Only the balance of loss remaining after any current year relief has been given and any relief made by aggregation is available for carry forward relief.[11]

This unused loss is to be set, as far as possible, against the assessable income of the same trade for the year of assessment immediately following the year of assessment in which the loss was incurred. Relief which cannot be so allowed because of an excess of loss over assessable income, is to be made in a similar manner in the *next* following year of assessment, then the next following year of assessment, and so on until the relief is exhausted.

It should be noted particularly that carry-forward relief extends only up to the amount of assessable income (excluding any Balancing Charge) from the same trade in which the loss was incurred. This is totally different from 'current year' relief which can be allowed against *total* assessable income from all sources, and Balancing Charges for the year of assessment in which the loss was incurred.

It may be that part or the whole of the capital allowances for the year are displaced by the loss relief.

(iv) Allowable losses

  (i) The loss must arise from the carrying on of a trade, profession, etc.

 (ii) The loss must be incurred during the year of assessment, and apportionments of figures for successive accounting periods may therefore be inevitable.

(iii) The loss must be computed in the same way as profits (already dealt with).

(iv) In the case of a partnership, the loss of each partner is personal to the partner who may claim a relief, which must be limited to the actual loss of the firm. For example, if a loss were ₦6000 and the shares of the partners were (A) ₦7000 (B) minus ₦1000, the first partner could only claim relief to the extent of the actual loss of the partnership.

(v) Losses incurred in the year of assessment may be set against total income from all sources, but a taxpayer wishing that such a loss should be set off against his total income must give notice in writing to the Tax Authority within twelve months after the end of the year of assessment.

While the incomes from other sources (excluding employment income) will be incomes of the preceding year, the loss is the loss during the year of assessment.

Notes

1 ITMA, s.2, s.6.
2 ITMA, s.21(2)(a).
3 ITMA, s.21(2)(b).
4 ITMA, s.21(2)(a) and (b).
5 ITMA, s.21(2)(a) proviso.
6 ITMA, s.21(1).
7 ITMA, s.21(2)(b), proviso(ii).
8 ITMA, s.21(2)(b), proviso(iv).
9 ITMA, s.21(2)(b).
10 ITMA, s.21(2)(b), proviso(ii).
11 ITMA, s.21(2)(b), proviso(i) and ITMA, s.21(4).

7 Capital Allowances

(i) Introduction

This chapter deals with the main aspects of the provisions of the Fifth Schedule to the Income Tax Management Act No. 21, 1961 and Companies Income Tax Act, 1979. The total capital allowances that may be claimed in any assessment year are now restricted to 75% of the year's profits for manufacturing companies and $66\frac{2}{3}$% in other cases.

It is important to understand that capital allowances are not deductions from income like the 'outgoings and expenses' covered by section 17 of ITMA. Capital allowances are *special deductions* from income under Schedule 2 of the Companies Income Tax Act, 1979: which refers to 'any deductions to be made or allowed in accordance with the provisions of section 26 of the 1979 Act and of the said schedule' (i.e. the Second Schedule). Capital allowances are not covered by the provisions of section 26 which relate to loss incurred by a taxpayer.

Capital allowances are amounts which are proportions of capital expenditure. Although it is a basic rule of income taxation that capital expenditure which has been charged against profit must be added-back, this does not mean that no capital expenditure whatever should be deducted from profit. On the contrary, it is correct to allow such deduction subject to strict rules.

Capital allowances are allowed *for years of assessment*. They are not like expenses incurred during the accounting period relative to a year of assessment. But in order to calculate the amounts of the allowances the concept of 'basis period' relative to each year of assessment is used. It is the capital expenditure incurred during such basis period which is used to calculate the amounts of the allowances for the relevant year of assessment. This basis period is normally the same as the accounting period, but it may be different in cases where any of the provisos to the definition of 'basis period' applies.

In order that capital expenditure may qualify for being used to calculate the amounts of the allowances it must fulfil the definition of '*qualifying expenditure*' in paragraph 2 of the Fifth Schedule to ITMA and Second Schedule to the 1979 Act. In order to determine the particular basis period during which qualifying expenditure was incurred, the date of payment is relevant. But where a liability for expenditure has been incurred in a particular basis period but payment is not made therein, the expenditure may be treated as incurred on the date it became due and payable by the owner of the asset acquired by such expenditure.

The assets acquired by qualifying expenditure are covered by the definition of this expression in paragraph 2 of the Fifth Schedule to the 1961 Act and paragraph 1 of the 1979 Act. Paragraph 9 of the Fifth Schedule to the 1961 Act lays down that such assets must be in use at the end of the *basis period*. If not, no capital allowances can be granted.

There are three kinds of capital allowances under the Fifth Schedule of ITMA and the Second Schedule of the Companies Income Tax Act, 1979 namely: Initial Allowances, Annual Allowances and Balancing Allowances. Capital Expenditure is the qualifying capital expenditure incurred during a basis period which is used to calculate the first or Initial Allowance. The full amount so calculated is allowable whether the expenditure was incurred on the first day of their basis period or any other day, or whether the basis period is a full year or shorter. The Initial Allowance is only allowable once, for the year of assessment relative to the basis period during which the expenditure was incurred.

It must, however, be pointed out that as from the 1969–70 assessment year a *Reconstruction Allowance*, referred to as *Investment Allowance*,[1] of 25 per cent based on capital expenditure is granted, on *new* assets bought to replace those certified as damaged or destroyed during the Civil War (16.7.67 to 15.1.70). This Investment Allowance is only granted once and it is additional to Initial Allowances. It is also not deductible from the cost of the asset but can be withdrawn if within a period of five years the following events took place:

The events referred to in sub-section (4) of section 27 of the 1979 Act are:

(a) any sale or transfer of the asset representing the expenditure made by the company incurring the expenditure otherwise than to a person acquiring the asset for a chargeable purpose or for scrap;

(b) any appropriation of the asset representing the expenditure made by the company incurring the expenditure, to a purpose other than a chargeable purpose;

(c) any sale, transfer or other dealing with the asset representing the expenditure by the company incurring the expenditure, being a case where it appears that the expenditure was incurred in con-

107

templation of the asset being so dealt with, and being a case where it is shown either –

(i) that the purpose of obtaining tax allowances was the sole or main purpose of the company for incurring the expenditure or for so dealing with the asset;

(ii) that the incurring of the expenditure and the asset being so dealt with were not *bona fide* business transactions, or were artificial or fictitious transactions, and were designed for the purpose of obtaining tax allowances.

Another form of Investment Allowances was introduced during the 1978–79 Budget Speech. All capital expenditure on plant and equipment incurred in agricultural production by companies and individuals will, apart from attracting the existing capital allowances on the assets, enjoy an investment allowance of 10 per cent. Like its counterpart, the Reconstruction Allowance, referred to previously, the investment allowance on plants and equipment used in agricultural industry is not deductible from the cost of the assets to arrive at its written-down value for tax purposes; it is tax-free.

As regards Annual Allowances[2], the taxpayer is also entitled to an Annual Allowance for the year of assessment relative to the basis period during which qualifying capital expenditure was incurred. Thus he is entitled to two allowances for that year with respect to the particular item of such expenditure.

Subject to the provisions of the Fifth Schedule, where in his basis period for a year of assessment, the owner of any asset has incurred in respect thereof qualifying expenditure wholly, exclusively, necessarily and reasonably for the purposes of a trade or business carried on by him whether or not an Initial Allowance may be made to him in respect of that qualifying expenditure, there shall be made to that individual for each year of assessment in his basis period for which that asset was used for the purposes of that trade or business an allowance (hereinafter called 'an Annual Allowance') at the rate specified in respect thereof in Table II of the Fifth Schedule of such expenditure after the deduction of Initial Allowance where applicable, provided that an amount of ₦10 shall be retained in the accounts for tax purposes until the asset is disposed of.

In the case of an asset in respect of which an allowance has been granted before the commencement of this sub-paragraph, an allowance shall be made in respect of the asset for the number of years of assessment which, if added to the number of years of assessment for which allowance has already been made, equals the number of years of assessment for which allowance is to be made under the provisions of the previous paragraph, provided that if an allowance has been made for a number of years which is equal to or more than the number of years specified in the previous paragraph, a single allowance shall be made for an amount which is ₦10 less than the residue of the qualifying expenditure for the year of assessment in which this sub-paragraph takes effect.

Balancing Allowance is covered by paragraph 9 of the Second Schedule to the 1979 Act. This arises where the asset acquired by qualifying capital expenditure is 'disposed of' at a time when there still remains some Residue of such expenditure. If the disposal 'Value of the Asset' is less than this Residue, the difference constitutes the amount of the Balancing Allowance. But it is to be noted that, under paragraph 13, Second Schedule to the 1979 Act, if the 'Value of the Asset' exceeds the Residue, the excess constitutes an amount to be added to income under Section 24 of the Law, and must be subjected to assessment by a 'Balancing Charge'. There are four important points to be noted:

(a) The excess of the Value of the Asset over the Residue may be large in some cases. For example, suppose capital allowances totalling ₦2200 have been allowed with respect to an asset costing ₦4000 with the result that the Residue is ₦1800. If the asset is disposed of for ₦4200, the excess of this amount over Residue is ₦2400. In such a case the whole ₦4200 is not subjected to the Balancing Charge, but only ₦2200 – which is the total amount of the capital allowances allowed at the time of disposal. The difference between the cost price ₦4000 and ₦42 000 sales proceeds, i.e. ₦200, will bear Capital Gains Tax at 20 per cent.

(b) Balancing Allowances and Balancing Charges are only to be operated where the asset was in use immediately prior to its disposal.

(c) The meaning of the expression 'disposal of' is covered by paragraph 12 of the Second Schedule of the 1979 Companies Income Tax Act.

(d) The 'Value of the Asset' is governed by paragraph 14 of the Fifth Schedule of ITMA.

Paragraph 21 of the Fifth Schedule to ITMA and paragraph 18 of the 1979 Act deal with lessors, i.e. persons who incur capital expenditure on assets and lease the assets to other persons. It is laid down that a lessor will be entitled to capital allowances in respect of such assets, if at the time the expenditure was incurred the lessor's purpose was to lease the asset for use wholly and exclusively for the purposes of a trade or business carried on by some other person. This applies to assets other than buildings, and means that, for example, in the case of a lorry, if the owner leases it to another person in its new condition without having used it himself, he may claim capital allowances. If, however, he leases it after having himself operated it for some time, he will not be entitled to claim allowances against the income from the lease arrangement.

This was the position on leased equipment up to 1977–78 assessment year. From the 1978–79 assessment year when the necessary Act on this issue was promulgated, if this is the intention of the pronouncement, all equipment leased out, whether or not this was the initial purpose for incurring the expenditure, enjoyed capital allowances at the appropriate rates as other plants and machinery used for the purposes of carrying on a trade.

The case of a building which is leased by the owner is covered as follows:

(a) if the capital expenditure incurred to acquire the building was incurred at any time not later than 31 March 1955, the owner must prove that he incurred the expenditure for the purpose of leasing the building (he will not able to prove this if he lived in the building himself after acquiring it);

(b) if the expenditure was incurred after 31 March 1955, then no such proof is required and the owner may claim allowances irrespective of the purpose he had when he first acquired the building (and whether he lived in it himself or not).

Paragraph 22 of the Fifth Schedule to ITMA deals with assets acquired partly for business purposes and partly for other purposes. For example, a trader constructs a building the ground floor of which he used for his business and the upper floor for his residence. In such cases, a proportion of the capital allowances on the whole building relative to the ground floor may be allowed.

Paragraph 29(2) of the same Schedule lays down that the total amount of Initial, Annual and Balancing Allowances for a year of assessment is to be allowed by deducting the amount from the 'Remainder' of the assessable income from all sources relevant to that year of assessment. Paragraph 29(3) of the schedule defines this 'Remainder' as follows:

Assessable Income from all sources *plus* addition for 'Balancing Charge' under paragraph 29(1) *minus* deduction for any loss allowable under section 17(2) of the Law.

It will be seen that the first step to be taken before granting any capital allowances whatever is to determine the 'Remainder'. In a case where there are several sources of income and there is a loss from one source and capital allowances are due in respect of assets used for that source, the amounts of loss and capital allowances must be kept entirely separate. Only the loss is to be used in determining the Remainder. The deduction of the loss is governed by section 17(2) paragraph (a) or (b) of ITMA as the case may be.

When the Remainder has been determined, the amount of the capital allowances should be deducted. It will be seen that there is no bar to deducting capital allowances from income of a different source, for example, capital allowances on buildings producing rental income can be deducted from employment income. Moreover, it is immaterial whether, in a loss case, section 17(2)(a) or section 17(2)(b) applies. These provisions have nothing to do with capital allowances, they merely govern loss. They only have an indirect effect on capital allowances because they must be applied first, to determine the Remainder from which the allowances are to be deducted. The fundamental point to be grasped is this: *Capital allowances are not to be deducted from the income of a particular source. They must be deducted from income of all sources.*

We must understand that in the computation of income inserted in the assessment file, we must first arrive at 'Remainder'. We must not compute assessable income from a particular source, deduct capital allowances relative to that source, and add the balance to income from other sources. We must first determine assessable income from all sources, fulfil the definition of 'Remainder' and lastly deduct any capital allowances, irrespective of the relevant source of income. The word 'Remainder' must be written in the computation.

With regard to paragraph 27 of the Fifth Schedule, the form of return of income provides an appropriate part in which claim for capital allowance is to be made by the taxpayer. If he leaves the part blank, officers must not assume that he does not wish to claim. On the contrary, the taxpayer must always be asked to state definitely whether or not he wishes to claim.

(ii) Qualifying expenditure

Types of qualifying expenditure

Capital expenditure which qualifies for capital allowances is of the following types, incurred on assets used for a trade or business:

(a) Capital expenditure incurred on plant machinery and fixtures;
(b) Capital expenditure incurred on the construction of buildings, structures or works of a permanent nature other than expenditure under (a) and (c);
(c) Capital expenditure incurred in connection with, or in preparation for, the working of mines, oil wells or other sources of mineral deposits of a wasting nature other than expenditure under (a);
(d) Capital expenditure incurred in connection with plantations on clearing land for planting and on first planting.

Plant, machinery and fixtures

In the absence of any statutory definition, the words 'plant, machinery and fixtures' must be given their ordinary meaning. Without attempting a definition, the technical terms may be said to include:

(a) motive power and engines, whether driven by electricity, gas, oil, steam, wind or water;

(b) shafting, pulleys, and banding conveying the power to the machines;

(c) actual running machinery whether operated by power or hand, e.g. lathes, pumps, drills, shuttles, rollers, sewing machines, comptometers and typewriters;

(d) stationary plant used for storage, processing, etc., for example, tanks, vats, pipes, refrigerators and containers;

(e) transporters driven by steam, oil, petrol, electricity, etc., for example, ships, locomotives, railway coaches, wagons, cars, vans, lorries, trucks, trolleys and cranes;

(f) carts, boats, bicycles, etc., hauled by animals or propelled by men;

(g) electrical, atomic and radiation devices used for industrial or professional purposes;

(h) fixtures and fittings of a permanent and durable nature including furniture but excluding soft furnishings.

Certain features, the absence or presence of which cannot be regarded as conclusive, may nevertheless be regarded as characteristic of plant and machinery: the generation or transmission of power or energy; movement or change as in transport or manufacture; and duration and permanence. It is at times difficult to draw a dividing line between plant and buildings, for example, gasholders or a shipyard slipway both of which are usually treated as plant.

A little guidance is available from case law in considering the meaning of plant and machinery.

In *Daphne v Shaw (11 TC 256)*, a solicitor was refused a wear and tear allowance on his library of professional books. Rowlatt, J. said: '... "plant and machinery" ... means apparatus, alive or dead, stationary or moveable, to achieve the operations which a person wants to achieve the operations which a person wants to achieve in his vocation.' This was over-ruled in *Mumby v Furlong* (1971)(2) All ER p.953.

An example of an asset which is on the borderline between machinery and buildings is in *Margrett v Lowestoft Water and Gas Co. (19 TC 481)*. The company claimed wear and tear on a water tower built, except for certain pumps, valves and pipes, of ferroconcrete. The tower was used for increasing the pressure of the water supply and replaced a gas engine and pumps. The UK Revenue admitted the claim as to the pumps, valves and pipes but not to the tower itself. The Court upheld that view.

Certain expenses, having the appearance of capital, are allowed as deductions in computing income and, under ITMA, Fifth Schedule, paragraph 18, are excluded from the scheme of capital allowances. Such expenses are:

(a) Sums expended on the renewal, repair or alteration of any implement, utensil or article employed in acquiring the income [ITMA s.17(1)(c)].

(b) Sums expended on the replacement of parts of machines or repair of machines [ITMA s.17(1)(c)] as opposed to the cost of renewal of complete machines which does qualify for capital allowances.

(c) Sums expended on collections of loose tools (e.g. hammers, spanners, jacks, jigs, patterns, picks and shovels) which are usually valued in the same way as trading stock, and if such valuation is reasonable the cost of 'consumption' is allowed as a deduction in computing income.

In this book, the word 'plant' is intended to cover plant, machinery and fixtures.

(iii) Buildings, structures or works of a permanent nature

The words 'buildings, structures or works of a permanent nature' in ITMA, Fifth Schedule, paragraph 2, are sufficiently broad to indicate that allowance can include, not only buildings of a conventional type (walls plus roof), but also any erection which is a permanent stationary structure (e.g. a loading ramp, a road, a tunnel).

In this book the word 'buildings' means buildings, structures or works of a permanent nature, and 'industrial buildings' means those industrial buildings or structures included in the main category.

Certain types of buildings are classified as 'industrial buildings or structures' for the purpose of higher allowances. These are defined as any building or structure in regular use:

(a) as a mill, factory, mechanical workshop, or other similar building, or as a structure used in connection with any such buildings;

(b) as a dock, port, wharf, pier, jetty or other similar building or structure;

(c) as an hotel with at least 20 bedrooms for guests;
(d) as a storehouse or shelter for plant and used in connection with:
  (i) a mill, factory, etc., [definition (a)],
  (ii) a dock, port, etc., [definition (b)],
  (iii) an hotel [definition (c)], or
  (iv) an employee's office or dwelling [definition (g)];
(e) for the operation of a public railway, waterworks or electricity undertaking;
(f) for the running of a plantation or the working of a mine;
(g) as an employee's office or dwelling used wholly, exclusively and regularly in connection with:
  (i) a mill, factory, etc., [definition (a)],
  (ii) a dock, port, etc. [definition (b)],
  (iii) an hotel [definition (c)],
  (iv) a store house, etc., [definition (d)],
  (v) a public railway, etc., [definition (e)], or
  (vi) a plantation or mine [definition (f)];
(h) as a warehouse or coldstore wholly, exclusively and regularly let out in storage spaces, and offices and dwellings of employees of the trade;
(i) as a bank. (ITMA Fifth Schedule, paragraph 6(b)).

Mines, oil wells or other sources of mineral deposit of a wasting nature

Expenditure qualifying for capital allowances under this heading is capital expenditure on:
(a) the acquisition of the deposits, or the acquisition of rights in or over the deposits, or the purchase of information as to the existence and extent of the deposits;
(b) the search for deposits, or the discovery and testing of deposits, or the approach to deposits;
(c) the construction of any works or buildings which are expected to have little or no value when the mine is no longer worked or when the concession to work the mine ends. (*Note* that offices or other buildings capable of further use when the mine is closed are treated as ordinary buildings.) (ITMA Fifth Schedule, paragraph 2).

The following special considerations are provided by ITMA, Fifth Schedule, paragraph 3:
(a) Where capital expenditure has been incurred on the purchase of information as to the existence and extent of the deposits, or on the search for deposits, or discovery and testing of deposits, or

the approach to deposits, by an individual for the purposes of a mining, etc., trade carried on by him; *or* expenditure has been incurred by an individual prior to commencing a mining, etc., trade, and would have qualified for an allowance if incurred after the trade had commenced; *and* such expenditure has not created an asset, then an asset owned by the individual for the purposes of his mining, etc., trade is deemed to have been created.

(b) Where an asset created by mining expenditure has not been disposed of, it is deemed to be in use for trading purposes for so long as the individual incurring expenditure carries on the trade.

(c) Where capital expenditure on the acquisition of rights in or over the deposits, or the purchase of information as to the existence and extent of the deposits, is higher than the original cost of acquisition or discovery, allowance is computed by reference to original cost only.

Plantations

A plantation is an estate used for growing cotton, rubber, sugar or other products of warm countries. Qualifying expenditure is capital expenditure on:

(a) clearing land for planting; and
(b) planting other than replanting.

Meaning of asset[3]

The term 'asset' as used in the Act includes a part of an asset and in the case of joint interests, an undivided part of an asset.

The general[4] rule is that if expenditure of the types defined is incurred for the purposes of a trade or business *in a basis period* of that trade or business then the expenditure gives rise to the right to capital allowances.

(iv) Basis period

The expression 'basis period' is fundamental to the scheme of capital allowances for it is in relation to his basis period that a claimant's title to an allowance or liability to a charge for any year of assessment is determined.

In the ordinary way the basis period of a trade or business is the period of account which is taken as the basis for the assessment on the profits of that trade or business. (ITMA, section 20 defines these basis periods.)

The granting of capital allowances depends upon the incurring of qualifying capital expenditure for the business. These allowances will be granted in the basis period; that is, the period of the profits or loss on which the assessment for that year is computed. The wear and tear of the assets during the year of assessment will be the deduction to be allowed in respect of the wear and tear. Where there is an overlapping in two basis periods, the period common to the two will be regarded as falling in the first basis period only.

In the case of employees, the basis period is the year of assessment, and in the case of lessors of plant and machinery, where hiring is not their trade, the year of assessment is also the basis period.

Paragraph 2 of the Fifth Schedule of the Income Tax Management Act, 1961, as amended, states that 'basis period' has the meaning assigned to it as follows:

(a) in the case of an individual to or on whom any capital allowance falls to be made, the basis period for any year of assessment is the basis period for computing the profits.

    (i) First year of commencing a trade – profits from the time of commencement to the following 31 December. In other words, if a trade commences on 1 June 1980, the first year of assessment will be 1 June 1980 to 31 December 1980 and the year of assessment will be 1980;

   (ii) Second year of trading – income to be taxed will be income of the first twelve months from the time of commencement of the trade, that is, from 1 June 1980 to 31 May 1981. The year of assessment will be 1981;

  (iii) Third year of trading – income of the preceding year, that is, income of 1 June 1980 to 31 May 1981 will be taxed in the year of assessment 1982.

  (iv) Fourth year of trading – income of 1 June 1981 to 31 May 1982 will be taxed in the 1983 year of assessment, that is, on a preceding year basis;

   (v) Fifth and subsequent years of trading – income of the preceding year. Election can be made under section 20(3) of the 1961 Act on giving notice to the relevant tax authority within two years after the end of the second year to have the second and third years of assessment based on 'actual', that is, the 1981 year of assessment to be based on income from 1 January 1981 to 31 December 1981, while 1982 will be based on income from 1 January 1982 to 31 December

1982. We could then ask whether any qualifying or capital expenditure was incurred by the taxpayer during the basis period and whether such an asset was in use during that basis period, and for how long.

(b) Where two basis periods overlap, the period common to both is treated as falling in the first basis period. [Paragraph (2)(b)(1) of the Schedule to the 1961 Act].

Overlaps and gaps in basis periods

Expenditure may be incurred, or an asset disposed of, in a period of account which is used as the basis for two years of assessment (e.g. in the commencing years) or which is not used as the basis for any year of assessment. This difficulty is eliminated by the following provisions:

(i) Where two basis periods overlap, the period of overlap is treated as only belonging to the first basis period except for annual allowance.

(ii) Where two basis periods coincide, the period is treated as the first basis period except for Annual Allowance.

(iii) Where there is an interval between basis periods of successive years of assessment, the interval is treated as part of the second basis period *unless* the year of assessment based on the second basis period is the year of permanent discontinuance of the trade or business, when the interval is treated as part of the first basis period.

Expenditure incurred prior to commencement

Where qualifying expenditure is incurred by an individual on an asset for the purposes of a trade or business which he is about to commence, the expenditure is regarded as incurred on the day the trade or business commences, that is, in the first basis period.

Example 1

From commencement to cessation of his business, a trader submits accounts as follows:

```
9 months from 1.6.82 to 28.2.83
12 months from 1.3.83 to 28.2.84
12 months from 1.3.84 to 28.2.85
12 months from 1.3.85 to 28.2.86
12 months from 1.3.86 to 28.2.87
5 months from 1.3.87 to 31.7.87
```

He claims for the second and third years of assessment to be based on actual profits. The assessment for 1986–87 (penultimate year) is also based on actual profits.

The basis periods for assessment of profit will be:

1982   7 months from 1.6.82 to 31.12.82
1983 12 months from 1.1.82 to 31.12.82
1984 12 months from 1.1.83 to 31.12.83
1985 12 months from 1.3.84 to 28.2.85
1986 12 months from 1.3.85 to 28.2.86
1987   4 months from 1.4.86 to 31.7.86

There is a period of overlap of the basis periods for 1982 and 1983.

Example 2

Adebisi commenced trading on 1 June 1980 and incurred qualifying expenditure as follows:

1980   2 June   ₦2400
1981   29 February   800
         31 May   1600
1982   30 April   400

You are required to show how the relevant expenditure will be allocated to years of assessment.

Year	Basis of Assessment	Qualifying expenditure
1980	1.6.80 to 31.12.80	Actual expenditure, i.e. ₦2400.
1981 (First 12 months)	1.6.80 to 31.5.81	There is an overlapping period of seven months, i.e. 1.6.80 to 31.12.80. The qualifying expenditure therefore is ₦800 + ₦1600 = ₦2400.
1982 (Preceding year)	1.6.80 to 31.5.81	There is no qualifying expenditure since no new one not yet dealt with was incurred in the basis period 1.6.80 to 31.5.81.
1983 (Preceding year)	1.6.81 to 31.5.82	The qualifying expenditure would be be ₦400, being expenditure incurred on 30 April 1982.

(c) Where there is an election to have both the second and third years of assessment based on actual, the position will be:

118

Income Tax year	Basis of assessment	Qualifying expenditure
1981	1.1.81 to 31.12.81	₦800 + ₦1600 = ₦2400
1982	1.1.82 to 31.12.82	₦400
1983	1.6.81 to 31.5.82	NIL (but there is an overlap with 1982)
1984	1.6.82 to 31.5.83	NIL (Basis period here overlaps with that of 1982).

Qualifying sources of income

In general, the capital allowances scheme is designed for trade and business only. ITMA, Fifth Schedule, paragraph 24, extends the relief of professions and vocations, however, in respect of items shown in the following table:

Source	Allowances which may be claimed
Trade	Plant: buildings, mines, plantations
Business	Plant: buildings, mines, plantations
Profession	Plant: buildings
Vocation	Plant

Relevant interest in buildings, etc.

Special consideration has to be given to the identification of the person entitled to capital allowances for buildings, structures, and works.

When a person incurs expenditure on a building, etc., his interest in the building at that time is called 'the relevant interest' in regard to that expenditure. Thenceforth, whoever holds that interest is the person entitled to allowance in respect of that expenditure. These provisions apply to 'buildings' and 'mines' allowances on buildings, structures or works, and are contained in ITMA the Fifth Schedule, paragraphs 4 and 5.

The primary definition of 'the relevant interest' is, in the words of the Act:

'in relation to any expenditure incurred on the construction of a building, structure or works, the interest in such building, structure or works to which the person who incurred such expenditure was entitled when he incurred it.'

119

Complex interests

'Lease' is defined in paragraph 2 of the Fifth Schedule as including any tenancy and any agreement for the letting or hiring out of an asset. Leasehold interest is to be construed accordingly. In this connection it must be remembered that a leaseholder is a person holding under a lease, not a person granting a lease.

If the person incurring qualifying expenditure on a building, etc., had two or more interests in the building at the time, the relevant interest is the interest which was reversionary on all the other, that is, the larger or superior interest.

If the relevant interest is sold after the building, etc., has been constructed, the buyer is treated as having incurred, on the day the purchase price becomes payable, capital expenditure of the lower of:

  (a) the price paid; or
  (b) the original cost of construction, *except* for Initial Allowance, which is not given.

If the relevant interest is sold after the building, etc., has been constructed *but before it has been used*, then Initial Allowance is given and the buyer is treated as having incurred capital expenditure equal to the original cost of construction. This provision applies only to the last buyer before the building is used.

Meaning of 'incurred'

The owner of an asset has to 'incur' capital expenditure in order to qualify for capital allowances. Expenditure is incurred when the bill becomes payable – *not* when the asset is ordered, and *not* when payment is made.

Expenditure becomes payable on the date on which it becomes due for payment, whether or not payment is actually made.

Hire purchase transactions – concession

Under a hire purchase agreement, payment is made by a number of instalments and the aggregate amount payable can be divided between:

  (a) capital cost, that is, the amount which would have been payable under a cash transaction; and
  (b) hire costs, that is, the balance.

Strictly, the capital cost is incurred as the instalments become payable. Capital allowances should be granted on this basis, that is,

120

not until the hirer becomes the owner at the conclusion of the hire purchase agreement. By concession, however, the hirer is treated as the owner and the full capital cost element of the total charges is treated as incurred on the date on which the agreement is made.

Relief in respect of hire costs under (b) above is to be granted under ITMA, section 17, as a deduction in computing profits and spread over the period of hire.

Initial Allowance

Qualifying conditions [5]

When in a basis period, a trader or businessman incurs qualifying expenditure wholly and exclusively for the purposes of his trade or business on an asset owned by him and in use in his trade or business at the end of the basis period he qualifies for Initial Allowance.

Grant of allowance

The Initial Allowance is given for the year of assessment in the basis period of which the asset was first used. It cannot be given more than once. It is not affected by length of basis period or of ownership.

Amount of allowance

The amounts of Initial Allowance which can be claimed are as follows (from the 1985 year of assessment):

Building Expenditure	5% of cost
Industrial Building Expenditure	15% of cost
Mining Expenditure	20% of cost
Plant Expenditure	20% of cost
Motor Vehicle Expenditure	20% of cost
Plantation Equipment Expenditure	20% of cost
Housing Estate Expenditure	20% of cost
Ranching and Plantation Expenditure	25% of cost

All companies and individuals engaged in agricultural production who incurred capital expenditure enjoy *in addition*, from 1.4.78, an investment allowance of 10%.

Example 3

Written-down value of capital assets, 31.12.81	₦657 500
Additions up to 31.12.82	750 000
	1 407 500

Less

Investment Allowance, 10% of ₦750 000 = ₦75 000
Initial Allowance, 20% of ₦750 000 = 150 000
Annual Allowance, $12\frac{1}{2}$% of ₦1 407 500 = 175 938   325 938
Written-down value of assets as at
1.1.83.   1 081 562
Total capital allowance granted ₦400 938

Investment allowance, like Initial Allowance, is a once and for all grant in respect of any new acquisitions but unlike Initial Allowance, it is not deductible in arriving at the written-down value of the capital assets. The lessors of plant and equipment in use in the agricultural sector are entitled to capital assets. Lessees of plant and equipment are not entitled to capital allowances but are entitled to deduct rental expenses from their profits.

Asset to be 'in use'[6]

To qualify for Initial Allowance, the asset has to be 'in use' at the end of the basis period. The asset is treated as 'in use' if:
  (a) it is out of use but the period of disuse is only temporary; or
  (b) the first anticipated use is expected to be in the trade or business. (Anticipated allowances thus given and not ultimately justified can be withdrawn.)

Extension of allowance

The allowance is extended not only to trades and businesses but also to professions for 'plant' and 'buildings', and to vocations for 'plant'.

Artificial transactions

Artificial transactions may arise where the buyer is controlled by the seller, or the seller is controlled by the buyer, or both are controlled by a third person. To prevent excessive Initial Allowance claims, the Act provides that in such transactions the Initial Allowance may be such a sum as the Commissioner of Internal Revenue thinks is just and reasonable but not exceeding the normal allowance.

Annual Allowance

Qualifying conditions

When, in a basis period, a trader or businessman has incurred qualifying expenditure wholly, and exclusively and reasonably for the purposes of his trade or business on an asset owned by him, he qualifies for Annual Allowance for each year of assessment at the end of which basis period the asset is in use in his trade or business. Act No. 65 of 1966 added the word 'necessarily' whilst Act No. 28 of 1974 added the word 'reasonably'.

Grant of allowance

The Annual Allowance is proportionately reduced if the length of the basis period to which it refers is less than one year. It is *not* proportionately increased if the basis period exceeds 12 months (the profit assessed for a full year of assessment is never greater than the profit of 12 months).

The Annual Allowance is not affected by the length of the period of ownership within the basis period.

Amount of allowance (Para. 8)

The rates of Annual Allowance which can be claimed are as follows: (percentage of cost or written-down value)

Qualifying Expenditure in respect of:	%
Building Expenditure	10
Industrial Building Expenditure	10
Mining Expenditure	10
Plant Expenditure	10
Housing Estate Expenditure	10
Ranching and Plantation Expenditure	15
Motor Vehicle Expenditure	25
Plantation Equipment Expenditure	$33\frac{1}{2}$

The amount of Annual Allowance for a year of assessment is the appropriate percentage of the residue of the expenditure at the end of the basis period for that year of assessment.

Residue of expenditure[7]

In giving effect to the provisions of sub-paragraph 2, the amount of capital allowances to be deducted from assessable income in any year of assessment shall not exceed 75 per cent of such assessable income in the case of an individual engaged in the manufacture of any product and $66\frac{2}{3}$ per cent in the case of any other business. Any individual in the agro-allied industry shall not be affected by this restriction.

For the purposes of this paragraph –

'an individual in the agro-allied industry' is a person who –
(a) establishes or manages a plantation for the production of rubber, oil palm, cocoa, coffee, tea, and similar crops;
(b) cultivates or produces cereal crops, tubers, fruits of all kind, cotton, beans, groundnuts, shea nuts, beniseed, vegetables, pineapples, bananas and plantains;
(c) establishes or manages animal husbandry, that is to say, poultry, piggery, cattle rearing and the like and fish farming;
(d) engages in food production.

Assets to be 'in use'[8]

To qualify for Annual Allowance, the asset must be 'in use' at the end of the basis period. The asset is treated as 'in use' if:
(a) it is out of use but the period of disuse is only temporary; or
(b) the first anticipated use is expected to be in the trade or business. (Anticipated allowances thus given and not ultimately justified can be withdrawn.)

Extension of allowance

The allowance is extended not only to trades and businesses but also to professions for 'plant' and 'buildings', and to vocations for 'plant'.

Example 4 (Initial and Annual Allowances)

Akunkunmi buys a vehicle qualifying for Initial Allowance and Annual Allowance in the basis period for the year 1981. He has been trading for some years and makes up accounts to 30 September. The cost of the vehicle is ₦1000.

The allowances due for the years 1981, 1982 and 1983 are:

1981	Cost	₦1000
20% Initial Allowance	₦200	
$12\frac{1}{2}$% Annual Allowance	125	325
Residue at 1.10.80		₦675

1982		
$12\frac{1}{2}$% Annual Allowance		84
Residue at 1.10.81		₦591

1983		
$12\frac{1}{2}$% Annual Allowance		74
Residue at 1.10.82		₦517

124

According to ITMA, 1961, Fifth Schedule, paragraph 12, the earliest date on which the residue of qualifying expenditure can be ascertained after making Initial and Annual Allowances for a year of assessment is the first day after the end of the basis period for that year of assessment.

Example of Initial and Annual Allowances

Yinka starts business on 1 October 1982 and makes up accounts first to 31 December 1983 and then annually to 31 December. He buys a vehicle qualifying for Capital Allowances on 1 December 1982. The cost of the vehicle was ₦800.

The basis periods for assessment of profits will be:

1982   3 months from 1.10.82 to 31.12.82
1983   12 months from 1.10.82 to 30.9.83
1984   12 months from 1.1.83 to 31.12.83
1985   12 months from 1.1.84 to 31.12.84

The allowances due will be:

1982	Cost	₦800
20% Initial Allowance (in full)	₦160	
$12\frac{1}{2}$% Annual Allowance (for 3 months although owned only 1 month)	25	185
Residue at 1.1.83		615
1983		
$12\frac{1}{2}$% Annual Allowance (for 12 months)		77
Residue at 1.10.83		538
1984		
$12\frac{1}{2}$% Annual Allowance (for 12 months)		67
Residue at 1.1.84		477
1985		
25% Annual Allowance (for 12 months)		467
Residue at 1.1.85		₦10

Example 5 (Initial and Annual Allowances)

Folasade starts business on 1 April 1982 and makes up accounts first to 31 December 1982 and then annually to 31 December. He buys two vehicles qualifying for capital allowance. The first was bought on 1 October 1982 for ₦1000 and the second on 31 January 1984 for ₦800. Calculate the allowances due up to 1986:

(a) if the normal basis of assessment applies; and

(b) if election is made for the second and third years to be assessed on actual profits.

(a) Where normal basis of assessment applies:

1982   9 months from 1.4.82 to 31.12.82
1983   12 months from 1.4.82 to 31.3.83
1984   12 months from 1.1.83 to 31.12.83
1985   12 months from 1.1.84 to 31.12.84
1986   12 months from 1.1.85 to 31.12.85

The allowances will be:

		Vehicle 1	*Vehicle 2*	
1982 Cost 1.10.82			₦1000	
20% Initial Allowance	₦200			
(in full)				
12½% Annual Allowance ($\frac{9}{12} \times$ ₦125)	94	294		
Residue at 1.1.83		706		
1983				
12½% Annual Allowance		88		
Residue 1.4.83		618		
1984				
12½% Annual Allowance		77		
Residue at 1.1.84		541		
1985 Cost 31.1.84			₦800	
20% Initial Allowance				
(in full)			160	
10% Annual Allowance				
(in full)	531	100	157	
Residue at 1.1.85	10	540	483	
1986				
12½% Annual Allowance			157	
Residue at 1.1.86			326	

(b) For the relief claimed for second and third years of assessment, the basis periods of assessment of profits will be:

1982   9 months from 1.4.82 to 31.12.82
1983   12 months from 1.1.83 to 31.12.83
1984   12 months from 1.1.84 to 31.12.84
1985   12 months from 1.1.85 to 31.12.85
1986   12 months from 1.1.86 to 31.12.86

The allowances will be:

		Vehicle 1		Vehicle 2
1982 Cost 1.10.82		₦1000		
20% Initial Allowance	₦200			
(in full)				
12½% Annual Allowance ($\frac{9}{12} \times$ ₦125)	94	294		
Residue at 1.1.83		706		
1983				₦800
20% Initial Allowance (in full)			160	
12½% Annual Allowance (in full)		88	100	260
Residue 1.1.84		618		540
1984				
12½% Annual Allowance		77		67
Residue at 1.1.85		541		473
1985				
25% Annual Allowance		531		231
Residue at 1.1.85		10		242
1986				
25% Annual Allowance				232
Residue at 1.1.86				10

Balancing Allowances and Balancing Charges

The Balancing Allowance or Balancing Charge is a final adjustment in the life of the asset in the particular trade or business (or profession or vocation in some instances). The object is to secure by a combination of Initial and Annual Allowances and a Balancing Allowance or Charge that the cost of the asset to the claimant, less any sum obtained when it is disposed of by sale or otherwise, and no more than this, is allowed over the period of use and is relieved from taxation.

Balancing Allowances and Balancing Charges

ITMA, Fifth Schedule, paragraphs 10 and 11, provides that when, in a basis period for a year of assessment, the owner disposes of a qualifying asset, there is made for that year of assessment:
   (a) *A Balancing Allowance* of the excess of the residue of qualifying expenditure over the value of the asset at the date of disposal; or

(b) *a Balancing Charge* of the excess of the value of the asset over the residue of qualifying expenditure at the date of disposal (but limited at its maximum to the total capital allowances given).

Residue of expenditure[9]

The residue of qualifying expenditure is the total; qualifying expenditure incurred less the total of Initial or Annual Allowances previously made.

Asset to be 'in use'[10]

A Balancing Allowance or Charge can only be made if, immediately before disposal, the asset was in use by its owner for the purposes of his trade or business. The term 'in use' covers the temporary disuse.

Disposal[11]

'Disposal' is defined as follows:
(a) *Plant, machinery and fixtures* – when:
   (i) sold;
   (ii) discarded or scrapped; or
   (iii) no longer used for the trade, etc.
(b) *Buildings, structures and works* – when:
   (i) relevant interest is sold;
   (ii) relevant interest ends on termination of a concession;
   (iii) relevant interest ends on termination of a lease unless lessee acquires superior interest;
   (iv) demolished or destroyed; or
   (v) no longer used for the trade, etc.
(c) *Mining Assets* – when:
   (i) sold;
   (ii) no longer used for the trade, etc., either on cessation of trading, or on receipt of insurance or compensation.

Value of asset[12]

In the normal way, the value of an asset on disposal is the net proceeds of sale of the asset or relevant interest in the asset. There may be no actual sale.

If insurance or compensation is received on disposal, the net proceeds are taken as the sale price. Otherwise, the net open market value at the date of disposal is taken as the value.

Allowances made[13]

The term 'allowance made' includes an allowance which would have been made had there been sufficient assessable income to absorb it.

Any balance of unused allowance qualifies for relief normally in a later year of assessment – see ITMA, the Fifth Schedule, paragraph 29 – and is thus not lost to the taxpayer.

Example 6 (Balancing Allowances and Charges)

Olufunmilayo buys a vehicle qualifying for capital allowances in his basis period for 1982 and sells it in his basis period for 1984. He has been trading for some years and continues to do so indefinitely. The vehicle cost ₦1000. Calculate the Balancing Allowance or Charge arising for 1984 if:

  (a) the vehicle was sold for ₦200;
  (b) the vehicle was sold for ₦400;
  (c) the vehicle was sold for ₦1100;
  (d) the vehicle was exchanged with ₦400 cash for another vehicle listed at ₦900;
  (e) the vehicle was destroyed and insurance of ₦300 was received;
  (f) the vehicle was taken out of use and its open market value was ₦250.

Assume that Initial Allowance was 40% and Annual Allowance was 25%

Solution

The allowances given on the vehicle will be:

1982		
	Cost	₦1000
Initial Allowance	₦400	
Annual Allowance	250	650
		350
1983		
Annual Allowance		88
Residue at sale		262

The computations are as follows:

(a) Vehicle sold for		₦200
Residue		262
Balancing Allowance 1984		₦62
(b) *Vehicle sold for*		₦400
Residue		262
Balancing Charge 1984		₦138

(c) *Vehicle sold for*   ₦1100
    Residue   262
    Excess   838
    Balancing Charge 1984 limited
    to allowances given   ₦738

(d) *Vehicle realised ₦900–₦400*   ₦500
    Residue   262
    Balancing Charge 1984   ₦238

(e) *Net insurance proceeds*   ₦300
    Residue   262
    Balancing Charge 1984   ₦38

(f) *Open market value*   ₦250
    Residue   262
    Balancing Allowance 1984   ₦12

For an example using the 1985 rates, see **Supplement (1985).**

Assets used only partially for trade or business

Qualifying expenditure may be incurred on the acquisition of an asset
which is not used wholly, exclusively, necessarily and reasonably for
the purposes of a trade, etc. Furthermore, an asset originally bought
for the purposes of a trade, etc. may be now only partly used for non-
trading purposes. Examples are:
  (a) a motor car bought for part use in a trade; and
  (b) a building originally constructed for full qualifying use and later
      only partly so used.

Restriction of allowances and charges[14]

In the circumstances outlined before, allowances and charges are first
calculated as though the assets were fully used for trading purposes.
Then the allowances and charges are restricted to a just and
reasonable figure, having regard to all the circumstances.

Example 7 (part business use)

Ayodele buys a vehicle qualifying for capital allowances in his basis
period for the year 1982 and sells it in his basis period for 1985. The
vehicle cost ₦800 and was sold for ₦200. Throughout the period of
ownership it was used $\frac{3}{4}$ for business purposes and $\frac{1}{4}$ for non-business
purposes. Calculate the allowances and any charge arising, assuming

130

that the trading was commenced some time before 1980 and went on after 1987. Assume that initial allowance was 40% and that annual allowance was 25% for those years.

1982		Cost	N800	
Initial Allowance	₦320			
Annual Allowance	200		520	($\frac{1}{4}$ non-business)
			280	₦390 allowable
				₦130 allowable

1983			
Annual Allowance		70	($\frac{1}{4}$ non-business)
Residue		210	₦53 allowable
			₦17 allowable

1984		
Residue	210	($\frac{1}{4}$ non-business)
Annual Allowance	52	₦39 allowable
		₦13 allowable
Residue at sale	158	

1985	
Sale	200
Cost	800
Net cost	600

Net business cost $= \frac{3}{4} \times$ ₦600 $=$ ₦450
Allowances given

1982	₦390	
1983	53	
1984	39	₦482
Excess of allowances given *over net cost*		32

₦32 would be a just and reasonable Balancing Charge to withdraw allowances given in excess of that part of the net cost of the vehicle appropriate to trading activities.

Disposal without change of ownership[15]

It can happen that a Balancing Allowance or Charge arises on disposal of an asset without any change of ownership (e.g. plant taken out of use in the trade.) If the owner later uses the same asset for a qualifying purpose, he is deemed to have bought it on the first disposal date at a

131

price equal to the value taken for Balancing Allowance or Charge purpose on the first disposal date.

Apportionment[16]

The purchase or disposal of any asset is taken to include a purchase or disposal which combines the asset under consideration with other non-relevant assets. In such cases, the purchase or sale price is apportioned on a just basis.

When assets are bought or disposed of together as one bargain, even though separate values are placed on the various assets, the whole purchase or sale price is still apportioned on a just basis to prevent excessive allowances being claimed on qualifying assets.

(v) Lessors

Normally the trader himself uses the assets in question and any allowances and charges are made in charging his profits to tax. But a person may spend money on plant, buildings, etc., that he hires out in order to make an income for himself. The Income Tax Management Act provides for allowances to, and charges on, the lessor in such a case.

Lessors of assets other than buildings[17]

In the case of a lessor of an asset other than a building, Capital Allowances and Charges may be made if it can be shown:
   (a) that the owner has incurred capital expenditure on an asset;
   (b) that the asset is leased to a person for use wholly, exclusively, necessarily, and reasonably in a trade or business carried on by him; and
   (c) that for the whole or part of the lease the asset is so used.

If these conditions apply, the owner is treated as using his asset in a trade commencing when the expenditure was incurred and as using his asset in the same manner as it was initially used.

Lessors of buildings[18]

The leasing of a building is to be regarded as a trade or business. In the case of a lessor of a building, Capital Allowances and Charges may be

132

made in respect of capital expenditure incurred after 31 March 1955 on the building irrespective of the use intended by the owner at the time he incurred that expenditure.

If the capital expenditure was incurred on or before 31 March 1955, the question of intended use at that time is a material factor.

Basis period[19]

The basis period of the notional trade carried on by any lessor is the year preceding the year of assessment.

(vi) Partnerships, settlements, trusts and estates

Partnerships[20]

There are special provisions as to Capital Allowances and Charges when a partnership is involved. These special provisions come into effect during the period (called the 'relevant period') which covers any of the following periods in succession:

(i) 'A' trading on his own;

(ii) 'A' in partnership with 'B' and 'C', carrying on the same trade;

(iii) 'A', 'B', and 'C' carry on another trade in partnership;

(iv) 'B' in partnership with 'D' and 'E' carrying on the second trade;

(v) 'E' carrying on the second trade on his own. It can be seen that the relevant period is a period of continuity with the same trade or business being carried on by different individuals or combinations of individuals having a common link when partnership charges occur, or when the same individuals successively carry on different trades.

During the relevant period, the trade is treated as carried on by one and the same person (the 'deemed person') and Capital Allowances or Charges are computed as though that person had done whatever was done by the person or persons in fact carrying on the trade.

Settlements, trusts and estates

The preceding instructions on Capital Allowances refer to individuals, corporations sole and bodies of individuals. In computing the income of a settlement, trust or estate, however, if that income includes the profits of a trade, business, profession or vocation, or any rents or premiums, then the Capital Allowances provisions are applied in a

133

special way but as though the income from the sources mentioned had been the income of an individual assessable on the preceding year basis.

Where any assets of a trade or business form part of the estate of a deceased individual, and Annual Allowances may be claimed by, or on behalf of, that individual for the year of assessment in which he died, then the following special provisions override the instructions generally applicable to individuals:

(a) no Balancing Allowance or Balancing Charge is made at the date of death;

(b) the residue of expenditure is treated as the amount of qualifying expenditure incurred by the estate on acquiring the assets on the day after death; and

(c) When the estate disposes of the assets the Balancing Charge or Balancing Allowance is computed by reference to the original cost and the allowances subsequently given to both the deceased individual and the estate.

Capital allowances in respect of assets bought under hire-purchase agreements or bank loans

What should be remembered is that Initial Allowance (where applicable) is claimable on each instalment paid, and an Annual Allowance is given on the cash price, that is, total instalments less interest, since the interest is an allowable deduction in computing adjusted profits.

It is essential to note that the interest chargeable under a hire-purchase agreement or a bank loan in respect of an asset that is used in producing a taxable income must be wholly, exclusively, reasonably, and necessarily incurred for the purpose of the business, and allowed as an expense in the profit-and-loss account.

A taxpayer only becomes the owner of an asset on a hire-purchase agreement after all the instalments have been paid, that is, at the end of the performance of the contract. Initial allowance is granted only on the instalments as they become payable, since the expenditure is deemed to have been incurred when due.

Since the interest claimed has been excluded, the Annual Allowance is only calculated on the cash price of the asset.

Example 8 (Hire-purchase)

Effiong purchased a television set on 1 August 1980 on the following terms:

134

Cash price	₦4000.00	
Hire-purchase price	4400.00	
Deposit	400.00	

(Monthly instalments commencing on 1 September were ₦166.67)
Interest element   10.67
Period of repayment: 2 years.
You are required to show the relevant capital allowance computation,
assuming that the following rates apply: Initial, 40%; Annual $33\frac{1}{3}$%.

Solution

1980 deposit paid	₦400		
Instalments, ₦166 × 4	664	1064	
1981 ₦166 × 12		1992	
1982 ₦166 × 8		1328	
		₦4384	

1980		
Cash price		4000.00
Initial Allowance, 40% × 1064	425.60	
Annual Allowance $\frac{1}{3}$ × $33\frac{1}{3}$% × 4000	444.44	870.04
Written-down value		3129.96
1981		
Initial Allowance 40% × ₦1992	796.80	
Annual Allowance $33\frac{1}{3}$% × ₦3129.96	1043.32	1840.12
Written-down value		1289.84
1982		
Initial Allowance 40% × ₦1328	531.20	
Annual Allowance $33\frac{1}{3}$ × ₦1289.84	429.95	961.15
Written-down value		328.69

Note

The Annual Allowance has been charged in full in 1982 instead of
apportioning it because the vehicle had been in use.

If the television had been bought by Bank Loan, the interest on the
loan would be an allowable deduction in computing the adjusted
profit but since the ownership of the television had vested in Effiong
on the basis of the agreement, unlike the position under a Hire
Purchase Agreement, the Initial Allowance would be on ₦4000, a
once and for all allowance. 1985 allowances do not apply.

Accelerated depreciation system

The most significant deductions are those granted by way of depreciation (or capital) allowances. These allowances are granted in order to write-off a company's assets for tax purposes. The technique of granting these allowances in Nigeria is such as to speed up this write-off process. In other words, it is an accelerated depreciation system. The advantages of an accelerated depreciation system, provided sufficient income is earned, cannot be denied. Accelerated depreciation has the related effects of enhancing the profitability and liquidity of the beneficiaries as well as reducing risks. These are of particular importance to potential investors. Moreover, the firm gains by the compound interest on the tax remission involved.

The accelerated depreciation system in Nigeria takes the form of Initial Allowances combined with the normal Annual Allowances. Initial Allowances enable a company to claim a prescribed proportion of the cost of the asset in the year of acquisition[21] in addition to the Annual Allowance due for that year. The residual value of the asset (that is, the original cost less the Initial and Annual Allowances already granted) is then amortised over the remainder of the estimated 'life' of the asset by way of Annual Allowances only. These Annual Allowances are calculated on a reducing balance[22] basis under which a fixed percentage of the residual value (i.e. cost less all previous allowance) is allowed each year. This method in fact yields a declining absolute amount of allowance each year. If profit in any year of assessment is less than allowances claimed, the unabsorbed allowances can be carried forward indefinitely against future profit. Where a company ceases operations but still has unabsorbed allowances, these can be carried backwards against previous income for as far back as five years. If an asset is sold before it has been completely amortised for tax purposes, a balancing charge[23] is imposed where the sale value exceeds the residual value, and a balancing allowance[24] is made if the sale value is less than the residual value.

The rates of Initial and Annual Allowances vary according to broad categories of capital expenditure. The rates introduced in 1952 remained unchanged (subject to an amendment in 1958) until December 1966 when they were changed, with effect from October 1966.

Since October 1966 there has been a general scaling down of the rates of Initial and Annual Allowances.[25] In most cases the rates are now about one-half of what they used to be. This general reduction to a large extent meets one of the major criticisms one could level against the rates as they existed before December 1966, namely, their over-generosity and hence their adverse effect on revenue. Also, it could be argued that the coverage of the tax has widened considerably, particularly since 1960, reflecting to some extent an increasing rate of investment, thus tending to reduce the need to continue to give the stimulus of liberal capital allowances as before.[26]

Although the general reduction of the rates of capital allowances is welcome, particularly from the point of view of revenue, it would seem to have come at a time when, for incentive reasons, reduction is hardly desirable given the current situation in the country. In comparison with previous years, the reductions have reduced the profitability, enhanced the risk and reduced the liquidity of a given amount of investment, all these in addition to the already depressive impact the current crisis is having on business investment. If the rates are to be reduced, the reduction should not be as drastic as it has been. Concern over revenue should not be allowed to impair incentives, particularly, as already mentioned, in view of Nigeria's dependence on private enterprise as the vehicle for rapid industrialisation.

In addition to the reduced incentives it now offers, the system of capital allowances continues to be grossly lacking as a tool of development policy. It is available to all companies, regardless of whether they are commercial or industrial, regardless of whether or not the investments involved are desirable and of high priority from the point of view of development, and regardless of the geographical location of the investments. Very few countries adopt such a neutral, almost supine, depreciation system as Nigeria does. Given the needs of development and the deficiencies of the price system as an allocative mechanism, there would seem to be a need for a differential capital allowances system. Generally, commercial companies should qualify for lower rates than their industrial counterparts, and investments of high priority should be eligible for higher allowances. A bias could also be created in favour of investments undertaken in less-developed areas of the country, whilst at the same time helping to break the bottlenecks increasingly evident in such industrially congested towns as Lagos, Ikeja, Ibadan, Port Harcourt, Kano and Kaduna. Apart from these towns, large areas of the country remain virtually untouched by industrialisation.

Obviously we are advocating a more complex system of capital allowances than now exists. The administration would consequently become more difficult and complex. But a simple system with very little impact on the development process has little to commend it. A moderately selective system of allowances would not be beyond the competence of the present tax administration, and it would constitute a potent fiscal weapon with which to deploy the country's resources in a more rational manner.

High tax rate and incentive[27]

At forty-five per cent the tax rate was high already by many standards. One wonders whether it is sound policy to maintain a high companies income tax rate in view of Nigeria's desire for rapid industrialisation and the dependence on private enterprise to bring this about. There is also the question of attracting foreign investment. Although the extent is not known, it is thought that even at forty-five per cent, the rate could have weakened Nigeria's competitive position *vis-à-vis* other developing countries in the market for private foreign capital.[28]

It could be argued that the array of generous tax incentives which Nigeria offers to companies, particularly accelerated depreciation, to a considerable extent compensates for the relatively high tax rate. This may be so. Indeed the higher the tax rate the more substantial the exemptions and reliefs from the tax, and the more significant the amount of discrimination in favour of the companies enjoying the exemptions and reliefs.[29] A low tax rate may not yield such results. In fact, if the rate is low, any revision of the rate is more likely to be upwards than downwards. Reliefs and exemptions granted at the lower rate therefore would lose some of their value in the future when the rate rises. Besides, the higher the tax rate, the smaller the margin for further increases, and the more stable will the rate be, particularly upwards. Investors cherish such 'permanence' in the tax structure.

However, faced with a choice between exemption from a high rate for a period of time and then being taxed at that rate thereafter, and being taxed at a low rate for all times, it would not be surprising if an investor chose to be taxed at a low rate throughout (provided of course, that the rate can be expected to be reasonably permanent).[30] In other words, a low rate of tax, with some degree of permanence, could be a more powerful incentive for investors than a high rate combined with a complex of generous incentives which can only by granted for some time. It ensures a low tax burden for companies for all times. Moreover it must be remembered that the grant of tax exemption is not necessarily a simple, trouble-free, and costless process, both for the company and the government. The entrepreneur has to bear with the delays, the uncertainties, the costs, and the interference with and restrictions on his activities, caused by his asking for and enjoying tax reliefs and exemptions. On the part of the government, the operation of the incentives means extra expenditure over and above that involved in the regular tax administration, not to mention the opportunity cost of personnel diverted to the operation of the tax exemption programme.

In sum, it would seem that a lower rate has much to commend it. A low rate with most, if not all, exemptions swept away, would considerably simplify the companies income tax system. Gains would be made from the point of view of the investor in terms of certainty, low tax burden, and so on. The system would become more predictable from the point of view of revenue and would be much simpler to administer.

Treatment of distributed and reinvested profits

The issue is whether it is sound policy not to discriminate, as at present, between distributed and undistributed profit in order to encourage retention and reinvestment of profits both by foreign-owned and indigenous companies.[31] The question is raised particularly because the bulk of modern economic activity in the economy is carried on in organisations with substantial foreign interests. Whether organised as subsidiaries or branches of foreign concerns, these organisations would naturally have a propensity to remit profits and dividends abroad. While the intention should not be to 'lock in' all the profits, appropriate discrimination in favour of undistributed and reinvested profits is necessary to ensure that the bulk of profits remains in the country.

In a country such as Nigeria where it is relatively difficult to obtain funds on the capital and money markets, retained earnings become a major source of investment finance, and compensate for the deficiencies of other sources. Moreover, they could give a fillip to the development of the capital market as retained earnings not used for expansion seek other investment outlets. Admittedly, even without tax discrimination in favour of undistributed profits, and in spite of Nigeria's open-door policy with regards to the repatriation of profits, foreign concerns were, in the early 1960s, in fact retaining in Nigeria about forty per cent annually of their total earnings[32] (excluding retentions by oil companies). Starting from this level it is not unlikely that a tax discrimination could increase the proportion of retained earnings, or, at least, prevent it from falling, other things being equal.

One or two points, however, must be emphasised. First, tax discrimination in favour of distributed profits is not the only, nor perhaps the most important, factor influencing retention and reinvestment of profits. If general business conditions are favourable companies will retain and reinvest a large proportion of their profit even in the absence of a positive tax incentive to do so. Secondly, even with tax discrimination against distributed profits, companies may still choose to distribute the same net amount after tax, in which case undistributed profits will decrease rather than increase. Where such distribution involves remission of profits abroad the problem of retaining within the country a high proportion of the profits of foreign companies still remains unsolved. Thirdly, implicit all along is the fact that retention of profits is not quite the same as reinvestment of profits. The fact that policy succeeds in stimulating retention of profits does not ensure that reinvestment will take place, whereas the aim of policy is principally the reinvestment of profits. Retained earnings may be held as idle reserves.[33] Even when they are invested, say in expansion, such investment may not be the most desirable form of investment from the point of view of the country's development. It may be better to channel the funds through the capital market into other investments (thus simultaneously aiding the development of the capital market itself).

The problem of retained earnings then is three-pronged: to ensure an increase in their volume, to ensure they are retained within the country, and to ensure that they are invested in desirable directions. These could be achieved within the companies income tax structure by, for instance, a differential rate structure in favour of undistributed and reinvested profits or through a higher taxation of dividends. But these would need to be supported with a tax on exported incomes or tighter exchange control to curb the outflow of profit, and with other measures to influence the direction of investment.[34]

Application of the Fifth Schedule to the Income Tax Management Act 1961 as amended to partnerships

Since members of a partnership are assessed to tax individually as if each were carrying on a trade, business, profession or vocation on his own, where the individuals commenced the said trade, business, profession, or vocation on the same day or where the partnership has been in existence for a long period of time, the capital allowance of the partnership for a particular year of assessment is shared among the partners in their profits and losses sharing ratio. However complications arise in the following cases:

    (a) Where a partnership succeeds a sole proprietorship.

    (b) Where a partnership precedes a sole proprietorship.

    (c) Where there is a change in the composition of an existing partnership.

The first two cases are to be considered since their treatment would cover all conceivable situations. The law relating to these cases is to be found under the Fifth Schedule to the Income Tax Management Act, 1961.

In the application of the Fifth Schedule to the ITMA to partnership, it is provided that whenever a change occurs in the membership of the partnership, the 'deemed person' should be considered as having ceased and recommenced the trade or business in which the partnership is engaged.

The application of the cessation and commencement provisions in this sense is for the purpose of determining the basis period for capital allowances only. Thus the computation of assessable income of the partners is not affected by this provision.

The aim of the provisions is, therefore, to regulate the division of the capital allowances due to the 'deemed person' among the individual members of the partnership in such a way as to reflect the change in the ownership of the assets used in the business without applying the commencement and cessation provisions to the profits.

A sole proprietor who later admits individual(s) to form a partnership, retains his normal basis period with respect to profits. This is because the trade, business, profession, or vocation does not actually cease before the establishment of the partnership.

However, with regard to capital allowances, paragraph 25(3) of the Fifth Schedule to ITMA requires that the allowances for both the year of change and the penultimate year should be calculated as if the change involves cessation and commencement.

Thus for the penultimate year (i.e. the year immediately preceding that in which the partnership commences), capital allowances are calculated with reference to a basis period running from the beginning of the normal basis period for the penultimate year to the last day of the actual penultimate year of assessment.

Capital allowances are computed in two parts for the year in which the change takes place or the partnership commences:

(a) The sole proprietor is granted the allowances based on a period running from the first day of the year of change to the actual date of change. The Annual Allowances are apportioned, taking into consideration the number of months involved in relation to full year.

(b) The members of the partnership are entitled to the allowances for the period running from the date of change to the last day of that year of assessment. Hence, the allowances involved are divided among them in their profit and losses sharing ratio. The Annual Allowances are similarly apportioned in relation to the period involved.

Example 9

As an illustration, assume Akin, who has been in business for several years preparing accounts to 31 December each year, took on Ayo as a partner with effect from 1 January 1982. It was agreed that profits and losses should be shared equally.

Plant and machinery are purchased as follows:

Purchased by	Cost	Date of Purchase
Akin	₦20 000	13.4.81
Akin	40 000	27.11.81
Akin & Ayo	30 000	2.2.82
Akin & Ayo	50 000	31.3.82
Akin & Ayo	11 000	30.11.82

1982 (year of change)

Basis period: 1.1.82–31.12.82		
Residue b/f		₦39 000
Additions (₦30 000 + 50 000 + 11 000)		91 000
		130 000
I/A (20% of ₦91 000)	18 200	
A/A (15% of ₦130 000)	19 000	
		37 200 (for Akin
		₦92 800 and Ayo)

The summary of allowances is as follows:

Akin	
1981	21 000
1982 ($\frac{1}{2}$ of ₦37 200)	18 600
Ayo	
1982 ($\frac{1}{2}$ of ₦37 000)	18 850

We are required to compute the capital allowances of Akin and Ayo for the 1981 and 1982 years of assessment. The rates of allowances are: Initial Allowance (I/A): 20%; Annual Allowance (A/A): 15%.

Solution

The year of change is the 1982 year of assessment. Hence the penultimate year is 1981. The computations of capital allowances for these two years are as follows:

1981 (Penultimate year)

Basis period: 1.1.80–31.12.81

Cost of asset (₦20 000 + 40 000)		₦60 000
I/A (20% of ₦60 000)	₦12 000	
A/A (15% of ₦60 000)	9 000	21 000 (for Akin only)
		₦39 000

In this case, the partners' capital allowances for the penultimate year of the partnership are re-calculated with reference to a basis period running from the beginning of the normal basis period to the last day of the actual penultimate year.

The partners will also share the allowances for the first part of the year in which the partnership changes to sole proprietorship and the remaining sole proprietor will take the allowances for the latter part of the year.

Example 10

To illustrate the above-mentioned case, assume that Funmi & Seyi have been trading as partners for several years, making up their accounts to 31 March each year and sharing profits and losses in the ratio Funmi:Seyi = 3:2. Seyi left the partnership with effect from 1 April 1982 and Funmi continued as a sole trader. The residue of their cars (used for the trading purposes) for capital allowances as at 31 March 1979 was ₦30 000. Acquisition of additional cars is as follows:

Tax management

Purchased by	Cost	Date of Purchase
Funmi & Seyi	₦8 000	20.12.80
Funmi & Seyi	12 000	10.11.81
Funmi	9 500	13.2.82
Funmi	9 700	11.11.82

As in the previous example, we are required to prepare the capital allowances computations of Funmi and Seyi for the 1981 and 1982 years of assessment, given that the rates of allowances are I/A = 20%, and A/A = 15%).

Solution

The year of change is the 1982 year of assessment and hence the

143

penultimate year is 1981. The capital allowances computations for these two years are as follows:

1981 (Penultimate year)

Basis period: 1.4.79–31.12.81

Residue b/f.		30 000	
Additions (₦8000 + 12 000)		20 000	
		50 000	
I/A (20% of ₦20 000)	₦4000		
A/A (15% of ₦50 000)	7500	11 500	(for Funmi & Seyi)
Residue c/f.		₦38 500	

Computations to 31.3.79 have been treated, hence basis period starts from 1.4.79.

1982 (Year of change)

Basis period: 1.1.82–31.12.82
1st Part (1.1.82–31.3.82)

Residue b/f.		38 500	
Additions		9 500	
		48 000	
I/A (20% of ₦9500)	1900		
A/A ($\frac{3}{12}$ of 15% of ₦48 000)	1800		
		3 700	(for Funmi & Seyi)
Residue c/f.		₦44 300	
2nd Part (1.4.82–31.12.82)			
Residue b/f.		44 300	
Additions		9 700	
		54 000	
I/A (20% of ₦9700)	1940		
A/A ($\frac{9}{12}$ m of 15% of ₦54 000)	6075	8 015	(for Funmi only)
		₦45 985	

The summary of allowances is as follows:

Funmi

1981 ($\frac{3}{5}$ of ₦11 500)	₦6 900
1982 1st Part ($\frac{3}{5}$ of ₦3700)	2 220
2nd Part	8 015
	10 235

Seyi

1981 ($\frac{2}{5}$ of ₦11 500)	4 600
1982 1st Part ($\frac{2}{5}$ of ₦3700)	1 480

Duration of relevant period

A word must now be said about the limits of the 'relevant period'. The 'relevant period' as defined under paragraph 25(1) of the Fifth Schedule to ITMA may be construed as the sum total of the period or series of periods, during which the trade or business is carried on by persons in partnership irrespective of any changes in the actual membership of the partnership from time to time.

The relevant period also includes a period during which only one person is engaged in a trade or business as a sole proprietor either before the commencement of a partnership of which he will be a member or after the termination of a partnership to which he had belonged. The question then is where to draw the boundary line between the 'relevant period' and the ordinary basis periods.

Generally, where a period of sole proprietorship comes at the beginning of the 'relevant period', such relevant period should be considered as extending to the penultimate year of the sole proprietorship.

Where, on the other hand, the period of sole proprietorship comes at the end of the 'relevant period' such relevant period should be considered as extending to the last year of assessment of the last partnership.

The strict procedure laid down in the provisions of paragraph 25 of the Fifth Schedule to ITMA has now been considered. However, the Joint Tax Board has discretionary power under paragraph 25(7) to modify this procedure.

Notes
1 CITA, 1979, s.27.
2 See para. 6 of Second Schedule to the 1979 Act.
3 ITMA, Fifth Schedule, para. 16.
4 ITMA, Fifth Schedule, para. 2.
5 ITMA, Fifth Schedule, paras. 7 and 9.
6 ITMA, Fifth Schedule, para. 7.
7 ITMA, Fifth Schedule, para. 12.
8 ITMA, Fifth Schedule, para. 17.
9 ITMA, Fifth Schedule, para. 12.
10 ITMA, Fifth Schedule, para. 17.
11 ITMA, Fifth Schedule, para. 13.
12 ITMA, Fifth Schedule, para. 14.
13 ITMA, Fifth Schedule, para. 26.
14 ITMA, Fifth Schedule, para. 22.
15 ITMA, Fifth Schedule, para. 23
16 ITMA, Fifth Schedule, para. 15.
17 ITMA, Fifth Schedule, para. 21(1).
18 ITMA, Fifth Schedule, para. 21(2).
19 ITMA, Fifth Schedule, para. 21(3).
20 ITMA, Fifth Schedule, para. 25.

21 Or, in practice, the following year, since Companies Income Tax in the country is imposed on the previous year's profits.

22 Another basis for calculating Annual Allowances (but which is not used in Nigeria) is the straight-line basis which grants annually a fixed amount representing a given proportion of the original cost.

23 That is, the excess of sale value over residual value is added to taxable income.

24 That is, the excess of residual value over sale value is deducted from taxable income.

25 The change in the structure of the rates of Initial Allowance in favour of mining expenditure is perhaps meant to compensate oil companies to some extent for the higher tax under the new Petroleum Profits Tax arrangement which came into being in January 1967.

26 The reduced rates are also welcome from another point of view, apart from revenue. By reducing the subsidy to capital intensiveness an incentive is given indirectly to use more labour. This is desirable, given the country's unemployment problem, but we do not wish to press this point.

27 The Super Tax was introduced, according to the authorities, as an interim measure to ease the pressure on government revenue during the period of emergency in the country. It is common knowledge, however, that 'temporary' levies such as this imposed during periods of war or emergencies have a way of becoming permanent items of the tax system. People get used to paying them. Expenditure catches up with the increased revenue. The administrative procedures would have become well advanced. All these factors tend to lead to the retention of such levies long after the period of emergency is over. It is necessary, therefore, to watch the situation and to ensure that the system is either eventually abolished, or if it is to remain (which is more likely), that it is improved in nature so that incentives and equity will not be sacrificed on the altar of revenue.

28 cf. P.O. Proehl: *Foreign Enterprise in Nigeria.* (Oxford University Press, 1965), p.118.

29 cf. J. Heller and K.M. Kauffman: *Tax Incentives for Industry in Less Developed Countries* (Harvard Law School, Cambridge, Massachusetts, 1963), p.99.

30 Such a permanence can be achieved by freezing the tax rate for particular companies as is done in Kleinsorge (ed.): *Public Finance and Welfare Essays in Honour of C. Ward Macy* (University of Oregon Books, 1966).

31 The only provision in the present law relating to undistributed profits is aimed at preventing tax evasion by persons who use the corporate form of business to escape high personal taxation by distributing only a small proportion of the company's profits in a given year. The Board of Inland Revenue can in such a case treat as distributed such proportion of the undistributed profits as it may think fit, and tax this under personal income tax (cf. section 24 of the Companies Income Tax Act, 1961).

32 Central Bank of Nigeria: *Economic and Financial Review*, July 1965, pp.9–11.

33 Increased retained earnings held as idle balances may be desirable during a period of inflation, as the neutralisation of capital which results would reduce the inflationary pressure. For development (as distinct from anti-inflationary) purposes, however, it is necessary that such balances be invested.

34 It should be mentioned that incorporating a differential treatment of reinvested profit into the companies income tax structure would necessarily make the system more complex and hence less simple to administer. Moreover, some inequity may arise. Retained earnings could enhance the value of the assets of a

company, and in the absence of a capital gains tax, inequity arises between shareholders and non-shareholders, or between rich and poor shareholders. cf. A.R. Prest: *Public Finance in Theory and Practice*, (Weidenfeld and Nicolson, 1963), pp.328–9. For an excellent analysis of the problems of distributed versus undistributed profits tax, see also pp.335–41.

8 Reliefs

(i) Introduction

Before 1 April 1974, each State operated different rates of reliefs.

Act Number 7, otherwise known as the Income Tax Management (Uniform Taxation Provisions, etc.) Act 1975[1] provided a large measure of uniformity in the taxation of the income of individuals throughout Nigeria by amending the Income Tax Management Act 1961 and the Armed Forces and Other Persons (Special Provisions) Act 1972. The Act takes effect as from 1 April 1974. There is, however, no uniformity with regard to exemptions, taxable persons, definition of expressions, and local rates.

Paragraph (b) of sub-section 1 of section 4 of the Income Tax Management Act is amended by the provision in the Act of a sub-paragraph (vi) which states that taxpayers will no longer pay tax on any amount of rent or allowance in lieu, paid to employers or on account of employees by employers up to a maximum of ₦720.

Schedule 1 to the Act provides a new section 20(A) to the Income Tax Management Act as amended by section 8 of the 1985 Decree, which gives the reliefs stated below. Apart from married allowance, husband or wife not separated by deed or by order of any court may claim any of the reliefs or the reliefs may be partly claimed by them provided the aggregate reliefs given to any husband and his wife or wives do not exceed the amount which would be allowed if such individuals were treated as one and the same individual[2] and the relevant tax authority is empowered to apportion as it deems fit[3].

After allowing for expenses against income and allowing for income exempted from tax, allowances are given for personal reliefs as follows:

(a) *Personal allowance*: ₦1200 plus $12\frac{1}{2}\%$ of earned income in excess of ₦6000. Earned income is income from employment, trade, vocation or profession, but does not include investment income such as rents or dividends.

(b) *Children's Allowance* of ₦250 per child up to a maximum of four children provided the child –

(i) is maintained by the individual during the year preceding the year of assessment;

(ii) has on the first day of the year preceding the year of assessment either not attained sixteen years of age; or

(iii) is receiving full time instruction in a recognised educational establishment; or

(iv) is under articles or indentures in a trade or profession.

A husband and his wife or wives not separated from the husband by deed or on order of any court shall be treated as one. No additional deduction is allowable in respect of costs incurred in connection with the education of any child. Where the cost of maintaining any child is shared between two or more persons, the relevant tax authority is entitled to apportion the sum of ₦250 per child as may deem to it to be equitable between such persons.

In the case of *Oram v Mapp* (1969) TR 269, decided in the House of Lords, it was said that the taxpayer was entitled to a child allowance in respect of his son, a boy over 16 years of age who was a full-time student at St Andrew's University. The son, on the advice of his tutor, took up a temporary teaching appointment in France to improve his French. He earned the equivalent of £150 in the $2\frac{1}{2}$ months that fell into the year of assessment concerned. The son spent the £150 in France on lodgings and incidental outgoings. Nothing was brought into the United Kingdom when the son returned.

The Revenue contended that the son, in the year under appeal, was entitled in his own right to 'an income' exceeding £115 and that therefore the amount of the child allowance was to be reduced by £150 minus £115, i.e. £35. The taxpayer contended that no such reduction should be made. The General Commissioners and the High Court decided in favour of the taxpayer. The Court of Appeal held in favour of the Revenue. The House of Lords held for the taxpayer and effectively changed the Revenue's practice, which had been followed for the previous forty years. The expression 'an income' means 'taxable income'. The child was taxable only on remittances to the UK and there were none. Thus he had no taxable income and no reduction in the child allowance was to be made.

(c) *Dependent Relative Allowance* of up to ₦400, provided –

(i) the relative is a close relative of the individual or his spouse and is maintained by him or assisted in maintaining the relative during the year preceding the year of assessment and the relatives' income does not exceed ₦600 per annum;

(ii) the close relative is incapacitated by old age or infirmity from maintaining himself;

(iii) the close relative is the widowed mother whether incapacitated or not, of the individual or the individual's spouse;

(iv) if two or more persons claim in respect of the same relative, the aggregate deductions to be allowed to two or more individuals for any year of assessment in respect of any one relative shall not exceed ₦400, the amount of the deduction to be allowed to any such individual shall be the same proportion of that sum as the costs so incurred by him bear to the total of the costs so incurred.

(d) *Married Allowance* of ₦300 to a married man who at any time during the year preceding the year of assessment has a wife living with or maintained by him or a deduction of the amount of any alimony not exceeding ₦300 paid to a former spouse under an order of a court of competent jurisdiction in the case of an individual whose marriage has been dissolved.

(e) *Life Assurance Relief* of up to 10% of the capital sum assured but not exceeding ₦2000 or $\frac{1}{5}$ of the total income of the individual exclusive of any additional benefits such as bonus, profits, etc., whichever is lower provided –

(i) the premiums were paid by the individual during the year preceding the year of assessment to any insurance company and the insurance is on the life of the individual or the life of his spouse or of any contract for a deferred annuity on his life or the life of his spouse;

(ii) the premiums are on policies securing a capital sum on the death, whether in conjunction with any other benefit or not.

The restriction above on a maximum claim of ₦2000 or $\frac{1}{5}$ of total income whichever is less apply in the case of husband and his wife or wives not separated from him by deed or an order of any court as though all such individuals were one and the same individual whose total income for any one year of assessment was equal to the aggregate total income for that year of such husband and his wife or wives.

Pension or Provident Fund – Approved Pension contribution that you pay will be a dedictable expense before calculating your tax; National Provident Fund falls into this category also. The total amount of reliefs allowed is in respect of Life Assurance and contribution to approved Pensions or Provident Fund subject to a maximum of ₦2000.

(f) *Rent Relief of 10% of rent paid.*

Rates of tax

For the first ₦2000 (after your reliefs) at 10k per ₦ = ₦200(10%)

For the next ₦2000 (after your reliefs) at 15k per ₦ = ₦300(15%)

For the next ₦2000 (after your reliefs) at 20k per ₦ = ₦400(20%)
For the next ₦2000 (after your reliefs) at 25k per ₦ = ₦500(25%)
For the next ₦2000 (after your reliefs) at 30k per ₦ = ₦600(30%)
For the next ₦5000 (after your reliefs) at 40k per ₦
   = ₦2000(40%)
For the next ₦5000 (after your reliefs) at 45k per ₦
   = ₦2250(45%)
For the next ₦10 000 (after your reliefs) at 55k per ₦
   = ₦5500(55%)
For the next over ₦30 000 (after your reliefs) at 70k per ₦
   = 1(70%)

Although paragraph 15 of Decree 4 of 1985 attempted to substitute a new table 2 of the Seventh Schedule to the Income Tax Management Act, 1961, the table inserted is the existing table as the Federal Military Government has not approved any change in the existing rates of tax for 1985. Notwithstanding the apparent impression given in this table that income over ₦60 000 appears not to have a rate, the correct interpretation is that, income over ₦60 000 is not free of tax but shall continue to be charged at 70 per cent since nothing to the contrary has been stated or suggested in the law.

(ii) 'Error or mistake'

Section 35 of the Income Tax Management Act, 1961, deals with this topic. The expression 'error or mistake' covers errors of omission as well as of commission, and errors arising from a misunderstanding of the law as well as erroneous statements of fact. Examples are:

(a) failure to deduct allowable expenses;
(b) arithmetical error;
(c) omission of claim for capital allowances; and
(d) failure to claim loss relief.

No relief is admissible on the ground of an alleged error or mistake in the basis of computation of liability if the return, statement, or account was made on the basis, or in accordance with the practice generally prevailing at the time the return, statement, or account was made. Thus a decision of the Courts given after the date of a return, statement, or account does not afford a title to the relief.

Similarly, no relief is admissible on the ground of an alleged error or mistake in the basis of computation of liability if the return, etc., was made on the basis which, though wrong in law, had been deliberately adopted by the taxpayer and gave a result which, having regard to all the relevant circumstances of the case, was reasonable and just.

(iii) Claim for overcharging

If a person has been overcharged, in an assessment made on him by reason of some error or mistake in the return, or statement of account made by him for the purposes of the assessment, he may, not later than six years after the end of the year of assessment in which the assessment was made, claim relief in respect of the overcharge.

Example 1

Olufumlayo has carried on a profitable business for some years in Ibadan. The following is a summary of her Profit and Loss Account for the year to 31 December 1984.

Salaries and wages	8 320	Gross Profit	₦15 435
Rent, rates & insurance	1 480	Surplus on sale	
Lighting	385	of investment	39
Repairs and renewals	420	Taxed dividends	
Carriage	215	(gross)	80
Audit fee	65		
Bad and doubtful debts	108		
General expenses	368		
Depreciation	680		
Net Profit	3 333		
	15 554		15 554

Details of general expenses were:

Printing and stationery	₦86
Legal Costs: Lease of new premises	35
Customer's claim on alleged	
defective goods	25
Luncheon Vouchers newly introduced	150
Subscriptions: Society membership	10
Trade Association	20
Sundries (all allowable)	42
	368

Details of repairs and renewals were:

Initial decorations of new office	120
Repairs to plant	90
Renewal of part of factory roof	210
	420

A copy of the Bad and Doubtful Debt Account is as follows:

Amounts written off			Balance 1.1.1983:	
Trade debts		65	Specific debts	₦60
Loan to former employee		50	2% of remaining debts	220
Balance 31.12.83:			Debts recovered	48
Specific debts	₦81		Profit and Loss	108
2% of remaining				
debts	240	321		
		436		436

Note

The bad debts recovered during the year had, in the past, been charged and allowed for tax purposes.

The loan interest related to ₦3000 advanced privately by a friend in 1970 at 6%.

The written-down values of the plant, including office furniture and typewriters, after deducting the 1983 allowances, are:

Plant purchased before 5.11.1980	2800
Plant purchased after 5.11.1980	500

The following expenditure has been incurred on the purchase of fixed assets in 1983:

New office furniture and equipment	₦800	
Less allowances on old typewriter		
bought new for ₦65		
in September 1970	10	₦790
Second-hand lathe (first		
used in 1979)		200
New car (purchased 10.5.1983)		850

You are required to calculate the adjusted profit and chargeable income of Olufumlayo for 1985. She is a spinster. Assume all capital allowance rates for the plant and machinery including typewriter are 10% and for the motor car 25%.

Solution 1

Olufunmilayo
Computation of adjusted profit
Year to 31 December 1984
Year of assessment 1985

Net Profit per Accounts				₦3333
Depreciation				680
General expenses:				
Legal costs – Lease of new premises				35
Subscription – Society membership				10
Loan Interest				180
Bad and doubtful debts				
Loan to former employee written off				50
Increase in general provision (₦240–220)				20
Repairs and renewals				
Initial decorations of new office				120
				4428
Less: Surplus on sale of investment		₦39		
Taxed dividends		80		119
Adjusted profit				4309

Capital Allowances

	Plant 10%		Plant 10%	Car 25%	All
Written-down values brought forward	₦2800		₦500		
Less: WDV of typewriter sold	32				
	2768				
Additions in 1984					
New			800	₦850	
New (after 31.3.84)				850	
Second hand (first used before 6.11.71)	200				
	2968		1300		
Capital Allowances 1985					
Initial 10%	₦20		80		
Annual 10%	297	317	130	210	213	₦740
Carried forward		2651		1090	637	740

Notes

1 Interest on loan has been added back because it is a private loan, otherwise loan interest is allowable under ITMA, 1961, s.17(1)(a).

2 Gross dividends are included in the chargeable income even though the recipient will be given tax credit. Chargeable income is therefore ₦4309 plus ₦80 = ₦4389.

Example 2

Mr Obioma, has been trading for some years, and his first Profit and Loss Account for the year ended 31 December 1983 was as follows:

Gross profit from trading		₦24 764
Profit on sale of motor vehicle		593
		25 357
Less: *Salaries* – employees	₦10 321	
– wife	600	
Light	130	
Rates	260	
Office expenses	140	
Car expenses	345	
General expenses	2 768	
Bad debts	48	
Depreciation	300	
Repairs and renewals of fittings (shop)	147	
Audit and accountancy	300	
Legal expenses	400	
Net profit for the year		15 759
		₦9 598

The following information is given:
(a) Mrs Obioma acts as book-keeper and works approximately 15 hours per week.
(b) Mr and Mrs Obioma live in a flat over the shop, the entire property having been purchased in 1974 for ₦12 000. One-third of the expenditure on rates and light is in respect of the flat.
(c) It is estimated that Mr Obioma does 15 000 kilometres per annum in the car, of which 4000 are for private purposes. Mr Obioma replaced his estate car on 1 July 1983 for a larger model. The new vehicle cost ₦1700, and the old car was traded in for ₦400. The written-down value for tax purposes at 1 January 1984 was ₦460.
(d) *General expenses include:*

(i) Staff Christmas party		₦50
(ii) Entertaining – Nigerian customers		155
– Overses customers		80
– Nigerian agent of overseas customers		20
(iii) Christmas gifts (overprinted diaries costing 50k each)		200
(iv) Charitable donations		30
(v) Telephones (15% private use)		60
(vi) Premium on Pensions Policy ignored by the Joint Tax Board		760

155

(vii)	Bank interest (on temporary overdraft to finance purchases)	110
(viii)	Other allowable expenditure	1 303
		₦2 768

(e) *Legal expenses*

(i)	*Legal expenses in successfully defending a charge of dangerous driving whilst delivering goods*	30
(ii)	*Bad debts*	180
(iii)	*Costs of a tax appeal*	190
		₦400

(f) *Bad debts*

Increase in general provision		₦180
Bad debts written off		120
		300
Less: Bad debts previously written off, now recovered	₦52	
Specific provision for bad debts no longer required	200	
		252
		₦48

(g) Fittings are dealt with on a 'renewals basis'.

You are required to:

  (i) compute the adjusted profit, clearly stating the fiscal year concerned.

  (ii) compute the capital allowances due for that year, assuming that maximum allowances are claimed. Assume writing-down allowance to be 25%.

Solution 2(i)

1984 Adjusted Profit Computation

Net profit, per accounts to 31.12.83	₦9 598
Add Cost of tax appeal (note 1)	190
Depreciation (note 2)	300
Bad debts (note 3)	180
Entertaining Nigerian customers (note 4)	155
Entertaining Nigerian (note 5)	20
Charitable donations (note 6)	30
Private telephone (note 7)	9
Premium on pensions annuity (note 8)	760
Car expenses $\frac{4}{15}$ *of ₦345* (note 9)	92
Private portion of rates and light (note 10)	130
Total	11 464

156

Deduct

    Profit on sale of vehicle (note 11)   <u>593</u>

                                      <u>593</u>

    Adjusted profit, 1984, (on preceding-year basis)   <u>₦10 871</u>

Notes

1 *Cost of Appeal:* This was disallowed in *Smith's Potato Estates Ltd v Bolland* (1947), 30 TC 267. These expenses were not wholly, exclusively, necessarily and reasonably laid out for trade, but were personal expenses of the company as taxpayers.
2 Prohibited as capital expenditure.
3 The adjustment of a bad debt account is a common feature of examination questions.

Bad debts account

Written-off	₦1232	*Balance b/f:*	
Balance c/f:			
General provision	1280	*General provision*	₦1500
Specific provision	204	*Trade debt recovered*	96
		Profit & Loss Account	<u>1120</u>
	<u>₦2716</u>		<u>₦2716</u>

In this case there would be a reduction in the taxable profit, since the general reserve has been reduced from ₦1500 to ₦1280, which means that the difference of ₦220 has been previously taxed. Another way of stating the same principle is to say that allowable bad debts for the accounting period were ₦1436, but only ₦1216 were charged, therefore, an additional allowance of ₦220 is due.

4/5 not necessary to earn income.
6 Prohibited as 'not being money wholly and exclusively laid out for the purpose of the trade'.
7 Prohibited as private expenditure.
8 Prohibited as personal or private expenditure, and not approved by Joint Tax Board.
9 Prohibited as private expenditure.
10 Prohibited as domestic expenditure.
11 Not a trading receipt, but a capital profit.

Solution 2(ii)

The written-down value of Mr Obioma's car was ₦460 on 1.1.84 He sold it on 1.7.83 (basis period for 1984) for ₦400

Loss on sale			₦60
Less: private use $\frac{4}{15} \times$ ₦60 =			16
Balancing allowance			44
Cost of new car	₦1700		
Writing-down allowance 25%	425	*Less:* private	
Written-down value	₦1275	use ($\frac{4}{15} \times$ ₦425	
		= ₦113) =	312
Capital allowances due to Obioma			₦356

Example 3

Mr Olayide, a pensioner, commenced a salaried employment of ₦6000 p.a. on 1.3.84. He regularly receives a pension from a previous employment of ₦2600 p.a. He received an interest of ₦66 on Federal Nigeria Development stock for the year ended 31.12.83.

On 12.9.84, he received royalties totalling ₦487.50 and on 12.9.83, a royalty of ₦52.

He leased his property situated at Ekiti Street, Bodija, Ibadan, with effect from 31.3.83 at an annual rent of ₦2000, and another property at Ekiti Street on 31.5.83 at an annual rent of ₦3500. The two properties are adjacent to each other and they cost ₦96 600.

During the period 1.1.83 to 31.12.83, a loan interest of ₦3466 was paid in respect of building loan.

He received interest of ₦1214 on his deposit account with a local bank for the year ended 31.12.83.

He paid a salary of ₦160 per month to his private secretary, without whom it would not have been possible to earn a substantial part of the assessable income declared.

Mr Olayide is assessed separately from his wife but he has two children attending universities in Britain. In addition, he regularly pays a life assurance premium of ₦480 and pays his dependent relative a sum of ₦100 every year.

You are required to compute the statutory total income of Mr Olayide for the 1984 fiscal year.

Solution 3

Assessable income

(a) *Salary* – Actual – 1.3.84 to 31.12.84	₦5000
(b) *Pension* – 1.1.84 to 31.12.84	2600
(c) *Interest* – Deposit Account, Year to 31.12.83	1214
(d) *Interest*, Federal Nigeria Development Stock	66
(e) *Royalty*, year ended 12.9.83	52

(f) *Net assessable rental income:*

Rent	₦3542	
Less Interest on loan	3466	76
Total income – ITMA, s.21(1) as amended		9008

Deduct Capital Allowances on buildings:

Cost	₦96 600	
Less Annual Allowance, 10%	9 660	9660
Written-down value	86 940	

Unrecouped capital allowance available for carrying forward	652

Notes

(a) Section 21(1) of the Income Tax Management Act 1961 specifically states that the total income of any individual should be aggregated and that capital allowance pursuant to the Fifth Schedule to the Act should be deductible therefrom.

(b) The royalty received on 12.9.84 is not assessable during 1984 but during 1985; reference should be made to the payment voucher. The payment of ₦487.50 was assessable on preceding year basis to 1985 since the payment voucher shows 31.12.84. Date on payment voucher is relevant.

There will be no point in setting out reliefs since there is no assessable income and the question does not ask for chargeable income which is NIL.

(c) Rental income of ₦3542 is arrived at as follows:

(i) Proportion due, 31.5.83 to 31.12.83 at ₦3500 p.a.		₦2041.67
(ii) Proportion due, 31.3.83 to 31.12.83 at ₦2000 p.a.		1500.00
		3542.00
		approx.

Example 4

On 29 September 1988, Fayose acquired a freehold shop and on the same day he granted a lease of the shop to Wilson Tobacconists for a term of 11 years from 29 September 1988. The yearly rental was to be ₦800 payable on the usual quarter days in arrear, the first payment being due on 25 December 1988. In consideration of the granting of the lease, Fayose received a premium of ₦8000.

Further information regarding Fayose is that:

159

1 He is married and has two children aged 13 and 9;
2 The wife and children have no income;
3 He has other income as follows:

	Years ended 31 December	
	1988	1989
Salary	₦5000	₦6000
Bank deposit interest		
(a/c opened 1968)	78	142
Dividends – amounts received	1040	1139

4 Fayose is assessable on a benefit from the use of a company car of ₦300 per annum.
5 There are no charges on income.
   You are required to:
   (a) compute the amount of premium assessable in 1988;
   (b) compute the total income of Fayose for the year 1988;
   (c) state the relief which would be available to Fayose in respect of the assessable premium (you are not required to compute the amount of the relief); and
   (d) state the deductions which Wilson Tobacconists Ltd may claim in respect of the lease in computing its taxable profits.

Solution 4

Fayose
The amount of premium assessable for 1988

Premium received	₦8000
Deduct: Capital element 2(11 − 1)% = 20%	1600
	₦6400

Taxation liability 1988

Earnings	₦6000		
Benefit in kind	300		₦6300
Rent ₦200 per quarter			
(Dec. 88 & Dec. 89)	400		
Premium as above	6400		
(Assumed no allowable			
expenditure incurred)		₦6800	
Bank deposit interest	78		
Dividends 1139 × $\frac{100}{67}$	1700	1778	8 578
			₦14 878

Deduct
Personal allowance

$\text{N}1200 + 12\frac{1}{2}\% \times \text{N}6300 =$	1988	
Wife allowance	300	
Children's allowance	500	
		2 788
Chargeable income		N12 090

Example 5

Quickly, a widow who remarried two years ago, owns a house of six flats which she inherited from her late father. Five of the flats are let at N120 per month per flat whilst the remaining one is occupied gratuitously by Quickly's late husband's mother.

Also inherited is a farmland which was being commercially run by the late husband until he died on 31 October 1981. The wife continued on that basis. The adjusted profits of the farm for income tax purposes were as follows:

Year ended 31 December 1980	N5000
Year ended 31 December 1981	6000
Year ended 31 December 1982	1000
Year ended 31 December 1983	2000
Year ended 31 December 1984	3000

The following expenditure was incurred by Quickly on the house:

September 1981	Repairs to roof	N500.00
December 1981	Widening of main drainage	250.00
March 1982	Repairs to soakaway and septic tank	50.00
April 1982	Construction of fence	150.00
June 1982	Repainting of the house	200.00
July 1982	Replacing the wooden German windows with louvre	600.00

Her other sources of income are as follows:
(1) Shares in limited liability companies on which the gross income, subject to deduction of tax at source has been as follows:

Year to 31 December 1981	N1000
Year to 31 December 1982	N1000
Year to 31 December 1983	N1500
Year to 31 December 1984	N1500

(2) Post Office Savings Account on which interest has been credited as follows:

Year to 31.12.83 ₦20.00
     31.12.83 ₦20.00

(3) Salary from her part-time appointment as a member of a committee charged with national assignment:

Year ended 31 December 1981   ₦1200
Year ended 31 December 1982   1200
Year ended 31 December 1983   1200
Year ended 31 December 1984   1200

You are required to calculate the net tax payable by or the tax refund due to Quickly for the three assessment years ended 31 December 1984.

Ignore Capital Allowances.

Solution 5

Quickly Computation of Assessment

	1982	1983	1984
Net Income from Rent (Note 1)	₦ 6450	₦ 6350	₦ 7200
Net Income from other sources (Note 2)	2200	2680	2680
Adjusted profit from commercial farming	6000	1000	2000
	14650	10030	11880

Computation of Tax Liability

		1982	1983	1984
For every Naira of the first	₦2000	₦ 200	₦ 200	₦ 200
For every Naira of the next	₦2000	300	300	300
For every Naira of the next	₦2000	400	400	400
For every Naira of the next	₦2000	500	500	500
For every Naira of the next	₦2000	600	600	600
For every Naira of the next	₦30	–	12	–
For every Naira of the next	₦1880	–	–	752
For every Naira of the next	₦4650	1860	–	–
		3860	2012	2752
Less: Withholding tax on dividends ($12\frac{1}{2}\%$)		125	188	188
Total tax payable		3735	1824	2564

Note 1   Computation of income from rent

Year of assessment	1983		1984	1985
Preceeding year basis	1982		1983	1984
Income	₦7200		₦7200	₦7200
Less: Allowable expenses:				
Repairs to roof 500				
Widening of main				
drain 250	750			
Repairs of				
soakaway		50		
Repainting of				
house		200		
Replacing of				
wooden				
windows with				
louvre		600	850	
	6450		6350	7200

Note 2   Computation of income from other sources

Year of assessment	1983	1984	1985
Preceeding year basis	1982	1983	1984
Dividends	₦1000	₦1500	₦1500
Salary from part-time			
appointment	1200	1200	1200
	2200	2700	2700
Less: Post Office Saving			
Interest	–	20	20
Net Income	2200	2680	2680

Example 6

Mr Akinkunmi, sole proprietor of Dabby Piano Electronics Enterprises, had been satisfied for a number of years with the best-of-judgement assessment served on him by the tax authority. However for 1979–80 assessment year as he again failed to present audited accounts to the Revenue, he was again served with an assessment notice with ₦40 000 as his chargeable income. You are to assume for this exercise, year ended 31 March as the basis period for all years.

He had approached your firm which accepted to act as his income tax advisers.

On investigation you discovered that Mr Akinkunmi does not keep a full set of account books but you were able to make out that:

(i) He buys solely from Emni Electronics Manufacturing Company. His total purchases at catalogue or list price amounted to ₦102 000 during the year, against which he was given 25% trade discount. He also received a total cash discount of ₦560. A certificate had been given to you to this effect by the suppliers.

(ii) In view of the scarcity of his wares and government restrictions on importations, he manages to dispose of his pianos at 15% above list price. There were no stocks at start and close of business.

(iii) He paid in December 1985 for a five-year period, ₦15 000 as rent for his warehouses.

(iv) Two shop assistants help him and each employee is paid ₦200 per month with ₦150 per head as Christmas bonus.

(v) He purchased on 5.10.78 a Toyota pick-up for ₦8000 for his business and he spent a total of ₦1300 as allowable expenses on the vehicle for the assessment year in question.

(vi) Mr Akinkunmi is married with two children aged 5 and 8 and he maintains his widowed mother whose income from her husband's estate is ₦600 p.a.

(vii) For the year ended 31 March 1979 and 1980 Mr Akinkunmi received ₦120 and ₦150 respectively as Post Office Savings Bank interest.

(viii) On your scrutiny of his investments you were informed that on 19.5.80 he sold 500 shares out of his total holdings of 1600 shares in Kadara Textile Mills ordinary shares. The shares cost him ₦700 in 1976, disposals fetched him ₦300, whilst the market value of part not disposed of, was 60k per share. (Ignore dividends.) Expenses on disposal were ₦50.

You are required to:
(a) object formally against the assessment;
(b) submit your own computations of Akinkunmi's income chargeable to tax.

Solution 6

(a)

Ola, Olayinka & Co.,
Chartered Accountants,
1, Christopher Ola Avenue,
Efon-Alaye.
20th November, 1981.

The Chief Inspector of Taxes,
Lagos State Internal Revenue,
216 Broad Street,
Lagos.

Sir,

Objection to the Notice of Assessment

We have been appointed to act on behalf of Mr. Akinkunmi, Sole Proprietor of Dabby Piano Electronics Enterprises in respect of the Best of Judgement Assessment Notice dated 12th November, 1981 served on him for a chargeable income of ₦40,000.

We therefore wish to raise an objection on behalf of our client on the following grounds:

(a) That the assessment was based on the Best of Judgement.
(b) That the total income of the enterprise for the year in question was below ₦40,000 (i.e. 1979–80 Year of Assessment).
(c) That proper reliefs have not been given in respect of:
    (i) Capital Allowances;
    (ii) Personal Reliefs, such as personal allowance, wife allowance, children allowance and dependent relative allowance.

In view of the above submission, we hereby attach a certified statement of accounts for the 1979/80 year of assessment, our computation of assessment thereof and would request you to review and revise the assessment accordingly.

Yours faithfully,

Ola, Olayinka & Co.,
Chartered Accountants.

(b) *Computations of Akinkunmi's chargeable income for 1979–80*

Sales		₦117 300
Less: *Purchases*	₦102 000	
Less: *Trade discount*	25 500	76 500
Gross profit		40 800
Gross profit b/d		₦40 800
Add: *Discount received*		560
		41 360
Less: *Allowable deductions*		
Rent	3 000	
Salary	4 800	
Xmas Bonus	300	
Motor Expenses	1 300	9 400
Net Profit		31 960
Less: *Capital Allowance*		2 100
		29 860
Less: *Reliefs*:		
Personal Allowance		

1200 + $12\frac{1}{2}\%$		
(31,960 – 6,000)	4 445	
Wife Allowance	300	
Children Allowance	500	
Dependent Relative	–	5 245
Chargeable Income		24 615

Capital Allowances Computation – Motor Vehicle

1979/80	*Cost*		8 000
	Initial Allowance		
	(20%)	1 600	
	Annual		
	Allowance		
	($12\frac{1}{2}\%$)	500	2 100
	WDV		5 900

Notes

1 Published in the Extra-Ordinary Federal Republic of Nigeria Official Gazette No. 9, Vol. 62, 24 February 1975.
2 Act No. 7, Schedule 1, para. 4(a)
3 Act No. 7, Schedule 1, paras 4(b), 4(c)

9 Partnerships

(i) Introduction

A partnership is an association of two or more persons agreeing to carry on business in common with a view to profit under some arrangement for the sharing of profits and losses. Partnerships consisting of more than ten persons in banking business and twenty in the case of other businesses, cease to be partnerships and must be registered under section 377 of the Companies Act 1968. In Nigerian and English Law, partnership is not a separate legal entity; it is, however, in Scottish law. Partnership is assessed jointly in one sum and a partner's tax liability is a partnership debt and each partner is jointly and severally liable to pay it. Section 6 of ITMA 1961, as amended reads:

(1) The gains or profits from a partnership of a partner therein shall be the sum of –
(i) any remuneration, interest on capital, or the cost of passages to or from Nigeria wholly or mainly undertaken for the purposes of leave or recreation, which is charged in the partnership accounts in respect of that partner; and
(ii) his share in the income of the partnership computed in accordance with the provisions of this Act after the deduction of charges to which the preceding sub-paragraph applies in respect of all the partners but before the deduction of any other expenses of the partnership referable to a partner which would have been private or domestic expenditure within the meaning of paragraph (a) of section 18 if incurred directly by that partner; and when the income computed under sub-paragraph (ii) results in a loss, his share therein shall be deducted from his gains or profits ascertained under the provisions of sub-paragraph (i), and he shall be deemed to have incurred a loss in the trade or business of the partnership to the extent, if any, by which the deductible share exceeds those gains or profits.
(2) For the purposes of the preceding subsection, the share of a partner in the computed income of a partnership shall be such proportion of that computed income as would accrue to him under the provisions of the partnership agreement if that computed income were wholly apportionable between the partners within the terms of the agreement, or, where the computed income results in a loss, such proportion of that loss as would be chargeable to him if that loss fell to be allocated between the partners in the terms of the agreement.

(3) The amount of the gains or profits or loss of a partner, ascertained under the foregoing provisions of this section of any period shall be deemed for all purposes of this Act to be his ascertained income or loss of that period from a trade, business, profession or vocation carried on by him during that period, and the provisions of Part III of this Act, other than of paragraph (g) of section 17, shall not apply to such partner with respect to such income or loss.

(4) The determination of the income or loss from a partnership of a partner therein shall be made by the relevant tax authority in relation to that partnership, and where any partner is taxable for a year of assessment in the territory of some other authority the relevant tax authority shall supply to that other authority particulars of that determination.

(5) An appeal against an assessment by any individual in so far as it relates to any partnership income or loss shall lie only to the appeal tribunal or court specified for income tax purposes in a law of the territory the tax authority of which is the relevant authority in relation to that partnership.

(6) For the purposes of paragraph 6 of the first schedule the income of a partner from a partnership in Nigeria shall be deemed to be derived from the territory of the relevant tax authority in relation to that partnership.

(7) On demand by the relevant tax authority addressed in writing to the principal office or place of business of a partnership in Nigeria, the partner, employee or agent in charge of that office shall register or cause to be registered with that authority a certified copy of the partnership deed or, where no written deed is in existence, particulars of any written or oral agreement under which the partnership is currently established, and where any such particulars have been so registered notice of any subsequent change therein agreed between the partners shall be similarly registered with that authority within thirty days of such agreement.

(8) Where the particulars of any partnership have been registered under the provisions of the foregoing subsection the computation under this section of the gains or profits of a partner therein may be made by the relevant tax authority on the basis of those particulars as they apply at any relevant time, and, in the event of failure by a partnership to comply with any demand made under the foregoing subsection, notwithstanding the provisions of subsection (2) of this section, tax may be assessed and charged by the relevant tax authority as though the whole gains or profits of such partnership accrued to any individual partner therein or were divisible between any partners therein as may appear just and reasonable to that authority.

(ii) Deed of partnership

A partnership can, and often does, exist without the term of such an arrangement being put into writting, but as a rule a legal document, called a 'Deed of partnership' is drawn up to define the rights, duties and interests of the partners. This agreement usually contains clauses relating, *inter alia*, to:

(a) partners' contributions of capital;

(b) interest, if any, to be paid to each partner on his capital;

(c) salaries, if any, to be paid to partners; and

(d) the agreed division of profits and losses.

A 'Deed of partnership' has effect only from the date of its execution. It may have a fixed period or be indefinite, and its terms may be varied by the consent of all partners.

No deed of partnership

If there is no formal partnership agreement:

    (a) partners share equally the profits and losses; and

    (b) they are not entitled to interest on capital or to salaries.

(iii) Existence of partnerships

Partnerships are usually found in trades, businesses and professions, and the letting of property. Income such as interest and dividends often forms part of the income of a partnership. Partnerships consisting of more than ten persons in the case of banking and twenty in the case of any other persons must be registered under the Companies Act 1968, section 377. In *Akinlose v AIT Co. Ltd* (1961), WNLR at page 213, it was held that a group consisting of more than 100 members was illegal as a partnership and should be registered under the Companies Act. Joint tenancy, tenancy in common, joint property, or part ownership does not create partnership.

The law relating to partnership in Nigeria can be found in the Partnership Act, 1890,[1] which is applicable to the whole of the Federation except Ondo, Oyo, Ogun and Bendel States where the Partnership Law[2] applies.

At common law, the participation in the profits of a business is strong but not conclusive evidence of partnership.[3] Each case must, however, be considered on its own merits. This common law rule has received statutory approval.[4] The Act has laid down the rules determining whether a partnership does or does not exist.

There is provision for the distribution of profits after the death or withdrawal of a partner, especially when the surviving or continuing partners carry on the business of the firm with its capital and assets. Without any final settlement of accounts as between the firm and the out-going partner by the surviving or continuing partners, there is no entitlement to any further share of profits.[5]

(iv) Partnership income and taxation

'Computed income' of partnership[6]

The income of a partnership for a period is computed in accordance with the provisions of the Income Tax Management Act as though the income of an individual were being computed, except that there is allowed the cost of:

(i) any partners' salaries;

(ii) any partner's interest on capital; and

(iii) any partner's leave or recreational passages.

Any partnership expenses referable to a partner which would have been private or domestic expenses if incurred by the partner himself are not allowed in computing the partnership income.

The income arrived at, as above, is called the 'computed income' of the partnership. It is *not*, however, assessed on the partnership or, collectively, on the partners. The partners are individually assessed, as though they were individually trading.

Income of partner[7]

The income of each partner is arrived at by adding:

(a) his salary, if any, charged in the partnership accounts;

(b) his interest on capital, if any, charged in the partnership accounts;

(c) his private passage costs, if any, charged in the partnership accounts; and

(d) his share of the 'computed income' of the partnership, apportioned on the basis that the whole of the 'computed income' is apportionable on the terms of sharing profits and losses laid down in the partnership agreement.

The amount so arrived at is taken to be the income, or loss, of the partner from a trade, business, profession or vocation for all *purposes*. No further deductions for expenses are made, and that income enters into the assessable income of the individual partner, on the same basis as would income from a trade.

Partners' capital allowances

Capital Allowances and Balancing Charges are applied to partners under the provisions contained in ITMA, Fifth Schedule, paragraph 25.

Partners' 'residence'[8]

If, because of the absence of superior income and a place of residence, the partnership income is the factor determining the residence of a partner, it should be noted that the partnership income is treated as arising in the territory of the 'partnership tax authority'.

Responsible tax authority[9]

It may happen that the head office of a partnership is situated in one territory while some of the partners are resident in other territories. In order to eliminate overlap of authority, it is laid down that the tax authority in which the principal office or place of business is situated on the first day of the year of assessment, or is first established during that year, is responsible for computing every partner's income from the partnership for that year and, where applicable, partner's profit or loss.

Appeal by partner[10]

Any appeal made by a partner against the amount of partnership income included in his total income assessed is dealt with by the 'partnership tax authority' which computed that income.

(v) Registration of partnership agreement

Particulars of partnership[11]

A certified copy of the partnership deed or particulars of any partnership agreement, if there is no deed, is to be supplied on demand by the 'partnership tax authority' from the head office of the partnership. Any later changes agreed between the partners are to be notified to the 'partnership tax authority' within 30 days of agreement.

No particulars supplied[12]

The apportionment of income between partners is normally based on the particulars supplied. If particulars are not supplied then the apportionment is made as the 'partnership tax authority' thinks just and reasonable.

Example 1

A partnership of Ayo, Bukola, and Christopher which has been in existence for some years submits accounts for the year ended 31

December 1987 showing a net profit of ₦4800 after the following charges:

	Ayo	Bukola	Christopher
Salaries	₦520	–	₦1040
Interest on capital	–	48	–
Passages on leave	180	180	–

The partners' shares under the deed of partnership are:
Ayo – $\frac{1}{2}$: Bukola – $\frac{3}{8}$: Christopher – $\frac{1}{8}$:

Solution 1

For the year 1988, the business income assessed on each partner is as follows:

	Ayo	Bukola	Christopher
Salaries	₦520	–	₦1040
Interest on capital	–	48	–
Share of passage	180	180	–
'computed income'	2400	1800	600
Assessable Incomes	₦3100	₦2028	₦1640

Example 2

Olufunmilayo and Olayinka have been in partnership for several years. Their principal office is situated at 25 Ekiti Street, Bodija, Ibadan, Nigeria.

The accounts of the partnership for the year ended 31 December 1982 show a net profit of ₦1200 after deducting salaries, interest on capital and depreciation. You ascertain that Olufumilayo received a salary of ₦500 and interest on capital of ₦90 and Olayinka, a salary of ₦300 and interest on capital of ₦70. Depreciation on partnership assets amounted to ₦600. The following information is also available:

(a) *Rent paid to Olufunmilayo*   ₦100
(b) *Repairs, including ₦250 for an additional shed*   450
(c) *Bad debt is arrived at as follows:*
    General Provision for bad and doubtful debts   ₦300
    Debts proved bad and written off   50
                                                                                                  350
    Less: Specific bad debt previously written off   30
                                                                                                  320

Capital allowances at 31 December 1982 are agreed at ₦400.

172

The partners share profits or losses in the ratio:
   Olufumilayo: 70%
   Olayinka: 30%
You are required:
(a) to compute the firm's adjusted profit for the year 1983; and
(b) to state clearly the amount of income each partner would show on
    her income tax return for that year.

Solution 2

Computation of Firm's Adjusted Profit for 1983

(a) *Assessment*

Net Profit per question		₦1200
Add back Depreciation	₦600	
Capital Expenditure in repairs	₦250	
General Provision for bad/ doubtful debts	300	1150
		2350
Less: Capital Allowance		400
Profit of the firm to be shared between partners in profit and loss sharing ratio		1950

(b) *Assessable income of each partner for that year may be computed as follows:*

	Total	Olufunmilayo	Olayinka
Salary from partnership	₦800	₦500	₦300
Interest on capital	160	90	70
share of partnership profit (7:3)	1950	1950	585
Rental income	100	100	–
	3010	2055	955

Example 3

A partnership of Debo and Letitia submits accounts for the year
ended 30 September 1988 showing a net loss of ₦2400 after the
following charges:

	Debo	Letitia
Salaries	1800	–
Interest on capital	60	30
Passages on leave	–	200

The partners share profits and losses as follows:
Debo – $\frac{1}{3}$: Letitia – $\frac{2}{3}$

Solution 3

The computations are:

	Debo	Letitia
Salary	₦1800	–
Interest on capital	60	30
Passage	–	200
	1860	230
Share of computed loss	800	1600
Profit of y.e. 30.9.88:	₦1060	
Loss of y.e. 30.9.88:		₦1370

Example 4

Okojie, Adebayo, Yusuf, and Chukwudi had been in partnership as Hotel Caterers and Entertainers, sharing profits in the ratio of 4:3:2:1 respectively since 1980.

On 30 September 1989 Okojie missed her footing at a show, fell down and died instantaneously. The remaining surviving partners immediately agreed to continue sharing profits in the same proportion as before.

On 30 December 1988 the partners covenanted in favour of the only surviving daughter Anne to pay her half yearly on 1 April and 1 October for a period of 10 years an annuity of ₦720.

A supplemental partnership deed was executed with effect from 1 January 1990 under which interest is to be allowed on Capitals of 6 per cent per annum. Chukwudi for his skill on the stage is to be paid a salary of ₦480 per annum, and the balance of profits is to be shared in the ratio 5:4:3 respectively.

The partners' capital accounts have remained unchanged and on 1 January 1990 were:

Adebayo	₦20 000
Yusuf	8 000
Chukwudi	4 000

The adjusted profits for Income Tax purposes were as follows:

Year ended 31 December 1987	₦15 810
Year ended 31 December 1988	15 680
Year ended 31 December 1989	14 556
Year ended 31 December 1990	15 336
Year ended 31 December 1991	14 274

All available reliefs have been claimed.

You are required:

(a) to set out the computation of the original and final Income Tax Assessment for each of the years from 1st of January, 1987 stating precisely which partners will share the assessment and

(b) to show the final division of the total income of the partnership for the year 1990.

Solution 4

Income Tax Assessments are: Okojie, Adebayo, Yusuf & Chukwudi

Original assessments 1988 on Okojie, Adebayo, Yusuf and Chukwudi ₦15 810, year to 31.12.87	Final assessments on Okojie, Adebaye, Yusuf & Chukwudi Assessment uncharged ₦15 810
1989 On Okojie, Adebayo, Yusuf and Chukwudi year to 31.12.88 ₦15 680 (1)	On Okojie, Adebayo, Yusuf & Chukwudi: Actual profit from 1.1.89–30.9.89 $\frac{9}{12} \times 14556$ = ₦10 917 On Adebayo, Yusuf & Chukwudi Actual profit from 1.10.89 to 31.12.89 = $\frac{3}{12} \times 14556$ ₦3 639 = ₦14 556
1990 On Adebayo, Yusuf & Chukwudi first twelve months' trading, 1.10.89–30.9.90 $\frac{3}{12} \times 14556 + \frac{9}{12} \times 15336$ = 15 141	*1990* Actual profit claim under sec. 20(3)(d)(e), ITMA 1961, 1.1.80–31.12.90 = ₦15 336
1991 On Adebayo, Yusuf & Chukwudi Year to 31 December 1990 ₦15 336	3rd year 1991, Actual profit claim under sec. 20(3)(d) & (e) ITMA 1961, ₦14 274
1992 Year to 31 December 1991 ₦14 274	Assessment uncharged PYB ₦14 274

Adebayo, Yusuf and Chukwudi Division of partnership Assessment for the year 1990

175

	Total	Annuity to	Adebayo	Yusuf	Chukwudi
Amended assessment					
Actual profit	₦15 336				
Proportion for 9 months to 31.9.90 $\frac{9}{12} \times 15336$	11 502				
Less:					
Annuity paid 1.4.90	720	₦720			
Shared by survivors	10 782				
			₦($\frac{1}{2}$)5391	($\frac{1}{3}$)3594	($\frac{1}{6}$)1797
Proportion for 3 months to December 1990 $\frac{3}{12} \times 15336$	3 834				
Annuity paid 1 Oct. 1990	(720)	720			
Salary to Chukwudi 3 months at 960 p.a. = 240	(240)				240
Interest on capital at 6% p.a. = 480	(480)	300	300	120	60
	2 394		997.5	798	($\frac{1}{4}$)598.50
	₦15 336	1440	6688.50	4512	2695.5

Notes

1. An English statute of general application in Nigeria.
2. Cap. 86 *Laws of Western Nigeria* (now Oyo, Ondo, Ogun and Bendel States) 1959.
3. See *Cox v Hickman* (1860) H.L. Cas. 268 followed also in *Badeley v Consolidated Bank* (1888) 38 Ch. D. 238 (CA).
4. s.2(3) Partnership Act, 1890, s.4(c), cap. 86.
5. s.42(2).
6. ITMA, s.6(1).
7. ITMA, s.6(1), (2), (3).
8. ITMA, s.6(6).
9. ITMA, s.6(4).
10. ITMA, s.6(5).
11. ITMA, s.6(7).
12. ITMA, s.6(8).

10   Corporate Taxation (1)

(i) Introduction

The recent development of this tax is attributable to the fact that until well after the Second World War the corporate form of business was practically non-existent in Nigeria. Being recent, it is not surprising that it has hitherto not received as much attention from writers and students of taxation in Nigeria as personal income tax has received.

However, with the growth of the economy, the corporate sector has expanded considerably, bringing more sharply into focus the problems of taxing corporate income, and of exploiting a potentially fruitful source of revenue. Over 1000 companies were subject to companies income tax in 1965 compared with only about 350 in 1960. The manner of taxing corporate incomes has become crucial not only from the point of view of revenue but also from the point of view of stimulating rapid industrialisation.

Prior to 1939, company income was not singled out as such for taxation. All incomes were treated either as personal income or partnership income. The few joint stock companies (almost all of whom were British) were either taxed in Great Britain or were subject to special tax arrangements. The Companies Income Tax Ordinance, 1939, imposed for the first time a tax specifically on company income 'accruing in, derived from or brought into Nigeria' at a proportional rate of $12\frac{1}{2}$ per cent. No specific rates for depreciation allowances were provided, but provision was made for the deduction of a 'reasonable amount for the exhaustion, wear and tear of the property owned by the company, including plant and machinery'.

The 1939 Ordinance was repealed by the 1940 Income Tax Ordinance. The 1940 Ordinance effected no change in the system (the rate, for example, remained at $12\frac{1}{2}$ per cent). All it did was to combine under the same law the provisions for the taxation of personal and company incomes. Indeed the same provisions applied in both

177

cases excepting that the rates differed, and companies were, naturally, not eligible for family allowances. Although the 1940 Ordinance was soon repealed in 1943 by that year's Income Tax Ordinance, the lumping together of personal and company incomes taxation under one single law remained unchanged for the following eighteen years. However, the system itself underwent significant changes over the years, particularly in the areas of rates, allowances, and reliefs. The changes were effected principally by the various amendments to the 1943 Income Tax Ordinance (which thus remained the original law for taxing company income for the next eighteen years).

The 1943 Ordinance doubled the tax rate to twenty-five per cent. This was further raised to forty-five per cent in 1949 by the Income Tax (Amendment) Ordinance of that year. This is the highest rate that ever obtained and it lasted for nine years. The 1949 Ordinance also made a significant addition to the system by granting tax relief to small companies.

There were two further signficant development in 1952. First, the Aid to Pioneer Industries Ordinance was passed granting full exemption from Companies Income Tax for up to five years to companies which have been certified 'pioneer companies'. Secondly, the Income Tax (Amendment) Ordinance of that year not only prescribed, for the first time, specific rates of Annual Depreciation Allowances (instead of leaving these to administrative discretion as previously), but also introduced Initial Allowances. In effect accelerated depreciation dated from 1952. Thus, plant expenditure attracted forty per cent Initial Allowances, mining expenditure twenty-five per cent, and building expenditure twenty-five per cent – all based on original cost. For Annual Allowances, building qualified for ten per cent, mining not less than fifteen per cent, whilst the rates for plant expenditure were left to administrative discretion.

In 1958 there was another major landmark. The Income Tax (Amendment) Ordinance of that year did two things. It reduced the tax rate to forty per cent. Secondly, it adjusted the system of initial and annual allowances by adding a new category of capital expenditure, namely plantation expenditure, to attract twenty per cent initial allowance, and annual allowance at rates to be determined by the administration. The Ordinance also isolated industrial building expenditure from other building expenditure, so that the former now attracted twenty per cent Initial Allowance and ten per cent Annual Allowance, whilst building expenditure attracted no Initial Allowance but qualified for five per cent Annual Allowance. In 1961 the rate of Annual Allowance for building expenditure was raised to ten per cent. The accelerated depreciation system thus amended remained significantly the same until December 1966.

1958 also saw the Industrial Development (Income Tax Relief) Act (repealing the Aid to Pioneer Industries Ordinance, 1952) which further liberalised the income tax relief provisions for pioneer companies.

The 'independence' which Companies Income Tax lost in 1940 was restored in 1961 by the Companies Income Tax Act. This Act ended the twenty-one-year-old unsatisfactory arrangement which combined the taxation of personal and company incomes under the same law, made more complex by so many amendments. It did not effect any significant change in the system, but it did collect together all the various companies income tax provisions that had littered the previous years. Indeed its aim was, according to the Minister of Finance, 'to provide a piece of legislation, without encumbering the reading material with extraneous personal income tax provisions as in the Combined Taxation Law (the 1943 Ordinance) at present in use.'[1] The 1961 Companies Income Tax remained up until 1979 the enabling law, although its rates of depreciation allowances were generally scaled down by the Income Tax (Amendment) Act of December 1966.[2] The current law is the Companies Income Tax Act, 1979.

One thing which emerges from this historical review is the continued liberalisation of companies income tax over the years, particularly in the areas of relief and allowances. These have become more generous and wider in scope. Losses could be carried forward against future income for only five years in 1940. Again, whereas in 1943 full payment was required within two months of service of notice of assessment, now payment could be in two instalments, the first within two months and the rest before the end of the financial year.

Also noticeable is that the system has remained relatively stable. The significant changes have not come in quick succession. Thus, the rate has changed on the average every nine years. Reaching its peak of forty-five per cent in 1949, it stood there for nine years before it was reduced to forty per cent in 1958. This stability has facilitated administration. Moreover, from the point of view of the companies, stability and liberality were two of the most desirable features of the system, at least until October 1966 when it seems a new phase of tightening-up began, with the general scaling down of Initial and Annual Allowances, and the addition of a Super Tax in 1967.[3]

(ii) Administration

The Federal Board of Inland Revenue, otherwise known as the Board, administers Companies Income Tax under section 2 of the Companies

Income Tax Act, 1979 published in the Federal Gazette Number 33 Volume 60 of 19 July 1979. The law repeals and re-enacts, with sundry amendments, the Companies Income Tax Act, 1961 and has effect from 1 April 1977.

The members of the Board are:

(a) a Chairman, who shall be the Director of the Federal Inland Revenue Department;

(b) four Deputy Directors of the Federal Inland Revenue Department;

(c) the most senior of those officers holding or acting in the posts of Legal Adviser and Assistant Legal Adviser in the Federal Inland Revenue Department who is available from time to time on duty in Lagos;

(d) the officer from time to time holding or acting in the office of Principal Assistant Secretary with responsibility for revenue matters in the Federal Ministry of Finance;

(e) a representative of the Nigerian National Petroleum Corporation;

(f) a representative of the Department of Customs and Excise; and

(g) the Registrar of Companies.

Any five members of the Board, of whom one shall be the Director or a Deputy Director, shall constitute a quorum. The Board nominates an officer of the Federal Inland Revenue Department as the Secretary to the Board.

Notwithstanding that the Legal Adviser to the Board is at any time a member of the Board, he may appear for and represent the Board in his professional capacity in any proceedings in which the Board is a party, and the Legal Adviser shall not in such circumstances give evidence on behalf of the Board.

The Secretary shall summon a meeting of the Board whenever the business requiring its attention so warrants, or upon any request of a member; and a majority decision of the members on any matter obtained by him in written correspondence shall be treated in all respects as though it were a decision of the Board in actual meeting unless any member has requested the submission of that matter to such meeting.

The Board[4] may do all such things as may be deemed necessary and expedient for the assessment and collection of the tax and shall account for all amounts so collected in a manner to be prescribed by the Minister of Finance. Whenever the Board shall consider it necessary with respect to any tax or penalty due, the Board may acquire, hold and dispose of any property taken as security for or in satisfaction of any such tax or penalty or of any judgement debt due in respect of any such tax or penalty and shall account for any such property and the proceeds of sale thereof in a manner to be prescribed by the Minister.

The Board may sue and be sued in its official name and, subject to any express provision under any subsidiary legislation or otherwise, the Board may authorise any person to accept service of any document to be sent, served upon or delivered to the Board. The Board may give notice in the *Gazette* or in writing to:

(a) authorise any person within or outside Nigeria to perform or exercise, on behalf of the Board, any power or duty conferred on the Board to receive any notice or other document to be given or delivered to, or served upon, the Board; and

(b) with the consent of the Minister, authorise the Joint Tax Board to perform or exercise, on behalf of the Board, any power or duty conferred on the Board.

The Minister shall not give any direction, order or instruction in respect of any particular person which would have the effect of requiring the Board to raise an additional assessment upon such person or to increase or decrease any assessment made or to be made or any penalty imposed or to be imposed upon or any relief given or to be given to or to defer the collection of any tax, penalty or judgement debt due by such person, or which would have the effect of altering the normal course of any proceedings, whether civil or criminal, relating either to the recovery of any tax or penalty or to any offence relating to tax.

In any claim or matter or upon any objection or appeal under the Law or under any subsidiary legislation made thereunder, any act, matter or thing done by or with the authority of the Board, in pursuance of any provisions of this Act or subsidiary legislation made thereunder, shall not be subject to challenge on the ground that such act, matter or thing was not or was not proved to be in accordance with any direction, order or instruction given by the Minister.

(iii) Jurisdiction

The Federal Board of Inland Revenue has powers to assess, in addition to limited liability companies:

(a) persons employed in the Nigerian Army, the Nigerian Navy or the Nigerian Air Force, other than in a civilian capacity;

(b) officers of the Nigeria Foreign Service;

(c) persons in receipt of Nigeria pensions where such pensions are payable overseas; and

(d) persons resident outside Nigeria who are shareholders of Nigerian companies.

Before the Act, civilian employees in the Nigerian Army, Nigerian Navy and the Nigerian Air Force were under the tax jurisdiction of the States in which they were resident. These will now be included in the category of persons who are subject to the personal income tax by the Federal Board of Inland Revenue. The salaries and allowances of members of the 'other ranks' in the Nigerian Armed Forces would be specifically exempt as established by convention in the past, which in effect means that only commissioned officers in the Nigerian Armed Forces, the Nigerian Navy and the Nigerian Air Force would be subject to the Act apart from those mentioned above. It is to be emphasised that the exemption of the salaries and allowances of members of the other ranks in the Nigerian Armed Forces should not preclude the taxation of any other income, e.g. rent, bank interest, etc., in their hands in the normal way and it is obligatory for them to inform the Federal Board of Inland Revenue of these other incomes.

Since its inception the taxation of company income had always been vested in the central government. The current constitutional disposition of taxing powers puts the tax within the exclusive jurisdiction of the Federal Government and the jurisdiction extends over the whole country.[5] Thus, regardless of the State of location of a company, it pays its tax to the Federal authorities. The right to retain the whole of the revenue yield of this tax goes along with the exclusive power to tax company income. Thus, the States[6] have no share whatever in the proceeds of the Companies Income Tax.

There is much to be said for having only one Companies Income Tax authority for the whole country. Already, without the taxing power over company income, there have been intense inter-state rivalries in the area of industrial development, which is constitutionally within the competence of each state government in its own area. State jurisdiction over Companies Income Tax can only worsen the situation. Moreover, it could do considerable damage from the point of view of attracting overseas investment. Not only would overseas investors face as many companies income tax systems as there are governments in the federation, it would also give them the opportunity to exploit inter-state rivalries to wring out as much tax concessions from each State as they could, but with little overall increase in investment to show for them.

Hitherto, it may have been fairly easy to defend the retention by the Federal Government of all the revenue derived from Companies Income Tax, owing to the insignificance of the tax as a source of revenue. It may not be easy to do so in the very near future. Not only has the company sector been expanding rapidly but the period of pioneering activities attracting various tax reliefs seems to be nearing its end. These two factors, among others, are bound to enhance the yield of Companies Income Tax in the future. The imbalance in the finances of the states and the centre with central revenues growing at a much faster rate than State revenues, has been one of the major weaknesses of Nigeria's federal fiscal system.[7] The continued retention of Companies Income Tax revenue by the centre may aggravate this imbalance, and cause further strains in the political and economic structure of the country. It would seem therefore that some sharing of Companies Income Tax revenue between the centre and the regions should be seriously considered.[8]

The Joint Tax Board

The Joint Tax Board was constituted under section 27 of the Income Tax Management Act, 1961. Members of the Board are civil servants, usually Directors of Internal Revenue, experienced in income tax matters. Each State of the Federation is represented on the Board. A member from each State is appointed by the Commissioner charged with responsibility for Income Tax matters in that State. The Federal Government is also represented on the Board by a similarly qualified civil servant appointed by the Federal Minister charged with responsibility for Income Tax matters. The Board has a Secretary, who is a civil servant appointed by the Federal Public Service Commission. The Secretary is not a member of the Board.

The Board exercises the power conferred upon it by the Act under which it was constituted. In addition, the Board:

(a) performs the functions such as may be referred to it by the Federal Minister (now Commissioner) for Finance in connection with the functions conferred on the Federal Board of Inland Revenue in relation to the Companies Income Tax;

(b) endeavours to promote uniformity both in the application of the Income Tax Management Act, 1961, and in the incidence of Income Tax on individuals throughout the Federation;

(c) advises the Federal Government on request by that Government, on matters connected with the introduction of amendment to the income Tax Acts, double taxation relief arrangements, and rates of capital allowances.

A major function of the Board, in its endeavour to promote uniformity, is the consideration and approval of benefits and pension schemes which may be submitted to it from time to time. Once the Board approves any scheme of such nature, the scheme is valid for Income Tax purposes throughout the Federation.

No one who is familiar with the working of the Board since it held its first meeting in 1963 will fail to be impressed by some of its accomplishments. It has served as a clearing-house for tax disputes, as an approving authority for pensions and provident fund schemes and as a forum for Heads of Inland Revenue Divisions of the Ministry of Finance for exchange of views.

Exemptions

Interest received by a company from the Federal Savings Bank is exempt from tax. The following are also exempted:
(1) (a) the profits of any company being a statutory or registered friendly society in so far as much profits are not derived from a trade or business carried on by such society;
   (b) the profits of any company being a cooperative society registered under the Cooperative Society Ordinance;
   (c) the profits of any company engaged in ecclesiastical, charitable or educational activities of a public character in so far as such profits are not derived from a trade or business carried on by such company.

The case of
1 Rev. M.F.Shodipo, and
2 T.R.B. Macaulay
   (Trustees of the Methodist Church Mission) ⎰ Plaintiffs[9]
3 Development Trust (Nig.) Ltd
and Federal Board of Inland Revenue (*Defendants*)
shows that where charitable, or religious bodies, trade and use commercial methods, they will be taxed, for whatever motive the business is carried on. By their writ of summons the plaintiffs claimed jointly and severally against the defendants as follows:
   (i) A declaration that the plaintiffs are exempt from liability to pay tax on the rents received or accruing from the property situate at Marina, Lagos and known as Wesley House.
   (ii) An injunction restraining the defendants, their servants and/ or agents from taking any steps or any further steps for the purpose of assessing, collecting or enforcing the payment of tax on the income received by or accruing to the plaintiffs from the properties aforesaid.

The property with which the court was immediately concerned was that owned by the third plaintiff company and known as Wesley House. It occupied a portion of the land registered as Title No. L06290 under the Registration of Title Act. The property was leased to various tenants and income derived therefrom was stated to be applied to charitable purposes. An agreement to this effect was contained in paragraph 6 of the Statement of Claim, to wit:

The income aforesaid is employed in maintaining the various Missionary establishments and Educational Institutions of the Methodist Mission in Nigeria, that is to say, for the advancement of Education.

In the Court's view, the purposes enumerated in paragraph 6 of the Statement of Claim to which the rental income was allegedly applied were charitable.

The third plaintiff company averred in paragraph 8 of the Statement of Claim that it 'is a company engaged in charitable or educational activities of a public character.' The defendant denied this and contended that since the third plaintiff company was involved in the activities of developing and letting property it could not be said that such activities were charitable. Because of the view the plaintiffs had taken of the seemingly charitable character of the third plaintiff company, they argued that it was exempt from tax under section 26(1)(c) of the Companies Income Tax Act, 1961. The defendants' view was that rental income received from ownership and development of property constituted 'trade or business' within the meaning of the relevant Income Tax legislation. Section 26(1)(c) of the Companies Income Tax Act mentions:

(c) the profits of any company engaged in ecclesiastical, charitable or educational activities of a public character in so far as such profits are not derived from a trade or business carried on by such company

The objects of the company as set out in Article 3 of its Memorandum of Association were, *inter alia*, as follows:

(a) To manage and develop the Methodist Marina site and building in accordance with Methodist tradition.
(b) As ancillary and incidental to the purposes and objects set out in sub-paragraph (a) above to carry on any other business which may seem to the company capable of being conveniently carried on in connection with its principal business or calculated directly or indirectly to enhance the value of or render profitable any of the company's property or rights.
(c) To purchase or by any other means acquire any freehold, leasehold or other property or any estate or other property or any estate or interest whatever, and any rights, privileges or easements over or in respect of any property, and any buildings, offices, factories, mills, works, wharves, roads, railways, tramways, machinery, engines, rolling stock, vehicles, plant live, etc.
(d) To improve, manage, cultivate, develop, exchange, let on lease or otherwise, mortgage, charge, sell, dispose of, turn to account, grant rights and privileges in respect of, or otherwise deal with all or any, part of the property and rights of the company.
(e) To sell, lease, let, mortgage or otherwise dispose of the land or other property of the company for such consideration of any kind as the company may determine.

Other objects of the company concerned dealings in shares, stocks, patents, trade marks and designs.

The question that arose was whether, looking at the objects for which the company was incorporated, it was not engaged in trade or business. In *Commissioner of Inland Revenue v The Birmingham Theatre Royal Estate Co. Ltd* 12 TC 580, the respondent company was formed in 1899 to acquire the leases of a theatre and other real estate. The lease of the theatre included certain theatrical properties and effects, but these ceased to exist on the rebuilding of the theatre in 1904, and from that date the company owned only certain investments, which remained unchanged after 1912, and the lease of the theatre and other real estate, which it let to five tenants under repairing leases for long periods. The company contended, on appeal to the Special Commissioners against assessments to Excess Profits Duty made upon it, that it did not carry on a trade or business, or alternatively that its income was excluded from liability under Rule 8 of Part 1 of the Fourth Schedule to the Finance (No. 2 Act 1915). The Special Commissioners discharged the assessments. It was held that the company was carrying on a trade or business within the charge to Excess Profits Duty and that its income was not excluded from liability under Rule 8 of Part 1 of the Fourth Schedule. At page 584 of the judgement Rowland, J., had this to say:

...looking at what the company were incorporated to do, they applied themselves to that, and they were fairly active in the early years in arranging their property, and during those years they enjoyed it and there is nothing more for them to do; but they have not gone out of their business and been left with the rents to collect.

Earlier in his judgement the learned Judge had observed that 'the form in which its revenue came in was the comfortable form of simply receiving rents'. In *The Balgownie Land Trust Ltd v The Commissioners of Inland Revenue* 14 TC 684, 'the owner of a landed estate at his death left his estate to trustees with a direction to realise.' The trustees, being unsuccessful in their efforts to sell the estate on the market, formed a company '*ex necessitate*' with general powers to deal in real property and transferred the estate to this company in exhange for shares which, with few exceptions, were allotted to the beneficiaries under the trustees and were, at the date of the appeal, still mainly held by those beneficiaries or their representatives. Shortly after its incorporation the company made a substantial purchase of other property with funds acquired by borrowing on the security of the orginal estate. The company received rents and paid a regular dividend on the capital. The company sold no property until 1921. In 1921, 1924, 1926 and 1927 parts of the original estate were sold and in 1925 the whole of the additional property. The company appealed against an assessment for the year 1926–27 in respect of profits from sales of land. The general commissioners held that the profits from the sales were the profits of a trade or business and that the company was liable to assessment. The company appealed to the First Division of the Court of Session in Edinburgh. It was held that the company was carrying on trade and was assessable to Income Tax. Giving his judgement in the case the Lord President said at page 692 as follows:

I cannot say that there is left in my mind any doubt that the company is doing precisely what it was formed to do, namely carrying on the business of a company dealing in real estate. As such it is assessable to Income Tax on its profits...

Again in *Carlisle & Silloth Golf Club v Smith* (1913) 3KB. 75 a golf club had permitted non-members to play upon the links and use the golf clubhouse on payment of the green fees fixed by the club. Hamilton, J., held that in the circumstances the golf club were carrying on an enterprise which was, in itself, outside the scope of the ordinary functions of the club, and distinct from its ordinary objects and activities, as to which it was possible to keep separate accounts, so as to ascertain whether there were any profits thereby realised, and that any profits derived from the green fees were therefore taxable.

Even if, as plaintiffs averred in paragraph 6 of their Statement of Claim, the income derived from the letting of Wesley House was wholly devoted to charity the third plaintiff company would still be assessable to tax on such income. It was found pertinent at this stage to refer, on this score, to the House of Lords case of *Rotunda Hospital, Dublin (Governors) v Coman* (1920) 7 TC 517. In that case the hospital, which was a maternity hospital, incorporated in 1956 for the care of poor women, owned certain rooms. These rooms were let by the governors of the hospital for concerts and other entertainments. It was contended that all the receipts from the hiring out of the rooms were devoted to the purposes of the charity and therefore not assessable to tax. Viscount Cave at page 586 of the judgement observed as follows:

No doubt the hospital, like other charities, yields no profit: but if the Governors in the course of their management carry on a profitable business, the profits of that business are subject to taxation.

In the Privy Council case of *Commissioner of Income Tax v Hanover Agencies Ltd* (1967) 1 AIIE.R. 954 Lord Guest, on the question whether the acquisition and letting of premises was a 'trade' or 'business', said at page 956 of the judgement that:

The word 'business' is of wide import and must be given its ordinary meaning, unless the context otherwise requires. The respondents' objects include *inter alia* acquiring of freehold property and the leasing of all or any of the company's property. If a company's objects are business objects and are in fact carried out, it carries on business.

It is not sufficient for a company to say that on an isolated letting of a property the profits derived therefrom are not assessable to tax. In the *Balgownie's* case cited *supra* the Lord President said:

A single plunge may be enough provided it is shown to the satisfaction of the Court that the plunge is made in the waters of trade.

Looking at the objects for which the third plaintiff company was incorporated as well as the Tax Office Copies of the Accounts (*Exhibits B and C*) for the years 1966 and 1967 it was clear to the Court that the company was doing precisely what it was formed to do, namely, carrying on the business of a company dealing in real estate. What was said about the liability of the third plaintiff company applied *mutatis mutandis* to the first and second plaintiffs, who could not claim to be exempted from the incidence of taxation under section 26(1)(c) of the Companies Income Tax Act or under paragraph (K) of the Third Schedule to the Income Tax Management Act once it was established that the relevant income was derived from a 'trade' or 'business' in which they were directly or indirectly involved.

It was said that the first and second plaintiffs hold practically all the shares in the third plaintiff company 'but they have not and cannot be paid any dividends accruing as profits from rents payable by the tenants'. It is an established principle of law that a company is a legal person separate and distinct from the individual members of the company – see *Salomon v Salomon* (1897) AC 22 at pages 42 and 51. It is also plain from the decision in *Ryhope Coal Co. Ltd v Foyer* (1881) 7 QBD 485 that assets transferred by the partners are now the shareholders', as a transfer to a distinct body. It was therefore immaterial that practically all the shares in the third plaintiff company were held by the first and second plaintiffs as Trustees of the Methodist Church Mission. On the question of payment of dividends to the first and second Plaintiffs as shareholders, this was a matter for the third plaintiff company alone to decide, and the court could not see its relevance to the liability of the third plaintif company to be assessed for tax under section 17 of the Companies Income Tax Act 1961.

Therefore, the court concluded that the plaintiffs were assessable to tax on the rents received or which accrued from the property situated at Marina, Lagos, and known as Wesley House. Accordingly the claim for a declaration and an Injunction that the plaintiffs were not assessable to tax on the said rental income was dismissed.

    (d) the profits of any company formed for the purpose of promoting sporting activities where such profits are wholly expendable for such purpose, subject to such conditions as the Board may prescribe;

    (e) the profits of any company being a trade union registered under the Trade Unions Ordinance in so far as such profits are not derived from a trade or business carried on by such trade union;

(f) interest received by a company from the Nigerian Federal Savings Bank;

(g) gains or profits from the business of operating ships or aircraft carried on by a company other than a Nigerian company in so far as in the case of ships the business is not carried on in inland waters only and by means of ships to which the provisions of Part IV of the Shipping and Navigating Ordinance apply; provided that the Board is satisfied that an equivalent exemption from tax is granted to Nigerian companies by the country in which such company is resident;

(h) the profits of any company being a body corporate established by or under the Native Authority Law, 1954, of Northern Nigeria, the Western Regional Local Government Law, 1952, or the Local Government Law, 1960, of Eastern Nigeria, as amended, or any law replacing any of those laws;

(i) the profits of any company being a purchasing authority established by the legislature of a Region and empowered to acquire any commodity in that Region for export from Nigeria from the purchase and sale (whether for the purposes of export or otherwise) of that commodity;

(j) the profits of any company being a corporation established by the legislature of a Region for the purpose of fostering the economic development of that Region, not being profits derived from any trade or business carried on by that corporation or from any share or other interest possessed by that corporation in a trade or business in Nigeria carried on by some other person or authority; the profits of any company engaged in petroleum operations within the meaning of section 2 of the Petroleum Profits Tax Act 1959 are exempt from Companies Income Tax since the company is liable to Petroleum Profits Tax.

(k) any profits of a company other than a Nigerian company which, but for this paragraph, would be chargeable to tax by reason solely of their being brought into or received in Nigeria.

(2) The Minister may also exempt by order –

(a) any company or class of companies from all or any of the provisions of this Act, or

(b) from tax all or any profits of any company or class of companies from any source, on any ground which appears to him sufficient.

(3) The Minister may by order amend, add to, or repeal any exemption, in so far as it affects a company, made by notice or order under the provisions of subsections (2) or (4) of section 9 of the Income Tax

Ordinance, and subject to the foregoing the following notices and order shall continue in force for all purposes of this Act –

   (a) The Income Tax Exemption (Interest on Nigerian Public Loans) Notice;

   (b) The Income Tax (Exemption)(Nigerian Broadcasting Corporation now Federal Radio Corporation) Order, 1957;

   (c) The Railway Loan (International Bank) (Exemption of Interest) Notice, 1958.

Western Nigeria Licensed Buying Agents Association (Appellant)[10] *v Federal Board of Inland Revenue (Respondent)*

This was an appeal against the assessment, particulars of which are as given below:

Notice of Assessment No.	Year of Assessment	Tax Charged
IBAC 1 63–64	1963–64	£1490
IBAC 5A 64–65	1964–65	1490
IBAC 7A 65–66	1965–66	1002
IBAC 23A 66–67	1966–67	800
IBAC 5 67–68	1967–68	1200
IBAC 7 68–69	1968–69	1200
IBAC 11 69–70	1969–70	1200

The grounds of appeal were based on the fact that the appellant company was a 'trade association' incorporated as a company limited by guarantee under the provisions of section 20 of the Companies Act, with no profit-making motive, although it transferred its annual surpluses into a deposit account with its bankers on which it received interest. It was further contended that the appellant was not a 'trading organisation' and that it did not, in fact, carry out a trade such as might bring it within the charging provisions of the Revenue Law.

Mr E.D. Alalade (Accountant for the appellant) with the assistance of his principal witness, Mr S.I. Abiodun, showed that the revenue of the Association derived principally from the levy of 3d per ton of produce handled by the members of the Association together with some interest received on the bank deposit account. By the provisions of its Memorandum of Association, the income of the Association was not available for the payment of dividends to members nor for eventual distribution to them in whatever form. While the interest received might be subject to tax (if the Association was deemed to carry on a trade in that regard), it was his opinion that the subscriptions of members cannot be so subject to tax. In return for the services to the members of the Association, members' levies were usually deducted by the Western Nigeria Marketing Board and passed on to the Association. The services of the Association were not available to non-members, while all produce-dealers had their subscriptions (or levies) deducted at source by the Marketing Board for the benefit of the Association. According to Mr Alalade, the Association did not come under the provisions of section 4 of ITMA, 1961, (*sic*) which seeks to tax any 'income from trade or business.' His opinion was that the appellant company was exempt from the income tax.

Mr Osholake, for the respondent, in turn submitted that the services normally rendered by the Association to its members constituted 'trade' within the meaning of the Revenue Law, since such services include 'bargaining on behalf of members with the Western Nigeria Marketing Board, training members in the use of equipment, etc.'; and that the contributions of members, in the circumstances, were payments for services rendered to them by the Association. In support of his contention, he cited the cases of *The Liverpool Corn Trade Association Ltd v Monks (Inspector of Taxes)*, 1926 (10 TC p.442) and *CIR v Cornish Mutual Assurance Co. Ltd*, 1926, (Appeal Cases, p.281). He said that it was held in the first case that the excess of members' contributions over the cost of the services provided by the Association constituted profit and should be assessed to tax accordingly. In the second case, he said it was the decision of their Lordships in that Appeal that 'it did not matter the description by which a person decides to call a particular 'payment', or 'receipt'; but that the point to note was whether such payments or receipts were in respect of services rendered.' He argued that instead of the appellant company asking for 'premiums' (that could have fallen within the charging provisions of section 17(1) of CITA, 1961) the Association merely preferred to ask its members for pay in the form of entrance fees, contributions, etc. He deposed further that the case of the appellant was similar to the substance of the two cases he had cited; and that the fact of the present case was that the appellant had 'performed for the promotion of the interest of its members – i.e., to assist its members generally and to represent them in their dealings with the Western Nigeria Marketing Board'. In return for these services, each member must pay an entrance fee and annual subscriptions in the form of income to the appellant company. He therefore urged the Commissioners to uphold the fact that the subscriptions and the entrance fees paid by members of the Western Nigerian Licensed Buying Agents' Association were in the form of payment services, that such services were in the nature of trade or business; and that such income was liable to tax in the hands of the Association. The Commissioners said,

191

We have reviewed all the evidence placed at our disposal in this case, and we have found, as a question of fact, that the appellant was incorporated as a company limited by guarantee on 11 August 1965, and that it received the approval of the appropriate Minister to dispense with the use of the word 'Limited' under the provisions of section 20 of the Companies Act, 1968 (which is the same as section 22 of the old Companies Act). The question at issue is whether the appellant can be exempted from the income tax by reference to part of the provisions of the tax statutes or could be deemed to be so exempt by reference to Case Law.

Section 26 of CITA, 1961, contained a list of incorporated business the profits of which are exempt from tax, while section 17(1) brought into charge to tax only the profits of a 'trade or business'. The real question, therefore, is whether the appellant's income is covered by the provisions of section 26 of CITA or whether or not it was carrying on a trade or business, within the meaning of the Law. It is not clear whether a company which has been granted a certificate of incorporation under the provisions of section 20 of the Company Act (because of its declared objective to promote 'commerce, art, science, religion, charity or any other useful object' and its intention to apply its profits or other income in promoting its object and to prohibit the payment of dividends out of its income to its members) automatically, because of that fact alone, qualifies for tax exemption under the provisions of section 26(1)(b) as a company 'engaged in ecclesiatical, charitable or educational activities of a public character.'

However, the main question of this appeal seems to have been answered in the case of 're-Duty on Estate of Incorporated Council of Law Reporting for England and Wales (1888)(3 TC p.105), where it was held that the 'profit motive' was not decisive in deciding whether or not a company was carrying on a trade or business, since 'there may be the carrying on of a trade for tax purposes even though there is no intention to make a profit. The question is whether or not a trade is or was being carried on; and once that question is answered in the affirmative, there is liability to tax on any resulting profit, irrespective of whether the trading activities were directed to the making of the profit, and irrespective of the purpose to which the profit is applied'. Also, although it was held in the case of Cornish Mutual Assurance Co. Ltd v IR Commissioners, 1926 (12 TC p.841)(to which Counsel for the respondent already referred) that the company did carry on a trade or business and that, as it was admittedly a mutual concern, it was expressly within the legislation in question and as such the surpluses arising from transactions with members were expressly made profits for the purpose of Corporaton Profits Tax; their Lordships also found 'that such a concern does not have profits which fall to be taxed unless, as in this case, the statute expressly treats surpluses as taxable profits.'

In view of the foregoing, it is the Commissioners' conclusion that the appellant company cannot be regarded as carrying on a trade or business (within the meaning of the existing Law) in so far as it continues to operate within the framework for which it was granted a special licence for pursuing a cause of 'public interest'. The interest received on the lodgement of its surplus funds with the Bank falls directly under the provisions of section 17(b) of CITA; and since the appellant does not appear to be exempted from tax on such income under the provisions of section 2626(c) of the Act, it is our view that income tax should be paid on the interest received in the various years.

It is the Commissioners' decision, therefore, to annul those portions of the assessments which related to the subscriptions and entrance fees of the members of the appellant company. They make the order that the respondent should revise its assessments on the appellant in the light of this decision and that the appellant (on its part) should continue to supply the respondent with its annual accounts as a means of indicating its various lines of activities from time to time.

(iv) Profit of income subject to tax

One of the most important provisions of the Companies Income Tax Act 1979 is section 8 which imposes tax on companies. It reads:

8   The tax shall, subject to the provisions of this Act, be payable at the rate hereinafter specified for each year as assessment upon the profits of any company accruing in, derived from, brought into, or received in Nigeria in respect of –

(a) any trade or business for whatever period of time such trade or business may have been carried on;
(b) rent or any premium arising from a right granted to any other persons for the use or occupation of any property;
(c) dividends, interest, discounts, charges or annuities;
(d) any source of annual profits or gains not falling within the preceding categories;
(e) any amount deemed to be income or profits under a provision of this Act or, with respect to any benefit arising from a pension or provident fund, of the Income Tax Management Act, 1961;
(f) fees, dues and allowances (wherever paid) for services rendered.

For the purposes of this section, interest shall be deemed to be derived from Nigeria if:

(i) there is a right to payment of the interest by a Nigerian company regardless of where or in what form the payment is made;
(ii) the interest accrues to a foreign company or person from a Nigerian company or a company in Nigeria regardless of whichever way the interest may have accrued.

As regards the current incentives, interest payable on foreign loan will be exempted from income tax as follows:[11]

Repayment period including moratorium	Grace period	Tax exemption allowed
(i) Above 7 years	Not less than 2 years	100%
(ii) 5–7 years	Not less than 18 months	70%
(iii) 2–4 years	Not less than 12 months	40%
(iv) Below 2 years		NIL

It should be noted that this tax incentive is applicable only to loans made available to Nigerian companies by foreign-based companies. The same incentives apply in respect of interest payable on loans granted by traditional lending authorities in respect of agriculture.

Whilst 'brought into' brings into the tax net profits from business carried on outside Nigeria, such taxable profits must be profits actually transferred from overseas into Nigeria or profits actually brought into Nigeria.

A Nigerian company is defined as one the management and control of which is exercised in Nigeria so that if the management or control is exercised outside Nigeria, the company becomes a non-Nigerian company. This provision raises an anomaly in the tax computations of limited liability companies. There is nothing preventing a company which is incorporated in Nigeria from becoming a non-Nigerian company for tax purposes. A company is controlled in the country in which the board of directors hold their meetings. The importance of control is emphasised because of the inequities it can create. In theory, if the board of directors of a Nigerian incorporated company hold its meeting in Ghana and if the Nigerian management is given directives in or from Ghana where it has branches, the profits from the Ghana branch will not be liable to Nigerian tax.

'Derived from' was held in *Commissioner of Taxation v Kirk*[12] to be synonymous with 'accruing in', 'derived from' means 'acquired', 'obtained' or 'got'. In *Toufic Karam v Commissioner of Income Tax*[13], Hooper J. said 'The words "accruing in" and "received" appear to me to import a clear territorial limitation to Nigeria. Among other things, cases where profits arise from transactions carried out in Nigeria by a non-resident taxpayer.'

Trade or business is a question of fact and not of law and it includes buying and selling, manufacturing or any other adventure in the nature of trade. When therefore a company's trade is on all fours with its objects clause in the memorandum association, the profits of such a trade or business must be taxed under section 8 of the Act. Isolated transactions that are related to the normal transactions of a business constitute trading. Thus isolated purchases with a view to resale at a profit even though such isolated transactions are not related to the company's normal business will constitute trade and its profits taxed under section 8. Where rental income accrues to a company normally carrying on its business, the company not being a dealer in properties, then the rental income will be taxed under section 8. If the company is a property-holding and property-dealing company, that is, buying land and buildings with a view to resale or letting such properties pending resale, and this fact is reflected in the company's objects clause in its memorandum of association, then the company's income will be assessable to tax under section 8.

No statute defines 'trade' and it is to judicial precedents that we must look for a solution. Lord Macmillan said, in *Van Den Berghs Ltd v Clark*,[14] that the definition 'only informs us with a fine disregard of logic, that it 'includes every trade, manufacture, adventure or concern in the nature of trade'.

His Lordship continued,

Consequently it is to the decided cases that one must go in search of light. While each case is found to turn upon its own facts and no infallible criterion emerges, nevertheless the decisions are useful as illustrations and as affording indications of the kind of consideration which may relevantly be borne in mind in approaching the problem.

In the leading case of *Edwards v Bairstow & Harrison*[15] the House of Lords, while accepting that the inference 'trade' or 'no trade' in a particular case was a question of fact, pointed out that the question what the statute means by 'trade' is a question of law, so that if a court is satisfied that the only reasonable conclusion to which it could come from the whole of the stated case contradicts the conclusion of the Commissioners, then the latter must have misdirected themselves in law and their finding will be set aside.[16]

Hence cases on this subject can be classified into four groups: (i) where a finding of 'no trade' is reversed; here the court decides that that facts must constitute trading,[17] (ii) where a finding of 'trade' is affirmed; here the court only decides that there was evidence to support the finding; it may, or may not, express its agreement with the conclusion, (iii) where a finding of 'no trade' is affirmed with the same result as in (ii), and (iv) where a finding of 'trade' is reversed; here the court says that the facts cannot constitute trading.[18]

Obviously the cases in groups (i) and (iv) are authorities on the limits of the meaning of trade in relation to a similar set of facts; those in groups (ii) and (iii) may contain some statement of law which is opposite to similar facts but must be closely scrutinised before being accepted as authorities on those facts.

In *Arbico Ltd v Federal Board of Inland Revenue*,[19] argued in the Federal Supreme Court, Lagos, the Supreme Court said:

We do not see that because there is no definition of 'trade' in our own law we must give that word a more restrictive meaning than has been given in the United Kingdom where by the definition trade includes any 'adventure or concern in the nature of trade.' It is of course not every sale under a power of sale, which is clearly an ancillary power to a main purpose of a Company, that is a transaction by way of trade. It is not only necessary to show that such a sale has been made at a profit, but it is necessary to go further and to show that the profit is attributable to a trading transaction rather than to merely capitalising a portion of the business which in this regard is not otherwise trading.

On further appeal to the Supreme Court, it was held, affirming the judgement of Sowemimo, J.:

1 That a single transaction may be a transaction by way of trade; and that in determining whether profit from such an isolated transaction is trading profit, the taxpayer's purpose or object cannot prevail over what he does, if what he does has all the characteristics of

trading; but if what he does is equivocal, his purpose or object may become very material;

2   That the fact that the memorandum of association of a company contains a power to sell property is an important consideration in determining whether the company's intention on a sale of property is to make a trading profit, but it is not conclusive; and where the power is exercised on a single occasion only, or where it is ancillary to the main purpose of the company and has not been used often enough to have become a main purpose itself, there is no presumption that a sale under a power is a trading activity rather than a mere capitalisation of portion of the business.

3   That there was no reason to upset the finding of the Appeal Commissioners that on the facts which they found established there was a transaction by way of trade within section 17(a) of the Act.

In *Aderawo's Timber Trading Co. Ltd v Federal Board of Inland Revenue*,[20] the applicant company, who had a concession to exploit a timber forest for 25 years, entered into an agreement to supply another company, A.T. & P. Ltd, with timber for five years. At the expiration of four years, the agreement was modified and A.T. & P. Ltd, paid £30 000 to the applicant and agreed to pay $5\frac{1}{2}$d per cubic foot of timber instead of $4\frac{1}{2}$ in the original agreement. The applicant therefore agreed not to terminate the contract before the end of five years from the time of the second agreement. The Revenue assessed the sum of £30 000 to tax of £7000 on the ground that the amount was a trading and not capital receipt. The applicant unsuccessfully appealed to the Revenue and applied for an order of *certiorari* to quash the decision on the ground that the assessment did not come under any of the items in section 17 of the Act. Ikpeazu, J., held that[21]

the structure of the applicant's business was not destroyed and no serious dislocation of the normal organisation of their business took place and nothing was lost by them and the payment cannot in my view be categorised as a capital receipt. It is income. . . .

It is clear . . . in the light of the evidence and the authorities that it is incidental to the Applicants' trade or business to enter into ordinary commercial beneficial contracts which would include the grant of licences to other persons to cut timber from their timber estate and to modify such contract, and the original agreement . . . as also the subsequent one modifying the original arrangments is one entered into by the Applicants in the ordinary course of their trade or business and any sum received for such modification, which was not destructive of the Applicants' profit-making machinery, is a sum which would go into ordinary trading receipt of the Company.[22]

The Supreme Court, affirming the judgement, said:

The applicants thought that it was a good bargain in their trading activities in timber to get a certain immediate large sum plus an extra penny per cubic foot in return for forgoing the possibility of achieving a modification, by giving six months' notice to terminate if it was refused, by the new term of five years certain. We do not think that this therefore was a single capital transaction, but was, though in a lump sum, in fact, profit derived from the trading activity of selling timber.[23]

Profit-making motive may not be necessary to come to a conclusion as to whether or not a particular transaction constitutes trading.[24] The test of trading is objective and not subjective. It is the method of trading[25] and not the profit motive that is essential. There are six tests or badges of trade listed by the Royal Commission[26] determining whether a transaction constitutes trading. These are:

1 Subject matter

Certain forms of property such as manufactured articles which are normally the subject of trading are only exceptionally the subject of investment. Property which does not yield to its owner an income or personal enjoyment merely by virtue of its ownership is more likely to have been acquired with the object of a deal than property that does.

This test is often a decisive one, as one transaction of purchase of a type of property yielding no income or personal enjoyment has, when followed by a profitable sale, in several cases been held to be trading. Thus, single purchases of a quantity of toilet paper,[27] of whisky,[28] of brandy,[29] and of linen,[30] far in excess of an individual's personal requirements, when coupled with a subsequent sale, have all been held taxable as trading operations; so has a single dealing in railway wagons,[31] and in a ship.[32]

2 Length of ownership

It is usual that property meant to be subject of trade is sold within a short time after acquisition. There are, however, many exceptions to this proposition.[33]

A quick resale no doubt helps to support a finding of trading where other elements of trading are present and a long period between acquisition and sale will only negative such a finding where other factors do not lead to an opposite conclusion.

This is emphasised by the provisions of Capital Gains Tax which impose a charge on short-term gains which depends on the length of time between acquisition and sale but does not apply where the gain is chargeable as a trading profit. As Capital Gains Tax, when it applies, is less favourable to the taxpayer than a charge under Income Tax there may be a number of cases in which a taxpayer who is *prima facie* chargeable under Capital Gains Tax may seek instead to establish that his acquisition and sale was a trading operation; but he will have to prove other circumstances besides a quick sale.

3 Supplementary work

Paragraph 116 of Cmd 9474 states:

If the property is worked up in any way during the ownership so as to bring it into a more marketable condition, or if any special exertions are made to find and attract purchasers, such as the opening of an office or large-scale advertising, there is some evidence of dealing. For when there is an organised effort to obtain profit there is a source of taxable income. But if nothing at all is done the suggestion tends the other way.

The decision in the case of *IRC v Livingston*[34] (1926) when three persons purchased a cargo vessel as a joint venture, converted her into a steam drifter and sold her, to the effect that they were not engaged in trading was overruled, as such a transaction was carrying on a trade. The court will attach great importance, as it did in the linen case,[35] to the elaborate selling organisation employed. Stress will also be laid on expenditure on the property as an indication of trade.[36] This test is not, however, by any means decisive; when a person with specialised knowledge with regard to cleaning stills bought two clogged stills, cleaned them and resold them at a profit to two companies which he controlled, a finding that he was not engaged in trading, although reversed at first instance, was restored by the Court of Appeal.[37]

4 *Frequency of similar transactions*
Paragraph 116 of Cmd 9474 states:

If realisations of the same sort of property occur in succession over a period of years or there are several such realisations at about the same date, a presumption arises that there has been a dealing in respect of each.

The test of frequency of similar transactions must be considered in relation to the subject-matter. One isolated transaction of purchase and sale may be treated as trading if the subject-matter is not something normally required for personal use or investment.[38]

Another feature of the doctrine that frequency of transactions may be the vital consideration in some cases is that a subsequent transaction may involve earlier ones becoming taxable, although they would otherwise not have been, in the same way that the thirteenth stroke of a crazy clock throws doubt on what has gone before.[39]

Purchasing of property in (say) 1979 and a farm in 1980 and selling in 1986, for example, of some of the property bought in 1979 and the farm bought in 1980 constitute trading.[40]

A man who spent a large part of his fortune in purchasing a number of endowment policies at various times with the intention of using the proceeds to live on as they matured, was held to be trading and assessed on the difference between the cost and amount received on each policy.[41] Although one sale of 'know-how' by a trading Company was held to be a sale of a capital asset, a number of sales of 'know-how' to different purchasers have been held to establish that the Company traded in 'know-how'.

5 Circumstances responsible for realisation

Even if the purpose of sale is inconsistent with trading, the fact that the taxpayer seized some emergency opportunity to sell the property is indicative of trading.[42]

Paragraph 116 of Cmd. 9474 states: 'There may be some explanation, such as a sudden emergency or opportunity calling for ready money, that negatives the idea that any plan of dealing prompted the original purchase.'

One cannot adequately discuss circumstances responsible for realisation without discussing the sixth badge of trade – the motive and purpose.

6 Motive and purposes

The test of trading, as we have seen, is objective[43] and the the intention of a man cannot be considered as determining what it is that his acts amount to.[44] The best approach to the problem in any given case is first to examine the taxpayer's acts and operations objectively to see whether they can fairly be called trading within the various decisions already discussed — or, to use Lord Buckmaster's phrase, 'do they disclose an operation of business in carrying out a scheme of profit-making?'[45] If the answer to this question is negative, then a second question should be posed. 'If it is not trading, what is it?'[46] Is there some satisfactory explanation, consistent with the facts as found, which shows that the *prima facie* inference of trading was wrong?

Paragraph 116 of Cmd. 9474 states:

There are cases in which the purpose of the transaction of purchase and sale is clearly discernible. Motive is never irrelevant in any of these cases. What is desirable is that it should be realised clearly that it can be inferred from surrounding circumstances in the absence of direct evidence of the seller's intentions and even, if necessary, in the face of that evidence.

Thus when a man purchased two farms and resold them in each case quickly, an inference by the Commissioners that he purchased with the intention of resale and was therefore engaged in trade, was affirmed.[47] In another case two men purchased a farm in 1930 and some additional land in 1932 and resold in 1936 at a profit; notwithstanding their evidence that they had bought the farm as a long-term investment, a finding by the Commissioners that they were engaged in trade was affirmed.[48] When two ladies purchased two houses, repaired them and sold them at a profit having lived in each of them for about two years, a finding that they had engaged in trade was affirmed.[49]

And as we have already observed, income from trade by charitable organisations is taxable even the purpose is ecclesiastical, charitable or educational.

(v) Business

The word 'businesses' is used as meaning an active occupation or profession continuously carried on, and it is in this sense that it is used in the Act with which we are concerned. (Rowlatt, J., in *Commissioners of Inland Revenue v Marine Steam Turbine Co. Ltd*, 12 TC 174.)

I think, with regard to the definition ... used by Mr Justice Rowlatt in *Commissioners of Inland Revenue v Marine Steam Turbine Co. Ltd* (*supra*), ... if any emphasis is attached to the word 'active', I think it would narrow the meaning of the word; for I see nothing to prevent a holding Company ... from carrying on business. It is unnecessary to consider the effect of the Act on such Companies, because it may be that they are protected in another way; but there is nothing in the Act which says that the business must be 'actively' carried on.
(Atkin, LJ, *in Commissioners of Inland Revenue v Korean Syndicate Ltd*, 12 TC 181)

When you come to look at four successive transactions you may hold that what was considered separately and apart, a transaction to which the words 'trade or concern in the nature of trade' could not be applied, yet, when you have that transaction repeated, not once, nor twice, but three times at least, you may draw a completely different inference from those incidents taken together.[50]

If, in such a transaction as we have here, the idea of an adventure in the nature of trade is negatived, I find it difficult to visualise any source of income, or to appreciate how such a transaction can properly be said to have been entered into for the purpose of producing income or revenue. Now there are many cases of course, in which a case not falling within Case I may well fall within Case VI; *Copper v Stubbs*, 10 TC 29, furnishes an example, but there are many others. In all those cases there is some element analogous to trade, and the distinction which seems to me to exist between those cases and the present one is that here we have an isolated transaction of a purchase and re-sale, and not a transaction or series of transactions which could properly be said to have been entered into for the purpose of producing revenue or income.
Lawrence, LJ, in *Leeming v Jones*, 15 TC 333.

The difficulty which can confront the courts is that the profit was the result of an isolated transaction of sale by way of trade, and it is not easy to see how the profit of an isolated sale which is not a trading transaction can be other than a capital accretion, and so outside the category of annual profits or gains.

There was much discussion as to the criterion which the Court should apply. It would not be possible to formulate a single criterion. The purchaser of a large quantity of a commodity like whisky, a commodity which yields no pride of possession, which cannot be turned to

200

account except by a process of realisation, can scarcely be considered to be other than an adventure in a transaction in the nature of trade. The fact that the transaction was not in the way of the business – whatever it was – of the respondent in no way alters the character which almost necessarily belongs to a trading transaction.

Most important of all, the actual dealings of the respondent with the whisky were exactly of the kind that takes place in ordinary trade. (Lord Normand, in *Commissioners of Inland Revenue v Fraser* 24 TC 498)

When a man deals with a subject such as whisky in bulk and bond, which he has acquired merely for the purposes of re-sale, and proceeds to effect a re-sale of the commodity, he engages, in trade and in trade only not in the investment of capital funds.

(vi) Flow of receipts

The 'flow of receipts' concept is adopted in Nigeria (as in most other countries) in defining the income of a company during a particular year. Thus, income includes income from the business itself as well as income from other sources such as rents, interests, dividends, premiums, etc., 'accruing in, derived from, brought into, or received in' Nigeria by the company. Defined this way, the change in the net worth of the company during a year is not taken into account except insofar as it is reflected in its flow of incomes during that year. Ideally, the change in the value of the company's assets should be included in its 'income' to give its total economic position during a year. But the resulting administrative problems of having to revalue assets annually are formidable enough to prevent such a procedure. Even most advanced countries, including the USA and the UK, which are more favourably situated to employ such an 'accretion' concept, nevertheless use the 'flow of receipts' concept as a matter of administrative expediency.

The taxable income of a company is arrived at by allowing certain expenses to be set off against the company's receipts during the relevant period. The principles governing the deductibility of expenses are crucial, since the effective burden of the tax depends on, *inter alia*, the extent to which various expenses are deductible for tax purposes. Moreover, an incentive or disincentive to investment would be built into the Companies Income Tax system depending on whether or not a liberal view is taken of what constitutes deductible expenses.[51] But, on the other hand, for equity, administrative and revenue reasons, it is necessary that provisions for deductible expenses should not be so generous and elastic as to afford simple opportunities for tax evasion. Such would merely leave the determination of the tax burden to the free choice of each taxpayer.

The existing law[52] provides for the deduction of all expenses incurred by the company wholly, reasonably, necessarily, and exclusively in producing its profits during the relevant period. Obvious items are the expenditure on wages, salaries, materials, fuels, etc. The Act specifically includes interest on money borrowed and employed in producing the profits, rents and premiums paid for use of lands and buildings, cost of repairing premises, plants, machinery and fixture, and bad debts incurred during the period. The law cannot of course, make the list exhaustive; considerable discretion can therefore be exercised by the administration as to which expenses are to be allowed.[53]

Capital and revenue receipts

In deciding whether a receipt is of a capital or income nature, both the substantial purpose of the transaction in question and the form adopted to carry it through are relevant. Those assets which form part of the permanent structure of the business and are the means whereby profits are made are to be regarded as capital assets[54] and that, as an accretion to capital is not taxable,[55] receipts in respect of such assets should not be brought into account. Another way of distinguishing capital from revenue receipts is to take the classical economists' distinction between fixed capital and circulating capital[56]; receipts in respect of the former are not brought into profit and loss account, whilst the latter are. The first test requires transactions relating to the subject-matter of the trade to be distinguished from those relating to the permanent structure by which the trade is carried on; the profits of the former are taxable but not of the latter. The second test has been judicially described by Lord Haldane in a case relation to expenditure[57]:

My lords, profit may be produced in two ways. It may result from purchases on income account, the cost of which is debited to that account, and the prices realised therefrom are credited, or it may result from realisation at a profit of assets forming part of the concern. In such a case a prudent man of business will no doubt debit to profit and loss the value of capital assets realised, and take credit only for the balance. But what was the nature of what the appellant had to deal with? He had bought as part of the capital of the business his father's contracts. These enabled him to purchase coal from the colliery owners at what we were told was a very advantageous price, about fourteen shillings per ton. He was able to buy at this price because the right to do so was part of the assets of the business. Was it circulating capital?

My lords, it is not necessary to draw an exact line of demarcation between fixed and circulating capital. Since Adam Smith drew the distinction in the Second Book of *The Wealth of Nations*, which appears in the chapter on the Division of Stock, a distinction which has since become classical, economists have never been able to define much more precisely what the line of demarcation is. Adam Smith described fixed capital as what the owner turns to profit by keeping it in his own possession, circulating capital as what he makes profit of by parting with it and letting it change masters. The latter capital circulates in this sense.

My lords, in the case before us the appellant, of course, made profit with circulating capital by buying coal under the contracts he had acquired from his father's estate at the stipulated price of fourteen shillings and reselling it for more, but he was able to do this simply because he had acquired, among other assets of his business, including the goodwill, the contracts in question. It was not by selling these contracts, of limited duration though they were, it was not by parting with them to other masters, but by retaining them, that he was able to employ his circulating capital in buying under them. I am accordingly of opinion that, although they may have been of short duration, they were nonetheless part of his fixed capital. That he had paid a price for them makes no difference. Indeed the description of their value by the accountants, in the words I have earlier referred to, as of doubtful validity in the hands of outsiders, emphasises this conclusion. The £30 000 paid for the contracts or its equivalent, therefore, became part of the appellant's fixed capital and could not properly appear in his revenue account.

In *Heavy Ferguson (Motors) Ltd v IRC*[58] (1951) Lord MacDermott, CJ said:

Whether a receipt is of capital or revenue nature is a question of fact. There is so far ... no single infallible test for settling the vexed question whether a receipt is of an income or a capital nature. Each case must depend upon its particular facts. . . .

We shall now deal with cases showing taxability or non-taxability of certain receipts.

Taxable receipt or trading receipt

This must be of a revenue nature and should not have any of the badges of a capital receipt. The distinction is one of fact. For example, although land, stocks and shares are of capital nature, being assets and an advantage for the benefit of a trade, the receipt by a trader who acquires land, etc. for the purpose of sale will be of revenue nature being profits of a business. The profits made by a liquidator disposing assets of a company for the purpose of meeting its liabilities will be capital because they do not arise from the trading operations of the company. Where, however, the liquidator carries on the trading operations of the company, profits made will be treated as revenue and will be subject to income tax. *IRC v Thompson* (1937) 1 KB 290.

We shall now deal with cases showing taxability or otherwise of certain receipts.

Taxation of income from illegal trade

Illegality of a trade or an operation does not make the income therefrom unlawful for tax purposes although the courts have disallowed expenditure on penalties for illegal trading.[59] Thus incomes from unlawful gaming,[60] illegal exportation of goods[61] have been held taxable.

Denman, J. said in *Patridge v Mallamdaine*[62]:

... if a man were to make a systematic business of receiving stolen goods, and to do nothing else, and he thereby systematically carried on a business and made a profit of £2000 a year, the Income Tax Commissioners would be quite right in assessing him as if it were in fact his vocation.

And Lord Morrison stated in the *Minister of Finance v Smith*:[63]

It is ... absurd that honest gains are charged to tax and dishonest gains escape. To hold otherwise would involve a plain breach of the rules of the statute, which require the full amount of the profits to be taxed and merely put a premium on dishonest trading. The burglar and the swindler, who carry on a trade or business for profit are as liable to tax as an honest business man, and, in addition, they get their deserts elsewhere.

Taxation of surplus arising from devaluation of Currency
In *Northern Nigeria Investments Ltd v Federal Board of Inland Revenue* (APP/COMM/134 of 17.3.72), the appellant's company contended that the surplus had not been realised and was therefore not taxable, and further that the surplus was of a capital nature which is not taxable as well.

The appeal was allowed. The Appeal Commissioners found that the profit had not been realised at the time the assessment was made.

In *Longmans of Nigeria Ltd v Federal Board of Inland Revenue* (APP/COMM/129 of 17.3.72), the appellant's contentions were:

(i) that the gain which accrued to the appellant on the devaluation of the £ sterling was not taxable as it did not arise from revenue transactions;

(ii) that management/consultancy fee was an allowable deduction – the appeal was allowed in part.

The Appeal Commissioners found that a proportion of the profit on exchange attributable to the goodwill of £400 000 be regarded as not taxable as there was no evidence

(i) that this sum or any part of it had been paid to the UK company,

(ii) that the balance of the profit on exchange should be regarded as profit on current accounts for goods and services obtained from the UK company and therefore taxable.

Longmans of Nigeria Limited was assessed by the Federal Board of Inland Revenue for tax in the 1969–70 year of assessment in the sum of £28 686.8/- and £6671.12/- on a total profit of £71 716 and £66 716 respectively. The assessment references being income-tax numbered IC5A for 1969–70 and Super Tax numbered IFC2A for 1969-70.

The grounds of appeal were:

(a) that the Inspector of Taxes erred in treating the gain of £67 684.17.4d. as being a profit liable to tax when it arose on devaluation of £ sterling in respect of amount due to Longmans Green and Company Limited (UK) whereas the total debt did not arise from revenue transactions but was in respect of capital assets acquired as follows: total assets – £684 547 less stock – included £170 199 leaving capital assets of £514 348 including goodwill of £400 000. The balance of the debt as at 19 November 1967, devaluation date, was £473 799 and the devaluation profit thereon was £67 685.

(b) that the Inspector of Taxes erred in failing to observe that £67 685 profit on devaluation was not payable and could not legally be payable unless and until exchange control approval had been granted for the transfer of funds to settle the debt to the holding company. Furthermore, that the Inspector of Taxes erred in failing to observe that the Consultancy and Management Fee of £12 039 was an allowable deduction in determining profit of the period liable to tax for the following among other reasons:

(i) The sum was shown as specific charge against the profit for the period concerned;

(ii) That the sum was not a reserve but was an expense, the liability for which had been incurred during the period and was not specifically referable to any other period within the terms of Section 27 of the Companies Income Tax Act, 1961. By consent, the second part of the appeal concerning Consultancy and Management Fee was heard first.

After listening to both sides the Commissioners decided that the appeal must succeed as the expense was an allowable deduction in the year for which it was made.

Arguing the first part of the appeal dealing with the treatment given by the Senior Inspector of Taxes to the profit on devaluation of £67 685, the appellant read paragraph 2 of the letter of 14 November 1969 written by Messrs Peat, Marwick, Casseleton Elliott and Company, Accountants to the Appellant, to the Chief Inspector of Taxes Ibadan, which read as follows:

CAPITAL RESERVE: We have already explained in our letter of 6 October that this arose from the capital items in the current account and as such is not taxable. The capital item in the current account arose originally with the payment of the goodwill £400 000 in Nigeria pound and the introduction of stock in the Nigerian Company on its formation by the holding Company.

This fact was contained in the letter of 6 October 1969 marked B. Counsel for the appellant then went on to say that the main point was that this particular item arose out of the devaluation of sterling and that the amount the Nigerian Company paid to the UK Company decreased because of devaluation of sterling. The profit arising from this was credited to capital reserve. In his opinion, there was no question of receipt of any income or anything of that nature. In cross-examination by Mr Osolake, counsel to the respondent, Mr Whittaker, a chartered accountant with Messrs Peat, Marwick, Caseseleton Elliot and Company, stated that the current account referred to in the balance sheet arose with the liability of the payment of goodwill and all the other assets which the Nigerian company took over from the holding company on its formation. It did not occur to Mr Whittaker that had he analysed the figure of £67 000 to the Inspector the latter would have been able to see how much of the currency profit was in respect of capital and how much was in respect of revenue items. Mr Whittaker stated that he was not requested to give the breakdown but if he had been asked to do so, he would have done it.

Taxation of income from agency services overseas and the question of irregular proceedings and unfair trial

Commissions received overseas are taxable in the hands of a Nigerian taxpayer. The question of irregular proceedings cannot serve any useful purpose, by giving an order for a rehearing of the entire case. The procedure for appeal is by itself a rehearing.

In *Reiss & Co. (Nigeria) Ltd* (Appellant)[64] *Federal Board of Inland Revenue* (Respondent), the appellants, a private limited liability company, incorporated in Nigeria under the provisions of the Companies Act, 1968 with its Headquarters Office at 47 Docemo Street, Lagos was concerned in the business of performing agency services and introducing customers in Nigeria to Handelsvereeninging V/H Reiss & Co. (Amsterdam), a private limited liability company incorporated in Holland, with Headquarters in Amsterdam. Reiss & Co. (Amsterdam) holds 60% of the shares of Reiss & Co. (Nigeria) Ltd. The company had been assessed to tax in respect of all the profits made by its principals on all businesses introduced to them by the company. This was an appeal against the decision of the Board of Appeal Commissioners delivered on 27 February 1976, dismissing their appeal against the revised assessment to tax for 1971–72 – 1974–75 made on them by the Federal Board of Inland Revenue in respect of income received in connection with their performing agency service of introducing customers to Reiss & Co. (Amsterdam). In support of their appeal, the appellants in paragraphs 20 of their amended grounds of appeal stated as follows:

(a) The body of Appeal Commissioners erred in law and on the facts holding that the appellants had not declared all their income for tax purposes when there was absolutely no evidence before them that the said appellants received any sum over and above those shown in its books of account and returns submitted to the respondent.

(b) The only profits chargeable to tax were the profits of the appellants and not those of the Overseas Company [Reiss & Co. (Amsterdam)].

(c) Even if (which was not admitted) the profits of the Overseas Company [Reiss & Co. (Amsterdam)] were or could be treated as the profits of the appellants, the expenses reasonably necessary and wholly incurred in earning the income must be deducted in order to determine the assessable profits.

The facts leading to this litigation are fairly simple, and there is substantial agreement on the part of both appellants and respondents on the material facts with the exception of the issues which will be mentioned later.

Before going into the question of the merits of the case, the court thought it important to consider and dispose of first, the contention of chief F.R.A. Williams, the appellant's counsel, who sought to open his argument with the contention that the trial before the Board of Appeal Commissioners was irregular and should be set aside because of the variation in its panel. This argument was based on paragraph 15 of the appellant's grounds of appeal which states:

(a) The Body of Appeal Commissioners who heard and determined the appeal of the appellant sat on

(i) 24 October 1975, when they had the opening remarks of appellant's counsel the evidence of Mr J.H. Doresteijn, the Managing Director of the Appellant Company, and received a number of documents in evidence.

(ii) 29 October 1975, when they heard the evidence of Mr K.A. Bankole, the Acting Senior Investigating Officer of the respondent, who tendered further documentary evidence.

(iii) 27 February 1976, when judgement was delivered.

(b) Mr Mojisola Oluwa, a member of the Board of Appeal Commissioners, sat at the hearing of the appeal on 24 October 1975 but did not sit at that of 29 October 1975.

(c) The appellant would contend at this appeal that the proceedings mentioned in sub-paragraph (i) hereof were irregular and judgement based thereon was irregular and judgement based thereon was illegal and ought to be set aside because Mr Mojisola Oluwa, who did not hear the proceedings held on 29 October 1975, participated in the unanimous judgement delivered on 27 February 1976.

Counsel contended therefore that being irregular a proper and valid trial in this Court cannot cure the irregularity, infringement arising from any of their constitutional right of absence of a fair trial.

The counsel relied on section 22(1) of the Constitution of the Federation Act No. 20 of 1963, and cited in support of his contention the cases of *Egba N.A. v Adeyanju* 13 NLR 77; *Timitimi v Amabebe* 14 WACA 374; *Adeigbe v Kushimo* (1965) 1 All NLR 248. Reference was made to *Durayapah v Fernando* (1967) AC.337 and *Leary v National Union of Vehicle Builders* (1971), ch. 34. Counsel submitted that if this contention was accepted, then the appeal failed *in limine*. In his reply, counsel for the respondent Board of Inland Revenue, contended that there was no infringement of the appellant's right to a fair trial as guaranteed under the constitution. The counsel admitted, however, that it is true the member complained of Mr Oluwa, who did not sit during one of the sessions of the trial, but signed the judgement. He, however, submitted relying on section 57(1) of the Companies Income Tax Act, 1961 and Rule 15(1) of the Income Tax Appeals Rules, 1958, that the judgement and trial were valid and regular. He argued that all that was required for the regularity of the trial was the presence of a quorum of three members of the Tribunal and this was present throughout even without counting the participation of Mr Oluwa. Counsel submitted that the proceedings in that court were in law regarded as new and could cure any irregularity in the earlier trial.

The court agreed with appellant's counsel that if the contention that the appellant did not have a fair hearing by reason of the variation in the composition of the members of the Board of Appeal Commissioners who tried the case were to succeed, then the appeal would be successful. The Court agreed with the view of Megarry, J., in *Leary v National Union of Vehicle Builders* (1970) 2 All ER 713 at page 720 that where there was a defect of natural justice in the trial court, this could not be cured only by sufficiency of natural justice in the appellate court. Section 22(1) of the Constitution Act No. 20/1973, so far as is relevant, provides that 'In the determination of his civil rights and obligations a person shall be entitled to fair hearing within a reasonable time *by a Court or other tribunal established by law and constituted in such manner as to* secure its independence and impartiality.' The relevant part is italicised. There is no doubt that the Board of Appeal Commissioners comes within this category having been established by section 57(1)(a)(b).

Section 57(1) reads:

(1) As often as may be necessary, Appeal Commissioners shall meet to hear appeals in any town in which is situated an office of the Federal Inland Revenue Department, and subject to the provisions of the next following subsection, at any such meeting –
   (i) any three or more Appeal Commissioners may hear and decide an appeal; and
   (ii) the Appeal Commissioners present shall elect one of their number to be the chairman of the meeting.

The Board of Appeal Commissioners will in accordance with the provisions of the above cited section be properly constituted where any three of its members are present to hear and decide an appeal. The appellant's contention was that even if there were three members, it must necessarily be at least three regular members who had to sit to hear and determine the appeal. It follows therefore that where more than three members have sat to hear and determine the appeal, the provision is satisfied if at least three of the members were present at all the sittings and also signed the judgement. In such a situation where the number at the sittings to determine the appeal was more than three, it is still possible to have three members who were present at all the sittings to hear and determine the appeal. In such a situation where any member who was not present at any one of the sittings signs the judgement, this does not necessarily contravene the provisions of s.57(1) such as to render the proceedings a nullity by the addition to the composition.

The problems of variation of adjudicating panels and the consequent validity or invalidity of decisions of such panels has in this country had a long and confused history. The problem has in many cases arisen from the decision of native Courts (Customary) whose panels were necessarily large and usually fluctuating. In many cases the number of persons entitled to sit in the Courts were provided in the warrants establishing the Courts, in others no limitation was placed. In any case these Courts were known to have allowed persons who did not hear the case to take part and sign the judgement. The problem has been very thoroughly discussed by Idigbe, Ag. CJ (as he then was), in *Chime & Ors v Elikwu & Ors* (1965) NMLR 71. After citing and discussing *Tawiah v Edwuzi* 3 WACA 52; *Otwiwa v Kwaseko* 3 WACA 320; *Damoah v Taibeth* 12 WACA 167; *Runka v Katsina NA* 13 WACA 98, and *Egba NA v Adeyanju* 13 NLR 77 in support of the contention that variation of panel rendered the decision a nullity; referred also to *Chapman v CFAO* 9 WACA 181, where the plea of *resjudicata* was rejected by the trial judge on the ground that the trial was a nullity because the composition of the tribunal altered between trial and judgement. In the West African Court of Appeal, their

Lordships admitted the fact of alteration in the composition of the tribunal, but held that the trial was not a nullity. The plea of *resjudicata* was rejected on other grounds. On the other hand in *Runka v Katsina NA* 13 WACA 98, the West African Court of Appeal regarded the statement made in *Chapman v CFAO* as *obiter* and quashed the decision of a Native Court reached in similar circumstances. In *Runka v Katsina NA* the Court did not declare that the decision of the Native Court was a nullity. This was the situation in which the law was when *Chime & Ors v Elikwu & Ors*, came before Idigbe, Ag. CJ. There were two conflicting decisions of the West African Court of Appeal, and the learned Ag. Chief Justice considered it not improper to review the law involved in the issue and to choose which line of decisions to follow. His Lordship followed *Chapman v CFAO* 9 WACA 181 and held in the case before him that variation in the composition of the panel should not be considered as having rendered their decision a nullity, but as an irregularity, so that if the irregularity was substantial, and occasioned a miscarriage of justice, and the point was specifically taken on appeal, that judgement should be set aside on appeal, but such judgement being merely voidable remains subsisting until set aside on appeal. Recent judicial developments have rendered it really unnecessary for me to follow the arduous line so excellently blazed by Idigbe, Ag. CJ. In *Adeigbe & Anor v Kusimo & Ors* (1965) NMLR 284, the Supreme Court had to consider this matter again and the arguments before the court followed the old familiar pattern. It was argued in support of the trial judge that the trial was a nullity because of the variation in the composition of the panel. The Supreme Court rejected the argument and in setting aside the decision of the lower Court made the distinction between jurisdiction of the Court and regularity of the proceedings. I set out the dictum of the Supreme Court *in extenso* because of its lucidity and clarity (pages 286–7):

We are in no doubt about the correctness of what the learned trial judge said in his judgement that there are abundant decisions in the High Court and in the West African Court of Appeal on the point that where a Court is differently constituted during the hearing of a case, or on various occasions when it met, or where one member did not hear the whole evidence the effect on the proceedings is to render then null and void. The learned judge obviously had in mind, among others, the following cases –
Egba N.A. v Adeyanju,
Tawiah III v Ewudzi,
Otwiwa v Kwaseko,
Damoab v Taibeth,
Runka v Katsina N.A.,
In the first of these cases, in which the defendant's witnesses were not heard by two members of the Court, the principle was enunciated that a judgement could not be allowed to stand which was given by judges who had not heard all the evidence; in the

other four cases, the Appeal Court held expressly that the proceedings were a nullity on that account. There seems to be a confusion of thought between jurisdiction and regularity, between the competence of the Court to hear the case and the propriety of a bench who had not heard all the evidence adjudicating on the case.

Their Lordships then cited the dictum of Bairamian, FJ, in *Madukolu v Nkemdilim* regarding the circumstance when a Court is competent and continued:

The complaint against the hearing that was not always before the same bench does not pertain to any matter that goes to the jurisdiction of the Court. It is at bottom a complaint that the judgement cannot be satisfactory on the ground that as the persons who gave it had not seen and heard all the witnesses, they could not appraise the evidence as a whole and decide the facts properly, thus it is a complaint on the soundness of the judgement itself, and not a complaint that is extrinsic to the adjudication, which is the test to apply when considering a submission on jurisdiction.

In concluding, their Lordships said:

We are therefore of the opinion that variations in the bench do not make the judgement a nullity; they make it unsatisfactory, and it may have to be set aside for this reason, but whether they do or not depends on the particular circumstances of the case.

This general principle as enunciated by their Lordships was applied to the case before them resulting in the absence of the two assessors during the hearing of the formal evidence, not making any difference to the soundness of the decision of the Court. *Adeigbe & Anor v Kusimo & Ors*, has clearly shown that the Supreme Court has chosen between the equal conflicting decisions of the Court, the line of decisions which it has to follow in subsequent cases. This is further supported by another decision of the Court in 1967. In *Ogiamien & Anor v Ogiamien & Ors* (1967) NMLR 245 Ademola, CJN delivering the judgement of the Court said, at page 249:

In the case of *Adeigbe & Anor v Salami Kusimo & Ors* (1965) NMLR 285, this Court has efficiently dealt with the state of the law on the question of variation in the panel of Judges and it was there laid down that variations in the Bench do not make the judgement a nullity ...

It can now be safely postulated that all the cases which hold that a variation in the panel of judges renders the trial a nullity are overruled by *Adeigbe & Anor v Kusimo & Ors*, that the law now as laid down by *Adeigbe v Kusimo & Ors* is that the variation in the panel of a tribunal *simpliciter* does not render the trial a nullity. It merely renders the trial irregular. Whether the nature of the irregularity is sufficient to set the trial aside will depend on the particular circumstances of the case.

It is therefore necessary in this case to look at the facts to determine whether the admitted variation in the composition of the Board of Appeal Commissioners was sufficient to affect the trial. The court had examined the record of proceedings before the Board of Appeal Commissioners, which were on 24 and 28 October 1975 on which evidence was taken, and on 27 February 1976, on which the Board delivered its judgement. The Chairman, Mr J.I. Obi, was present on all the occasions. There were in addition five other members including Mr Oluwa, on the 24th. On 28 October 1975, Mr Oluwa was absent; there were, including the Chairman, four other members. On 7 February 1976, when Mr Oluwa again appeared, there were also four members including the Chairman, and three members excluding Mr Oluwa. Thus even if it were to be conceded that Mr Oluwa who was not present on 28 October 1976, should not sign the judgement, the presence of the other three members would still comply with the provisions of section 57(1) of the Companies Income Tax Act 1961. However, in strict legal theory and in the absence of any statutory provision, justice may appear not to have been done to a litigant if any of the judges who gave the judgement did not hear all the evidence. In the case before the court, it is not difficult to appreciate how Mr Oluwa could have subscribed to the judgement of the court when he did not take part in all the proceedings. It has been held that this omission is a mere irregularity. (See *Adeigbe's case*.) Apart merely from the objection that Mr Oluwa did not hear all the evidence, how substantial is the irregularity to vitiate the trial as a whole? To vitiate the trial the irregularity must be regarded as resulting in a miscarriage of justice. It is well settled that a judge cannot give a decision in a proceeding in which he has not heard evidence – See *Coleshill v Manchester Corporation* (1928) 1 KB 785. In unusual circumstances and with the consent of the parties, a judge may proceed with notes of evidence taken by another judge and can give judgement – see *Chua Chee Chor v Chua Kiai Yen & Ors* (1936) 1 All ER 102.

In circumstances where a judge who did not hear evidence had taken part in the decision the proceedings have been regarding as irregular and not void – See *Whittle v Whittle* (1939) 1 All ER 737, and the cases could be remitted for rehearing. The court thought that cases under the provisions of section 57(1) of the Companies Income Tax Act, 1961 are a statutory exception to s.22(1) of the constitution and clearly different and intended to be so. The reasons for providing for a quorum to decide such cases is to provide for contingency situations and enable a valid trial where all the members might not be present. In such cases where the minimum number required by the statute is present, it was of little moment in the court's view that the excess in the number is made up of a person whose presence would otherwise vitiate the proceedings. The court agreed with respondent's counsel and held therefore that since there were three members of the Board of Appeal Commissioners who heard all the evidence and signed the judgement, the interposition of Mr Oluwa would not render the proceedings contrary to the provisions of section 22(1) of the constitution. The facts of this case are covered by the Supreme court decision of *Adeigbe & Anor v Kushimo & Ors*. In the court's view there is necessarily a fair trial in accordance with s.57(1) of the CITA 1961 before the Board of Appeal Commissioners when the provisions of the statute is satisfied. There is no doubt that this had been done in this case. The view the court had taken of this case precludes its giving any consideration to *Leary v National Union of Vehicle Builders* (1970) 2 All ER 713, cited by counsel for the appellant. Leary's case is based on the ground that the decision of the initial tribunal was invalid and irregular and cannot be cured by a subsequent valid trial in another tribunal. It was therefore said that a lack of natural justice before the trial body generally cannot be cured by a sufficiency of natural justice before an appellate body. There was no lack of natural justice in the trial body in the instant case. The provisions of the enabling statute were complied with throughout the trial. Leary's case therefore does not apply to the case before the court: and it therefore held that there was a fair hearing and the trial was valid, and not irregular. This ground of appeal therefore failed.

The other contention of Chief Williams was that the respondent's amended answer offended against the requirement of order XXXI r.5 of the Federal Revenue Court (Civil Procedure) Rules, 1976 which provides:

Every pleading shall contain a statement of all the material facts on which the party pleading relies, but not the evidence by which they are to be proved, such statement being divided into paragraphs numbered consecutively, and each paragraph containing as nearly as may be a separate allegation.

Alternatively it was contended that the respondent's answer did not contain any specific traverse of material facts – counsel cited and relied upon *Service Press Ltd v Nnamdi Azikiwe* 13 WACA; *Warner Bros v Sampson* (1959) 1 OB 297, 310–311; and *Bullen & Leake's Precedents of Pleadings* 12th ed., page 83. Counsel submitted on the authority of NIPC v Thompson Organisation (1969) 1 All NLR 138 that the respondent's answer contained no averments and that all the respondent's amended answer would therefore be inadmissible.

Mr Akinloye, counsel for the respondent, asked for an adjournment to enable him reply to the points of pleading which did not appear on the grounds of appeal. On 20 June 1977 when the respondent continued his address, he applied by virtue of Order XXXII of the Federal Revenue Court (Civil Procedure) Rules 1976, to amend the numbering of the paragraphs of the respondent's amended answers. He applied that the general traverse be numbered 1, and the remaining paragraphs to be renumbered consecutively in that order. The counsel submitted that the pleadings sufficiently disclose the issues in controversy and that the amendment raised no new issues. He relied on *Ratcliffe v Evans* (1892) 20 B 524 at page 533.

The court accepted the submission that non-compliance with a mandatory provision of a procedural legislation is fatal. But this is only where such provision is not equivocal as to the effect of non-compliance. It will seem that the mandatory requirement of r.5 Order XXXI will apply to numbering paragraphs consecutively in pleadings. The court agreed with the appellant's counsel that the respondent's answer as it was, if not amended, did not contain any specific traverse of the material facts in the appellant's grounds of appeal – See *Service Press Ltd v Nnamdi Azikiwe*, 13 WACA. Again if the amended answer was not amended by renumbering the paragraphs in the manner respondent had applied, this would be an infringement of Order XXXI r.5, and the provision being mandatory, there would be no valid answer before the court.

Counsel for respondent had applied for the amendment of the answer under Order XXXII of the Federal Revenue Court (Civil Procedure) Rules, 1976. The court agreed with Mr Akinloye, that the amendment sought would not raise new issues, or introduce new facts in the case. It would not embarrass the appellant who had already argued his case. In fact the amendment was aimed at bringing out the issues in controversy in line with the pleadings and arguments already in support of them.

In *Amadi v Thomas Aplin & Co. Ltd* (1972) 1 All NLR 409, the Supreme Court in similar circumstances as the present case held to reversing the ruling of the trial judge who refused leave to amend as follows:

It appears that the amendment sought was necessary and proper such as the Court was bound to make as, in the language of the provisions of Order XXXIV (similar to Order XXXII), 'all such amendments as may be necessary and proper for the purpose of determining in the existing suit the real questions or question in controversy between the parties shall be so made' (see *England v Palmer* 14 WACA 659; *Oquntimeyin v Gubere* (1964) 1 All NLR 176.

It had not been argued that the amendment sought would delay the trial of the action or was in any way prejudicial to the defence of the appellants. The appellant had only raised the issue in his address after contesting the case on the basis of the respondent's answer. The court was of the opinion that the interest of justice required granting the amendment which obviously was not sought *mala fide* – See *Tiddesley v Harper* 10 Ch. D 896. The court appreciated the fact that the respondent had not formulated the amendment as he was required to do by practice. This was meant to facilitate understanding of the matter sought to be amended. The court was aware of the fact and that the appellant had not been misled by what was sought to be amended, and it exercised its discretion to waive that requirement and allow the amendment. It therefore granted leave to respondent to further amend his amended answers, by now renumbering the paragraphs starting from number I, that is, the unnumbered paragraph and progressing consecutively in the ascending order. The respondent's amended answer was hereby accordingly further amended – See *Amadi v Thomas Aplin & Co.* (1972) 1 All NLR at page 417.

This amendment did not include any other than the renumbering of the amended answer. Counsel for the respondent had no argument against the contention of Chief Williams that the respondent had not specifically denied the material allegations in paragraph 10 of the appellant's grounds of appeal. The court agreed with Chief Williams that the claim must be deemed to have been admitted.

In *Thorp v Holdsworth* (1876) 3 Ch. D 637, Jessel, M.R., said,

> (The defendant) is bound to deny that any agreement or any terms of arrangement were ever come to, if that is what he means, if he does not mean that he should say that there were no terms of arrangement come to, except the following terms and state what the terms were ...

Paragraphs 10 and 11 of the appellant's grounds of appeal contain material allegations as to the profits made by the overseas company and the agency remuneration payable to the appellants in respect of each of the transactions. These were never specifically denied by the respondent's answer, and it is only fair that they should be deemed to have been admitted. All that the respondent did was to plead as follows:

> The respondent is not in a position to admit or deny paragraphs 3 to 11 of the amended grounds of appeal and therefore puts the appellant to the strictest proof thereof.

This was not acceptable to refute the specific allegation in paragraph 10 of the appellant's ground of appeal. In *Lewis & Peat (NRI) Ltd v Akhimien* (1976) 7 SC at page 163, the Supreme Court said:

> We must observe, however, that in order to raise an issue of fact in these circumstances there must be a proper traverse; and a traverse must be made either by a denial or non-admission either expressly or by necessary implication. So that if a defendant refused to admit a particular allegation in the statement of claim he must state so specifically; and he does not do this satisfactorily by pleading thus, the defendant is *not in a position* to admit or deny (the particular allegation in the statement of claim) and will at the trial put to plaintiff to proof. As was held in *Harris v Gamble* (1878) 7 Ch.D 877, a plea that defendant *puts plaintiff to proof* amounts to insufficient denial, equally a plea that the defendant *does not admit* correctness (or a particular allegation in the statement of claim) is also an insufficient denial – see *Rutter v Tregent* (1879) 12 Ch. D 758.

215

The court now proceded to consider the appeal before it on the merits and to decide whether or not the appellant had satisfied it that:

(i) The Body of Appeal Commissioners erred in law and on the facts that the appellants have not declared all their income for tax purposes when there was absolutely no evidence before them that the said appellants received any sum over and above these shown in its books of account and returns submitted to the respondent.

(ii) The only profits chargeable to tax are the profits of the appellants and those of the overseas company.

(iii) Even if (which is not admitted) the profits of the overseas company are or can be treated as the profits of the appellants, the expenses reasonably, necessarily and wholly incurred in earning the income must be deducted in order to determine the assessable profits.

The facts which had led to the assessment of the appellants to tax by the respondents were simple. And they were the subject matter of the appeal both before the Board of Appeal Commissioners and in this Court. They were substantially set out in the grounds of appeal and were not materially controverted by the respondent's answer.

The facts are that the appellants, who are a Nigerian incorporated private limited liability company, are agents in Nigeria to Messrs Handelsvereeninging v/h Reiss & Co. NV [hereinafter referred to as Reiss & Co. (Amsterdam)], a company incorporated in Holland with its Head Office at Amsterdam. Reiss & Co. (Nigeria) Ltd introduces customers to Reiss & Co. (Amsterdam) for the purposes of enabling such customers to make purchases from overseas manufacturers through Reiss & Co. (Amsterdam). In this arrangement Reiss & Co. (Nigeria), accepts orders from such customers, and a deposit in respect of such orders. The orders are transmitted to Reiss & Co. (Amsterdam), who decides to accept or reject the orders. When such orders are received from Reiss & Co. (Nigeria), Reiss & Co. (Amsterdam) thereafter communicates directly with the Nigerian customer. Reiss & Co. (Amsterdam) charges the Nigerian customers for its services in selling the goods to them. It also pays to Reiss & Co. (Nigeria) a mutually agreed percentage in return for its agency services of introducing customers to it. Reiss & Co. (Amsterdam) in the course of its business sends the invoices of each Nigerian customer directly to such customer and to Reiss & Co. (Nigeria). The invoices contain particulars of cost of the goods, the percentage of commisson chargeable to the buyer, and the commission allowed to the seller. At best the appellants acted as intermediaries between Nigerian customers and Reiss & Co. (Amsterdam).

The respondent had contended that the entire commission appearing on the face of the invoice was due to the appellants and should be subject to tax. It was the contention of the appellants that the only percentage of commission due to them was 50% of the profits after deduction of sundry expenses made in connection with the transaction, and that the other 50% went to Reiss & Co. (Amsterdam) who undertook the larger part of the trading and bore all the financial burdens of the transaction.

The chief argument before the court was that the entire buying commission was due to the appellants. Mr Akinloye, counsel for the respondents, was at pains to point out that the extra commission of 10% in addition to the mandatory 4% on all the invoices had been earned by the appellants. He referred to s.17 of the Companies Income Tax Act 1961 and submitted that tax was levied at the source. Counsel also referred to the provisions of section 18(1) of the Companies Income Tax Act 1961. Mr Akinloye argued that a reading together of the two sections supported his contention. The Counsel referred to the case of *Barclays Bank Ltd v Inland Revenue Commissioners* (1960) 2 All ER 817. He contended that the fact that the money was being paid to Reiss & Co. (Amsterdam) was immaterial, the income belonged to the appellants having been derived from Nigeria. Whilst not disputing that the appellants were assessable to tax, counsel for the appellants contended that they were only assessable in respect of earned income and no more. Chief Williams pointed out that the circumstances in which the Nigerian and the overseas company were assessable to tax were clearly stated in section 18 of the Companies Income Tax Act, 1961. He argued that the appellants shared the profits with Reiss & Co. (Nigeria) and could not be assessed to tax in respect of the whole.

In order to understand the situation, it is necessary to state the relationship between Reiss & Co. (Nigeria) and Reiss & Co. (Amsterdam) apart from the agency arrangement. In his evidence, the Managing Director of Reiss & Co. (Nigeria) stated on oath that the company's founder and principal shareholder was Reiss & Co. (Amsterdam). He said that the appellant company was incorporated on 23 September 1960. Mr Jacob Dirk Moraal, Assistant Managing Director of Reiss & Co. (Amsterdam) owned 55% of the shares in Reiss & Co. (Nigeria). Notwithstanding this controlling shareholding both witnesses stated in their evidence that Reiss & Co. (Amsterdam) did not control the affairs or management of the appellant company in any way. The agency relationship was remunerated on the basis of a 'gentleman's agreement.' There was no formal contract embodying the percentage due to the appellants, although there was the understanding that 50% was due to the appellants.

It was vital in the circumstances to determine from where the source of income had accrued and to whom. Section 17(a) of the Companies Income Tax Act 1961 provides:

The tax shall, subject to the provisions of the Act, be payable at the rate hereinafter specified for each year of assessment upon the profits of any company accruing in, derived from, brought into or received in Nigeria in respect of –
(a) any trade or business for whatever period of time such trade or business may have been carried on ...

This enables profits of Nigerian companies to be assessed to tax wherever they have been made, if they are derived from, brought into or received in Nigeria. The profit must be made in trade or business carried on by such company. Wherever such profits have arisen and whether or not they have been brought into or received in Nigeria they shall be deemed to accrue in Nigeria.

On the other hand the situation with respect to a non-Nigerian company is different. Section 18(2) of the CITA 1961 provides:

The profits of a company other than a Nigerian Company from any trade or business shall be deemed to be derived from Nigeria to the extent to which such profits are not attributable to any part of the operations of the company carried on outside Nigeria.

The evidence that the appellant was an intermediary of Reiss & Co. (Amsterdam) for the purposes of introducing Nigerian customers had not been controverted. There is no evidence that the appellant did anything more with respect to such customers. This was clearly brought out by evidence in chief and answers to cross-examination of the appellant's Managing Director. The Assistant Managing Director of Reiss & Co. (Amsterdam) in his evidence gave a full description of the duties of the appellants and Reiss & Co. (Amsterdam) in respect of orders of customers. All the appellant did was to take a proforma invoice from the customer and send this to Reiss & Co. (Amsterdam). The deposit received by the appellant was refunded to the customer, if Reiss & Co. (Amsterdam) rejected the order. Every other activity in respect of the transaction, and financial obligations thereon was carried on in Amsterdam by Reiss & Co. (Amsterdam). Simply put, all operations relating to the transaction were carried on outside Nigeria by Reiss & Co. (Amsterdam). It therefore followed that it was not a trade or business carried on in Nigeria; by a Nigerian company in accordance with s.17. Rather it was a trade or business carried on by a company other than a Nigerian company, and no part of its profits was attributable to operations of the company in Nigeria in accordance with section 18(2) of the Companies Income Tax Act, 1961. Considerable importance has been attached and emphasis laid on the relationship between the appellants and Reiss & Co. (Amsterdam). It was in evidence that the appellant was before 23 September 1960 only an overseas branch of Reiss & Co.

(Amsterdam). Following upon the promulgation of the Companies Decree, 1968, and in compliance with the provisions of Part X of that Decree, the Nigerian branch became incorporated as a separate legal entity with its own Managing Director and Board of Directors. There was, however, evidence before the court that Reiss & Co. (Amsterdam) still had a controlling shareholding of 55% of the shares of the appellant company. There was no evidence before the court of any actual control of the affairs of the appellant company by Reiss & Co. (Amsterdam). The only evidence before the court which had remained uncontroverted was the oral evidence of a sharing agreement in respect of commissions payable to the appellant company on profits of business introduced to Reiss & Co. (Amsterdam). Although there was a considerable dark cloud of suspicion regarding the genuineness of this transaction, especially the two companies being the same before the legal separation, the natural philosophical variety in the arrangement is more indicative of the arrangement generally understood of companies within the same group. The separate legal identity of the appellants and Reiss & Co. (Amsterdam), cannot be denied, *Salomon v Salomon & Co.* (1892) AC 22. The respondent cannot impugn the legal situation successfully without adducing sufficient evidence to the contrary. It is not sufficient to allege that the profits in the transaction accrue to the appellants. It must be shown how it so accrued notwithstanding the clear words ef s.18(1) of CITA 1961.

In *Smith & Co. v Greenwood* S. Tax Cases 193, the facts are similar to this case. The appellants carried on business at Copenhagen in Denmark, as manufacturers of and dealers in cement-making and other allied machinery. All the partners were resident in Copenhagen, where they had their head office. They had an employee in London, who was paid a salary and a bonus based on the profits of the entire turnover of the business. The appellants rented an office in London where the employee, whose duty was to ascertain the requirements of intending purchasers, inspect the proposed site of any proposed installation of machinery, and take samples of earth, used to report to the appellants in Copenhagen. Otherwise, the employee had no responsibility for the negotiation of contracts which were made directly with the appellants in Copenhangen. All machinery purchased was sent FOB from Copenhagen. Samples of earth were tested in laboratories in Copenhagen. During the war the appellant purchased parts of the machinery in the United Kingdom in order to complete installations or to carry out repairs. It was admitted that the appellant was liable to tax in respect of the profits arising from the resale of the goods so purchased.

It was held that apart from the goods locally purchased and resold in the United Kingdom, the evidence before the Commission did not

219

justify the conclusion of fact that the firm exercised a trade within the United Kingdom.

In the High Court, Rowlatt, J, gave a definition of where the trade or business is exercised which is acceptable to the court, and was indeed accepted by the Court of Appeal and the House of Lords. He said:

... The real place where the trade is exercise is where the transactions forming the alleged business are closed, in the case of a selling business, by the sale of commodity and the profit thereby realised. It seems to me that is a clear principle. Until the sale is effected the trade is incomplete. Trading is buying or making and selling, and if I am right that one single place has to be treated as the place where the business is exercised, it seems to me it must be where the profit bearing transactions are closed.

On the same point, Lord Atkin in the court of Appeal said:

To my mind, there is no evidence in the present case of any place other than Denmark. No doubt operations of importance take place here, orders are solicited, and the successful adapting of the goods bought for the purpose of the buyer's business is supervised here. But in the words of Lord Watson in the case cited at page 340: 'There may, in my opinion, be transactions by or on behalf of a foreign merchant in this country, so intimately connected with his business abroad that without them, it could not be successfully carried on, which are nevertheless insufficient to constitute an exercise of his trade here within the meaning of schedule D.'

These dicta largely support the agreed facts of the case before the court which was that the appellant's only duty was to introduce customers to Reiss & Co. (Amsterdam). This function has been aptly described by Herschell, LJ, in *Sulley v AG 3 TC* 467, as:

... only ancillary to the exercise of his trade in the Country where he buys or makes, stores and sells his goods.

On examination of the facts, the appellant company in *Smith's case* had been more involved in the transaction than the appellant in this case.

It will seem from the cases referred to above as if the place of the conclusion of the contract of sale is of itself decisive of the test of the place where business is carried on. This is not so. As was said by Atkin, LJ, in *Smith & Co. v Greenwood* 8 Tax Cases 193 at page 204, there is no exhaustive test as to what consitutes trading within or outside a place by a non-resident. Attention must be paid to the whole circumstances of the case in order to understand the basis of operations where the profits in substance arise. In *Firestone Tyre & Rubber Co. Ltd (as agents for Firestone Tyre & Rubber Co. of Akron, Ohio USA) v Lewellin* (HM Inspector of Taxes) 37 Tax Cases III, the facts of which are a bit complicated, Firestone Tyre & Rubber Co. of Akron, Ohio, USA, a corporation established in Maine, USA has a wholly-owned subsidiary, the Firestone Tyre & Rubber Co. Ltd registered in

England. The English Company at first sold tyres manufactured in Ohio, USA, but subsequently manufactured and sold tyres in England. It also sells tyres abroad on an agreement with the American company. The profits received from this latter business were assessed to tax but the English company contending that they were not liable argued that they were not profits of a trade carried on within the United Kingdom. This was based on the agreement with the parent company which was not made in the United Kingdom, Harman, J., rejected this argument and held:

I agree at once that a contract between Akron and the Swedish company was made when the letter was posted in Stockholm but that was a contract under which Akron was not bound to deliver tyres but was bound to procure someone else to do so. It is the kind of contract which warranted out A, B or C would deliver the goods. The contract for the purchase and sale of the goods themselves was not made, in the court's view, until the letter from the Swedish distributors reached Bradford, and the latter company either accepted it in writing or appropriated the goods in fulfilment of it; and that contract it seems to me was made in England. Therefore if that be the case, the relevant contract was a contract made in England; and if so, the trade was exercised in England.

His Lordship therefore held that although the business was done as an agent, by the English company, the business was that of the American company, who was the principal, and can be regarded as carrying on business in England. It was therefore assessable to tax for that business. The court had to add that the facts of the case before were different.

The appeal of the company to the Court of Appeal and House of Lords were dismissed. The facts of *Mitchell's Case*, a divided decision of the House of Lords, are very similar to the facts of *Reiss & Co. (Nigeria) v FBIR* if all the evidence necessary to establish the relationship between the appellants and Reiss & Co. (Amsterdam) had been adduced. There was nothing in the Articles of Association of the appellant's company or Reiss & Co. (Amsterdam). Exhibit 3 which was an excerpt of Reiss & Co. (Amsterdam) reveals nothing of the relationship. It was, however, not disputed that it had controlling shares in the appellant company. The facts of Mitchell's case, *Mitchell (Supervisor of Taxes) v Egyptian Hotels Ltd* (1915) AC 1022 is that the Appellant Company incorporated in England owned and carried on a hotel business in Egypt. In 1908, the company altered its articles of association by providing for a local board in Egypt to manage its Egyptian business including the hotel to the exclusion of any board of directors of the company itself. The local board was to exercise all the powers of the company in regard to the hotel. They were to retain all the profits made by the hotel and remit to the company in England only so much as was necessary to pay dividends to shareholders resident in England and for expenses incurred by the London Board. The accounts of the company were kept in London, which recommended dividends and controlled the capital. The company was assessed to tax upon the full amount of its profits, on the basis that the controlling power of the company remained with the London Board. The assessment was upheld on appeal by the Revenue Commissioners, and Horridge, J., dismissed the appeal of the company to the High Court. His decision was reversed by the Court of Appeal. On a further appeal to the House of Lords, the decision of the Court of Appeal was affirmed by the House being equally divided.

It was clear from the evidence that a considerable part of the essential management of the income producing capital was in London. In affirming the Court of Appeal, Lord Parker of Waddington reviewed the facts and came to the conclusion on the facts that (at page 1038):

Under these circumstances it appears to me indisputable that no single act has been done in or directed from this country by way of participation in or furtherance of the trade or business of the company from which the profits or gains said to be chargeable to income tax since August 1980, have arisen.

On this reasoning his Lordship came to the conclusion (at 1039) as follows:

In the absence of any act done or directed by any person resident here in participation or furtherance of the business operations in Egypt from which the profits and gains in question arose, I think your Lordships are bound to come to the conclusion that this trade or business was carried on wholly outside the United Kingdom ...

Sumner, LJ, at page 1041, Loreburn, Parmoor LJJ, held the contrary. The decision of the Court of Appeal therefore was affirmed.

The court thought that the view of the Court of Appeal affirmed by this decision ought to be followed. The court applied that decision as consistent with judicial authority and more in consonance with the express provisions of the enabling statutes. There was no doubt that the participation of the appellant in the profit-earning business in Amsterdam was not significant or existent. The appellant could conveniently be regarded as a sleeping partner in the context of *Colquhon v Brooks*. Again from the evidence before the court, there was nothing to show that any part of the transaction was carried on in this country. Apart from introducing customers who thereafter dealt directly with the principal, the appellant did not feature again in any other important aspect of the transaction. In *Grainger & Son v Gough (Surveyor of Taxes)* (1896) AC 325, one of the Champagne cases, whose essential facts were fairly similar to the case before the court, it was held that a foreign merchant who canvasses through agents in the United Kingdom for orders for the sale of his merchandise to customers in the United Kingdom, does not exercise a trade in the United Kingdom, within the meaning of the Income Tax Acts, so long as all contracts for the sale and all deliveries to merchandise are made in a foreign country.

So in this case all that the appellants did was to canvass for customers in Nigeria, as Grainger & Sons did to Louis Roedorer, the French wine merchant in that case, who was held not to have exercised any trade in the United Kingdom. On the court's findings of fact on the evidence no trade or business was carried on in Nigeria either by the appellants or by Reiss & Co. (Amsterdam). This was because the acceptance of the order was by Reiss & Co. (Amsterdam). The purchase of the goods was made outside Nigeria and the invoice was prepared outside Nigeria, and from there sent directly to the customer in Nigeria. Payment was made to Reiss & Co. (Amsterdam) in Amsterdam. That they were paid in Nigeria through Nigerian banks is a convenient manner and in accordance with modern commercial practice to pay the seller. The delivery was also made in Amsterdam outside the country. In the circumstances, the court was of the opinion that whenever profitable contracts are habitually made in this country, by or for foreigners, with persons in this country because they are here to do something for or supply something to those persons, such persons are exercising a profitable trade in the country even though everything to be done by them to fulfil the contracts is done abroad. It is otherwise when the same result is achieved through an agent without coming into this country. It was held in *Colquhon v Brooks* 14 App. Cas. 493, that where, there is resident in a country a sleeping partner with respect to a business carried on abroad, the management of which he does not take part, such partner is only liable to be assessed on such parts of the profits as are remitted to him from abroad. This accentuates the two different situations of trading in a country and carrying on a trade within the country. It seemed to the court that Reiss & Co. (Amsterdam) in exporting goods to Nigerians or persons in Nigeria, through the appellant who only introduces customers to it, does not thereby carry on business in Nigeria. If, as the court held, Reiss & Co. (Amsterdam) did not carry on business in this country, the court did not see how the appellant whose only association and participation in the transaction was to introduce customers would amount to carrying on business. This was because the appellant cannot be credited with what his principal could not and did not do.

It follows therefore that all the profits shown in the invoices complained of were profits which were due to Reiss & Co. (Amsterdam) and not to the apellants. Counsel for the respondent has contended that the source of this income being Nigeria, it was taxable. The court could not subscribe to that proposition. It agreed with Chief Williams that the only taxable income is that due to the appellants.

The appellant is a Nigerian company and is caught by the provisions of s.18(1) of the CITA 1961 – see *Colquhon v Brooks* 14 App. Cas. 493.

In *Mitchell v Egyptian Hotels Ltd* (1915) AC 1022, it was held that where the business of a company was wholly carried on abroad, it is not assessable to income tax. The facts of the case before the court itself excluded, by virtue of s.18(2) of the CITA, the possibility of imposing taxes on foreign companies not carrying on any trade or business within this country. Counsel for the respondent has contended that the provisions of s.18(1) can be construed by virtue of the meaning of the word deemed used therein to include the profits of the foreign company. He relies for this interpretation on *Barclays Bank Ltd v Inland Revenue Commissioners* (1960) 2 All ER 817 at page 820. The court did not accept this view. The provisions of the two sub-sections of section 18 of CITA 1961, are intended to achieve similar objectives but with different subject matters and circumstances in contemplation. Where a Nigerian company is contemplated it is not allowable to transpose the situation and include a non-Nigerian company. If it was intended to apply the same standard it would not have been necessary to place them in two different sub-sections. It could be observed that the expression 'deemed' was also used in s.18(2) but in different circumstance. The court was of the opinion that the construction contended for cannot be enlarged to bring foreign earned income by foreign companies operating entirely outside this country within the scope of s.18(1), as this is clearly within the provisions of s.18(2). See *Alluminium Industries Aktien Gesellschaft v FBIR* (1971) NMLR 339. In *Alluminium Industries Aktien Gesellschaft v Federal Board of Inland Revenue* (1971) NMIL 339 where the obligation itself did not arise from this country, but in Switzerland, the Supreme Court held:

That being so on that ground we must decide that the claim for tax could not be brought within the first deeming provision of section 17 of the Companies Income Tax Act 1961 which only deems interest to be derived from Nigeria and so be liable to tax if there is a right to payment of that interest in Nigeria.

The court hoped that the appellants could only be caught within the deeming provisions of section 17 of the CITA 1961 for carrying on trade or business in this country. The facts of this case did not fall within the provision and it was therefore not applicable. The court therefore rejected the contention of counsel for the respondent that the appellant could be brought within the provisions of s.18(1).

The court came to the more important and decisive aspect of this case which was the basis on which appellants had been assessed to tax. The court had held that on the evidence before it the transactions between Reiss & Co. (Amsterdam) and its Nigerian customers produced income for Reiss & Co. (Amsterdam). It therefore rejected the contention of the respondents that the whole commission earned on those transactions was income arising from Nigeria and therefore deemed to accrue to the appellants. It was income derived from Nigeria to a company entirely based outside Nigeria and arising out of transactions carried out wholly outside Nigeria. In dismissing the appeal of the appellants before the Board of Appeal Commissioners the Board in their judgement said:

It is difficult to say with absolute certainty that all the commission due to Reiss & Co. (Nigeria) Limited are being credited in full. The appellant company has not proved conclusively that all the commission due to Reiss & Co. (Nigeria) Limited, has been accounted for fully in their books for tax purposes. The second ground of appeal therefore fails. On the first ground of appeal we are not convinced that the appellant company has declared all their income for tax purposes and therefore this ground also fails.

Chief Williams attacked this finding on two grounds. First, that the Board had no evidence before them, that appellants received any sum over and above those shown in the books of accounts and returns of the company submitted to the respondents. Secondly, that the standard of proof required for the appellants was too high. The appellant is only required to show on the balance of probabilities that the matters alleged might be so.

The assessments which the appellant's complained of and appealed against were set out in paragraph 19 of their amended grounds appear as follows:

Number	Year	Tax charged	Super-tax Charged	Total Profits
IB/LCBA 11	1971–72	₦35 706.40	—	₦ 89 266.00
IB/LCBA 1	1971–72	—	₦21 869.00	120 000.00
IB/LCBA 12	1962–73	61 821.00	—	137 380.00
IB/LCBA 13	1973–74	72 980.00	—	162 178.00
IB/LCBA 14	1974–75	88 884.45	—	197 521.00

It was the contention of the appellants that they were assessable to tax only in respect of the commission received by them in the transaction. It was the contention of appellants before the Board, and in court that the appellant had declared and paid tax on their own share of the buying commission. This contention was rejected by the Board. The appellant had called additional evidence before the court to satisfy it that the appellant was only entitled to 50% of the buying commission due to Reiss & Co. (Amsterdam). The respondent's counsel endeavoured to establish that there was a discrepancy in the rates of buying commission as indicated in the selling price of ₦2400, excluding buying commission, whereas Exhibit P indicated the selling price as N2740 which on calculation clearly shows that 14% buying commission was included in the selling price. The respondent's counsel contended that the appellant was allowed to remit to Reiss & Co. (Amsterdam) only 4% buying commission, and argued that the motive for indicating a higher selling price was to enable the remittance of sums more than the 4% buying commission allowed. Both Mr Dorresteijn, the Managing Director of the appellant company and Mr Moraal, assistant Managing Director of Reiss & Co. (Amsterdam) were only able to explain the discrepancies in Exhibits M and P, by pointing out that the invoice Exhibit P contained the charges incurred by Reiss & Co. (Amsterdam) in the entire transaction. This included, credit insurance, legalisation expenses, bank charges and forward premium. It was claimed that the charges on the forward cover did not appear on the invoice. The appellant tendered documents Exhibits 6 and 7, the rate of forward cover at the relevant time, Exhibit 8 the premium paid on the *del credere* insurance. Mr Kalkman, a qualified accountant and the auditor of Reiss & Co. (Amsterdam) and the fourth appellants' witness and Mr Moraal, the third witness, admitted that it was impossible to determine the profits at the time the invoice was raised, and that what was indicated was at best a pre-estimated profit and not actual profit. He also stated that the 14% indicated in Exhibit M was the aggregate percentage to cover the profits both of the appellants and Reiss & Co. (Amsterdam). Mr Moraal tendered in evidence as Exhibit 9, the total payments and expenses made in respect of order 73512. The court accepted that there was a discrepancy in the rate of commissions indicated on the invoices. It is possible the motive for this was to deceive. But this is not a consideration relevant to the determination whether the profits arising from the transaction was due to the appellant company on the test of where the transaction actually took place. Although admitting that 14% commission was charged and this was contrary to the regulations, Mr Bankole, the only respondent's witness and a Senior Investigation Officer of the Respondent Board conceded that Mr Dorretsteijn told him that the excess of 10% over the approved 4% was being shared between the appellants and Reiss & Co. (Amsterdam). Mr Bankole could not trace any correspondence relating to the sharing agreement, and such agreement was not indicated anywhere in the accounts of the company. Mr Bankole said that on discovering the extra 10% commission he raised an additional assessment against the appellants as indicated in Exhibits E1 to E5.

As I have indicated above, the Board of Appeal Commissioners appear to have held the view that it was not possible to extricate the accounts of the two companies, namely, the appellants and Reiss & Co. (Amsterdam) Ltd. On a careful examination of the evidence before the court, it would seem the Board was in error. It would seem that it was not realised that the status of the appellants in the transaction, and the nature of their participation rendered the entire transaction and its profits those of Reiss & Co. (Amsterdam) subject to the 5% commission due to appellants, whom the court had held did not carry on any trade or business in Nigeria, and were therefore not liable to tax. Chief Williams had submitted, and the court agreed with him, that the accounts of the appellant company had never been challenged. The only doubt raised was in respect of the sharing agreement which had been said to have been arrived at on a gentleman's basis. There is before the Court evidence of a sharing arrangement which is not controverted. It is revealing to review the evidence of Mr Bankole under cross-examination by Chief Williams on this point. Mr Bankole had said that by taxing the 10% he was taxing the whole commission due.

Chief Williams: I suggest to you that you gave the impression that the tax was imposed on 10% commission as against 5% already declared.
Mr Bankole: No.
Chief Williams: Do you accept the contents of Exhibit 'C'? (This is a letter written by Mr Bankole to the appellants' accountants admitting the percentage of commission due to the appellants.)
Mr Bankole: Yes.
Chief Williams: Is it right to say that additional tax was raised because the books of the company showed 5% commission?
Mr Bankole: Yes.
Chief Williams: Is there any difference between the gross receipts upon which you computed income and gross receipts in the books of Reiss & Co. (Nigeria) multiplied by two?
Mr Bankole: Yes, there is.
Chief Williams: Will the difference be more or less?
Mr Bankole: The difference will be the result of the amount held by Reiss & Co. (Nigeria). The assessment was made on the best of judgement assessment principle.
Chief Williams: You admitted that the Nigerian company had half the commission and the Dutch company the remaining half?
Mr Bankole: Yes.
Chief Williams: This was a reason for the additional assessment?
Mr Bankole: Yes.
Chief Williams: You examined the accounts of Reiss & Co. (Nigeria)?
Mr Bankole: Yes.

These answers of Mr Bankole, the only respondent's witness, in cross-examination, sufficiently disclosed that the denials of the respondent are unfounded. It was obvious from Mr Bankole's answers that at the time of the additional assessment, he knew that the appellants had been assessed and paid tax on 5% commission regarded as 50% of 10% commission shared between appellant and Reiss & Co. (Amsterdam). It was because the respondent later considered that the whole 10% commission was due to the appellant that the additional assessment was made. Even if this was true, the appellant could only be assessed on an additional 5% and not 10%. In the circumstances it is not true that the respondent was not aware of the sharing agreement. If the respondent was not aware of the sharing agreement and did not accept and apply it, the appellant would not have been assessed on 5% commission.

The counsel for the respondent had contended that the appellant was assessed to additional tax on the best of judgement principle. The court did not think that that principle should apply to this case. The principle applies where the company has not delivered a return, and the board is of the view that such a company is liable to tax s.49(3). The company must have failed or neglected to deliver a return. Although no guidelines are laid down for the exercise of the judgement, in the opinion of the court provisions of s.49(3) of CITA 1961 cannot be exercised where the company has rendered returns which have neither been rejected as inadequate nor challenged as incorrect. The court held therefore that there is no basis for the exercise of the discretion conferred on the Board by section 49(3) of the CITA 1961. The case of *D.R. Fraser & Co. Ltd v Minister of National Revenue* (1949) AC 36 did not apply to this case.

On the above evidence it was difficult to appreciate how the Board of Appeal Commissioners arrived at their decision that the appellant was assessable to additional tax on the basis of 10% commission. The Board was obviously in error in holding that the appellants were entitled to 10% as the whole of the commission, when the invoice indicated 14%; and that all that Reiss & Co. (Amsterdam) was entitled to was the 4% buying commission approved by the regulation of the Central Bank. This was notwithstanding that it was understood and accepted by the Board that the appellant was entitled to 50% of the profits of the transaction. This ground of appeal therefore succeeded.

However, the court was not satisfied from the evidence in this case that the appellant's accounts reflected the payment to them of 50% of the total profits earned in its agency commission. On the evidence before court it had not been disputed that the total profit of the company was 14% of the cost of the invoice prices. If on this view the appellants were entitled to 50% of the profits, then they should be assessable to tax at 7% and not the 5% on which tax had already been paid. Chief Williams in his third ground of appeal, had contended that conceding for the purposes of argument that the profits of the Reiss &

Co. (Amsterdam) are the profits of the appellants, reasonable expenses necessarily and wholly incurred in earning the income must be deducted. The court agreed with Chief Williams that the profits were those of Reiss & Co. (Amsterdam) alone. The only claim of the appellants was as to 50% of such profits declared by Reiss & Co. (Amsterdam). The court, however, did not agree with the appellants that they had been assessed to tax on the total commissions payable to them in their agency relationship with Reiss & Co. (Amsterdam). The Board was obviously in error in assessing the appellants on the whole of the profits earned by Reiss & Co. (Amsterdam), and not as to the percentage of profits which by agreement accrued to the appellants by virtue of their agency commissions payable to them on the transactions, namely 50% of the profits of the commission payable to their principals, namely Reiss & Co. (Amsterdam) in the transactions introduced by the appellants. This ground of Appeal also succeeds section 28 of the Federal Revenue Court (Civil Procedure) Rules empowers the courts:

On the hearing of an appeal under section 27 to draw any inference of fact and either —
(a) confirm, vary or set aside the judgement or order of the Court or body mentioned therein (this includes in S.27(a) the decisions of Appeal Commissioners established under the CITA 1961 and PITA 1961 so far as applicable as Federal Law); or
(b) order a rehearing and determination on such terms as the Federal Revenue Court may think just; or
(c) order judgement to be entered for any party; or
(d) make a final or other order on such terms as the Federal Revenue Court may think proper to ensure the determination on the merits of the real questions in controversy between the parties.

The appellant had contended that to order a rehearing if the court found the trial was irregular would itself be unconstitutional. The court did not find the trial to be irregular. Indeed, on the contrary the Court found it was in compliance with the provisions of section 57(1) of the Companies Income Tax Management Act, 1961. The authorities relied upon by Chief Williams therefore did not apply to enable the court to have the assessments discharged.

However, where the assessment had been made on the basis of a wrong principle of law, as in this case, it was the duty of the court to set aside the judgement or order of the court and make a final order it thought proper to ensure the determination on the parties – see s.28(d) Federal Revenue Court Decree No. 13 of 1973, or in the alternative order a rehearing and determination on such terms as the Court may think just.

The court gave careful consideration to the facts of the case, the evidence tendered, and the arguments in support of the case of the parties. It did not think in the circumstances any useful purpose would be served by an order for a rehearing. The procedure for appeal in these cases is by itself a rehearing. The error committed by the Board of Appeal Commissioners was one of law. The evidence necessary and required for the court to come to a correct finding was before it. In *Nader v Board of Customs* (1965) 1 All NLR 33, it was stated that where the evidence the parties chose to present was before the court, and if the trial court approach in law was wrong and the ultimate decision found to be wrong, it should have been corrected on appeal in the High Court and the right decision given. In *Nader's case*, the Supreme Court allowed the appeal by the prosecutor and reversed the decision of the Chief Magistrate ordering a retrial. The Supreme Court did not think the case was a proper one for an order of retrial. Furthermore the case of the respondent as presented before the Board, had not failed *in toto* –*Ayoola v Adebayo & Ors* (1969) 1 All NLR 159. Although the appellant had succeeded in showing that the Board of Appeal Commissioners had dismissed his appeal by applying the wrong principles, the court was entitled to draw such inferences of fact from the evidence before it and to come to such conclusions of law supported by the inferences.

In the circumstances, the court held that the appellant is liable to be assessed for tax in respect of the commissions received on the agency transactions with Reiss & Co. (Amsterdam). It agreed with the Board that the appellant had not shown that all the commission due to them was being credited in full. It accepted that the agreed percentage of commission payable to the appellants was 50% of the profits of the entire transaction payable to Reiss & Co. (Amsterdam). The court found from the evidence that Reiss & Co. (Amsterdam) had received 14% commission on each of the transactions in respect of which commission was payable to the appellants. It therefore held that the appellant was entitled to 7% of the entire commission payable to Reiss & Co. (Amsterdam) and was assessable to tax on the sum equivalent thereto, as profits accruing assessable to tax on the sum equivalent thereto, as profits accruing in respect of any trade or business in Nigeria. See s.17(a) CITA 1961.

It was admitted that the appellant had been assessed and had paid tax on 5% commission before the further assessment of the appellant to 10%. The court held therefore that the appellant was only assessable to 7% of the profits of the transactions, and not on 10%.

The appeal of the appellants against the judgement of the Board of Appeal Commissioners was allowed to the extent that the judgement was varied as follows:

The Appellant is entitled to a refund of any tax assessed and paid on the profits of the entire transactions in respect of the agency commission in excess of 7% of the profits due to the appellant by the agreement. Otherwise if the tax assessment on 10%

commission has not been paid for the relevant period, the respondent shall proceed to take steps to recover from appellant the the balance of the tax payable on the basis of 50% of the commission of 14% due to Reiss & Co. (Amsterdam), less what has already been paid by the appellants.

Taxation of government subsidies or grants

The test appears to lie in deciding what is the main purpose of the subsidy; if the purpose is to assist the trader to enable him to perform his trading operations more profitably it will be a trading receipt.

The House of Lords has held that a subsidy payable to a railway company to enable it to meet income charges was a trading receipt,[65] and that a subsidy from district councils to a water board to enable it to meet deficits on its water supply operations was also a trading receipt.[66] Similarly a ploughing grant made to a farmer under the Agricultural Development Act, 1939, was held to be a trading receipt.[67] Advances made to a sugar-beet company under the British Sugar Industry (Assistance) Act, 1931, which might have been but did not in fact become repayable, were also held by the House of Lords to be trading receipts.[68] On the same principle payments made under a deed of covenant to meet the losses of a trading company were held to be trading receipts of that company and so were not annual payments.[69] Another example is the deficiency payment scheme for farmers; this is now dealt with by an extra-statutory concession.

On the other hand when grants were made to a dock company by the Unemployment Grants Committee to assist it in extending its dock and thus provide employment in its area, the House of Lords held that these were not trading receipts, although the amount of the grants had been arrived at on the basis of two years' interest on the cost of the work.[70] When a farmer received payments under the Coastal Flooding (Emergency Provision) Act, 1953, which covered both damage to his land and loss of profit, it was held that as the predominant purpose was to replace capital, they were not trading receipts, it being impossible to apportion between the two purposes.[71]

Taxation of income from sale of 'know-how'

In several cases there have been sales of secret processes or 'know-how' usually accompanied by provisions under which the vendor agreed to assist the purchaser in exploiting the knowledge acquired. When a manufacturer of dyes agreed to communicate patents and secret processes relating to dyes to an American dye company and received in return annual sums of £25 000 it was held that these were trading receipts.[72] In another case, the Court of Appeal held that when the owner of a secret process disclosed it during war to the government and thence to other competitors, so that it was no longer secret, the sum received by him as compensation was capital.[73]

The case of *IRC v Rolls-Royce Ltd*,[74] dealt with a case where engineering 'know-how' was sold on a number of occasions to different countries. In this case the Rolls-Royce Company embarked on a deliberate policy of licensing persons in other countries to manufacture its engines on terms which involved payments of capital sums (so called) and royalties. The Commissioners held that the lump sums were capital receipts of the company and not taxable but the House of Lords held that this finding was wrong in law and that the only reasonable conclusion was that the lump sums were trading receipts on revenue account. The engineering 'know-how' sold in this case was regarded as a regular product of the trade and was treated as more transient and less permanent than the 'know-how' relating to medical supplies in *Evans Medical Supplies v Moriarty*[75] which could be applied in manufacture for a long time. Also the number of sales in the second case, which were clearly part of a deliberate policy, distinguished it from the first case where there was only one sale.

Somewhat similar problems have arisen in connection with patent rights and copyright payments.

Taxation of compensation for loss of beneficial contract

Except where the compensation can be regarded as capital on this basis, the normal rule is that compensation for the non-performance of a business contract is taxed on the same footing as the profits for the loss of which the compensation is paid.[76] Thus when shipbuilders were paid £100 000 for cancellation of two contracts to build ships it was held by the Commissioners and affirmed by the Court of Appeal that the receipt was part of the company's trading profits[77] and this decision has been followed in a series of cases.[78]

Sums received as compensation for loss or variation of some basic agreement on which the whole structure of a business depends have been held to be capital receipts.[79] In an earlier case Rowlatt, J, expressed the view that a payment to make up for the cessation in the future of annual taxable profits is not itself an annual profit at all,[80] but this dictum is now considered to be too wide.[81] His decision, however, that a sum of £50 000 compensation paid to a firm of ship managers, for loss of office as managers of a steamship company, was a capital receipt is well within the general principle, as the main business of the ship managers consisted in managing the ships of the steamship company in question.[82] As a result of a number of later cases[83] a general principle has now been enunciated as follows:

The sum received by a commercial firm as compensation for the loss sustained by the cancellation of a trading contract or the premature termination of an agency agreement may in the recipient's hands be regarded either as a capital receipt or as a trading receipt forming part of the trading profit. It may be difficult to formulate a general principle by reference to which in all cases the correct decision will be arrived at since in each case the question comes to be one of circumstance and degree. When the rights and advantages surrendered on cancellation are such as to destroy or materially to cripple the whole structure of the recipient's profit-making apparatus, involving the serious dislocation of the normal commercial organisation and resulting perhaps in the cutting-down of the staff previously required, the recipient of the compensation may properly affirm that the compensation represents the price paid for the loss or sterilisation of a capital asset and is therefore a capital and not a revenue receipt.[84]

Taxation of Income from compensation for breach of contract

The treatment of this item as either revenue or capital receipt will depend upon the nature of payment. In *Sommerfelds Ltd v Freeman* (Ch 1966, TR 381) S owned virtually the whole of the share capital of two engineering companies, K Company and the taxpayer company. In March 1950, K Company purchased the whole of the issued share capital of the taxpayer company which thus became its wholly-owned subsidiary. Immediately afterwards K Company transferred its business as a going concern to the taxpayer company and itself ceased to trade. At that time K Company had a contract with the Ministry of Supply under which it had an option to buy or a right of pre-emption in respect of so much of certain material known as Sommerfeld Track which might be declared surplus by the War Office. Shortly after March 1950, the Ministry of Supply broke its contract by disposing of 9000 tons of this material elsewhere. Following negotiations between the parties the Ministry of Supply made good 3000 tons and paid £50 000 compensation in respect of the remaining 6000 tons by a cheque drawn in favour of K Company. This cheque was endorsed over to the taxpayer company and was paid into that company's bank account on 29 January 1952. In the books of the two companies the transaction was shown as a loan by K Company to the taxpayer company. The taxpayer company claimed that the £50 000 was a post-cessation receipt of K Company, but the Special Commissioners decided that it belonged to the taxpayer company and fell to be treated as a revenue receipt in computing the profits of its trade. The taxpayer company appealed.

The case for the taxpayer company had been put in three ways: (i) that the £50 000 never belonged to it; (ii) that if it did belong to it, it was never available to the taxpayer company and therefore, on the authority of such cases as *Dewar v CIR* (1935) 19 TC 561 and *Woodhouse v CIR* (1936) 20 TC 673 was not taxable as the taxpayer company's income, and (iii) that if the £50 000 did belong to the taxpayer company and was available to it, the £50 000 was a capital and not a revenue receipt.

On the first point, the agreement by the Ministry of Supply to pay the £50 000 compensation was made in favour of K Company, but even so it did not follow that as between the two companies the £50 000 did not belong beneficially to the taxpayer company, whatever may have been the position of those companies *vis-à-vis* the Ministry of Supply. Ministry of Supply surpluses were one of the sources of supply of the business which K Company sold as a going concern to the taxpayer company, and if the Ministry of Supply, instead of breaking its contract, had offered the 9000 tons of surplus Sommerfeld Track to K Company, which had ceased to trade, K Company would have been bound under its agreement with the taxpayer company to accept the offer for the taxpayer company's benefit if that company had wanted the material. The £50 000 which was paid in order to put K Company in the same position as it would have been in if the offer had been made by the Ministry of Supply and accepted, belonged in equity to the taxpayer company.

On the second point the short answer was 'Yes', because the taxpayer company obtained the money, and when it received the money it was entitled to keep it. The payment was not in reality a loan to the taxpayer company at all. The third point was whether the £50 000 was a capital or a revenue receipt. The fact that the money was paid as compensation or damages was not of itself conclusive of the question. Damages might be capital or income according to the circumstances in which they were paid. Broadly, damages paid to replace a capital sum were capital, and damages paid to replace income were themselves income. It is difficult to determine into which category a payment fell, but damages for breach of contract paid to replace profits which the taxpayer would or might have made under the contract were *prima facie* a revenue receipt: *Bush, Beach and Gent Ltd v Road* (1939) 22 TC 519. It was plain that the compensation agreement with the Ministry of Supply concerned the loss of profit which would have been made if the Ministry had not broken its contract as regards 6000 tons of Sommerfeld Track.

234

Taxation of receipts by a trader in return for contractual restrictions

When a film actor who had taken the leading part in a film, for which he had been paid separately, was also paid £15000 in return for a covenant not to act in any other film for eighteen months, it was held that this payment was a capital sum and outside the ambit of his profession.[85] On the other hand, when magnesium manufacturers, desiring to obtain a supply of chlorine, entered into a bargain with a chemical manufacturer for future supplies, of which one term was that they would not themselves manufacture chlorine in return for certain sums of money, it was held that these sums were trade receipts as they were part of a general arrangement for obtaining supplies required for their trade.[86] The main distinction between these two cases appears to lie in the restrictive agreement in the first case being quite separate and later in date than the agreement to make the film; had it been collateral to the latter agreement it appears that this would have been a taxable profit.

Following the last case was one where a garage proprietor made an agreement with an oil company, under the latter agreed to supply him with petrol for ten years and promised to pay him certain sums towards his advertising and selling expenditure, in return for his undertaking to buy petrol only from the company and to give the company the first refusal of his business if he sold it. Here it was held that the agreement was basically one for the supply of petrol and that receipts under it were on revenue account and were taxable.[87] This case can be contrasted with another, which also dealt with an agreement between a garage proprietor and an oil company, where the garage proprietor gave a similar undertaking in return for sums of money. Here, however, the sums were paid towards capital expenditure in extending the garage building and premises and the court held they were capital, and not taxable, as the agreement altered the capital structure of the garage proprietor's business and was not merely a long-term commercial contract for supply of petrol.[88] In an earlier case a company which had developed a special process for renovating tyres entered into an agreement with a motor dealer under which a plant for executing this process was erected on the dealer's premises. One of the terms provided for a payment by the dealer to the company in return for the company not introducing a similar plant in a specified area (the dealer's territory) and not canvassing for direct orders in that territory. The Commissioners held that the company received the payment as capital and the court held there was evidence to support that finding.[89]

Taxation of income from sales of business assets

Such a profit may be taxable when the sale can itself be regarded as a trading operation. The test here was stated by Bankes, LJ:

The real question, looking at the matter, is the transaction in substance a parting by the Company with part of its property for a purchase price, or is it a method of trading by which it acquires this particular sum of money as part of the profits and gains of that trade?[90]

The test, however, is easier to state than to apply and a number of cases have arisen in which decision has been a narrow one. These can be considered in two categories; first, where the asset sold is a tangible asset or consists of rights which are equivalent to some tangible asset; secondly, when the asset sold is intangible, such as a secret process.

In the first category may be mentioned the case of a builder who built some houses to hold as an investment and some for resale, these latter only being originally treated as part of his trade. Later on he decided to sell the others and did so through the same organisation that sold his trading houses. The Commissioners held that he had thereby brought the investment houses within the ambit of his trade and that his profit on this was taxable. The Court of Appeal reversed this finding as it was satisfied that he had decided to sell the investment houses for reasons unconnected with his trade.[91]

Normally when a trader sells all the assets of his business this does not give rise to a taxable profit except in so far as a profit is made thereby on trading assets such as stock.[92] But if the operation consists of a sale of part of the assets and the trader continues his trade, a part or the whole of any profit made by the sale may be taxable in one of two ways.[93] First, although the asset sold is a capital asset, the terms of sale may contain what is, in effect, a collateral trading bargain and receipts under that bargain may be taxable. Thus when partners in a wine and spirit business sold a secret formula, a trademark and the goodwill relating to a particular type of liqueur on terms, *inter alia*, that they were entitled to a commission on future sale of the liqueur, it was held that the commission was a trading receipt.[94] Similarly when shipowners sold shares in another company upon terms, *inter alia*, that they received a commission on certain future purchases of oil it was held that this commission was a trading receipt.[95] In another case steel manufacturers paid a railway company a large sum by instalments to shut down its steel works and to agree to take its steel requirements from them for ten years. They then subcontracted some of the steel supplied under the contract and took a commission from the subcontractor which was held to be a trading receipt.[96]

236

Taxation of appropriation of unclaimed money

Money due from a company to a third party who has not claimed it remains the property of the third party and transfer of such money by the company to its current bank account does not make it income since the money was not a trading receipt[97] unless such money becomes vested in the legal person by statute when it becomes a taxable trading receipt.[98] An example of this is where the surplus of the proceeds of the sale of a pledge became vested in the pawner under the Pawnbrokers Act, 1872.[99]

Taxation of misappropriated sums

In *Gray v Lord Penrhyn*,[100] the negligent auditors of a company failed to detect a falsification of wages sheet by the company's employees. They paid to the company a sum to cover the defalcations which took place after their audit. It was held that the amount paid by the auditor was a revenue receipt. The payment would have been capital if it related to a capital expenditure.

Taxation of insurance receipts

Again, the taxation of this type of receipt will depend on the nature of the income. If the money is received under an insurance policy for the loss of trading stock, this will be a taxable trading income.[101]

Where a company insured its employees against some risks which later occurred and the company was paid by the insurers, the sum received was held to be a taxable trading receipt.[102]

Where, however, the nature of the payment is capital as when a company took up insurance policies to receive a certain sum if the ships it ordered arrived late, the sum received when the ships did arrive late was held to be a capital receipt since the payment was a reduction on the price payable for the ship delivered late.[103]

Taxation of income from investment and foreign exchange transactions

If a trader purchases goods abroad and buys foreign currency to do so, any profit he makes on exchange transactions is part of his trading operations and taxable. Thus when trading agents purchased dollars as advances against goods which they were selling on commission and the dollars had appreciated when they finally settled with their principals, the resultant profit was held to be earned in the course of their trade and so taxable.[104]

If a transaction in foreign exchange can be regarded as a temporary investment of money or a speculation outside the trade, any profit made is not taxable as a trading profit. Thus stone merchants purchased lire in anticipation of having to buy marble in Italy some six months ahead and when the lire appreciated, sold them; they repurchased lire again at a lower price when they actually bought the marble. It was held that the profit on the original purchase and sale was merely the appreciation of a temporary investment and not a profit of their trade.[105] Similarly a company trading in China took deposits in Chinese dollars from its Chinese agents as security for any sums due from them and transferred those deposits into sterling. Later they shut down their agencies and repaid the deposits in depreciated Chinese dollars. The profit thus made was held to be a capital profit and not a trading profit.[106]

A trader who has money in hand and temporarily invests it in shares is not regarded as performing a trading operation; if he later wants the money and realises his investment at a profit, such profit is not taxable. But if he carries on a trade in which investing money is a normal part of that trade, then any profits or losses he makes on investments will be brought into his tax computation. Thus an insurance company[107] and a bank[108] have been held taxable on profits made on realising investments as the buying of investments is part of insurance or banking business; conversely any loss may be deducted.[109] Interest received by a trading company from its bankers on its daily bank balances has been held to be part of its trading profits.[110]

Taxation of income from damages

If the damages represent arrears of salary or commission due to the claimant under a contract of employment, they will be taxable as emoluments; if they represent compensation for breach of a contract of employment they will not be taxable under the general law,[111] even though assessed by reference to the income lost. Similarly arrears of pension will be taxable, but a sum paid for loss of pension rights will not be taxable under the general law.[112] It seems clear that damages for personal injuries paid by someone other than the employer cannot be taxed even though they compensate the employee for loss of earnings. They are paid because he could not work and cannot arise from his contract of employment.[113] It is submitted that the same result occurs

238

if damages are paid by an employer, unless the sum awarded is payable under an express term of the contract and not for breach of it.

Arrears of interest and annual payments will be taxable by deduction even though included in damages.[114] In calculating sums due for interest for inclusion in a court order it is customary to deduct tax and only give judgement for the net amount.

It is an open question whether damages for personal injuries received by a trader or professional based on loss of profits should in any circumstances be included in his profits; there is a *dictum* to the effect that compensation for a loss of profit due to absence from the trade or profession for a short period may be taxable although compensation for a permanent disablement would not.[115] It is clear that a sum paid to a trader under a loss of profits insurance policy is taxable; on the other hand, a sum paid to an actor for not acting was held to be capital and outside the ambit of his profession.[116]

In many cases damages for compensation for a number of items will be awarded in a lump sum; if the damages for some items, if paid separately without an order or award, would have been taxable, but for others would not, the total sum must be apportioned to find out how much is taxable.[117]

(vii) Trading expenditure

Income tax is to be charged without any deduction other than that allowed by statute and no other deductions shall be made than such as are expressly enumerated. The effect is that a deduction which is neither within the terms of an express statutory prohibition, nor such that an express allowance must be taken as the exclusive definition of its area, is one to be made or not to be made, according as it is, or is not, on the facts of the case a proper debit item to be charged against incomings of the trade when computing the balance of profits:

It has long been well settled that the effect of these provisions as to deduction is that the balance of the profits and gains of a trade must be ascertained in accordance with the ordinary principles of commercial trading, by deducting from the gross receipts all expenditure properly deductible from them on those principles, save in so far as any amount so deducted falls within any of the statutory prohibitions contained in the relevant Rules, in which case it must be added back for the purpose of arriving at the balance of profits and gains assessable to tax.[118]

Section 20 of the 1979 Act, which deals with Ascertainment of Loss of Taxable Profits states that for the purpose of ascertaining the profits or loss of a company, there shall be deducted all expenses wholly, exclusively, necessarily and reasonably incurred in the earning of the income. Deductible or allowable expenses include:

(a) any sum payable by way of interest on any money borrowed and employed as capital in acquiring the profits;

(b) rent for that period, and premiums the liability for which was incurred during that period, in respect of land or buildings occupied for the purposes of acquiring the profits, subject, in the case of employees of the Company to a maximum of ₦28 000 p.a. for each building and ₦14 000 p.a. for each plot in Lagos;

(c) any expense incurred for repair of premises, plant, machinery or fixtures employed enquiring or for the renewals, repair or alteration of any implement, utensils or articles so employed;

(d) bad debts incurred in the course of a trade, or business proved to be bad;

(e) any contribution to a pension, provident or other retirement benefits fund approved by the Joint Tax Board;

(f) expenses that are wholly, exclusively, necessarily and reasonably incurred for trade purposes; and

(g) any such deduction as may be approved by the Minister for Finance.

Deductions allowed

Expenses wholly, exclusively, necessarily and reasonably incurred

These are all expenses which are wholly, exclusively, necessarily and reasonably incurred during that period and ultimately borne by that individual in the production of the income including:

(a) interest payable upon money borrowed and employed as capital in acquiring the income and interest on loans for developing an owner-occupied residential house where the value of such property does not exceed ₦100 000.

(b) rent for that period payable in respect of land or buildings occupied for the purpose of acquiring the income, subject, in the case of residential accommodation so occupied, to a maximum of –

    (i) ₦28 000 per annum for each building and ₦4000 per annum for each flat in the Lagos area, and

    (ii) ₦20 000 per annum for each building and ₦5000 for each flat in any other part of Nigeria.

(c) any expense incurred for repair of premises, plant, machinery or fixtures employed in acquiring the income, or for the renewal, repair or alteration of any implement, utensil or article so employed.

(d) bad debts incurred in any trade, business, profession or vocation proved to have become bad during the period for which the income is being ascertained and doubtful debts to the extent that they are respectively estimated to have become bad during the said period.

The test for allowable expenses is that they must have been incurred, wholly exclusively, necessarily and reasonably for the production of the income.

The words 'necessarily', and 'reasonably' were added to the test because of the general tendency towards high spending. In Simon's *Taxes*, revised edition, it was expressed: 'In many cases it may be difficult to establish as a fact that the expenditure was given wholly and exclusively for the purposes of the trade, rather than satisfying the moral obligation felt by the trader'.

The problem is, when a businessman decides to buy two cars instead of one for his business, how does the tax official contend the reasonableness of the expenditure?

It is unreasonable to pay a messenger a clerical officer's salary in order to claim a deduction and pay less tax. The excess will be added to the profits. The revenue will only allow reasonable expenses.

All allowable deductions must also be necessary for the purpose of earning profits. It is unnecessary to pay the club subscriptions of a bank manager even though the employer expects him to join such a club,[119] neither is it necessary to pay an employee's travelling expenses from his home to his place of work since expenses at or from his place of work for official purposes are necessary to earn profits.[120]

Any disbursements or expenses, not being money wholly and exclusively laid out for the purpose of the trade, profession or vocation, are specifically disallowed. These words have been considered by the courts on numerous occasions and in the leading case the words 'for the purpose of the trade' were translated by Lord Davey to mean 'for the purpose of enabling a person to carry on and earn profits'.[121] In that case damages had been paid by an innkeeper to a customer of the inn who had been injured by a chimney falling on him as a result of negligence by the innkeeper's staff, and the House of Lords held that such damages were not deductible for tax. It is, however, well established that a payment made voluntarily, on grounds of commercial expediency and in order indirectly to facilitate the carrying on of the business, may be held to be wholly and exclusively expended for the purpose of the trade.[122]

The courts have disallowed expenditure on penalties for illegal trading[123] (although illegal trading is a taxable trade), on costs of defence of a criminal prosecution arising from professional activities,[124] on damages and costs awarded against a trader for libel in a business communication,[125] on costs of prosecuting an income tax appeal,[126] on costs of reducing a company's capital,[127] on income taxes paid abroad,[128] on losses on loans made by a solicitor to his client for the purpose of obtaining business,[129] on fire insurance premiums paid on premises abroad and owned by the taxpayer but occupied by a third party under a trading arrangement[130] and on travelling expenses of a barrister between his study at home (where he did much of his work) and his professional chambers.[131]

On the other side of the line expenditure has been allowed for solicitor's expenses in entertaining clients,[132] for a sum paid to settle an action for misrepresentation on sale of shares by a company which traded in shares,[133] for losses made by brewers on loans to their tied tenants,[134] and for sums paid by brewers for repairs and insurance of tied houses owned by them and let to tenants, although they were under no legal obligation to repair them.[135]

In *IBM World Trade Corporation, Nigerian Branch v Federal Board of Inland Revenue*, the Appeal Commissioners, in their judgement APP/COMM/95, disallowed a revenue expenditure since it was not wholly and exclusively incurred for the purpose of earning profit. The appeal before the Commissioners centred on the disallowance by the Board of the expenditure incurred by the appellant on the African Educational Centre in the accounting years ended 31 December 1964 and 1965, on the ground that the expenditure was capital and not revenue.

There appeared to the court to be no dispute between the appellant and the Board on the facts of this appeal. In short, the appellant incurred certain expenses on the African Educational Centre which is situated at the campus of the University of Ibadan. The appellant commenced business in Nigeria in 1961 and the Educational Centre was opened in 1964. After operating and running the centre for about two years the appellant gave up the centre to the University in December 1965; the expenses incurred in 1964 were £38 960, and for 1965 £31 596. The centre was maintained for the purpose of teaching persons from the eight African countries in which the appellant operates the use of its IBM data processes and equipment. The cost of maintaining the centre was appointed between the eight countries concerned on the basis of the ratio of the gross revenue earned by the appellant in each of the countries. The arrangements with the university contemplated that the appellant would finance the courses

242

of two years during which members of the university staff would be trained to take over the total training assignments. The purpose of the centre, as far as the appellant was concerned, was to turn out graduates who would be capable of being employed as managers, systems engineers or salesmen. The students were, however, not contractually obliged to work for the appellant at the end of their courses.

The appellant tendered the following report which appeared in the *Wall Street Journal*, a well-known newspaper in the financial world, which on 14 July 1965 acknowledged the likely benefit to the appellant's trade:

IBM's computer centre in Nigeria could yield important benefits to the company. Some of the graduates will undoubtedly have sufficient stature for the companies and government agencies they get jobs with to do the computer ordering for their employers. (*sic*) These IBM-trained men are bound to be kindly disposed to the company that financed their schooling.

The question, therefore, was whether the expenses of this character should be classified as capital expenditure and not revenue expenditure.

It was the submission of the appellant that the expenses on the African Educational Centre are revenue expenses and therefore allowable as expenses wholly and exclusively incurred in the production of the profits now being assessed. That the benefit to the appellant's trade from the expenditure on the African Educational Centre not being referable specifically to any particular accounting period or periods, the expenditure is by virtue of section 27(g)(1) of the Companies Income Tax Act, 1961 deductible from the profits of the period in which the liability for the expenditure was incurred.

The Board, however, took a different view and cited the case of *British Insulated and Helsby Ltd v Atherton*, reported in *1926 Appeal Cases* – page 205, at page 213 where Lord Cave asserted that

when an expenditure is made, *not only once and for all* but with a view to bringing into existence an asset or an advantage for the enduring benefit of a trade, there is very good reason in the absence of special circumstances leading to an opposite conclusion – for treating such expenditure as properly attributable not to revenue, but to capital.

Although the expenditure was of a recurrent nature, it was not incurred wholly and exclusively in the production of the income as provided by section 27 of CITA 1961.

In *Mr S. E. Ola v Federal Board of Inland Revenue*, (APP/COMM/98), the appellant, who was a UAC sales agent who ran a fleet of lorries, was assessed on PAYE basis as no disclosure was made of his business as transporter. The appeal was against additional assessments raised on his undisclosed income. The appellant's contention was that the additional assessment was excessive. The appeal was dismissed.

The Appeal Commissioners found that the accounts submitted were inaccurate and unreliable as a full disclosure of the appellant's income.

We shall now discuss some of the specific deductions allowed for tax purposes.

Misappropriations by subordinate employees

These have been allowed as deductions but not when they were committed by a managing director.[136] Fees to directors are normally allowed as paid, but if they are unduly high for reasons unconnected with the trade these may be disallowed;[137] remuneration paid by a trader to relatives employed in his business is similarly treated.[138]

Salaries, wages etc.

Salaries including payments to employees after a certain number of years' meritorious service and payments to directors are *prima facie* sums paid for the purpose of earning profits, but payments made to employees as wedding gifts are given on personal grounds.[139] Lord Cave, LC said in *Seymour v Reed*:[140]

salaries, fees, wages, perquisites of office whatever include all payments made to the holder of an office or employment as such, that is to say, by way of remuneration for services, even though such payments may be voluntary, but that they do not include a might be that a payment by a company to the Tariff Reform League might be of great advantage to its trade. It might be that a payment by a company to a political party

Payment by a company of a lump sum by instalments to a director who retired, to avoid publicity and injury to the company, where circumstances had arisen which might possibly have justified the director's dismissal, was an admissible deduction.

Payments for political purposes

The question how far payments for political purposes are allowable has been judicially discussed in several cases:

Payments for political purposes might conceivably be for the purposes of trade. It might be that a payment by a Company to the Tariff Reform League might be of great advantage to its trade. It might be that a payment by a Company to a political party which was supposed to be identified with the interests of a particular trade might be to the advantage of the trade; but one can easily imagine cases, such as a payment by a company to the National Service League, where it would be impossible to conceive that anybody could find that such money was wholly and exclusively laid out or expended for the purposes of the trade.[141]

244

In a later case the expense of distributing a chairman's speech containing general political propaganda was disallowed because the protection of the business from injury was plainly not the sole object[142] but when a sugar company was faced with a threat of nationalisation and spent large sums in a national propaganda campaign to convince the public that nationalisation of their industry was unwise, the House of Lords held that these expenses were allowable.[143]

The financing of political parties

This has become a highly contentious issue.

In fact one course is to require companies to seek the prior agreement of a shareholders' meeting before making political donations. It is also suggested that individual companies should be permitted to finance political action only from a separate fund to which shareholders would have a right not to contribute. A similar system already operates in the United States.

If the right of shareholders to contract out of the political action of their respective companies is becoming a highly sensitive issue, an even more fundamental question is raised by company political donations: are they lawful?

If the answer to that is in the negative, it could be open to an aggrieved shareholder to take legal action to prevent any political use of his company's money and to require the directors to account for any contribution unlawfully made to a political party or in pursuit of a political object. The traditional view of Company secretaries, supported by famous decisions (albeit not directly in point) such as *Morgan v Tate & Lyle Co. Ltd*, 1955 AC 21 is that such payments are perfectly lawful.

It is to be noted, that no decision of the Courts expressly authorises the making of political donations. Publicity and disclosure in the accounts are vital so that shareholders may take steps to stop what is an unlawful practice.

Recent developments tend to suggest that the received wisdom may need to be re-examined and that in most cases political payments will be *ultra vires*. The starting point of any discussion of company powers is the objects of the individual companies. Here we find that none of the large companies is expressly authorised by its objects to make political donations. However, several donors would no doubt wish to claim that they had an implied power based on wide general objects which typically permit the company 'To support and subscribe to any charitable or public object, and any institution, society or club which may be for the benefit of the Company or its employees ...'

The fact that a company can point to a wide express power of this kind does not place its political donations beyond legal challenge. Although it is true that the courts in the past have construed these wide powers generously in favour of companies, that approach has been shaken by a number of recent cases. Acts done under express objects in the memorandum are beyond judicial challenge only insofar as these objects are substantive, and not ancillary objects of the company concerned.

If the object is an ancillary one (even though express) then any donation made under it will be lawful only if it is reasonably incidental to the substantive objects of the company.

It could no doubt be argued that donations to the Conservative Party in the UK are reasonably incidental to the objects of most commercial companies in the sense that the payments will finance the Party; this will help its election prospects; if elected this will be conducive to the healthy operation of the free enterprise system; and this in turn will be a benefit to each and every company. But although superficially attractive, this argument may not be enough and ultimately may be unconvincing. Not all corporate investors are convinced that they perform better under Conservative administrations. But more important, it is claimed by political scientists that, as is not the case in the United States, money has no bearing on the outcome of elections in many countries.

If this view is correct it may be questioned how donations – particularly in election years, when they tend to be highest – are reasonably incidental to the objects of commercial companies. If the payment will not affect the likelihood of the supported party being elected, it can hardly be claimed that it will promote the objects of the company, unless it is rewarded with lucrative government contracts – in which case serious questions of corruption would arise. Further support for the view that political payments would fail the test of *ultra vires* is provided by a recent unreported (1983) decision of the UK High Court, *Simmonds v League Against Cruel Sports*. In that case Mrs Simmonds successfully challenged payments made by the League (a limited Company) to the Labour Party's 1979 General Election Campaign Fund.

The Court held that the only payment which was lawful was one of £30 000 which the Labour Party undertook to use in order to promote the express aims of the League. A general donation of £50 000 to the Party's election fund for unspecified purposes was held to be *ultra vires*. It was not authorised by the express objects of the League even though one of these permitted the Company 'to affiliate, to combine or cooperate with, subscribe to or support any institution having objects similar to the main objects of the League'. Nor could the payment of £50 000 be authorised as being reasonably incidental to the objects of the League. In delivering judgement, Mervyn-Davies, J., said that the payment had not been made 'in the pursuit of, or to extend, an express authorised object.'

Translated into language appropriate to commercial companies, the League Against Cruel Sports case suggests that a donation to the Conservative Party will be lawful only if it is used subsequently to promote the express objects of the company, whether that is trading in baked beans or machine tools. It is even doubtful whether a payment through British United Industrialists to the Conservative Party's Free Enterprise Account would withstand legal challenge. Following the Cruel Sports case, that would be too remote from the substantive objects of the company.

It not the business of either trade unions or companies to support particular political parties or promote particular political policies.

As the law now stands, companies are extremely vulnerable to legal action at the suit of disgruntled and perhaps even politically inspired shareholders. The League Against Cruel Sports case provides a timely reminder that such an action could serve to stop any political payments by a particular Company in the future. In that case the Labour Party was required to repay the money wrongly donated to it by the League. A run of successful cases against trading companies could well be embarrassing, and would certainly cause major damage to the Conservative Party if it was to repay money received from companies over a number of years.

In these circumstances the safest course for many companies may well be to hold fire until the government intervenes to remove the very serious doubts about the power of companies to make political donations.

Section 20 of CITA 1979 deals with the following deductions.

(i) *Interest on money borrowed*

In order that the interest may be deductible, the money borrowed may be for a short or a long period. It may be an overdraft for a short term. The money borrowed which will normally be capital must be employed as capital in acquiring profits.

(ii) *Rent and premium*

Rent for the accounting period and premiums the liability for which was incurred during that period, in respect of land or building occupied for the purposes of acquiring the profits, subject, in the case of residential accommodation occupied by employees of the company, to a maximum of:

(a) ₦28 000 per annum for each building and ₦14 000 per annum for each flat in the Lagos area, and

(b) ₦20 000 per annum for each building and ₦5000 per annum for each flat in any other part of Nigeria; and the provisions of this paragraph shall be deemed to have come into effect on 1st April 1976, is allowable.' (Section 20(b) CITA 1979)

Section 20 also allows, in the case of a holding company, expenses on maintenance of property. Any rent actually paid for the business premises and not payable under a 'long lease' is deductible as an expense exclusively incurred in order to earn the profits[144] even though it may be paid by a partnership to one of the partners.[145] Where a 'short lease' of another building is taken because its control is essential to the use of the trade premises themselves, the net rent of the building is deductible.[146] The reason for the deduction has been variously put upon the grounds that that deduction is 'an essential element to be taken into account in ascertaining the amount of the balance of profits,' that it is 'included in a very broad construction of the provision relating to disbursements and expenses.'[147]

Repairs, replacement, renewals, etc.

Section 20(c) states that 'any expense incurred for repair of premises, plant, machinery or fixtures employed in acquiring the profits, or for the renewals, repair or alteration of any implement, utensil or articles so employed' is allowable. Buckley, LJ, said in *Lurcott v Wakely and Wheeler*:[148]

repair is restoration by renewal or replacement of a subsidiary part of a whole. Renewal as distinct from repair is restoration of the entirety, meaning by the entirety not necessarily the whole but substantially the whole subject-matter under discussion ... question of repair is in every case one of degree; and the test is whether the act to be done is one which in substance is the renewal or replacement of defective parts or the renewal or replacement of substantially the whole.

The first problem is to ascertain, as a question of degree, what is the 'entirety' of the premises in question, i.e. is what has been replaced substantially a complete entity in itself, or is it more properly regarded as only a part of larger premises?[149] If the premises, so regarded, have been replaced, then the expenditure is capital; if, however, what has been replaced is only a part of larger premises and the replacement does not involve substantial improvements or extensions, then the expenditure can properly be regarded as a revenue expense.

Expenditure on repairs can be disallowed when premises have been newly acquired by a trader in a state of disrepair and the cost of putting them in repair is treated as part of the capital cost of the acquisition. Thus when a company took a lease of business premises at a low rent but covenanted to put the premises in repair, it was held that the cost of doing so was a capital item;[150] if, however, the landlords had done the repairs and exacted a higher rent the rent would have been deductible.[151] If a man takes over a business from another and replaces trading fixtures and fittings with new ones, such expenditure is not deductible, even though the expenditure would have been allowed on a renewals basis if incurred by the predecessor.[152]

On similar principles no deduction was allowed for the cost of removal of machinery from smaller to larger premises,[153] nor for the cost incurred by multiple shopkeepers in fitting up a new shop,[154] nor for the expenses incurred in surrendering a lease of a shop they have given up.[155]

Whilst the cost of normal repairs to business premises is allowed as a revenue expense it may not be so allowed if the work done is substantially an improvement[156] or amounts to a replacement of the premises.[157] The line between a repair which involves a replacement of some part of the premises and a replacement of the premises is a narrow one; it has been held by the Privy Council that replacement of a part of a railway's running track which was worn out was an allowable expense and was not to be regarded as a replacement of the whole track.[158]

Bad debts

The onus is on a trader who seeks such a deduction to show that the debt is bad or doubtful; this is a question of fact and there is no justification for refusing to treat a debt as bad because the debtor is still trading.[159] The substitution of a new debt for an old one does not alter the quality of the debt and a proper allowance may be made if the new debtor cannot pay.[160]

Apart from any question whether a debt is bad or doubtful, a debt which is not payable until a future date and does not carry interest may be discounted[161] and a debt payable at a distant date by a person of little financial means and secured only by a second mortgage should be valued having regard to all these circumstances and brought into account at that valuation.[162]

There is, however, no relation back when a trader receives less than the debt due to him, owing to the failure of his debtor to pay, and no provision was made for this in the year the debt arose. The statutory rule prohibiting any deduction except for bad and doubtful debts only allows a deduction according to the facts known at the end of the trading period in which a deduction is sought[163] but it has been held to allow a deduction in a later year when a debt, formerly thought to be good and for which no deduction was taken earlier, turns out to be bad.[164] Similarly if a deduction for a bad or doubtful debt is taken in one year and subsequently the debt is paid in full, the proper course is to treat the excess over the written-down value of the debt as a receipt for the year when it is paid[165] and not to relate it back to the year when the deduction was taken.[166] In effect, debts carried forward for several years should be adjusted each year according to their then degree of badness and any increase or decrease from their previous values should be added or subtracted in each year of valuation.[167]

Contribution to pensions and other benefit funds

These funds, set up for the benefit of employees are maintained by contributions by both employees and employers, and are allowed provided the scheme is approved by the Joint Tax Board under powers section 17(f) of the Income Tax Management Act, 1961, subject to the provisions of Schedule 4 to the Income Tax Management Act, 1961 (s.27)(e) and any conditions that the Board may impose.

The amount to be deducted will be the amount contributed by the company to the scheme during the relevant period and, if the aggregate of the contributions (other than contributions made with the approval of the Board in respect of past services of the employees with the company) exceeds 25 per cent of the remuneration paid to the employees by the employer for that period, the excess will be excluded from the amount to be deducted. In the case of any pension or provident fund, if the company as employer becomes entitled to any benefit such as bonus, the value of the benefit is deemed to be income of the trade, or business.

Donations

Section 21 of CITA 1979 states:

1   Subject to the provisions of this section and notwithstanding anything contained in section 20 of this Act, for the purpose of ascertaining the profits or loss of any Company for any period from any source chargeable with tax under this Act, there shall be deducted the amount of any donations made for the period by that Company to any donations fund, body or institution in Nigeria to which this section applies.

2   Without prejudice to section 22 it is hereby declared for the avoidance of doubt that the provisions of subsection 1 of this section shall have effect if, but only if, the donations are made out of the profits of the Company, and are not expenditure of a capital nature.

3   Except to such extent (if any) as the Federal Executive Council may by order in the Gazette otherwise direct, any deduction to be allowed to any Company, under subsection (1) of this section, for any year of assessment shall not exceed an amount which is equal to ten per centum of the total profits of that Company for that year as ascertained before any deduction is made under this section.

4   There shall be excluded from the sum allowable as a deduction under this section any outgoings and expenses which are allowable as deductions under section 20.

5.   This section shall apply to:

  (a) the public funds;

  (b) the statutory bodies and institutions;

  (c) the ecclesiastical, charitable, benevolent, educational and scientific institutions, established in Nigeria, which are specified in Schedule 5,

6   The Commissioner may by order in the Gazette amend the said Schedule in any manner whatsoever:

Provided that no fund, body or institution shall be added to that Schedule, in exercise of the powers conferred under the foregoing provisions of this subsection, unless the fund is a public fund established in Nigeria, or the body or institution is a statutory body or institution, or is a body or institution of a public character, established in Nigeria.

7   In this section references to donations made by a Company do not include references to any payments made by the Company for valuable consideration.

The list specified in Schedule 5 is as follows:

1   The Boys' Brigade of Nigeria.
2   The Boy Scouts of Nigeria.
3   The Christian Council of Nigeria.
4   The Cocoa Research Institute of Nigeria.
5   Any educational institution affiliated under any law with any University in Nigeria or established under any law in Nigeria and any other educational institution recognised by any Government in Nigeria.
6   The Girl Guides of Nigeria.
7   Any hospital owned by the Government of the Federation or of a state or any University Teaching Hospital or any hospital which is carried on by a society or association other than for the purpose of profits or gains to the individual members of that society or association.
8   The Institute of Medical Laboratory Technology.
9   The National Commission for Rehabilitation.
10   The National Library.
11   The Nigerian Council for Medical Research.
12   The Nigerian Council for Science and Technology.
13   The Nigerian Institute for International Affairs.
14   The Nigerian Institute for Oil Palm Research.
15   The Nigerian Institute for Trypanosomiasis Research.
16   The Nigerian Museum.
17   The Nigerian Red Cross.
18   A public fund established and maintained for providing money for the construction or maintenance of a public memorial relating to the civil war in Nigeria which ended on 15 January 1970.
19   A public institution or public fund (including the Armed Forces Comfort Fund) established or maintained for the comfort, recreation or welfare of members of the Nigerian Army, Navy or Air Force.
20   A public fund established and maintained exclusively for providing money for the acquisition, construction, maintenance or equipment of a building used or to be used as a school or college by the Government of the Federation or a

251

State or by a public authority or by a society or association which is carried on other than for the purpose of profit or gain to the individual members of that society or association.

21 The National Youth Council of Nigeria.
22 National Sports Commission and its State Associations.
23 The Nigerian Society for the Deaf and Dumb.
24 The Society for the Blind.
25 The Nigerian National Advisory Council for the Blind.
26 Associations or Societies for the Blind in Nigeria.
27 Training Centres and Residential Schools for the Blind in Nigeria.
28 The National Braille Library of Nigeria.
29 The Nigerian Youth Trust.
30 Van Leer Nigerian Educational Trust.
31 Southern Africa Relief Fund.
32 Islamic Education Trust.
33 The Institute of Chartered Accountants of Nigeria Building Fund.
34 Any public fund established or approved by the Government of the Federation or established by any of the State Governments in aid of or for the relief of drought or any other national disaster in any part of the Federation.

Entertainment allowance, employees' medical and miscellaneous expenses

In *Messrs Victors Ltd (Kokodome Restaurant & Night Club) v Federal Board of Inland Revenue*, the appellant's contention was that all the expenses charged were *bona fide* business expenses and were therefore allowable deductions.

The appeal was allowed. The Appeal Commissioners found:

(i)   that the expenses were reasonably incurred for the purpose of earning the company's profits,

(ii)   the cash said to be introduced was actually introduced and did not represent undisclosed income.

The Commissioners dismissed this appeal, but asked the respondent to issue fresh notices of assessments which would allow as deductions a portion of each year's expenses. The deductions should be in equal proportion to the income from loan interest and any chargeable income to the overall profits of the appellant for each year of assessment. There was no order as to costs; and all Exhibits were to be returned to the respondent thirty days after the delivery of this judgement if no valid appeal was made to the High Court.

Disallowable deductions

Section 22, CITA 1979 lists the following:

(a) Capital repaid or withdrawn and any expenditure of a capital nature;

(b) any sum recoverable under an insurance or contract of indemnity;

(c) taxes on income or profits levied in Nigeria or elsewhere, other than tax levied outside Nigeria on profits which are also chargeable to tax in Nigeria where relief which are also chargeable to tax in Nigeria where relief for the double taxation of those profits may not be given under any other provision of this Act;

(d) any payment to a savings, widows and orphans, pension, provident or other retirement benefits fund, society or scheme except as permitted by paragraph (e) of section 20;

(e) the depreciation of any asset;

(f) any sum reserved out of profits, except as permitted by paragraph (d) of section 20 or 21 or as may be estimated to the satisfaction of the Board, pending the determination of the amount, to represent the amount of any expense deductible under the provisions of that section the liability for which was irrevocably incurred during the period for which the income is being ascertained;

(g) any expense of any description incurred outside Nigeria for and on behalf of any Company except of the nature and to the extent as the Board may consider allowable; and to the extent as the Board may consider allowable; and

(h) any expense of any description incurred within or outside Nigeria for the purpose of earning management fees.

Whilst section 23 which deals with Waiver or refund of liability or expenses states:

When a deduction has been allowed to a Company under the provisions of section 20 or 21 in respect of any liability of, or any expense incurred by, that Company and such liability is waived or released or such expense is refunded to the Company, in whole or in part, then the amount of that liability or expense which is waived, released or refunded as the case may be shall be deemed to be profits of the Company on the day on which such waiver, release or refund was made or given.

These disallowable expenses are more or less the opposite of the principles we learnt under allowable deductions and are not deductible partly because they are not wholly, exclusively, reasonably and necessarily incurred in the earning of the profits, and partly because they are of a capital nature or because capital allowance is grantable in lieu. Whenever an expenditure is incurred once and for all with a view to bringing into existence an asset or an advantage of an enduring nature, it is a capital expenditure. It is sufficient if there is an intention to bring about an asset or advantage. Revenue or allowable expenditure usually recurs annually.[168] We shall now discuss some of these disallowable expenses.

(a) *Capital repaid or withdrawn and any expenditure of a capital nature.*

Capital expenditure, capital paid, and capital withdrawn, as we have been already observed, are of a capital nature.

(b) *Any sum recoverable under an insurance or contract of indemnity.*

This, again, is of capital nature, being in respect of capital assets.

(c) *Taxes on income or profits levied in Nigeria or elsewhere, other than tax levied outside Nigeria on profits which are also chargeable to tax in Nigeria where relief for the double taxation of those profits may not be given under any other provision of the Companies Income Tax Act.*

Where tax is paid abroad, the full income without the tax deducted should be disclosed. Thus where a Nigerian company pays tax on its income from abroad, the income already taxed should be disclosed in full.

(d) *Payments to a savings, widows and orphans, pensions, provident, or other retirement benefit funds, society or scheme.*

Unless these are approved by the Joint Tax Board under s.17(f) of ITMA 1961, these will be disallowed.

(e) *The depreciation of any assets.*

Since capital allowances are granted under schedule 2 to CITA 1979, depreciation is not allowed.

(f) *any sum reserved out of profits.*

If the sum reserved is not a bad debt, it is not deductible unless it is a liability irrevocably incurred.

(g) *Any expense incurred for and on behalf of any company as head office expenses.*

The disallowance is to prevent drainage on foreign funds by companies with a foreign Head Office since the Companies Act, 1968, provides for the registered office but not the head office to be in Nigeria.

Directors' remuneration

In Habis Travels Ltd v Federal Board of Inland Revenue App/COMM/131, the appellant's ground of appeal was that the director's remunerations were allowable deductions under CITA, sections 27, and also that they were not excessive.

The Appeal Commissioners overruling the preliminary objection found (i) that payment on behalf of a director to settle that director's obligation to a third party was not an expense wholly and exclusively incurred for the purpose of earning the profit being taxed and was therefore not allowable; (ii) that a tenfold increase in director's remunerations was not justified, and therefore the allowable remuneration was limited to the sum allowed in the previous year.

254

Ferrostall AG v Federal Board of Inland Revenue, App/COMM/of 8 to 12 May 1974, the appellant's contention was that the management agent expenses were properly incurred under the agreement between it and its principal, and they were deductible under section 27 CITA, 1961. The appeal was dismissed.

The Appeal Commissioners found that the respondents acted properly in disallowing the expenses claimed by the appellants and that a subsequent memorandum purported to be executed by the appellant 'is a very clumsy device to evade tax payable by the appellant.'

(viii) Business changes

In this section it is proposed to examine the factors which are to be considered in deciding:
1 whether a trade has been newly set up and commenced;
2 whether there has been an expansion of an existing trade;
3 whether a trade has ceased; and
4 the treatment of book debts on a change of proprietorship.
An ancillary problem arises in deciding the effective date of commencement, change or cessation.

1 Trade newly set up and commenced

Whether a trade has commenced and the date of commencement are questions of fact. It may be said that trading has commenced when the principal assets are worked out, e.g. when the private shopkeeper opens his shop and exposes goods for sale, or when a manufacturing concern commences to manufacture. A company cannot trade before the date of registration which gives it legal existence, but trade is not, of course, necessarily commenced even on that date.

In *the Birmingham and District Cattle by-Products Co. Ltd v CIR*, 12 TC 92, the company was incorporated on 20 June 1913 and was interested in claiming that it commenced trading on that date so that there would be available a full year's trading before war broke out in August 1914, and therefore a more favourable standard for the computation of Excess Profits Duty. The Commissioners found as fact that arrangements for erection of works, engagement of foreman, and purchase of machinery and materials were not completed until October 1913, and it was only then it began to finished products.

From this they concluded that trading did not commence until October 1913. Their determination was supported by Rowlatt, J.; he reviewed all the facts and confirmed that the Commissioners had come to a proper conclusion from them. As a subsidiary point it may be noted that though the minutes of the company stated that it commenced in October, Rowlatt, J., did not hold the company to these, drawing a distinction between a formal recognition of events and the substance of the matter.

A person can carry on more than one trade. This is true of companies, though ownership by a single limited company is presumptive evidence that only one trade is carried on. Where a person carrying on one business opens an additional business in other premises the question arises whether the additional business is merely an extension of the first business, or whether a new trade has been set up and commenced. It may happen for instance that an existing business is taken over in the new premises. The question is always decided on the facts of the particular case under review.

In *Fullwood Foundry Company Ltd v CIR* 9 TC 101, the company wished to manufacture a new line of goods. For this purpose it purchased a foundry from another company together with the goodwill, but it did not take the books, the debtors, the creditors, or any orders from the former owner's customers. It retained the existing working staff at the foundry, but transferred the management to its original premises.

The Special Commissioners held that a new business had been commenced, and the Court did not interfere with the decision, agreeing that it was one of fact, and that the Commissioners were entitled to come to the conclusion that a new business had commenced:

> ... that is a question of fact. If it had been my duty to form an opinion of my own upon the facts which appear in this case, I really do not know what judgement I might have arrived at. The facts are not many and the arrival at a definite conclusion is a question, therefore, of inference from these facts, such as they are.

2 Expansion of trade

In ordinary language a trade may be said to continue even if there is a complete change of proprietorship, but in the United Kingdom there is a special rule that where one owner succeeds another the trade shall, for the purpose of computing assessments, be regarded as ceasing and recommencing. A complete change in proprietorship occurs, for example, when a business carried on by an individual is sold or transferred to another individual or a company, when a business

256

carried on by one company is sold or transferred to another company or when a business carried on by a partnership is sold or transferred to a company.

In the case of partnerships a somewhat different situation can arise – there can be a change of proprietorship with at the same time an element of continuity in personnel. Here again, there is a special rule in the United Kingdom for cases of this kind.

This explanation is given in order that it may be understood why there are so many United Kingdom cases on 'succession'. It is obvious that if 'succession' cannot be proved, a new proprietor already carrying on a business in the United Kingdom and taking over another will not be charged under the 'commencing' provisions. His new acquisition will be treated only as an extension of his existing business and will escape tax until caught on the preceeding year basis.

Under the Nigerian Acts the position is different; the emphasis is on the permanent cessation *by an individual or company* of a trade, etc., and not, as in the United Kingdom, on the *permanent discontinuance of the trade, etc.* Also, as regards partnerships, the Nigerian Acts recognise that it is not the firm but the individual partners in common who carry on the trade, etc., thus section 6 of ITMA provides that a partner's income for any period is his share of the total income of that period and that his assessable income is to be computed by treating that share as if it were the income of a trade, etc., carried on by him.

In short, it has to be remembered that, while in the United Kingdom a successor of a trade *must be* assessed as if a new business has been set up and commenced, in Nigeria we are only concerned to know whether on the facts a new or additional business has been acquired.

There are at least four ways in which a person can expand an existing trade:

(a) By taking over an existing business as a going concern. There is a strong presumption that a new trade has commenced side by side with the old, particularly if it is a different trade, or in a different locality, but the facts must decide.

(b) By acquiring part only of an existing business. The presumption here is not so strong.

(c) By acquiring separate assets. The trader is doing no more than if he bought additional plant in his existing premises.

(d) By opening up business in newly-built premises, or in premises in which either a different kind of trade has been previously carried on, or, even if a similar trade has been previously carried on there, it has now ceased so that the trader gets no benefit from it.

It is a question of fact whether the new venture constitutes a new trade or not. Generally, if there is centralised control and the same kind of trade is carried on at the new premises as at the old, the new venture will be a mere branch and there will be one calculation based on all activities of the preceeding year.

The only case it is proposed to mention in this subject is that of *Geo. Humphries and Co. v Cook*, 19 TC 121. Two individuals each carried on a separate trade, the one (Humphries) undertaking to get film processed for film companies, the other performing the technical work of processing on his behalf. They formed a partnership to carry on the same activities jointly. Humphries maintained that his trade had not been discontinued, but previously carried on as an individual. The Court, however, upheld the Commissioners' finding that Humphries' trade was discontinued when the partnership was formed and that a new trade was set up and commenced. Singleton, J., remarked:

... prior to the date of the partnership the business of Mr Humphries ... was purely a business of clerical nature, the getting of orders and the arranging for somebody else by contract to execute those orders. From the time the partnership began the business was of an entirely different nature. It was making things and doing work; it involved the employment of a considerable quantity of machinery ...

The point in this exceptional case was the identity of the trades which had been merged. The partnership was engaging in a new kind of trade which combined processing with the supply of processed film to film companies.

It is to be noticed that although the case was one of partnership, the principle that identity can be lost and some new merged trade commenced is not confined to partnership, but is of general application. [See Section 20(8) of ITMA as regards the sameness of the trade carried on before and after an individual or company becomes or ceases to be a partner in a partnership.]

Date of change

In most changes of proprietorship of business, there is a vending agreement which usually gives the date on which the change is assumed to take place. The agreement may provide for the change to be regarded as taking place at some date prior to the date of the agreement. In such a case the date of the agreement is usually to be taken as the date of change: the purchaser was not the proprietor before that date and the antedating merely secures that the profits for a period are included in the price of the transfer. On the other hand, the purchaser may be able to show that he did take effective possession of a business before the date of the vending agreement. In that case the date of change of ownership can be taken as preceding the date of the agreement.

In considering a relevant case when the business commenced regard must be had to the date any vending agreement was signed and the date shown in the agreement as the date of transfer. Either of these dates may be the date when possession was effectively transferred, or there may be evidence to show that transfer took place on some other date.

Where a business is transferred to a newly registered company it may happen that the company is not registered until after the date of the vending agreement. In such a case, provided that the company when formed immediately adopts the vending agreement, the date of the company's registration will be taken as the effective date of transfer. An earlier date is not possible, as the company has no legal existence before registration, and therefore, no contractual capacity.

In practice, a difficulty may occur when a new business added to another fails to keep separate records during the initial period of trading of the combined businesses. Once it is established a new business was commenced, however, the legal position is clear and the business taken over must be assessed as a new trade. It may be necessary to apportion the combined figures on such evidence as is available until the point is reached when both businesses are assessable on the preceding year basis

3 Discontinuance or cessation of a trade

The Acts refer to an individual or company permanently ceasing to carry on or exercise a trade, etc. It sometimes happens that because of bad trade or for some other reason, a person's business dwindles to practically nothing and is regarded as dormant. After some years of inactivity, however, it revives. Has the business continued, or has it ceased and recommenced?

The case of *Kirk and Randall Ltd v Dunn* 8 TC 633 was concerned with the 1914-18 War. The company took over from a firm in 1912 the trade of building contractors and completed existing contracts. The premises were closed in 1913 and were taken over by the War Office in 1914. The company, though without works or plant, maintained a registered office, continued to try for contracts, held meetings, and paid salaries, fees and expenses. New capital was raised in 1920, fresh plant acquired, and active business started. The Special Comissioners held that trade had been discontinued but Rowlatt, J., although admitting that the changes in 1920 might have been of such a kind, 'as clearly to indicate that there was a new business altogether' stated that the facts showed only that more money came in and more energetic people got hold of the business. He held that it could not be argued that 'they began their business in 1920 merely because for the first time somebody yielded to their solicitations for a contract'. He decided, therefore, that the business continued. As a secondary point he held that the point was one of law. He was considering the rules applicable to the basis of assessment:

> it is not really a question of fact or even of mixed fact and law. I thnk it is a question of law, because all the facts are quite clearly stated as far as they are thought to be relevant and to have been acted on in the case.

It is possible that when part of a trade is sold, what appears to be only a part of a trade is really a separate trade. The situation at the date of change must be considered on the available facts at that date. It is not necessarily relevant that the part now disposed of was originally acquired either as a separate business or as a part; the facts may have changed since that time. On the other hand, earlier history may offer some clue to the present situation.

In *Howden Boiler and Armaments Co. Ltd v Stewart,* 9 TC, it was considered whether a section of trading activity was a part of another trade or was a separate trade. The company was engaged in boiler making. For a period, it was also manufacturing shells but later it reverted to boiler-making only. The shell manufacture was carried on in specially erected premises, adjacent to the original works, but having no intercommunication. There were separate plant, separate workmen and technical and clerical staff, and a separate set of books and trading accounts, but the same general direction and management. There was a common profit and loss account and balance sheet, and bank interest and management expenses were charged against the company generally. In the Court of Session the decision of the General Commissioners that there was only one business carried on in two departments was upheld. The commissioners were held to have had sufficient evidence before them to reach their determination.

In *Scales v Geo. Thompson & Co. Ltd,* 13 TC 83, a similar problem arose. The company had a ship owner and broker. It also carried on the trading activity of underwriting. To conform to the rules of Lloyds the underwriting was actually in the hands of two 'partners' who acted as nominees and agents of the company. The underwriting was given up when these persons ceased to be connected with the company. The Special Commissioners found that two separate businesses were carried on, and Rowlatt, J., saw no reason to interfere with their decision. He attached no importance to the fact that the income from both sources was put into a common profit and loss account.

> ... [the] method of book-keeping does not seem to me to throw any light upon this matter at all. I think the real question is, was there any inter-connection, any

interlacing, any interdependence, any unity at all embracing these two businesses, and I should have thought ... that there was none. I think the Commissioners had ample evidence upon which they could decide.

This case clearly shows that there may be two separate businesses in fact, although a composite account is submitted. It also illustrates the point that a company can carry on more than one trade or business.

In each of these cases it is noticeable that the court, being satisfied that the Commissions' decision was well-founded on fact, did not interfere with it.

Finally, it is worth remembering that, although a business *acquired* by an individual or a company already in business might have been dealt with on commencing lines when taken over, it does not follow that the closing down or cessation of the acquisition at some later date will mean the automatic application of the ceasing provisions. The facts may be such that the acquisition has, by the time it ceases, become such an integral part of the whole that it can only be regarded as the closing down of a mere part of an existing business in such circumstances that the preceding year basis remains undisturbed.

4 Book debts

The treatment of book debts of a continuing business was dealt with earlier. When there is a change in proprietorship the question arises whether the new owner, if he takes the book debts over at a valuation, is to include as a trading profit or loss any difference between the valuation and the amount eventually realised. It is to be treated as a capital profit or loss, even though the business is transferred as a going concern, unless there is evidence that the acquisition of the debts was a trading operation, e.g. where the new owner can provide reasonable evidence to show that he is trading in book debts.

(ix) Ascertainment of assessable profits
Assessments – basis and procedure

Section 24 of the Companies Income Tax Act, 1979, governs the position. The Government year begins on 1 January and ends on 31 December. The basis of assessment of income from trade, business, profession or vocation is the profits or gains of the year preceding the year of assessment. The year preceding the year of assessment is either the financial year preceding the year of assessment or the accounting year of the taxpayer ending any time during the financial year preceding the year of assessment. Businessmen and companies usually prepare the annual accounts of their business up to any date they consider suitable. The Act provides that if the relevant tax authority is satisfied that accounts will be made to a date other than 31 December, it shall direct that the assessable income from that source be computed on the amount of the gains or profits of the year ending on that day in the year preceding the year of assessment.

Business accounts are prepared on normal accounting principles and are adjusted for tax purpose in accordance with the rules mentioned above.

The normal basis of assessment is the preceding year basis. Section 24 of the Companies Income Tax Act, 1979, provides the following rules:

(a) in respect of new business, assessable profits must fall into the period commencing from the date of commencement of the new business to the following 31 December;

(b) the assessable profits for the second year are those of twelve months from the date of commencement;

(c) in respect of the third year, the profits of the accounting year ending in the previous year are the assessable profits for that year;

(d) the assessable profits of the fourth and succeeding years are those of the preceding year.

Election in writing to have the second and third years but not just one of those years, assessed on actual adjusted profits of those years must be within two years of the end of the second year of assessment.

Provided that the company may, by notice in writing given to the Board within twelve months after the end of the third year revoke the notice, and in such case the assessable profits both for the second year and the third year shall be computed as if the first notice had never been given.

Where such notice has been given or revoked, such additional assessments or such reductions of assessments or repayments of tax shall be made as may be necessary. Provided that if the company fails to agree with the Board as to the amount of any reduction of an assessment or repayment of tax, the Board shall give notice to the company of refusal to admit such reduction or repayment.

Where a company has permanently ceased to carry on its trade or business the basis of assessment is:

(a) the profits of the final year of cessation from 1 January of the year of assessment of the date of cessation will be the assessable profits of the final year;

(b) in respect of the penultimate year, the assessable income is the income or profits of the year preceding the year of cessation or the profits previously computed, whichever is greater.

262

(x) Ascertainment of total profits and capital allowances

The total profits of any company for any year of assessment shall be the amount of its total assessable profits from all sources for that year together with any additions thereto to be made in accordance with the provisions of Schedule 2, less any deductions to be made or allowed in accordance with the provisions of section 27 and of the Second Schedule.

Section 26 of CITA 1979, states:

Subject to the provisions of subsection (4) of this section 26 there shall be deducted –
(a) the amount of a loss which the Board is satisfied has been incurred by the Company in any trade or business during any preceding year of assessment –
Provided that –
(i) in no circumstances shall the aggregate deduction from assessable profits or income in respect of any such loss exceed the amount of such loss; and
(ii) a deduction under this section for any particular year of assessment shall not exceed the amount, if any, of the assessable profits, included in the total profits for that year of assessment, from the trade or business in which the loss was incurred and shall be made as far as possible from the amount of such assessable profits of the first year of assessment after that in which the loss was incurred and, so far as it cannot be so made, then from such amount of such assessable profits of the next year of assessment, and so on;
(iii) the period for carrying forward any unabsorbed losses shall be limited to four years after which period any unabsorbed losses shall lapse;
(b) the amount of any loss which, under paragraph (d) of subsection (10) of section 24 is deemed to be a loss incurred by the Company during the year of assessment in which its trade or business commenced, so however that any deduction in respect of that loss shall be made as provided under paragraph (f) of that subsection.
The amount of loss incurred by a Company engaged in an agricultural trade or business shall be deducted as far as possible from the assessable profits of the first year of assessment after that in which the loss was incurred and so far as it cannot be so made, then from such amount of such assessable profits of the next year of assessment, and so on (without limit as to time) until the loss has been completely set off against the Company's subsequent assessable profits.
For the purposes of subsection (2) of this section the loss incurred during any year of assessment shall be computed, where the Board so decides, by reference to the year ending on a day in such year of assessment which would have been adopted under subsection (2) of section 24 for the computation of assessable profits for the following year of assessment if such profits had arisen.
Where under the provisions of subsection (6) of section 24 for the purpose of computing the profits of a period from a source chargeable with tax under this Act, being a period the profits of which are assessable profits from that source for any year, it has been necessary to allocate or apportion to specific periods which fall within that whole period both profits and losses, then no deduction shall be made under the provisions of subsection (2) of this section in respect of the loss or apportioned part thereof referable to any such specific period except to the extent that such loss or part thereof exceeds the aggregate profits apportioned to the remaining specific period or periods within that whole period.

Capital allowances

We have already dealt with capital allowances in Chapter 7. Section 27 of the 1979 Act, states:

(1) Subject to the provisions of this section, where –

(a) any asset in respect of which a Company has incurred qualifying expenditure is damaged or destroyed in any part of Nigeria at any time during the period commencing on 16th July 1967 and ending with 15th January 1970, as a direct result of any military or other operations which in the opinion of the Board are connected with the civil war in Nigeria; and

(b) the Company, on or after 1st April 1969, incurs expenditure in acquiring a new asset as a replacement of the asset which is so damaged or destroyed;

there shall be allowed to that Company a reconstruction allowance in respect of the expenditure incurred on the new asset (hereinafter in this section referred to as 'an investment allowance').

(2) An investment allowance shall be calculated at the rate of twenty-five per centum of the expenditure in respect of which it is made, and shall be in addition to an initial allowance under Schedule 2 to this Act.

(2A) An investment allowance shall be calculated at the rate of 10 per cent of the expenditure incurred on plant and equipment in use in agricultural production and shall be in addition to an initial allowance under Schedule 2 to this Act;

(3) Any provisions of Schedule 2 applicable to an initial allowance shall also apply to an investment allowance under this section, except that an investment allowance shall not be taken into account in ascertaining the residue of qualifying expenditure, in respect of an asset, for the purpose of the said Schedule.

(4) If in the case of any qualifying expenditure incurred on the new asset any such event as is mentioned in the next following subsection occurs within a period of five years beginning with the date on which the expenditure incurred, no investment allowance shall be made in respect of the expenditure or if such allowance has been made before the occurrence of the event it shall be withdrawn.

(5) The events referred to in subsection (4) of this section are –

(a) any sale or transfer of the asset representing the expenditure made by the Company incurring the expenditure otherwise than to a person acquiring the asset for a chargeable purpose or for scrap;

(b) any appropriation of the asset representing the expenditure made by the Company incurring the expenditure to a purpose other than a chargeable purpose;

(c) any sale, or transfer or other dealing with the asset representing the expenditure by the Company incurring the expenditure, being a case where it appears that the expenditure was incurred in contemplation of the asset being so dealt with, and being a case where it is shown either –

(i) that the purpose of obtaining tax allowances was the sole or main purposes of the Company for incurring the expenditure or for so dealing with the asset; or

(ii) that the incurring of the expenditure and the asset being so dealt with were not *bona fide* business transactions, or were artificial or fictitious transactions, and were designed for the purpose of obtaining tax allowances.

(6) A company incurring any expenditure in respect of which an investment allowance has been made and has not been withdrawn shall give notice to the Board if, to the knowledge of the Company, any of the events as is mentioned in subsection (5) of this section occurs at any time before the expiration of five years beginning with the date when the expenditure was incurred.

(7) Any notice of a sale or transfer given under subsection (6) of this section shall state the name and address of the person to whom the sale or transfer is made.

(8) Where an asset in respect of which an investment allowance has been made is sold or transferred it shall be the duty of the purchaser or transferee, and of the personal representatives of any such person on being required to do so by any officer duly authorised by the Board to give that officer all such information as he may require, and as they have or can reasonably obtain, about any sale or transfer of the asset representing the expenditure or about any other dealing with the asset.

(9) Any person who, without reasonable excuse, fails to comply with this section shall be guilty of an offence and liable on conviction to a penalty not exceeding ₦100 plus the amount of tax lost by the granting of the investment allowance made in respect of the expenditure in question.

(10) All such additional assessments and adjustments of assessments shall be made as may be necessary in consequence of the withdrawal of any investment allowance, and may be so made at any time.

For further details, reference should be made to chapter 7; the Supplement (1985) gives the rates for Initial Allowances and Annual Allowances.

Example 1

Progressive Ltd, a private limited company, has had a successful business for many years in Benin City. The following is a summary of its Profit and Loss Account for the year to 31 December, 1987.

Progressive Ltd
Profit and Loss Account to 31 December, 1987

Salaries & wages	₦16 640	Gross profit	₦30 870
Rents, rates &		Surplus on sale of	
insurance	2 960	investment	78
Lighting	770	Dividends	
Repairs &		received (gross)	160
renewals	840		
Carriage	430		
Loan interest	360		
Audit fee	130		
Bad & doubtful			
debts	216		
General expenses	736		
Depreciation	1 360		
Net profit	6 666		
	31 108		31 108

The general expenses were broken down as follows:

Printing & stationery		₦172
Legal costs: lease of new premises	₦70	

Customer's claim on alleged defective goods	50	120
Luncheon Vouchers (newly introduced)		300
Subscriptions: Economic Society	20	
Trade Association	40	60
Sundry expenses (all allowable)		84
		736

The repairs and renewals were broken down as follows:

Initial decorations to new premises	₦240
Repairs to plant	180
Renewal to part of roof of old factory	420
	840

The Bad & Doubtful Debts Account comprised the following entries:

Accounts written off:			Balance at 1 Jan. 1987:		
Trade debts	₦130		Specific debts	₦120	
Loan to former employee	100	₦230	2% of Remaining debts	440	₦560
			Debts recovered		96
Balance at 31 Dec. 1987:			Profit & Loss Account		216
Specific debts	162				
2% of Remaining debts	480	642			
		872			872

Note: The bad debts recovered during the year had, in previous years, been charged and allowed for tax purposes.

The loan interest shown in the Profit and Loss Account related to ₦3000 advanced by a friend in 1983 at 12% p.a. and is not for business purposes.

The written-down value of the plant, including office furniture and typewriters, after deducting the 1987 allowances, was ₦6600 and the written-down value of the motor car as at 1 January 1988 was ₦1700. Capital allowances have been claimed on the assets in 1986 and 1987 assessment years.

The following expenditure was incurred on the purchase of fixed assets during 1987:

New office furniture and equipment	₦1600
Less: Proceeds on sale of old typewriter bought new for	

₦130 in September, 1984		20
		₦1580
Second-hand lathe		400
		1980

You are required to calculate Progressive Ltd's adjusted profit and chargeable income for 1988.

Solution 1

Progressive Ltd
Computation of Adjusted Profit 1988 Year to 31 December 1987

Net Profit per Account			₦6,666
Add: Depreciation		₦1,360	
General Expenses:			
Legal cost (lease)	₦70		
Subscription (Econ. Soc.)	20	90	
Loan interest		360	
Bad & doubtful debts:			
loan to former			
employee written off	100		
Increase in general provision			
(480 less 440)	40	140	
Repairs & renewals:			
Initial decorations			
to new premises		240	
			2,190
			8,856
Less: Surplus on sale of investment		78	
Dividends received (Gross)		160	238
Adjusted profit:			8,618

Capital Allowances

		Plant	Car	Total Allowances
Written-down values				
(1st January 1987)		₦6,600	₦1,700	
Less: Typewriter –				
WDV (see note)	85			
Less: Proceeds	20	85		₦65
Balancing				
Allowance	65	6,515		

Additions:
   New office
    Furniture and
     equipment   1,600
    Second-hand lathe   400
                          2,000

Less: Initial Allowance
    (20%)   400   8,515
    Annual Allowance
    (10% – plant)   963
    (25% – car)   –

	1,363	845	2,208
Written-down values	7,152	855	2,273

Note: The balancing allowance on the old typewriter is arrived at as follows:

Cost of typewriter		₦130.00
1985 *Less*: Initial Allowance (20%)	₦26.00	
Annual Allowance (10%)	9.50	
		35.50
1986 Written-down value		94.50
Less: Annual Allowance (10%)		9.50
1987 Written-down value		85.00
Less: Sale proceeds		20.00
		65.00

Chargeable Income	
Adjusted profit	₦8,618
Less: Capital Allowances (total)	2,208
Total income for 1988 year of assessment	6,410

Note: Chargeable Income 1988 is ₦6410 since a limited liability Company, though a legal person, cannot get married and cannot produce children.

Capital Allowance Computations

Plant: Additions – ₦2000 at 20%
Initial Allowance – ₦400
Annual Allowance on the additions
= 2,000 – (400 + 10) = 1590
to be spread over 10 years = 159 (A)
(to make calculations easier, this has been rounded down to ₦150).

Annual Allowance on Residue
brought forward less disposal
(₦6,515) = 6,515 − 10 = ₦6505
to be spread over eight years

$$= \frac{6,505}{8} = 813 \text{ (B)}$$

Total Annual Allowance (A & B) 150 + 813 = ₦963
Cars:
Annual Allowance on Residue b/f ₦1700 was calculated as follows:

Residue b/f		₦1700
Less: Residue b/f		10
		1690
Spread over 2 years	$\frac{(1690)}{2}$ =	845

Example 2

The Income Tax account of Sundeb Academical Ltd at 1 January 1985 showed the following credit balances:

Income Tax	*1983*	₦500
Income Tax	*1984*	5000
Income Tax	*1985*	7000

The tax agreed, assessed and paid during the year ended 31 December 1985 was as follows:

Income Tax	*1983*	₦370
Income Tax	*1984*	6200
Income Tax	*1985 (one half only)*	3000

During the year ended 31 December 1985 you are informed that the trading profit was ₦8000; after allowing the following:

Depreciation	₦3000
Legal retainer fees	500
Profit on surrender on leasehold property	2500

The balance sheet at 31 December 1985 included the following items:

Stock reserve at 5%	₦8000	(1984 – 6000)
Leave passage provision	3200	(1984 – 5000)
Bad debt at 10%	4000	(1984 – 3000)

Assume that the rate of tax is 40%. You are required to write up the Income Tax account in the books of Sundeb Academical Company Ltd at 31 December 1985, and indicate how the balance would be shown in the balance-sheet. Ignore capital allowances.

Solution 2

Sundeb Academical Company Ltd
Income Tax account, 31 December 1985

	Dr.	Cr.
1.1.85 Balance brought down		
Income Tax 1983	–	₦500
Income Tax 1984	–	5 000
Income Tax 1985	–	7 000

Tax paid in the year

1983 (agreed)	370	
1984 (agreed)	6 200	
1985 (agreed) (one half only)	3 000	

Profit and loss account

Income Tax on profits for the year per workings (Note 1)		3 880

Adjustment in respect of prior year's tax:

	Under/over provision	
1983		₦130
1984	₦1200	
1985		1000
	₦1200	₦1130

Net under-provision ₦1200–₦1130 70

31.12.85 balances carried down:

1985 half only	3 000	
1986 full	3 880	
	₦16 450	₦16 450

31.12.85 Balances brought down:

Income Tax 1985	3 000
Income Tax 1986	3 880
	₦6 880

31.12.85 Balances that would appear in the balance sheet are:

Current taxation 1985	₦3000
Future taxation 1986	3880
	₦6880

270

Note 1 Computation of 1986 Income Tax

Net profit per accounts year to 31 December 1985		₦8 000
Add: Depreciation	3 000	
Increase in general stock reserve	2 000	
Increase in bad debts provision	1 000	6 000
		14 000
Less: Decrease in general		
Leave passage provision	1 800	
Profit on surrender of Leasehold property (Note 2)	2 500	4 300
		₦9 700

Income Tax thereon at say 40% ₦3880

Note 2 Profit on surrender of leasehold property will be liable to Capital Gains Tax, but this is not asked in the question.

Example 3

Akinzeye Ltd commenced business on 1 February 1984 and ceased on 30 June 1988. You are required to show the necessary Income Tax computations:

(a) on normal basis;
(b) if the taxpayer elected to have the second and third years based on actual; and
(c) on cessation, assuming the Inland Revenue exercised its option to reduce the assessment preceding the year of cessation to actual.

The following profit figures are given:

Accounts for the 11 months ending	*31.12.84*	₦1200
Accounts for the year ending	*31.12.85*	1500
Accounts for the year ending	*31.12.86*	1900
Accounts for the year ending	*31.12.87*	2000
Accounts for the 6 months to	*30.6.88*	2100

Solution 3

First year; 1984 year of assessment; 1.2.84–31.12.84
   (actual; date of commencement to the following
   31st December)   ₦1200

Second year; 1985 year of assessment 1.2.84–31.1.85
   (first 12 months from date of commencement)

   i.e. ₦1200 + ($\frac{1}{12}$ × ₦1500)   1325

Third year; 1986 year of assessment; preceding year;
   accounts ended 1985   1500

271

Fourth year; 1987 year of assessment; preceding year
    accounts ended 1986   1900

Fifth year 1988 year of assessment; accounts ended 1987   2000

On election, the first three years' assessments will be
    1984 year of assessment (no option)   ₦1200

1985 year of assessment; actual; 1.1.85–31.12.85   1500

1986 year of assessment; actual; 1.1.86–31.12.86   1900
    (He may not make an election.)

On cessation, its
1988 assessment will be based on profits from 1.1.88
    to 30.6.88; actual; (instead of the former assessment
    on ₦1909)   2100

1987 assessment will be revised to actual i.e. 1.1.87–
    31.12.87 (instead of the former assessment on ₦1900)   2000

It should be noted that the power to revise to actual, on cessation belongs to Inland Revenue Authorities exclusively.

Partnership income

Income or loss of a company arising from partnership with any person in Nigeria is a separate income/loss and will be determined in accordance with s.6 of ITMA, 1961, as amended – i.e. the proportion of the income/loss accruing under the partnership agreement.

Example 4

Afrotec (Nigeria) Ltd, a private company, distributes drugs for major pharmaceutical companies in the country. Its trading results for the second year to 31 December 1981 are as follows:

Commissions received		₦55 200
Dividends received (Gross)		8 000 ₦63 200
Staff salaries	₦10 500	
Rent and rates	2 500	
Printing and stationery	1 480	
Telephone and postage	550	
Transport and travelling	3 200	
Medical expenses	1 320	
Insurance	550	
Legal and professional fees	4 500	
Subscriptions and donations	350	
Depreciation	950	

Provision for bad debts	250	
Income Tax	1 250	27 400
Net profit		35 800

The following details are available:

(a) *Legal and professional fees include:*

Retainer's fees	2 400
Cost of acquiring a fixed asset	1 000
Penalty	1 100

The Company is presently constructing a warehouse at Isolo.

(b) *Subscriptions & donations*

Lagos Chamber of Commerce	₦200
Ikoyi Club	₦150

(c) Provision for bad debts
The company failed to recover the balance of ₦250 from loan given to a former employee.

(d) Tax written-down values of the company's assets as at the end of the immediately preceding tax year were:

Motor vehicles	₦11 700
Furniture and fittings	₦2 700

(e) Cost to date of warehouse under construction ₦80 000.

You are required to compute the company's Income Tax liability for the relevant year of assessment.
    Assume the rate of tax to be 45%.

Solution 4

Afrotec (Nigeria) Ltd
1982 year of assessment
Computation of tax liability

Net profit as per accounts		₦35 800
Add: *Income Tax*	₦1 250	
Provision for bad debts	250	
Depreciation	950	
Subscriptions and donations	150	
Legal cost	2 100	4 700
Adjusted Profit		40 500
Less: *Capital Allowances for the year*		1 800
Assessable profits		38 700

273

Tax at 45%
   on ₦38 700   ₦17 415
Less tax deducted
   at source on div.   1 000
   Tax liability   16 415

Capital Allowances

                                    WDV
   Motor vehicles   11 700
   Furniture and fittings   2 700
                                   14 400

Annual Allowances at $12\frac{1}{2}$%   1 800
WDV c/f   12 600

Example 5

Adaralegbe Technical (Nigeria) Ltd is an engineering construction company. The company makes up its accounts to 30 June of each year.

The following information is provided in respect of the year ended 30 June 1983.

(a) *Turnover*   ₦2 750 000
(b) *Net profit before taxation*   800 000
(c) But after charging and crediting the following items
     in the profit and loss account:
     (i) *Depreciation*   135 000
     (ii) *Rent paid*   75 000
     (iii) *Profits on sale of fixed assets*   23 760
(d) A sum of ₦15 000 stolen by the paymaster was included in salaries and wages and this was covered by an insurance policy.
(e) *Rent on residential accommodation:*
     (i) *paid on a building in Victoria Island*   ₦45 000
     (ii) *paid on a building in Warri*   30 000
(f) *Tax written-down value of assets at 1 July 1982 are:*
     Industrial building   78 000
     Plant and machinery   475 680
     Office furniture and equipment   31 975
     Motor vehicles   601 675
   Disposals during the year were as follows:
   (i) Industrial building bought on 1 June 1979 for
        ₦51 212 and sold for ₦65 000
   (ii) Motor vehicles bought on 16 February 1982 for
        ₦44 445 and sold for ₦25 000

Additions during the year were:
  (i) *Industrial buildings*   278 000
  (ii) *Office furniture and equipment*   4 000
(g) *Unabsorbed capital allowances brought forward*
    amounted to   31 750

You are required to compute the company's tax liability including tax on capital gains, if any, for the relevant year of assessment.

Solution 5

Adaralegbe Technical (Nigeria) Ltd
Computation of company's tax liability, 1984

Net profit as per accounts for the year ended 30 June 1983

			₦800 000
Add:			
Non-allowed deductions			
Depreciation			
Rent		₦135 000	
Victoria Island	45 000		
Less: Allowable rent			
(Note 1)	28 000	17 000	
Warri	30 000		
Less: Allowable rent			
(Note 1)	20 000	10 000	
Stolen Cash s.22(b) CITA 1979			
(Note 2)		15 000	177 000
			977 000
Less:			23 760
Profit on disposal of fixed assets			953 240
Less: capital allowances			
Initial Allowance		42 500	
Annual Allowance		168 216	
Balancing Allowance		5 000	
Balancing Charge		(23 212)	
		192 504	
Capital allowances brought forward		31 750	224 254
Taxable profits			728 986

Company tax (at 45%) chargeable	₦328 043.70	(A)
Minimum tax based on 2½% of Turnover		
= 2½% of ₦2 750 000	₦68 750	(B)
Company tax payable		
= Higher of (A) and (B)	₦328 043.70	

Notes

1 Section 20 of CITA, 1979 dealing with ascertainment of profits states *inter alia*:

Save where the provisions of subsection (2) or (3) of section 12 or of section 14 apply, for the purpose of ascertaining the profits or loss of any Company of any period from any source chargeable with tax under this Act there shall be deducted all expenses for that period by that Company wholly, exclusively, necessarily and reasonably incurred in the production of those profits including, but without otherwise expanding or limiting the generality of the foregoing –

(a) any sum payable by way of interest on any money borrowed and employed as capital in acquiring the profits;

(b) rent for that period, and premiums the liability for which was incurred during that period, in respect of land or building occupied for the purposes of acquiring the profits, subject, in the case of residential accommodation occupied by employees of the company, to a maximum of –

(i) ₦28 000 per annum for each building and ₦14 000 per annum for each flat in the Lagos area, and

(ii) ₦20 000 per annum for each building and ₦5000 per annum for each flat in any other part of Nigeria; and the provisions of this paragraph shall be deemed to have come into effect on 1st April, 1976; ...

Whilst section 22 states, *inter alia*:

Notwithstanding any other provision of this Act, no deduction shall be allowed for the purpose of ascertaining the profits of any Company in respect of –

(a) capital repaid or withdrawn and any expenditure of a capital nature;

(b) any sum recoverable under an insurance or contract of indemnity.

Adaralegbe Technical (Nigeria) Ltd
Computation of Balancing Allowance/Charge

				Total allowance claim
Industrial building				
Cost of building, 1 June 1979			₦51 212	
1980–81 Initial Allowance	*15%*	7 682		
Annual Allowance	*10%*	5 121	12 803	₦12 803
			38 409	
1981–82 Annual Allowance	*10%*		3 841	3 841
			34 568	
1982 Annual Allowance	*10%*		3 457	3 457
			31 111	
1983 Annual Allowance	*10%*		3 111	3 111
1984 written-down value			28 000	23 212
Proceed of sale in 1984			(65 000)	
Balancing Charge			₦(37 000)	

276

Adaralegbe Technical (Nigeria) Ltd
Computation of capital allowances for 1984

	Industrial buildings	Plant and machinery	Office furniture and equipment	Motor vehicles	Total
Written-down value b/f	₦78 000	₦475 680	₦31 975	₦601 675	₦1 187 330
Disposals	(28 000)			(30 000)	(58 000)
	50 000	475 680	31 975	571 675	1 129 330
	278 000	–	4 000	–	282 000
	328 000	475 680	35 975	571 675	1 411 330
Allowances					
Initial (based on allowable percentage on additions) 15%	(41 700)	–	20% (800)	–	(42 500)
Annual (based on allowable percentage on cumulative balance after additions) 10%	(32 800)	12½% (59 460)	12½% (4 497)	12½% (71 459)	(168 216)
	74 500		(5 297)		(210 716)
Written-down value carried forward	253 500	416 220	30 678	500 216	1 200 614

Summary:

Initial Allowance	42 500
Annual Allowance	168 216
Balancing Allowance	5 000
Balancing Charge	(23 212)
Total	192 504

277

Note

Balancing Charge is limited to capital allowances claimed to date of
sale – ₦23 212 – section 10, para. 2, Schedule 2, CITA 1979.

Motor vehicles

Cost of 16 February 1982			₦44 445
1983 Initial Allowance 20%		₦8 889	
Annual Allowance $12\frac{1}{2}\%$		5 556	14 445
1984 Written-down value			30 000
Proceed of sale in 1984			(25 000)
Balancing Allowance			5 000

Adaralegbe Technical (Nigeria) Ltd
Computation of Capital Gains Tax

Sales proceeds of industrial buildings	₦65 000
Less: Cost 1 June 1979	51 212
Chargeable gain	13 788
Capital Gains Tax at 20%	₦2 757.60

Subject to the company applying for roll-over relief which in this case
is to the company's advantage because the cost of newly-acquired
asset is in excess of the entire sale proceeds of the old asset.

Example 6

Funlayo & Sons Ltd, a textile manufacturing company commenced
production on 1 March 1981 and incurred qualifying expenditures as
follows:

Factory premises erected	₦330 000
Production plant installed	130 000
Vehicles	52 400
Furniture and fittings	32 000

The first set of accounts was prepared for 14 months to 30 June 1982.
Adjusted profits for the period were ₦12 500.

(a) You are required to compute the assessable profit of the company
for the first three years and state the option if any that is available to the company under CITA 1979.

(b) What are the conditions precedent to the granting of capital
allowances?

Solution 6

(a) *Funlayo & Sons Ltd, assessments*

First year assessment (10 months)   (1981)
Second year assessment (12 months)   (1982)
Third year assessment   (1983)

Preceding year basis or actual (1983)
1981 Assessment, first year

Profit as per a/c ₦ $\frac{10}{14}$ × 12 500)	₦8 929
Deduct	
Capital allowances for period	(165 588)
Chargeable income for 1982	Nil
Tax payable	Nil
Unabsorbed capital allowances c/f to 1982	₦(156 659)

1982 Assessment, second year

Profit for first 12 months' operation ₦ $\frac{12}{14}$ × 12 500)		10 714
Deduct		
Capital allowances for period	(47 352)	
Unabsorbed capital allowances b/f from 1981	(156 659)	(204 011)
Chargeable income for 1982		Nil
Tax payable		Nil
Unabsorbed capital allowances c/f to 1982		(193 297)

1983 Assessment, third year

Profit for the period (preceding year basis)		₦10 714
Deduct		
Capital allowances for period	₦(41 433)	
Unabsorbed capital allowances b/f for 1982	(193 297)	(234 730)
Chargeable income for 1983		Nil
Tax payable for 1983		Nil
Unabsorbed capital allowances c/f to 1983		224 016

(b) Conditions precedent for granting of capital allowances:
- (i) There must be a formal claim by the taxpayer before capital allowances are granted.
- (ii) Assets on which capital allowances are claimed must be in use as at the end of the basis period.
- (iii) Capital allowances can be granted to the person on whom wear and tear falls.
- (iv) Capital allowances granted will be limited to the ascertained wear and tear for the basis period.
- (v) Capital allowances will not be granted on assets suspected to have been purchased by artificial transactions.

Example 7

Yinka (Nigeria) Ltd decided to move their production facilities from Lagos to Ogun State. Having acquired land for the new factory premises, they sold their Lagos warehouse which cost ₦750 000 seven years earlier for ₦1 750 000 in January 1981. This amount was applied in constructing what would be one of the two new factories in the new premises. Construction was completed in December 1981 at a cost of ₦1 900 000.

In January 1982 the Lagos factory, built at a cost of ₦2 100 000, was disposed of for ₦2 500 000. Of the proceeds only ₦2 200 000 was invested in the second factory building in Ogun State; the management having decided to retain the balance as working capital.

Compute the capital gains arising from the disposals of the Lagos properties and state what Yinka (Nigeria) Ltd should do to minimise or defer capital gains taxation.

Solution 7

(a) *Capital Gains Tax computation: Yinka (Nigeria) Ltd*

Sale of warehouse	₦1 750 000
Less: Cost	750 000
Capital gain	1 000 000
Amount reinvested	1 900 000
Chargeable gain	Nil
(roll-over relief or s.32 relief)	

(b) *Sales of Lagos factory*	₦2 500 000
Cost	2 100 000
Capital gain	400 000
Amount reinvested	2 200 000
Capital gain	400 000
Less: Amount included in the original cost of	
₦2.1m to acquire the new assets at ₦2.2m	100 000
Chargeable gain	300 000
CGT payable at 20%	₦60 000

Note 1

Section 32(1) states that if the consideration for disposing of old assets is used to acquire new assets which are to be used in the business and the old and the new assets are with the same class of assets, the consideration for the disposal of the old assets if in excess of costs is to be imputed neither as a loss nor as a gain. The assets concerned are heavy plant and industrial equipment to encourage Nigerian industrialists to invest in heavy plant and equipment.

280

This treatment is not to apply to the purchaser if and when he disposes of the old assets in future.

Section 32(2) states: if part of the consideration for the disposal of the old assets is used in acquiring new assets or reinvested then the gain is to be reduced to the amount reinvested and the amount reinvested is reduced by the amount by which the gain is reduced above. The value of the asset bought or newly invested in is thus reduced and this will reduce its cost and increase its capital gains when sold in future.

General

The fact that an asset has a written-down value, Balancing Allowance or Balance Charge is for capital allowances computation only. The asset will be liable to Capital Gains Tax since this is concerned with original cost and other costs and sale price. Capital losses are not to be offset against capital gains.

(xi) Change of accounting date

The basis period for a year of assessment is the preceding 1 January to 31 December. If a continuing business whose assessable income falls to be assessed under section 24(1) of the Companies Income Tax Act, 1979, makes up its accounts up to a date other than 31 December, its accounting period of twelve months ending within the year preceding the year of assessment is adopted as its basis period.

If, for instance, the accounting year-end of a business is 30 September 1980, that date is before 31 December 1980 which is the end of the basis period for the 1981 year of assessment. The basis period of the business for the 1981 year of assessment is therefore 1 October 1979 to 30 September 1980. The twelve months to 30 September continues to be recognised as the basis period of the business as long as that terminal date remains unaltered.

A business is at liberty to change its accounting year-end if for any reason it finds it necessary to do so. In such case, the assessable profits of the year of assessment in which there is a failure to make up accounts to the former terminal date and for the two years following are to be computed on such basis as the Board in its discretion may direct.

As soon as it is known that a business has changed or intends to change its accounting date, it should be requested to state the reason for the change and whether the change will be permanent. If the change is temporary, the assessments of the business should continue to be based on the results of twelve months ended on the old terminal date.

Where it is stated that the new accounting date is permanent, the three discretionary years of assessment under section 24(2) of the Companies Income Tax Act, 1979, should be determined and recorded in the permanent note jacket of the assessment file. It is not possible at the outset to determine what the assessable profits of the three years will be, but the new terminal date should be adopted provisionally for the earliest convenient assessment year and should thereafter be maintained. In many cases the assessable profits for the first of the three years would have been determined by reference to the accounting year ended on the old terminal date before the change is notified. In that case the assessment of the first year of change should not be revised in the meantime but the new date should be adopted at the earliest opportunity and subsequently. The business should, however, be made to understand that any assessments made for the first and possibly the second years should be regarded as provisional and would be subject to review when the accounts for the third year have been received.

It is to be understood that the Board has no power to refuse to accept a permanent change and must prepare the computations of the assessments of the business for the three years concerned. On the other hand, the Board is given power to exercise its discretion as to how the computations should be made. The only reason for the discretion is to ensure that the Government obtains the best terms possible revenue-wise from the transaction provided that none of the affected assessments is based on the profits of more than twelve months. If the business considers that the change does not pay off, it has the option to revert to the old accounting year.

It is to be noted that where a permanent change is desired during the commencement years, the three basis periods should be reworked from commencement of business. A change involving the year of cessation as the third relevant year should be rejected. A change involving the penultimate year should be referred to Headquarters for consideration.

As a result of the adoption of the new accounting period one of two things must happen:

(a) If the new date is later in the income tax year than the old date, the profits of some period will not come into the assessment at all.

(b) If the new date is earlier in the income tax year than the old, the profits of some period will come into assessment twice.

The amount of the profits excluded or brought in twice and the related period should be ascertained and recorded prominently in the permanent note jacket of the assessment file. The ultimate objective is to determine the assessable profits of the first relevant year or of the second relevant year. It is to be noted that only the periods forming the basis for the year of assessment affected should be used in the determination of the assessable profits of the business for the relevant years.

As soon as the accounts for the period of twelve months to the terminal date which forms the basis for the third relevant year of assessment have been agreed, the following computations should be made:

(i) the profits of all accounting periods which could enter into the computation of assessable profits for the three relevant years on the old and new basis together with the number of months falling within those periods should be aggregated and reduced or increased proportionately as the case may be to the profits of thirty-six months.

(ii) the profits of the accounting periods which could enter into the computation of assessable profits for the first two relevant years on the old and new basis should be aggregated and reduced or increased proportionately as the case may be to the assessable profits of twenty-four months.

(iii) the profits of the accounting periods which could enter into the computation of assessable profits for the last two relevant years on the new basis should be increased proportionately to the assessable profits of twenty-four months.

(iv) the profits of the accounting periods which could enter into the computation of assessable profits for the first relevant year on the old and new basis should be reduced proportionately to the assessable profits of twelve months.

The following examples illustrate the points above:

(A) The accounts of a company have been made up annually to 31 March, the last accounts have been made up to 31 March 1980. The first accounts of the new date are made up to 31 December 1980.

The trading results are:

12 months to 31.3.80 profits	₦8 000
9 months to 31.12.80 profits	3 000
12 months to 31.12.81 profits	10 000
12 months to 31.12.82 profits	9 000

The company failed to make up accounts to 31 March 1981. The year in which the failure occurred is the 1981 year of assessment. The three relevant years are therefore 1981, 1982 and 1983.

In this case the change of the company's accounting year coincides with change in government fiscal year, the determination of the assessable profits is straightforward and admits of no alternatives. The assessable profits are determined as follows:

1.4.79–31.12.79	*1980 profits*	₦6 000
1.1.80–31.12.80	*1981 profits*	5 000
1.1.81–31.12.81	*1982 profits*	10 000
1.1.82–31.12.82	*1983 profits*	9 000

No part of the profits is included twice or left out of assessment. (B) The accounts of a company have been made up annually to 31 March, the last accounts have been made up to 31 March 1981. The first accounts of the new date are made up to 31 December 1981.

This change is subsequent to the change in government fiscal year. The determination of the company's assessable profits for the relevant years is therefore not the same as that in (A).

The trading results are:

12 months to 31.3.81 profits	₦10 000
9 months to 31.12.81 profits	7 000
12 months to 31.12.82 profits	12 000
12 months to 31.12.82 profits	15 000

The company failed to make up accounts to 31 March 1982. The year in which the failure occurred is the 1982 year of assessment. The three relevant years are therefore 1982, 1983 and 1984. Note that the new date is later in the tax year than the old date, as explained above.

(i)
21 months to 31.12.81		₦17 000
12 months to 31.12.82		12 000
12 months to 31.12.83		15 000
45 months' profit is		₦44 000
$\frac{36}{45} \times$ ₦44 000 *is*		₦35 200
Profits for 1984 year of assessment are	₦15 000	
Profits for 1983 year of assessment are	₦12 000	27 000
∴ *Profits for 1982 year of assessment are*		₦8 200

(ii)
21 months to 31.12.81	17 000
12 months to 31.12.82	12 000
33 months profits are	₦29 000
$\frac{24}{33} \times$ ₦29 000 *is*	21 090
Profits for 1983 year of assessment are	12 000

$\therefore$ *Profits for 1982 year of*
assessment are ₦9 090

(iii) *21 months to 31.12.81* ₦17 000
$\frac{12}{21} \times$ ₦17 000, *i.e. 1982 profits are* ₦9 714

(iv) *Profits for 1982 year of assessment*
    1.1.81 to 31.3.81 $\frac{1}{4} \times$ ₦10 000 is   2 500
    1.4.81 to 31.12.81   7 000
    ₦9 500

(v) *Profits for 1982 year of assessment*
  Profits of 1982 original
  assessment are ₦10 000

The amount to be left out of assessment is   ₦44 000
Less 1982   ₦10 000
    1983   12 000
    15 000   37 000
    7 000

The highest assessable profits for 1982 obtained in this exercise are lower than the original assessable profits which should not be revised but should be communicated to the company's auditors along with the figures for 1983 and 1984 years of assessment.

(C) The accounts of a company have been made up annually to 31 March, the last accounts being to 31 March 1981. The first accounts of the new date are made up to 30 September 1981.

The trading results are:

12 months to 31.3.81 profits	₦8 000
6 months to 30.9.81 profits	6 000
12 months to 30.9.82 profits	9 000
12 months to 30.9.83 profits	12 000

The company failed to make up accounts to 31 March 1982. The year in which the failure occurred is the 1982 year of assessment. The three relevant years are 1982, 1983 and 1984 years of assessment.

(i) *18 months to 30.9.81*   ₦14 000
  12 months to 30.9.82   9 000
  12 months to 30.9.83   12 000
  42 assessable profits   35 000
  36 months' profits, i.e.
  $\frac{36}{42} \times$ ₦35 000 *are*   ₦30 000
  Profits for 1984 year of
  assessment are   ₦12 000
  Profits for 1983 year of

assessment are	9 000	₦21 000
∴ Profits for 1982 year of assessment are		₦9 000
(ii) 18 months' profits to 30.9.81		₦14 000
12 months' profits to 30.9.82		9 000
30 months' profits		₦23 000
24 months' profits, i.e. $\frac{24}{30}$ × ₦23 000 are		18 400
Profits for 1983 year of assessment are		9 000
∴ Profits for 1982 year of assessment are		₦9 400
(iii) 18 months' profits to 30.9.81		₦14 000
Profits for 1982 year of assessment, i.e. $\frac{12}{18}$ × ₦14 000, are		₦9 333
(iv) Profits for 1982 year of assessment 1.10.80 to 31.3.81, i.e. $\frac{1}{2}$ × ₦8000		₦4 000
are 1.4.81 to 30.9.81		6 000
(v) The original assessment for 1982 is		10 000
		₦8 000

The highest assessable profits for 1982 obtained in this exercise is (iv), that is ₦10 000. Assessable profits for 1982 should be revised upwards to this figure and should be communicated to the company's auditors along with the assessable profits for 1983 and 1984.

The amount left out of assessment is		₦35 000
Less 1982	₦10 000	
1983	9 000	
1984	12 000	31 000
		₦4 000

(D) The accounts of a company have been made up annually to 31 December, the last accounts being to 31 December, 1980. The first accounts of the new date are made up to 30 June 1981.

The trading results are:

12 months to 31.12.79 profits	₦8500
12 months to 31.12.80 profits	7000
6 months to 30.6.81 profits	2000
12 months to 30.6.82 profits	5000

The company failed to make up accounts to 31 December 1981. The year in which the failure occurred is the 1981 year of assessment. The three relevant years are therefore 1981, 1982 and 1983 years of assessment.

286

(i) *12 months to 31.12.81 profit*   ₦7 000
    6 months to 30.6.81 profits   2 000
   12 months to 30.6.82 profits   5 000
   30 months assessable profits is   ₦14 000
   36 months profits, i.e. $\frac{36}{30} \times$ ₦14 000 *is*   ₦16 800
   Profits for 1981 year of
   assessment are   ₦7000
   Profits for 1983 year of
   assessment are   5000   12 000
   ∴ *Profits for 1982 year of*
   assessable are   ₦4 800

(ii) *18 months to 30.6.81 profits*   ₦9 000
   24 months' profits $\frac{24}{18} \times$ ₦9000   12 000
   Profits for 1981 year of assessment are   7 000
   ∴ *Profits for 1982 year of assessment are*   ₦5 000

(iii) *18 months profits to 30.6.82 are*   ₦7 000
   24 months' profits $\frac{24}{18} \times$ ₦7000 *are*   9 333
   Profits for 1983 year of assessment are   5 000
   ∴ *Profits for 1982 year of assessment are*   ₦4 333

(iv) *Profits for 1981 year of assessment*
   6 months to 31.12.79 $\frac{1}{2} \times$ ₦8500   ₦4 250
   6 months to 30.6.80 $\frac{1}{2} \times$ ₦7000   3 500
                                    ₦7 750

   Profits for 1982 year of assessments
   6 months to 31.12.80   i.e. $\frac{1}{2} \times$ ₦7000   ₦3 500
   6 months to 30.6.81   2 000
                                    ₦5 500

The highest assessable profits for 1981 are ₦7770 and for 1982, ₦5500. Since the original 1981 and 1982 assessable profits are less than the above, they should be revised to these figures and should be communicated to the company's auditors along with the assessable profits for 1983, ₦5000.

The amount brought twice into assessment is calculated as follows:

   1981   ₦7750
   1982   5500
   1983   5000   ₦18 250
   Assessable profits for 30 months are   14 000
   Amount brought in twice is   ₦4 250

Where losses are involved in any of the relevant accounting periods the following procedure should be followed:

(a) both profits and losses of all the relevant accounting periods should be aggregated together with the number of months falling within these periods.

(b) where the aggregate figure arrived at in any of the computations is a loss, such computation should not be used for comparison. In any case the assessable profits provisionally determined for the three relevant years should either be left unchanged or should be revised in such a way that any method adopted should ensure that all profits in the relevant accounting periods are brought into assessment and all losses are absorbed by aggregation with profits or are relieved once only in accordance with the provisions of section 26.

The following example illustrate the points made above:

(A) The accounts of a company have been made up annually to 31 March; the last accounts were made up to 31 March 1981.

The first accounts of the new date were made up to 31 December 1981.

The trading results are:

12 months to 31.3.80 profits	₦2000
12 months to 31.3.81 profit	4000
9 months to 31.12.81 loss	3000
12 months to 31.12.81 profit	5000
12 months to 31.12.83 profit	6000

The company failed to make up accounts to 31 March 1982. The year of assessment in which the failure occurred is the 1982 year of assessment. The three relevant years are 1982, 1983 and 1984.

(i)

21 months to 31.12.81 profit	₦1 000
12 months to 31.12.82 profit	5 000
12 months to 31.12.83 profits	6 000
45 months' profits are	₦12 000
$\frac{36}{45} \times$ ₦12 000 *is*	7 200
1984 assessable profits are ₦6000	
1983 assessable profits are 5000	11 000
∴ *1982 assessable loss is*	₦3 800

(ii)

21 months to 31.12.81 profit	₦1 000
12 months to 31.12.82 profit	5 000
33 months profits are	₦6 000
$\frac{24}{33} \times$ ₦6000 *is*	₦4 363
1983 assessable profits are	5 000
∴ *1982 assessable loss is*	₦637

(iii) *Assessable profits for 1982 year of assessment*

21 months to 31.12.81 profit	₦1 000
$\frac{12}{21}$ × ₦1000, i.e.	571
(iv) *3 months to 31.3.81 $\frac{1}{4}$ × ₦4000 profits*	₦1 000
9 months to 31.12.81 loss	3 000
Assessable loss for 1982 is	₦2 000

Sub-paragraphs (i), (ii), (iv) cannot be used for comparison because they result in losses. The following alternative should therefore be considered and compared with sub-paragraph (iii).

(v) *Assessable profits for 1982*	
Profits for 12 months to 31.3.81	₦4 000
Less losses for 9 months to 31.12.81	3 000
Assessable profits allocable to 1982	
year of assessment are	₦1 000

Sub-paragraph (v) produces the higher assessable profits for the 1982 year of assessment and should therefore be communicated to the company along with the assessable profits for 1983, ₦5000 and for 1984, ₦6000. The original assessable profit of ₦4000 should therefore be vacated.

(B) The accounts of a company have been made up annually to 31 December, the last accounts being to 31 December 1980. The first accounts of the new date are made up to 30 June 1981.

The trading results are:

12 months to 31.12.79 loss	₦3000
12 months to 31.12.80 profits	2000
6 months to 30.6.81 loss	1000
12 months to 30.6.81 profit	4000

The company failed to make up accounts to 31 December 1981. The year in which the failure occurred is the 1981 year of assessment. The three relevant years are therefore 1981, 1982 and 1983 years of assessments.

(i) *12 months to 31.12.80 profit*		₦2000
6 months to 30.6.81 loss		1000
12 months to 30.6.82 profit		4000
30 months aggregate profit		5000
$\frac{36}{30}$ × ₦5000, *i.e. 36 months profit is*		₦6000
Profits for 1981 year of assessment	₦2000	
Profits for 1983 year of assessment	4000	6000
Profit/loss for 1982 year of assessment		Nil

(ii) *18 months to 30.6.81 profits*   ₦1000
24 months' profits, i.e. $\frac{24}{18} \times$ ₦1000   1333
Profits for 1981 year of assessment   2000
Loss for 1982   ₦667

(iii) *18 months' profits to 30.6.82*   ₦3000
24 months' profits,i.e. $\frac{24}{18} \times$ ₦3000   ₦4000
Profits for 1983 year of assessment are   4000
∴ Profits for 1982 year of assessment are   Nil

(iv) *Profits for 1981 year of assessment*
6 months to 31.12.79 loss   ₦1500
6 months to 30.6.80 profit   1000
                            Loss   500

(v) *Profits for 1982 year of assessment*
6 months to 31.12.80 profits   ₦1000
6 months to 30.6.81 loss   1000
                               Nil

Sub-paragraphs (i) to (v) show either nil profit or a loss. The following should therefore be considered.

The 1980 assessment is nil with ₦3000 loss carried forward and set against the profit of ₦2000 for the 1981 assessment. The 1982 assessment is also nil with the loss ₦1000 incurred in that year added to the unabsorbed loss of ₦1000 carried forward from the 1981 year of assessment. The loss of ₦2000 is set off against the assessable profits of ₦4000 shown in the 1982 year of assessment. The profit of ₦2000 which remains is assessed in that year.

This chapter is designed to give assessing officers the opportunity of exploring a wide range of possibilities in determining the assessable profits of a business under the proviso to section 24(2). It is to be emphasised, however, that the case should be referred to Headquarters by the Head of the District after he has had the opportunity of reviewing the case himself if:

(a) the amount left out of or brought twice into assessment is more than 20 per cent of the assessable profits of the first or the second relevant year respectively;

(b) the business objects to his determination and it becomes inevitable that a notice of refusal to review his determination has to be issued to the business;

(c) he has any reason to believe that the accounting date is being manipulated with the object of tax avoidance.

(d) the penultimate year is involved in any of the relevant years.

(e) the case presents some difficulty to the Head of the District.

Example 8

Yinka & Co. (Nigeria) Ltd, has been in business for several years and makes up its accounts regularly to 31 March each year.

In 1981, it was decided to make up accounts to 31 December in future. The adjusted profits were:

12 months to 31 March 1981	₦95 000
9 months to 31 December 1981	80 000
12 months to 31 December 1982	86 000
12 months to 31 December 1983	90 000

Compute the profits assessable to tax for the last 3 years
  (a) on the normal basis
  (b) on the change of accounting date.

Solution 8

Yinka & Co. (Nigeria) Ltd
Change of accounting date

(a) *Year of assessment*

1982 21 months to 31.12.81	₦175 000		
1983 12 months to 31.12.82	86 000		
1984 12 months to 31.12.82	90 000		
45 months' profit	351 000		
$\frac{36}{45} \times$ ₦351 000 *is*			280 800
Less profit for 1984 year of assessment	90 000		
Profit for 1983 year of assessment	86 000	176 000	
		104 800	

(b)

21 months to 31.12.81	175 000
12 months to 31.12.82	86 000
33 months' profits	261 000
$\frac{24}{33} \times$ ₦261 000 *is*	189 818
Less profits for 1983	86 000
Profits for 1982 =	103 818

(c)

21 months to 31.12.81		175 000
$\frac{12}{21} \times$ 175 000 *profits*	100 000	
1982 profits =	100 000	

(d) *Profits for 1982 year of assessment (y/a)*

1.1.81–31.3.81, i.e. $\frac{1}{4}$ of 95 000 =	23 750
1.4.81–31.12.81	80 000
	103 750

(e) *Profit for 1982 y/a are*   104 800
      Amount to be left out of   351 000
       1982   104 800
       1983   86 000
       1984   90 000   280 000
                                                          70 200

The highest assessable profit for 1982 obtained in this exercise is (a).
Assessable profit for 1982 should be revised upwards to this figure.

Points to note

1   Only in respect of a trade, etc. is the Board obliged to accept
accounts made up to a permanent accounting date in the year preceding the year of assessment. For all other sources of income – rent,
dividend, etc., i.e. all those mentioned in section 4(1) of ITMA, except
employment and pension – the income for assessment is that of
the year to the 31 December immediately preceding the year of
assessment.
2   The commencing or ceasing provisions apply only where an
individual or a company commences or ceases to trade, etc. in Nigeria,
and not in any particular territory. In other words, a change of
territory does not in itself mean the cessation and recommencement of
any trade, etc. carried on.
3   The commencing or ceasing provisions do *not* apply where an
individual becomes or ceases to be a partner in a partnership, if the
trade carried on by him and the partnership before and after the
change is the same. The provisions do seemingly apply, however, if
there is a change of partnership in a partnership carrying on a profession or vocation.
4   If a company becomes a partner with any other person, the trade,
etc. activity is regarded as a separate source of profits to be determined as if the provisions of section 6, etc. of ITMA apply. (As for
the granting of capital allowances in such cases, see paragraph 25 of
the Fifth Schedule of ITMA.)
5   Where the whole or a part of a trade of business carried on by a
company is sold or transferred to a *Nigerian* company for the purposes of better organisation or the transfer of its management to
Nigeria, the Board is authorised to direct that neither the commencing
nor the ceasing provisions shall apply and that the capital allowances
shall be computed in a special manner (Schedule 2 CITA 979).
6   Any change in a basis period demands a review and almost certain
recomputation of any capital allowances (see paragraph 2 and

paragraph 1 of the Fifth Schedule of ITMA and the Third Schedule of CITA respectively.)

7   Receipts and payments after the date of permanent cessation of trade, etc. are to be regarded as the receipts and payments of the last day of trading, etc.

8   The Joint Tax Board has a limited right of determination under section 20(2) of ITMA where, during the three relevant years of assessment involved in a 'change-of-accounting-date' adjustment, the individual is deemed to be resident in more than one territory for any part of the period.

Any appeal against the Joint Tax Board's determination is direct to the Federal Supreme Court.

9   No matter what the source, the basis of assessment of the income of a trust or estate is always the income of the preceding year ended 31 December.

Example 9

Finished Paper Ltd manufactures paper, paperboard and converts the paper into other household products. It has been in this trade for several years. But in 1982 it decided to close down its factory permanently. Its adjusted profits (loss) and agreed capital allowances were as follows:

		Profit/(loss)	
Year ended *30 Sept. 1978*		₦6 400	
Year ended *30 Sept. 1979*		10 500	
Year ended *30 Sept. 1980*		18 000	
Year ended *30 Sept. 1981*		(8 500)	
Capital allowances	*1979–80*		4500
	1980		3000
	1981		3500
	1982		4100

At 30 June 1982 the trading results gave a net loss of ₦34 000. There was in 1982 the following additional information.

Depreciation	₦9400
Donations to a political party	5000
Doubtful debts	2500
of which ₦900 related to specific debts.	
Defalcations by cashier	1400

During the year, a vehicle with tax written-down value of ₦350 at the end of the 1981 year of assessment was sold for ₦510 capital allowances for the other assets were ₦3960.

You are required to compute the terminal loss and show what relief would be given in respect of losses in the last two years of the business.

Solution 9

Finished Paper Ltd

	Adjusted profits ₦	Capital allowances ₦	Net assessments ₦
Assessments			
1979–80	6 400	4000	2 400
1980	10 500	3000	7 500
1981	18 000	3500	14 500
1982	–	3800	–

Terminal loss claim computation

$$1.10.81-30.9.82$$

1982: *1.1.82–30.6.82 (6 months)*

$$\text{Loss} \quad \tfrac{6}{12} \times 18\,000 = \quad ₦9\,000$$

Capital allowances	3 800
	12 800

1981: 1.10.81–31.12.81 *(3 months)*

$$\tfrac{3}{12} \times 18\,000 = \quad ₦4\,500$$

Capital allowances for period Nil	–
Claimed in 1981 original assessment	
Available loss relief	17 300

Application for Loss Relief

Y/a	Net assessment ₦	Terminal Loss ₦	Revised assessment ₦
1981	14 500	14 500	–
1980	7 500	2 800	4 700
1979–80	2 400	–	–
		17 300	

Terminal loss is granted against previous net assessments until the entire terminal loss has been utilised.

Workings
Adjusted profit for 1982

Loss per question		₦(34 000)
Add depreciation	₦9400	
Donation	5000	
Doubtful debts	1600	16 000
Adjusted loss		18 000

Capital allowances as agreed		₦3960
Disposal		
Motor vehicles WDV	₦350	
Sale value	510	
Balancing Charge		160
		3800

(xii) Claims for losses

Normally, losses are computed on the same basis as profits, that is, on preceding-year basis. A loss can be set off against future profits and cannot be set off against the profits of the accounting year. The possibility of refunding tax already paid is thus eliminated.[169] Under Act no. 47 of 1972, any company which has made losses in its trading activities in any preceding year could claim the amount of such losses in the current year and could carry any unabsorbed losses forward indefinitely until such losses are wiped out completed by succeeding annual profits. With effect from 1.4.76, the period for the carry-forward of any unabsorbed losses is restricted to four years.[170] Under no circumstances should the aggregate deduction from assessable profits in respect of any loss exceed the amount of such loss.

The losses incurred after commencement of agricultural production can be carried forward indefinitely and set off against future profits in the same time.

In *Elder Dempster Agencies (Nigeria) Limited v Federal Board of Inland Revenue* (APP/COMM/190 of 15 May 1974), Companies Income Tax Act, 1961, the Commissioners were to determine:

1 loss arising from the operation of the banking obligation (Eastern States) section 8(2) of Decree no. 56 of 1970;
2 whether section 8(2) of Decree no. 56 of 1970 expressly disallowed the deduction of irrecoverable bank balances from taxable profit;
3 whether the loss so sustained amounted to a bad debt and, if so, whether section 8(2) of Decree no. 56 of 1970 extinguished such bad debt;

4 whether loss arising under Decree no. 56 of 1970 could be regarded as a trade loss.

The appellant contended that the amount which it lost as a result of the irrecoverability of certain bank balances should be allowed as deduction.

The appeal was allowed: the Appeal Commissioners found that section 8(2) of Decree no. 56 of 1970 only barred the right to recover and to sue for recovery; it did not bar the right to deduct the loss from assessable profit.

In *Tin and Associated Minerals Ltd* (Appellant) *v Federal Board of Inland Revenue* (Respondent) (APP/COMM/213 of 18 October 1974, Companies Income Tax Act 1961), the Commissioners were to determine:

1 whether trade loss includes capital allowance section 31(2)(a) CITA, 1961;

2 capital allowance Third Schedule, paragraph 24 CITA, 1961.

The appellant's contention was that the respondent erred in failing to take into consideration balancing allowance and capital allowance which the appellant wanted to set off against profits.

The appeal was dismissed: the Appeal Commissioners found that what is contemplated to be set off by way of loss incurred by the company is its trading loss which does not include capital allowances.

Incar (Nigeria) Ltd (Appellant)[171] *v Federal Board of Inland Revenue (Respondents)*

This was an appeal by Incar Nigeria Limited against the decision of the Appeal Commissioners dated 1 December 1976 refusing to allow the deduction of losses sustained by the appellant company in the Eastern States during the civil war.

The appellant company was a limited liability company incorporated under Nigerian laws. It had branches in many parts of Nigeria including the Eastern States. The appellant company's main business was the purchase and sale of motor vehicles and spare parts. It also sold motor vehicles on a hire purchase basis.

It appeared that all the branches outside Lagos, the Head Quarters, sent their returns to the Head Office which was in Lagos. The last returns received by the Head Office from the Eastern State was in June 1967. That was immediately before the last civil war. Both the appellant and respondent agree that during the civil war years, that is, 1967, 1968 and 1969, the accounts for assets and liabilities in respect of the Eastern States branches of the appellant company were shown in separate schedules. 'Reserves' for possible loss or damage to those assets were made as follows:

Year ended 31 December 1967	₦52 000
Year ended 31 December 1968	96 000
Year ended 31 December 1969	96 000
	₦244 000

At the end of the civil war in January 1970, the damage and losses suffered by the appellant company were stated as follows:

Fixed assets at written-down value	₦53 420
Stocks of motor vehicles, spare parts and material in transit	228 426
Vehicles and spare parts in transit	23 446
Hire purchase debtors	341 320
Sundry debtors and prepayment	18 032
Cash at hand	28 500
Cash at hand	1 268
	694 432
Less: deferred income	17 614
	₦676 818

For the year of assessment 1970–71 the sum of ₦244 000 was deducted from taxable profits as specific reserve for Eastern States assets while the balance of ₦432 818 was treated as a legitimate expense in arriving at profit for year ending 31 December, 1970.

On 15 June 1972, the respondent sent to the appellant an amended assessment in respect of Income and Super Tax for the year 1971–72 as per Exhibits A and B. This brings in the sum of ₦694 432 which had been written off by the appellant for 1970–71 and 1971–72 years of assessment as losses and damage in the Eastern States during the civil war years.

Before arguing his grounds of appeal, learned counsel for the appellant applied under Rule 15(2) of the Income Tax Appeal Rules 1957 to call Mr Folarin A. Pearse to give evidence.

Mr Pearse, a partner in the firm of Pannell Fitzpatrick and Co., testified that they were the auditors of the appellant company and that he was very familiar with the facts of this appeal. It was he who prepared the grounds of appeal before the Appeal Commissioners. He stated that the point of conclusiveness of 1970–71 assessment which he argued before the Appeal Commissioners was not one of the grounds he filed. The omission was inadvertent, he said.

Under cross-examination by Dr Akintan, learned counsel for the respondent, Mr Pearse admitted giving evidence before the Appeal Commissioners. He admitted the correctness of his testimony as recorded.

After this witness evidence, Mr Bab Williams then proceeded to argue his appeal. He took the grounds one by one. The first point taken by Mr Bab Williams was ground 11(a) of his grounds of appeal. It reads:

(a) The decision of the majority of the Appeal Commissioners, as regards the tax payable, was not, as required by law, definitive with respect to the 1971–72 assessment, namely YC 234A and YS 95A.

The said assessments were contained in Exhibits A and B. YC 234A was Exhibit A and YS 95A was Exhibit B. Exhibit B was an amendment to Exhibit A. Learned counsel contended that the finding of the Appeal Commissioners as contained in page 11 of the majority decision was inexact and contrary to section 57(9) of the Companies Income Tax Act 1961. The sub-section provides:

57(9) the Appeal Commissioners may confirm, reduce, increase or annul the assessment or make such order thereon as they see fit.

At page 11 of the majority decision the Appeal Commissioners stated as follows:

If section 33A is read as forming part of the whole companies Income Tax Act 1961 as amended, it would be obvious that the appellant must fail. I would take this opportunity to commend Mr Pearse for the appellant who ably argued the appellant's case before us. In the light of his argument I hope the respondent would take another look at section 33A and make whatever amendments may be deemed necessary, if only to remove any doubt as to the issue raised in this appeal.

However I would dismiss this Appeal for the reason which I have already given. I would confirm the assessment made by the respondent for 1971–72 year of assessment.

The court did not see any thing wrong or vague or 'not definitive', in this statement. By this decision they had confirmed the assessment for the year 1971–72. There was nothing novel in the observation made by the Appeal Commissioners. The Supreme Court made a similar observation in the famous case of the *African Continental Bank Ltd v Jammal Steel Structures Ltd* SC 322/73 page 77. At page 97 the Supreme Court observed as follows:

We would say at once that the Decree is inelegantly drafted in a number of provisions including sections 7 and 33, and that a pruning knife would improve it.

The judgement in *African Continental Bank Ltd v Jammal Steel Structures Ltd* was a decision of high authority. No one would find any fault with the judgement because of this observation which is hereby *obiter dictum*. The court did not see anything wrong with the judgement of the Appeal Commissioners based on this ground.

The next grounds argued by Mr Bab Williams were grounds 11(b) and (c). He took up ground 11(c) first which stated:

11.(c) That the said Body of Appeal Commissioners contradicted themselves in confirming the aforesaid assessment of 1971–72, having regard to their decision that the relevent assessment years and amounts assessable were as claimed by the appellants, as follows: –

1970–71	₦244 000.00
1971–72	₦379 398.00
	₦623 398.00

Instead of –

1971–72	₦600 030.00
1972–73	94 402.00
	₦694 432.00

The Appeal Commissioners in their majority judgement stated that the amount which the appellant ought to deduct under section 27 of the Companies Income Tax Act was ₦623 398.00 and not ₦694 532 as maintained by the respondent. The court did not see any contradiction here. They only stated the amount which in their view should be deducted under section 27. The years of assessment were different; hence the appellant's claim for the years 1970–71 and 1971–72. Mr F.A. Pearse testified in his evidence before the court as follows:

The point of conclusiveness of 1970–71 assessment which I argued before the Appeal Commissioners was not one of the grounds filed. The reason for the omission to file this particular ground was not wilful. It was inadvertent.

The court supposed this evidence was given in order to enable Mr Bab Williams to file and argue ground 11(c) stated above. Exhibit B was clearly stated as an amendment to Exhibit A which was the assessment for 1971–72. The court did not see any contradiction in the judgement of the Appeal Commissioners for that year of assessment. At page 14 of the record of proceedings Mr Pearse while giving evidence for the appellants said among other things as follows:

Here is the assessment and the letter of objection. We therefore submit that the respondent is wrong in law in re-opening an assessment which was final and conclusive in respect of an issue on the same facts previously known and determined. We therefore submit that the issue in 1970–71 is part of the whole of an amount of ₦23 398. If therefore a part, that is, in naira ₦244 000, has been determined as allowable, the remaining part of the whole, that is, ₦379 398 claimed in 1971–72 must be allowed. On the foregoing grounds our case must rest.

This evidence as far as the court was concerned answered Mr Bab Williams' argument in respect of ground 11(c).

Mr Pearse who appeared and gave evidence for appellants before the Appeal Commissioners by his testimony reproduced above had explained how the figures came about and the years of assessment to which each figure related. This ground of appeals therefore failed.

Mr Bab Williams contended that it was improper to re-open an assessment which had been closed. He referred to Exhibit C. The sum of ₦94 402.00 was originally claimed and allowed in Exhibit D but was later refused. On this issue of re-opening an assessment Dr Akintan referred the court to sections 50 and 60 of the Companies Income Tax Act, 1961. He relied mainly on section 50 which stipulates:

50(1) If the Board discovered or is of the opinion at any time that any company liable to tax has not been assessed or has been assessed at a less amount than that which ought to have been charged, the Board may, within the year of assessment or within six years after the expiration thereof and as often as may be necessary assess such company at such amount or additional amount, as ought to have been charged, and the provisions of this act as to notice of assessment, appeal and other proceedings shall apply to such assessment or additional assessment and to the Tax Charged thereunder.

Provided that where any form of fraud, wilful default or neglect has been committed by or on behalf of any taxable person in connection with any tax imposed under this Act or under the Income Tax Act, the Board may at any time and as often as may be necessary for the purpose of making good loss of tax attributable to the fraud, wilful default or neglect.

Dr Akintan contended that the various amounts allowed by the respondent were improperly described in the Exhibits and when the discovery was made the respondent had to disallow these sums of money. He referred to Exhibits D, E, F, and G. This contention, in the court's view, was valid. The court held that the respondent searched closely the Exhibits D to G and made some discoveries and properly in the court's view acted under section 50 of the Companies Income Tax Act, 1961. The case of *Parkin v Cattel (HM Inspector of Taxes)* 48 Tax cases 462 at pages 472 to 475 is appropriate. At page 474 of the Report Lord Denning, MR, put the matter very clearly in this way:

The word 'discover' simply means 'find out'. That is what Lord President Normand said in *Commissioners of Inland Revenue v Mackinlay's Trustee* 22 TC 305 (at page 312) with approval of Tucker, LJ, in *Commercial Structures Ltd v Briggs* (1948) 30 TC 477 (at page 492). An Inspector of Taxes discovers (that an Income has not been assessed when it ought to have been assessed), not only when he finds new facts out, *new facts* which were not known to him or his predecessor, but also when he finds out that he or his predecessor drew a wrong inference from the facts which were then known to him, and further, when he finds out that he or his predecessor got the law wrong and did not assess the Income when it ought to have been. That appears in *Cenlon Finance Co. Ltd v Ellwood (1962)* AC 182. I venture to quote what I said at page 799. 'Every Lawyer who, in his researches in the books, finds out that he was mistaken about the law, makes a discovery. So also does an Inspector of Taxes'.

The Appeal Commissioners were right in dismissing the appeal with regards to the 1972–73 assessment as it was not in fact argued before them. Before the court it was not argued with any conviction. This ground of appeal therefore failed. Having considered ground 11(b) of the grounds of appeal, the court thought it convenient to consider ground 11(g) below. It read:

(g) That the Appeal Commissioners were wrong in failing to consider the appellants' submission that section 60 of the Act precludes the respondents from re-opening the assessments which form the subject matter of this appeal.

Learned Counsel for the appellants argued grounds 5 and 6 of the grounds of appeal with ground 11(g). For these grounds Mr Bab Williams placed much reliance on section 60 of the Act which provides as follows:

60. Where no valid objection or appeal has been lodged within the time limited by section 53, 56 or 59 of this Act, as the case may be, against an assessment as regards the amount of the total profits assessed thereby, or where the amount of the total profits assessed thereby, or where the amount of the total profits has been determined on objection, revision under the proviso to subsection (3) of section 53 of this Act, or on appeal, as the case may be, shall be final and conclusive for all purposes of this Act as regards the amount of such total profits; and if the full amount of the tax in respect of any such final and conclusive assessment is not paid within the appropriate period or periods prescribed in this Act, the provisions thereof relating to the recovery of tax, and to any penalty thereof subject only to the set-off of the amount of tax repayable under any claim, made under any provision of this Act, which has been agreed to by the Board or determined on any appeal against a refusal to admit any such claim

Provided that:
    (a) where an assessment has become final and conclusive any tax over-paid shall be repaid;
    (b) Nothing in section 53 or in part XI of this Act shall prevent the Board from making any assessment or additional assessment for any year of assessment which does not involve re-opening any issue; on the same facts, which has been determined for that year of assessment under subsection (3) of section 53 of this Act by agreement or otherwise or on appeal.

In Exhibit D page 9 the appellants stated that the sum of ₦48 000.00 was reserved for damaged and lost Assets in the Eastern States. It was contended on behalf of the appellants that the respondent in Exhibit O accepted the account and computation submitted by the appellants for 1970–71 year of assessment. Exhibit P also supported the computation. It appeared to the court that Exhibit O was a reply to Exhibit V. It read:

(see over)

File IMC.301/70–71/34
Principal Inspector of Taxes
Federal Inland Revenue Department
Mainland District,
223 Herbert Macaulay Street,
PMB 2002,
Yaba

Dear Sir,

Incar (Nigeria) Limited
1968–69 to 1970–71 assessment

We were much impressed by the encouraging remarks contained in your letter of 27th March and are indeed thankful.

We now enclose schedules of Rent and Rates for 1968 and 1969 which are outstanding points as we promised to forward to you. The delay in sending these schedules is regretted and was due to the difficulty in obtaining the information from Kano and Kaduna.

Yours faithfully,

Exhibit O states:

File No. IMC.301/70–71/40   27 April 1971
Messrs Pannell Fitz Patrick, & Co,
Wesley House,
PO Box 2047,
Lagos.

Gentlemen,

Incar (Nigeria) Ltd
1970–71 assessment

I thank you for your letter dated 22 April 1971 and the enclosed schedules showing as requested, the details of Rent and Rates paid by your client for 1968 and 1969.

2 I am pleased to finalise the accounts which, together with your computation are agreed.

3 A nil assessment has been registered in favour of your client after discharging my best of judgement assessment of £40 000 tax payable.

4 Thank you for your co-operation.

Yours faithfully,
I.O. Adebekun
for Principal Inspector of Taxes, Mainland District (Yaba)

Exhibit P was a Tax Clearance Certificate for the tax years 1969–70 and 1970–71 issued to the appellants by the respondent.

The court did not see how Exhibits O, P and V related to the losses subtained by the appellants in the Eastern States during the civil war years. The Appeal Commissioners stated in their judgement that the last returns from Eastern States were received in June 1967. In accounts for the years ended 1971, 1968 and 1969, the assets and liabilities in respect of the Eastern States branches were shown as amounting to ₦244 000.00. They disallowd this figure as they said it was 'not based on certainties.' At page 3 of the judgement the Appeal Commissioners made a detailed analysis of the figures. The court did not see anything wrong with the figures, or how they arrived at them. The appellants had no complaint against this either. They only challenged the competence of the respondent to re-open an assessment which had been concluded in Exhibits O and P.

The court had reproduced above the contents of Exbibit O. It dealt with 'the details of Rent and Rates' paid by the appellants for 1968 and 1969. The last returns received from the Eastern States were in June 1967. Exhibits O and P could not therefore relate to the transction in the Eastern States which were the arrears whose accounts were in issue. The respondent contended that the figures disallowed by them were shown in Exhibit D pages 3, 6 and 9, the same amount of £48 000, that is, ₦69 000.00 was shown at page 9 of Exhibit E. Learned Counsel for the respondent, Dr Akintan, also referred to Exhibit F page 5 and Exhibit G page 5. He maintained these were improperly described and they discovered the error after writing Exhibits O and P. Dr Akintan submitted that the details of the losses sustained by the appellant company were not stated.

The court had already referred to section 60 of the Act. It was clear to the court that the respondent was competent to re-open the assessment in view of the wrong description which they discovered. See *Parkin v Cattel (HM Inspector of Taxes) supra*.

Mr Bab Williams, Learned Counsel for the appellant company, argued with considerable force that his clients based their claim on section 27 and not on section 33A of the Companies Income Tax Act, 1961. In the court's view, this appeared to be one of the main points of this appeal. At this juncture, it was pertinent to reproduce the two sections under consideration. Section 27 provides as follows:

Section 27 of the Companies Income Tax
Save where the provisions of subsections (2) or (3) of section 19, or section 21 apply, for the purpose of ascertaining the profits or loss of any company of any period from any sources chargeable with tax under this Act there shall be deducted all expenses incurred for that period by that company wholly exclusively necessarily and reasonably in the production of those profits including, but without otherwise expanding or limiting the generality of the foregoing –
(a) any sum payable by way of interest on any money borrowed and employed as capital in acquiring the profits;
(b) rent for that period, and premiums the liability for which was incurred during that period, in respect of land or buildings occupied for the purposes of acquiring the profits;
(c) any expense incurred for repair of premises, plant, machinery or fixtures employed in acquiring the profits, or for the renewal, repair or alteration of any implement, utensil or article so employed;

(d) bad debts incurred in the course of a trade or business proved to have become bad during the period for which the profits are being ascertained, and doubtful debts to the extent that they are respectively estimated to have become bad during the said period notwithstanding that such bad or doubtful debts were due and payable before the commencement of the period.

Provided that –

(i) where in any period a deduction under this paragraph is to be made as regards any particular debt, and a deduction has in any previous period been allowed either under the Income Tax Ordinance or this cap.85 of the Act in respect of the same debt, the appropriate reduction shall be made in the deduction to be made for the period in question;

(ii) all sums recovered during the said period on account of amounts previously written off or allowed either under the Income Tax Ordinance or this Act in respect of bad or doubtful debts shall for the purposes of cap.85 of this Act be deemed to be profits of the trade or business of that period;

(iii) it is proved to the satisfaction of the Board that the debts in respect of which a deduction is claimed either were included as a receipt of the trade or business in the profits of the year within which they were incurred or were advances not falling within the provisions of paragraph (a) of section 28 made in the course of normal trading or business operations;

(e) any contribution to a pension, provident or other retirement benefits fund, society or scheme approved by the Joint Tax Board under the powers conferred upon it by paragraph (f) of section 17 of the Income Tax Management Act, 1961, subject to the provisions of the Fourth Schedule to that Act and to any conditions imposed by that Board; and any contribution other than a penalty made under the provisions of any Act establishing a national provident fund or other retirement benefits scheme for employees throughout Nigeria;

(f) in the case of the Nigerian Railway Corporation such deductions as are allowed under the provisions of the Authorised Deduction (Nigerian Railway Corporation) Rules, 1959, which rules shall continue in force for all purposes of this Act;

(g) in the case of profits from a trade or business, any expense or part thereof –

(i) the liability for which was incurred during that period wholly, exclusively, necessarily and reasonably for the purposes of such trade or business and which is not specifically referable to any other period or periods; or

(ii) the liability for which was incurred during any previous period wholly, exclusively, necessarily and reasonably for the purposes of such trade or business and which is specifically referable to the period of which the profits are being ascertained which is not deductible under any other provision of this section;

(h) such other deduction as may be prescribed by the Minister under the rule.

Section 33A stipulates –

(1) Subject to the provisions of this section every company which had suffered a civil war damage in respect of its trade or business or any other operations carried on in Nigeria shall to the exclusion of the operation of section 31 and the Third Schedule to the Act, be granted relief from tax in the manner and to the extent provided hereunder, so however that, where a claim for such relief is made no deduction shall be made or allowed to that company as regards any assets damaged or destroyed during the civil war under section 31 and the schedule aforementioned;

(2) In respect of any such company, relief from tax under this section for any relevant year of assessment mentioned in subsection (3) of this section shall be granted upon the total profits assessed for that year and the amount of profits to be relieved of

tax shall be a sum which is equal to forty per cent of the total profits of the company for the year of assessment. Provided however that, in the case of any such company, the aggregate amount of profits to be relieved under this section for all relevant years of assessment shall not exceed a sum which is equal to the amount of the civil war damage suffered by that company.

(3) Relief from tax under this section shall be granted to a company only in the following cases and for the duration hereinafter specified, that is –

(a) if the amount of the civil war damage suffered by the company (whether a Nigerian company or not) is not less than the sum of £100 000, the relief shall be granted for the years of assessment 1970–71, 1971–72 and 1972–73;

(b) if the company is a Nigerian company and the amount of the civil war damage suffered by it is less than £100 000 but is not less than £10 000, the relief shall be granted for the years of assessment 1970–71 and 1971–72;

(c) if the company is not a Nigerian company and the amount of the civil war damage suffered by it is less than £100 000 but is not less than £50 000, the relief shall be granted for the years of assessment 1970–71 and 1971–72.

(4) Notwithstanding anything in subsection (3) above, relief under this section shall be granted in the case of a company other than a Nigerian company if, but only if, the accounts of that company for any relevant period or periods are made up separately and are completely isolated from the accounts of any other company which has control over the first mentioned company and in this subsection 'relevant period or periods' means the period or periods which under Part V of this Act are to be taken as the basis period or periods in ascertaining the amount of the profit or loss of the company for any relevant year of assessment.

(5) A claim by a company for relief from tax under this section shall be made by it in writing to the most senior officer in the Industrial Inspectorate Division of the Federal Ministry of Industries (hereinafter in this section referred to as 'the Director') not later than six months after the end of the year of assessment to which the claim relates; and a copy of the claim shall forthwith be delivered to the Board by the company.

(6) Where a claim has been made under the provisions of subsection (5) of this section, then –

(a) if the Director is satisfied that the total amount of the claim should be allowed in accordance with the provisions of this section, he may admit the claim and give notice of the admission to the Board;

(b) if the Director is not satisfied with the full amount of the claim, he shall determine the claim in such amount as he thinks fit and shall give the Board notice of the amount so admitted, and of the amount which is refused;

(c) if the Director is not satisfied that the claimant is entitled to make the claim, he shall give notice to that effect to the Board.

(7) Where a notice of admission of a claim or part thereof, or of refusal of a claim, is given to the Board under section (6) of this section, the Board shall cause to be served on the claimant a notice of refusal to admit the full amount of the claim (specifying the amount which is admitted, or a notice of refusal of the claim, as the case may be.

(8) Where a notice of refusal to admit a claim or to admit the full amount of a claim is given to a claimant under subsection (7) of this section, the provisions of Part XI of this Act shall apply accordingly with any necessary modifications as if the notice were a notice of assessment.

(9) The provisions of subsection (5)(c) of section 31 of this Act shall apply in relation to a claim under this section as it is applied in relation to a claim under the said section 31, with any necessary modifications.

(10) In this section –

'civil war damage' means any damage or destruction caused by any military or other operations connected with the civil war in Nigeria;

'civil war in Nigeria' means the civil war in which Nigeria was engaged and which ended on 15 January 1970;

'1970–71' indicates the year of assessment beginning on 1 April 1970 and ending 31 March 1971; and '1971–72' and '1972–73' shall be construed accordingly.

Learned counsel stressed that the two sections were not incompatible. Section 27, he argued, covers all Revenue losses whilst section 33A covers only capital losses for tax relief at 40 per cent for future profits. According to Learned Counsel section 33A does not apply to all civil war damages. There are qualifications to the applicability of section 33A to civil war damages.

Mr Bab Williams strongly submitted that what his clients, the appellants, sustained were Revenue losses and they were covered by section 27. The cost of acquiring stock-in-trade, he maintained, is an expense legally deductible under section 27. Section 33A concerns only capital assets.

On this point Dr Akintan, learned counsel, submitted that the losses suffered by the appellants were not in production of profit and were therefore not covered by section 27 under which the appellants based their claim. Section 27 deals with expenses not with losses. The procedure laid down by section 33A must be complied with. He further contended that without the introduction of section 33A the claim by the appellant company would have come under section 31 of the Companies Income Tax Act, 1961, and not under section 27.

In as much as the court disagreed with the Appeal Commissioners that sections 27 and 31 were amended by section 33A, it was of the view that these sections were for different purposes. Section 27 covers expenses in business for profits. The court talked of 'all expenses incurred for that period by that company wholly, exclusively, necessarily and reasonably in production of those profits'. Section 31 deals with total profits from all sources whilst section 33A provides for losses suffered during the period of the Nigerian Civil War.

Mr Bab Williams strongly contended that what his client lost were revenue losses and therefore covered by section 27 of the decree. Dr Akintan, on the other hand, submitted with equal force that what the appellant company sustained were capital losses and therefore should be claimed under section 33A.

This appeal depended on whether the loss suffered by the appellant company could be described as a revenue expenditure or capital expenditure. The answer to this is not always an easy one. In the case of *Heather (Inspector of Taxes) v PE Consulting Group Ltd* (1973) 1 All ER 8, Lord Denning, MR, at page 12 quoted the *dictum* of Viscount Cave, LC, with approval as a solution or rather a guideline. It reads:

... when an expenditure is made, not only once and for all but with a view to bringing into existence an asset or an advantage for the enduring benefit of a trade, I think that there is very good reason (in the absence of special circumstance leading to an opposite conclusion) for treating such an expenditure as properly attributable not to revenue but to capital.

(*See British Insulated and Helsby Cables Ltd v Atherton (Inspector of Taxes)* 1926) A C. at pages 213 and 214. Mr Bab Williams, in his argument, submitted quite rightly that section 27 covers revenue losses and section 33A covers only capital losses. The appellant company, in the court's view, sustained capital losses during the period now in question. Their claim should be under section 33A not under section 27.

Section 27 clearly provides for deduction of all 'expenses incurred for that period by that company wholly, exclusively, necessarily and reasonably in the production of those profits ...' (See *Woodcock v Inland Revenue Commissioners, Times Law Report*, 22 June 1977.) Section 33A, on the other hand, deals with 'civil war damage' suffered by every company in respect of its trade or business or any other operations carried on in Nigeria. There are many other conditions to be satisfied before any company can claim under this section. Sub-sections (5) to (9) of section 33A show the procedure to be followed before any claim for relief is presented to the Board of Inland Revenue. The reasons for procedural safeguards are obvious. They are meant to enable the Director in the Industrial Inspectorate Division of the Federal Ministry of Industries to investigate claims made under this section and report his finding with recommendations to the Board. The appellant company had deliberately decided not to apply under this section but rather under section 27 which in the court's judgement did not apply to them in the instant case.

The court had carefully considered all the points and legal authorities cited by both counsel. The court was disposed to think that Dr Akintan, Learned Counsel for the respondent, is right in his contention that the appellant company claim should be brought under section 33A of the Companies Income Tax Act, 1961 (*supra*). For this and other reasons given above the court would dismiss this appeal. The judgement of the Appeal Commissioner is hereby confirmed.

(xiii) Objections, appeals, offences and penalties

Revision of assessment in case of objection

Section 50 of the Companies Income Tax Act 1979 states that an aggrieved taxpayer may object to a tax assessment in writing, stating the grounds of objection within fifteen days from the date of the service of the notice of assessment.

Establishment of Appeal Commissioners

Section 52 of the Companies Income Tax Act, 1979, empowers the Federal Minister of Finance to establish by notice in the *Gazette* a body of Appeal Commissioners consisting of not more than twelve persons, none of whom shall be a public officer. Each Appeal Commissioner holds office for a period of three years. Any three of them shall form a quorum.

Appeals to Appeal Commissioners

Where notice of refusal to amend is served by the Board under s.50, a taxpayer may appeal against the assessment to the Secretary to the Appeal Commissioners within fifteen days after the date of service upon such company a notice of the refusal of the Board to amend the assessment. Such a notice must specify the following particulars:

    (a) official number of the assessment and the year of assessment.

    (b) amount of tax charged by the assessment.

    (c) the amount of the total profits upon which the tax was charged.

    (d) date of Notice of Refusal to amend.

    (e) grounds of appeal which must be limited to the grounds stated by the appellant in the former notice of objection.

Where the tax chargeable in accordance with the decision of the Appeal Commissioners does not exceed ₦400, no further appeal is allowed except with the consent of the Board. An award or judgement of the Appeal Commissioners is enforceable as if it were a judgement of the Federal High Court.

Either the Board or the taxpayer can appeal against the decision of the Appeal Commissioners to the Federal High Court[172] on a point of law by giving notice in writing to the Secretary to the Appeal Commissioners within fifteen days after the date on which the decision was given upon the receipt of a notice; the Secretary to the Appeal Commissioners shall send all records of proceedings to the Chief Registrar of the Federal High Court.

Appeal from the Federal High Court goes to the Federal Court of Appeal where the tax determined by the Federal High Court exceeds ₦1000.

(xiv) Time within which tax is payable

Section 58 deals with the position. Every company shall, not later than three months after the end of each year of assessment, pay in a lump sum or not more than six monthly instalments, provisional tax of an amount equal to the tax paid by such company in the immediately preceding year.

Tax raised in an assessment which is not disputed shall be paid within two months after service of such advice upon the company. The Board may, in its discretion, extend the time within which payment is to be made.

Imposition of penalty

Section 60 of the CITA 1979 empowers the Board to impose 10% penalty for tax unpaid on its due date. If payment is not made within a month, payment may be enforced. The Board, in its discretion, can remit the whole or part of the penalty.

Power to distrain for non-payment of tax

Section 61 of the 1979 Act gives the Board power to distrain the taxpayer by his goods, chattels, or other securities, distrain upon any land, premises or place in respect of which the taxpayer is the owner for the purpose of recovering the amount of tax due.

Artificial transaction

Section 18 of the Companies Income Tax Act, 1979, states that where a tax authority is of opinion that any disposition is not in fact given effect to or that any transaction which reduces or would reduce the amount of any tax payable is artificial or fictitious, the authority may disregard such disposition or direct that such adjustments shall be made in respect of the income of an individual or an executor, or a trustee, as the authority considers appropriate so as to counteract the reduction of liability to tax affected, or reduction which would otherwise be affected by the transaction.

Where it appears that the interests of more than one tax authority are affected thereby, the exercise of any power conferred on a tax authority by subsection (1) shall be performed by the Joint Tax Board

Offences and penalties under s.66–69 of the Companies

Income Tax Act, 1979

Nature of offence	Penalties
1 Offence against any of the provisions of the law	₦1200 fine: s.66(1)
2 Failure to keep records or furnish statement	₦200 fine and ₦40 for each and every day during which failure occurs and in default of payment, 6 months' imprisonment: s.66(1)
3 Failure to comply with the requirements of a notice served or failure to answer questions by law fully put	₦200 fine: s.66(2)
4 Failure to file audited accounts and returns within 6 months after the end of the company's accounting year (s.40)	₦5000 fine (s.40); penalty of tax charged in the preceding year: s.66(4)
5 Failure to answer the Board's call for further returns (s.41)	Penalty of tax charged in the preceding year.
6 Making of incorrect returns, omitting or understating profits	₦200 fine and double the amount of tax which has been undercharged (s.67(1)). The complaint must be made within six years of the date the offence was committed.
7 Aiding, abetting, assisting, counselling, inciting or inducing others to deliver false returns or keep false accounts, preparation of false accounts, refusal or neglect to pay tax.	₦1000 fine or 5 years' imprisonment or both: s.68.
8 Corruption by Federal tax officials, demanding more tax than due, incorrect return of tax collected.	₦600 or 3 years' imprisonment or both: s.69.

Note: The Board may compound any offence and no prosecution may be commenced except at the instance of or with the sanction of the Board (s.71).

alone and any decision or direction of the Board under this section shall be binding on all tax authorities.

For the purpose of section 18,

  (i) 'disposition' includes any trust, grant, covenant, agreement or arrangement;

  (ii) transactions between persons one of whom either has control over the other or, in the case of individuals, who are related to each other or between persons both of whom are controlled by some other person, shall be deemed to be artificial or fictitious if in the opinion of the tax authority those transactions have not been made by independent persons engaged in the same or similar activities dealing with one another at arm's length.

Appointment of agent

Under s.37 of the Companies Income Tax Act, 1979, the Board may by notice in writing appoint any person to be the agent of any company for the purpose of preparing tax and the person so appointed is indemnified against any person for tax payments made. Section 39 of the 1979 Act empowers a liquidator, when a company is wound up, to pay any tax due before distributing assets to any of the shareholders.

In *ACM of Nigeria Ltd v Federal Board of Inland Revenue* (APP/ CCMM/204 of 15 May 1974), the appellant appealed on the grounds that the year of assessment was incorrectly stated, that the respondent was wrong in assessing gross receipt to tax without making proper deduction for expenses incurred in earning the gross receipt, and finally that it was improper to appoint the appellant as agent.

The appeal was allowed. The Appeal Commissioners found that the power of the respondent to tax the profits of a foreign company is not absolute. It is limited to such profits as are attributable to the operation of the company within Nigeria only. The appellant can be appointed an agent where there is evidence that there are moneys in the hands of the appellant due to the company whose agent the appellant has been declared to be.

Refer also to Supplement (1985).

Notes

1 *House of Representatives Debates*, 2 April 1961, Federal Government Printer, Lagos, 1961.
2 *Federal Republic of Nigeria Gazette*, 6 December 1966.
3 A point also worth mentioning is that from the inception of the tax a sizeable

proportion of taxable profit was assessed in the UK by agents of the Nigerian Government. In fact as late as 1960–61 about 50 per cent of taxable profits were assessed in the UK. The ratio has declined rapidly since then, so that since 1964–65 all taxable profits have been assessed in Nigeria, thus reducing administrative costs.

4 The Federal Board of Inland Revenue is now authorised to post assessment notices to the last-known address of a company, or by advertising in a single issue of the *Federal Gazette* where personal service has proved difficult or impossible. Any person found guilty of obstructing, or of using violence against an officer of the Board in the performance of his duties is to be heavily penalised.

5 Section 76 of the Constitution of the Federal Republic of Nigeria, Lagos, 1963.

6 In May 1967 the four Regions of Nigeria were replaced with twelve States. The constitutional position of Companies Income Tax, however, remains unchanged. Although the former Federal structure is assumed throughout this book, many of the conclusions reached can apply to the new Federal set-up.

7 See O. Teriba: 'Nigerian Revenue Allocation Experience 1952–65, in *Nigerian Journal of Economic and Social Studies*, November 1966; and B.J. Dudley: 'Federalism and the Balance of Political Power in Nigeria', *Journal of Commonwealth Political Studies*, March 1966.

8 In the alternative, increases in the State shares of other federally-raised revenue may be considered.

9 Suit No FRC/L/15/1973 of 11 Feb, 1974, before S.O. Lambo, J., in the Federal Revenue Court, Lagos. Similarly the business of selling hymn books has been held to be a trade although the profits were distributed among widows and orphans of ministers and missionaries: *Trustees of Psalms and Hymns v Whitwell* (1890) 3 TC 7; so was that of a restaurant whose proceeds supported an institution for social and religious improvement: *Grove v Young Men's Christian Association* (1903) 4 TC 613 and that of a hospital which let rooms for entertainments and meetings: *Coman v Rotunda Hospital, Dublin* (1921) 1 AC 1. A society for Advancement of Agriculture was held to be trading by an annual show: *Royal Agricultural Society v Wilson* (1924) 9 TC 62. This decision has been followed by the enactment of a specific exemption – see ITA 1952 s.452.

10 APP/COMM/146 of 11.5.72.

11 Schedule 3, Companies Income Tax Act, 1979. See C.S. Ola's 'A Nigerian decision on interest paid to a foreign investor' in the *British Tax Review* No. 6, 1971 published by Sweet and Maxwell, London.

12 (1900) AC.

13 WACA, 25 May 1948.

14 (1935) 19 TC 390.

15 (1956) AC 14; 36 TC. 207; see particularly Lord Simonds (1956) AC 14, at p.30, and 36 TC 207, at p.224, and Lord Radcliffe at p.36 (AC) and at p.229 (TC).

16 See Lord Reid's dictum 'The question is not whether the Commissioners were wrong but whether their decision was unreasonable,' in his dissenting speech in *Griffiths v J.P. Harrison (Watford) Ltd* (1982) 2 WLR 909 at p.916.

17 *Edwards v Bairstow & Harrison, supra,* is a good example.

18 *Cooksey & Bibby v Rednall* and *Harvey v Caulcott,* (1949) 30 TC 514 (farm purchased in 1924 and sold in 1938 at a profit, having been let meanwhile; held, no evidence to support a finding of trading); *Harvey v Caulcott* (1952) 33 TC 159.

19 (1968) 1 All NLR 263.

20 (1966) LLR 195.

312

21　See *Murray v Commissioner of Inland Revenue* (1923) 32 TC 238; *Kelsall-Parsons & Co. v Commissioner of Inland Revenue* 21 TC 608 and *Commissioner of Inland Revenue v Fleming & Co. (Machinery) Ltd* (1951) 33 TC 57.

22　*Aderawo's Timber Trading Co. Ltd v FBIR* (1966) LLR 195 at p. 206.

23　SC 398/1967, of 13 June 1969, unreported.

24　*Jennings v Middlesborough Corporation* (1953) 34TC, 447 and *IRC v Incorporated Council of Law Reporting* (1888) 22 QBD, 279.

25　e.g. a commercial method of trading is a proof of trading.

26　Cmd 9474 (1954).

27　*Rutledge v CIR* (1929) 14 TC 490.

28　*IRC v Fraser* (1942) 24 TC 498 (finding of no trading by Commissioners reversed on appeal).

29　*Cape Brandy Syndicate v IRC* (1921) 2 KB 403; 12 TC 358 (here the brandy was blended before resale).

30　*Martin v Lowry* (1927) AC 312; 11 TC 297.

31　*T. Beynor & Co. Ltd v Ogg* (1918) 7 TC 125.

32　*IRC v Livingston* (1926) 11 TC 538.

33　Cmd 9474, para. 116.

34　11 TC 538.

35　*Martin v Lowry* (1927) AC 312; 11 TC 297.

36　See *IRC v Toll Property Co. Ltd* (1952) 34 TC 13, as distinguished in *IRC v Reinhold* (1953) 34 TC 389. Another ground of distinction was the form of the Memorandum of Association. There is, however, one significant difference between an individual and a company in that the latter's objects have to be stated in its memorandum of association; if those objects clearly include the acquisition of a particular type of property for the purpose of resale at a profit, this is an indication that it acquired that property by way of trade. If, however, the objects of a company are primarily to acquire and hold property as an investment, changes or realisation of investments will not necessarily constitute trading. *(Scottish Investment Trust Co. v Forbes* (1893) 3 TC 231; *California Copper Syndicate v Harris* (1904) 5 TC 159; (cf. *Tebrau (Johore) Rubber Syndicate Ltd v Farmer* (1910) 5 TC 658). *Balgownie Land Trust Ltd v IRC* (1929) 14 TC 684; (cf. *IRC v Hyndland Investment Co. Ltd)*; *IRC v The Korean Syndicate* (1921) 3 KB 258; 12 TC 181; *St Aubyn Estates Ltd v Strick* (1932) 17 TC 412; *IRC v Toll Property Co. Ltd* (1952) 34 TC 13; *Granville Building Co. Ltd v Oxby* (1954) 35 TC 245; *IRC v Highams (Saftex) Ltd* (1956) 37 TC 39; *Griffiths v J.P. Harrison (Watford) Ltd* (1962) 2 WLR 909). *IRC v Hyndland Investment Co. Ltd* (1929) 14 TC 694; *Dunn Trust Ltd v Williams* (1950) 31 TC 477. There is an intermediate type of case when a Company which trades in some other way (e.g. shipping) buys land and the problem is whether it is also trading in land; see *Cayzer, Irvine & Co. Ltd v IRC* (1942) 24 TC 491).

37　*Jenkison v Freedland* (1961) 39 TC 636. It appears that if he had sold the stills to an outside buyer the Court of Appeal would have held that he was trading (per Lord Evershed at p.643); the real object of the transaction was to obtain larger capital allowances than if the companies had originally purchased the stills and the Court of Appeal did not regard this fiscal motive as an element in trading (per Harman L.J. at p.646). On the last point, see now the House of Lords decision in *Griffiths v J.P. Harrison (Watford), Ltd* 1962 2 WLR 909.

38　See s.1–424. Another type of case where trading may be excluded is when a trader buys some asset with a view to using it as capital in his trade and then changes his mind and sells it; see *McLellan Rawson & Co. Ltd v Newall* (1955) 36 TC 117.

39   See *Pickford v Quirke* (1927) 13 TC 251, *supra*.

40   *Rellim Ltd v Vise* (1951) 32 TC 254; see also *Hudson v Wrightson* (1934) 26 TC 55; *Foulds v Clayton* (1953) 34 TC 382; *Emro Investments Ltd v Aller* (1954) 35 TC 305; *Mitchell Bros v Tomlinson* (1957) 37 TC 224.

41   *Smith Barry v Cordy* (1946) 28 TC 250.

42   *West v Phillips* (1958) 38 TC

43   See ss.1–414.

44   Per Lord Buckmaster in *J. & R. O'Kane & Co. v IRC* (1922) 12 TC 303, at p.347.

45   See ss.1–423. For a case where the court held that a series of operations involving a large number of companies formed for the purpose were completely artificial and not trading, see *Johnson v Jewitt* (1961) TR 321. This case should be compared with *Griffiths v J.P. Harrison (Watford) Ltd* (1962) 2 WLR 909, where the transactions were held to be trading although the object was to make a profit by dividend stripping. See ss.1–1333.

46   See *Griffiths v J.P. Harrison (Watford) Ltd* (1962) 2 WLR 909, at pp.912, 929.

47   *Reynolds' Executors v Bennett* (1943) 25 TC 401; cf. *IRC v Reinhold* (1953) 34 TC 389 (where one house was bought and sold three years later, having been expressly purchased with a view to resale; held, no trading).

48   *Gray & Gillitt v Tiley* (1944) 26 TC 80; *Cooke v Haddock* (1960) 39 TC 64; cf. *Williams v Davies* (1945) 26 TC 371 (where the land purchased was given by the purchasers to their wives who then resold at a profit; finding of no trading affirmed) and *Dunn Trust Ltd. v Williams* (1950) 31 TC 477 (where shares were purchased and resold four years later but special reasons were given for the sale; finding of trading reversed). The decision in *Sharkey v Wernher* (1956) AC 58; 36 TC 275, considered in ss.1–583, throws doubt on *Williams v Davies (supra)*.

49   *Macmahon and Macmahon v IRC* (1951) 32 TC 311. See also *Sharpless v Rees* (1940) 23 TC 361.

50   *Pickford v Quirke*, 13 TC 251.

51   cf. D. Walker: 'Fiscal measures to promote foreign investment' in E.F. Jackson (ed.): *Economic Development in Africa*, Blackwell, Oxford, 1965, pp.223–4.

52   Section 20, Companies Income Tax Act, 1979.

53   Before the Income Tax (Amendment) Act, December 1966, the extent of administrative discretion was even wider because the law did not provide that the expenses should be 'necessary', in other words unavoidable for carrying on the activities of the company. Therefore, to the extent that expenses which were not necessary or inevitable were allowed as deductible, to that extent the government had been subsidising such expenses to the tune of the tax which otherwise would have been payable. Apart from the fact that such hidden subsidies may be quite unjustifiable economically, some inequity inevitably arises when similar expenditures are treated differently for deduction purposes. The Act has now rectified the situation by providing that deductible expenses should also be 'necessary'.

54   *Van den Berghs v Clark* (1935) AC 431; 19 TC 390 (sum received for cancellation of pooling agreement on which the business was based not included in taxable profit); *Sabine Lookers* (1958) 38 TC 120 (sum received for variation of basic agreement of motor dealers treated similarly). See also *IRC v Coia* (1959) 38 TC 334; *McLaren v Needham* (1960) 39 TC 37 and *Walter W. Saunders Ltd v Dixon* (1962) TR 99.

55   *Hudson's Bay Co. Ltd v Stevens* (1909) 5 TC 434.

56   See Lord Haldane's observations cited below and Romer L.J.'s observations in *Golden Horse Shoe (New) Ltd v Thurgood* (1933) 18 TC 280, at pp.300, 301, which are often cited on this topic; for the distinction in Company law see

Ammonia Soda Co. v Chamberlain (1918) 1 Ch. 266. But cf. Lord Macmillan's comment in *Van den Berghs v Clark, supra,* at pp.433 (AC) and Lord Reid's comments.

57   In *John Smith & Son v Moore* (1921) 2 AC 13, at pp.19, 20; 12 TC 266, at p.282.

58   33 TC 15 at p.42.

59   *IRC v E.C. Warnes & Co. Ltd* (1919) 2 KB 444; 12 TC 227.

60   *Mann v Nash* (1932) 1 KB 752; 16 TC 523; see also *Southern v A.B. Ltd* (1933) 1 KB 713; 18 TC 59 at p.73.

61   *Lindsay and others v IRC* (1932) SC 33; 18 TC 43 at p.56.

62   (1886) 18 QBD 276; 2 TC 179 at p.181.

63   (1927) AC 193, p.198.

64   Suit No FRC/L/1A/76 Before A.G. Karibi – Whyte Federal Revenue Court Lagos on 15 July 1977.

65   *Seaham Harbour Dock Co. v Crook* (1931) 16 TC 333.

66   *Ostime v Pontypridd & Rhondda Joint Water Board* (1946) AC 477; 28 TC 261; the effect of this decision as regards joint authorities is now reversed by ITA, 1952, s.454.

67   *Higgs (Clyde) v Wrightson* (1944) 26 TC 73. See also *Charles Brown & Co v IRC* (1930) 12 TC 1256 (subsidy to millers in wartime calculated by 'standard profit'; finding that it was paid to make good a deficiency of profits, and so a trading receipt, affirmed).

68   *Smart v Lincolnshire Sugar Co. Ltd* (1937) 20 TC 645. See also *Severne v Dadswell* (1954) 35 TC 649.

69   *British Commonwealth International Newsfilm Agency v Mahany (1962) 1 WLR 560.*

70   *Pretoria-Pietersbury Ry Co. Ltd v Elwood* (1908) 6 TC 508. See also *Laird v IRC* (1929) 14 TC 395 (US soldier resident in England who received compensation from US government for war injuries paid on a monthly basis; finding that payments were income under Case V, reversed).

71   *Watson v Samson Bros* (1959) 38 TC 346.

72   *British Dyestuffs Corporation (Blackley) Ltd v IRC* (1924) 12 TC 586. See also *Harry Ferguson (Motors) Ltd v IRC* (1951) 33 TC 15 (Payments made to a trading Company by its managing director in return for assistance in developing his patents; finding that these were payments received in a commercial enterprise for joint exploitation of the patents and so were trading receipts, affirmed); *(Boyce v Whitwick Colliery Co.* (1934) 18 TC 655 (payments made to a colliery company by the local UDC towards the cost of erecting waterworks held to be capital receipts, whilst payments for water under the same agreement were trading receipts).

73   *Handley Page v Butterworth* (1935) 19 TC 328; see particularly the judgement of Romer, LJ, at p.359. The House of Lords upheld the Court of Appeal on a different point and their judgements did not deal with this aspect.

74   *IRC v Rolls-Royce Ltd* (1962) 1 WLR 425; see also *Musker v English Electric Co. Ltd* (1962) TR 199.

75   (1957) 37 TC 540.

76   See the Australian case Re *Meeks, Taxation Commissioners v Meeks* (1915) 19 CLR 568, at page 580. In an Irish case, *O'Dwyer v Irish Exporters and Importers Ltd* (1943) IR 176, compensation was paid to a parent company for the cancellation of a favourable contract held by its subsidiary and as the parent company was not engaged in the trade of promoting companies, the payment was held not to be a trading receipt.

77   *Short Bros Ltd v IRC* (1927) 12 TC 955.

78 *IRC v Northfleet Coal & Ballast Co. Ltd* (1927) 12 TC 1102.

79 *Van den Berghs Ltd v Clark* (1935) AC 431; 19 TC 390;

80 *Chibbett v Joseph Robinson & Sons Ltd* (1924) 9 TC 48, at p.61; following *Cowan v Seymour* (1919) 7 TC 372.

81 See *Hunter v Dewhurst* (1932) 16 TC 605, at p.653 (another employment case) and *Bush, Beach & Gent, Ltd v Road* (1939) 22 TC 519, at p.524.

82 See also *Barr Crombie & Co. Ltd v IRC* (1945) 26 TC 406 (compensation paid to ship managers, who only managed the ships of one shipping company, when that company went into liquidation; finding that this was a trading receipt, reversed). In this case the compensation was payable under a clause in the original contract for management and the distinction in the employment cases between sums paid under a contract of service and sums paid for cancellation of the contract.

83 *Kelsall, Parsons & Co. v IRC* (1938) 21 TC 608 (£1500 paid for termination, a year early, of one agency agreement out of several; finding that this was a trading receipt, affirmed).

84 Per Lord Rusell in *IRC v Fleming & Co. (Machinery) Ltd* (1951) 33 TC 57, at p.63; cited by Birkett, LJ in *Wiseburgh v Domville* (1956) 36 TC 527, at p.541.

85 *Higgs v Olivier* (1951) 33 TC 136.

86 *Thompson v Magnesium Elektron Ltd* (1943) 26 TC 1.

87 *Evans v Wheatley* (1958) 38 TC 216.

88 *IRC v Coia* (1959) 38 TC 334; *McLaren v Needham* (1960) 39 TC 37; *Walter W. Saunders Ltd v Dixon* (1962) TR 99 for the converse problem in relation to the oil company's trade.

89 *Margerison v Tyresoles Ltd* (1942) 25 TC 59.

90 *Bitish Dyestuffs Corporation (Blackley) Ltd v IRC* (1924) 12 TC 586, at p.596; approved as the test in the House of Lords in *Evans Medical Supplies v Moriarty* (1957) 37 TC 540, at pp.579, 584, and in *IRC v Rolls-Royce Ltd* (1962) 1 WLR 425, at p.428. For these cases see also *Crole v Lloyd* (1950) 31 TC 338.

91 *West v Phillips* (1958) 38 TC 203; *Seaward Brothers v Varty* (1962) TR 65; *J. & C. Oliver v Farnsworth* (1956) 71 TC 51.

92 *Doughty v Commissioner of Taxes* (1927) AC 327 (PC).

93 *Jones v IRC* (1919) 7 TC 310.

94 *Orchard Wine and Supply v Loynes* (1952) 33 TC 97.

95 *Lamport & Holt Line v Langwell* (1958) 38 TC 193. See also *IRC v 36/49 Holdings Ltd* (1943) 25 TC 173.

96 *United Steel Companies Ltd v Cullington* (No. 1) (1939) 23 TC 71.

97 *Morley v Messrs Tattersall* (1938) 159 LT 197; 22 TC 51.

98 *Jays the Jewellers Ltd v IRC* (1947) 2 All ER 762.

99 An English Act.

100 (1937) 3 All ER 468; 21 TC 252.

101 See *Green v Glisbten & Son Ltd* (1929) AC 381; 14 TC 364; a timber company insured its premises for £477 838, the current value of the property when the book value was £160 824. On the occurrence of a fire, the insurance company paid £477 838 and it was held that the whole sum received was taxable trading receipt.

102 *Williams v IRC* (1943) 1 All ER 318.

103 *Crabb v Blue Star Line Ltd* (1961) 39 TC 482.

104 *Landes Brothers v Simpson* (1934) 19 TC 62.

105 *McKinlay v H.T. Jenkins & Son Ltd* (1926) 10 TC 372.

106 *Davies v The Shell Company of China Ltd* (1951) 32 TC 133.

316

107   *Scottish Union & National Insurance Co. v Smiles; Northern Assurance v Russell* (1889) 2 TC 551.

108   *Westminster Bank Ltd. v Osler* (1933) AC 139; 17 TC 381, *Frasers (Glasgow) Bank Ltd v IRC* (1962) TR 165.

109   *Royal Insurance Co. v Stephen* (1928) 14 TC 22; *Thompson v Trust & War Loan Company of Canada* (1932) 1 KB 517; 16 TC 394.

110   *IRC v Imperial Tobacco Co. Ltd* (1940) 2 KB 287; 29 TC 1.

111   *Beach v Reed Corrugated Cases Ltd* (1956) 1 WLR 807; *Phipps v Orthodox Unit Trusts* (1958) 1 QB 314; *Barber v Manchester Regional Hospital Board* (1958) 1 WLR 181; *Shindler v Northern Raincoat Co.* (1960) 1 WLR 1038.

112   See *Re Houghton Main Colliery Ltd* (1956) 1 WLR 1219.

113   *See Higgs v Olivier* (1951) 33 TC 136.

114   See *Riches v Westminster Bank Ltd* (1947) AC 390.

115   Per Lord Clyde, LP, in *Renfrew Town Council v IRC* (1934) 19 TC 13 at p.19; Lord Clyde based that *dictum* on *Burmah SS Co. v IRC* (1930) 16 TC 67.

116   *Higgs v Olivier* (1951) 33 TC 136.

117   See *IRC v Barnato* (1936) 20 TC 455.

118   Per Jenkins, LJ, in *Morgan v Tate & Lyle Ltd* (1954) 35 TC 367, at p.393, approved by Lord Morton at p.407.

119   *Brown v Bullock* (1961) 1 WLR 1095 10 TC 118.

120   *Ricketts v Colquhoun* (1962) AC 1

121   *Strong & Co. v Woodifield* (1906) AC 448; 5 TC 215.

122   See *Incorporated Council of Law Reporting v Smith* (1914) 3 KB 674; 6 TC 477.

123   *IRC v E.C. Warnes & Co. Ltd* (1919) 2 KB 444; 12 TC 22.

124   *Spofforth & Prince v Colder* (1945) 26 TC 310.

125   *Fairrie v Hall* (1947) 28 TC 200.

126   *Rushden Heel Co. Ltd v Keene* (1948) 30 TC 298.

127   *Archibald Thomson Ltd v Batty* (1919) 7 TC 158.

128   *IRC v Dowdall, O'Mahoney & Co. Ltd*

129   *Hagart & Burn-Murdoch v IRC* (1929) AC 21; 14 TC 433.

130   *Union Cold Storage Co. Ltd v Jones* (1924) 8 TC 725.

131   *Newsom v Robertson* (1952) 33 TC 452.

132   *Bentleys, Stokes & Lowless v Beeson* (1952) 33 TC 491.

133   *Golder v. Great Boulder Proprietary Gold Mines Ltd* (1952) 33 TC 75.

134   *Reid's Brewery Co. Ltd v Male* (1891) 2 QB 1; 3 TC 279.

135   *Smith v Lion Brewery Ltd* (1911) AC 150; 5 TC 568; *Usher's Wiltshire Brewery Co. Ltd v Bruce* (1915) AC 433; 6 TC 399.

136   *Roebank Printing Co. Ltd v IRC* (1928) 13 TC 864; *Curtis v J. & G. Oldfield* (1925) 9 TC 319.

137   *Copeman v William Flood & Sons Ltd* (1941) 1 KB 202; 24 TC 53; *Dracup v Dakin* (1957) 37 TC 377.

138   *Johnson Brothers & Co. v IRC* (1919) 2 KB 717; 12 TC 147.

139   *Weston v Hearn* (1943) 2 All ER 421; 25 TC 425.

140   (1927) AC 554; 11 TC 625.

141   Per Scrutton J. in *Smith v Incorporated Council of Law Reporting* (1914) 3 KB 674.

142   *Boarland v Kramat Pulai, Ltd* (1953) 35 TC 1.

143   *Morgan v Tate & Lyle, Ltd* (1955) AC 21; 35 TC 367; where *Ward & Co. v Commissioner of Taxes* (1923) AC 145.

144   *Union Cold Storage Co. Ltd v Adamson* (1931) 16 TC 293. *IRC v Falkirk Iron Co. Ltd* (1933) 17 TC 625; *Hyett v Lennard* (1940) 2 KB 180; 23 TC 346.

145 *Heastie v Veitch* (1934) 1 KB 535; 18 TC 305.

146 *Allied Newspapers Ltd v Hindsley* (1937) 21 TC 422.

147 *Per* Ltd Herschell in *Russell v Town and County Bank* (1888) 13.

148 (1932) 17 TC 93.

149 See the judgement of Donovan, J., in *Phillips v Whielden Sanitary Potteries Ltd*, where he indicates that the size of the expenditure may be a decisive factor.

150 *Jackson v Laskers Home Furnishers Ltd* (1956) 37 TC 69, following *Law Shipping Co. v IRC* (1924) 12 TC 621.

151 See *Jackson v Laskers Home Furnishers Ltd.*

152 *Bidwell v Gardiner* (1960) 39 TC 31.

153 *Smith v Westinghouse Brake Co.* (1888) 2 TC 357; *Granite Supply Association v Kitton* (1905) 5 TC 168.

154 *Eastmans Ltd v Shew* (1928) 14 TC 218, *Hyam v IRC* (1929) 14 TC 479.

155 *Cowcher v R. Mills & Co. Ltd.* (1927) 13 TC 216.

156 See ITA, 1952, s.137(g), which prohibits deduction of 'any capital employed in improvements of premises occupied for the purpose of trade.' The question whether particular work is an 'improvement' is one of fact: *Thomas Wilson (Keighley), Ltd v Emmerson* (1960) 39 TC 360.

157 See *Fitzgerald v IRC* (1926) IR 182 (cost of replacing buildings burnt down and salvaging safes, etc., held to be capital expenditure).

158 *Rhodesia Railways Ltd v Bechuanaland IT Collector* (1933) AC 368 (PC). See also *Caledonian Ry v Banks* (1880) ITC 487. The possible use of the 'renewals basis.'

159 *Dinshaw v Bombay Commissioner* (1934) 50 TLR 527.

160 *Calders Ltd v IRC* (1944) 26 TC. 213

161 *Absalom v Talbot* (1944) AC 204; 26 TC 166.

162 *Absalom v Talbot* (1944) AC 204; 26 TC 166.

163 *Lock v Jones* (1941) 23 TC 749.

164 Per Viscount Simon, LC in *Absalom v Talbot* (1944) AC 204, at p.213; 26 TC 166, at p.190 (dispproving a contrary decision on a Jamaican statute in *Gleaner Co. Ltd v Assessment Committee* (1922) 2 AC 169 (PC), concurred in by Lord Akin and Lord Porter and followed in *Bristow v Dickinson Ltd* (1946) KB 321; 27 TC 157.

165 *Bristow v Dickinson Ltd* (1946) KB 321; 27 TC 157.

166 *Anderton and Halstead v Birrell* (1932) 1 KB 271; 16 TC 200.

167 See *Absalom v Talbot* (1944) AC 204; 26 TC 166

168 *Atherton v British Insulated and Helsby Cables Ltd* (1926) AC 25; 10 TC 155.

169 s.31 as amended by section 1 of Finance (Miscellaneous Taxation Provisions) 1972, otherwise known as Act no. 47 published in the *Federal Gazette* no. 63, vol. 59, 28 December 1972.

170 s.24, Act no. 28 of 1979

171 Suit No PPL/L/3^A/77 before F.O. Angaegbunam, J, Federal Revenue Court, Lagos on 29 June 1977.

172 Appeal used to be to the Federal Revenue Court; see section 230 (2) of the 1979 Constitution.

11   Corporate Taxation (2)

(i) Taxation of banks' excess profits

Section 28 of the Companies Income Tax Act, 1979 states:

28. (1) There shall be levied and paid for each year of assessment in respect of the total profits of every Company tax at the rate of forty-five kobo for each naira, so however that for the year of assessment 1978–79 it shall be at the rate of fifty kobo for every naira.

(2) In addition to any levy made pursuant to subsection (1) of this section, there shall, as from the assessment year commencing on 1st April 1978, be levied and paid a special levy of ten per cent on excess profits of every bank (as defined in section 41 of the Banking Act, 1969) and for the purposes of this subsection, excess profits means the difference between total profits as computed in accordance with section 26 and normal profits as calculated in accordance with subsection (3) of this section.

(3) For the purposes of subsection (2) of this section, normal profit shall be determined by the addition of the amounts arrived at after applying the percentages specified below to the amount of capital employed at the end of the accounting year of the Company.

Paid-up capital	40%
Capital or statutory reserve	20%
General reserve	20%
Long-term loans	20%

(4) Subject to the provisions of section 25, if a Company is engaged in the building or construction industry, the Company shall be assessed and charged for each year of assessment tax either –

(a) at the rate of $2\frac{1}{2}$% per centum of the turnover of the trade or business of that Company or, as the case may be, of that part of the turnover of the trade or business attributable to the operation carried out in Nigeria; or

(b) at the rate provided for in subsection (1) of this section, whichever is higher.

(5) For the purposes of paragraph (a) of subsection (4) of this section, any unabsorbed capital allowance brought forward shall be suspended until normal assessment is made; but a notional allowance shall be deemed to have been granted for the assessment year in which a turnover tax is payable.

Example 1

(i) Paid-Up capital		₦500 000
(ii) Capital or statutory reserve		250 000
(iii) General reserve		100 000
(iv) Long-term loan		800 000
(v) Total profits		650 000

Excess profit is calculated thus:

Total profits	=		₦650 000
40% of ₦250 000	=	₦200 000	
20% of ₦250 000	=	50 000	
20% of ₦100 000	=	20 000	
20% of ₦800 000	=	160 000	430 000
Excess Profit			220 000
10% on ₦220 000	=	₦22 000	

Example 2

Go-Ahead Bank Limited is a commercial bank registered in Nigeria. The bank makes up its accounts to December 31 of each year. The following information was extracted from the balance sheet for the year ended December 31 1986.

	1985	1986
Paid-up capital	15 000 000	18 500 000
Statutory reserve	2 500 000	6 100 000
General reserve	1 750 000	2 500 000
Debenture loan	9 000 000	12 000 000

A summarised statement of the company's profit and loss account for the year ended December 31 1986 is as follows:

Income

Interest and discount	₦20 450 000
Commission and exchange	4 000 000
Income on investments	1 500 000
Other income	7 000 000
	32 950 000

Expenses

Interest paid to other banks	₦3 000 000
Staff advances written off	50 000
Other expenses (allowable)	6 240 000
Interest paid to depositors	1 350 000
General provisions for loan loss	1 000 000

Depreciation	600 000	
Provision for possible loss in		
respect of loans and advances	3 000 000	
		15 240 000
Net Profit		17 710 000

The following additional information was provided:
(a) The written-down values of fixed assets as at January 1 1987 are:

(i) *Office building*	₦3 000 000	
(ii) *Motor vehicles*	800 000	
(iii) *Office furniture and equipment*	1 260 000	

(b) Additions to fixed assets during the year:

(i) *Land*	750 000	
(ii) *Motor vehicles*	410 000	
(iii) *Office furniture and equipment*	2 000 000	

(c) Income from banking operations included interest on agricultural loan amounting to ₦365 000.

A breakdown of the interest is as follows:

Period of loan	Grace period	Amount of interest
Over 7 years	Not less than 2 years	–
5–7 years	Not less than $1\frac{1}{2}$ years	₦230 000
2–4 years	Not less than 1 year	100 000
Below 2 years	Nil	35 000
		₦365 000

Compute the total tax liability of the Bank for the relevant year of assessment.

Solution

Go-Ahead Bank Ltd
Income Tax Computation, 1984

Net Profit as per audited financial statements for the year ended Dec. 31 1983		₦17 710 000
Add: Depreciation	₦600 000	
General provision for loan loss	1 000 000	
		1 600 000
		19 310 000

Deduct: Agricultural loan interest (Workings 1) s.59(7) of CITA 1979		201 000
Adjusted Profit		19 109 000
Less: Capital allowances for the year (Workings 2)		1 350 000
Taxable Profit		17 759 000
(i) Tax payable at 45%		₦7 995 712.50

Excess levy:		
Normal profit calculation		
40% paid up capital on	18 500 000	₦7 400 000
20% of statutory reserves on	6 100 000	1 220 000
20% of general reserve on	2 500 000	500 000
20% of debenture loan	12 000 000	2 400 000
		11 520 000
Excess profit calculation		
Taxable profit per s.26 CITA, 1979		17 759 000
Deduct: normal profit		11 520 000
		6 239 000
(ii) Excess levy at 10%		₦623 900
Normal tax		₦7 991 550
Income Tax		
Excess levy		623 900
Total tax due		8 615 450

Workings

(1) *Qualifying interest on agricultural loan exempted from tax:*

Loan Exemption	Over 7 yrs	5–7 yrs	2–4 yrs	Below 2 yrs
	100%	70%	40%	NIL
	–	230 000	100 000	
Tax exempt				
70% on ₦230 000		₦161 000		
40% on ₦100 000		40 000		
		₦201 000		

322

(2) *Capital Allowances Computation for 1987 Assessment Year*

	Buildings	Motor Vehicles	Furniture & Fittings	Total
Written-down value at 1/1/87	₦3 000 000	₦800 000	₦1 260 000	₦5 060 000
Additions	–	410 000	2 000 000	2 410 000
A	3 000 000	1 210 000	3 260 000	7 470 000
Capital Allowances:				
Initial (20%)	–	(82 000)	(400 000)	(482 000)
Annual	(10%) (300 000)	(25%) 282 000	(10%) (286 000)	(868 000)
B	(300 000)	(364 000)	(686 000)	(1 350 000)
WDV Carried forward to 1988: (A − B)	2 700 000	846 000	2 574 000	6 120 000

Note: Annual allowances on buildings, motor vehicles and furniture/fittings were calculated using Current rates and after deducting the initial allowances. This has been done for illustration purposes since the question does not state the dates of purchase of assets or which capital allowances have been claimed in the past.

Distribution of interim dividends

It is required that, not later than thirty days after the declaration of an interim dividend, the company declaring the dividend should pay the tax element of the interim dividend to the Board.

It should be noted that the intention is not to levy Income Tax on dividends. Any Income Tax paid is regarded as an instalment of the tax which the company declaring the dividend should normally pay during the year of assessment to which the dividend relates.

Part X companies

Section 24 of the Companies Income Tax Act, 1979 governs the position.

In pursuance of Part X of the Companies Decree, 1968, where a company is incorporated and carries on trade or business not substantially different in nature from that carried on in Nigeria by the branch of the foreign company, the following provisions will apply:

(a) the assets vesting in accordance with section 24(10) the Companies Act, 1979, shall be deemed to have been sold at tax residual values.

(b) Any revenue loss incurred by the foreign company prior to 18 November can be carried forward by the deemed company but the deemed company must proved to the satisfaction of the most senior officer in the Industrial Inspectorate Division of the Federal Ministry of Trade (the Director) that the loss was not the result of any damage or destruction caused by any military or other operations connected with the civil war.

(c) Any losses are first to be set off against assessable profits made by the deemed company in its first accounting year and any loss not so utilised can be carried forward indefinitely.

(d) the commencement and cessation provisions of the Act are not applicable.

(e) the deemed company and the reconstituted company (which are to be treated as the same entity for all purposes) shall not be entitled to initial allowances on assets vesting and shall be deemed to have received all allowances earlier granted to the foreign company. Thus when an asset is later sold by the company at a value in excess of tax residue value, the balancing charge is to be computed on the difference between the sale price and tax value at the date of sale restricted where appropriate to the total allowances given to the deemed company. Also, the new company can carry forward any unabsorbed capital allowances applicable to the former branch.

(f) Claims for the carry-forward of losses must be made to the Director within three years of the date of formal incorporation of the deemed company.

In *Reynolds Construction Company (Nigeria) Ltd v Federal Board of Inland Revenue* (APP/COMM/160 – 11 May 1972)

Companies Income Tax Act, 1961 – Additional assessment CITA sec. 50 – sections 30(3) and 30(4) of CITA as amended by Act No. 19 of 1970 – whether re-registration under part X of the Companies Decree 1968 amounted to permanent cessation.

The appellant's case was that as it ceased operation in November 1968, it ought to have been assessed under CITA sec. 30(4), in which case the additional assessment would not have arisen.

The appeal was dismissed. The Appeal Commissioners found that as the appellant had not taken steps to wind up its operations, it could not be regarded as having permanently ceased operation and must therefore fall within the provisions of the new section 30(10)(a) of CITA 1961 as amended.

(ii) Trade or business sold or transferred

Under section 24(a) of the Companies Income Tax Act, 1979, where a business carried on by a company is sold or transferred to a Nigerian company for the purposes of better organisation and the Federal Board of Inland Revenue is satisfied that one company has control over the other or that both are controlled by some other person or are members of a recognised group of companies, the Board may, in its discretion, direct that: –

(a) the commencement and cessation provisions shall not apply,

(b) for the purposes of making capital allowances or charges, any asset sold or transferred shall be deemed to have been sold for an amount equal to the residue of the qualifying expenditure there on the day following such sale or transfer,

(c) the company acquiring each such asset shall not be entitled to initial allowances with respect thereto and shall be deemed to have received all allowances given to the vendor company in respect of that asset.

(iii) Cable undertakings

Section 13 of CITA 1979 states that where a foreign company carries on the business of transmission of messages by cable or by any form or wireless apparatus, it shall be assessable to tax as though it operates ships or aircraft, and the provisions of section 12 (Companies engaged in shipping or air transport) shall apply. In other words, its earnings from abroad shall be deemed to be derived in Nigeria as though the transmission of messages abroad was equivalent to the shipping or loading of passengers, etc. in Nigeria.

(iv) Shipping and air companies

Section 12(1) of the Companies Income Tax Act, 1979, states that the profits or loss of a foreign company which carries on the business of transport by sea or by air, and any ship or aircraft owned or chartered by it calls at any sea port or airport in Nigeria its income or loss deemed to be derived from Nigeria shall be the full profits or loss arising from the carriage of passengers, mails, livestock or goods shipped, or loaded into an aircraft, in Nigeria. This subsection does not apply to passengers, mails, livestock or goods which are brought to Nigeria solely for transhipment or for transfer from one aircraft to another or in their direction between an aircraft and a ship. Where the Board is satisfied that the tax authority of any foreign country computes and assesses, on a basis not materially different from that prescribed by the Act, the profits of a company which operates ships or aircraft, and that authority certifies: (a) the ratio of profits or loss, before any allowance by way of depreciation, of an accounting period to the total sums receivable in respect of the carriage of passengers, mails, livestock or goods; and (b) the ratio of allowances by way of depreciation for that period to that same total, then the full profits or loss of that period shall be taken to be that proportion of the total sums receivable in respect of the carriage of passengers, mails, livestock or goods shipped or loaded in Nigeria which is produced by applying the first mentioned ratio to that total and in place under the provisions of Schedule 2 relating to capital allowances there shall be allowed the amount produced by applying the second ratio mentioned above to that same total. (subsection 2).

Where the provision of subsection 2 cannot be applied at the time of the assessment, the profits which should be deemed to be derived from Nigeria may be computed on a first percentage in the full sum receivable in respect of the carriage of passengers, mails, livestock and goods shipped or loaded in Nigeria. Where any company has thus been assessed for any year by reference to such percentage, it can claim that its liability for that year be recomputed on the basis provided by subsection 2 at any time within six years after the end of such year.

Where such claim has been made and a certificate produced to the satisfaction of the Board, a tax repayment shall be made but if the company does not agree with the Board's repayment of tax computation, notice of refusal of the claim shall be served on the company by the Board and the rules on objections and appeals shall apply with any necessary amendments.

The following is an illustration of this. British Caledonian operates several international airlines, some of which call in Nigeria. Accounts to 31 December 1981 show that:

Income for passenger traffic into Nigeria is ₦400 000.

Income for passenger traffic out of Nigeria is ₦100 000.

It is clear that income which is deemed to be derived from Nigeria is ₦100 000.

Under section 12 of the Companies Income Tax Act 1979, the profit element of income derived from Nigeria is arrived at as follows:

Adjusted profit/loss before depreciation allowance divided by total sum receivable in respect of carriage or passengers, mails and livestock.

This is known as the gross adjusted profit of the accounting period, before any allowance is made on account of depreciation relief. This second method ascertains the required ratio for the depreciation relief. Assume that the following information is given:

Income from passenger flights on other routes	₦2 600 000
Income from passenger flights into Nigeria	400 000
Income from passenger flights out of Nigeria	100 000
	3 100 000

Deduct:
Depreciation	₦310 000	
Salaries	2 325 000	
Other expenses disallowed	185 000	2 820 000
		280 000

Adjusted profit for the period:
Net profit per accounts	280 000
Add depreciation and other disallowed expenses	495 000
	775 000

Ratio is arrived at as follows:

$$\frac{\textit{Adjusted profit before depreciation allowance}}{\text{Total sum receivable for carriage of passengers, and livestock}} \times 100$$

$$= \frac{775\,000}{3\,100\,000} \times 100 \qquad = 25\%$$

The ratio for depreciation allowance is arrived at as follows:

$$\frac{\textit{Depreciation}}{\text{Total sum receivable for carriage of passengers, mails \& livestock}} \times 100$$

$$= \frac{310\,000}{3\,100\,000} \times 100 \qquad = 10\%$$

If these ratios are applied to the ₦100 000, the assessable profit of British Caledonian will be,

Gross adjusted profit, 25% of ₦100 000	₦25 000
Less depreciation relief, 10% of ₦100 000	10 000
Total Profit	15 000

(v)   Insurance companies

(a) *Non-life insurance companies*

As stated in CITA 1979 14(1), a non-life insurance company or a Nigerian company (whether proprietary or mutual) which carried on business through a permanent establishment in Nigeria, and whose profits accrue in part outside Nigeria, the profits on which tax may be imposed shall be ascertained by taking the gross premium and interest and other income receivable in Nigeria (less any premium returned to the insured and premiums paid on re-insurances), and deducting from the balance so arrived at a reserve for unexpired risks at the percentage adopted by the company in relation to its operations as a whole for such risks at the end of the period for which the profits are being ascertained, and adding a reserve similarly calculated for unexpired risks outstanding at the commencement of such period, and from the net amount so arrived at deducting the actual losses in Nigeria (less the amount recovered in respect thereof under reinsurance), the agency expenses in Nigeria and a fair proportion of the expenses of the head office of the company.

Example 3

Insurance Company, 1984

Non-Life Insurance Company

	₦000	₦000
Reserve for unexpired risks		
(at the commencement of the accounting		
period)		400
Gross Premium received	1000	
Less: Premium returned to the insured	(200)	
Premium paid on reinsurance	(300)	500
		900
Other Incomes		
Rent	20	
Fines	20	
Assignment fees	10	
Interest	30	
Dividend (gross)	100	180
Less:		
Reserve for unexpired risks		1080
(at the end of the accounting period)		380
		700

Deduct allowable items	₦000		
Actual losses	15		
Less: Recovery under			
reinsurance	(5)	10	
Agency expenses		10	
Head office expenses			
Management expenses		200	220
Taxable Income			₦480

Notes
(1) Reserve for unexpired risk should be calculated using the percentage adopted by the company to the operations.
(2) Dividend: Franked Investment Income was not law in 1984 and as such dividend should be added gross into the computation.
(3) In arriving at the tax due, deductions should be made for tax suffered at source.

The chargeable profit of an insurance company, in accordance with section 14(1)(a) of the CITA 1979, is computed as follows:

Example 4

Gross premium and interest received in Nigeria, 1983		₦2 200 000
Less:		
Premium returned to insured	80 000	
Premium paid on reinsurance	204 000	284 000
		1 916 000
Less:		
Reserve for unexpired risks at year end	600 000	
Less: Unexpired risks at beginning of year	560 000	40 000
		1 876 000
Less:		
Actual losses in Nigeria	80 000	
Less: Amounts recovered under reinsurance	16 000	
	64 000	
Add:		
Agency expenses in Nigeria	720 000	
Head Office expenses	240 000	1 024 000
		852 000

Only reasonable Head Office expenses are allowed, and this is at the discretion of the Board.

Income Tax computation will then be as follows:

Net profit per account	₦852 000
Add:	
Depreciation in agent expenses	40 000
Other disallowed expenses	24 000
	916 000
Deduct:	
Capital allowances (assumed to be)	80 000
Chargeable income	₦836 000

Example 5

	₦000	₦000
Reserve for unexpired risks (at the commencement of the accounting period)		400
Gross premium received	1000	
Less: Premium returned to the insured	(200)	
Premium paid on reinsurance	(300)	500
		900

Other Income	20	
Rent	20	
Fines	10	
Assignment fees	10	
Interest	30	
Dividend (Gross)	100	180
Less		
Reserve for unexpired risks		1080
at the end of the accounting period		380
		700
Deduct Allowable items	₦000	
Actual losses	15	
Less: Recovery under		
reinsurance	(5)	10
Agency expenses		10
Head office expenses		
Management expenses	200	220
Taxable income		₦480

(i) Reserve for unexpired risk should be calculated using the percentage adopted by the company to the operations.

(ii) Dividend: Franked investment income was not yet law and as such dividend should be added gross into the computation.

(iii) In arriving at the tax due, deductions should be made for tax suffered at source.

(b) *Life Assurance companies*

Section 14(1) CITA 1979 states that profits on which tax may be imposed shall be the total investment income of the company less the management expenses, including commission. This is upon the assumption that where the profits of such a company accrue, in parts, outside Nigeria, the profits shall be that proportion of the total investment income of the company as the premiums receivable in Nigeria bear to the total premiums receivable, less the agency expenses in Nigeria and a fair proportion of the expenses of the head office of the company. In addition, the Board may substitute some basis other than that prescribed for ascertaining the required proportion of the total investment income for the purposes of the foregoing provision in the case of such an insurance company having its head office abroad. In other words, where a life insurance company declares a dividend to be paid to the shareholders from the increase arising from actuarial revaluation, the company shall pay tax on the dividend as if such dividend is the total profit of the company. In practice the formula to be adopted can be discussed and agreed with the Revenue and will be subject to review from time to time.

Permanent establishment: in relation to an insurance company means a branch, management or other fixed place of business in Nigeria, but does not include an agency in Nigeria unless the agent has, and habitually exercises, a general authority to negotiate and conclude contracts on behalf of such company.

Example 6

Ade Company Limited
(No income has accrued outside Nigeria)

Total investment income		₦140 000
Less:		
Management expenses		40 000
Net profit per accounts		100 000
Add back:		
Disallowable expenses in management expenses		10 000
Adjusted profits		110 000
Less:		
Capital allowances		50 000
Chargeable income		60 000

	₦000	₦000
INVESTMENT INCOME		
Premiums received		1000
(Or amount transferred from actuarial valuation of any unexpired risks to its profit and loss Account ₦500 000		
Other income		
Dividend	20	
Interest	15	
Fines	15	
Rent	30	
Assignment Fees	20	100
	–	1100
Less		
Management expenses	80	
Commission	20	100
Taxable income		1000

Note

1 Where dividend is declared from the increase arising from an actuarial valuation, the company is liable to pay tax on the dividend as if the dividend were the profit of the company.

2 There is no provision in the Act s.14(b) CITA 1979 as to which amount to take in respect of premiums or amount transferred to profit and loss account due to actuarial valuation. It is safer to take the higher of the two for examination purposes with a note for the examiner.

3 There is no provision in the Act as to whether premiums paid to the insured or on reinsurance should be deducted. A note should be made for the examiner in this respect.

Example 7

Part of the income accrued outside Nigeria.

(a) *Additional information:*

    1 Total premium receivable is ₦80 000, of which ₦20 000 is receivable in Nigeria.

    2 Agency expenses in Nigeria ₦14 000.

    3 Head office expenses chargeable to Nigerian Branch, ₦6 000.

    4 Disallowable expenses in agency expenses amount to ₦2 000.

    5 Capital allowances available are ₦6 000.

(b) Computation of chargeable profit:

$$\frac{\text{Premiums receivable in Nigeria}}{\text{Total premiums receivable}} \times \text{total investment income}$$

$$= \frac{20\,000}{80\,000} \times \frac{140\,000}{1} = \text{₦}35\,000$$

Less:		
Agency expenses in Nigeria	₦14 000	
Head office expenses	6 000	20 000
		15 000
Add back:		
Disallowable expenses		2 000
		17 000
Less		
Capital allowances		6 000
Chargeable profit		11 000

Special provision relating to Nigerian insurance companies:
In the case of a Nigerian insurance company, the profits liable to tax shall be the whole investment and premium income of the company less all expenses and other outgoings of the company (section 14(2)(c) of CITA 1979).

Example 8

Bell Company Ltd		
Investment income		₦50 000
Premiums received less		
returned to insured		110 000
Other income		20 000
		180 000
Less:		
Management expenses	₦80 000	
Depreciation	30 000	
Other expenses		
(all allowable)	50 000	160 000
Net Profit		20 000
Add back:		
Depreciation		30 000
		50 000
Less		
Capital allowances		16 000
Chargeable income		34 000

The format is as below:

Example 9

Insurance Company, 1984

Life Insurance Company	₦000	₦000
Investment Income		
Premiums Received		1000
(Or amount transferred		
from actuarial valuation		
of any unexpired risks		
to its Profit and Loss		
Account ₦500 000		
Other Income		
Dividend	20	
Interest	15	
Fines	15	
Rent	30	
Assignment fees	20	100
		1100
Less		
Managment expenses	80	
Commission	20	100
Taxable Income		₦1000

Notes

(1) Where dividend was declared from the increase arising from actuarial valuation, the company was liable to pay Income Tax on the dividend as if the dividend is the total profit of the company.
(2) There is no provision in the Act, s.14(b) CITA 1979 as to which amount to take in respect of premiums or amount to take in respect of premiums or amount transferred to P & L due to actuarial valuation. It is suggested one takes the higher for examination purposes and makes a note for the examiner.
(3) There is also no provision in the Act as to whether premiums paid to the insured or on reinsurance should be deducted. A note should be made for the examiner in this respect.

Section 14 of the Companies Income Tax Act 1979, as amended by s.19 of Decree No.4 of 1985 states that Life Insurance Companies should carry out, annually, actuarial valuation of their life business and submit full particulars of any such valuation or revaluations to the Board.

Unlike in the past when only the surplus on actuarial valuation (after deducting amounts distributed as dividends) was transferred to the Profit and Loss account (and hence taxable), such distributed surplus resulting from valuation should now be accounted for in respect of company taxation.

(vi) Pioneer companies

The Industrial Development (Income Tax Relief), Act 1971 repeals the Industrial Development (Income Tax Relief) Act, 1958, and is deemed to have come into effect on 1 April 1970.

The Decree empowers the Federal Executive Council to publish a list of industries and products as pioneer industries or products where it is satisfied that:

(a) the industry is not carried on in Nigeria on a scale suitable to the economic development of Nigeria, or
(b) there were favourable prospects of further development of such industries in Nigeria or,
(c) it is expedient in the public interest to encourage the development or establishment of such industries in Nigeria.

Application may also be made to the Federal Commissioner for Industries (the Commissioner) by any company or individual for any industry to be included in the list of pioneer industries and pioneer products.

Application may be made to the Commissioner by a company incorporated in Nigeria or by a group of persons on behalf of a company yet to be incorporated for the issue of a pioneer certificate in respect of any industry published as a pioneer industry provided that the qualifying capital expenditure to be incurred on or before the production day is in excess of:

(a) ₦50 000 in respect of an indigenous controlled company;

(b) ₦50 000 in respect of any other company.

Where the Council approves an application made on behalf of a proposed company that company must be incorporated within four months of approval, and the pioneer certificate will not be issued until the company has been incorporated.[1]

Not later than one month after production in marketable quantities, the pioneer company must apply in writing to the Director[2], Industrial Inspectorate Division, Federal Ministry of Industries (The Director) to certify a date as its production day and give the reason for proposing such date. Where the Director certifies that the date of production day is more than one year later than the date estimated in its application for pioneer certificate, the pioneer certificate may be cancelled unless the company can show sufficient cause.

Within one month after the certificate of production day has been given, the company shall apply in writing to the Federal Board of Inland Revenue (the Board) to certify the qualifying capital expenditure incurred prior to the production day. Where any asset is sold before the date of value of such asset, which must be at arm's length, or where the Board certifies that the qualifying capital expenditure incurred on or before the production day is:

(a) less than ₦50 000 in the case of an indigenous controlled company; or

(b) less than ₦50 000 in any other case;

the pioneer certificate shall be cancelled.

The company may voluntarily apply[3], or in the case of any contravention of the decree, the Council may direct that the pioneer certificate be cancelled.

The effective day of cancellation shall be the pioneer date (production day) or the last anniversary thereof, whichever is the later.

The tax relief period is three years[4], commencing from the date of the production day. The Council may, on an application in writing within one month of the end of initial relief period, and on fulfilment of certain conditions by the pioneer company, extend the tax relief period to a maximum of five years.

335

The conditions to be fulfilled concern satisfaction as to the company's rate of expansion, efficiency, utilisation of raw materials, training of Nigerian staff, etc.

At the end of its pioneer period the company is treated as though it had commenced a new business and the normal tax 'commencement' provisions apply.

During its pioneer period a company must not carry on any business other than its pioneer enterprise[5], and if it derives any other earnings they are subject to tax.

The profit[6] of a pioneer company for any accounting period is to be ascertained in accordance with the provisions of sections 27 and 28 of CITA. For the purpose of ascertaining the profit during the pioneer period, however, the Board is empowered to direct that receipts which have been treated as part of the pioneer profits but which properly should have been treated as profit of the following period, be so treated.

The Board may likewise direct that any expense incurred in the first year of the post-pioneer period is properly attributable to the tax relief period. The profits of the company for the tax relief period and the post pioneer period will be accordingly adjusted.[7]

In ascertaining the loss for any accounting period the Board may only allow reasonable amounts in respect of:

(a) directors' remuneration;

(b) interest, agency and service charges paid to a shareholder or anyone controlled by the shareholder.

Where a loss has been so ascertained, the Board shall issue a certificate. Losses certified in any accounting period can only be allowed to be carried forward in so far as they exceed the aggregate of all the pioneer profits. The 'net' loss is deemed to have been incurred on the first day after the cessation of the pioneer period and is available as a set-off against the total profits in the first year of the new business 14(3). Where the net loss exceeds the total profits of the new business in the first year such excess cannot be carried forward to the second year. The reason is that the net loss is deemed to be incurred (in computing total profit) by the company on the first day on which the new business commenced. We are not told that the net loss is deemed to be incurred by the company in its new trade or business. It follows therefore that the net loss of the old business is a distinct source from the profits of the new business. Any deduction of the loss from the total profit in these years must not exceed 'the amount, if any, of the assessable profits, included in the total profits, from the trade or business in which the loss was incurred.' Since the trade or business on which the loss was incurred is the pioneer business which ceased at the end of the tax relief period, it appears that the unabsorbed net loss cannot be set off against the total profits of the second and subsequent years of the new business.

The wordings of section 14(3) of the Pioneer Development (Income Tax Relief) Act may here be compared with those of section 24 of CITA (which deals with Part 'x' companies). In the latter, it is clearly spelt out that 'any loss incurred during any year of assessment by the foreign company in the said business previously carried on by it shall be deemed to be a loss incurred by the reconstituted company in its trade or business during the year of assessment in which its trade or business commenced ....'

It might have been the intention of the Government that the provisions of section 14(3) of the pioneer legislation should be construed just as those of section 24; however on the strength of the former section, I cannot see how pioneer companies can carry their losses forward indefinitely. The best way out is to amend section 14(3); otherwise all pioneer companies with heavy losses incurred during the pioneer period should seek Government approval to cancel their pioneer status *ab initio* so that their losses may be carried forward indefinitely.

Capital expenditure during the pioneer period is regarded for capital allowance purposes to have been incurred on the first day after the end of the period.

The profit of a pioneer company for any accounting year shall be certified by the Board (section 14(4) and such profit is exempt from Income Tax.[8]

Profits exempted from tax must be credited to an account, called the 'section 17 Account' and any dividends, or distributions in the form of bonus shares, shall be debited to that account and such dividends shall be exempt from tax in the hands of the recipients.

Where however; (a) as a result of a direction made under section 13 or (b) the pioneer certificate is cancelled so that profits and dividends which have been exempted from tax ought not to have been so exempted, additional assessments will be made on the pioneer company or the shareholder, as the case may be, within six years of the direction or cancellation.

It may not grant loans without the permission of the Minister.
Pioneer Certificates granted under Industrial Development (Income Tax Relief) Act, 1958 (i.e. under previous pioneer legislation)
Any pioneer certificate which has not expired on 3 May 1971, and which was granted under the Industrial Development (Income Tax Relief) Act, 1958, shall have effect as if it were granted under the Act. Where the initial relief period of two years has not expired at 3 May

1971 and the qualifying capital expenditure incurred by the company on or before its production day is:

(a) in the case of an indigenous controlled company not less than ₦25 000; or

(b) in the case of any other company not less than ₦75 000; then the initial tax relief period is construed as if it were three years instead of two years and any extension of the tax relief period shall be in accordance with the provision of section 10(2).

Where the initial tax relief period of two years has expired on 3 May 1971 but the company is still within its old pioneer period, it may apply for an extension of its tax relief period in accordance with the provisions of section 10(2).

In no circumstances, though, can the total tax relief period granted under both acts combined exceed five years.

Termination of pioneer period as a result of industrial development (Income Tax Relief) Act, 1971:

There are some pioneer companies which have their original pioneer periods (granted under the previous Act) extended beyond five years as a result of losses sustained in any accounting period. In some cases, the periods are extended to 31 December 1970 or 31 March 1971.

The new Act is deemed to come into effect on 1 April 1970 and the old Act was repealed on that date. It has been suggested by some authorities that in the cases mentioned above, the pioneer period must terminate at the later of:

(a) five years from the production date; or

(b) 1 April 1970 (the date the new Act came into force).

I submit that the fact that the new Act repealed the old does not mean that actions done under the old Act are automatically invalidated. Section 6 of the Interpretation Act, 1964, says that

The repeal of any enactment shall *not*

(a) revive anything not in force or existing at the time when the repeal takes effect.

(b) affect the previous operation of the enactment or anything done or suffered under the enactment.

It follows, therefore, that if the Board of Inland Revenue through one of its Inspectors of Taxes issued a certificate extending the pioneer period of a company to a date beyond 1 April 1970, the repeal of the old Act does not invalidate that extension. However, the date of the extension cannot go beyond 3 May 1971. The provisions of the Interpretation Act, 1964, do not affect certificates in existence at 3 May 1971, and since under section 24(5) of the new Act, the tax relief period cannot exceed five years from production date, it appears that where the date of extension goes beyond 3 May 1971 the certificate must lapse on that date.

338

The provisions relating to assessment and appeals shall apply in the following cases:

(a) certificate of production day issued by the Director, Industrial Inspectorate Division, Federal Ministry of Industries and certificate issued by the Federal Board of Inland Revenue as regards qualifying capital expenditure incurred on production day (section 6(6);

(b) certificate issued by the Board of Inland Revenue in respect of qualifying capital expenditure as regards application for extension of tax relief period (section 10(7);

(c) ascertainment of profit or loss for any accounting period.[9]

Agro-allied Projects, whose raw materials were produced locally, will not enjoy pioneer status.

Federal Revenue Court (now the Federal High Court)

A federal Revenue Court was established under Federal Revenue Court Act 1973 published in the *Federal Gazette* No. 22, Vol. 60 of 13 April 1973.

The Act establishes the Federal Revenue Court as a High Court of Justice with certain special powers.

The court consists of a President and other judges, not being less than four, as the Head of State may prescribe by an order. As in the case of a High Court of a State, the President and the other judges shall be appointed by the Federal Executive Council acting after consultation with the Advisory Judicial Committee.

The Federal Revenue Court's original jurisdiction lay in certain specified matters, including taxation of companies, customs and excise duties, banking, foreign exchange, currency and fiscal measures of the Government of the Federation, and priority is to be given to all such revenue cases.

The Head of State is empowered under the Act to increase the jurisdiction to include other matters which he may specify and to confer jurisdiction on the High Court of a State in respect of causes and matters which he may specify generally or specially.

For the purposes of the Act the area of the Federation will be divided into judicial Divisions, not being less than four, and the court may sit in any one or more of the Judicial Divisions as the President of the Federal Revenue Court may direct, and the court may exercise appellante jurisdiction in the circumstances mentioned in the Act. There is a right of appeal from the decisions of a Federal Revenue Court by any aggrieved person to the Federal Appeal Court and from there to the Surpreme Court. The FRC has now been abolished.

(vii) Revision of assessment in case of objection

Section 50 of the Companies Income Tax Act, 1979, states that an aggrieved taxpayer may object to a tax assessment in writing, stating the grounds of objection within fifteen days from the date of the service of the notice of assessment.

Establishment of Appeal Commissioners

Section 52 of the Companies Income Tax Act, 1979, empowers the Federal Minister of Finance to establish by notice in the *Gazette* a body of Appeal Commissioners consisting of not more than twelve persons, none of whom shall be a public officer. Each Appeal Commissioner holds office for a period of three years. Any three of them shall form a quorum.

Appeals to Appeal Commissioners

Where notice of refusal to amend is served by the Board under s.50, a taxpayer may appeal against the assessment to the Secretary to the Appeal Commissioners within fifteen days after the date of service upon such company a notice of the refusal of the Board to amend the assessment. Such a notice must specify the following particulars:
(a) official number of the assessment and the year of assessment.
(b) amount of tax charged by the assessment.
(c) the amount of the total profits upon which the tax was charged.
(d) date of Notice of Refusal to amend
(e) grounds of appeal which must be limited to the grounds stated by the appellant in the former notice of objection.
Where the tax chargeable in accordance with the decision of the Appeal Commissioners does not exceed ₦400, no further appeal is allowed except with the consent of the Board. An award or judgement of the Appeal Commissioners is enforceable as if it were a judgement of the Federal Revenue Court (now the Federal High Court).

Either the Board or the taxpayer can appeal against the decision of the Appeal Commissioners to the Federal Revenue Court on a point of law by giving notice in writing to the Secretary to the Appeal Commissioners within fifteen days after the date on which the decision was given upon the receipt of a notice. The Secretary to the Appeal Commissioners shall send all records of proceedings to the Chief Registrar of the Federal Revenue Court (now the Federal High Court).

Appeal from the Federal High Court goes to the Federal Court of Appeal where the tax determined by the Federal High Court exceeds ₦1000.

Time within which tax is payable

Section 58 deals with the position. Every company shall, not later than three months after the end of each year of assessment, pay in a lump sum or not more than six monthly instalments of provisional tax of an amount equal to the tax paid by such company in the immediately preceding year.

Tax raised in an assessment which is not disputed shall be paid within two months after service of such advice upon the company. The Board may, in its discretion, extend the time within which payment is to be made.

Imposition of penalty

Section 60 of the CITA 1979 empowers the Board to impose a ten per cent penalty for tax unpaid on its due date. If payment is not made within a month, payment may be enforced. The Board, at its discretion, can remit the whole or part of the penalty.

Power to distrain for non-payment of tax

Section 61 of the 1979 Act gives the Board power to distrain the taxpayer by his goods, chattels, or other securities, distrain upon any land, premises or place in respect of which the taxpayer is the owner for the purpose of recovering the amount of tax due.

Appointment as agent

A.C.M. of Nigeria Ltd vs Federal Board of Inland Revenue APP/ COMM/204 of 15 May 1974
Companies Income Tax Act, 1961: Assessment to tax of income of a non-Nigerian company, section 18(2) CITA, 1961; Appointment of appellant as agent, section 41 CITA.
The appellant appealed on the grounds that the year of assessment was incorrectly stated, that the respondent was wrong in assessing gross receipt to tax without making proper deduction for expenses incurred

Offences and penalties under s. 66–69 of the Companies Income Tax Act, 1979

Nature of offence	Penalties
1 Offence against any of the provisions of the law	₦1200 fine: s.66(1)
2 Failure to keep records or furnish statement	₦200 fine and ₦40 for each and every day during which failure occurs and in default of payment, 6 months' imprisonment: s.66(1)
3 Failure to comply with the requirements of a notice served or failure to answer questions of law fully put	200 fine: s.66(2)
4 Failure to file audited accounts and returns within 6 months after the end of the company's accounting year (s.40)	₦5000 fine (s.40); penalty of tax charged in the preceding year: s.66(4)
5 Failure to answer the Board's call for further returns (s.41)	Penalty of tax charged in the preceding year.
6 Making of incorrect returns, omitting or understating profits	₦200 fine and double the amount of tax which has been undercharged: s.67(1). The complaint must be made within six years of the date the offence was committed.
7 Aiding, abetting, assisting, counselling, inciting or inducing others to deliver false return or keep false accounts, preparation of false accounts, refusal or neglect to pay tax.	₦1000 fine or 5 years' imprisonment or both: s.68.
8 Corruption by Federal tax officials, demanding more tax than due, incorrect return of tax collected.	₦600 or 3 years' imprisonment or both: s.69.

Note:
The Board may compound any offence and no prosecution may be commenced except at the instance of or with the sanction of the

in earning the gross receipt, and finally that it was improper to appoint the appellant as agent.

The appeal was allowed. The Appeal Commissioners found that the power of the respondent to tax the profits of a foreign company is not absolute, but is limited to such profits as are attributable to the operation of the company within Nigeria only, and that the appellant can be appointed an agent where there is evidence that there are moneys in the hands of the appellant due to the company whose agent the appellant has been declared to be.

Ely Bernard Properties Ltd v Federal Board of Inland Revenue
Companies Income Tax Act 1961 – Imposition of penalty CITA s.62(1)(a) – Preliminary objection to the hearing of the appeal on the ground that the appeal was against the Board's discretionary power to remit – s.62(1) CITA, 1961.

The appellant's grounds of appeal were that the respondent was wrong in not accepting its excuse for the delay in settling the tax, that the respondent was unreasonable in not using its discretionary power to the appellant's advantage CITA s.62(3), and that it was within the jurisdiction of the Commissioners to hear the case in spite of the respondent's preliminary objection. The preliminary objection was upheld and the appeal was dismissed.

The Appeal Commissioners found (i) that the respondent had absolute discretion to impose penalty for non-payment of tax that had become final and conclusive, (ii) that it does not fall within the jurisdiction of the commissioners whether or not the exercise of the discretionary power under CITA s.61(3) should be in favour of the taxpayer.

Ely Bernard Properties Ltd   (Appellant)
Federal Board of Inland Revenue   (Respondent)

The question was that relating to Imposition of Penalty under s.62(1)(a)

This was an appeal by the appellant company against the penalty of £983 imposed imposed by the respondent under the provisions of section 62(1)(a) of the CITA, 1961, for failure to pay within the stipulated time the tax of £9780 which had been raised in the assessment No. KC 1012 for the 1966–67 Income Tax year. The grounds of appeal were stated by counsel for the appellant in the following terms:

(1) that the Board erred in not accepting as constituting good cause shown the fact that late payment (of the tax in question) had only occured by reason of the absence of a member of the staff of the appellant company's paying agents occasioned by the disturbed situation in the country;
(2) that the Board erred in failing to take into account the before-mentioned and to consider that payment, in any event, was only overdue by 13 days; and
(3) that the Board's refusal to remit the whole or part of the addition charged under

343

section 62(1) of the Companies Income Tax Act, 1961 cannot be supported by the facts put before it.

At the opening of the submissions in this appeal, Counsel for the respondent, Mr R.O. Egbeyemi (on Tuesday, 25 March 1966) raised preliminary objection to the hearing of the appeal on the ground that the appeal was against a penalty imposed by the respondent after an assessment had become final. According to him, the appeal did not therefore fall within the jurisdiction of the Commissioners.

At the subsequent hearing, which took place on Friday, 20 November 1970, counsel for the appellant sought, by reference to a case previously decided in *FBIR v Nigerian Insurance Co. Ltd* (No. LD 578/65), to show that it was not only within the jurisdiction of the Commissioners to hear the appeal but also that the notice of objection or appeal by the appellant should have stopped the collection of the tax and the penalty that was imposed for the late payment of the tax. He contended that it was unreasonable for the Board to have refused to take congnizance of the facts at the material time before imposing the penalty, particularly at a time that the whole nation was in a state of civil war. He deposed that it was also unreasonable for the Board to have refused to remit the penalty after it had been notified of the reasons that led to the delay. Counsel for the appellant referred to the discretion conferred on the Board by section 62(3), which discretion it had refused to exercise in favour of the appellant. He further deposed that it was because of the refusal of the respondent to exercise its discretion of remission that this appeal was brought before the Commissioners.

The court examined both sides to this appeal and found itself in agreement with the view expressed by counsel for the respondent that the Board has absolute discretion under section 61(1)(a) to impose an addition for the non-payment of tax that has become final and conclusive, subject only to the provisions of paragraph 3 of that section, which states that 'the Board may, for any good cause shown, remit the whole or any part of the addition due under subsection (1)'. The court was also of the opinion that whether or not the Board exercise this discretion in favour of a taxpayer is a matter that does not fall within the jurisdiction of the Commissioners.
(APP/COMM/87 of 22 March 1973)

Example 10

ADO-EKITI Progressive Ltd was formed on 1 January 1982, and started to operate immediately.

The adjusted profits for the next five financial years were as follows:

Year ended 31 December 1982	₦400
Year ended 31 December 1983	800
Year ended 31 December 1984	1200
Year ended 31 December 1985	1500
Year ended 31 December 1986	1150

You are asked to compute the assessable profit for the relevant years of assessments.

Solution

ADO-EKITI Progressive Ltd
Computation of assessable profits 1982 to 1987

Year of assessment	Basis of assessment	Amount
1982	Commencement; date of commencement to following 31 December	₦400
1983	Income of the first 12 months	400
1984	Preceding year basis	800
1985	Preceding year basis	1200
1986	Preceding year basis	1500
1987	Preceding year basis	1150

Example 11

BOLA Ltd is a manufacturing company registered in Nigeria making up its accounts to 31 December every year. The net profit for the year ended 31 December 1983 is ₦28 893 after charging the following expenses:

Salaries	₦4 800
Provision for bad debts	335
Mortgage interest (net)	115
General expenses	800
Legal and professional fees	180
Directors' salaries	4 000
Secretary's salary	950
Depreciation	475
Provision for discount allowed	75
Income tax	2 300
Repairs and renewals	2 000
	₦16 230

The following additional information is supplied.

(i) *General expenses* include an item of ₦100 embezzled by a cashier.

(ii) *Repair and renewals* include:

(a) Repainting of administrative offices	₦500
(b) Building improvements to Isolo Branch Sales Office	₦1500
	₦2000

(iii) *Legal and professional fees* include:

(a) Preparation of service agreement	₦15
(b) Collection of book debts	30
(c) Payment of customer for compromise or an action	40
(d) Cost of a successful appeal against income tax assessments	45
(e) Audit fee paid in connection with the appeal	20
(f) Preparation of leasehold agreement	30

(iv) *Provision for Bad Debts* 15, ₦335. This amount contains bad debts written off, ₦130; bad debts recovered, ₦25; and percentage provisions brought down, ₦415; and carried forward, ₦655.

(v) *Provisions for discount allowed* include ₦30 allowed as discount in respect of actual receipts during the year.

Assuming that the rates of capital allowances are:

	Initial	Annual
Industrial buildings	15%	10%
Non-industrial buildings	–	5%
Plant and machinery	20%	$12\frac{1}{2}$%

You are required to compute the chargeable income of BOLA Ltd. Assume that the rate of tax is 40% on the first ₦10 000 and 45% on the rest.

Solution

BOLA Ltd
Income Tax computation for 1984

Net profit per account for year ended 31 December 1983   ₦28 893
Add items of expenses not allowable for tax purposes:

Income Tax	2 300
Depreciation	475
Improvements to building	1 500
Legal cost of appeal against Income Tax assessments	45
Audit fee paid in connection with the appeal	20

Legal fee for preparation of leasehold agreements	30
Increase in provisions for bad debts	395
Staff Pension Fund	1 000
Provision for discount allowed	15
Adjusted profit	₦34 673
Deduct: Capital allowances (say)	1 332
	₦33 341

Income Tax on ₦10 000 at 40% =	4 000.00
Income Tax on ₦23 341 at 45% =	10 503.45
Total Income Tax payable =	₦14 503.45

Notes

1. Section 3.
2. Section 6.
3. Section 7.
4. Sections 10 and 11.
5. Section 12.
6. Sections 13 and 14.
7. Section 13(a)(b).
8. Section 16.
9. Section 14(4).

347

12 The Law and Practice of Petroleum Profits Tax in Nigeria

(i) Introduction

It is an open secret that the bulk of the nation's revenue is now being derived from Petroleum Profits Tax. To the man in the street and even to more detached observers, the work of assessing and collecting tax from companies engaged in petroleum operations may appear as simple as calculating the cost of six bottles of cooking oil at 10k per bottle. But like the taxation of trading companies and business entrepreneurs, implementation of Petroleum Profits Tax Provisions requires a high degree of intelligence and imagination, capacity for hard work and a sense of responsibility.

The relative Principal Act is the Petroleum Profits Tax Ordinance No. 15 of 1959 published as a supplement to the *Official Gazette* No. 26, Vol. 46 of April 1959 and took effect as from 1 January 1958.

The search for oil dated back to 1937 when licence was granted to Shell d'Arcy Company Limited which later became known as Shell BP Petroleum Development Company of Nigeria Limited. The first oil find in commercial quantity was struck in 1956 and production for export began in 1958. Because of the special and complicated nature of the oil industry generally, companies engaged in the business of oil winning are not taxed under the Companies Income Tax Act (1961) but under the Petroleum Profits Tax Ordinance No. 15 of 1959 referred to above as amended since 1966 by the following Acts:

(a) Income Tax (Amendment) Act No. 65 of 1966;

(b) Petroleum Profits Tax (Amendment) Act No. 1, 1967;

(c) Oil Terminal Dues Act No. 9, 1969;

(d) Petroleum Profits Tax (Amendment) Act No. 22, 1970;

(e) Petroleum Profits Tax (Amendment) Act No. 15, 1973;

(f) Petroleum Profits Tax Amendment Act No. 55 of 1977

(g) Petroleum Tax Amendment Act No. 4 1979

(h) Petroleum Profits Tax (Amendment) (No. 2) Act 1979.

(ii) Interpretation

It is extremely important to master the exact meaning of every word, expression or phrase as defined in section 2 of the Principal Act. Some of the most important are:

   (i) 'accounting period' which, in petroleum operation means:

      (a) a period of one year commencing on 1 January and ending on 31 December of the same year; or

      (b) any shorter period commencing on the day the company first makes a sale of bulk disposal of chargeable oil under a programme of continuous production and sales, domestic, export or both and ending on 31 December of the same year; or

      (c) any period or less than a year being a period commencing on 1 January of any year and ending on the date in the same year when the company ceases to be engaged in petroleum operations.

Note

In the event of any dispute with respect to the date of the first sale of chargeable oil or with respect to the date on which the company ceases to be engaged in petroleum operations, the Director of Petroleum Resources shall determine the same and no appeal shall lie therefrom.

   (ii) 'assessable profits' means the adjusted profits of an accounting period after the deduction of any amount of any loss incurred by the company during any previous accounting period – see section (14);

   (iii) 'adjusted profits' means the profit of an accounting period after the deductions allowed by sub-section (1) of section (10) and any adjustment to be made in accordance with provisions of section (12);

   (iv) 'chargeable profits' means the amount of assessable profits of an accounting period after deduction of *any amount and allowances due to the company under the provisions of the second schedule to the Petroleum Profits Tax Act 1959* – see section (15);

   (v) 'assessable tax' means the chargeable profits of the accounting period multiplied by the current rate of tax – see section (16);

   (vi) 'chargeable tax' means the assessable tax for that period after the deductions allowed under section (17) shall have been made;

(vii) 'chargeable oil' in relation to a company engaged in petroleum operations, means any one or more of the following, namely casinghead petroleum spirit, crude oil or natural gas, as the case may be, *won or obtained* by the company from such operation;

(viii) 'casing-head petroleum spirit' means any liquid hydrocarbons obtained in Nigeria from natural gas by separation or by any chemical or physical process but before the same has been refined or otherwise treated;

(ix) 'petroleum operations' means the winning or obtaining and transportation of petroleum or chargeable oil in Nigeria by or on behalf of a company for its own account by any drilling, mining, extracting or other like operations or process, not including refining at a refinery in the course of a business carried on by the company engaged in such operations, and all operations incidental thereto and any sale of or any disposal of chargeable oil by or on behalf of the company;

(x) 'royalties' means and includes (a) the amount of any rent as to which there is provision for its deduction from the amount of any royalties under an oil-prospecting licence or oil-mining lease to the extent that such rent is so deducted; and (b) the amount of any royalties payable under any such licence or lease less any such rent deducted from those royalties;

(xi) 'tax' means chargeable tax;

(xii) 'oil-mining lease' means a lease granted to a company under the Mineral Oils Ordinance, for the purpose of winning petroleum, or any assignment of such licence;

(xiii) 'oil-prospecting licence' means a licence granted to a company under the Mineral Oils Ordinance for the purpose of winning petroleum or any assignment of such licence;

(xiv) 'natural gas' means gas obtained in Nigeria from bore holes and wells and consisting primarily of hydrocarbons;

(xv) 'petroleum' means any mineral oil or relative hydrocarbon and natural gas existing in its natural condition in Nigeria but does not include coal or bituminous shales or other stratified deposits from which oil can be extracted by destructive distillation;

(xvi) 'intangible drilling costs' means all expenditure for labour, fuel, repairs, maintenance, haulage and supplies and materials (not being supplies and materials for well-cement, casing or other well-fixtures) which are for or incidental to drilling, cleaning, deepening or completing wells or the preparations thereof incurred in respect of:
(a) determination of well-locations, geological studies and

topographical and geographical surveys preparatory to drilling;

(b) drilling, shooting, testing and cleaning wells;

(c) cleaning, draining and levelling land, roadbuilding and the laying of foundations;

(d) erection of rigs and tankage assembly and installation of pipe lines and other plant and equipment required in the preparation or drilling of wells producing petroleum.

Note

Wells are classified into development/appraisal and exploration wells.

(xvii) 'non-productive rents' means and includes the amount of any rent as to which there is provision for its deduction from the amount of any royalties under an oil-prospecting licence or oil mining lease, to the extent that such rent is not so deducted.

The whole of section 2 of the Principal Act should be read over and over to ensure that the correct meaning of every defined expression is fully grasped. It is also to be emphasised that the Inspector must amend his copy of the Principal Act of 1959 to date by getting copies of all the amendment Acts referred to above.

(iii) Administration

Section 3 of the Act deals with administration. The powers and duties of the Board are clearly set out in section 3(a) to (h) but attention is invited to 3(e)–(i) which precludes the Board from authorising any person within or without Nigeria from performing on its behalf the duties specified in the First Schedule. These duties and powers which must not be delegated are contained in sections 3(b), (d) and (e), 6(2), 10(i)–(f), 11(2)(b)(iii), 13, 25(2), 27(i), 42, 45, 46 and 49. Each of these sections should be looked up in the Act, and its provisions carefully noted.

It should be noted, of course, that oil-marketing and oil-transportation companies as distinct from oil-producing companies are not subject to tax under the Petroleum Profits Tax Act but under the Companies Income Tax Act. In other words only oil-producing companies are taxed under the Petroleum Profits Tax Act because of the special peculiarities inherent in profits assessment.

An important peculiarity is that liability to tax arises over the accounting period of a company engaged in petroleum operation and is not related to a year of assessment as is the case with Companies Income Tax.

Anything required to be done under the Act should be done under the signature of the Chairman or any officer of the Federal Board of Inland Revenue Department so authorised by the Board. Even then, such authorisation should be under the signature of the Chairman, unless the authorisation is published in the *Gazette.*

Any notice or document from the Board is valid if it is signed by the Chairman of the Board or any officer authorised by him or such document or notice is printed and the offical name of the Board is only printed or stamped on it.

Service of notices

Service may be effected personally. In this respect, it is important that the notice is entered into a despatch book and signed for by the taxpayer, his agent, staff or representative.

Service may also be effected by registered post and the notice would be deemed to have been served on the day after which the post office informs the taxpayer that a registered letter is awaiting him at a post office, usually by registered slip.

A notice should be addressed to the registered office of a Nigerian limited liability company and, in the case of an overseas limited liability company, to the person authorised under the Companies Act to accept notices at the address filed with the Registrar of Companies or to the registered office of the company.

Thus a notice may be left at the office or address filed with the Registrar of Companies. The address at which the notice is left or served should not be a registered box number.

The Petroleum Profits Tax Act, 1959, as amended by the Petroleum Profits Tax (Amendment) Act No. 2 of 1977 imposes tax annually on every company engaged in petroleum operation.

The profits of a petroleum company are all its incomes which are incidental to its petroleum operations, arising from petroleum operations, the worth of chargeable oil sold by the company during the year and sales by the company of all chargeable oil.[1]

Sections 9–15 deal exhaustively with the procedure to be followed in ascertaining the chargeable profits of an oil company for any accounting period. The following stages will be reached step by step before finally arriving at the chargeable profits on which assessable tax at the rate of 85 per cent of chargeable profits is imposable under section (16).

First stage The proceeds of sales and other incidental income of the company must first be ascertained under section 9(1) which provides that in relation to any accounting period, the profits of that period of a company shall be taken to be the aggregate of:

(a) the proceeds of sale of all chargeable oil sold by the company in that period;

(b) the value of all chargeable oil disposed of by the company in that period; and

(c) all income of the company of that period incidental to and arising from any one or more of its petroleum operations.

Second stage After ascertaining the proceeds of sales and other income of an accounting period the next thing is to compute the adjusted profit. *This is done by making all deductions allowed by section 10 from the total of the proceeds and other income as ascertained under section 9.* These deductions include 'all out-goings and expenses wholly and exclusively and necessarily incurred, whether within or without Nigeria, during that period by such company for the purpose of those operations, including but without otherwise expanding or limiting the generality of the foregoing:

(a) any rents (excluding rents included in the definition of royalties and non-productive rents) incurred in respect of land or buildings occupied for its petroleum operations or compensation incurred under an oil-prospecting licence or an oil-mining lease for disturbance of surface rights or for any other like disturbance;

(b) all royalties the liability for which was incurred by the company during that period in respect of crude oil exported from Nigeria (whether by the company or otherwise) or of casinghead petroleum spirit so exported after injection into such crude oil;

(c) sums incurred by way of interest upon money borrowed by such company; where the Board is satisfied that the interest was payable on capital employed in carrying on its petroleum operations. It should be noted that interest on loan from any of its subsidiary companies is not allowable as a deduction. See section 11 (ii);

(d) any expense incurred for repair of premises, plant, machinery or fixtures employed for the purpose of carrying on petroleum operations or for the renewal, repair or alteration of any implement, utensils or articles so employed;

(e) debts directly incurred to the company and proved to the satisfaction of the Board to have become bad or doubtful in the accounting period for which the adjusted profit is being ascertained notwithstanding that such bad or doubtful debts were due and payable prior to the commencement of that period. There are three provisos:

    (i) this provision restricts the deduction of doubtful debt to the allowed to the portion of the debt which is proved to have become doubtful;

    (ii) requires that sums recovered by the company during a particular accounting period in respect of previously allowed bad or doubtful debts shall, for the purposes of section 9, sub-section (1)(c) be treated as income of that company for that period;

(iii) requires that it must be proved to the satisfaction of the Board that the debts in respect of which a deduction is claimed were either;

(a) included as a profit from the carrying on of petroleum operations in the accounting period in which they were incurred; or

(b) the debts were advances made in the normal course of carrying on petroleum operations not being advances on account of any item falling within the provisions of section 11 which deals with deductions not allowed. Still in the second stage of ascertaining the adjusted profit of a company under section 10 we have to grant deduction in respect of expenditure including intangible drilling costs directly incurred in connection with drilling an appraisal or development well but not an exploration well. Deduction in respect of contribution to approved provident, pension or other society or scheme or fund. Adjustment required to be made by section 12, if necessary, will then be made.

At this point the stage is reached of Adjusted Profit.

Third stage The third stage is the assessable profit stage and this is arrived at after deduction under section 14 of any unrelieved loss sustained in the previous period from the adjusted profit of the new accounting period.

Fourth stage The fourth and last stage is the chargeable profit stage. This is arrived at after deducting from the assessable profit capital allowances granted on fixed assets in accordance with the provisions of the Second Schedule and section 15 to the Principal Act as amended by Act 65 of 1966. In calculating the deduction to be allowed for an accounting period a limitation is imposed to ensure that the amount of any tax chargeable on the company for that period shall not be less than 15% of the tax which would be chargeable if no deductions were to be made under section 15. The amount of deduction allowable shall be:

(a) the full amount of capital allowances due, or

(b) 85% of assessable profits less 170% of the total amount of set-off under section 17 whichever is the less. Where there is an insufficiency of or no assessable profits, the total amount or part thereof which has not been so deducted shall be added to the aggregate amount to be computed for the following accounting period.

354

Deductions not allowed

(1) Section 11(i) of the Principal Act sets forth the following as disallowable items of expenditure in ascertaining the adjusted profit of any company of any accounting period from petroleum operations:

(a) any disbursements or expenses not being money wholly and exclusively laid out or expended, or any liability not being a liability wholly or exclusively incurred for the purpose of those operations;

(b) any capital withdrawn or any sum employed or intended to be employed as capital;

(c) any capital employed in improvements as distinct from repairs;

(d) any sum recoverable under an insurance or contract of indemnity;

(e) rent of or cost of repairs to any premises or part of premises not incurred for the purpose of those operations;

(f) any amounts incurred in respect of any income tax, profits tax or other similar tax whether charged within Nigeria or elsewhere;

(g) the depreciation of any premises, buildings, structures; works of a permanent nature, plant, machinery or fixtures;

(h) any payment to any provident, savings, widows and orphans or other society, scheme or fund, except such payments as are allowed under subsection (i)(f) of section 10;

(i) any royalty or other sums deductible in ascertaining the tax under section 17;

(j) any expenditure for the purchases of information relating to the existence and extent of petroleum deposits.

(2) (a) Notwithstanding the provisions of subsection (1) (b) of section 10, in computing the adjusted profit of any company of any accounting period no deduction shall be allowed in respect of such sums incurred by way of interest during that period upon any borrowed money where such money was borrowed from a second company if during that period –

(i) either company has an interest in the other company, or

(ii) both have interests in another company either directly or through other companies, or

(b) For the purposes of this subsection –

(i) a company shall be deemed to be a subsidiary of another company if and so long as an interest in it is held by that other company either directly or through any other company or companies;

355

(ii) an interest means a beneficial interest in issued share capital (by whatever name called); and

(iii) the Board shall disregard any such last mentioned interest which in their opinion is insignificant or remote, or where in their opinion that interest arises from a normal market investment and the companies concerned have no other dealings or connection between each other.

Section 12 says that where a company engaged in petroleum operations is engaged in the transportation of chargeable oil by ocean going oil-tankers operated by or on behalf of the company from Nigeria to another territory then such adjustments shall be made in computing an adjusted profit or a loss as shall have the effect of excluding therefrom any profit or loss attributable to such transportation.

Section 13 lays down that (1) where the Board is of opinion that any disposition is not in fact given effect to or that any transaction which reduces or would reduce the amount of any tax payable is artificial or fictitious, the Board may disregard any such disposition or direct that such adjustments shall be made as respects liability to tax as the Board considers appropriate so as to counteract the reduction of liability to tax effected, or reduction which would otherwise be effected, by the transaction and the companies concerned shall be assessable accordingly. In this sub-section the expression 'disposition' includes any trust, grant, covenant, agreement or arrangement.

(3) For the purpose of this section, the following transactions shall be deemed to be artificial or fictitious, namely transactions between persons one of whom has control over the other or between persons both of whom are controlled by some other person which, in the opinion of the Board, have not been made on terms which might fairly have been expected to have been made by independent persons engaged in the same or similar activities dealing with one another at arm's length.

Sub-section (3) provides: nothing in this section shall prevent the decision of the Board in the exercise of any discretion given to the Board by this section from being questioned in an appeal against an assessment in accordance with Part VIII of this Ordinance and, on the hearing of any appeal, the appropriate Appeal Commissioners or the court may confirm or vary such decision including any directions made under this section.

(iv) Ascertainment of assessable tax and chargeable tax

Section 16 The assessable tax for any accounting period of a company shall be an amount equal to:

(a)   (i) 1958 to 19.3.71: 50% of its chargeable profits

     (ii) 20.3.71. – 30.9.74: 55% of its chargeable profits

    (iii) 1.10.74 – 30.11.74: 60.78% of its chargeable profits

    (iv) 1.12.74 – 31.3.75: 65.78% of its chargeable profits

     (v) 1.4.75 – to date: 85% of its chargeable profits

(b)   (i) 65.75% of its chargeable profits where a company commenced production on or after 1 April 1977 until the production costs are fully amortised, and

    (ii) 65.75% of chargeable profit on crude oil locally disposed off for domestic consumption.

Section 17 1 The chargeable tax for any accounting period of a company to be charged, assessed and paid, shall be the amount of assessable tax after the deduction of the following:

Sub-section 2 (a) all royalties the liability for which was incurred by the company during that period in respect of the *chargeable oil* won during that period to the extent that these royalties are not deductible under section 10(1)(aa) of the Act in computing the adjusted profit of the company for that period;

Sub-section 2 (aa) all non-productive rents the liability for which was incurred by the company during that period;

Sub-section 2 (b) all sums the liability for which was incurred by the Company during that period to the Federal Government of Nigeria by way of customs or excise duty or other like charges levied in respect of plant, storage tanks, pipelines, tools, machinery and equipment *'essential'* for use in the company's petroleum operations, and in the event of a dispute as to whether any item is essential, the Director of Petroleum Resources shall determine the matter and no appeal shall lie therefrom;

sub-section 2(c) the amount of investment tax credit due to the company. This is only from 1 April 1977 onwards.

Note

An agreed list of such essential equipment is available in the office of the Chief Inspector of Taxes, Petroleum and Pioneer Branch. Custom Duties on equipments etc. outside the list will be expensed under section 10(g).

3 Where the total sums allowed to be deducted under this section 17 exceed the assessable tax, such excess or such total amount shall be

carried forward for deduction from the assessable tax for the next following accounting period and so on until the excess or total amount has been so deducted. In case of any repayment or refund or waiver or release, of any or part of the deduction, the total deduction will be so reduced by the amount of that repayment, refund etc.

4 Liability incurred by a company engaged in petroleum operations in the business of transportation of chargeable oil by oil tankers or has any other source of income not chargeable under the PPTA, then any such liability attributable to such transportation, oil tankers or source (which would but for this subsection be allowed to be deducted under this section 17) shall not be allowed to be deducted under the provisions of this section.

Section 17A This section deals with the calculation of additional chargeable tax in any accounting period by multiplying the number of barrels known as the posted price applicable to that crude oil reduced by such allowance (if any) as may from time to time be agreed in writing between the Federal Government and the company. The excess of the figure so obtained over the sale proceeds referred to in section 9(1)(a) in an accounting period will form the basis of the additional chargeable tax. *Posted price[2] in relation to any crude oil exported from Nigeria by a company means the price f.o.b. at the Nigeria port of export* for crude oil of the gravity and quality.

Example 1

To illustrate implementation of
Petroleum Profits Tax Act, section 15 restriction

Assessable profit, say   ₦10 000 000   (CA's ₦800 000)
   Less capital allowance   8 000 000
   Chargeable profit   ₦2 000 000

Assessable Tax (50% of chargeable profit =   ₦1 000 000
  (royalties say ₦800 000)
   Less royalties, etc. (section 17)   800 000
                             ₦200 000

Under section 15(3) the amount of tax chargeable must not be less than 15% of the tax which would be chargeable if no capital allowances were given. (It should be noted that tax means 'Chargeable tax' i.e. after section 17 deductions).

Applying the formula in section 15(4)(b) capital allowances to be:

85% of assessable profit of ₦10 000 000   =   ₦8 500 000
Less 170% of section 17 deductions
   (₦800 000) (i.e. royalties, etc.)   1 360 000
                             ₦7 140 000

Example 2

Computation of profit and tax for the accounting period
1 January–31 December of Ajasa Oil Company Ltd

Income	section 9 and 17A	The next fiscal value of sale of chargeable oil is based on section 17A, That is, total barrels multiplied by posted price – see section 170. Section 9 will produce less as it deals with proceeds which will be calculated using realised price per barrel.			485 350 455
Deductions	section 10(1)	*Recurrent administrative and production expenditure*		24 999 782	
		Gross royalty	60 159 635		
		Less gross royalty on local sales of crude oil and gas	1 420 605		
		Balance being gross royalty on export sales	58 739 030	58 739 030	
		Intangible drilling expenditure		25 470 692	109 209 504
		Adjusted assessable profit			375 140 951
Capital allowance	section 14	*1977 allowances*			
	section 15	*Building*		415 047	
		Drilling		2 394 792	

359

85% of assessable profit of ₦376 140 951
Less 170% of deduction of ₦6 132 680
from assessable tax (See below for
the deductions from assessable tax)

=

Total 1977 allowances	9 689 236	12 499 075
	12 499 075	
Chargeable profit		363 641 876
	₦319 719 808	
	10 425 556	
	₦309 294 252	

Since the aggregate amount computed under section 15(2) is less than 85% of assessable profit less 170% of deduction from assessable tax, deduction of capital allowance under section 15(4) is claimed in full.

Assessable tax	section 16	85% of chargeable profit of	₦363 641 876		₦262 900 111
Statement No. 1	Assessable Tax	brought forward			262 900 111
Chargeable Tax	section 17	*Deduction from Assessable Tax*			
		1977 items rentals	5 169 658		
		Less Rentals offset against royalty	2 489 457		
			2 680 201	2 680 201	
		Balance Rentals qualifying as tax offset		1 420 605	
		Royalty on gas and crude oil local sales		2 031 874	6 132 680
		Custom duties qualifying as tax offset			
		Chargeable tax			₦256 767 431

Note

No allowance has been made in this computation for local sales of crude and gas which now attracts tax of 65.75% of chargeable profits.

360

As ₦7 140 000 is less than capital allowances computed of ₦8 000 000 capital allowances have to be restricted. The fresh computations then become:

Assessable profit	₦10 000 000	
Less CA's as recommended	7 140 000	(Balance CA of
	₦2 860 000	₦860 000 for carry-
		forward under
		section 15(5)
Assessable tax (50% of CA)	1 430 000	
Less section 17 deductions	800 000	
Chargeable tax	₦630 000	

Proof:
If no CA's were due
Assessable profit and chargeable profit would be:

	₦10 000 000	
Assessable tax (50%)	5 000 000	
Less section 17 deductions	800 000	
	4 200 000	
Chargeable tax, i.e.		
15% of ₦4 200 000	630 000	(agreeing with the above).

Other taxes offsettable are in respect of expenditure incurred on custom duty, non-productive rent and investment tax credit – see section 17.

Question

(a) In relation to Petroleum Profits Tax, state briefly the basis of computing capital allowances on qualifying petroleum expenditure as contained in section 15 of the Petroleum Profits Tax Act, 1959, as amended and Second Schedule to the same Act for any given accounting period.

(b) List nine of the items which are specifically disallowed in ascertaining the adjusted profit of a petroleum company.

Answer

Section 15 of PPTA, 1959, provides that the chargeable profits of any company of any accounting period shall be the amount of the assessable profits of that period after deduction of any amount to be allowed in accordance with the provisions of this section.

There shall be computed the aggregate amount of all allowances due to the company under the provisions of the Second Schedule for the accounting period.

In calculating the amount of the deduction to be allowed, under this section, for the accounting period, it should be ensured that the amount of any tax chargeable on the company for that period shall not be less than 15 per cent of the tax which would be chargeable on the company for that period had not capital allowances been claimed.

The amount to be allowed as a deduction for capital allowances shall be:

(a) the aggregate amount of the allowances

or

(b) a sum equal to 85 per cent of the assessable profits of the accounting period, less 170% of the total amount of the deductions as tax offsets under s.17 of PPTA, 1979, whichever is the less.

Where the total amount of the allowances under (a) above cannot be deducted owing to there being an insufficiency of or no assessable profits of the accounting period or to the limitation referred to above, such total amount or the part thereof which has not been so deducted as the case may be shall be added to the aggregate amount to be computed under sub-section (2) for the following accounting period of the company and thereafter shall be deemed to be an allowance due to the company under the provisions of the Second Schedule for that following accounting period.

Second Schedule to PPTA, 1959, para. (5) provides that where in any accounting period of a company, the company owing any asset has incurred in respect thereof qualifying expenditure wholly, necessarily and exclusively for the purposes of petroleum operations carried out by it, there shall be due to that company for the accounting period in which such expenditure was incurred an investment tax credit for the purposes of s.17(2)(c) at the rates specified below:

1 qualifying expenditure in respect of on-shore operations   5%
2 operations in territorial waters and continental shelf areas up to and including 100 metres of water depth   10%
3 operations in water depth between 100–200 metres   15%
4 operations beyond 200 metres of water depth   20%

With reference to annual allowances, the qualifying expenditure is to be written off at the rates specified below subject to retention in the books of 1% of the initial value of each qualifying expenditure:

First year	20%
2nd year	20%
3rd year	20%
4th year	20%
5th year	19%
6th year and after	nil

Any asset or part thereof in respect of which capital allowances have been granted may only be disposed of on the authority of a certificate of disposal issued by the Commissioner or any person authorised by him.

Any unrecovered capitalised expenditure prior to 1 April 1977 shall be deemed to have been capitalised with effect from 1 April 1977 and shall as provided for above, be amortised in five equal instalments subject to the provisions of sub-paragraphs (2) and (3) of the Second Schedule to PPTA, 1959.

The following items are specifically disallowed in ascertaining the assessable profit of a company engaged in petroleum operations:

  (i) capital withdrawn or any sum employed or intended to be employed as capital;
  (ii) capital improvements as distinct from repairs;
  (iii) depreciation of fixed assets;
  (iv) sums recoverable under an insurance or contract of indemnity;
  (v) any amount incurred in respect of income tax or profits tax charged within Nigeria or elsewhere;
  (vi) rent of or cost of repairs of any premises not incurred for petroleum operations;
  (vii) royalties treated as tax offset in accordance with the provisions of section 17(2)(a);
  (viii) non-productive rents, customs duties, and tax treated as tax offset;
  (ix) any expenditure for the purchase of information relating to the existence and extent of petroleum deposits.

The following is the format of the Petroleum Profits Tax Computation with full cognisance of the tax introduced since the Petroleum Profits Tax (Amendment) Act, 1977.

	Export	Domestic	Total for year
(a) *Tax value of crude oil sales*			
Incidental revenue			
(sect. 9–17A)			
(b) *Less: section 10 deductions*			
Royalty			
Operating costs			
Repairs and maintenance			
Office service & general charges, etc.			
Intangible drilling costs			
Wildcat and appraisal wells (tangible costs)			
Customs duties (non-essentials)			

Crude oil inventory charges
(storage, pipeline hire or
use charges)
(c) *Assessable profits*
Deduct: (section 15)
Capital allowances
Chargeable profits
Tax rate   85%   65.75%
Assessable tax
(d) *Deduct:* (offsettables under
sect. 17)
Customs duties
(essentials)
Non-productive rents
(on leases)
Royalty (domestic crude
oil)
Investment tax credit
(e) *Chargeable tax*   ₦____   ₦_____   ₦_____

(v) Payments

Payments of Petroleum Profits Tax for any accounting period of twelve months shall be payable in twelve instalments together with a final instalment which shall be due and payable within 21 days of the date of service of the notice of assessment. It shall be for the amount of the assessment, less the sum already paid.

The first monthly payment shall be due on the last day of the third month of the accounting date, that is, 31 March, and shall be an amount equal to one-twelfth of the amount of tax estimated to be chargeable for such accounting period.

Offences and penalties

The following are the offences against the Act to which a company may be guilty:
(a) failure to comply with the requirements of a notice served under the Act;
(b) failure to render returns;
(c) failure to attend in answer to a notice or summons or having attended, failure to answer any question lawfully put; and

(d) failure to submit any return of estimated tax.

Any company guilty of an offence against the Act of or any rule made thereunder for which no penalty is specifically provided, shall be liable to a fine of ten thousand naira.

For a failure to submit a return, or to deliver accounts, particulars or information or to keep records required, a further sum of two thousand naira for each and every day during which such offence or failure continues and in default of payment, to imprisonment for six months, the liability for such further sum to commence from the day following the conviction or from such day thereafter as the court may order.

Miscellaneous

In respect of any income or dividends paid out of any profits charged, assessed and paid under the provisions of the Petroleum Profits Tax Act, no tax shall be further charged under the Companies Income Tax Act or any other Act.

Example 3

Sales within Nigeria of crude oil and gas		₦2 000 000
Fiscal value of chargeable oil exported		82 000 000
Miscellaneous income		120 000
		84 120 000
Less		
Production and administrative costs	₦16 000 000	
Intangible drilling expenditure	10 000 000	
Surveys preparatory to drilling	2 000 000	
Rents and royalties on exports	10 800 000	38 800 000
Assessable profits		45 320 000
Less: Capital allowances		26 000 000
Chargeable profits		19 320 000
Assessable tax at 60.78%		11 742 696
Less tax offsets:		
Royalties on local sales for local refining purposes	₦300 000	
Unabsorbed concession rentals (Non-productive rents)	1 200 000	
Customs duties on essential supplies	3 700 000	4 200 000
Chargeable tax		7 542 696

Act No. 24 of 1979 published in the *Federal Gazette* No. 27, Vol. 66 of 28 June 1979 amends the Petroleum Profits Tax Act, 1959, by giving certain incentives by way reduced taxation to companies prospecting for oil in Nigeria. The Act takes effect from 1.4.77. For example Investment Tax Credit is now given as follows:

(a) For land operations, 5%
(b) For offshore operations in areas up to and including 100 metres of water depth, 10%
(c) For offshore operations in water depth beyond 100 metres and up to 200 metres, 15%
(d) for operations in areas beyond 200 metres, 20%.

Investment Tax Credit (formerly Initial Allowance) is deducted from the cost of the asset to arrive at the amount of qualifying expenditure and before calculating the Annual Allowance. Investment Tax Credit is a charge against tax payable and not a charge against income.

Example 4

Ikeja Oil Producing Company
Accounts for year ended 31.12.88

The above-named company, submitting its accounts for the second accounting year, showed the following:

Aggregate revenue for the year: ₦8 591 000; section 10 expenses (all allowable): ₦2 300 000; loss sustained in its first year and which was carried forward to the second year; ₦95 000; capital allowances for the year: ₦4 726 000. The rate of tax was 85%. Relief allowable under section 17 (as offsettables), ₦500 000.

You are required to compute the chargeable tax of the company for the year.

Solution

Revenue	₦8 591 000
Less section 10 expenses	2 300 000
	6 291 000
Less Loss brought forward	95 000
	6 196 000
Deduct capital allowances	4 726 000
Chargeable profit	1 470 000
Assessable tax at 85%	1 249 500
Less offsettables (section 17)	500 000
Chargeable Tax	749 500

This is the tax payable.

Example 5: to illustrate implementation of Petroleum Profits Tax Act, section 15 restriction

Assessable profit, say ₦10 000 000   (CA's ₦800 000)
   Less capital allowances   8 000 000
   Chargeable profit   ₦2 000 000
Assessable Tax (50%³ of chargeable profit) = ₦1 000 000
   Less royalties, etc. (section 17)   800 000
      ₦200 000

Under section 15(3) the amount of tax chargeable must not be less than 15% of the tax which would be chargeable if no capital allowances were given. (It should be noted that tax means 'chargeable tax', i.e. after section 17 deductions). Applying the formula in section 15(4)(b) capital allowances to be:

85% of assessable profit of ₦10 000 000 = ₦8 500 000
   Less 170% of section 17 deductions
     (₦800 000, royalties, etc.)   1 360 000
      ₦7 140 000

As ₦7 140 000 is less than capital allowances computed of ₦8 000 000 capital allowances have to be restricted. The fresh computations then became:

Assessable profit   ₦10 000 000 (Balance CA of
Less CA's as recommended   7 140 000 ₦860 000 for carry-
   Chargeable profit   ₦2 860 000 forward under
          section 15(5))

Assessable Tax (50%³ of CP   1 430 000
Less section 17 deductions   800 000
   Chargeable tax   ₦630 000

Proof:
If no CA's were due
   Assessable profit and chargeable profit would be:

               ₦10 000 000
Assessable tax (50%)³   5 000 000
Less section 17 deductions   800 000
            4 200 000
Chargeable tax, i.e. 15% of ₦4 200 000   630 000
          (agreeing with the above.)

Other Tax Offsettables are in respect of expenditure incurred on custom duty, non-productive rent and investment tax credit – see section 17.

Question 2

Majasan Oil Producing Company operated since 1950 as a division of a private company owned 100% by its parent company – Majasan Oil Producing Company Limited. By the Companies Act, 1968, this Company was deemed to have been incorporated on 18 November, 1968 in Nigeria. As enjoined under the provisions of the Petroleum Profits Tax Act, 1959, as amended by the various Acts up to date, this company compiled the following accounts from its 1988 operations in Nigeria:

	Crude oil; exported crude	Domestic disposal
Revenue sales	₦467 534 040	₦5 568 924
Incidental income	33 146	3 159
Section 10 deductions claimed		
Export royalty	87 102 462	–
Operating costs	7 484 452	713 195
Repairs & maintenance costs	3 520 689	335 487
Office service & general expenses	4 275 822	407 444
Intangible drilling cost	11 243 198	1 071 367
Wildcat & appraisal wells (tangible costs)	322 923	30 771
Customs duties – non-essential	212 307	20 231
Crude oil inventory net charge	34 357	–
Capital allowances (section 15)	7 750 100	738 509
Offset-tables claimed under section 17A		
Customs duties – essential goods	240 448	18 383
Non-productive – lease rentals	1 006 950	96 848
Royalties on domestic crude only	–	1 200 999
Investment tax credit	358 940	33 800
Ruling tax rates	85%	65.75%

From the above accounts, prepare a schedule of Petroleum Profits Tax Computation of Majasan Oil Producing Company for the year ended 31 December 1988 indicating the following with separate totals in respect of:

(a) (i) exported crude oil, and
    (ii) domestically-disposed crude;
(b) aggregate revenue for the year (1988);
(c) total section 10 allowable deductions;
(d) aggregate assessable profit;
(e) aggregate chargeable profit;
(f) aggregate assessable tax;
(g) aggregate offsettable charges; and
    the chargeable tax (for the solution, see pp. 371–2).

Example 6

Computation of profit and tax for the accounting period
1 January–31 December of Ajasa Oil Company Ltd

Income	section 9 and 17A	The next fiscal value of sale of chargeable oil is based on section 17A, that is, total barrels multiplied by posted price – see section 170. Section 9 will produce less as it deals with proceeds which will be calculated using realised price per barrel.			485 350 455
Deductions	section 10(1)	Recurrent administrative and production expenditure		24 999 782	
		Gross royalty	60 159 635		
		Less gross royalty on local sales of crude oil and gas	1 420 605		
		Balance being gross royalty on export sales	58 739 030	58 739 030	
		Intangible drilling expenditure		25 470 692	
					109 209 504
		Adjusted assessable profit			375 140 951
Capital allowance	section 14	1977 allowances		415 047	
	section 15	Building		2 394 792	
		Drilling		9 689 236	

85% of assessable profit of ₦376 140 951
Less 170% of deduction of ₦6 132 680
from assessable tax (See below for
the deductions from assessable tax)

		Total 1977 allowances	12 499 075
			363 641 876
	=	Chargeable profit	₦319 719 808
			10 425 556
			₦309 294 252

Since the aggregate amount computed under section 15(2) is less than 85% of assessable profit less 170% of deduction from assessable tax, deduction of capital allowance under section 15(4) is claimed in full.

Assessable tax	section 16	85% of chargeable profit of	₦363 641 876		₦262 900 111
Statement No. 1	Assessable Tax	brought forward			262 900 111
Chargeable Tax	section 17	Deduction from Assessable Tax			
		1977 items rentals		5 169 658	
		Less Rentals offset against royalty		2 489 457	
		Balance Rentals qualifying as tax offset	2 680 201	2 680 201	
		Royalty on gas and crude oil local sales	1 420 605		
		Custom duties qualifying as tax offset	2 031 874		6 132 680
		Chargeable tax			₦256 767 431

Note:
No allowance has been made in this computation for local sales of crude and gas which now attracts tax of 65.75% of chargeable profits.

Answer to Question 2 on p. 368

Majasan Oil Producing Company Ltd
Petroleum Profits Tax Computation for the year ended 31 December 1988

	Export		Domestic		Total for the year	
Tax value of crude oil sales	₦467 534 040		₦5 568 924		₦473 103 964	
Incidental revenue	33 146		3 159		36 305	(i)
		₦467 567 186		₦5 572 083	₦473 139 269	(i)
Less: section 10 deductions						
Royalty	₦87 102 462		–		87 102 462	
Operating costs	7 484 452		713 195		8 197 647	
Repairs & maintenance	3 520 689		335 487		3 856 176	
Office service & general charges	4 275 822		407 444		4 683 266	
Intangible drilling costs	11 243 198		1 071 367		12 314 565	
Wildcat & appraisal wells (tangible costs)	322 923		30 771		353 694	
Customs duties – non-essentials	212 307		20 231		232 538	
Crude oil inventory – net charges	34 357	114 196 210	–	2 578 495	34 357	(ii)
					116 774 705	(ii)
Assessable profit		353 370 976		2 993 588	356 364 564	(iii)

371

Deduct (section 15)					
Capital allowances		7 750 100	738 509	8 488 609	
Chargeable profit		345 620 876	2 255 079	₦347 875 955	(iv)
Tax rate @		85%	65.75%		
Assessable tax		293 777 745	1 482 714	₦295 260 459	(v)
Deduct (offsettables under section 17)					
Customs duties – essential	240 448	18 383			
Non-productive – lease rental	1 006 950	96 848			
Royalty – domestic crude only	–	1 200 999			
Investment tax credit	358 940	33 800	1 350 030	2 956 368	(vi)
		11 606 338	132 684		
Chargeable tax		292 171 407		₦292 304 091	(vii)

Note:
There is only one ruling tax rate in Petroleum Profit Taxation. The current rate is 85%; the rate of 65.7% mentioned above is a temporary concession.

Question 3

Spectacular developments as incorporated in the Petroleum Profits Tax (Amendments) Act, 1979, have occurred with effect from April 1977 in the Federal Government Petroleum Tax policy and have boosted the morale of foreign investors and companies prospecting for oil in Nigeria.

Write notes in defence of this observation on each of these new measures.

Answer

The most spectacular development in the taxation of crude oil from the period 1 April 1977 to date is embodied in the package of incentives incorporated in the Petroleum Profits Tax (Amendment) No. 2, Act 24 of 1979.[4]

The purpose of this Act is to amend the Petroleum Profits Tax Act (1959)) tax policy by giving certain incentives by way of reduced taxation to oil companies prospecting for oil in Nigeria.

The measures of the new tax policy include the following:

(i) *exploration incentives:*

Exploration drilling costs and those of the first two appraisal wells whether successful or not are to be expensed.

(ii) *tax incentives:*

Companies holding oil concessions and commencing oil production on or after the effective date should pay tax at 65.75% until their pre-production costs were fully amortised less the 1% residual book retention, when the company would be taxed at the rate of 85%.

(iii) *investment tax credit:*

All capitalised expenditure made on or after the effective date, 1.4.77, shall qualify for Capital Investment Tax Credit as follows only in the year of such expenditure:

(a) operations on land – 5%

(b) operations on offshore areas of water depth up to and including 100 metres – 10%

(c) for operations in offshore areas in water depth beyond 100 metres and up to 200 metres – 15%

(d) for operations in areas beyond 200 metres – 20%.

(iv) Royalty rate modification:

As against the uniform existing rate of 20%, royalty is henceforth graded as follows:

(a) operation on land – 20%

(b) operation in offshore areas up to and including 100 metres – $18\frac{1}{2}$%, and

(c) operation in offshore areas beyond 100 metres – $16\frac{2}{3}$%.

373

(v) Capital allowances:

Annual allowances – all capitalised expenditure be amortised in five equal annual instalments. There shall be retained in the books in respect of each asset 1% of the initial cost of the asset which may only be written off on the authority of a Certificate of Asset Disposal issued by the Federal Commissioner for Petroleum. This applies to all unrecovered capitalised expenditure as at the effective date.

(vi) Company Profit Margin:

The Company Profit Margin has been increased from 70¢/bbl. to 80¢/bbl. for higher oils and 77¢/bbl. for medium with effect from the effective date.

It is too early to assess the effect of these new measures but already there is a gradual improvement in production as illustrated by the following statistical data:

Crude oil production: a rise from 2 071 231 bbls per day to 2 098 779 bbls and

Crude oil exports: a rise from 2 013 115 bbls per day to 2 039 487 bbls (324 253 cubic metres per day).

APP/COMM/225 – 18 April 1975
The Shell-BP Petroleum Development Co. Nigeria Ltd v Federal Board of Inland Revenue

Petroleum Profits Tax Act (PPTA) 1959 – Disallowance of demurrage/ deadfreight charges – Interpretation of 'Petroleum Operations' – section 2 PPTA 1959 – Whether the sale of crude oil come within the definition of 'petroleum operations' – Allowable deductions – section 10 PPTA, 1959 – Additional assessment section 17A PPTA.

The contention of the appellant was that the word 'sale' in section 2 of the PPTA includes sale of crude oil and such sale comes within the definition of 'petroleum operations' as defined, and therefore the demurrage and dead freight disallowed ought to be allowed.

The appeal was dismissed. The Appeal Commissioners found (*i*) that the sale or the disposal of chargeable oil does not come within the definition of 'petroleum operations' as defined in section 2 PPTA 1959 and consequently demurrage/dead freight charges were not allowable deductions under section 10 of PPTA. (*ii*) that the respondent should make a comparison of accounts computed under two different sections of the Act – that is, sections 9 and 17A. It is only where these two sets of accounts are available to the respondent that a comparison could be made with a view to raising an additional assessment pursuant to section 17A(1) of the Act.

Notes

1   Crude oil reserves existing under the ground are of importance to the country. The cost of finding whether or not crude oil exists should be treated as cost of operation and should be treated as a tax-offset and not as a tax deduction since these costs will improve the country's oil reserve basis. The questions relating to the quantity of crude oils available in the country and for how long they will last are crucial to an oil-producing developing country.

    Some schools of thought think that since the operations of a petroleum company are different and since the revenue regulated for them is based on posted price which they do not obtain, they should be exempted from tax on dividends. The limit of allowable expenditure an oil company can claim at the time of writing is restricted to technical cost which is a dollar and ten cents (regulated by NNPC). Petroleum companies, in addition, have specified for them, the profit they can make, i.e. 53k a barrel. It would therefore appear unfair for these companies to pay a dividend withholding tax as long as these constraints are on.

2   Posted price is an artificial or deemed price, about 10% higher than actual price of crude oil which is sold abroad. No one can tell at any given time what the price of crude oil is. It appears therefore that the Federal Board of Inland Revenue is using an artificial price to assess petroleum companies on the profits they do not make. It is suggested that realisation price, which is the price at which the company actually sells, should be substituted for posted price.

3   Assessable tax is presently at 85%.

4   Otherwise known as Petroleum Profits Tax (Amendment) (No. 2) Act, 1977, published in the *Federal Gazette* Vol. 66, No. 29, 28 June 1979.

375

13 Double Taxation Relief

Nigeria, like other countries, seeks to tax the global income of persons resident here and to tax the incomes of non-residents where the incomes arise here. Because other countries adopt similar policies an income may be taxed by two or more different countries.

The question of residence has been dealt with. In employment cases, the earnings of an employed person are exempt if:

(a) the employer is in a country other than Nigeria;

(b) the employer is not in Nigeria for 183 days in the year of assessment;

(c) the remuneration is taxable in the other country. If the duties are wholly or mainly performed in Nigeria, the remuneration is taxable during temporal absences from Nigeria. If the duties are wholly or mainly performed outside Nigeria, the remuneration relating to the duties performed in Nigeria is taxable.

In order to ensure alleviation of payment of tax in two or more countries on one income, double taxation relief is granted provided there is a double taxation agreement between this country and the other country. Section 16 of the Act empowers the Minister of Finance (now Commissioner) to extend the Third Schedule which is an exemption schedule, following agreement with another country or international body with Nigerian State governments. The Nigerian Federal Government can add to the list of exemptions and this it has done by, for example, exempting interest accruing to the Commonwealth Development Corporation and salaries of technical assistants so that even if there is no right under the Double Taxation Agreement, it may be wise to ensure that the income is specifically exempted either under section 16 or the Third Schedule.

376

Type of exemptions provided by Double Taxation Agreements

1   Article 3 of the Double Taxation Agreement[1] between this country and the United Kingdom provides that unless a permanent establishment is maintained in Nigeria, the profits of a United Kingdom enterprise in Nigeria are not taxable in Nigeria, and *vice versa*. By permanent establishment' is meant, 'a branch management or other fixed place of business.' A place of business maintained merely for purchase of goods is not a permanent establishment. The activities of a *bona fide* commission broker's agent do not consitute permanent establishment neither does an agency unless the agent habitually concludes contracts on behalf of his principal or has a stock or merchandise from which he regularly fills orders on behalf of his principal.

2   The remuneration of a professor or teacher[2] who is resident for not more than two years in the other country for the purpose of teaching is exempt from Nigerian tax.

3   Shipping and aircraft profits are exempt.[3]

4   Government pensions are not taxable unless the recipient is ordinarily resident here.[4]

5   Dividends[5] paid by a United Kingdom company to a Nigerian resident who has no permanent establishment in the United Kingdom are exempt from United Kingdom tax. The same rule applies when a Nigerian company pays dividends to a United Kingdom resident.

6   Payments to a student or apprentice for his full-time education or training here are exempt.

7   Under article 9, the income of a resident in the United Kingdom is exempt

   (a) if he is not in Nigeria for 183 days;
   (b) the services are rendered for a UK employer.

The exemption does not extend to entertainers such as pop stars.

Similar agreements with Ghana, Gambia, Sierra-Leone, the USA, New Zealand, Denmark, Sweden, etc. have been concluded. Those agreements should be consulted whenever difficulties are encountered. For example, incomes earned in the United States of America by Nigerian visiting lecturers or Professors are exempt from US tax under Article XIX of the First Schedule to the Income Tax (Double Taxation Relief) (USA) Order 1958.[6]

Double tax is not an easy subject. The definitive picture of its complexity is to be found in *England, Their England,* A.G. Macdonnell's small masterpiece which so brilliantly caught the desperate and brittle gaiety of the years following the First World War, when the survivors attempt to return to normal peace-time activities, and responsibilities were impeded by economic catastrophe. One of the shorter-lived jobs acquired by the book's hero was in a chartered accounting firm, working for the senior partner 'across whose eyes a blind would fall if anyone mentioned double taxation, and who would not rejoin the conversation until it got back to safer subjects of which he had at least some comprehension.'

Little is different today. The economic situation is no better, chartered accountancy in general and senior partners in particular are just as difficult, and double taxation even more so. That does not mean, however, that we need make no effort to discover anything about the discipline, and about the principles on which it operates.

There are two completely separate strands to double taxation, and confusion of the two is the single greatest cause of difficulties. The difference can best be pointed up in an illustration.

Assume that a UK company sends one of its junior executives to work for eight months for its US subsidiary. His UK tax position is straightforward; he is not out of the UK long enough to lose his resident status, or to achieve complete exemption for his earnings, but those earnings for the eight-month period will only be taxed on three-quarters of their total amount.

US taxes are also a relevant factor. The individual being in the US for more than 90 days and earning more than $3000 is taxable as a non-resident alien. His salary for the period in the US is treated as US source income, whether or not it is actually paid in the US because it is in their terminology effectively connected with the US trade or business of the subsidiary there. Not only is his salary taxable in the US but so also, in strictness, are any other amounts paid by his employer. The US recognises, however, a *per diem* allowance, within lmits, for 'away from home expenses,' and it is therefore reasonable to assume that no liability will arise under this head.

A non-resident alien does not qualify for all the categories of deductions available to a citizen. If our man's salary is £6000 per annum, so that the eight month proportion of it is £4000, his US liability will be slightly less than £700, an average rate of 17 per cent. He is required before leaving to file a US tax return in order to obtain a tax compliance certificate – often called a sailing permit. Failure to produce such a certificate can give rise to income tax examination at the point of departure, and a demand for taxes at that time.

The first meaning of 'double tax' can now be outlined, that dealt with in the tax treaty between the UK and the US, which is properly called the 'Convention for the Avoidance of Double Taxation and the Prevention of Fiscal Evasion.' The existing treaty dates substantially from 1946. Its provisions have the status of an international treaty, and to the extent that they conflict with the domestic law of either party, override that domestic law.

378

The tax treaty states that a resident of the UK is exempt from US tax on earnings unless he is in the US for more than 183 days in the year and is working for the benefit of a company other than a UK one. This exemption can be seen to be considerably wider than the 90-day and $3000 exemption which is all that US law would give without the treaty enlargement. But our individual (given certain assumptions about how his eight months fall into one or more tax years), has exceeded even these enlarged limits, and is taxable in the US.

One note of warning needs to be sounded on the subject of tax treaties. Words and phrases in them are frequently similar to those in the domestic laws of the parties but can have significantly different implications. In the existing US/UK treaty, individuals are referred to as resident of, not resident in, one of the countries. The definition of this phrase embodied in the treaty restricts the treaty's operation to cases where an individual is either a UK resident under UK law, or a US resident under US law: it is perfectly possible for an individual to be both at once, and if so the treaty would give him no protection.

All treaties are different. The proposed new US treaty, if it is ever ratified by the Senate, will work differently – actually identifying the dual resident, and then deciding by a set of more or less arbitrary rules in which country to locate him for treaty purposes. The new treaty will also redefine the criteria for the exemption of earnings. Instead of basing it on the residence status of the company benefiting from the individual's labours, the new treaty looks to the status of the company actually paying the salary, and if different the company to whom that salary is charged. Treaties usually deal with dividends, interest and royalties.

We are now able to look at the second meaning of double tax, namely double tax relief. In the UK this is in 99 cases out of 100 governed solely by UK domestic law which provides for the giving of credit against UK tax liabilities in respect of overseas income. In this case, the $700 of US tax would reduce the taxable 75 per cent of the eight months earnings in the UK.

Credit is the word invariably used to denote the selling of tax against tax. Double tax credit relief, and Unilateral credit relief are used to distinguish cases where there is or is not a treaty with the other country involved. Provisions of UK law for each are in fact identical, and it is therefore a distinction without a difference except in the minds of the Revenue statisticians charged with working out the costs and benefits of each tax treaty.

Other possible methods of affording relief for overseas tax are treating that tax as an expense in computing UK income or treating the income which is taxable or deemed taxable abroad as consequently exempt in the UK. Exemption in the home country of foreign income

379

is commonly provided for in a tax treaty, but it is a form of relief only exceptionally given in the UK so that most of our treaties are silent on this matter.

Credit relief is the more common UK rule. Its effect can be neatly summarised by saying that the higher of the two tax rates always remains the payer's effective burden.

Method of calculation where the Double Taxation Agreement does not exempt an income that has been doubly taxed

Direct overseas tax

Example 1

Overseas company dividend	₦100
Overseas tax paid at 25%	25
No. dividend received	₦75

Assume the taxpayer is chargeable to UK tax on the dividend at the UK basic rate of Income Tax, (say) 30%. *Without a claim* for tax credit relief, the taxpayer would be assessed on ₦75 at 30% = ₦22.50 UK tax. *With a claim* for relief, the figures are:

UK assessment ₦100 at 30%	₦30
Less: tax credit relief	25
net UK tax payable	₦5

Total tax borne by the taxpayer is, therefore,

overseas tax	₦25
UK tax	5
	₦30

Example 2

Overseas company dividend	₦100
Overseas tax paid at 40%	₦40
Overseas company dividend	100
Net dividend received	₦60

A claim is made for tax credit relief. Assume the taxpayer is liable at the UK basic rate of Income Tax (say) 30%

UK assessment ₦100 at 30%	₦30
Less: tax credit relief	30
net UK tax payable	NIL
Total tax borne by the taxpayer:	
Overseas tax	₦40

Example 3 (Marginal Rate)

Taxpayer's income

	UK earnings	₦6000	
Dividend from country X		1500	(less overseas tax at 55% = ₦825)
Dividend from country Y		1000	(less overseas tax at 35% = ₦350)
	Total income	₦8500	
	Less: personal allowances (say)	1000	
	Taxable income	₦7500	

Calculating relief for country X dividend first:

(i) *UK tax chargeable on total income*

(say) Basic rate	₦5000 at 30%	=	₦1500
Higher rates	1000 at 40%	=	400
	1000 at 45%	=	450
	500 at 50%	=	250
₦7500*			₦2600

Investment Income surcharge ₦500
at 15%   75

UK tax chargeable   ₦2675

(ii) *UK tax on total income excluding X dividend*

UK earnings	₦6000
Dividend from country Y	1000
	₦7000
Less: personal allowances	1000
Taxable income	₦6000
Basic rate ₦5000 at 30% =	₦1500
Higher rate 1000 at 40%	400
	₦1900

Marginal rate on country X dividend (₦2675 − ₦1900)   ₦775
Tax credit relief given for ₦775 overseas tax (out of ₦825)

381

(iii) *UK tax on total income excluding X and Y dividend:*

UK earnings	₦6000
Less personal allowances	₦1000
Taxable income	₦5000

Basic rate ₦5000 at 30% =	₦1500
Marginal rate on	
country Y dividend (₦1900 − ₦1500)	₦400
Tax credit relief	
limited to overseas	
tax payable in country Y	₦350
Total tax credit relief (₦775 + ₦350)	₦1125
UK tax chargeable on total income	2675
Less: tax credit relief	1125
Net UK tax payable	₦1550

Example 4 (Marginal rate)

Facts as in Example 3, but giving relief for country Y dividend first.

(i) UK tax on total income ₦2675

(ii) *UK tax on total income excluding Y dividend*

UK earnings	₦6000
country X dividend	1500
	₦7500
Less: personal allowances	1000
Taxable income	₦6500
Basic rate ₦5000 at 30% =	₦1500
Higher rate 1000 at 40% =	400
500 at 45% =	225
	₦2125

Marginal rate on country Y dividend (₦2675 − ₦2175) = ₦550.
Tax credit relief limited to overseas tax payable in country Y = ₦350

(iii) *UK tax on total income excluding X and Y dividends*

UK earnings	₦6000
Less: personal allowance	1000
Taxable income	₦5000

Basic rate ₦5000 at 30% =	₦1500

Marginal rate on country X dividend (₦2125 − ₦1500) ₦625
Tax credit relief *given for* ₦625 overseas tax (out of ₦825)

Total tax credit relief (₦350 + ₦625)	₦975
UK tax chargeable on total income	₦2675
Less: tax credit relief	975
Net UK tax payable	₦1700

Example 5 (Indirect effect of underlying tax)

A dividend of ₦2000 is received from company X resident in an overseas country by a UK resident company which controls 15% of the voting power in company X. Overseas tax at 10% is deducted from the dividend and company X has paid tax at a rate of 20% on its profits. Tax credit relief is claimed by the UK resident company.

The underlying tax on the dividend, arrived at by grossing the dividend at the rate of tax borne by company X,

	is 2000 × 1.25 =	₦2500
Less: Dividend paid		2000
Underlying tax		₦500

The total overseas tax borne on the dividend is

Direct withholding tax	₦200	(₦2000 at 10%)
Underlying tax	500	
	₦700	

The UK Corporation Tax figures will be

₦2500 at (say) 50% =	₦1250
Less: tax credit relief	700
Net Corporation Tax payable	₦550

'Income accruing in, derived from, brought into or received in Nigeria'

This is regarded as income chargeable to tax by section 4(1) of the 1961 Act. For example, a Nigerian student in London qualifies as a lawyer in the United Kingdom. He practises for some time and brings into Nigeria ₦900 of his savings from his professional earnings. This income has been taxed in London. Since the money is 'brought into' Nigeria, in accordance with section 4 and could not have been exempted under the double taxation agreement because it is not the profit of a Nigerian business enterprise undertaken on behalf of Nigerian residents, it will be taxed again in Nigeria.

The same income having been taxed twice, double taxation relief will be given in Nigeria.

Under section 11 of the 1961 Act as amended by section 3 of Act 65 of 1966, interest on money lent by a person outside Nigeria to a person in Nigeria is deemed to be derived from Nigeria and taxable in Nigeria:

(i) if there is a right to payment of the interest in Nigeria including a person who is resident or present in Nigeria at the time of the loan;

(ii) the interest is by deed, will or otherwise charged upon or reserved out of real or personal estate situated in Nigeria the property of the person paying the same, or as a personal debt or obligation, by virtue of any contract which is entered into in Nigeria;

(iii) in the case of money lent to a Nigerian company the loan is evidenced by mortgage, debenture, loan or other stock, whether secured or unsecured, issued by the company in recognition of its debt;

(iv) the interest is payable on money lodged at interest in Nigeria.

Thus borrowing money by a Nigerian resident from abroad and paying the interest from Nigeria may not be advantageous to the foreign lender who may have to pay local tax on the interest received and Nigerian tax as well. Of course, if there is a double taxation agreement between Nigeria and the foreign country, double taxation relief may be claimed.

Computation of the taxable income and double taxation relief

Having shown that the income is subject to Nigerian tax, the next step is to compute the amount of the income liable to such tax.

1 Trading income is arrived at on the normal basis previously discussed.

2 A dividend paid by a Nigerian company[7] is deemed to be derived from Nigeria and the net dividend paid should be grossed up and included in the total statutory income.

3 The portion or whole of dividend[8] paid by a company other than a Nigerian company or from a foreign company remitted, or brought into or received in Nigeria is part of the statutory total income that is taxable here.

4 Where an individual outside Nigeria deals with a person in Nigeria ('person' includes a limited liability company), and the transaction produces less than normal commercial profits, the individual shall be assessed in the name of the person.[9] Where the profits of the individual cannot be ascertained, he will be charged on a fair and reasonable percentage of the turnover of business with that person.

5 The profits of a foreign business controlled in this country are taxable here.

6 The profits of a company[10] other than a Nigerian company from any trade or business shall be deemed to be derived from Nigeria to the extent to which such profits are not attributable to any part of the operations of the company carried on outside Nigeria. This will apply in cases where a foreign company has branches in Nigeria.

7 The method of computing profits of insurance companies has been explained.

8 Where a company other than a Nigerian company carries on a shipping or air transport business, the profit on passengers or freight-loading in Nigeria is taxable here.[11]

9 Where a UK enterprise has a permanent establishment in this country thereby making its profits taxable in Nigeria, its profits shall be computed as if it were an independent business dealing at arm's length so that in the case of a United Kingdom Company having a branch in Nigeria, its profits cannot be reduced by inflating branch purchase, etc.[12]

Computation

Part VI of the 1961 Act and Part VII of the Companies Income Tax Act govern the position.

Double taxation relief will be given where:

1 the income is subject to Nigerian tax;

2 the income is also subject to tax in another country;

3 the other country has concluded a double taxation agreement with this country.

Where the relief is by reason of a similar enactment in a Commonwealth country, the relief is determined thus:[13]

1 if the rate in the foreign country does not exceed one-half of the Nigerian rate, the rate in the other country applies;

2 otherwise, half of the Nigerian rate applies.

The Nigerian rate is the individual's total income from all sources divided by the Nigerian tax payable.[14] The Commonwealth or foreign rate of tax is determined in the same way. By 'total income'[15] is meant all incomes from all sources after allowing for capital allowances, losses and Balancing Charges.

Example 6

Sunday has a Nigerian income of ₦24 000, including a Commonwealth income of ₦400. He pays Nigerian tax of ₦12 000 and a Commonwealth tax of ₦100 on his Commonwealth income of ₦400.

The Nigerian rate is $\dfrac{12\,000}{24\,000}$ = 50k in the ₦

The Commonwealth rate is $\dfrac{100}{400}$ = 25k

385

Since the rate in the other country does not exceed half the rate of Nigerian tax, he will get a relief of 25k on ₦400.

Non-residence in Nigeria

Where an individual is not resident[16] in Nigeria and he has paid or is liable to pay Nigerian tax for any year of assessment on any part of his income and has to pay Commonwealth income tax on the same part of his income, he will be entitled to relief from tax paid in Nigeria as follows:

(a) if the Commonwealth rate of tax does not exceed the Nigerian rate of tax, the rate at which relief is to be given shall be one half of the Commonwealth rate of tax.

(b) if the Commonwealth rate of tax exceeds the Nigerian rate of tax, the rate at which relief is to be given shall be equal to the amount by which the Nigerian rate of tax exceeds one half of the Commonwealth rate of tax.

Example 7

Ajala, who is not resident in Nigeria, has a Nigerian income of ₦4000 and a Commonwealth income of ₦2000. He pays tax of ₦1000 on his foreign income and a Nigerian tax of ₦1170.

Nigerian rate $\qquad \dfrac{1170}{6000} \ = \ 19\frac{1}{2}k$

Commonwealth rate $\qquad \dfrac{700}{2000} \ = \ 35k$

Since the Commonwealth rate exceeds the Nigerian rate, the relief is calculated as follows:

$19\frac{1}{2}k - \frac{35}{2} \ = \ 2k$

₦2000 at 2k $\ = \ $ ₦20.00

Since there must have been a similar legislation in the Commonwealth, his relief in the Commonwealth country would be ₦2000 $\times \frac{35}{2}$ = ₦350. Total reliefs enjoyed would therefore be ₦390.

Cases where there is a double taxation agreement

Section 25, subsections (1) (2) (3) of the 1961 Act sets out the method of calculating relief to be allowed for double taxation. The claimant must be resident in Nigeria, that is, must be in Nigeria for more days than in the other country.

Example 8

Mr Andrew, a British Civil Servant resident in Efon Alaye in Ondo

State, was seconded by the British government to the University of Ife in July 1964 on the following terms:

(1) that the University will pay the UK Treasury the salary Mr Andrew will draw as a British Civil Servant, that is ₦3000.

(2) that the salary will be paid to Mr Andrew by the UK Treasury less UK Income Tax.

(3) that the University will pay Mr Andrew in Nigeria the difference between his British salary and the salary of ₦4200.

(4) that the amount payable under (3) shall be subject to Nigerian Income Tax.

It will be observed that article VIII (i) of the Double Taxation Agreement between the United Kingdom and Nigeria affords Mr Andrew exemption on the salary paid from the UK government funds. He will be entitled to double taxation relief if he pays UK tax on any part of the income assessed in Nigeria. The UK tax paid on ₦3000 is ₦280.

Assume he was entitled to married man's allowance of ₦400, three children's allowances, together with ₦134 in respect of education and life assurance relief. Assume wife's allowance was ₦400, life assurance ₦380 and children including education totalled ₦374.

Solution

Salary paid in Nigeria		₦1200
Salary paid in UK but earned in Nigeria		₦3000
Total income		₦4200
Less Children, including education	374	
Wife	400	
Life assurance	380	1154
Chargeable income		₦3046

Nigerian tax payable (say)   ₦319.52

Rate of Nigerian tax $\dfrac{319.52}{₦412.00}$ $= 7\frac{1}{2}$k in the ₦

Tax payable on ₦3000 (which has also borne UK tax) at the Nigerian rate of $7\frac{1}{2}$k in the ₦ = ₦225. Since the UK tax paid on ₦3000 was ₦280, then credit to be given to Mr Andrew under section 25(3) of the 1961 Act is ₦225, that is, Nigerian tax payable on ₦3000. If the UK tax paid on ₦3000 were ₦200, then the credit to be given will be ₦200. In other words, where foreign (UK) tax and Nigerian tax are paid on the same portion of income, credit will be given in Nigeria for the lesser of the two amounts of tax paid.

Treatment of dividends

Dividends paid by a UK company to a Nigerian resident who does not carry on a trade in the UK through a permanent establishment is exempt[17] in the UK from tax on dividends other than tax leviable on the profits of the company. Similarly, dividends paid by a Nigerian company to a UK resident is exempt in Nigeria from any tax on dividends. A Nigerian who derives income including dividends from the UK would not be subject to tax in the UK.

Section 10(ii) of the 1961 Act provides that the profits tax relating to the dividend paid by a UK company shall be added to the income in computing relief but not in arriving at the Nigerian rate[18]. A deduction shall be allowed of the amount by which the foreign tax in respect of income exceeds the credit therefor. The preceding provisions provide that no foreign tax shall be deducted in computing the income. Under article 13, the credit for double taxation relief on a dividend paid by a UK company shall include UK profits tax paid or payable by the company.

Cases of local double taxation – dividends

Section 26 of the 1961 Act covers cases of local double taxation, that is, without any element of foreign income. Dividends are assessed on preceding year basis.

The material date a state Revenue Department should watch is the date the dividend was declared and *not* the date the dividend was received by the taxpayers or the accounting year of the company. Ascertainment of the proper date is relevant to determine the preceding year basis.

Relief is given in respect of tax suffered on the dividends and each state is entitled under section 26(3) of the 1961 Act to claim the amount of relief from the Federal Government.

Example 9

Dr Dynamic, resident in the Ondo State of Nigeria, received incomes as follows:

Salary: 1.4.67 – 31.3.68	₦7190.00
Dividends (gross) from Guiness (Nig.)	
Ltd, preceding year, declared 31.3.67	527.50
Total income	7717.50
Less reliefs (5n7)	1078.00
Chargeable income	6639.50

388

He suffered PAYE tax of ₦1200 on his salary and tax of ₦89.80 on dividends.

Tax due	₦1164.17
Tax suffered on dividends and PAYE	1289.80
Refund due	1115.63

The Western State Internal Revenue will in turn claim tax of ₦89.80 back from the Federal Government.

Companies

Under a Double Taxation Agreement, a company may enjoy double taxation relief[19] if it is a Nigerian company for at least part of the year of assessment under section 38(2) of the Companies Income Tax Act. 'Nigerian company' and 'company other than Nigerian company' should be substituted for 'resident' and 'non-resident' in Nigeria.

Net Nigerian Rate (Companies)

This is dealt with by section 34(3) of the Companies Income Tax Act, 1961. If the profit from which the dividend is declared is the basis period, the net Nigerian rate is the tax payable by the company after deducting double taxation relief dividend by the distributable profits before deducting tax but after deducting (1) any capital profit or (2) exempted profits from which dividends are distributable, otherwise the Federal Board has power to determine the rate.

Section 35 of the Companies Income Tax Act, 1961, contains similar provisions for dividends received by companies. A company which is not a Nigerian company and not in business in Nigeria but which receives a dividend from a Nigerian company is not entitled to repayment[20] The net Nigerian rate is therefore:

tax payable by the company less double taxation on relief allowed, divided by: distributable profits of the company; and, relief will be the rate so found multiplied by the gross dividends received.

Non-comprehensive double taxation arrangements and unilateral double taxation provisions

Where there is intercourse between two countries *to warrant the granting of some double taxation reliefs but not warranting the entering into a* comprehensive double taxation arrangement between the two countries, what is normally done is to make 'unilateral double taxation provisions' in the tax code. Such a unilateral relief was introduced by section 36 of the United Kingdom Finance Act, 1960.[21] Under this legislation, relief is given by the UK by way of credit against the UK on overseas income for taxes charged on the income in an overseas country even though there is no double taxation agreement between the UK and that country.

The overseas taxes for which this unilateral relief may be given are taxes which are charged on income or profits and which correspond to taxes levied in the UK. The relief extends to taxes levied in Commonwealth countries but not elsewhere. The relief is essentially the same as the relief by way of credit granted under comprehensive Double Taxation Agreements.

The effect of a unilateral relief of this nature is that one country gives relief by way of credit in respect of income which remains taxable in that country and in another Commonwealth country where the taxpayer is resident in the first country or in both countries even though a reciprocal relief is not granted in that other country.

Similar provisions to those of section 348 of the United Kingdom Income Tax Act, 1952 are made in section 23 of the 1961 Act and, just as in the UK, the unilateral reliefs are granted only in respect of Commonwealth income tax. It has not been considered fit to extend the unilateral reliefs to territories outside the Commonwealth.

Difficulties have occured in respect of individuals who live in Nigeria and travel to the Cameroons in pursuit of their occupations. These problems are similar to those of the Nigerian 'itinerant worker' which have been dealt with satisfactorily by the special provisions of section 3(3) of the 1961 Act. In such case, it may be desirable in view of absence of any double taxation agreement, to enter into a non-comprehensive double taxation agreement with that country. Without amendment to section 23, it is possible for a state in Nigeria to provide in its law for the grant of such unilateral relief with the consent of the Joint Tax Board. All existing double taxation agreements have been scrapped, notably those with UK and USA. New treaties based on the Nigerian standard draft are to be negotiated with any interested countries.

On the basis of the old agreements, a typical computation will merely reflect deduction of offsettable items which have borne tax in either of the two territories.

Notes

1 Article 1 (K) of the Double Taxation Agreement.
2 Article 2.
3 Article 5.
4 Article 8.

5   Article 6.
6   Published as Legal Notice 207 of 1958 in the Supplement to the *Federal Gazette*
    No. 84, 24 December 1958.
7   Section 9 of the 1961 Act.
8   Section 10 of the 1961 Act and section 22, Companies Income Tax Act.
9   Section 5(2) of the 1961 Act.
10 Companies Income Tax Act, section 18(2).
11 Companies Income Tax Act, section 19.
12 Article 3(3) Double Taxation Agreement with the UK.
13 Section 23 of the 1961 Act.
14 Section 23(3) of the 1961 Act.
15 Section 2 of the 1961 Act.
16 Section 23(2) of the 1961 Act.
17 Article 6 of the Double Taxation Agreement with the UK.
18 Section 25(5)(c) of the 1961 Act.
19 Section 36 and 37 provide similar relief for companies.
20 Section 23.
21 Now section 348 of the United Kingdom Income Tax Act, 1952.

14   Capital Gains Tax

Act (formerly Decree) No. 44[1] introduced the taxation of capital gains in the country. The Act resembles the Capital Gains Tax of the United Kingdom[2] although it takes into account the prevailing conditions in Nigeria.[3] Losses are not relieved and there is no distinction between long-term and short-term gains.

Rate of tax and persons liable to the tax

Section 2(1) of the Act provides that the rate of Capital Gains Tax shall be 20 per cent of the capital gains accruing within the Federal territory.

Section 2(2) states that the rate of 20 per cent already mentioned shall apply to the capital gains accruing to any person in a year of assessment. Section 46 of the Decree is more helpful and provides that (1) individuals and (2) all companies throughout the Federation (since they are all dealt with by the Federal Board of Inland Revenue) are deemed to be resident in the Federal territory irrespective of their location. All sources of income are taxable under part V and section 24 of the Personal Income Tax (Lagos) Act, 1961 irrespective of location of assets.

Section 45(1) states that references to a company include any body corporate but do not include a partnership or a corporation sole and, subsection 2 of section 45 goes on to say that 'company' includes any company or body corporate established by or under any law in force in Nigeria or elsewhere to whom capital gains accrue; references to an 'individual' include any individual or body of individuals or any corporation sole, trustee, executor, partnership to whom the gains accrue and in respect of whom in a year of assessment the Federal Board of Inland Revenue is the relevant tax authority within the meaning of section 2 of the 1961 Act.

Exemptions

The Act[4] exempts:

1 capital gains accruing to ecclesiastical, charitable or educational institutions of a public character (s.27(1)(a))
2 any statutory or registered friendly society (s.27(1)(b))
3 any trade union registered under the Cooperative Societies Act or any trade union registered under the Trade Unions Act, provided (s.27(1)(d)):

(a) that the gain or profit is not derived from any disposal of any assets acquired in connection with any trade or business carried on by the institution,

(b) the gain or profit is applied solely for the purpose of the institution or society,[5]

(c) if any property held on trust ceases to be subject to that trust, the trustees will be regarded as having disposed of and immediately reacquired the property for a consideration equal to its market value and any gain will not be treated as accruing to the institution or society.

Section 27 to 42 of the Act exempt the following from Capital Gains Tax:

(i) the main or only private residence of an individual
(ii) motor cars suitable for private use
(iii) life assurance policies
(iv) chattels disposed of for not more than ₦1000 in any year of assessment (s.37, Capital Gains Tax Act, 1967)
(v) compensation for wrong or injury suffered by an individual
(vi) gifts, not being an acquisition or a devolution on death (s.39)
(vii) benefits from superannuation funds approved by the Joint Tax Board
(viii) land disposed of to an authority having compulsory powers
(ix) disposal of decorations and sale of Nigerian government securities.

Capital losses are not deductible from Capital Gains Tax (s.5).

Chargeable assets

Options, stocks and shares, goodwill, patents, trademarks, ships, aircraft, paintings, debts and foreign currency are subject to Capital Gains Tax. Land and buildings, plant and machinery apart from those discussed under Exemptions are the only chargeable assets. The asset must have been disposed of before capital gains can arise. Sections 6 to 24 of the Act deal with disposal. The assets are chargeable whether

393

they are situated in or outside Nigeria (s.3). Debt, for example, is chargeable where the creditor is resident in Nigeria.

Disposal

Disposal must, however, be given its literal meaning. 'Disposal' occurs when ownership changes or when the owner divests himself of his rights or interest over the property. The receipt of a capital sum from the assets is deemed to be a disposal. Thus receipt of compensation from an insurance company for loss or damage in cases of fire accidents is a disposal. There is disposal where there is a loss or total destruction of an asset (s.19) or death of an individual.

The gains or disposal but not the acquisition of the asset must have occurred on or after 1 April 1967.[6] The gains or disposal must have accrued to taxpayers within the Federal territory of Lagos in the case of individuals.[7]

If the landed property is given in exchange for another landed property of lesser value, the transaction will be deemed to have been at the market value[8] on the date of the exchange and tax will be paid on the chargeable gains. The person with whom the exchange was made would also be deemed to have disposed of his own landed property at the market value at the date of exchange and he too will pay Capital Gains Tax.

If the disposal of an asset is to a 'connected person', sections 23 and 24 will apply. Section 24 defines a 'connected person' in this way:

(1) A person is connected with an individual if that person is the individual's spouse or a relative or spouse of a relative of the individual's spouse.

(2) A trustee of a settlement is connected with any individual who in relation to the settlement is a settler and with any person who is connected with such an individual.

(3) A person is connected with any person with whom he is in partnership and with the spouse or relative of any individual with whom he is partnership.

(4) A company is connected with another company if:
   (a) the same person has control of both or a person has control of one and a person connected with him, or he and persons connected with him, have control of the other or,
   (b) if a group of two or more persons has control of each company, and the groups either consist of the same persons or could be regarded as consisting of the same persons by treating (in one or more cases) a member of either group as replaced by a person with whom he is connected.
   (c) a company is connected with another person if that person has

394

control of it or if that person and persons connected with him together have control of it.

(d) any two or more persons acting together to secure or exercise control of a company shall be treated in relation to that company as connected with one another and with any person acting on the directions of any of them to secure or exercise control of the company.

In this connection section 24(8) defines a 'relative' as 'brother, sister, ancestor or lineal descendant'.

If a taxpayer sells his property at an under-value to, say, his sister-in-law, this will be a transaction between 'connected persons' and the chargeable gains will be calculated on the market value of the property at the date of the transfer. Sales by husband to wife will be treated in the same way, that is, as a transaction otherwise than by way of bargain made at arm's length.[9]

Computation of Capital Gains Tax

The chargeable gain is arrived at by deducting the cost of acquisition from net proceeds of sale or net market value.

The Capital Gains Tax will then be levied at 20%.

Sections 12 to 16 deal with computations of capital gains. The allowable expenses under section 14 are:

(a) expenses incurred wholly, exclusively, reasonably and necessarily for the acquisition of the asset.

(b) expenses incurred wholly, exclusively, reasonably and necessarily for the purposes of enhancing the value of the asset, being expenditure reflected in the state or nature of the asset at the time of the disposal.

(c) expenses incurred wholly, exclusively, reasonably and necessarily for the purpose of establishing, preserving or defending his title to, or a right over, the asset.

(d) incidental expenses of making the disposal, e.g. professional charges of any accountant, lawyer, surveyor, valuer or auctioneer, costs of advertising to find a seller or a buyer.

Section 5 of the Act provides that in the computation of chargeable gains, the amount of any loss which accrues to a person on a disposal of any asset, shall not be deductible from gains accruing to any person on a disposal of such asset.

Under section 41 of the Act, sections 22, 23 and 24 of the 1961 Act and sections 36 and 37 of the Companies Income Tax Act, 1961, dealing with double taxation relief apply to Capital Gains Tax as well.

Example 1

Bola, resident in the Federal territory of Lagos, sold on 3 April, 1987 his house at Yaba, not being his principal private residence, for ₦7500. He paid agents' commission of ₦310, and in addition incurred the following expenses:

Advertisement in the Daily Times	₦90
Cleaning	25
Allowable legal expenses	75
	190

He bought the house on 16 July, 1982 for ₦4500 and on that day incurred the following expenses:

Solicitor's fees re conveyance	₦100
Re-roofing	150
Purchase of tiles for flooring	250
	500

Compute the amount of Capital Gains Tax due from Bola.

Solution 1

Proceeds of sale	₦7500	
Less: Expenses on sale	500	₦7000
Cost of acquisition	4500	
Add: expenses – all capital	500	5000
Chargeable gain		2000

1988 Capital Gains Tax thereon, 20% of ₦2000, ₦400 payable by Bola.
1   If the house sold by Bola had been in Kaduna or any place outside the Federal Territory of Lagos, no Capital Gains Tax would have arisen.
2   If the proceeds of sale are unknown, then market value will be substituted in accordance with section 7 of the Decree.
3   If the house had been sold at an under-value to a connected person, and a 'loss' had been sustained, market value would have been substituted for 'proceeds' to arrive at a capital gain.
4   The date of acquisition is immaterial but the date of disposal should be on or after 1.4.87.
Administration of the tax: The Federal Board of Inland Revenue administers the tax. Power to call for information and to appoint agents are contained in sections 28 to 30 of the 1961 Act and Part IX of the 1961 Act dealing with returns. Part XII of the 1961 Act deals with collection, recovery and repayment.

Part XIII, dealing with offences and penalties also applies to the administration of the Capital Gains Tax. The Board has power under section 21 of the Decree to disregard any artificial disposition in relation to Capital Gains Tax. States are responsible for assessment of individuals resident in them.

Appeal

Section 43(2) of the Act provides that an appeal shall lie against any assessment to Capital Gains Tax made in accordance with section 49 of the Companies Income Tax Act, 1961, to the body of Appeal Commissioners established under section 55 of the Companies Income Tax Act, 1961.

McCorquodale and Company Ltd v Federal Board of Inland Revenue
APP/COMM/139
Companies Income Tax Act 1961 – Capital Gains Tax Decree 1967, assessment arising thereunder – Whether surplus arising from sterling devaluation constituted an income under CITA sec. 17 – Whether the surplus not yet realised could constitute a taxable profit – Basis of assessment CITA sec. 30.

The appellant's grounds of appeal were (i) that the devaluation surplus did not amount to a capital gain under Capital Gains Tax Decree 1967, (ii) that the surplus had not been realised at the time of the assessment and could not be realised until the appellant's creditors were repaid, (iii) that the assessments were hypothetical.

The appeal was allowed. The Appeal Commissioners found that liability to capital gains did not arise as there was no chargeable disposal within the meaning of the provisions of the Capital Gains Tax Decree, 1967, and that as devaluation surplus had not been realised, no liability to tax could arise.

Example 2

Ayodele purchases fixed plant in March 1980, for ₦40 000, and sells this in June 1986 for ₦45 000, replacing the plant sold with similar equipment costing ₦48 000 which was sold in March 1987 for ₦50 000. The position is as follows:

1986		₦	
Sale proceeds		45 000	
Less: cost		40 000	
Gain		₦5000	not assessed as plant has been replaced.

1987	₦	₦	
Sale proceeds		50 000	
Cost	48 000		assessable to
Less: Gain 1986	5 000	43 000	Capital Gains
Chargeable gain		₦7000	Tax.

Example 3

Olufunmilayo purchases a building (which is used solely for her trade purposes) on 1 January 1964 for ₦5000, and sells it on 6 July 1989 for ₦24 000. Olufunmilayo replaces this building with a similar building costing ₦24 000 on 22 August 1990.

This position is as follows:

1989	₦
Sale proceeds	20 000
Less cost	5 000
Gain	₦15 000

Time apportionment:

$$\frac{14\frac{1}{2}}{25\frac{1}{2}} \times ₦15\,000 = ₦8\,529 \text{ chargeable gain (not assessed as building}$$

replaced).

The cost of the new building to be brought into account when considering disposal will be ₦15 471 (₦24 000 − ₦8 529).

Example 4

Mr and Mrs Investor returned the following income for the year ended 1.3.79.

	Mr Investor	Mrs Investor
Salaries	₦6000	₦8000
Benefit in kind	120	–
Dividends received	670	2010
Net rents due	–	1400
Bank interest	130	–

Mr Investor paid professional fees of ₦50 and mortgage interest of ₦1600 in the year ended 31.3.79. Mrs Investor pays her sister ₦660 per annum. During 1978–79 Mrs Investor sold the following:

1.5.78   A parcel of land. Net proceeds received ₦6000. The land was part of a larger piece purchased for ₦4000 in 1967. The value of the remaining piece of land at 1.5.78 was ₦8000.

10.6.78   2000 shares in Guinness. Proceeds of sale were ₦1500 and the shares cost ₦600 in 1968.

1.8.78   Sold 3000 shares in C. Ltd for ₦4500. Mrs Investor had originally purchased 1000 shares in 1963 for ₦500, a further 2000 shares in 1967 for ₦1200. The company had made a rights issue of 1:4 at 60k each in 1964 and a bonus issue of 1:2 in 1970. C's shares were quoted on the Lagos stock Exchange at 55k each on 1.4.65.

5.12.78   Sold 1000 shares in Algol Ltd, an unquoted company for ₦4000. The shares were acquired on 1.8.51 for ₦4000. The shares were acquired on 6.8.51 for ₦800. The value of the shares in April 1965 was ₦2.30 each.

Mr Investor had capital losses brought forward of ₦1200 at 1.4.78.

You are required to compute Mr and Mrs Investor's capital gain on the assumption that they make any elections which may reduce their liabilities.

Solution 4

Mr and Mrs Investor: Capital Tax Gains computation 1979–80.

			Gains
		₦	₦
1.5.78	Sale of proceeds of land		
Cost	$\dfrac{6000}{(6000 + 8000)} \times \dfrac{4000}{1}$	6000 (1714)	
			4286
10.6.78	Sale proceeds, Guinness shares	1,500	
	Cost	(600)	
	Chargeable gain		900
1.8.78	Sale proceeds, C. Ltd shares	4500	

	Cost	1.4.65
	₦	₦
1963 1000 shares	500	550
1964 250 rights @ 60k	150	150
1250		
1970 625 bonus 1:2	—	—
1875	₦650	₦700
1967 2000 shares	1200	
1970 1000 Bonus 1:2	—	
3000	₦1200	

1st Acquisition: Sale proceeds

$$\frac{1875}{3000} \times \frac{4500}{1}$$

	2812
	(700)
Cost 1.4.65 value	2112

2nd Acquisition: Sale proceeds

$$\frac{1125}{3000} \times \frac{4500}{1} \qquad\qquad\qquad 1688$$
$$\qquad\qquad\qquad\qquad\qquad\qquad\qquad (450)$$
$$\text{Cost } \frac{1125}{3000} \times \frac{1200}{1}$$
$$\qquad\qquad\qquad\qquad\qquad\qquad\qquad 1238$$

5.12.78	*Cost*	*1.4.65*
	₦	₦
Sale proceeds, Algol	4000	4000
Cost	(800)	(3300)
Gain	3200	1700

Time apportionment

$$\frac{1.4.65 - 5.12.78}{6.8.51 - 5.12.78} \times 3200 = 1600 \qquad\qquad\quad 1600$$
$$\qquad\qquad\qquad\qquad\qquad\qquad\qquad\quad 10136$$
Capital losses brought forward: $\qquad\qquad\qquad\qquad 1200$
$$\qquad\qquad\qquad\qquad\qquad\qquad\qquad ₦8936$$

Part disposal

Sections 6(2)(b)(i) and 6(2)(b)(ii) deal with part disposal of an asset where apportionment is applicable. Thus the cost of acquisition of the asset and expenses for enhancing the value of the asset are apportioned in accordance with sections 17(1) and 17(2).

The cost of part disposal is arrived at as stated below:

$$\frac{\text{Consideration for the part disposal}}{\substack{\text{Value of the disposal plus market value} \\ \text{of the part yet to be disposed of}}} \times \substack{\text{Cost of acquiring} \\ \text{the whole asset}}$$

and the chargeable gain on part disposal is arrived at as follows:

Full Proceeds of the part disposed of less expenses of sale less cost of part disposed of.

$$\frac{\text{Sale of Part Disposal}}{\text{Proceeds of part disposal plus market value}}$$

will give the fraction or apportionment to be used for the cost of the entire cost of the asset before part disposal, and multiplying the cost of the whole asset by this fraction gives the cost of part disposal which should be deducted from proceeds of part disposal to arrive at chargeable gain. Year of sale determines the year of assessment. Where assets are lost or destroyed, whether under a policy of insurance or otherwise, and the capital sum received by way of compensation is applied within three years of receipt in buying

400

another asset in replacement of the asset lost or destroyed, the owner may claim under s.19(1) that the consideration for the disposal of the asset is such that neither a loss nor a gain acrues on disposal, i.e. payment by the insurance company even if in excess of cost will be restricted to the cost in calculating capital gain which will be Nil. To do this, the whole but not part of the capital sum should be applied in acquiring the new asset.

Exemptions and reliefs

Reliefs

These include legally delayed remittances or gains which will become assessable in the year of assessment in which it becomes remittable s.42(2), Double Taxation Relief where the law of the other country has double taxation arrangements with Nigeria (s.41) and replacement of Business Assets Relief where the disposal results in a gain and the entire proceeds are reinvested in the purchase of another asset for use in the business: s.32(1). Section 32(6) stipulates that the old and the new assets must fall within the same class of assets. Provided that the trade carried on is not one dealing in or developing land, occupied land for the purpose of the trade and building or any part thereof used for the purpose of the trade will fall within the same class of Lands and Buildings.

The new assets must not have been purchased for speculative reasons and the claimants must have been carrying on a trade and the acquisition of the new assets or interest therein or unconditional contract for the acquisition must be entered into within the period commencing 12 months before and ending 12 months after the disposal of the old asset. This relief is also called Roll-over Relief.

Example 5

A B C bought a plant in 1985 costing ₦200 000 and sold it in 1986 for ₦212 000 replacing the plant with a similar asset costing ₦230 000. This was sold in 1987 for ₦255 000. This capital gain will be calculated as follows:

1986 Sale proceeds	₦212 000
Less cost	200 000
Capital gain	12 000

Capital gain will not be levied as there is a roll-over gain since the asset was replaced.

1987 Sale proceeds		₦255 000
Less cost	₦230 000	
1985 gain	12 000	
Notional cost		242 000
Chargeable gain		13 000

1987 Capital gains tax 20% of ₦13 000 = ₦2600

If only part of the proceeds were used for acquisition of new assets, only part of the gain spent on replacement will be deducted from the cost of the new asset whilst the remainder will attract Capital Gains Tax.

Example 6

Machinery was bought in 1983 for ₦35 000. In 1984, it was sold for ₦38 000 and replaced with machinery costing ₦36 000.

Proceeds of sale	₦38 000
Cost of replacement	36 000
Sale proceeds not re-invested	2000

The ₦2000 not re-invested is assessable to Capital Gains Tax at 20% = ₦400. The roll-over gain will be:

Sale proceeds	₦38 000
Less cost	35 000
	3000
Less: Sale Proceeds not re-invested	2000
Roll-over gain	1000

Partial Use of Asset

Where the asset is not used for trade purposes for some time s.32(8) and where part of the asset is not used for trade purposes, apportionment applies [s.32(2)].

Example 7

A bought an asset on 1.7.86 for ₦50 000 and sublet 30% of the building as from 1 July 1990. He sold the asset on 1.7.1996 replacing it with one costing ₦47 500.

The periods of ownership when the asset was used are 1.7.86 – 30.6.1990, i.e. 4 years whereas the period of subletting was 1.7.90 – 30.6.96, i.e. 6 years.

Cost is apportioned as follows:
(Total period = 10 years)

402

	Total	Trade use	Other
First 4 years			
$\frac{4}{10} \times 50\,000$	₦20 000	₦20 000	
Next 6 years			
$\frac{6}{10} \times 50\,000 \times 70\%$	21 000	21 000	
$\frac{6}{10} \times 50\,000 \times 30\%$	9 000	–	₦9 000
	50 000	41 000	9 000

Proceeds Apportionment

	Total	Trade use	Other
First 4 years			
$\frac{4}{10} \times$ ₦60 000	₦24 000	₦24 000	–
Next 6 years			
$\frac{6}{10} \times 60\,000 \times 70\%$	25 200	25 200	–
$\frac{6}{10} \times 60\,000 \times 30\%$	10 800	–	₦10 800
	60 000	49 200	10 800

Capital Gain for 1996

Proceeds of trade use	₦49 200
Less cost of replacement	47 500
Gains not re-invested	1 700

Capital Gains Tax thereon at 20% = ₦340.

Example 8

(a) Mr Resettled's family residence was recently compulsorily acquired by one of the State governments in Nigeria. It had cost ₦50 000 to build. He was paid compensation in the sum of ₦100 000. He took advantage of the resettlement scheme of the Government whereby low-cost houses was offered simultaneously in addition to the cash compensation. For this he had to pay ₦75 000 to the Government. Discuss the Capital Gains Tax implications.

(b) Property Ltd is an estate management company. Included amongst its string of houses is a property situated in Ikoyi area of Lagos which was acquired ten years ago at a cost of ₦80 000. The legal expenses of ₦5000 incurred at the time of purchase had been completely written off into the company's profit and loss account. On 28 February 1983 this property was sold for ₦450 000. The total legal expenses incurred of ₦10 000 and sales commission of ₦9000 were borne by the purchaser, but before the property was put on the market it was valued at ₦400 000 by one of the leading estate valuers in Nigeria at a fee of ₦10 000. Calculate the Capital Gains Tax and designate the year of assessment to which it relates.

Solution 8

(a) Section 36(2) of the Capital Gains Tax Act, 1967 specifically exempts gains from the disposal of an individual's main or only residence.

According to section 9(1) of the Act, 'a person shall not be chargeable to tax under the Act, in respect of any acquisition and the disposal to an authority exercising or having compulsory powers, if that person had neither:
  (i) Acquired the land at a time when he knew or might reasonably have known that it was likely to be acquired by the authority; nor
  (ii) Taken any steps by advertisement or otherwise to dispose of the land or to make his willingness to dispose of it known to the authority, or others.'

In addition to this section 36, subsections (1) and (2) provide that gain accruing to an individual so far as attributable to the disposal of, or of an interest in a dwelling-house or part of a dwelling-house which is, or has at any time in his period of ownership been, his only or main residence, shall not be a chargeable gain if the dwelling-house or part of a dwelling-house has been the individual's or main residence throughout the period of ownership, or throughout the period of ownership except for all or any part of the last twelve months of that period.

Section 36(3) provides that so far as it is necessary for the purposes of this section to determine which of two or more residences is an individual's main residence for any period –

(1) The individual may conclude that the question by notice in writing to the Board given within two years from the beginning of that period, or given by the end of 1967–68, if that is later, but subject to a right to vary that notice by a further notice in writing to the Board as respects any period beginning not earlier than two years before the giving of the further notice.

(2) Subject to paragraph (1) above, the question shall be concluded by the determination of the Board, in which may be as respects either the whole or specified parts of the period of ownership in question.

If the above enumerated conditions apply in the case of Mr Resettled, the gains accruing to him from the compulsory acquisition irrespective of the fact that he was simultaneously given a Government low-cost house, shall not be chargeable to tax.

(b) *Property Limited*
Computation of Capital Gains Tax
1983 Year of Assessment

Gross sales proceeds		₦450 000
Less: Payments by vendor (Allowable		
Deductions):		
Estate valuer's fees	₦10 000	
Original cost of property	80 000	
Legal charges on acquisition	5 000	95 000
Capital gains		355 000

Capital Gains Tax payable at 20% on
₦355 000 = *₦71 000.*

Sections 27 to 42 of the Act state:

27 (1) Subject to subsection 2 of this section a gain shall not be chargeable if it accrues to –

(a) an ecclesiastical, charitable or educational institution of a public character;

(b) any statutory or registered friendly society;

(c) any cooperative society registered under the Cooperative Societies Act; or

(d) any trade union registered under the Trade Unions Act;

in so far as the gain is not derived from any disposal of any assets acquired in connection with any trade or business carried on by the institution or society and the gain is applied purely for the purpose of the institution or society as the case may be.

(2) If any property to which subsection (1) above relates which is held on trust ceases to be subject to such trust –

(a) the trustees shall be treated as if they had disposed of, and immediately reacquired, the property for a consideration equal to its market value, any gain on the disposal being treated as not accruing to the institution or society; and

(b) if and so far as any of that property represents, directly or indirectly, the consideration for the disposal of assets by the trustees, any gain accruing on that disposal shall be treated as not having accrued to such institution or society, and, notwithstanding anything in this Act limiting the time for making assessments, any assessment to capital gains tax chargeable virtue of paragraph (b) above may be made at any time not more than three years after the end of the year of assessments in which the property ceases to be subject to such trusts.

28 (1) There shall be exempt from Capital Gains Tax any gains accruing to any local or native authority.

(2) Gains accruing to any of the bodies mentioned in this subsection shall be exempt from Capital Gains Tax, that is to say –

(a) gains accruing to any company, being a purchasing authority established by or under any law in Nigeria, empowered to acquire any commodity in Nigeria for export from Nigeria; or

(b) gains accruing to any corporation established by or under any law for the purpose of fostering the economic development of any part of Nigeria in so far as the gains are not derived from the disposal of any assets acquired by the corporation in connection with any trade or business carried on by it or from the disposal of any share or other interest possessed by the corporation in a trade or business carried on by some other person or authority.

29 (1) A gain shall not be a chargeable gain –

(a) if accruing to a person from any disposal of investments held by him as part of any superannuation fund but so that where part only of that fund is approved under section 17 of the Income Tax Management Act, 1961, the gain shall be exempt from being a chargeable gain to the same extent only as income derived from the assets would be exempt under that section;

(b) if accruing to a person from his disposal of investment held by him as part of any national provident fund or other retirement benefits scheme established under the provisions of any Act for employees throughout Nigeria,

and such gain shall be exempt from tax under this Act in the same manner as investment income of any of those funds is exempt under paragraph (w) of the Third Schedule of the Income Tax Management Act, 1961.

(2) No chargeable gain shall accrue to any person on the disposal of a right to, or to any part of any sum payable out of any superannuation fund.

(3) In this section, 'superannuation fund' means a pension, provident or other retirement benefits fund, society or scheme approved by the Joint Tax Board under section 17 (1) (f) of the Income Tax Management Act 1961.

30   A gain shall not be a chargeable gain if it accrues on the disposal by any person of a decoration, awarded for valour or gallant conduct which he acquires otherwise than for consideration in money or money's worth.

31   Gain accruing to a person from a disposal by him of Nigerian government securities shall not be chargeable gains under this Act.

32   (1) If the consideration which a person carrying on a trade obtains for the disposal of, or of his interest in, assets (in this section referred to as 'the old assets') used, and used only, for the purposes of the trade throughout the period of ownership, is applied by him in acquiring other assets, or an interest in other assets (in this section referred to as 'the new assets') which on the acquisition are taken into use, and used only, for the purposes of the trade and the old assets and new assets are within one, and the same one, of the classes of assets listed in the section, then the person carrying on the trade shall, on making a claim as respects the consideration which has been so applied, be treated for the purposes of this Act –

(a) as if the consideration for the disposal of, or of the interest in, the old assets were (if otherwise of a greater amount of value) of such amount as would secure that on the disposal neither a loss nor a gain accrues to him, and

(b) as if the amount or value of the consideration for the acquisition of, or of the interest in, the new assets were reduced by the excess of the amount or value of the actual consideration for the disposal of, or of the interest in, the old assets over the amount of the consideration which he is treated as receiving under paragraph (s) above.

But neither paragraph (a) nor paragraph (b) above shall affect the treatment for the purposes of this Act of the other party to the transaction involving the old assets or of the other party to the transaction involving the new assets.

(2) Subsection (1) of this section shall not apply if part only of the amount or value of the consideration for the disposal of, or of the interest in, the old assets is applied as described in that subsection but if all of the amount or value of the consideration except for a part which is less than the amount of the gain (whether all chargeable gain or not) accruing on the disposal of, or of the interest in, the old assets is so applied, then the person carrying on the trade, on making a claim as respects the consideration which has been so applied, shall be treated for the purposes of this Act –

(a) as if the amount of the gain so accruing were reduced to the amount of the said part (and, if not all chargeable gain, with a proportionate reduction in the amount of the chargeable gain), and (b) as if the amount or value of the consideration for the acquisition of, or of the interest in, the new assets were reduced by the amount by which the gain is reduced under paragraph (a) of this subsection,

406

but neither paragraph (a) nor paragraph (b) above shall affect the treatment for the purposes of this Act of the other party to the transaction involving the old assets or of the other party to the transaction involving the new assets.

(3) This section shall only apply if the acquisition of, or of the interest in, the new assets takes place, or an unconditional contract for the acquisition is entered into, in the period beginning twelve months before and ending twelve months after the disposal of, or of the interest in, the old assets, or at such earlier or later time as the Board may be notice in writing allow:

Provided that, where an unconditional contract for the acquisition is so entered into, this section may be applied on a provisional basis without waiting to ascertain whether the new assets or the interest in the new assets, is acquired in pursuance of the contract, and, when that fact is ascertained, all necessary adjustments shall be made by making assessments or by repayment or discharge of tax, and shall be so made notwithstanding any limitation in this Act on the time within which assessments may be made.

(4) If two or more persons are carrying on a trade in partnership, this section shall not apply in relation to any one of them unless he is, under this Act, to be treated both as making disposal of a share in, or the interest in, the old assets, and as acquiring a share in, or in the interest in, the new assets; and if those shares are different, that partner's share shall be taken for the purposes of this section to be the smaller share.

(5) This section shall not apply unless the acquisition of, or of the interest in, the new assets was made for the purpose of their use in the trade, and not wholly or partly for the purpose of realising a gain from the disposal of, or of the interest in, the new assets.

(6) The classes of assets for the purpose of this section are as follows –

Class 1. Assets within the heads A and B below.

A. Except where the trade is a trade of dealing in or developing land, or of providing services for the occupier of land in which the person carrying on the trade has an estate or interest –

(a) any building or part of a building and any permanent or semi-permanent structure in the nature of a building, occupied (as well as used) only for the purposes of the trade, and

(b) any land occupied (as well as used) only for the purposes of the trade.

B. Fixed plant or machinery which does not form part of a building or of a permanent or semi-permanent structure in the nature of a building.

Ships	*Class 2*
Aircraft	*Class 3*
Goodwill	*Class 4*

(7) If, over the period of ownership or any substantial part of the period of ownership, part of a building or structure is, and any part is not, used for the purposes of a trade, this section shall apply as if the part so used, with any land occupied for purposes ancillary to the occupation and use of that part of the building or structure, were a separate asset, and subject to any necessary apportionments of consideration for an acquisition or disposal of, or of an interest in, the building or structure and other land.

(8) If the old assets were not used for the purposes of the trade throughout the period of ownership this section shall apply as if a part of the asset representing its use for the purposes of the trade having regard to the time and extent to which it was, and was not, used for those purposes, were a separate asset which had been wholly used for the purposes of the trade and this subsection shall apply in relation to that part subject to any necessary aportionment of consideration for an acquisition or disposal of, or of the interest in, the asset.

(9) This section shall apply in relation to a person who, either successively or at the same time, carries on two trades which are in different localities, but which are concerned with goods or services of the same kind, as if, in relation to old assets used for the purposes of the one trade and new assets used for the purposes of the other trade, the two trades were the same.

(10) This section shall apply with the necessary modifications in relation to a business, profession, vocation or employment as it applies in relation to a trade, and in this section the expression 'trade', 'business', 'profession', 'vocation', and 'employment' have the same meanings as in the Income Tax Acts, but not so as to apply the provisions of the Income Tax Acts as to the circumstnances in which, on a change in the persons carrying on a trade, a trade is to be regarded as discontinued, or as set up and commenced.

(11) The provisions of this Act fixing the amount of the consideration deemed to be given for the acquisition or disposal of assets shall be applied to this section.

(12) Without prejudice to the provisions of this Act providing generally for apportionments, where consideration is given for the acquisition or disposal of assets some or part of which are assets in relation to which a claim under subsection (1) or subsection (2) of this section applies, and some or part of which are not, the consideration shall be apportioned in such manner as is just and reasonable.

33 (1) This section has effect as respects any policy of assurance or contract for a deferred annuity on the life of any person.

(2) No chargeable gain shall accrue on the disposal of, or of an interest in, the rights under any such policy of assurance or contract except where the person making the disposal is not the original beneficial owner and acquired the rights or interests for a consideration in money or money's worth.

(3) Subject to subsection (2) above, the occasion of the payment of the sum or sums assured by a policy of assurance or of the first instalment of a deferred annuity, and the occasion of the surrender of a policy of assurance or of the rights under a contract for a deferred annuity, shall be the occasion of a disposal of the rights under the policy of assurance or contract for a deferred annuity, and the amount of the consideration for the disposal of a contract for a deferred annuity shall be the market value at that time of the right to that and further instalments of the annuity.

34 (1) The rights of the insured under any insurance effected in the course of a capital redemption business shall constitute an asset on the disposal of which a gain may accrue to the person making the disposal but subject to that neither the rights of the insurer nor the rights of the insured under any policy of insurance whether the risks insured relate to property or not shall constitute an asset on the disposal of which a gain may accrue.

(2) Notwithstanding subsection (1) above sums received under a policy of insurance of the risk of any kind of damage to, or the loss or depreciation of assets are for the purposes of this Act and in particular for the purposes of section 6 of this Act sums derived from the assets.

(3) In this section –

(a) 'capital redemption business' means the business (not being life assurance business or industrial assurance business) of effecting and carrying out contracts of insurance, whether effected by the issue of policies, bonds or endowment certificates or otherwise, whereby, in return for one or more premiums paid to the insurer a sum or a series of sums is to become payable to the insured in the future;

(b) 'industrial assurance business' means the business of effecting and carrying out contracts of insurance in connection with any industrial assurance whereby in return for one or more premiums paid to the insurer a sum or a series of sums is to become payable to the insured in the future; and

(c) 'policy of insurance' does not include a policy of assurance on human life.

35 (1) Subject to subsection (2) below, sums obtained by way of compensation or damages for any wrong or injury suffered by an individual in his person or in his profession or vocation shall not be chargeable gains within the meaning of this Act; and the foregoing provision of this subsection shall extend to compensation or damages for personal or professional wrong or injury including wrong or injury for libel, slander or enticement.

(2) Sums obtained by way of compensation for loss of office shall not, however, be chargeable gains, except where the amount of such compensation or damages exceeds ₦10 000 in any year of assessment.

36 (1) This section applies to a gain accruing to an individual so far as attributable to the disposal of, or of an interest in –

(a) a dwelling-house or part of a dwelling-house which is, or has any time in his period of ownership been, his only or main residence, or

(b) land which he has for his own occupation and enjoyment with that residence as its garden or grounds up to an area (inclusive of the site of the dwelling-house) of one acre or such larger area as the Board may in any particular case determine, on being satisfied that, regard being had to the size and character of the dwelling-house, the larger area is required for the reasonable enjoyment of it (or of the part in question) as a residence.

In the case where part of the land occupied with a residence is and part is not within this subsection, then (up to the permitted area) that part shall be taken to be within this subsection which, if the remainder were separately occupied, would be the most suitable for occupation and enjoyment with the residence.

(2) The gain shall not be a chargeable gain if the dwelling-house or part of a dwelling-house has been the individual's only or main residence throughout the period of ownership, or throughout the period of ownership except for all or any part of the last twelve months of that period.

(3) So far as it is necessary for the purposes of this section to determine which of two or more residences is an individual's main residence for any period –

(a) the individual may conclude that question by notice in writing to the Board given within two years from the beginning of that period, or given by the end of the year 1967-68, if that is later, but subject to a right to vary that notice by a further notice in writing to the Board as respects any period beginning not earlier than two years before the giving of the further notice,

(b) subject to paragraph (a) above, the question shall be concluded by the determination of the Board, which may be as respects either the whole or specified parts of the period of ownership in question,

and notice of any determination of the Board under paragraph (b) above shall be given to the individual who may appeal to the Appeal Commissioners against that determination within thirty days of service of the notice.

(4) This section shall not apply in relation to a gain unless the acquisition of, or of the interest in, the dwelling-house or the part of a dwelling-house was made for the purpose of residing in it and not wholly or partly for the purpose of realising a gain from the disposal of it, and shall not apply in relation to gain so far as attributable to any expenditure which was incurred after the beginning of the period of ownership and was incurred wholly or partly for the purpose of realising a gain from the disposal.

(5) Apportionments of consideration shall be made wherever required by this section and, in particular, where a person disposes of a dwelling-house only part of which is his only or main residence.

37 (1) Subject to this section a gain accruing on a disposal of an asset which is tangible

moveable property shall not be a chargeable gain if the total amount or value of the consideration for the disposal does not in a year of assessment exceed ₦1000.

(2) The amount of capital gains tax chargeable in respect of a gain accruing on a disposal of an asset which is tangible moveable property for a consideration the total amount or value of which exceeds ₦1000 shall not exceed half the difference between the amount of that consideration and ₦1000.

For the purposes of this subsection the Capital Gains Tax chargeable in respect of the gain shall be the amount of tax which would not have been chargeable but for that gain.

(3) If two or more assets which have formed part of a set of articles of any description all owned at one time by one person are disposed of by that person, and –

(a) to the same person, or

(b) to persons who are acting in concert or who are, in terms of section 24 above, connected persons,

whether on the same or different occasions, the two or more transactions shall be treated as a single transaction disposing of a single asset, but which any necessary apportionments of the reductions in tax under subsection (2) of this section, and this subsection shall also apply where the assets, or some of the assets, are disposed of on different occasions on the first of April 1966, but not so as to make any gain accruing on that date a chargeable gain.

(4) If the disposal is of a right or interest in or over tangible moveable property –

(a) in the first instance subsections (1) and (2) of this section shall be applied in relation to the asset as a whole, taking the consideration as including the market value of what remains undisposed of, in addition to the actual consideration;

(b) where the sum of the actual consideration and that market value exceeds ₦1000 the limitation and the amount of tax in subsection (2) above shall be of half the difference between that sum and ₦1000 multiplied by the fraction equal to the actual consideration divided by the said sum.

(5) The foregoing provisions of this section shall apply in relation to a gain accruing on a disposal of two or more assets (not necessarily forming part of a set of articles of any description) which are tangible moveable properties in the same manner as they apply in relation to a gain accruing on a disposal of an asset, or two or more assets which formed part of a set of articles, if in a year of assessment the total amount or value of the consideration is ₦1000 or more.

(6) This section shall not apply in relation to a disposal of currency of any description.

38 A mechanically-propelled road vehicle constructed or adapted for the carriage of passengers shall not be an asset for the purposes of this Act unless it is a vehicle of a type not commonly used as private vehicle and is unsuitable to be so used.

39 Subject to the provisions of this Act where a person disposes, by way of a gift, of an asset acquired by him by way of a gift or otherwise (not being an acquisition on a devolution on death), the person making the disposal shall not be chargeable to Capital Gains Tax under this Act by reference to that disposal.

In this section, 'gift' has the same meaning as in section 37 (2) above.

40 (1) Gains shall not be chargeable gains if the gains accrue to a diplomatic body, and such gains shall be exempt from Capital Gains Tax under this Act in the same manner as the income of a diplomatic body is exempt from Income Tax under paragraphs (b) and (i) of the Third Schedule of the Income Tax Management Act, 1961, and sections 9, 10 and 11 of the Diplomatic Immunities and Privileges Act, 1962, and those provisions shall be construed accordingly.

(2) In this section 'diplomatic body' includes a diplomatic representative, a foreign

envoy, a foreign consular officer and an employee of any foreign state, or any organisation the members of which are foreign Powers to which section II of the Diplomatic Immunities and Privileges Act, 1962, applies.

41　(1) For the purposes of giving relief on double taxation, in relation to Capital Gains Tax and tax on chargeable gains charged under the law of any country outside Nigeria, in sections 22, 23 and 24 of the Income Tax Management Act, 1961, and sections 36 and 37 of the Companies Income Tax Act, 1961 (double taxation relief and unilateral relief), for references to income and profits there shall be substituted references to capital gains, and for references to income tax there shall be substituted references to Capital Gains Tax, meaning (as the content may require) tax charged under any law in force in Nigeria or tax charged under the law of a country outside Nigeria; and the enactments mentioned as aforesaid in this subsection shall apply accordingly.

(2) Any arrangement set out in order made under the said section 24 of the Income Tax Management Act, 1961, and section 37 of the Companies Income Tax Act, 1961, after the commencement of this Act shall, so far as they provide (in whatever terms) for relief from tax chargeable in Nigeria on capital gains by virtue of this section have effect in relation to Capital Gains Tax.

(3) So far as by virtue of this section Capital Gains Tax charged under the law of a country outside Nigeria may be brough into account under the said provisions of the Income Tax Management Act, 1961, and the Companies Income Tax Act, 1961, as applied by this section, that tax, whether relief given by virtue of this section in repect of it or not, shall not be taken into account for the purposes of those provisions of the Income Tax Management Act, 1961, and the Companies Income Tax Act, 1961, as they apply apart from this section.

(4) Section 24(3) of the Income Tax Management Act, 1961, and section 37(3) of the Companies Income Tax Act, 1961 (which relate to disclosure of information for purposes of double taxtion) shall without prejudice to the foregoing provisions of this section apply in relation to Capital Gains Tax as they apply in relation to Income Tax.

42　(1) A person charged or chargeable for any year of assessment in respect of chargeable gains accruing to him from the disposal of assets situated outside Nigeria may claim that the following provisions of this section shall apply on showing that –

　　(a) he was unable to transfer those gains to Nigeria, and

　　(b) that inability was due to the laws of the country where the income arose, or to the executive action of this government, or to the impossibility of obtaining foreign currency in that territory, and

(2) If he so claims then for the purposes of Capital Gains Tax –

　　(a) there shall be deducted from the amounts on which he is assessed to Capital Gains Tax for the year in which the chargeable gain accrued to the claimant the amount as respects which the conditions in paragraphs (a), (b) and (c) above are satisified, so far as applicable, but

　　(b) the amount so deducted shall be assessed to Capital Gains Tax on the claimant (or his personal representatives) as if it were an amount of chargeable gains accruing in the year of assessment in which the said conditions cease to be satisfied.

(3) No claim under this section shall be made in respect of any chargeable gain more than six years after the end of the year of assessment in which that gain accrues.

(4) The personal representatives of a deceased person may make any claim which he might have made under this section if he had not died.

Notes

1 Known as the Capital Gains Tax Act, 1967. See *Federal Republic of Nigeria Official Gazette* No. 91, Vol.54, 24 October 1967.

2 Finance Act, 1965 (as amended)

3 See section dealing with stocks, shares and gifts. Recipients of gifts are taxable under the Act, *not* the donor of the gifts as in the United Kingdom. Unlike the position in the UK stocks and shares were formerly excluded by the Act to encourage Nigerians to invest in Stock Exchange securities. The exemption of gains arising from a disposal of stocks and shares was deleted by the Finance (Miscellaneous Taxation Provisions) Act, 1972, which amended section 31 of the Capital Gains Tax Act, 1967.

4 Sections 27 to 42.

5 Section 37(2).

6 In spite of section 3 of the Act which provides that all forms of property are assets for the purpose of the Act. The reason for the limitation of chargeable assets is obviously because land and buildings are the main income-yielding assets in Nigeria in view of the concentration of government, commercial, industrial and private offices in Lagos.

7 Section 1.

8 Section 46(3): It is thought desirable to include 'death' in the definition of 'disposal' in order to bring in more revenue.

9 Section 23(2).

15 Capital Transfer Tax Act

The Capital Transfer Tax Act empowers the 'relevant tax authority' to impose Capital Transfer Tax on the value of the property of those who died after 31 March 1979 at graduated levels above the ₦100 000 mark. The Act is published in the *Federal Government Gazette* No. 18, Vol. 66 of 12 April 1979, and is aimed at discouraging young people from relying on the wealth of their parents.

Any property valued at more than ₦1 million will be taxed at the rate of 60 per cent.

But where Capital Transfer Tax becomes payable on the same property within 10 years, following the death of the first benefactor, the tax in respect of the second death will reduced.

For instance, where the second death occurs within twelve months of the first death, the tax will go down by 80 per cent. The tax chargeable in such circumstance is graduated till the tenth year, when the tax is reduced to only 10 per cent.

Transfer

The Act stipulates that anyone who is accountable for Capital Transfer Tax would be required to notify the tax authorities within twelve months after the death of the owner of the property, or six months after the transfer of the property.

It also says that the market price of any property as estimated by the relevant tax authority shall be taken as the value of the property.

Any person who falls foul of the law will pay a fine equal to twice the amount of the Capital Transfer Tax.

For false declaration a person risks a fine of ₦10 000 or two years in jail.

The Act makes allowance for certain deductions in determining the value of property of the dead.

A total of ₦1000 for a tombstone and ₦3000 for funeral expenses are allowable in evaluating the property of the dead for tax purposes.

Valuations

The value of any property for the purposes of determining the tax due is the price which, in the opinion of the relevant tax authority, the property would attain if sold on the open market at the time of death or at the time of transfer. The Act permits the relevant tax authority to appoint and remunerate a sufficient number of qualified persons to act as valuers on its behalf.

In determining the value of the estate of a deceased person for tax purposes, an allowance can be made for reasonable funeral expenses and debts and encumbrances, providing such debts or encumbrances were incurred or created *bona fide* for a full consideration for the deceased's own use or benefit and where there is no right for reimbursement from other sources in whole or in part.

The phrase 'reasonable funeral expenses' includes any expenditure on embalming and transporting the deceased to a burying place up to a maximum of:

(i) ₦1000 in respect of a tombstone; and,

(ii) ₦3000 in respect of all other funeral expenses.

Payment of the tax

The person accountable is required to pay the tax due to the relevant tax authority when the Capital Transfer Tax form is delivered to the authority or on the expiry of twelve months after the death or six months after the transfer, whichever is the sooner. (The person accountable will be either the executor or equivalent of a deceased person or the transferee of property transferred *inter vivos.)*

Where the relevant tax authority is satisfied that the payment in respect of any tax due cannot be made at once without causing excessive hardship (due, for instance, to the tax being due on illiquid assets), then it may allow payment to be delayed for as long as it sees fit, although interest not exceeding 3 per cent will be payable on the outstanding tax due. However, a similar rate of interest is payable by the authority where it is proved that an overpayment of tax has been made by the person accountable, providing such overpayment was made as a result of an over-valuation by the authority.

414

The relevant tax authority may, where it sees fit, accept the payment of the tax due in the form of property where the person accountable applies to pay the tax in whole or in part in such a manner.

Power to distrain

The relevant tax authority may enforce payment of any tax which any person accountable fails, neglects or refuses to pay by distraint on the assets on which the tax was charged or the goods and chattels of the person charged.

Appeals

Any person accountable who does not agree with the decision of the relevant tax authority either on the grounds of the value of the property or on the rate of tax charged may, on payment of 50 per cent of the tax assessed, appeal to the High Court of the State concerned. The matter is then determined by that court or by further appeal to a higher authority as laid down by the rules of that court.

Quick succession

The rate of capital transfer tax is reduced on a sliding scale on any property which has borne tax during the previous ten years as a result of an earlier death. The concession is designed to reduce the cumulative effect of successive deaths within a family (or group of connected people) over a short space of time which – in the normal operation of the tax – would cause a potentially harsh tax charge on property passing from person to person as a result of the deaths.

Where property has been the subject of a death within the preceding twelve months, then, on the second death, the tax charge is reduced by 80 per cent, although the value of the property at the time of second death is taken as its value for tax purposes. For each succeeding twelve months after the first death, the tax charge is:

Death within years	Tax charge reduced by %
2	75
3	60
4	55
5	50
6	45
7	30
8	20
9	15
10	10

The rates[1] of Capital Transfer Tax are according to the following scale:

Net value of the estate or property transferred %	Rate of Capital Transfer Tax %
First 100 000	Nil
Next 150 000	10
Next 150 000	20
Next 250 000	30
Next 500 000	40
Next 1 000 000	50
Thereafter	60

Gifts by way of creation of burden or release of right[2]

The creation by a person or with his consent of a debt or other right enforceable against him personally or against property of which he was or might become competent to dispose, or to charge or burden for his own benefit, shall be deemed to have been a disposition made by that person, and in relation to such a disposition the expression 'property' in the Act shall include the debt or right created.

The extinguishment at the expense of the deceased of a debt or other right shall be deemed to have been a disposition made by the deceased in favour of the person for whose benefit the debt or right was extinguished, and in relation to such a disposition the expression 'property' includes the benefit conferred by the extinguishment of the debt or right.

Insurance Premiums[3]

Where by way of gift a person pays a premium under a policy of assurance on his life in circumstances where the payment does not fall to be treated for Capital Transfer Tax purposes both as a gift and as one of money, and, by reason of assignment or otherwise the payment operates to keep up the policy for the benefit of another person or the donee, then, for Capital Transfer Tax purposes, the payment shall be treated as a gift to the donee of rights under the policy, and the property comprised in the gift shall be treated for those purposes as standing at the payer's death (whether or not the policy continues on foot till that time) at a value equal to the proportion of the value of the policy which the amount of the premium bears to the aggregate amount of all relevant premiums.

Where by reason of any dealing with a policy of life assurance property[4] would be deemed to have passed on the death of the assured, the property so deemed to have passed shall be treated as standing at the assured's death (whether or not the policy continues on foot till that time) at a value equal to the proportion of the value of the policy which the aggregate amount of all premiums paid under the policy before the dealing with the policy bears to the aggregate amount of all relevant premiums.

Charge on company's assets in respect of deceased's benefits therefrom[5]

Where a person dying after the commencement of the Act has made to a company to which section 4 applies, a transfer of any property (other than an interest limited to cease on his death or property which he transferred in a fiduciary capacity), and any benefits accruing to the deceased from the company accrued to him during his life time, the assets of the company shall be deemed for the purposes of Capital Transfer Tax to be included in the property passing on his death to an extent determined, in accordance with sub-paragraph (2) below, by reference to the proportion of that aggregate amount of the benefits accruing to the deceased from the company bore to the net income of the company.

Matters to be treated as benefits to deceased from company

The following shall be treated as benefits accruing to the deceased from the company[6] –

(a) any income of the company, and any periodical payment out of the resources or at the expense of the company, which the deceased received for his own benefit whether directly or indirectly, and any enjoyment in specie of land or other property of the company or of a right thereover which the deceased had for his own benefit whether directly or indirectly;

(b) any such income or payment or enjoyment which the deceased was entitled to receive or have; and

(c) any such income or payment or enjoyment which the deceased could have become entitled to receive or have by an exercise of any power exercisable by him or with his consent;

and where the deceased could, by an exercise of any such power, have become entitled to receive any payment out of the resources or at the expense of the company not being a periodical payment, but did not in fact receive or become entitled to receive that payment, there shall be treated as benefit accruing to the deceased from the company interest on that payment at the average rate from the earliest date on which he could have become entitled to receive it.

The expression 'periodical payment' means a payment by way of dividend or interest, a payment by way of remuneration not being a single lump sum payment, and any other payment being one of a series of payments, whether interconnected or not, whether of the same or of varying amounts, and whether payable at regular intervals or otherwise.

Determination of income of company[7]

The income of the company for any accounting year or for the period between the end of the last accounting year and the death of the deceased, shall be determined by computing the amount of the income of the company from each source in accordance with the provisions of the Companies Income Tax Act, 1961, relating to the computation of income from such a source (subject to the modification that the computation shall be made by reference to the actual income for that year or period, and not by reference to the income for any other period), and the net income of the company for any accounting year shall be determined by deducting from the income of the company for that year the aggregate of the amounts of –

(a) the liabilities of the company for that year in respect of any kind of payment from which income tax is deductible, or which is assessable to income tax, but excluding liabilities in respect of any dividend on shares of or interest on debentures in the company and liabilities incurred otherwise than for the

purposes of the business of the company wholly and exclusively;
(b) any deduction or set-off that could have been claimed for income tax purposes if the computation of the income of the company had been made by reference to the assessable income for that year and not to the actual income:

Provided that there shall be excluded from the computation of the income of the company any income thereof which was neither *bona fide* earned in the ordinary course of business nor the produce of income-yielding assets held by it.

Collection and incidence of Capital Transfer Tax[8]

The following persons shall be accountable for the tax payable on the death of the deceased:
(a) the company;
(b) any person (other than a *bona fide* purchaser for full consideration in money or money's worth received by the company for its own use and benefit) who receives, whether directly from the company or otherwise, or disposes of, any assets which the company had, whether as capital or as income, at the death or at any time thereafter;
(c) any person who received any distributed assets of the company on their distribution:

Provided that a person shall not –
(i) be accountable in respect of any assets for any captial transfer tax in excess of the value of those assets, or
(ii) be accountable in respect of any assets for more than a part of the Capital Transfer Tax bearing to the whole thereof the same proportion that the value of the distribution of those assets bears to the principal value of the assets of the company passing on the death after making the allowance to be made under the law.

For this purpose the expressions 'distributed assets' and 'assets of the company passing on the death' do not inclue any distributed assets of the company which the deceased received on their distribution; and a person who, having received any distributed assets of the company, has died before the deceased shall be deemed to have been a person accountable.

A person accountable for any capital transfer tax shall, for the purpose of raising and paying the tax, have all the powers conferred on accountable parties by the Act.

On a winding up of the company subsection (1) of section 297 of the Companies Act, 1968 (which determines what debts shall have priority over other debts in a winding-up) shall have effect as if there were included a reference to any tax payable in respect of assets of the company passing on a death.

The tax payable on the death of the deceased shall be a first charge by way of floating security on the assets which the company had at the death or has at any time thereafter, any part of the tax for which any person is accountable in respect of any distributed assets shall be a first charge also on those assets:

Provided that nothing shall operate to make any property chargeable as against a *bona fide* purchaser thereof for valuable consideration without notice.

Where any tax has been –
(i) paid by a person accountable therefor by virtue only of paragraph (c) of sub-paragraph (1) above; or
(ii) raised by virtue of sub-paragraph (5) above out of any distributed assets charged therewith;

that person or, as the case may be, the person who was entitled to those assets subject to the charge, may (without prejudice to any right of contribution or indemnity which he may have apart from this sub-paragraph) recover the amount of the tax so paid or raised as aforesaid from any person who is accountable therefore otherwise than by virtue of the said paragraph (c).

No part of the tax paid by the company shall be recoverable by it from any person on the ground only that he is entitled to any interest in, or to any sum charged on, the assets which the company had at the death of the deceased.

The following provisions of the Act shall not have effect in relation to the tax payable:
(a) so much of section 12 (2) of this Act as relates to payment of Capital Transfer Tax on personal property of which the deceased was competent to dispose at his death; and
(b) so much of section 11 (1) of this Act as relates to the accountability of the executor of the deceased in respect of personal property of which the deceased was competent to dispose at his death, and subsection (2) of that section;

and section 11 (1) of the Act shall have effect in relation to the estate as if the property passing had been property passing to the executor as such.

Example 1

Mr Ben Olowolagba died on 10 April 1979. He made a will before his death which stated that his landed properties should pass to his dependants as follows;

(a) a house valued at ₦72000 to his wife;

(b) his eldest son, who is a legal practitioner, is to have a bungalow worth ₦40000;

(c) a storey building valued at ₦35000 should go to his married daughter;

(d) a sawmill valued at ₦150000 passed to another son who is a mechanical engineer;

(e) sundry other properties valued at ₦120000 he had passed to relatives and dependants in February 1979;

(f) the house he lived in up to the time of his death should be treated as family house. This was completed in December 1978 at a cost of ₦80000.

All these items were declared and agreed to by the Tax Authority. You are required to determine the Capital Transfer Tax due resulting from the death of Mr Ben Olowolagba.

Solution 1

Assets subject to Capital Transfer Tax:

(a)	*a house valued at*	72000
(b)	*a bungalow valued at*	40000
(c)	*a storey building valued at*	35000
(d)	*a sawmill valued at*	150000
(e)	*a family house valued at*	80000
		₦377000

Tax due:

1st ₦100000	Nil
Next ₦150000 @ 10%	₦15000
Next ₦127000 @ 20%	₦25400
	₦40400

Other properties transferred before 1 April 1979 are not caught by the Act. Cash gifts are chargeable to CTT but where the gift is in the form of paintings, works of art, etc; to, say, a University, exemption which will be supported by section 17 (3) of the Capital Transfer Act, 1979, will be allowed.

Example 2

Mr John Jolaiya at the time of his death passed to his only son Mr Ben Jolaiya properties which cost ₦720000 to acquire. These properties were passed to him by his deceased mother. Mr John Jolaiya died within two years of his mother's death.

421

Although John's mother had established residence in Ondo State before she died, only one-quarter of the properties were in the State, while the rest were in Lagos State where she lived most of her life.

Assuming that Capital Transfer Tax took effect from the time John's mother was alive, what is the tax due and payable by Mr Ben Jolaiya?

Solution 2

The second death occurred within two years, therefore 60% is subject to tax, that is, ₦432 000.

Amount subject to tax in Lagos State – $\frac{3}{4}$ of ₦432 000 that is, ₦324 000.

Tax due:

1st ₦100 000	Nil
Next ₦150 000 @ 10%	₦15 000
Next ₦174 000 @ 20%	₦14 800
	₦29 800

Amount subject to tax in Ondo State – one-quarter of ₦432 000, that is, ₦108 000.

Tax due:

1st ₦100 000	Nil
Next ₦8 000 @ 10%	₦800

Tax payable by Mr Ben Jolaiya:

(a)	*to Lagos State*	₦29 800
(b)	*to Ondo State*	₦ 800
	Total	₦30 600

Example 3

When James Bennedict wished to resign from the service, he decided to pass part of his assets to his relations. The house in which he lived and some undistributed assets were valued at ₦200 000. These he wished to leave to his wife at death. The value of his assets which passed to his junior brother was ₦110 000; his son was to have ₦90 000, while his daughter was to have ₦75 000. He died two months after. The Internal Revenue Department's valuation of assets which passed *inter vivos* were ₦150 000, ₦120 000 and ₦100 000 respectively.

How much Capital Transfer Tax is due from his assets?

Solution 3

(i) The assets which he passed to relations were:
    (a) *to brother*   ₦150 000
    (b) *to son*   ₦120 000
    (c) *to daughter*   ₦100 000
(ii) The assets which passed at death   ₦200 000
                Total   ₦570 000

Tax due:
1st ₦100 000   Nil
Next ₦150 000 @ 10%   ₦15 000
Next ₦150 000 @ 20%   ₦30 000
Next ₦170 000 @ 30%   ₦51 000
              Total   ₦96 000

Significant Differences between the Capital Gains Tax and the Capital Transfer Tax:

(i) Capital Gains Tax is charged separately in respect of specific assets or a group of assets sold or disposed of as and when the disposal takes place. Capital Transfer Tax is cumulative. This means that Capital Transfer Tax (CTT) is chargeable at progressive rates on the cumulative total of all the gifts made by a donor both during his lifetime and on death.

(ii) Capital Transfer Tax usually arises on the death of an individual whose estate passes to others by reason of death. Liability to capital gains does not merely arise by reason of an individual's death except to the extent of a sale or other chargeable disposition made before the date of death.

(iii) Capital Transfer Tax relates to all gratuitous transfer of wealth made by an individual whether *inter vivos* or on death. The charge arises whether an individual either makes or is deemed to make a transfer of value without an equivalent consideration. On the contrary, any transfer of asset for full valueable consideration attracts Capital Gains Tax but not Capital Transfer Tax.

(iv) Liability to Capital Gains Tax falls directly on the vendor or transferor of an asset sold or disposed of.
In respect of Capital Transfer Tax, liability to tax falls, as a rule on the transferee and not on the transferor.

(v) A company does not become liable to Capital Transfer Tax but can be to Capital Gains Tax in respect of any of its transactions resulting in chargeable gains, such as a sale or disposal of an asset.

Example 4

Mr Koku died on 15 June 1979 at Akure in Ondo State where he had been resident for a number of years. The assets he left were at the date of death valued as follows:

Only private residence at Akure occupied by his widow and family	₦5 000
Business at Akure	150 000
Freehold hospital premises at Akure	80 000
Other properties in Akure	15 000
2 houses in Lagos with a mortgage of ₦55 000 still outstanding	260 000

His death and funeral expenses amounted to ₦5500.

The hospital premises were to be transferred to the second son on the completion of his medical training which he finished in October 1981, when eventually the capital transfer tax was paid on the interest in expectancy. By this time however, the premises were valued at ₦110 000.

Calculate the Capital Transfer Tax payable at death and the amount of tax which had to be paid on the interest in expectancy when it fell into possession.

Apply the following rates for Capital Transfer Tax.

1st	₦100 000	Nil
Next	150 000	10%
Next	150 000	20%
Next	250 000	30%
Next	500 000	40%
Next	500 000	50%
There after		60%

Solution 4

Capital Transfer Tax payable at death

Business at Akure		₦150 000
Other properties in Akure		15 000
Freehold hospital premises		80 000
2 houses in Lagos	₦260 000	
Less mortgate	55 000	205 000
		450 000

Deduct:

Death and funeral expenses
reduced to ₦4000 (maximum)

	4 000	4 000
		446 000
Less *statutory exemption*		100 000
Aggregate value transferred		346 000

Capital Transfer Tax payable at death
Tax payable

Next 150 000 at 10%	15 000
Next 150 000 at 20%	30 000
Next 46 000 at 30%	13 800
	58 800

(b) The amount of tax which has to be paid on the interest in expectancy when it falls into possession shall be calculated according to its value when it falls into possession.

Value of property in October 1981		₦110 000
Business at Akure		150 000
Other properties in Akure		15 000
2 houses in Lagos	₦260 000	
Less mortgage	55 000	205 000
		480 000
Less funeral expenses		4 000
		476 000
Less statutory exemption		100 000
Aggregate value transferred		376 000

Capital Transfer Tax chargeable:

150 000 at 10% =	₦15 000
150 000 at 20% =	30 000
76 000 at 30% =	₦22 800
	₦67 800

CTT payable on property transferred in October 1981.

$$\frac{110\,000}{480\,000} \times 67\,800 = ₦15\,537.50$$

Since there was no mention as to whether the remaining properties are to be transferred to any other beneficiary, the executor should apply to Ondo State Internal Revenue Department for deferment of Capital Transfer Tax payable until the properties are transferred to the beneficiaries or Capital Gains Tax would be paid if the properties are disposed of for valuable consideration (i.e. in transactions made at arm's length).

Capital Transfer Tax is payable on the property transferred to Mr Koku's son in October 1981.

Notes

1   Section 18, Capital Transfer Tax, 1979.
2   Section 2.
3   Section 3.
4   Section 5.
5   Section 4.
6   Section 5.
7   Section 7.
8   Section 12.

16 Settlements, Trusts and Estates

Definitions

A 'settlement' is an agreement by which a sum of money is set aside to make provision for another person (e.g. a marriage settlement).

A 'trust' is the conveying of property (both real and personal) to one or more persons in confidence that it will be applied for the benefit of others or to some specified purpose. A trust may be created by will, by deed, or occasionally by an Order of the Courts.

The administration of a settlement or trust is placed in the hands of one or more 'trustees' who hold the property to take care of it and apply it for the benefit of those entitled to it, i.e. the 'beneficiaries'. A trustee may also be a beneficiary.

An 'estate' is the aggregate of the things possessed by a person, including his goods, money and property of every kind.

When a person dies, his estate passes into the possession of his personal representatives, 'executors' or 'administrators', whose duties, briefly, are to meet the necessary funeral expenses and then, after having any will legally proved, to realise the estate and pay debts and legacies. They deal with the residue of the estate as directed by the will, if any, or if none, according to the rules of intestacy; e.g. they set up a trust to administer the income, or distribute the residue among the persons entitled to benefit. In these Instructions the term 'executor' includes any person administering the estate of a deceased person.

The period between the date of death and date on which the executor is able to set up a trust or distribute the residue of the estate is known as the 'administration period'.

After the administration period the estate of a deceased person, so far as it has not been distributed, remains in trust and is in the same position as any other trust estate, e.g. one established by deed.

The types of persons who may benefit from the income of an estate are:

(a) A person receiving a specific bequest (e.g. investments) from the estate. He is known as a 'legatee', i.e. one to whom a legacy is bequeathed. This part of these instructions is not concerned with legatees.

(b) A person receiving an annuity which may be charged on the income of the estate, on income and capital, or on particular assets. He is known as an 'annuitant'.

(c) A person entitled both to income and capital (or a part of it) at the end of the administration period. He holds an absolute interest and is known as a 'residuary legatee' or 'residuary devisee'. This part of the instructions is not concerned with such persons, but the will may direct that the capital should be held in trust for a period during which they would be called 'beneficiaries'.

(b) A person entitled to income and capital (or part of it). He holds a limited interest and is known as a 'beneficiary'. At the end of a specified period, usually at the death of such a beneficiary, the capital passes to some other person, the 'remaining'.

Anti-avoidance provisions

General: ITMA Second Schedule, para. 1

To prevent avoidance of tax by the creation of an 'artificial' settlement or trust, it is provided that the income shall be treated as being that of the settlor or person creating the trust if:

(a) that settlor or person can direct the disposition of the capital or income; or

(b) that settlor or person has any right to any of the income; or

(c) the settlement or trust is revocable and that settlor or person, or the spouse of that settlor or person, may resume control over the capital or income; except where such reversion is planned to take place on the prior death of a beneficiary, or the happening of an uncertain event by which the settlement or trust is limited.

If any of the conditions set out above apply then this section of the instructions is not relevant to such a settlement or trust.

Trustees and executors chargeable

Trustees: ITMA, section 3(6)

Income Tax may be charged on a trustee of a settlement or trust only if:

(a) the seat of administration of the settlement or trust was situated in a State on 1 April 1961; *or*

(b) the first seat of administration was in a State in the case of a settlement or trust created after 1 April 1961.

Executors: ITMA, section 3(6)

Income Tax may be charged on an executor of a deceased individual's estate only if the deceased individual was deemed to be resident in a State, or would have been deemed to be resident in Northern Nigeria had the ITMA been in force when he died.

Assessments

Assessments on trustees or executors are made only in the territory of the relevant tax authority. The responsibility of the tax authority of any other territory is determined by the same factors.

Income arising from settlements, trusts and estates

Income arising: ITMA s.13; ITMA Second Schedule, para.2(1)

Income arising from a settlement, trust or estate, made, created or administered in Nigeria, is that income derived from any source in Nigeria and any income brought into or received in Nigeria.

Apportionment of income

The income arising may be apportioned between the following classes:

(a) an annuitant;

(b) a beneficiary;

(c) a trustee or executor.

The income of a settlement, trust or estate is first computed. The 'computed income' is then allocated between the beneficiaries and trustees or executors.

The 'Computed income' of a settlement, trust or estate

'Computed income': ITMA Second Schedule, para.2(2)

The 'computed income' is the income of the year ending on 31 March, arrived at under the following provisions (a) to (e):

(a) *Income subject to Income Tax*

The provisions of ITMA, Part II, apply in the way they apply to individuals.

(b) *Deductions in computing income*

The provisions of ITMA, Part III apply in the way they apply to individuals.

(c) *Special deductions*

There are also deducted:

(i) any *expenses* of the trustee or executor connected with the settlement, trust or estate which are authorised by the deed or will;

(ii) any fixed annual *annuity* paid out of income under the deed or will.

(d) *Loss relief*

If the income includes profits from a trade, business, profession or vocation, or any rents or premiums, there is deducted the same sum as would have been allowed as loss relief in the *next* year of assessment to an individual carrying on that trade, etc. and assessed on the preceding year basis.

(e) *Capital allowances and Balancing Charges*

If the income includes profits from a trade, business, profession or vocation, or any rents or premiums, there is deducted or added the same sums as would have been allowed as capital allowances or charged as Balancing Charges in the *next* year of assessment to an individual carrying on that trade, etc. and assessed on the preceding year basis.

Special capital allowances provisions

The following special provisions apply under TECH. 7560(a) in relation to the assets of a trade or business of a deceased individual transferred to his estate where capital allowances may be claimed on behalf of that individual for the year of death. The normal capital allowances provisions are modified to the extent that:

(i) no Balancing Allowances or Balancing Charges are made in respect of assets transferred on death to the estate;

(ii) the estate is treated as having incurred qualifying expenditure, on the acquisition of each asset, equal to the residue of expenditure as on the day following the date of death;

(iii) when each asset is disposed of, any Balancing Charge arising is computed by reference to the net total capital allowances given to both the deceased individual and the estate.

430

Apportionment of 'Computed income'

Apportionment rules: ITMA, Second Schedule, para.3

The 'computed income' of any year of assessment is apportioned for assessment purposes in accordance with the following rules:

Rule 1
Where the deed or will lays down that the *whole* of the net income, after authorised expenses and fixed annuities have been paid, is to be divided in *specific* proportions between the beneficiaries the 'computed income' is *wholly* apportioned on a similar basis to each of those beneficiaries.

Rule 2
Where the deed or will gives the trustee or executor a *discretionary* power to make *any payment* out of income to a beneficiary that payment is income in the hands of that beneficiary for the year of payment.

Rule 3
Where the deed or will lays down that the balance of the net income after authorised expenses, fixed annuities and discretionary payments (as under Rule 2) is to be divided in specific proportions between the beneficiaries the balance of the 'computed income' is apportioned on a similar basis to each of those beneficiaries.

Rule 4
Any balance of the 'computed income' after deducting the sums allocated to beneficiaries under Rule 2 and Rule 3 is assessed on the trustee or executor in his name as trustee or executor.

It should be borne in mind that:

(a) The whole of the 'computed income' may not be apportioned, e.g.

'computed income'	₦1 000
discretionary payments made	200
specific payments $= \frac{1}{4} + \frac{1}{2}$	750
Non-apportioned balance	50

(b) The aggregate apportioned may exceed the 'computed income', e.g.

'computed income'	₦1 000
discretionary payments made	500
specific payments $= \frac{1}{4} + \frac{1}{2}$	750
Excess	250

In this case the payments made to *all* beneficiaries are proportionally reduced so that the total amounts equal the 'computed income'. This would be achieved in the example by reducing the payments to:

discretionary payments to 'A'	₦400
specific payment to 'B' $(\frac{1}{4})$	200
specific payment to 'C' $(\frac{1}{2})$	400
Total = 'computed income'	₦1000

Double taxation relief: ITMA, Second Schedule, para.6

Where double taxation relief is due on any income of a settlement, trust or estate, the relief due is computed as though the whole of the doubly-taxed income were receivable by the beneficiaries, trustees or executors to whom the 'computed income' of the year was apportioned, under Rules 1 to 4, in proportion to their respective shares.

If, by chance, the income of the settlement, trust or estate is exhausted by expenses, annuities, etc. and there is no 'computed income' the relief is to be given to the trustee or executor.

Basis of assessment

Basis of assessment – annuitant: ITMA, Second Schedule, paras. 4 & 5

Any individual who receives a fixed annual annuity out of the income of a settlement, trust or estate, is assessed on the full amount of that annuity for the year preceding the year of assessment. This income is included in his Income Tax assessment.

Basis of assessment – beneficiary, trustee or executor: ITMA, Second Schedule, para.5

Any beneficiary, trustee or executor to whom part of the 'computed income' has been apportioned under Rules 1 to 4 is assessed on that part of the 'computed income' for the year preceding the year of assessment.

The income of a beneficiary is included in his Income Tax assessment in the same way as income from any other source.

The income of a trustee or executor is not included in any assessment on him as an individual but is assessed separately in his name as trustee or executor. No personal reliefs are allowed: instead the graduated rates of tax are charged directly on the assessable income.

432

Settlement, trust or estate accounts

Accounts: ITMA Second Schedule, para.8

It is the responsibility of the trustee or executor of a settlement, trust or estate in Nigeria to prepare accounts of the trust, etc. income. These accounts are to be made up to each 31 March and to the date on which the assets are finally distributed.

Appeals

Responsible territory: ITMA, Second Schedule, para.9

Assessments on beneficiaries and annuitants may be made in territories other than that in which the trustee or executor is assessed. In any event, an appeal against the assessment of income from a settlement, trust or estate is to be dealt with by the tax authority for the territory in which the trustee or executor is assessable.

17 The Cases for Taxation of Savings and Expenditure, and for a Value Added Tax

Some form of taxation of savings and consumption is already in existence in Nigeria. Interest on savings in excess of ₦15 per annum is a taxable income. Comsumption or expenditure to a small extent is rarely taxed because only 5% of the taxable self-employed population prepare accounts and the taxation is in the form set out below where the assessing officer is trained and displays honesty, integrity and professionalism.

A person's assessable income during a given period is also to be arrived at (especially in the absence of complete records of business and other accounts year by year) by deducting from his capital at the end of the said period his capital at the beginning of that period and adding to the figure obtained the amount of his living expenses during the period in question. Here is a simple illustration:

(1) At the end of year one, a person's assets totalled ₦300 and his liabilities ₦100. His capital at the end of year one was, therefore ₦300 − ₦100 = ₦200.

Suppose this person declared ₦300 as his income from all sources for each of years two, three, four and five and that he spent ₦220 per annum on living expenses of himself and family and his liability at the end of year five was ₦150 then his capital at the end of year five would be ascertained as follows:

Capital at the end of year one (as above)	₦200
Total income for four years @ N300 p.a.	1200
	1400
Less: living expenses for four years @ N200 p.a.	880
	520
Less liability at the end of year five	150
Capital at the end of year five	₦370

His capital increase in four years was only ₦170 i.e. ₦370 − ₦200 = ₦170.

There are import duties on selected goods but my main concern is the reform of income tax laws, and the co-operation of the Customs and Excise Department in inter-governmental co-operation in taxation by circularisation of tax districts throughout the Federation on details about importers is a condition precedent.

It is time self-employed taxpayers were statutorily compelled to submit audited accounts annually to avoid confusion for themselves and the Internal Revenue. This would lead to correct payment of tax.

An increase in the saving-investment rate is one of the conditions of economic progress in Nigeria. Most of the developing countries have accepted the goal of a mixed economy and are seeking means of increasing saving and capital formation in both the public and private sectors. Even in a country which assigns to the state the major share of investment, private saving may be an important source of finance for public investment. The USSR, for example, has not been oblivious to the advantages of promoting private saving and the sale of government bonds.

Tax revenues are the principal source of government saving, and taxation influences private saving because it affects incentives and capacity to save. Owing to the heavy responsibilities that governments are assuming, not only for capital formation, but also for the provision of current services, Nigeria cannot promote saving merely by maintaining low taxes. Most less developed countries need to raise more revenue, many of them, much more. Tax policy has the delicate responsibility of obtaining large amounts of revenue without unduly impairing private saving or, if feasible, by means that will stimulate private saving.

This chapter considers the question whether Nigeria can advise and administer tax systems that will raise adequate amounts of revenue in socially and politically acceptable ways and at the same time allow or encourage desired increases in private saving.

By concentrating on taxation I do not intend to imply that it is the most important influence on private saving or that variations of the tax system are the most efficient means of modifying the saving-income ratio. But, even if other policies are more significant, it does not follow that taxes exert only a trivial influence on saving.

Alternative approaches

Programmes for fostering private saving by means of the tax system range from broad prescriptions regarding the distribution of the tax load through detailed schemes of tax incentives and penalties. A general admonition that is heard from time to time is that the progressive taxes should be minimised. A positive recommendation, which is usually thought to be practically identical with this advice although theoretically distinguishable, is that major reliance be placed on indirect taxes. Lately there has been considerable discussion of proposals for partial or complete exemption of saving under the Income Tax and for the imposition of a direct tax on personal consumption expenditures.

This idea is intended to concentrate taxation on consumption and to leave private saving either free of taxation or subject to lower rates of tax. It is usually taken for granted that this policy will promote private saving, but the basis of the belief is not obvious and is worthy of attention. There is no ground for supposing that even full tax immunity of saved income would eliminate the influence of taxation on the amount saved. Savers would make their decisions in the light of their position after allowance for consumption taxes and other taxes, and it would be surprising if these taxes did not affect both saving and consumption. Preferential taxation of saving by reliance on consumption taxes or other means may encourage saving for two reasons. First, the possible reward for saving will be higher than under a different tax system. Second, the capacity to save will be greater in the sense that potential savers will have more resources at their disposal.

Progressive taxation of income will cut more deeply into the return on saving than will proportional or regressive taxation, if interest and profits receipts are a rising fraction of income as size of income increases. This is true in capitalistic countries but is less clearly so in pre-industrial societies, where landowners are often the richest members of the community.

The terms of exchange between present and future consumption are more favourable to the latter under a system of consumption taxation than under a general income tax and in this sense the reward for saving is greater under a consumption tax. Consider the alternatives open to a person subject to (say) 50 per cent Income Tax or a 100 per cent Consumption Tax. If in year one he receives 100 of income he will be liable for 50 of tax under the Income Tax. He can either consume the remaining 50 immediately or save and invest it and, at a market rate of interest of 5 per cent, realise a net return of 1.25 in one year (2.50 gross return minus 1.25 of income tax). Thus, by giving up 50 of present consumption he can enjoy 51.25 of consumption one year later. Under the Consumption Tax he can save and invest 100 in year one and have available 105 a year later, which will allow him to consume 52.50 at that time. In this case he exchanges 50 of present consumption for 52.50 of future consumption. The advantage to the saver under the Consumption Tax is due to the fact that postponement of consumption also postpones tax payment and allows the saver to receive interest on the postponed tax.[1] A 100 per cent Consumption Tax will yield less revenue than a 50 per cent Income Tax, if there are positive savings; but it can be shown that adjustment of rates to make the yields of the two taxes equal will not eliminate the advantage enjoyed by savers under the Consumption Tax.

It is by no means certain, however, that an increase in the net rate of return obtainable on savings will stimulate additional saving. The effect is not clearly indicated by either economic theory or statistical observation.[2] Whereas some individuals might be induced to save more, others might save less because a smaller capital sum would satisfy their demands for retirement income, family security, and dowries. Many might not respond at all. Total personal saving might increase, decrease, or remain unchanged.

The uncertainty of the influence of the rate of return on the volume of saving may justify the neglect of the possibility of stimulating saving by preferential taxation of interest and profit income. The absence of proposals of this nature, however, is probably due more to broad political considerations than to doubts about their effectiveness. The prevailing opinion throughout the world seems to be that justice demands that any differentiation in tax rates should run in favour of earned income rather than property income. Selective tax exemption of interest and profits from strategic sources is more acceptable on political grounds and is widely practised.

The capacity-to-save argument holds that aggregate saving can be increased by transferring taxation from those who are most inclined to save to those who are least inclined to do so; the capacity to save is increased where the inclination to save is strongest. It is not necessary that anyone change his attitude toward present and future consumption or accumulation. The community's saving ratio can be raised without altering the saving ratio of any individual, provided high savers are given command over a larger fraction of the resources available to the private sector.

This reasoning suggests that a tax on consumption will be more favourable to private saving than an equal-yield tax on income because the Consumption Tax will leave a larger proportion of real disposable income in the hands of those with higher-than-average saving rates. The argument, although plausible, is not conclusive. Differences in individuals' liabilities for the Consumption Tax and the Income Tax depend on the ratio of their total taxable consumption to their taxable income, whereas the impact on saving is governed by the use to which individuals will put comparatively small changes in their real disposable income. In short, the marginal propensity to save rather than the average propensity is the relevant characteristic.

Persons with high average propensities to save may also have high marginal propensities to save. The assumption that this is true implies only a certain continuity of behaviour, after any initial lags associated with a change in disposable income have been overcome. No doubt, however, there are individuals who save a large fraction of their income at a certain time who would save little if any of an increment to income. They may have been accumulating for a specific purpose which has been satisfied, or they may have been paying off a mortgage or other long-term debt (a form of saving) and feel free to consume more after getting out of debt or meeting contractual instalments. On the other hand, some families who have consumed all of their income may save a large part of an increase in income. But such sharp changes in behaviour seem exceptional. Average saving ratios reflect age and family composition, tastes, habits, opportunities, and other factors which change slowly, and presumably these influences also determine marginal saving ratios.

It is easy to form an exaggerated impression of what can be accomplished by reallocating taxes between high and low savers. Differences between the impacts of alternative tax formulae will not be as great as differences between the marginal propensities to consume of high and low savers, provided that the choice of tax formula does not itself influence individual propensities to save. This is true because all feasible measures impose taxes on both high and low savers; hence the effect on saving is a weighted average of high and low marginal propensities to save, with the weights depending on the amounts of tax paid. To illustrate, consider A and B, who have equal incomes but different saving behaviour. Assume that A's marginal propensity to save is 0 and that B's is 20 per cent. If A is taxed while B goes free, private saving is unaffected; if B is taxed and A is not, saving is curtailed by 20 per cent of the revenue. There is, however, no feasible and socially acceptable means of taxing A while exempting B, unless they differ in characteristics other than saving behaviour. The realistic alternatives are to tax both A and B on income, total consumption, selected items of consumption, or property. If A and B are taxed in proportion to their total consumption, A will pay $\frac{5}{9}$ of the aggregate tax and B $\frac{4}{9}$; private saving will be reduced by approximately 8.9 per cent of the revenue.[3] By selective consumption taxes, it may be possible to allocate a still larger share of taxes to A and other low savers; but B and other frugal people will have to bear part of the load.

The argument that regressive taxation (measured with respect to income) is more favourable to private saving than is progressive taxation may be viewed as an alternative approach to allocation of taxes between high and low savers. The assumption is that the marginal propensity to save rises with income size. This hypothesis has been supported by two kinds of evidence: (1) the commonsense belief that saving is hard for the poor but easy for the rich; and (2) the observation that national saving ratios tend to vary directly with income per head.

To a middle-class observer from North America or Western Europe it often seems that the poor in many less-developed countries live at the subsistence level and could not save if they wished to do so, whereas the rich must save inasmuch as there is positive private saving in most˙ countries. This impression may be misleading. Social convention is probably more important than physiological necessity as a limitation on the saving capacity of a large majority of the population. Anthropologists tell us that in virtually all societies appreciable amounts of resources are used for ceremonial and other purposes that cannot be classified as physical necessities. These outlays often place heavy demands on the rich as well as the poor.[4]

The extravagant standards of personal consumption and hospitality of the rich in Nigerian societies are notorious. In these conditions it seems naive to suppose that saving habits are predictably related to size of income. Heavy saving may reflect deviant behaviour rather than a large income; or, as the classical economists usually assumed, saving may be done almost exclusively by receivers of profits and interest.[5]

It is doubtful whether the findings of family budget studies in high-income countries have much value as an indication of saving behaviour in the underdeveloped countries. Studies in Puerto Rico and Delhi, India, it is true, agree with American and British surveys in indicating negative saving ratios in the lowest income classes and increasing saving ratios in higher income classes.[6] These data, however, measure average saving ratios rather than marginal propensities to save. They are not necessarily inconsistent with the existence of a uniform marginal propensity to save in the range where most income is found.[7] It has been cogently argued, moreover, that the cross-section data provided by the single-year budget studies which are available give a misleading impression of the normal relationship between income and saving, exaggerating the difference between low and high incomes.[8] Although important differences of opinion exist, there seems to be agreement among research workers in the field that, in the United States and Great Britain, the marginal propensity to save differs less between income classes than was formerly assumed on the basis of family budget surveys.[9]

The fact that the ratio of aggregate household saving to aggregate disposable income tends to be considerably higher in countries with high income per head than in low-income countries[10] is constent with the hypothesis that the marginal propensity to save within countries varies directly with size of income. The correlation between national saving ratios and income per head is by no means perfect, however. Differences among countries may be due, not only to the level of income per head, but also to differences in the industrial composition of production, the factor distribution of income, social values, customs, and the security of property.

Even if we conclude that the weight of evidence – or intuition – indicates that the marginal propensity to save rises with size of income in all countries, we should recognise the existence of differences in saving patterns of families in the same income class. 'The' saving ratio for an income class is an average derived from a distribution including some families with lower ratios and some wtih higher ratios. The distributions for adjacent income classes – and perhaps also for widely separated classes – overlap. In the United States, for example, the Survey of Consumer Finances indicates that in 1950 consumer units making up the highest one-fifth of income recipients had an average net saving ratio twice the national average; nevertheless, 38 per cent of these units had saving ratios below the national average, and 22 per cent of them were negative savers. About 23 per cent of consumer units in income classes below the top fifth had saving ratios equal to or higher than the average ratio for the top income group.[11] Size of income is at best a rough method of classifying individuals according to saving propensities. A decrease in tax progressively will augment the disposable income of rich spendthrifts as well as high savers.

None of the approaches, it seems, can confidently be expected to bring about a significant increase in private saving. All rest on questionable assumptions. Proposals for concentrating taxes on consumption and exempting saving or taxing it lightly are perhaps more firmly based than suggestions for preferential taxation of interest and profits and the avoidance of progressivity. The former, moreover, clash less openly with political values that have been spread around the world by the same social currents.

Tax design and administration

Difficult problems are encountered in the design of direct-tax provisions to favour saving. Less serious but still genuine problems are involved in the refinement of indirect taxes to help advance the social and economic objectives of the less-developed countries. The challenge is to design measures that are as consistent and logical as possible in allocating taxes in a manner calculated to achieve the objectives and which are within the administrative and compliance capabilities of the country. This includes the devising of tax forms and information reports and the drawing up of detailed rules of tax assessment as well as the clarification of grand policy issues and the explanation of proposals to political leaders and the general public. Lack of attention to tax design may result in action or the adoption of measures that fail to produce the desired results and that have harmful side-effects on economic progress, respect for law, and political maturity.

General economists have displayed great interest in tax policy but have usually left questions of tax design to the specialists. Most Commissioners of Internal Revenue and tax officials, like specialists in many other fields, tend to resist innovations. Neither the general economists nor the technicians have given enough thought to the irksome details that determine the practicability of fundamental revisions of the tax system.

Kaldor is a conspicuous exception to the statement that economists have not worked out the details of measures to put into effect their broad tax proposals.

Exemption of saving under the Income Tax

The suggestion that saving be exempt from Income Tax or taxed at lower rates than other income may appear to be simple but on closer examination will be seen to entail complications. It would not be easy to define and measure saving to prevent tax evasion, and to assure equitable treatment of persons who save in some years and dissave in other years.

Let us consider first a broad scheme providing tax exemption or preferential rates for the part of current income that is saved regardless of the form in which the savings are held. If taxable income were measured as recommended by Haig, Simons, and other students, as the algebraic sum of consumption and changes in net worth,[12] no special difficulty would be involved in putting into effect this scheme. The general practice, however, is to define taxable income by enumeration of includable receipts and allowable deductions. The assessment of income does not produce a figure for saving. Therefore, the authorities and taxpayers would have to go through all of the steps that are now required for the determination of taxable income and the additional steps necessary to measure saving.

In principle, saving could be measured as the difference between current income and consumption outlays or by the identification of increases in various forms of asset during the year. Few families, however, keep records of their consumption expenditures and even when available such accounts could not easily be verified. There is general agreement that the subtraction method is not practicable and that saving would have to be measured by the increase in asset.

The authorities would have to require taxpayers to present evidence on all holding of securities, real property, direct investment in business enterprises, cash balances and perhaps other assets.

It would not be sufficient merely to ascertain new purchases of assets or increases in bank balances during the year. The scheme would be defeated if taxpayers could gain tax exemption by converting assets, that is, by selling one kind of asset and buying another or by borrowing and purchasing an asset. A measure of the net increase in all capital transactions – purchases and sales of assets, gifts received and given, debts contracted and repaid, increases and decreases in cash balances, and certain other items would be required. A better method, and indeed the only way of making sure that no changes were omitted, would be to examine complete balance sheets of each taxpayer for the beginning and end of the year. Comparative balance sheets would be highly useful also for the determination of net income and would be helpful in the assessment of an ordinary income tax. However, the authorities have not considered it feasible to require balance sheets of individual taxpayers who are not engaged in trade or business even in the countries with the most advanced tax administrations.

It would be especially important to obtain accurate balance sheets at the time the new plan went into effect. Taxpayers would have an incentive to conceal cash and other liquid assets because by converting these assets over a period of years they could appear to be accumulating new savings and could thus qualify for tax benefits. In addition, many persons would be reluctant to divulge their true assets because of fear of revealing past tax evasion and of exposing themselves to exchange controls and back duty by Internal Revenue.

In the Western State, that does not tax capital gains, information on capital transactions is not generally required from employees for assessment of income tax. Thus, the introduction of an exemption for saving would greatly increase the scope of reporting and verification.

Lagos and Midwest which now tax capital gains would not have to undertake a completely new activity, but they would face enforcement problems. One of the most difficult points would be the ascertainment of changes in cash balances, not required for assessment of Capital Gains Tax but essential for the measurement of net saving.[13]

The exemption of saving from the Income Tax would increase incentives for omitting transactions in which gains occurred and for understating gains. Taxpayers who did so would not only escape Capital Gains Tax but would also acquire funds that could be used to purchase other assets or increase cash balances and thus to serve as evidence of 'saving' that would entail a reduction in regular income tax liability. Of course, some moderation would have to be exercised in taking advantage of this means of evasion. Alert tax officials would become suspicious of persons who reported a high rate of saving if their living habits were obviously inconsistent with the indicated scale of consumption.

The saving and consumption elements cannot be readily distinguished in some transactions. Examples are purchases of jewellery and other durable consumer goods, purchases and maintenance of dwellings, payments of life insurance premiums and expenditures for education. More or less arbitrary rules already apply to several of these items under the income tax, and similar conventions would have to be worked out to separate consumption and saving elements. An acceptable treatment would complicate administration but would not present unique or insurable difficulties. [14]

Administration could be simplified by limiting the tax exemption to savings invested in a few kinds of asset, say government bonds, shares and bonds or debentures of quoted securities on the Lagos Stock Exchange, and savings accounts in banks and similar institutions. It would be possible to require that all eligible securities be in registered form rather than bearer form in order to facilitate verification of claimed changes in holdings. This scheme would not provide tax exemption for net saving as such but for the acquisition of the designated assets. There would be nothing to prevent the taxpayer from acquiring the eligible assets by converting other assets.

Nigeria should be concerned with the form in which savings are held as well as with the rate of total saving. As already noted, a decree of selectivity in tax concessions for saving would no doubt be regarded as an advantage by most governments. Too narrow and rigid a provision governing eligibility for special treatment, however, would sacrifice much of the advantage of private saving and investment compared with direct state investment, while retaining the conditions making for economic and social inequality. On the other hand, extension of the list of eligible assets would lead toward the problems associated with a general exemption.

A serious difficulty that is often overlooked relates to the length of the assessment period. [15] The purpose of a tax concession for saving is to encourage a permanent – or at least a long-term – increase in savings or in holdings of certain assets. This purpose would not be served by acts of saving which were soon reversed or offset by dissaving. Some means would have to be found to prevent a taxpayer from qualifying for an exemption say every second year by alternatively building up and drawing down his savings. Opportunities of this kind would be limited by the desire to avoid violent fluctuations in consumption, but many possibilities of illegal evasion and legal avoidance would suggest themselves to imaginative taxpayers, for example the use of personal loans or open accounts not revealed to the tax assessor to finance consumption in the years of nominally high saving and the scheduling of vacation trips and other postponable expenditure in alternate years.

Three means suggest themselves for dealing with ascertainable dissaving that follows a year in which an exemption has been granted for saving. The return of the earlier year could be reopened and tax reassessed, the dissaving could be added to taxable income in the year in which it occurred, or Income Tax could be assessed on the basis of a cumulative averaging plan covering several years or perhaps the taxpayer's whole life. Reopening of returns is troublesome, and most tax administrators like to minimise the extent to which it is necessary. The addition of dissaving to current taxable income seems preferable but, with progressive rates, could result in hardships for taxpayers or opportunities for manipulation. Cumulative averaging is an attractive idea even in an undifferentiated Income Tax; however, most countries have considered it too complex.

Expenditure Tax

The Expenditure Tax would be administered in almost the same way as an Income Tax with all saving exempt. The assessment procedure recommended by Kaldor is as follows: (1) all receipts from current net income, sale of assets, borrowing, gifts, inheritances, and other sources would be aggregated; (2) deductions would be allowed for gross saving in the form of additions to cash balances, investment outlays, and debt repayment; (3) deduction would also be allowed for any consumption expenditures exempt from tax and for certain direct tax payments, and (4) tax would be assessed on the balance, representing taxable consumption expenditures. As under the Income Tax with saving exempt problems would arise in obtaining complete and accurate balance sheets (or comprehensive statements of capital transactions), in identifying the consumption and saving elements of certain transactions, and in fairly assessing tax on fluctuating levels of consumption.

The point of departure for a successful Expenditure Tax would be an accurate determination of net income. The addition of balance sheet data, essential for the Expenditure Tax, would facilitate the determination of income. On the other hand the imposition of a steeply graduated Expenditure Tax to an Income Tax would increase incentives to classify personal consumption items as business expenses in the form of entertainment, travel expenses, and the like – an especially troublesome form of Income Tax evasion.

Provision for spreading outlays for consumer durables over a period of years, by means of averaging or capitalisation and taxation of the annual imputed service value, would be necessary for equity under a graduated expenditure tax.

***

The remainder of this paper will be devoted to direct and indirect taxes on consumption and plans for exempting saving from income taxes. Although the extent of the influence on private saving of these measures is uncertain, they can be presumed to have some favourable effect, and they would at least leave the way open for an increase in private saving due to other policies and to social and economic change.

Methodology for taxing consumption

Methods of taxing consumption are (1) an Income Tax with saving partially or wholly exempt; (2) a personal Expenditure Tax or Spendings Tax; and (3) indirect taxes in the form of excises, sales or turnover taxes, and customs duties. A policy of attempting to foster private saving involves not only reliance on taxes on consumption but also avoidance of taxes that are especially destructive of saving. In as much as the latter taxes will not yield large sums, the fact that a government raises a large proportion of its revenue from consumption taxes is not necessarily a proof that it offers favourable treatment to private saving.

The indirect taxes on consumption are well known. Exemption of saving from the Income Tax is not so familiar, but the general import of this proposal is easily visualised. The personal Expenditure Tax is a direct tax on consumption expenditure; like the Income Tax, it can incorporate personal exemptions, allowances for dependants, and graduated rates. Irving Fisher was a well-known advocate of such a tax, although he insisted on calling it an Income Tax since he defined personal income as equal to consumption.[16] More recently, Kaldor revived interest in the idea through a book published in 1955 and reports to the governments of India and Ceyon.[17] These two countries adopted expenditure taxes of limited scope, India in 1957 and Ceylon in 1959.[18]

A personal Expenditure Tax and an Income Tax with saving exempt are similar in that both are direct taxes falling on consumption. As explained in a later section, the two taxes would be assessed in much the same way. In practice, however, there are likely to be differences in coverage and rate structures.

In as much as indirect taxes are traditional in most less-developed countries, the question may be raised how the policy under discussion differs from existing practice. Although this method of attempting to foster saving would be less novel than the other two, its consistent application would involve revision of the tax system of Nigeria. Indirect taxes are now often imposed on capital goods as well as consumption goods. This is particularly true of import duties and not solely or even mainly for protectionist reasons.

Coverage and selectivity

The Expenditure Tax, in pure form, distinguishes only between consumption and saving and, when graduated, amounts of personal consumption; it does not differentiate between kinds of consumption and forms of saving. The same tax rates apply to spending for imports and home goods, goods that are plentiful and those that are in short supply, items whose production competes directly with the development programme and other items. Expenditures for education and cultural activities are taxed in the same way as spending for luxurious cars, social ceremonies and fashionable clothes. The expenditure tax exempts all non-consumption uses of income and wealth, including hoarding, real estate purchases, capital flight, and other activities that the authorities may wish to discourage rather than stimulate.

A system that exempts all saving from Income Tax is as unselective as the Expenditure Tax. In practice, however, exemption is likely to be granted only for forms of saving that are considered desirable or innocuous. For example, a tax remission may be allowed for purchases of government securities or shares in approved industries and for bank deposits but denied for saving embodied in currency hoards, gold, and foreign securities.[19] Desirable forms of consumption can be favoured allowing the taxpayer to deduct specified personal expenses when he computes his taxable income, but this method of differentiation has limited flexibility. It can be applied only to items for which reasonably accurate information on individual expenditures is available; furthermore expenses are usually deductible in full or not at all and hence are subject either to the regular Income Tax rate or a zero rate.

The pure Expenditure Tax of course, may be modified to exempt certain consumption outlays, but, like the Income Tax, it lacks flexibility as a means of differential taxation of consumption. Distinctions between forms of saving are less likely under the Expenditure Tax than under the modified Income Tax since the Expenditure Tax focuses on consumption as the tax base rather than on the concession offered to saving.

A difference in coverage of the Expenditure Tax and an Income Tax with saving exempt is that the expenditure tax base includes consumption financed by disposal of wealth as well as that supported from current income whereas the modified Income Tax may not reach this part of consumption. The importance of this difference depends largely on the length of the period for which tax is assessed. The longer the averaging period, the less the difference in coverage of the two taxes. With lifetime averaging, the principal difference would be that the Expenditure Tax would strike consumption financed by using up inherited wealth whereas the Income Tax with saving exempt would not. Another difference in coverage, which may be more significant, is that the Expenditure Tax will reach consumption financed from capital gains, gifts and other receipts which are not included in taxable income. In India, the possibilities of broader coverage of the Expenditure Tax have not been fully exploited. The tax does not apply to persons who, together with their dependents, receive from all sources an annual income of less than Rs. 36 000 after deduction of Indian Income Tax.[20] Thus the expenditure tax does not reach certain extreme forms of dissaving or consumption financed from gifts but presumably does apply to consumption paid out of tax-exempt income.

Indirect taxes are necessarily selective or discriminatory regarding forms of consumption and nonselective regarding means of finance. They apply unequally to different items of consumption but equally to expenditures financed from capital and those made out of income. Indirect taxes may also apply to capital goods and to certain forms of financial saving. Special taxes on security transactions are common. In the Federal Republic of Germany the general turnover tax applies to gold transactions.[21]

Selectivity with respect to both items of consumption and forms of saving can be attained by combining indirect taxes with exemptions for enumerated forms of saving under the income tax.

Selectivity of taxation is not universally approved. According to one view, selectivity or discrimination should be decided because it distorts the allocation of resources through the market. Formally stated, the argument identifies selectivity as the source of an 'excess burden' attributable to taxes that alter relative prices. Economic planning, however, is a process of selection even when not comprehensive or highly detailed. Few officials or legislators will be much impressed

447

by a general argument against selectivity. They will be concerned with the political acceptability and efficiency of selective measures.

Progressivity

Much of the appeal of the Expenditure Tax and of the Income Tax with certain forms of saving exempt is due to the fact that these taxes can incorporate personal exemptions and graduated rates. The taxes are progressive with respect to consumption and are likely to be progressive also with respect to income. Whether they are more or less progressive with respect to income than an ordinary Income Tax depends on the rate structures and the relation between income and consumption expenditures over the relevant range of the income distribution. There seems to be a fair presumption that the maximum nominal rates of an Expenditure Tax would exceed the top rate of the modified Income Tax. Income Tax rates are limited by a strong aversion to rates in excess of 100 per cent, but this tradition does not exist for the Expenditure Tax and rates above 100 per cent presumably would be less objectionable in an Expenditure Tax than in an Income Tax.

Most indirect taxes of large yield are commonly believed to be regressive. In the less-developed countries there is a strong presumption that the traditional levies on salt and sugar are decidedly regressing (except possibly where these items are extensively produced in the non-monetised sector). Taxes on articles such as common cloth, matches, tobacco, and beer are probably also regressive over middle and upper income ranges but may not be regressive at the lower end of the income distribution, expecially in countries where a considerable part of the population is employed mainly in subsistence agriculture or village economies with only limited participation in the monetised sector. Consumption of items such as luxurious cars, radios and other electrical appliances, lace and the better grades of textiles, most cosmetics and distilled spirits is still confined mainly to a fairly small and prosperous class in Nigeria. Taxes on such items may be progressive up to a rather high income level.

A judgement that the whole system of indirect taxes is regressive need not depend on the assumption that the marginal propensity to consume declines as income rises. Indirect taxes are usually low or non-existent on many items that are important in the consumption patterns of upper income groups in this country, including, for example, personal services of household servants and others, luxury foods of local origin, and foreign travel.

448

Although it may not be feasible to impose taxes on many services, it may be possible to devise indirect tax systems which are not highly regressive. One of these is Value Added Tax.

Value Added Tax

Value Added Tax, commonly referred to as VAT, is a form of taxation levied on various commodities consumed by people. It is widely used in the UK. VAT is highly necessary where collection taxes from the self-employed is virtually impossible.

It will generate a lot of income for the Federal Government to execute its gigantic programmes since it will be levied on all items consumed and it will greatly relieve the Inland Revenue of its present difficult task of collecting tax from traders. The introduction of VAT must reduce considerably the impact of heavy taxation being experienced by Pay-As-You-Earn employees by government reduction of the rate payable on PAYE, otherwise PAYE employees will experience more suffering by paying two forms of taxation at the same time. This will not only be unfair but will cause poverty.

Under the present direct tax system many traders are far better off than civil servants or private sector employees and pay virtually nothing.

Most PAYE people do not understand how the government spends the heavy monthly deductions from their pay, particularly when they cannot telephone, have light, water and good roads. Little do they realise that less then 20 per cent of the population pay direct tax, yet all of us enjoy the available scarce facilities.

In order to alleviate the sufferings of the PAYE class, it is desirable for the government to introduce VAT or any form of indirect taxation from where it can generate reasonable income. There must be a unified market and receipt system.

VAT is charged on the supply of all goods and services within the country and on the import of goods. VAT attaching to goods or services accumulates as they pass through the production chain and is borne by the ultimate consumer as part of the purchase price of the goods or services.

VAT differs from a purchase tax, or a customs or excise tax, or a sales tax, in two respects. In the first place VAT, in the ideal system, applies equally to all goods and services and to all suppliers of goods or services. This avoids the distortions of trade patterns inherent in a more narrowly based tax. Secondly, it is not a cumulative or cascade tax. It avoids the distortions caused by a sales tax where the sales at one stage of production (plus tax) enter into the cost of production of the next stage and thus eventually tax is levied upon tax.

In an ideal form, VAT is levied at only one rate (leaving aside the zero rate applied, for example, to exports). It is thus entirely neutral in its effect upon price structure. However, a VAT system with only one effective rate is too blunt an instrument for most governments; a government wishing to raise further income is obliged to apply an across-the-board increase which adds the same percentage to a suit of clothes as to a string of pearls. The UK had only one rate of 8% (plus a zero rate) until November 1974 but most other nations have moved to a three or four rate structure taxing luxuries at high rates and leaving essentials at very low rates. The UK has been warned to prepare for the possibility of three rates (plus a zero rate) and indeed, in November 1974 a rate of 25% was introduced for petrol. Any accounting system should probably allow for four rates and for four significant figures in each rate (e.g. 12.75%).

In its ideal state, therefore – one rate and all embracing – VAT is a neutral tax and ideally suited for fiscal reform. However, it does affect the cost of living and therefore governments will be tempted to achieve three or four rates to sharpen what is otherwise a blunt fiscal weapon.

The operation of the tax

Broadly speaking VAT operates by making each and every trader a collector of tax. Each trader is obliged to add VAT at the appropriate rate every time he sends out a bill and to account for that VAT (his 'output tax') to the government. However, in accounting to the government he is able to deduct the VAT which he himself has suffered on the invoices sent to him by other traders (his 'input tax') and to account only for the difference. Thus, in effect, he accounts for tax only to the extent that he has added value.

Traders with a very small turnover are usually not required to register. In addition there are usually exceptions for particular goods or services dealt with either by exemption or by zero rating. Leaving aside all such complications the following is an example of the operation of VAT in respect of the manufacture and sale of a particular article (using a 10% VAT rate):

	Basic value ₦	Add VAT at 10% ₦	Total invoice ₦		VAT payable at each stage ₦
Raw material supplier					
Imported materials	4	0.40	4.40		0.40
Home materials	8	0.80	8.80		0.80
	12	1.20	13.20		1.20
Other costs and profit	8			(2.00	
Sale price to manufacturer	20	2.00	22.00	− 1.20)	0.80
Manufacturer's costs and profit	30			(5.00	
Sale to wholesaler	50	5.00	55.00	− 2.00)	3.00
Wholesaler's costs and profit	15			(6.50)	
Sale to retailer	65	6.50	71.50	− 5.00)	1.50
Retailer's costs and profit	30				
Basic price to consumer	₦95				
Add VAT at 10%		₦9.50		(9.50 − 6.50)	3.00
Total invoice price			₦104.50		
Total VAT paid at all stages					₦9.50

In the above example four traders are concerned in manufacturing the article and getting it to the ultimate consumer :

   (a) the raw material supplier, who has borne 10% VAT on his imports and on his home trade purchases. He has borne a total of ₦1.20 VAT. His basic selling price is ₦20 to which he adds ₦2 VAT. He pays the 80p difference (₦2 − ₦1.20) to the authorities;

   (b) the manufacturer, who incurs further costs not liable to VAT (e.g. wages), adds his profit and sells to the wholesaler at a basic

451

price of ₦50. He adds £5 VAT. Having paid ₦2 VAT to the raw material supplier he now pays the £3 difference to the authorities;

(c) the wholesaler, whose selling price is ₦65 so that he charges £6.50 VAT and pays £1.50 to the authorities;

(d) the retailer, whose basic selling price is ₦95, charges ₦9.50 VAT and accounts for ₦3.

The VAT paid over by each trader is 10% of the value added by him. None of them bears the tax which added by him. None of them bears the tax which rolls forward to fall on the ultimate consumer.

The above example usefully illustrates the incidence of VAT but is not a practical example. In practice a trader does not identify at the time of sale the particular VAT costs incurred in making that sale. There is no question of keeping meticulous records of the VAT 'inputs' incurred in connection with a particular sale. In practice, each trader accounts for VAT on a total basis by what is known as the invoice system. The invoice is therefore fundamental; it is the voucher for the tax.

The invoice system

The invoice system turns what could be a complicated tax into a tax which is very simple indeed to operate.

The invoice system ignores completely the VAT costs entering into the cost of a particular sale and has regard only to the total invoices issued and total invoices received by the trader during an accounting period. All the VAT added to sales and to other charges to customers is simply credited to one VAT account. All the VAT suffered on purchases and on other expenses is simply debited to that same VAT account and the difference is paid to the authorities.

An example is given below in the most simple form of the transactions for one accounting period of a manufacturer of furniture.

(a) *Purchase ledger entries*	*Basic purchase price*	*VAT (10%)*	*Total invoice payable*
Timber	1500	150	1650
Audit fee	200	20	220
Stationery	10	1	11
Machinery	2000	200	2200
Debited to expenses and asset accounts	₦3710		
Debited to VAT account		₦371	
Credit to suppliers			₦4081

(b) *Sales ledger entries*

	Basic sale price	*VAT (10%)*	*Total receivable*
Sale of goods	1100	110	1210
Sale of goods	1000	100	1100
Sale of goods	2500	250	2750
Goods returned	(60)	(6)	(66)
Credited to sales	₦4540		
Credited to VAT account		₦454	
Debited to customers			₦4994

(c) *VAT account* — 371 *Added*

Suffered on purchases		*to sales* 454
Cash due to the Government	₦454	₦454

The example, suitably modified, would apply equally to a supplier of services. His inputs would be fewer (since wages and salaries do not normally attract VAT; however he would add VAT to his fees or commission charges and credit that VAT to his VAT account. After deducting any VAT on inputs he would pay any balance to the Government.

The example brings out a number of points which are important in considering VAT as an instrument of fiscal reform:

(a) There is no attempt to relate VAT suffered on purchases to the corresponding sale. A trader simply totals the VAT account at the end of each period and pays the government the difference on the basis of invoices received and invoices issued.

(b) VAT is not related to profit. It is payable regardless of profit or loss on the particular sale.

(c) VAT does not normally enter into the calculation of the trader's profit or loss for the accounting period. The VAT on purchases is taken to the separate VAT account and set off against the VAT added to sales. The profit and loss account is credited only with the VAT exclusive value of sales and debited with the VAT exclusive cost of purchases.

(d) Once an invoice has been issued to a customer, VAT is payable whether or not the customer pays the invoice. VAT is payable by reference to goods or services supplied and credit is given by reference to invoices received. There is normally no provision for the reduction of VAT for bad debts. The official view in the UK is that the debtor will have used the invoice to reduce his own VAT payments and the government would thus be out of pocket if VAT relief was allowed on the bad debts. Some other countries do allow relief for VAT on bad debts.

(e) VAT does, however, affect cash flow. It also affects the balance

453

sheet in that it will increase both debtors and creditors, but it does not increase the balance sheet cost of fixed assets.

(f) VAT makes no distinction between capital goods (e.g. the machinery purchase) and revenue goods (e.g. timber stock). VAT is payable in each case. Moreover the entire VAT suffered on capital goods purchases is available to reduce the VAT payable to the authorities on outputs. A large capital goods purchase could lead to a repayment of VAT at the end of the accounting period. Similarly sales of second-hand capital goods by a trader attract VAT. The system of allowing an immediate deduction for VAT on capital goods is not common to all countries. Relief is often given only over a period of up to say five years following the expenditure.

(g) It will be noted from the example that the VAT suffered on the purchases of stock has had the effect of reducing the VAT payable to the authorities. (Indeed, under the UK system, had there been no sales in the period the VAT account would have shown a credit balance which would have been repaid by the authorities.) It is clear therefore that all raw material stocks, all work in progress and indeed all equipment is held free of VAT. This is an improvement upon sales taxes or customs and excise duties from a cash flow point of view.

(h) An invoice showing VAT (a tax invoice) is a very important document in the hands of a trader; the VAT shown on the face of the invoice directly reduces his own liability to account for VAT. A tax invoice in the hands of the ultimate consumer is, however, of no such significance. The control of invoices is therefore fundamental.

On these points, VAT emerges with reasonable credit as an instrument of fiscal reform.

The principal exceptions

1 Zero rating

There are normally three different circumstances where VAT is not payable. They must be carefully distinguished from each other. The most important is zero rating.

Zero rating means that the trader is within the VAT system but that the rate of VAT on the particular transaction is nil. Zero rating applies to exports and to a number of other items.

It is important to any sales tax system that exports and other special categories of goods and services should be free of tax. The whole VAT charge on the value of exports is eliminated by applying a zero rating.

If a trader's entire sales were export sales the application of a zero rate would mean that no VAT was credited to the VAT account in his books. Nevertheless, VAT would continue to be debited to the VAT account by reference to his purchases and other costs. Therefore, on balance, the authorities would owe the trader money and would in practice repay him periodically. In this way it is possible to relieve exports from the whole burden of VAT.

An illustration is given below of the transactions for one accounting period of a trader with exports or other zero rated sales. This example uses the same basic information as in the example on pages 452–3.

(a) Purchase ledger entries	Basic purchase price	VAT (10%)	Total invoice payable
Timber	1500	150	1650
Audited fee	200	20	220
Stationery	10	1	11
Machinery	2000	200	2200
Debited to expense and asset accounts	₦3710		
Debited to VAT account		₦371	
Credited to suppliers			₦4081

(b) Sales ledger entries	Basic sale price ₦	VAT (10%) ₦	Total receivable ₦
Sale of goods (UK)	1100	110	1210
Sale of goods (export)	1000	—	1000
Sale of goods (export)	2500	—	2500
Goods returned (export)	(60)	(—)	(60)
Credited to sales	₦4540		
Credited to VAT account		₦110	
Debited to customers			₦4650

(c) VAT account			
Suffered on purchases	371	Added to sales	110
		Cash from the government	261
	₦371		₦371

A number of points emerge from this example:
(a) Again there is no attempt to relate VAT suffered on purchases

to the corresponding sale. In particular there is no attempt to relate export sales to the relevant purchases.

(b) Accordingly, zero rating requires no special book-keeping techniques. There will simply be fewer credits to the VAT account and thus possibly a debit balance which is repayable.

(c) Again VAT is not related to profit.

(d) Zero rating is very valuable in that it keeps down the sale price of the goods or service without affecting the trader's profit or loss. The trader is simply relieved from the task of adding VAT to the cost of his goods or services and accounting for the VAT to the authorities.

(e) The existence of zero-rated sales does not affect the trader's suppliers and therefore the input tax is unchanged from the earlier example.

Under this heading, therefore, VAT again emerges with credit. It is an improvement on most systems of sales or purchase taxes.

The benefit of zero rating is applied in all VAT countries to the export of goods and, insofar as possible, to services to persons not resident in the taxing country. Zero-rating is also applied to a number of other goods or services for either social or political reasons. Zero rating in the UK is extended to the supply of food (but not catering), water, fuel and power, public transport (but not freight), books, and newspapers and newspaper advertisements and services, gold bullion and bank notes. It also extends to the construction of new buildings and caravan homes and, from November 1974, to purchases of building materials by energetic 'do-it-yourself' homebuilders.

2 The small unregistered trader

It would be uneconomic to oblige all traders to register for VAT purposes and accordingly in the UK, registration is not obligatory for a trader whose turnover in VAT goods and services does not exceed £5000 per annum. The unregistered trader suffers VAT on his purchases but is otherwise outside the VAT system and therefore keeps no special records and does not charge VAT on sales or recover VAT on purchases.

The advantages of non-registration are that the trader is not involved with VAT administratively and that his goods will be slightly cheaper in that although he has suffered VAT on his purchases he does not need to add VAT in respect of his own value added.

It will bear repeating that:

(a) the unregistered trader still suffers VAT on his own purchases. His suppliers are not affected by his unregistered position.

(b) since he cannot pass on VAT as a separate item, he is obliged to bear it as an expense, or to add it to the cost of his fixed asset purchases. Thus if he buys stock costing ₦10 to which has been added VAT of ₦1 he will simply treat the stock as having cost ₦11. If he buys a typewriter consting ₦100 to which has been added VAT of ₦10 he will simply add ₦110 for a typewriter to his fixed assets.

(c) the unregistered trader will need to increase his basic sale prices in order to absorb the VAT on his purchases and other costs. The VAT cannot be recovered from the authorities or passed on to purchasers and must therefore enter into the profit and loss account costs (either directly or in consequence of depreciation).

The unregistered trader is at a disadvantage in that he is unable to pass on a VAT invoice to a customer who is a registered trader. Thus, although the goods that he sells might to some extent have a VAT content (by reason of his own purchases and other costs) the invoice to his customer will not show VAT. The customer will therefore be unable to claim credit for the VAT suffered. This is not important to the unregistered trader who incurs few VAT costs but an unregistered trader in the middle of the production chain is in an extremely difficult position. Whilst suffering VAT himself, he is not in a position to charge VAT on his sales invoices and therefore cannot pass on to his purchasers the benefit of the VAT which he himself has suffered. In addition, the customer will know that he is dealing with a very small trader. Accordingly, nonregistration will be unattractive for the trader who deals with other traders. It will only be attractive to the small trader (e.g. a window cleaner, street trader, etc.) who suffers little VAT on his expenses or whose customers, broadly speaking, are themselves consumers who have no use for an invoice showing VAT.

An example showing the effect of the interposition of an unregistered trader in the production chain is given below:

	Basic value ₦	Add VAT at 10% ₦	Total Invoice ₦	VAT payable ₦
(a) Goods sold by a registered trader to an unregistered trader	100	10.0	110	10.0
Add unregistered trader's costs and profit			20	—
Price to customers			130	—

If bought by a registered trader	130			
Add costs and profit	40			
Ultimate price	170	17.0	187	17.0
				₦27.0

(b) Goods sold by a registered trader to another registered

trader	100	10.0	110	10.0
Add costs and profit	20			
	120	12.0		2.0
Price to customers			132	
If bought by another registered trader				
Add costs and profit	40			
Ultimate price	₦160	16.0	176	4.0
				₦16.0

It will be seen from the first part of the example that the sale to the unregistered trader is at a basic value of ₦100 plus VAT of ₦10 giving a total invoice price ₦110. The unregistered trader's own price to the public, after adding costs of ₦20, is only ₦130. The similar cost in the second part of the example, where VAT has been added, is ₦132. At this point, therefore, the unregistered trader has an advantage. However, if at this stage,the goods are bought by a registered trader from the unregistered trader it will be seen from the first part of the example that the registered trader can take no account of the VAT so far suffered of ₦10 because he cannot be issued with a tax invoice. He is thus obliged to add a further ₦17 VAT giving a total invoice price of ₦187.00. On the other hand, if the purchase by the registered trader had been from another registered trader (as in the second part of the example) the VAT at that point accumulated of ₦10 could have been deducted from the VAT ultimately payable. The price disadvantage (i.e. in terms of the price he has to charge so as to preserve his profit) of the trader buying from an unregistered trader is thus ₦11.

The disadvantage to another trader of dealing with an unregistered trader lies only in the unregistered trader having suffered VAT on his own supplies and being unable to 'pass on' that VAT. There is therefore no such disadvantage in dealing with an unregistered trader, e.g. a freelance model or barber or a window cleaner, who has suffered little or no VAT and whose prices are therefore no more than the ex-VAT prices of a registered trader.

In an emerging country there is presumably a higher proportion of small traders. The registration limit would therefore need more study if VAT was not to be the reverse of a reform.

3 Exemption

There is a number of categories of services and, less commonly, goods which are exempt from VAT. This is because the particular service is inappropriate for a VAT. For example, a dealer in securities is exempt. VAT on his turnover would effectively impose a very heavy stamp duty on stock and share transactions. The provision of finance or insurance is similarly exempt because of the inevitable inequities. Some countries impose a special tax on such exempt financial industries; the UK does not.

The principal exempt items in the UK are rents, insurance premiums and commissions, postal services (but not telephones), betting, financial services, education, health services, burial and cremation.

Exemption is not as attractive as zero rating. A trader who supplies nothing but exempt services and goods will not register (because he will have no turnover in taxable goods and services). He will not add VAT or pass a tax invoice and will obtain no relief for the VAT which he may have suffered incidentally on his purchases going to make up the exempt supply. An insurance broker in the UK may be used as an example. Commissions earned are exempt from VAT. However the business will no doubt have suffered VAT on stationery, on office cleaning and on other goods and services. That VAT is simply an expense in the same manner as the VAT of the small trader. Again, therefore, the trader dealing in exempt services and goods will find that he is left bearing the VAT and that his prices rise marginally (except to the extent offset by sales tax reductions).

It will be noted that, with minor exceptions, all rents are exempt. The private householder therefore pays no VAT on his rent. The trader pays no VAT on rent of any premises but, having suffered less input tax, thereby pays over a correspondingly greater amount of VAT on sales, etc. so that the exemption does not help him. The property owner letting his premises is left to bear VAT on his costs except in so far as they relate to services. A property owner letting for a rent which includes services (e.g. cleaning) will need to charge VAT on the services but not on the rent.

Exemption is nowhere near as favourable as zero rating. A supplier of exempt services like a supplier of zero-rated services does not add VAT to his price. But the exempt supplier is left to bear the VAT on his purchases; the zero-rated trader is not. There is, thus, a form of taxation on the exempt supplier which slightly increases his prices.

It is in the area of exemptions that the symmetry of the VAT system begins to be distorted.

The partly exempt trader

Exemption may begin to disturb the symmetry of the VAT system but it presents few accounting problems.

The more difficult case is the partly exempt trader. Many shopkeepers will sell a range of goods which includes exempt items. Professional men will carry out exempt services. In the case of the partly exempt trader only the taxable sales or services attract VAT which is credited to the VAT account. That account, however, would normally have been debited with VAT (input tax) suffered on all purchases and other costs incurred whether those purchases and costs relate to taxable sales and services or to exempt sales and services. VAT suffered on purchases and other costs relating to taxable (including zero-rated) sales and services should properly be debited to the VAT account. However, in so far as a transaction is exempt, it is not proper for the trader to debit to the VAT account VAT incurred in relation to that item. It is necessary therefore to apportion the total input tax so as to debit to the VAT account only that part which relates to taxable supplies of sales or services.

Appointment gives rise to problems. Should it be on the basis of turnover, or volume of transactions, or some more scientific approach – or a bit of each?

The authorities are usually given very wide powers to make regulations to deal with this question, to determine what fraction of input tax may be deducted, to ignore trifling amounts, to distinguish between various trades and so on. They may also approve special schemes for individual businesses; this may be very important for traders with special problems.

It is largely in the field of exemption and part-exemption that the simplicity of VAT breaks down. The instrument of fiscal reform has led to much discussion under this heading in the UK, leading often to an unsatisfactory compromise until finally the economic objectives are lost in a search for a practical solution.

Accounting and book-keeping

In the UK each trader accounts for VAT in three-monthly periods, the VAT being payable not later than by the end of the following month. Persons constantly in a position of reclaim (e.g. exporters) may complete a monthly return. The three-monthly periods are staggered to give the authorities a monthly collection.

Other countries collect the tax at more frequent intervals and indeed, the Sixth Directive for the EEC suggests a monthly collection.

The obligation to make a quarterly or monthly return within one month following the end of the period and the detail required by that return imposes a very severe accounting discipine upon all trading organisations including many who have been used to a more leisurely pace in the past. There is no doubt that in the UK at least the introduction of VAT has made a significant contribution towards better record-keeping in the case of the smaller trader. However, if a good, but simple, system of book-keeping exists, VAT is not a complicated tax to deal with.

It is essential from the authorities' point of view that it be possible for their inspectors to check that the tax invoices for which credit is claimed by one trader have each entered into the calculation of the VAT liability of another trader. It follows that a VAT Act will always provide for proper records to be kept.

Whatever the form of the trader's records they must be sufficient to enable him to complete the quarterly or monthly return. For this purpose he must be able to total separately where applicable to his trade:

(a) outputs (e.g. sales, commissions, gifts, loans, self supplies etc.); chargeable at each VAT rate;
(b) credit notes allowed in respect of outputs in (a);
(c) exports (and the corresponding credit notes);
(d) other zero-rated outputs (and the corresponding credit notes);
(e) exempt outputs (and the corresponding credit notes);
(f) taxable inputs including zero-rated inputs and goods imported or removed from a bonded warehouse;
(g) credits against taxable or zero-rated inputs;
(h) output tax;
(i) deductible input tax.

Each trader must also redesign his invoices to give the essential VAT information.

VAT therefore imposes on some businesses accounting disciplines which are further-reaching than the business has been used to previously. In particular great care must be taken of all tax invoices received since they may be required to support a claim for credit. Whilst therefore VAT is relatively simple for a trader to deal with, it is another example of the transfer of part of the costs of collection of tax from the Exchequer to the trader.

Special types of trader

The large trader dealing entirely in goods taxed at the standard rate has few special accounting problems.

Similarly, the small shop-keeper dealing only in goods taxed at the standard rate will not find VAT difficult. A separate invoice is not required of him for each retail sale, unless it is especially demanded. Generally, therefore, he accounts for VAT by reference to total turnover. For example with VAT at 8% each ₦108 of sales represents ₦100 of sales exclusive of VAT and ₦8 of VAT. Therefore his output tax payable to the government is simply 8/108 parts of his turnover.

The retailer's problems multiply where he deals in standard rate items (e.g. notepaper, pens, pencils), plus zero-rated items (e.g. newspapers) on which no VAT is payable. Some retailers may use separate tills. Others have agreed one of a variety of special schemes with the authorities to allow them to estimate the proportion of sales attracting VAT.

There are also special schemes for second-hand cars and for antiques where goods tend to pass out of the trading cycle to an ultimate consumer and then back into the hands of a trader who, having bought from a non-trader, does not receive a tax invoice.

VAT is attracted by many activities which would not normally be regarded as businesses. For example, a golf club charges VAT on its subscriptions, its bar takings, etc. VAT applies to all suppliers of goods or services.

During the twelve months prior to the introduction of VAT in the UK – and indeed for some months after its introduction – the authorities held discussions with almost every trade organisation to iron out special problems. Very many trades, therefore, now have unique variations of the VAT structure to allow for their special problems. There is no doubt that the authorities in the UK took great pains to 'sell' VAT and to make sure that people understood its operation. That was certainly well worth while; any other country considering introducing VAT must devote considerable governmental talent to that selling and teaching operation if chaos is to be avoided.

The effect of VAT on the economy

There was certainly a shift in the UK price structure at the time of introduction of VAT at an overall flat rate in place of both a very selective purchase tax and a selective employment tax. Luxury goods became somewhat cheaper (although private cars did not because of the simultaneous introduction of a car tax). Services, previously free of consumption taxes (except for the indirect effect of selective employment tax) became dearer.

The simultaneous abolition of purchase tax and selective employment tax in the UK was relatively simple. Individual state (as opposed to federal) sales taxes could cause more problems.

In March 1974 the UK rate of VAT dropped from 10% to 8% thus bringing about an estimated 1% reduction in the cost of living. The effect was immediate but so long as the UK had only one effective rate of VAT, the room for the government to manoeuvre in rate changes was relatively small. What is more, any increase has a noticeable effect on the cost of living.

It is particularly fascinating therefore to look at the UK November 1974 Budget where a 25% VAT rate was introduced for petrol. The government achieved a sharp increase in the price of petrol, thus both raising revenue and controlling consumption by the private individual. However, the registered trader was not affected because, as explained earlier, the additional VAT suffered on petrol will simply reduce the trader's own VAT payment at the end of the quarter. Therefore, the additional VAT on petrol does not affect the cost of production of goods and services. VAT is in this sense far superior to a customs or excise duty.

The reduction of the UK standard rate in March 1974 and the increase in the rate on petrol in November 1974 also demonstrate the superiority of VAT in its immediate effect without harm to the retailer. Since stocks are carried free of VAT and VAT is payable by reference to sales, a reduction in VAT is immediate in effect yet does not leave the retailer with expensive pre-Budget stock. Similarly an increase is immediately effective yet does not give the retailer an undeserved profit.

Exports have been aided by the introduction of VAT. Their price structure is free of all VAT whereas purchase tax (and any equivalent sales tax) inevitably creeps into the price structure of exports. A developing economy must benefit from a system of tax which keeps export prices down. Export zero rating is dealt with later.

The trader dealing with other traders is little affected by VAT. The trader dealing with the general public is much affected. For exemple, the accountancy profession deals with both traders and private individuals. The average audit client, paying VAT himself does not object to the addition of VAT to his audit bill because that reduces his own liability to account for VAT by a similar sum. On the other hand, the private client paying a private bill of ₦40.00 for the preparation of his tax return finds that the cost is increased to ₦44.00 by a 10% VAT. The tax always falls upon the ultimate consumer. This is perhaps a principal feature of VAT, that it is collected continually throughout the production chain by traders, none of whom bears the tax; each passes it on to the ultimate consumer.

VAT has quickly become a very important tax in the UK. The November 1974 Treasury estimates show that in 1974-75 it will yield £2560 million – a third of the total yield of indirect taxes. On the other hand, it is much more expensive to collect than its predecessor, purchase tax. That tax was collected from relatively few wholesalers; VAT is collected from about 1 250 000 traders. The advantage of so many collection points is that no one trader can, by his default, greatly affect the overall collection. Collection is controlled by a central computer which, after initial problems, is functioning well.

The main disadvantage of VAT is its relatively high collection, administration and avoidance-prevention cost. It is far less cheap to collect than say Income Tax. The instrument of fiscal reform fails under this heading.

VAT has had very little effect upon business decisions in the UK. That is because it replaced purchase tax plus selective employment tax (a form of poll tax on the number of employees). Both were indirect taxes operating in the same field as VAT. Obviously a shift to VAT from say Income Tax or any other direct tax would have a more noticeable effect.

There are, however, areas where the borderline between attracting a zero rate or exemption and not attracting such relief is hard to discern and where therefore business decisions may be determined by the VAT consequences. The most popularly quoted (and yet least important) example is that a cooked meal sold across a shop counter and consumed at home is food, attracting a zero rate. The same meal eaten on the shop premises is catering, chargeable to VAT. There will always be such anomalies.

The quarterly collection of VAT at the end of the fourth month means that businesses giving no more than two months' credit and issuing bills evenly through the month will neither gain nor lose cash in consequence of VAT. There must be a temptation to issue bills very early in the VAT quarter. The pattern of payment of creditors' invoices also distorts the picture. Any business entering into a VAT era must prepare careful cash flow forecasts; inevitably whatever the overall advantage or disadvantage, there will be serious peaks and troughs of cash with a three-monthly collection. But generally speaking a business with good control of cash will gain in cash flow from VAT on a quarterly collection – but lose on a monthly collection basis. Cash flow is also improved to the extent that VAT replaces Customs and Excise duties.

The introduction of VAT depends upon a reasonably sophisticated standard of book-keeping throughout the tax-paying community (or a relatively high turnover exemption limit). It also depends upon a rigorous and continuous check by the authorities both on the gross VAT collections by traders and on the deductions claimed for VAT invoices received. This is essential since basically VAT in Europe works on the self-assessment principle, each trader making his quarterly return and sending his cheque with the return. It is this check system which adds considerably to the total collection cost.

The introduction of VAT in the UK was managed very smoothly. An outline of the tax was published in 1971 and a draft bill in March 1972. That draft bill became law late in July 1972. VAT was introduced on 1 April 1973. The authorities carried out a very extensive and essential campaign of publicity and education.

The accountancy profession did a great deal to educate its clients in the twelve months to March 1973, many firms holding seminars for their clients. Now I am sure that the average businessman forgets that VAT exists – until he buys his girl-friend a private meal in a restaurant.

Does VAT succeed as an instrument of fiscal reform?

One can do no more than give a personal opinion but in my opinion, provided the economy is capable of accepting a workable system, VAT is an excellent form of indirect taxation. I think that is brought out by the earlier paragraphs of this paper. VAT will never rival or replace taxes based on income such as income tax and corporate tax. It will never replace customs and excise duties where there is a political or social reason for a special rate of tax. Nevertheless, in the field of indirect taxes, it is superior to a purchase or sales tax both theoretically and in practice.

But has the UK achieved a useful reform? Certainly the zero-rating system has produced the right answer for exports and for necessities such as food. But can one call it a reform when essential clothing attracts the same rate of VAT as does an imported gold watch? From the point of view of accounting simplicity it certainly is a reform. Economically, however, the answer must be different. From the authorities' point of view, a VAT with only one effective rate is too blunt as an instrument of fiscal reform; we must therefore expect three or four rates and the inevitable further complication of accounting records.

VAT has achieved the further advantage that in practice for the average businessman it is simple to operate and has an entirely neutral effect on his business decisions. It is also easy to collect in that the tax is paid to the authorities by the trader but the trader does not bear it and is not normally harmed in a cash flow sense by it. He is, therefore, less interested in its reduction or avoidance.

In essence, VAT is a form of Expenditure Tax. It falls on the ultimate consumer and if he cares to refrain from spending or is unable to spend, he will avoid the tax. Home consumption may therefore be greatly affected by the rate(s) of VAT. But exports never suffer.

There is no doubt, however, that VAT is an expensive tax to collect, compared with the UK predecessor system of purchase tax levied at the wholesaler stage. The collection, checking and anti-avoidance cost of VAT is its greatest disadvantage. However, if it replaces a complicated sales tax with existing collection problems, then VAT would compare more favourably.

Perhaps from the accountants' point of view the questions to be answered in a country like Nigeria, seeking to impose a VAT are:

(a) What tax is it to replace and is it in that direct sense an improvement?

(b) Will it aid exports?

(c) Will it be possible to collect VAT from possibly millions of collection points?

(d) Is the individual accounting system sufficiently sophisticated to provide the information and proof of liability required (or is the turnover exemption limit high enough?)

(e) Bearing in mind that VAT is a consumer tax is it falling on the right consumers and are the poor sufficiently protected (either within the structure of the tax or separately?)

(f) Is the cost of collection justified?

In the case of Nigeria, the answers to (c), (d) and (f) are 'No', but through education and legislation we must make a start.

As a final note, there are, of course, those who will argue that VAT in the UK was never intended as a fiscal reform, that it was imposed as part of the process of going into the Common Market. If so, then the UK is not a good example to give you. Nevertheless, I hope that the example has given an idea of what VAT looks like once it is introduced.

Notes

1 See A.R. Prest, 'The Expenditure Tax and Saving', *Economic Journal,* LXIX (Sept. 1959), 483–90.

2 There seems to be a growing tendency toward scepticism. Mill, Marshall, and Taussig conceded that individual reactions may differ but argued that on balance the total value of saving is positively correlated with the interest rate. Wicksell,

Knight, Keynes, and Joan Robinson stress the complexity and uncertainty of the relationship between thriftiness and interest rates. See John Stuart Mill, *Principles of Political Economy*. Book I. Chap. XI and Book IV. Chap. IV, sec. 3 ed. W.J. Ashley (London: Longmans, Green, 1929), pp.163–75, 729; Alfred Marshall, *Principles of Economics*, 8th ed. (London: Macmillan, 1938) pp. 230–36; F.W. Taussig. *Principles of Economics*, 3rd rev. ed. (New York: Macmillan, 1923). Vol. 11, pp.20–33; Knut Wicksell, *Lectures on Political Economy*, trans. by E. Cassen, Vol. 1 (London: Routledge, 1934), pp.207–18; Frank H. Knight, *The Economic Organization* (New York: Augustus M. Kelly, 1951), p.115; John Maynard Keynes, *The General Theory of Employment, Interest, and Money* (New York: Harcourt, Brace, 1936), pp. 93–94; Joan Robinson, *The Accumulation of Capital* (Homewood, Ill.: Irwin, 1956). p.252.

3   Let y = Income Tax rate, c = Consumption Tax rate, 100 = income of A = income of B. The yield of the Income Tax will by $100y + 100y = 200y$: saving will be reduced by $[0(100y)] + 20(100y) + 20(100y) = 20y$; $20y/200y = .10$. Under the Consumption Tax A will pay 100c and B will pay $(1–0.2) 100 + 80c$; the total yield will be 180c. The reduction in saving will be $[0(100c)] + 20(80c)] – 16c$ 16c/180c 0.888 + , Note that. 10 and 0888 + are weighted averages of 0 and .20, with weights varying with the proportion of total tax yield paid by A and B.

4   Melville J. Herskovits, *Cultural Anthropology* (New York: Knopf, 1955) pp.160–64. *Economic Anthropology* (New York: Knopf, 1952).

5   W. Arthur Lewis takes the classical view. He asserts, 'The ratio of savings to national income is a function not just of inequality, but more precisely, of the ratio of profits to national income.' In his opinion landed aristocrats, peasants, and members of the wage and salary earning classes do not save much, except possibly in situations in which there is a 'capitalist example to imitate.' *The Theory of Economic Growth* (London: Allen & Unwin, 1957). pp.227–28.

6   Commonwealth of Puerto Rico, Department of Labour, Bureau of Labour Statistics, *Ingresos y Gastos de las Familias*. Puerto Rico 1953 (San Juan, 1960); Eleaner E. Maccoby and Frances Fielder, *Saving Among Upper-Income Families in Puerto Rico* (University of Puerto Rico Press, 1953); National Council of Applied Economic Research, Delhi *Saving Survey* (Bombay: Asia Publishing House, 1960): P.S. Lokanathan, 'A Study of Saving in India,' American Statistical Association, 1959 *Proceedings* of Business and Economics Section pp.236–241 L. The Delhi survey indicated that, if household income is measured as a multiple of mean income and net investment in consumer durables is classified as saving, saving ratios in that Indian city in 1959 were as high as ratios for comparable incomes in the United States in 1950 and higher than in the United Kingdom in 1951–52 (*Delhi Saving Survey* p.23, 24).

7   If saving is a linear function of income and the interest of the saving curve is negative (indicating dissaving at zero income), saving will be a larger fraction of high incomes than of low incomes, but the marginal propensity to save will be the same for all income levels. Under these conditions the degree of tax progressively will not affect the amount of private saving.

8   William Vickrey, 'Resource Distribution Patterns and the Classification of Families,' in Conference on Research in Income and Wealth, *Studies in Income and Wealth,* Vol. X (New York: National Bureau of Economic Research, 1947). pp.272–74, 287–95; Milton Friedman. *A Theory of the Consumption Function* (Princeton: Princeton University Press, 1957). France Modigliani and Richard Brumberg. 'Utility Analysis and the Consumption Function: An Interpretation of Cross-Section Date,' in *Post-Keynesian Economics*, ed. Kenneth K. Kurihare (New Brunswick, N.J.: Rutbers University Press, 1954), pp. 383–436.

9 An extensive literature has grown up in recent years. Several valuable papers have appeared in the *Bulletin of the Oxford University Institute of Statistics*, 1956–69, and in *Consumption and Saving*, ed. Irwin Friend and Robert Jones (Philadelphia: University of Pennsylvania, 1960).

10 Simon Kuznets, 'Quantitative Aspects of the Economic Growth of Nations: Capital Formation Proportions; International Comparisons for Recent Years,' *Economic Development and Cultural Change,* VIII (July 1960, Pt. II) 74, 95–96.

11 Derived from 1951 Survey of Consumer Finances, *Federal Reserve Bulletin,* August 1951, September 1951.

12 Robert Murray Haig. 'The Concept of Income – Economic and Legal Aspects' in *The Federal Income Tax,* ed. Haig (New York: Columbia University Press, 1921),pp.1–28, reprinted in American Economic Association, *Readings in the Economics of Taxation* (Homewood, III: Irwin, 1959) pp.54–76; Henry C. Simons, *Personal Income Taxation* (Chicago University of Chicago Press, 1938)

13 In my opinion William Vickrey overstates the case when he asserts that for high-income persons, there is 'Very little difference' between the administrative complications of an expenditure tax and an income tax including capital gains and losses ('Expenditure, Capital Gains and the Basis of Progressive Taxation.' *Manchester School of Economic and Social Studies* XXV, Jan. 1957, 18–20.

14 See William Vickrey, *Agenda for Progressive Taxation* (New York: Ronald Press, 1947) for a discussion of such items under the Income Tax and the expenditure tax.

15 Chelliah; op. cit., pp.72–73, recognises the existence of these problems but does not examine them in detail.

16 Irving Fisher, 'Income Theory and Income Taxation in Practice,' *Econometrica.* V (Jan. 1937), 1–55; Irving Fisher and Herbert W. Fisher, *Constructive Income Taxation* (New York: Harper & Brothers, 1942). The book contains a bibliogrphy at pages 249–60.

17 Nicholas Kalder, *An Expenditure Tax* (London: Allen and Unwin, 1955). *Indian Tax Reform, Report of a Survey* (New Delhi; Ministry of Finance, Government of India, 1956); *Suggestions for a Comprehensive Reform of Direct Taxation* (in Ceylon), Sessional Paper IV, 1960 (Colombo: Government Press, Ceylon, 1960).

18 Harvard Law School, International Programme in Taxation , World Tax Series, *Taxation in India* (Boston: Little Brown & Co. 1960). pp.421–34; Richard Goode, New System of Direct Taxation in Ceylon', *National Tax Journal*, XIII (December 1950), 329–40.

19 See the suggestions of Raja J. Chelliah, *Fiscal Policy in Under-developed Countries* (London: Allen and Unwin, 1960). pp.65–75.

20 *Taxation in India*. p.425 Rs. 36,000 is more than 100 times the national income per head (*International Financial Statistics*, July 1961, p.150; United Nations, *Monthly Bulletin of Statistics,* June 1961, p.2).

21 International Monetary Fund, *Annual Report,* 1959, p.157.

468

18 Guidelines for a Suggested Tax System under the Presidential System of Government

Below are some of the taxes levied in the United States with an indication of the authorities responsible for the levies and collections.

Source of tax	Authority that can make levy and collect
1 Income of individual	The Federal Government and State Governments
2 Income of partnership (taxed in the hands of individual partners as in Nigeria)	The Federal Government and State Governments
3 Income of corporations	The Federal Government and the State Governments
4 Value of estate of a deceased person	Federal Government only
5 Inheritance derived from estate left by a deceased person	State Governments and, in some states Local Governments also
6 Gift (other than donation to charities) taxed in the hands of beneficiary	Federal Government and State Governments
7 Sales tax (on almost any merchandise or service other than raw food)	State Governments only
8 Property tax (including landed property and other properties like car, inventories of goods for sale etc.)	Local Governments mostly (in some states, State Governments also levy and collect the tax)
9 Excise tax (tax on manufacture, and use of goods)	Federal, State and, in some cases, Local Governments
10 Use of goods and services produced by utility companies	Federal and State Governments

469

(telephone, for example; one pays
tax on telephone calls)

11 Use of highways (sometimes heavy duty vehicles plying inter-state roads may pay as much as 3000 dollars per annum for right to use highways.	Federal Government
12 Use of motor vehicles (Vehicle licences)	State Governments
13 Pay roll (social security tax)	Federal Government
14 Betting and gambling	Federal and State Governments
15 Manufacture of gambling devices	Federal Government

(i) Income Tax

The Federal Government as well as States Governments have the right under the US Constitution to impose tax on income of individuals and companies. In determining income chargeable to tax under the Federal tax law, Income Tax paid to any State Government is allowable as deduction. While the Federal rate of tax can be as much as 70% of chargeable income at the upper segment of income, the states' rates of tax are low and vary from State to State.

In Nigeria, each State has the power to levy tax on the income of individuals resident within the State. This is not so in the United States. Here, each State has the power to levy tax on the income of corporations, partners (in the hands of individual partners) and individuals derived from the territory of the State. This means that a person may file return to the Federal Government on his or her income from all sources for a year and to a State on income derived from the State for that year.

(ii) Excise Tax

Excise tax is payable on goods manufactured in the United States. Excise tax may also be charged on the use and distribution of some goods. For example both the Federal and State Governments levy tax on the distribution and use of tobacco, alcohol and gas (petrol).

(iii) Sales Tax

Sales tax is generally levied and collected by the State Governments. The sellers are generally the collecting agents. Hardly any good or service can be purchased in the United States without payment of sales tax. Raw food is, however, exempted from sales tax.

470

Administration of the Internal Revenue Service

The Internal Revenue Service of the United States is a Division of the Treasury Department. The Division is headed by the Commissioner of Internal Revenue who is a political appointee. There is also a Deputy Commissioner of Internal Revenue. This officer is the most senior civil servant and he is on special grade level.

The functions of the IRS are grouped into two major sections, namely, the operational section and the service section.

(1) Operational section

The operational section is called the Compliance Section. It is this section that actually performs the functions of tax assessment and collection. The section is sub-divided into:

- (a) Taxpayers' Service and Returns Processing Division
- (b) Appeals Division
- (c) Collection Division
- (d) Criminal Investigation Division
- (e) Examination Division

(2) Service section

The service or supporting functions are grouped together as follows:

- (a) Data Service
- (b) Employee Plans and Exempt Organisations
- (c) Inspection
- (d) Planning and Research
- (e) Resources management
- (f) Technical

The whole of the United States is divided into 7 tax regions and the tax administration in each of the regions is headed by a Regional Commissioner on grade level 18. The Regional Commissioner reports directly to the Commissioner and Deputy Commissioner in Washington. There are eight heads of functional departments in Washington. These officers are also on grade level 18 and they report to the Commissioner and the Deputy Commissioner. The heads of functional departments are staff officers who give advice to the Commissioner of Internal Revenue.

It is pertinent to say that the highest level that a civil servant can attain in the United States public service is the grade level 18, and fifteen officers of the Internal Revenue Service are on that grade.

Scope of the operations of the IRS

The IRS has about 86 000 employees or 86% of the total employees of the Treasury Department. The scope of the IRS operations may be illustrated by recapitulation of its performance during 1978 Federal Income Tax Year.

Total actual tax collection for the year is as shown hereunder:

Source of revenue	Actual collection as a percentage of total collection	Actual collection in thousands of dollars
1 *Income Tax*:		
(i) Corporations (companies)	16.4%	65 380 145
(ii) Individuals:		
(a) employees (withheld at source by employers like PAYE tax)	41.3%	165 254 230
(b) self-employed	12.0%	47 803 913
2 *Employment taxes* (social security tax contributed by employers and employees)	24.3%	97 291 653
3 *Estate and Gift Taxes*	1.3	5 381 499
4 *Excise Taxes*		
(i) Alcohol	1.4	5 612 715
(ii) Tobacco	0.6	2 450 913
(iii) Others	2.7	10 601 321
Total	100.00	399 776 389

(Source: IRS Commissioner of Internal Revenue, *Annual Report* for 1978)

A total sum of 399 776 389 000 or almost 400 billion dollars was collected during 1978. (The American billion is 1 000 000 000 or one thousand million, while the British billion is 1 000 000 000 000 or one million million. In other words, the total collection would be 400 thousand million dollars according to the British numeral system.)

The Voluntary Compliance System

The IRS operates on what it describes as the 'Voluntary Compliance System'. According to this system every taxpayer files his tax return at the beginning of each tax year without being given any notice to do so. The taxpayer also calculates what his tax liability for that year should be on the basis of the return filed. He also pays the tax so calculated simultaneously with the filing of the return.

The principle behind this system is that the objective of the IRS tax administration is not necessarily to collect revenue but mainly to make the taxpayer comply with the tax law. The more the taxpayers comply with the tax law, the more revenue will be collected and if every one complies with the tax law, maximum revenue will be collected. This being so, the best and most efficient way the IRS can make the taxpayers comply with the law is to make them do so voluntarily. The only problem is that every person will comply with the law only in a perfect society and as the United States is an imperfect society, as any other community of men, there are controls and checks devised to make the system work. When the achievement of the IRS both in terms of revenue collected and in terms of the efficiency with which the collection is achieved are considered, one can only conclude that the system works. More than 90 per cent of the tax collected is paid voluntarily and only about 2 per cent of the tax returns are examined for accuracy and error. This situation explains why the cost of collection for 1978 is only 49 cents of every one hundred dollars of tax collected or 0.5 per cent.

Administrative devices that make the system work

Among the administrative devices that make the system work, the following may be noted:

(1) Use of social security number to identify the taxpayer

Every taxpayer in the United States is required to obtain a social security number. If an infant has taxable income, no matter the age of the infant, the infant's parent or guardian must obtain a social security number for the infant. A taxpayer is required to quote his social security number in his tax return and in all documents relating to his tax matters.

Informations rendered by banks, government agencies, companies, etc. about the sources of income of taxpayers and other matters concerning taxes must indicate the social security numbers of the taxpayers affected. The use of the social security number facilitates collection, analysis and use of information for tax purposes. It also facilitates identification and location of taxpayers. Since the social security number must be obtained and produced before any person can be employed for any job and since the production of the social security number is required before one can enter into certain commercial transactions like opening a bank account, one can not run away successfully from the taxman for any length of time. Law enforcement officers, including the taxmen, make extensive use of social security numbers in locating lawbreakers, including tax evaders and defaulters.

(ii) Efficient organisation and management of the Internal Revenue Service

The actual functions of the revenue collection involve the criminal investigation and prosecution of tax offenders, the examination of tax returns and the assessment of taxpayers and tax collection. There are supporting services like data collection, analysis and records, administration, the taxpayers' service and employee plan and exempt organisation matters.

These functions may be discussed in detail as hereunder:

(a) Criminal investigation

Tax evasion is a very serious offence in the United States. A tax offender can go to jail for a maximum term of 30 years and may pay tax and penalties that may be valued in millions of dollars. There is a well-trained corps of officers responsible for criminal investigation of tax offenders: Criminal Investigation Agents. These officers are highly trained in police and detective duties. They have permission to carry guns. They are also responsible for the security and protection of tax officers generally. They have a web of informers. An informer is paid 10 per cent of the tax which directly results as collection from his information. Ninety-eight per cent of cases they recommend for criminal prosecution are usually resolved in favour of the IRS. The activity of the Criminal Investigation Division contributes in no small way to the voluntary compliance to tax law by taxpayers since the possibility of detection of a tax crime is very high and the penalty on conviction is severe.

(b) Tax records and information (Data Service)

Tax and other IRS records are very reliable and efficiently kept. There are three types of computer services in the IRS. These are:

1 *National Computer Centre*

The National Computer Centre, located in Martinsburg, West Virginia, is responsible for maintaining and updating the master file of individual and business tax accounts. In addition to producing output data, used for refund cheques, bills, notices etc., the National Computer Centre assists the enforcement of the tax law by conducting delinquency checks – providing information about taxpayers who have failed to file returns, evaded tax or are tax defaulters or those who have made false claims for tax refunds. The Centre also classifies returns for audit checks or examination.

2 *Data Centre*

The Data Centre, located in Detroit, Michigan, handles all the non-tax data processing operations, including pay rolls processing for the entire Treasury Department, preparation of fiscal and personnel analysis reports, tax research and other statistical and budget work.

3 *Regional Service Centres*

There are ten Regional Service Centres in the United States. Each centre is a computer centre. Taxpayers within an area covered by a service centre are required to file their tax returns to that service centre. The computer screens each tax return, receives and stores vital information about a taxpayer and selects returns which have high probability of inaccuracies for examination. Only about 2 per cent of total returns filed for a year are selected for examination. This means that the self-assessment made by 98 per cent of the American taxpayers are accepted as final and conclusive by the IRS.

(c) Examination

Although only about 2 per cent of the total returns filed in a year are examined, the total returns examined runs to millions. For example, 100 775 000 Income Tax returns were filed during the year 1978 and out of this total, 2 015 500 were examined. There is corps of highly-trained revenue agents who are charged with the duty of examining tax returns. They are usually university graduates with an accounting bias or members of the American Certified Public Accountants (CPA). Out of the seven or so divisions of the Internal Revenue Service, the Examination Division is the only division where accounting skill is absolutely required, though it is of advantage in other divisions. The examination agents work mostly in the field, at the taxpayers' offices or places of business to examine their records. When an examination is concluded and the tax payable is determined, the taxpayer and the examination agent who examines the record will jointly sign a form to indicate that the taxpayer agrees with the final tax as determined.

A unique provision recently made into the American tax law is that the 'preparer' of a tax return is made responsible for the inaccuracy in the return he prepares. A preparer can be penalised administratively by being asked to pay a sum of money for any inaccuracy or he may be prosecuted in a court and may even go to jail if found guilty.

(d) Appeal

The Appeal Section is part of the Operational Section. There is no appeal body outside the Internal Revenue Service. But the revenue agents who hear appeals are highly experienced senior agents who have no hand whatever in the examination and assessment process. A taxpayer who is not satisfied with the decision of the appeal board may appeal to the court without having to satisfy any condition. There are tax courts which deal mainly with tax cases.

(e) Tax collection

Taxpayers who fail to file a return or who file a return but fail to pay tax are called delinquent taxpayers. As noted earlier, the overwhelming majority of Americans file returns and pay their tax at the time of filing returns but some big taxpayers like corporations may delay payment of tax or pay by instalments. Returns are required to be filed in January but the whole of the tax liability is due for payment on the first of April of the year for which the return is filed. Any tax due but not paid from then attracts interest ranging from 5 per cent. The interest and penalty may rise to as much as 50 per cent of the tax due depending on when it is finally paid. There is a corps of well-trained collection agents who are also field workers. They impose penalties and interest on tax arrears, may seize properties of tax defaulters and sell them to settle tax due without going to court or may seize the bank account of a tax defaulter similarly. They are knowledgeable in business and commercial transactions. They primarily encourage taxpayers to comply voluntarily and only enforce payment as a last resort.

(f) Taxpayers' Service

The objective of the Taxpayers' Service is to educate taxpayers no tax laws and procedures. The tax agents in the Taxpayers' Service Division may help taxpayers fill tax forms, answer taxpayers' queries, make speeches at organisational meetings to interpret tax laws and procedures and produce hand-notes and pamphlets for the guidance of taxpayers. At every tax district, batteries of telephones connected to computer centres are installed to answer taxpayers' queries.

(g) Employee plan and exempt organisation matters

There is a division responsible for considering and approving

476

employee pension plans and retirement benefit plans. This division is also responsible for the approval of tax-exemption for organisations devoted wholly to charities, non-profit religious, sporting, social, educational and such other activities. The tax agents from this division inspect and examine employers' records and the records of exempt organisations to ensure that they comply with the conditions which make them tax-exempt.

(h) Inspection
The Inspection Division is responsible for internal security and internal audit. Like the criminal investigation agents, the inspection agents may carry guns. They are responsible for the investigation of:
1 misconduct by any IRS employee which is considered as likely to prejudice the integrity and good image of the IRS;
2 embezzlement of funds by IRS employees;
3 threat to and assault on any IRS employee.

They also act to prevent commission of fraud and to ensure efficient utilisation of resources.

(iii) Competence and high professional integrity of the taxpayers' advisers

Taxpayers in the United States are generally advised by tax lawyers and accountants. The accountants who prepare taxpayers' returns try as much as possible to ensure that the returns prepared by them reflect the 'true and correct view' of the affairs of taxpayers.

(iv) Staff training and development

The employees of the IRS are required to attain a very high standard of proficiency and integrity. To this end, about 40 000 dollars is spent for the training of every revenue agent in each of the major divisions of the IRS. Employees are not merely promoted for length of service when there is a vacancy. Whenever a vacancy is declared, any qualified person within a specified grade in the organisation is required to apply for the post. It is deemed that any qualified person who fails to apply is not interested in the vacant post. The officers responsible for appraising the work of those who apply will be required to complete a special promotion appraisal form, a copy of which must be given to the candidate affected. On the basis of this and the periodical appraisals previously made in respect of each candidate, consideration for promotion will be made. By and large, the officers of the IRS are incorruptible. They are highly motivated and measure their career success by their professional accomplishment rather than in terms of dollars.

A university graduate usually enters the IRS on grade level 7. After completing training, he moves to grade level 9 and a year thereafter he moves to grade level 11. On this grade, he is considered a fully-fledged agent. Promotion from grade 11 to higher grades depends on vacancies, merit of the officer and his willingness to assume managerial responsibility.

Importance of tax as source of revenue to the Federal, State and Local Governments

(i) Federal Government

For the fiscal year 1978, the estimated sources of revenue to the Federal Government are listed as below:

Source	Amount in billions of dollars (net)	Percentage of total
1 Income Tax – individuals	181.00	40.00
2 Income Tax – corporations	60.00	13.00
3 Social Security and other insurance and retirement taxes and contributions	123.40	27.00
4 Excise Tax	18.40	4.00
5 Others	19.30	5.00
6 Borrowing	48.80	11.00
Total revenue for 1978	450.90	100.00

(Source: IRS, *Your Federal Income Tax*, 1979)

From the above statistics, it may be seen that the main source of revenue to the United States Government is from taxes and the most important tax is Income Tax which accounts for 53 per cent of the total revenue.

(ii) State Government

The main source of revenue to the State Government is revenue from income tax. As already noted, a State Government has power under the constitution to levy tax on the income of every person derived from its area. In fact, taxpayers pay tax twice on the same amount of income – both to the Federal and State Governments. The State Governments also levy sales and purchase taxes.

Although there is no opportunity to study State finances, it is

478

asserted that the State of California has a substantial revenue surplus – more than 100 million dollars.

(iii) Local Government

Revenue of the Local Government is derived mainly from property taxes. For example, the County of San Diego – the second largest county in California after Los Angeles, though not necessarily the second richest – collected about 350 million dollars from property taxes in 1978. This amount could have been as high as 500 million dollars but for proposition 3, a constitutional amendment voted in a referendum by the voters of the State of California a year ago to limit property tax to not more than 1 per cent of the market value of the property. Property tax is easy to collect as the law allows the property of a tax defaulter to be sold without recourse to the court of law.

Conclusions and recommendations

Income Tax

The Voluntary Compliance System works in the United States mostly for the reasons stated. The main advantage of the system is that the bulk of tax revenue is assessed and paid voluntarily by taxpayers and the effort and resources of the tax authority are free to be concentrated in tracking down delinquent taxpayers and in improving the quality of service. The system also assures that tax law is equitably administered since the bulk of the taxpayers assess themselves.

The question is whether the system can work in a country such as Nigeria. When the record of tax payment in Nigeria is considered, it might be concluded that a voluntary compliance system cannot work in Nigeria because the Nigerian taxpayers are more unwilling to pay tax than the American taxpayers. On the other hand, the rate at which Nigerians contribute effort and resources voluntarily to community development projects generally suggests that Nigerians are not less willing to make sacrifices and contribute to development efforts than the Americans. If there is sufficient motivation and if there is greater control and better management in tax administration, the system of voluntary compliance will work in Nigeria and this may lead to payment of tax without tears if the Obas or Chiefs are involved in Tax administration.

Some of the measures that may be taken to enforce tax compliance in Nigeria may be examined as follows:

479

(i) Identification of taxpayers

This is necessary for the following reasons:

(a) to bring into the tax net every person who ought to pay tax in accordance with the provisions of the tax law;

(b) to facilitate collection, analysis and use of data not only for the purpose of determining the correct tax liability of taxpayers but also for the purpose of control of operations;

(c) to trace tax defaulters, obtain evidence against and prosecute them so as to secure a credible impression in the minds of taxpayers that there is a high probability of detection and punishment of tax evasion and other tax crimes.

In the United States, the social security number is used to identify taxpayers, as already noted. There is no social security administration in Nigeria. The only Nigerian system which has a similarity to the social security system is the National Provident Fund. This, however, applies to casual workers and the National Provident Fund number cannot be universally applied for the purpose of identifying taxpayers in Nigeria. Some time ago, the newspapers reported that Nigerians would soon have identification numbers. It is not yet clear whether that is the firm policy of the Federal Government. It is very desirable now that Nigerians, at least the taxpaying population, should have identification numbers not only for use by the tax authorities but also by the taxpayers to identify themselves to their bankers, the post office savings bank and other bodies who may need their identification. Such identification will also help the law enforcement agents in solving crimes. It will also improve national security measures. I will call such an identification number 'tax code number' for the purpose of this report.

The Federal Government should introduce an 'identification of taxpayers' Act. The Act should be made applicable throughout the Federation, and should require:

1 every individual, whether exempted from payment of tax or not under any tax law in Nigeria, who is 16 years old or above; and

2 every person not being up to 16 years old but who, for the first time in his life, is in receipt of taxable income;

3 to register and obtain a registration card from the tax authority relevant to him under the First Schedule of the Income Tax Management Act, 1961, at the time of registration.

The registration card should show the photograph of the person registered and the photograph should be endorsed by the relevant tax authority or its representative. Each tax authority should maintain a register of taxpayers.

The provision which requires tax officials not to disclose information about taxpayers should not apply to the register of taxpayers. This will make it possible for the tax authorities to disclose the name and address of any person in whose name any tax code number is registered.

The Income Tax Management Act, 1961, should be amended to require any person who has an obligation to furnish or render returns or information to any tax authority for the purpose of determining the tax liability of any person to state in that return or information the name and the tax code number of the person in respect of whom the return or information is being issued.

In order to simplify registration procedure, two block digits may be allocated to each State as follows:

Anambra	01	Kwara	11
Bauchi	02	Lagos	12
Bendel	03	Niger	13
Benue	04	Ogun	14
Bornu	05	Ondo	15
Cross River	06	Oyo	16
Gongola	07	Plateau	17
Imo	08	Rivers	18
Kaduna	09	Sokoto	19
Kano	10		

Each State will register the number of tax districts within the State in alphabetical order and allocate to each of the tax districts two digits as is done in the case of States.

The taxpayer's actual number will then come as the third block of digits after the first two blocks.

Example

Assuming that Ado-Ekiti in Ondo State is number 01 tax district in Ondo State and that taxpayer X is registered as number 109 in Ado-Ekiti tax district register, his tax number will be 1501109.

A taxpayer will be registered only once in his lifetime. If he moves from the place where he is registered to any other tax district or State, his original tax code number will remain unchanged.

(ii) Administrative actions by the Ondo State separately or in conjunction with the Joint Tax Board

(a) Investigation and prosecution of tax crimes and offences. There are two types of tax crimes and offences. These are:
1 offences committed by the taxpayers
2 offences committed by the employees of the Internal Revenue Division in connection with their official duties.

There are provisions in the State Income Tax Law for offences and penalties for those offences. The offences that a taxpayer may commit include:

   (i) failure to pay tax;
  (ii) false declaration of income for the purpose of securing reduction in tax liability;
 (iii) failure to make declaration of income or make return or give information to the State Tax Board when there is obligation to do so.
 (iv) advising or inciting any person not to pay tax.
  (v) failure to do any other thing that the tax law requires to be done.

Taxpayers on flat rate tax are known to have been taken to court at one time or the other for failure to pay flat rate tax. A few taxpayers on assessment may also have been taken to court on criminal charge for 'failing to pay tax'. No taxpayer either in the old Western Nigeria or in Ondo State has ever been taken to court for any of the other tax offences since 1957 when the State tax law was first enacted. Of course, no one can say that the taxpayers of the old Western Nigeria as a whole or of the Ondo State have never violated the provisions of the tax laws. On the contrary, it is more the exception than the rule for most self-employed taxpayers either to declare their true income or to furnish a return when obliged to do so and also for the taxpayers under PAYE to claim no more reliefs than they are entitled to. At present, it seems that the Nigerian taxpayers take the provisions of the tax laws no more seriously than they take the law against bigamy, and people will not change unless the tax laws are enforced.

It is desirable that concerted action should be taken at the national level to vigorously enforce the tax law. It is to be pointed out, however, that any State may embark on this exercise without any serious problem. The Ondo State Government may start the enforcement programme by taking the following steps:

1 Taxpayers' guide and education

A pamphlet should be produced for the guidance and education of taxpayers. There should be a list of tax offences and penalties with the warning that the State Tax Board will vigorously enforce the provisions as from a convenient 1 April. A copy of the pamphlet should be sent to each taxpayer along with his tax form for that tax year. There should be a radio and press announcement as a follow-up.

2 Tax enforcement and security section

Consideration should be given to the setting up of a 'tax enforcement and security section' to be responsible for the investigation of tax crimes and tax offences and misconduct by the employees of the Internal Revenue Division. This section will be at the headquarters under the supervision of the Commissioner of Internal Revenue.

3 Training of the employees of the Internal Revenue Division
Tax duties in Nigeria today have gone a long way from purely administrative and clerical duties connected with the collection of flat rate tax. Tax laws are complex and the complexity is exacerbated by a welter of tax amendments made since 1957. Business organisations are expanding and becoming more complex. Tax duty today is therefore a highly technical duty involving accounting, legal and business management skills. The tax officers and clerks require more training than before. Investment in the training of tax personnel should therefore be regarded as worthwhile.

4 Publication of Annual Report by the Commissioner of Internal Revenue
Although the Commissioner of Internal Revenue for Ondo State publishes a monthly statement of activities and an annual statement of revenue collection, this is not enough, especially as tax statistics are vitally necessary as indicators for social and economic development and planning. There are statisticians of the United States Statistics Department in the Internal Revenue Service. They provide assistance and expertise in statistical collection and presentation. This should also obtain in this State.

(iii) Administrative action by the Joint Tax Board with application throughout Nigeria
(a) Liaison with the Institute of Chartered Accountants of Nigeria
As of now, many professional accountants in Nigeria believe that their duty is to secure minimum tax liability for their clients and to this end, they prepare and present to tax authorities accounts which do not represent a 'fair and correct view' of the financial affairs of their clients. Some accountants are of high integrity, however. As a result of the adverse experience which some tax authorities have with the work of some accountants, the working relations between accountants and tax authorities is not cordial, to say the least.

The Joint Tax Board should open a dialogue with the Nigerian Institute of Chartered Accountants on:

1 promoting and maintaining an acceptable level of integrity on the part of the accountants in preparing the accounts of taxpayers for tax purposes.

2 developing appropriate tax law provisions and regulations for greater operational efficiency and for exposing and penalising

unethical and unprofessional practices by accountants in relation to preparation of taxpayers' accounts.

Each tax authority should report to the Joint Tax Board any unprofessional action such as errors, inaccuracies and falsification of figures in accounts presented by a professional accountant on behalf of any taxpayer. The Joint Tax Board should investigate such reports and, if satisfied that such a report has merit, make formal allegation of the misconduct to the Institute of Chartered Accountants of Nigeria. Specific informations about the taxpayer may not, however, be disclosed as this will be against the provisions of the tax law.

In the United States, a law enacted in 1978 makes it a criminal offence for an accountant or preparer of tax return to prepare a false or inaccurate tax return. The taxpayer and the preparer are also required to sign a tax return if it is not prepared by the taxpayer himself.

(b) Establishment of National Computer Centre for tax information, control and records

The Joint Tax Board should make recommendation to the Federal government to establish a national data centre which will serve all the tax authorities in Nigeria. Information regarding tax code number, rental income paid by any government or body other than an individual, bank interest, dividend, registration of business names and companies and other important information about taxpayers or their sources of income should be fed into the computer and retained as an 'information bank'. Each tax authority will then have the benefit of receiving and using such information for locating taxpayers and assessing them.

(c) Establishment of National Tax Library

There should be a tax library with up-to-date copies of all the tax laws of the Federation, tax cases, comparative tax laws and tax publications including books and magazines.

With these measures and controls, voluntary compliance to tax law in Nigeria may become a reality in a few years' time.

Property Tax

It has already been noted that Local Governments in the United States derive the bulk of their revenue from property taxation. Apart from the fact that property tax is easy to collect, if the collection machinery is properly organised, the concept that government expenditure on infrastructures, such as roads, electricity and water supply and public security, improves and enhances the value of property and makes it politically attractive. It is another way of redistributing income and promoting egalitarianism since only the more fortunate members of the society have and are likely to have property of taxable value.

There is already tenement rates law operating in Ondo State. The Local Governments charged with the responsibility of enforcing the law are, however, unable to do so mainly because of the method of valuation and because the rate of tax is so low that it can hardly cover the cost of collection. In order that the tenement rate law should be more effective, the following suggestions are made:

(a) Minimum rate

There should be established a minimum rate and the rate should be applied to any building:

    (i) that is not more in value than the minimum value set;

    (ii) that is occupied by individuals who have no assessable income or are exempt from payment of tax;

    (iii) that is not built by any person that has assessable income in excess of ₦2000 p.a. in the year of assessment for which the tenement rate is payable.

These three conditions will ensure that a high burden of tenement rate does not fall on peasant farmers, and the possibility of agitation by the poor will be obviated. Most of the occupiers of rural buildings are either flat rate taxpayers who have no assessable income, or women and old men who have no income and do not even pay flat rate tax.

The minimum value may be ₦10 000 and the minimum tenement rate in respect of building of ₦10 000 or less in value may be fixed at ₦3.00 per annum. Tenement rate in respect of any other building should be 0.5 per cent of the market value of the building or 5 per cent of annual rent received, whichever is the higher.

(b) Collecting agents

The Internal Revenue Division of the Ministry of Finance should for the time being be charged with the responsibility of collecting tenement rate throughout the State. The proceeds, less administrative expenses of collection, should be returned to the Local Governments on the basis of derivation. This recommendation is made in view of the fact that the Local Governments have not been administering the tenement rate encouragingly – to say the least.

Sales Tax

The need to impose sales tax on items of goods like tobacco, cigarettes, alcoholic drinks, motor vehicles including motorcycles, boats, timber sawmills, guns for which a licence to carry is required, buildings and landed property, should be considered as a start. This will be in addition to any sales tax which may already be under consideration. The items of goods listed are such that sales tax on them will be easier to collect than others not listed. Besides, the peasant farmers will bear the least of the burden.

Appendix 1
Tax Clearance Certificates

Tax Clearance Certificates have become more important as a means of raising revenue, especially in an age where there is an oil glut on the world market.

Tax Clearance Certificates are not only used by the banking industry to conserve the country's reserve fund, to stop fraudulent transfer of funds by importers and exporters, but also by other companies and individuals including sufferers who 'suffer' by its use.

The following Notes are used by the Federal Board of Internal Revenue.

Guidance notes on individual's request for Tax Clearance Certificate

1 The demand for Tax Clearance Certificate for a number of purposes by various organisations throughout the country was introduced by the Federal Government as a measure to reduce tax evasion and improve tax collection generally.

2 While introducing the measure, care was taken in accordance with Federal Government intentions to ensure that only tax evaders are inconvenienced, where they cannot produce an up-to-date Tax Clearance Certificate for whatever purpose it is demanded. For example, in the case of employees who wish to obtain Basic Travel Allowance from banks, the regulation stipulates that such employees may either produce a certificate of total pay and tax deducted for the last assessment year immediately preceding the date of application for a Basic Travel Allowance. Assessment years now run from 1 January – 31 December, so if, for example, an employee applies for a Basic Travel Allowance in January 1981 or February or even September 1981, he is only expected to produce a Certificate of total pay and tax deducted issued by an 'authorised and directed' employer for the year ended 31 December 1980 or in the alternative a Tax Clearance Certificate up to that date. 'Authorised and directed employer' means any employer authorised and directed by any Tax Authority in the country to operate the PAYE tax deduction scheme. Such employers are usually given reference numbers which they are supposed to quote in the prescribed certificates they issue. This certificate is known as Form H2 in both Federal and Lagos State.

3 Employees are taxed on their income on current year basis under the PAYE system, that is to say, employment incomes received in a year of assessment (1 January–31 December) are taxed in that year. Whereas other income of the employee and claims for allowances and reliefs are dealt with on previous years basis.

4   Personal reliefs and allowances are not usually apportioned as they are given for each year of assessment.

5   Obtaining a Tax Clearance Certificate

   (a) A Tax Clearance Certificate may be obtained from the relevant tax authority after a taxpayer has paid his tax assessed for the relevant years or he has entered into satisfactory arrangement with the relevant tax authority for the settlement of tax for the relevant years.

   (b) Relevant tax authorities are not expected to raise additional best-of-judgement assessment other than the one which might have been settled before an application for a tax clearance certificate is lodged.

   (c) Arbitrary best-of-judgement assessments quickly raised only after the taxpayer has requested a Tax Clearance Certificate are not in accordance with proper procedure and should be discouraged. Procedure for issuing assessment notices and time within which such assessments should be paid are adequately laid down in the law. However, a reasonable and scientific assessment may be raised on an individual by a relevant tax authority where there is sufficient reason to believe that the individual is liable to tax, but for some reason or other, the taxpayer has successfully escaped tax. Such assessments, however, are expected to have been thoroughly computed, based on the information, available to the tax authority, in addition to the personal circumstances of the individual for tax purposes.

   (d) A Tax Clearance Certificate should be issued on demand and as promptly as possible if the taxpayer who is requesting it has in fact paid all existing assessments and no further assessments need be raised except on substantiated evidence warranting an additional assessment, e.g. new evidence of rental income not previously included in the original assessment.

   (e) The request for a tax clearance certificate should not be regarded as an invitation to raise new assessments, additional assessments or even assessments in advance. It has been observed, for instance, that some taxpayers were asked to pay 1981 tax in January 1981. This amounts to assessing in advance, because the taxpayer is expected to be given an opportunity to make a return of his income up to December 1980 and has a right to object to the assessment when raised. Because of this normal process of assessment, which is clearly stated in the Income Tax Laws, the Tax Clearance Certificate which is valid for 1981 is that which shows that all taxes have been paid for the three assessment years up to 1980 or that no tax is due for those years or that the person is not liable to tax for all or any of those years.

   (f) A Tax Clearance Certificate may be demanded only for the purposes already listed in the Federal Government Budget. However, for Basic Travel Allowance only, a Certificate of total pay and tax deducted for employees subjected to an approved PAYE tax deduction scheme is acceptable.

   (g) Where Tax Clearance Certificates are suspected to be forged, reference should be made to the relevant tax authority, but a Tax Clearance Certificate issued by any tax authority of a State in Nigeria is tenable for all the selected transactions throughout the country. There is therefore no reason for any State not to honour a Tax Clearance Certificate issued by another State tax authority of competent jurisdiction.

(h) Tax Clearance Certificates are classified documents and should be treated as such.

(i) Taxpayers are advised to apply for their Tax Clearance Certificates well in advance of the time when the certificates are required for any of the purposes for which the certificates may be demanded. This will give sufficient time to the tax authorities to issue such certificates without inconvenience. Taxpayers are advised to avoid rush and congestions in tax offices by adhering to this practice.

Appendix 2
Exempted Income

1   Certain income from employments and pensions which would otherwise be chargeable to Income Tax is exempted by the taxing Acts (Appendix B).

2A   Under the adaptation of Laws (Miscellaneous Provisions) Order, 1965, certain modifications were made to the income exemption provisions of the Income Tax Management Act, 1961. As a result, substantive changes are required in paragraphs 6 and 16 below. Please contact the relevant Revenue Department for details where required.

3   The official emoluments of the Governor, and of any person performing the functions of the Governor, received by such person in his capacity as such.

4   The establishment allowance of a chief.

5   Allowances paid to any member of the Executive Council or the Legislative Houses of a State or of the Council of Minister or Parliament for attendance at meetings of any such body or of any committee thereof.

6   The remuneration of any consular officer or employee of a foreign State except where:
   (a) the employee is engaged on domestic duties or
   (b) the employee ordinarily resides in Nigeria and is not also a national of that foreign State.

7   The emoluments payable from United Kingdom funds to an individual in the permanent service of the United Kingdom government in Nigeria in respect of his office under the United Kingdom government except where:
   (a) the employee is a citizen of Nigeria; or
   (b) the employee ordinarily resides in Nigeria.

8   The remuneration of any employee, other than a citizen of Nigeria, of any government, organisation or agency between which and the Government of the Federation or of a State there exists an arrangement for technical assistance, in so far as and to the extent only the employment is solely in pursuit of such technical assistance arrangement.

9   The income of any national of the United States of America from employment by the Internal Cooperation Administration, being an administration or agency formed and directed by the government of that country.

10   The income of any national of the United States of America from employment by the International Development Services as agent for the International Cooperation Administration.

11   The income of any individual from employment by the Ohio University of Athens, Ohio, as agent for the International Cooperation Administration,

in connection with any scheme for the training of teachers in Nigeria.

12   Wound and disability pensions granted to members of the armed forces or of any recognised national defence organisation or to persons injured as a result of enemy action.

13   Pensions granted to any person under the provisions of Widow's and Orphans' Pensions Ordinance.

14   Gratuities payable to a public officer by the Government of the Federation or of a State in respect of services rendered by him under a contract of service with such government and described as gratuities either in such contract or some other document issued by or on behalf of such government in connection with such contract:

Where, however,

(a) the period of service (if continuous) does not amount to five years; or

(b) the aggregate period of service in any 63 consecutive months (if gratuities exceed a sum calculated at the rate of ₦1000 per annum for such period or aggregate period), the amount of any such excess shall be exempt but shall be deemed to be income of the last day of the employment including any terminal leave arising from the employment.

15   Gratuities payable to a member or former member of the staff of the Nigerian College of Arts, Science and Technology by the College in respect of service in with the college and described as gratituties either in such contract or in some other document issued by or on behalf of the College in connection with such contract. 'Member of the staff' means here an individual appointed to an office specified in the Second Schedule to the Nigeria College of Arts, Science and Technology Ordinance.

Where, however:

(a) the period of service (if continuous) does not amount to five years; or

(b) the aggregate period of service in any 63 consecutive months (if service is not continuous) does not amount to five years, and the total gratuities exceed a sum calculated at the rate of ₦1000 per annum for such period or aggregate period, the amount of any such excess shall be exempt but shall be deemed to be income of the last day of the employment including any terminal leave arising from the employment.

16   Gratuities payable to an employee or former employee under a contract of service with a body established by any of the following:

West African Institute for Trypanosomiasis Research Ordinance,

West African Institute for Oil Palm Research Ordinance,

West African Council for Medical Research Ordinance, being a gratuity so described either in his contract of service with such body or in some other document issued by or on behalf of such body in connection with that contract, subject to the following conditions:

(a) Where the service of an employee with any such body terminates then if the gratuity or aggregate gratuities paid or payable in respect of that service exceed one-quarter of the whole income arising to him from that employment including such gratuity or aggregate gratuities, that excess shall not be exempt but shall be deemed to be income of the employee of the last day of his employment including any terminal leave arising from that employment;

(b) where the service of an employee with any such body (or the aggregate service under two or more contracts within any period of 63 months) does not amount to five years, then upon the employee permanently ceasing such service with the body, if the gratuity or aggregate of the gratuities paid or payable in respect of that service exceeds a sum calculated at ₦1000 per annum for the period or day of such service in Nigeria or, if he is entitled to terminal leave following such service in Nigeria, of the last day of such leave.

(c) If any part of a gratuity paid or payable to an employee fails to be deemed to be his income under both conditions (a) and (b) then such part shall be deducted in ascertaining the excess under condition (b).

17   Any sums received by way of death gratuities or as consolidated compensation for death or injuries.

18   Any sum withdrawn or received by an employee from a pension, provident or other retirement benefits scheme established under the provisions of any Act for employees throughout Nigeria.

19   Any income from an employment or pension which is not derived or not deemed to be derived, from Nigeria and chargeable to tax solely by reason of it being brought into or received in Nigeria during any year preceding a year of assessment if the employee or pensioner is not in Nigeria for a period or any time during that year of assessment, or is not in Nigeria for a period or periods amounting to 183 days or more during that year of assessment.

Appendix 3   Tax deduction card

FEDERAL INLAND REVENUE DEPARTMENT
TAX DEDUCTION CARD 19........

(a)	NAME	(b) INITIALS	(c) FIRD REFERENCE
Mr			
Mrs			
Miss			

(c) MIN/DEPT	(d) EMPLOYER'S REF.

(e)	(f)						
1 MONTH	2 Total Gross Pay in Month	3 Total Gross Pay to Date	4 Total Free Pay to Date	5 Total Taxable Pay to Date	6 Total Tax Due to Date	7 Tax deducted in Month	8 Tax refunded in Month
1. April	₦	₦	₦	₦	₦	₦	₦
2. May							
3. June							
4. July							
5. Aug.							
6. Sept.							
7. Oct.							
8. Nov.							
9. Dec.							
10. Jan.							
11. Feb.							
12. Mar.							
TOTALS							

9. If employee engaged during Year deduct pay and Tax in respect of previous Employment	10. Checked	11. If a net refund Mark entry in this column "P" and use red ink
	Inits........	
	Date........	

Reminder being Pay and Tax of this
Employment

12. Contribution to Approved Pension Funds should be included
in entries in Col.2.   ₦

Instructions to employer

1 If there is any doubt as to the identity of this employee please return this card without delay to the Tax Office.

2 The Department and Branch, Division, or Section at which the Tax Deduction Card is completed should be entered in space (e).

3 Any special instruction will be shown by the Tax Office in space (f).

4 This card must be written up once a month to cover all payments made to the employee during that month.

5 In column (2) enter all the salary, etc. (see paragraph 1 of Employer's Guide) paid during the month, after the deduction of the employer's contribution to the National Provident Fund.

6 Column (3) in April repeats the column (2) figure but after that shows the total of all the entries to date in column (2).

7 Column (4) will show the amount of free pay to date, on a cumulative basis, to be allowed each month. These figures will be inserted in the Tax Office.

8 Column (5) is for the remainder when the figure in column (4) is subtracted from the figure in column (3) and is the figure to be looked up in the Tax Tables for the month concerned as the taxable pay to date.

9 Column (6) is for the figure found in the Tax Tables against the column (5) figures; if that figures is not shown, take the next smaller figure.

10 Column (7) in April repeats the column (6) figure but thereafter is for the difference between the column (6) figure for the current month and that for the previous month.

11 If the current month's figure in column (6) is less than that for the previous month, a refund will be due to the employee and the difference should be entered in column (8). In all other cases column (8) is left blank.

12 If the employee leaves your employment, mark the card "Left ... (date)" and retain it until the end of the financial year. You must also prepare a leaving certificate, send Part I to the Tax Office and give Part II to the employee. If the employee dies send both copies to the Tax Office.

13 If you engage a new employee, send form IR 144 to the Tax Office, prepare an Emergency Card IR 137 and act on the instructions thereon.

14 Never hand this card to the employee, to whom it refers.

15 At the end of each month the tax deducted must be paid to the Revenue.

16 At the end of the financial year this card must be sent to the Tax Office accompanied by a reconciliation with the monthly remittances. Remember that for employees who have come to you from a previous employment you will have to fill in the bottom two lines of columns 3 and 6 overleaf to arrive at your net deduction (or refund) for reconciliation purposes.

Appendix 4
The Capital Gains Tax Act, 1967

Capital Gains Tax – General

Gains chargeable to tax

Capital Gains – Computation

Computation – Miscellaneous

Exemptions and reliefs

Administration provisions, etc.

Schedule

Provisions of certain Income Tax Acts applied to Capital gains Tax.

Capital Gains Tax – General

1 (1) Subject to the provisions of this Act there shall be charged a tax to be called capital gains tax for the year of assessment 1967-68 and for subsequent years of assessment in respect of any capital gains, that is to say, gains accruing to any person on or after 1st April 1967 on a disposal of assets.

(2) Every such gain shall, except so far as otherwise expressly provided, be a chargeable gain.

(3) In this Act, unless the context otherwise requires, any reference to

person shall include a reference to any person to whom the Income Tax (Armed Forces and Other Persons) (Special Provisions) Act 1972 applies.

2   (1) The rate of capital gains tax shall be twenty per cent.

(2) Capital gains tax shall be chargeable at the rate mentioned in subsection (1) above on the total amount of chargeable gains accruing to any person in a year of assessment after making such deductions as may be allowed under this Act in the computation of such gains.

(3) Capital gains tax to be assessed on any person under this Act shall be computed and charged in accordance with the provisions of this Act.

3   Subject to any exceptions provided by this Act, all forms of property shall be assets for the purposes of this Act whether situated in Nigeria or not, including —

(*a*) options, debts and incorporeal property generally;

(*b*) any currency other than Nigerian currency; and

(*c*) any form of property created by the person disposing of it, or otherwise coming to be owned without being acquired;

(*d*) stocks and shares of every description,

and without prejudice to the foregoing provisions, this section shall have effect, notwithstanding that —

(i) the property is an eligible property within the meaning of the Income Tax (Rents) Act 1965 or the Act repealed by that Act; or

(ii) the property is an asset in respect of which qualifying expenditure had been incurred under the Fifth Schedule of the Income Tax Management Act 1961, the Third Schedule of the Companies Income Tax Act 1961 or Petroleum Profits Tax Act 1959.

4   Without prejudice to the foregoing provisions of this Act, as respects any chargeable gains accruing in the year 1967-68 or a later year of assessment from a disposal of assets situated outside Nigeria—

(*a*) where the disposal of assets is by an individual —

(i) who is in Nigeria for some temporary purpose only and not with any view or intent to establish his residence in Nigeria; and

(ii) if the period or sum of the periods for which he is present in Nigeria in that year of assessment exceeds 182 days; or

(*b*) where the disposal is by any trustee of any trust or settlement and the seat of administration of the trust or settlement is situated outside Nigeria during the whole of that year of assessment; or

(*c*) where the disposal is by a company, which is not a Nigerian Company within the meaning of section 2 of the Companies Income Tax Act 1961, that is to say, a company whose activities are managed and controlled outside Nigeria during the whole of that year of assessment,

capital gains tax shall be charged on the amounts (if any) received or brought into Nigeria in respect of any chargeable gains, such amounts being treated as gains accruing when they are received or brought into Nigeria.

5   In the computation of chargeable gains under this Act the amount of any loss which accrues to a person on a disposal of any asset shall not be deductible from gains accruing to any person on a disposal of such asset.

Gains chargeable to tax

6 (1) Subject to any exceptions provided by this Act there is, for the purposes of this Act, a disposal of assets by a person where any capital sum is derived from a sale, lease, transfer, an assignment, a compulsory acquisition or any other disposition of assets, notwithstanding that no asset is acquired by the person paying the cpaital sum, and in particular —

(*a*) where any capital sum is derived by way of compensation for any loss of office or employment;

(*b*) where any capital sum is received under a policy of insurance and the risk of any kind of damage or injury to, or the loss or depreciation of, assets;

(*c*) where any capital sum is received in return for forfeiture or surrender of rights, or for refraining from exercising rights,

(*d*) where any capital sum is received as consideration for use or exploitation of any asset; and

(*e*) without prejudice to paragraph (*a*) above, where any capital sum is received in connection with or arises by virtue of any trade, business, profession or vocation.

(2) In this section and elsewhere in this Act —

(*a*) 'capital sum' means any money or money's worth which is not excluded from the consideration taken into account in the computation under section 12 below; and

(*b*) references to a disposal of assets include, except where the context otherwise requires, references to a part disposal of assets, and there is a part disposal of assets —

(i) where an interest or right in or over the assets is created by the disposal, as well as where it subsists before the disposal; and

(ii) where, on a person making a disposal, any description of property derived from the assets remains undisposed of.

7 (1) Subject to the provisions of this Act, a person's acquisition of an asset and the disposal of it to him shall, for the purposes of this Act, be deemed to be for a consideration equal to the market value of the asset –

(*a*) where he acquires the asset otherwise than by way of a bargain made at arm's length; or

(*b*) where he acquires the asset wholly or partly for a consideration that cannot be valued, or in connection with his own or another's loss of office or employment or diminution of emolument, or otherwise in consideration for or recognition of his or another's services or past services in any office or employment or of any other service rendered or to be rendered by him or another; or

(*c*) where he acquires the asset as trustee for creditors of the person making the disposal.

(2) Where person disposes by way of gift of an asset acquired by him by way of a gift or otherwise (not being an acquisition on a devolution on death) the person acquiring the asset on that disposal shall, for all purposes of this Act, so far as relates to the interest taken by him, be deemed to have acquired the asset –

(*a*) in a case where the amount of the consideration for which the asset was last disposed of by way of a bargain made at arm's length is ascertainable, for a consideration equal to that amount; and

(*b*) in any other case, for a consideration equal to the market value of the asset on the date of that disposal.

In this subsection 'gift' does not include a donatio mortis causa.

(3) In relation to any asset held by a person as nominee for another person, or as trustee for another person absolutely entitled as against the trustee, or for any person who would be so entitled but for being an infant or other person under disability (or for two or more persons who are or would be jointly so entitled), this Act shall apply as if the property were vested in, and the acts of the nominee or trustee in relation to the asset were the acts of, the person or persons for whom he is the nominee or trustee (acquisitions from or disposals to him by that person or persons being disregarded accordingly).

(4) The conveyance or transfer by way of security of an asset or of an interest or right in or over it, or transfer of a subsisting interest or right by way of security in or over an asset (including a re-transfer on redemption of the security), shall not be treated for the purposes of this Act as involving any acquisition or disposal of the asset.

(5) Where a person entitled to an asset by way of security or to the benefit of a charge or incumbrance on an asset deals with the asset for the purpose of enforcing or giving effect to the security, charge or incumbrance on an asset deals with the asset for the purpose of enforcing or giving effect to the security, charge or incumbrance his dealings with it shall be treated for the purposes of this Act as if they were done through him as nominee by the person entitled to it subject to the security, charge or incumbrance; and this subsection shall apply to the dealings of any person appointed to enforce or give effect to the security, charge or incumbrance as receiver and manager or judicial factor as it applies to the dealings of the person entitled as aforesaid.

(6) An asset shall be treated as having been acquired free of any interest or right by way of security subsisting at the time of any acquistion of it, and as being disposed of free of any such interest or right subsisting at the time of the disposal; and where an asset is acquired subject to any such interest or right the full amount of the liability thereby assumed by the person acquiring the asset shall form part of the consideration for the acquisition and disposal in addition to any other consideration.

(7) Where an asset is acquired by a creditor in satisfaction of his debt or part thereof, the asset shall not be treated as disposed of by the debtor or acquired by the creditor for a consideration greater than its market value at the time of the creditor's acquisition of it, and if a chargeable gain accrues to the creditor on a disposal by him of the asset the amount of the chargeable gain (where necessary) shall be reduced so as not to exceed the chargeable gain which would have accrued if he had acquired the property for a consideration equal to the amount of the debt or that part thereof.

8 (1) On the death of an individual any assets of which he was competent to dispose of shall for the purposes of this Act be deemed to be disposed of

by him at the date of his death and acquired by the personal representatives or other person on whom the assets devolve for a consideration equal to —

(a) in a case where the amount of the consideration for which the asset was last disposed of by way of a bargain made at arm's length is ascertainable, that amount; and

(b) in any other case the market value of the asset at that date.

(2) The gains which accrue in consequence of subsection (1) of this section shall not be chargeable to capital gains tax under this Act.

(3) In relation to property forming part of the estate of a deceased person the personal representatives shall for the purposes of this Act be treated as being a single and continuous body of persons (distinct from the persons who may from time to time be the personal representatives), and that body shall be treated as having the deceased's residence and domicile at the date of death.

(4) On a person acquiring any asset as legatee —

(a) no chargeable gain shall accrue to the personal representatives, and

(b) the legatee shall be treated as if the personal reprentatives' acquisition of the asset had been his acquisition of it.

(5) In this section references to assets of which a deceased person was competent to dispose of are references to assets of the deceased which (otherwise than in right of a power of appointment) he could, if of full age and capacity, have disposed of by his will assuming that all the assets were situated in Nigeria and, if he was not domiciled in Nigeria, that he was domiciled in Nigeria.

(6) If not more than two years after a death any of the dispositions of the property of which the deceased was competent to dispose of whether by will, or under the law relating to intestacies, or otherwise, are varied by deed of family arrangement or similar instrument, this section shall apply as if the variations made by the deed or other instrument were effected by the deceased, and no disposition made by the deed or other instrument shall consitute a disposition for the purposes of this Act.

(7) In this section —

'legatee' includes any person taking under a testamentary disposition or on an intestacy or partial intestacy whether he takes beneficially or as trustee, and a donatio mortis causa shall be treated as a testamentary disposition and not as a gift:

'personal representatives' means —

(a) the executor, original or by representation, or administrator for the time being of a deceased person under any law in force in Nigeria;

(b) persons having in relation to the deceased under the law of another country any functions corresponding to the functions for administration purposes under any law in force in Nigeria of personal representatives as defined under paragraph (a) above,

and references to personal representatives as such shall be construed as references to the personal representatives in their capacity as having such functions as aforesaid.

9 (1) A person shall not be chargeable to tax under this Act in respect of

500

any acquisition and the disposal of land by reference to a disposal to an authority exercising or having compulsory powers, if that person had neither —

(a) acquired the land at a time when he knew or might reasonably have known that it was likely to be acquired by the authority; nor

(b) taken any steps by advertisement or otherwise to dispose of the land or to make his willingness to dispose of it known to the authority, or others.

(2) In this section 'authority exercising or having compulsory powers' means, in relation to any disposal of land, an authority, a person or body of persons acquiring the land compulsorily under the Public Lands Acquisition Act, the Land and Native Rights Act or any other enactment, or law of a country other than Nigeria, or who has or have been, or could be, authorised to acquire it compulsorily for the purposes for which it is acquired, or for whom another authority, person or body of persons has or have been, or could be, authorised so to acquire it.

10 (1) Subject to the provisions of this section where a person disposes of shares in a company and immediately before the disposal either—

(a) the company is or has control of a land-owning company, and is under the control of not more than 5 persons, and in which he has a substantial interest; or

(b) the company or a company of which it has control, has a substantial interest in a land-owning company under the control of not more than five persons of which he and persons connected with him have control;

then he shall be chargeable to tax under this Act by reference to his disposal of the shares, whenever he acquired them, and notwithstanding that he acquired them as legatee.

(2) Where, but for this section, a person would not be chargeable to tax under this Act by reference to disposal of shares in a company, then —

(a) he shall not be chargeable unless chargeable gains would have accrued to the company, being a land-owning company, or to a land-owning company referred to in paragraph (a) or (b), as the case may be, of subsection (1) above, on the company disposing of its land at market value at the time of his disposal and any such land-owning company disposing likewise of the land of that company; and

(b) he shall not, if a gain accrues to him on that disposal, be chargeable by reference to it to tax on an amount greater than the amount of the chargeable gains which would have to tax on an amount greater than the amount of the chargeable gains which would have so accrued, or such part of that amount as is attributable to the shares disposed of by him.

(3) For the purposes of this section, 'chargeable gains' means gains chargeable to tax by reference to a disposal of shares in a company.

(4) In this section 'land-owning company' means a company not carrying on a trade or dealing in or developing land, but entitled to land, being chargeable assets, to a value equal to or exceeding one-fifth of the net value of all its assets (that is to say their value less the value of the debts

and liabilities of the company); and for this purpose the value of the said land shall be taken to be the value of the company's interest free of any liability charged thereon, and to include the value of interests which the company has unconditionally contracted to acquire, but not that of interests which the company has unconditionally contracted to dispose of.

For the purposes of this subsection 'value' in relation to a company's land means market value, and the net value of a company's assets is the net value they would have on a sale in the open market of the company's business as a going concern.

(5) For the purposes of this section a person shall be deemed to have a substantial interest in a company if one-tenth or more in market value of the issued shares in the company is held by him or is held partly by him and partly by persons connected with him.

(6) In this section 'shares', in relation to a company not limited by shares (whether or not it has a share capital) shall include the interest of a member of the company as such, whatever the form of that interest, and this section shall apply in relation to any disposal of rights attached to or forming part of a share as if the rights included in the disposal and those not included were separate shares.

11 For the purposes of this Act any asset acquired or disposed of by any person chargeable to capital gains tax shall subject to section 21 (1) be deemed to have been so acquired or disposed of at the date of the contract to acquire or dispose of the asset or at a date at which there is an enforceable right to acquire or a binding duty to dispose of the asset or any right or interest therein, and in particular —

(a) where any contract is to be performed subject to any condition the date of acquisition or disposal of the asset shall be deemed to be the date when the condition is satisfied, but where a consideration of such a contract does not depend solely or mainly on the value of the asset at the time the condition is satisfied, the acquisition or disposal shall be treated as if the contract had never been conditional, in which case the date of the acquisition or disposal of asset shall be the date of the contract;

(b) where an option is conferred by virtue of any contract, the date of the acquisition or disposal of asset shall be the date when the option is exercised.

Capital Gains – Computation

12 In the computation of any chargeable gains under this Act such gains as may be chargeable to tax shall, subject to the provisions of this Act, be the difference between the consideration accruing to any person on a disposal of assets and any sum to be excluded from that consideration, and there shall be added to that sum the amount of the value of any

502

expenditure allowable to such person on such disposal by virtue of this Act.

13 (1) There shall be excluded from the consideration for a disposal of assets taken into account in the computation of the gain accruing on that disposal any money or money's worth charged to income tax as income of, or taken into account as a receipt in computing income or profits or gains or losses of the person making the disposal for the purposes of the Income Tax Management Act 1961, the Companies Income Tax Act 1961 or the Petroleum Profit Tax Act 1959, which Acts are hereafter jointly referred to as 'the Income Tax Acts'.

(2) Subsection (1) above shall not be taken as excluding from the consideration for the disposal of an asset any money or money's worth which is taken into account in the making of a balancing charge under the Income Tax Acts.

14 (1) In the computation of capital gains the sums allowable as a deduction from the consideration accruing to a person on the disposal of an asset shall be restricted to —

(a) the amount or value of the consideration, in money or money's worth given by him or on his behalf wholly, exclusively and necessarily for the acquisition of the asset, together with the incidental costs to him of the acquisition or, if the asset was not acquired by him, any expenditure wholly, exclusively and necessarily incurred by him in providing the asset;

(b) any amount of an expenditure wholly, exclusively and necessarily incurred on the asset by him or on his behalf for the purposes of enhancing the value of the asset being expenditure reflected in the state or nature of the asset at the time of the disposal;

(c) the amount of any expenditure wholly, exclusively and necessarily incurred on the asset by him or on his behalf in establishing, preserving or defending his title to, or a right over, the asset; and

(d) the incidental costs to him of making the disposal.

(2) For the purposes of this section and any other provision of this Act the incidental costs to the person making the disposal of the acquisition of the asset or of its disposal shall consist of expenditure wholly, exclusively and necessarily incurred by him for the purposes of the acquisition or , as the case may be, the disposal, being fees, commission or remuneration paid for the professional services of any surveyor or valuer, or auctioneer, or accountant, or agent, or legal adviser and costs of transfer or conveyance (including stamp duties) together —

(a) in the case of the acquisition of an asset, with costs of advertising to find a seller; and

(b) in the case of a disposal, with costs of advertising to find a buyer and costs reasonably incurred in making any valuation or apportionment required for the purposes of the computation of the capital gains, including in particular, expenses reasonably incurred in ascertaining market value where required under this Act.

15 (1) There shall be excluded from the sum allowable under section 14 as a deduction in the computation under this Act any expenditure allowable as

a deduction in computing the profits or gains or losses of a trade, business, profession or vocation for the purposes of income tax or allowable as a deduction in computing any other income or profits or gains or losses for the purposes of the Income Tax Acts and any expenditure which, although not so allowable as a deduction in computing any losses, would be so allowable but for an insufficiency of income or profits or gains: and this section applies irrespective of whether effect is or would be given to the deduction in computing the amount of tax chargeable or by discharge of payment of tax or in any other way.

(2) Without prejudice to the provisions of subsection (1) above there shall be excluded from the sums allowable under section 14 as a deduction in the computation under this Act any expenditure which, if the assets, or all the assets to which the computation relates, were, and had at all times been, held or used as part of the fixed capital of a trade or business the profits or gains of which were (irrespective of whether the person making the disposal is a company or not) chargeable to income tax would be allowable as a deduction in computing the profits or gains or losses of the trade for the purposes of income tax.

(3) The foregoing provisions of this section shall not require the exclusion from the sums allowable as deduction in the computation under this Act of any expenditure as being expenditure in respect of which capital allowances are granted under the Income Tax Acts.

16 Without prejudice to section 14 above there shall be excluded from the sums allowable as a deduction in the computation under this Act of the gain accruing to a person on the disposal of an asset any premiums or other payments made under a policy of insurance against the risks of any kind of damage or injury to, loss or depreciation of, any asset.

Computation: Miscellaneous

17 (1) Where there is a part disposal of an asset within the meaning of section 6 (2) above and generally wherever on the disposal of an asset any description of property derived from that asset remains undisposed of, the sums representing the amount or value of the consideration for the acquisition of the asset (in this Act referred to as the cost of acquisition of the asset) together with any amount of expenditure wholly, exclusively and necessarily incurred on the asset for the purposes of enhancing the value of the asset as are attributable to the asset shall, both for the purposes of the computation under this Act and in relation to the property which remains undisposed of, be apportioned.

(2) Apportionment shall be made by reference —
(a) to the amount or value of the consideration for the disposal on the one hand (call that amount or value A), and
(b) to the market value of the property which remains undisposed of on the other hand (call that market value B),
and accordingly the fraction of the said cost or sums allowable as a deduction in computing under this Act the amount of the

gain accruing on the disposal shall be $\dfrac{A}{A + B}$ and the remainder shall be attributed to the property which remains undisposed of.

(3) Where there is a disposal of an interest or right in or over a chargeable asset created by the disposal or where it subsists before the disposal, and on the making of the disposal any description of property derived from the asset remains undisposed of, there shall be apportioned the amount or value of the consideration in money or money's worth given by him or on his behalf wholly and exclusively for the acquisition of the asset together with the incidental costs to him of the acquisition or any expenditure wholly or exclusively incurred by him in providing the asset as against the market value of the property.

18 (1) If the consideration, or part of a consideration, taken into account in the computation of capital gains under this Act is payable by instalments over a period beginning not earlier than the time when the disposal is made, being a period exceeding 18 months, the chargeable gain accruing on the disposal shall be regarded for all the purposes of this Act as accruing in proportionate parts in the year of assessment in which the disposal is made and in each of the subsequent years of assessment down to and including the year of assessment in which the last instalment is payable.

(2) The proportionate parts to be recorded as accruing in the respective years of assessment shall correspond to the proportions of the amounts of the instalments of consideration payable in those respective years of assessment.

(3) The time in the year or accounting period when any such part of a chargeable gain is deemed to accrue under this section shall be the last day in that year of assessment.

(4) Subsection (1) above shall not apply to any part of the consideration which has effectively passed to the person making the disposal by way of a loan made to that person by the other party to the transaction.

(5) In the computation of chargeable gains under this Act consideration for the disposal shall be brought into account without any discount for postponement of the right to receive any part of it and, in the first instance, without regard to a risk of any part of the consideration being irrecoverable, or to the right to receive any part of the consideration being contingent; and if any part of the consideration so brought into account is subsequently shown to the satisfaction of the Board to be irrecoverable, such adjustment, whether by way of discharge, or repayment of tax or otherwise, shall be made as is required in consequence.

19 (1) If an asset, whether under a policy of insurance or otherwise, is lost or destroyed, and a capital sum received by way of compensation for the loss or destruction is applied within 3 years of receipt in acquiring another asset in replacement of the asset lost or destroyed, the owner shall if he so claims be treated for the purposes of this Act —

(a) as if the consideration for the disposal of the old asset were (if otherwise of a greater amount) of such amount as would secure that on the disposal neither a loss nor a gain accrues to him, and (*b*) as if the amount of the consideration for the acquisition of the new asset were reduced by the excess of the amount of the capital sum received by way of compensation or under the policy of insurance, together with any residual or scrap value, over the amount of the consideration which he is treated as receiving under paragraph (*a*) of this subsection.

(2) A claim shall not be made under subsection (1) above if part only of the capital sum is applied in acquiring the new asset but if all of that capital sum except for a part which is less than the amount of the gain (whether all chargeable gain or not) accruing on the disposal of the old asset is so applied, then the owner shall if he so claims be treated for the purposes of this Act —

(*a*) as if the amount of the gain so accruing were reduced to the amount of the said part (and, if not all chargeable gain, with a proportionate reduction in the amount of the chargeable gain), and

(*b*) as if the amount of the consideration for the acquisition of the new asset were reduced by the amount by which the gain is reduced under paragraph (*a*) of this subsection.

20 (1) Where a single bargain comprises two or more transactions whereby assets are disposed of, those transactions shall be treated for the purposes of computing capital gains as a single disposal.

(2) Where separate considerations are agreed or purported to be agreed for any two or more transactions comprised in one bargain (whether transactions whereby assets are disposed of or not) those considerations shall be treated as altogether constituting an entire consideration for the transactions and shall be apportionable between them accordingly.

(3) Where any apportionment under this section shall result in lesser consideration than that agreed (or purported to be agreed) in the bargain being attributable to the disposal of the assets, the separate considerations agreed (or purported to be agreed) in respect of those assets shall be deemed to be the consideration for which those assets are disposed of.

21 (1) Subject to the provisions of this Act where the Board is of the opinion that any disposition is an artificial or fictitious transaction or where any transaction which reduces or would reduce the amount of any capital gains tax is artificial or fictitious the Board shall disregard such disposition and may direct that such adjustments shall be made with respect to the liability of any person for the payment of capital gains tax as it considers appropriate so as to counteract the reduction of liability to capital gains tax effected or reduction which would otherwise be effected, by the transaction and any person concerned with such transaction shall be assessable accordingly.

(2) Any person in respect of whom any direction is made under this section shall have a right of appeal in like manner as though for the purposes of this Act such direction were an assessment to capital gains tax.

(3) For the purposes of this section—

(*a*) 'disposition' includes any trust, grant, covenant, agreement or arrangement;

506

(*b*) transactions between connected persons (within the meaning of section 24 below) shall be deemed to be artificial or fictitious if in the opinion of the Board those transactions have not been made on terms which might fairly have been expected to have been made by persons engaged in the same or similar activities dealing with one another at arm's length; and

(*c*) in relation to any direction made under this section the provision of this Act as to appeals against an assessment shall have effect as if such direction were an assessment.

22 (1) For the purposes of computing capital gains, unless the context otherwise requires, 'market value' in relation to any assets (whether chargeable assets or not) means the prices which those assets might reasonably be expected to fetch on a sale in the open market.

(2) In estimating the market value of any asset no reduction shall be made in the estimate on account of the estimate being made on the assumption that the whole of the assets is to be placed on the market at one and the same time.

(3) In re-estimating the market value of any assets acquired, if the market value exceeds the consideration actually paid by the acquirer, the assets shall be deemed to have been acquired for the amount actually paid by the acquirer.

23 (1) This section shall apply where a person acquires an asset and the person making the disposal is connected with him.

(2) Without prejudice to the generality of section 7 of this Act the person acquiring the asset and the person making the disposal shall be treated as parties to a transaction otherwise than by way of a bargain made at arm's length.

(3) In a case where any asset mentioned in subsection (1) above is subject to any right or restriction enforceable by the person making the disposal, or by a person connected with him, then (the amount of the consideration for the acquisition being, in accordance with subsection (2) of this section, deemed to be equal to the market value of the asset) that market value shall be—

(*a*) what its market value would be if not subject to the right or restriction, minus—

(*b*) the market value of the right or restriction or the amount by which its extinction would enhance the value of the asset to its owner, whichever is the less:

Provided that if the right or restriction is of such a nature that its enforcement would or might effectively destroy or substantially impair the value of the asset without bringing any countervailing advantage either to the person making the disposal or a person connected with him or other right to acquire the asset or, in the case of immovable property, is a right to extinguish the asset in the hands of the person giving the consideration by forfeiture or merger or otherwise, that market value of the asset shall be determined, and the amount of the gain accruing on the disposal shall be computed, as if the right or restriction did not exist. This subsection shall not apply to a right of forfeiture or other right exercisable

507

on breach of a covenant contained in a lease of land or other property, and shall not apply to any right or restriction under a mortgage or other charge.

24 (1) Any question whether a person is connected with another shall for the purposes of this Act be determined in accordance with this section (any provision that one person is connected with another being taken to mean that they are connected with one another).

(2) A person is connected with an individual if that person is the individual's husband or wife, or is a relative, or the husband or wife of a relative, of the individual or of the individual's husband or wife.

(3) A person, in his capacity as trustee of a settlement, is connected with any individual who in relation to the settlement is a settlor, and with any person who is connected with such an individual.

(4) A person is connected with any person with whom he is in partnership, and with the husband or wife or a relative of any individual with whom he is in partnership.

(5) A company is connected with another company—

(a) if the same person has control of both, or a person has control of one and persons connected with him, or he and persons connected with him, have control of the other; or

(b) if a group of two or more persons has control of each company, and the groups either consist of the same persons or could be regarded as consisting of the same persons by treating (in one or more cases) a member of either group as replaced by a person with whom he is connected.

(6) A company is connected with another person, if that person has control of it or if that person and persons connected with him together have control of it.

(7) Any two or more persons acting together to secure or exercise control of a company shall be treated in relation to that company as connected with one another and with any person acting on the directions of any of them to secure or exercise control of the company.

(8) In this section 'relative' means brother, sister, ancestor or lineal descendant.

25 For the purposes of this Act—

(a) the situation of rights or interests (otherwise than by way of security) in or over immovable property is that of the immovable property,

(b) subject to the following provisions of this subsection, the situation of rights or interests (otherwise than by way of security) in or over tangible movable property is that of the tangible movable property,

(c) subject to the following provisions of this section, a debt, secured or unsecured, is situated in Nigeria if and only if the creditor is resident in Nigeria,

(d) shares or securities issued by any governmental, municipal, local or native authority, or by any body created by such an authority, are situated in the country of that authority or place where the authority is situated,

(e) subject to paragraph (d) above, registered shares or securities are situated where they are registered and, if registered in more than one register, where the principal register is situated,

(f) a ship or aircraft is situated in Nigeria if and only if the owner is then resident in Nigeria, and an interest or right in or over a ship or aircraft is situated in Nigeria if and only if the person entitled to the interest or right is resident in Nigeria,

(g) the situation of good-will of a trade, business or professional asset is at the place where the trade, business or profession is carried on,

(h) patents, trade-marks and designs are situated where they are registered, and if registered in more than one register, where each register is situated, and copy-right, franchises, rights and licences to use any copy-right material, patent, trade-mark or design are situated in Nigeria if they, or any rights derived from them, are exercisable in Nigeria,

(i) a judgment debt is situated where the judgment is recorded.

26 (1) No deduction shall be allowable in a computation under this Act more than once from any sum or from more than one sum.

(2) Reference in this Act to sums taken into account as receipts or as expenditure in computing profits or gains or losses for the purposes of income tax shall include references to sums which would be so taken into account but for the fact that any profits or gains of a trade, profession, employment or vocation are not chargeable to income tax or that losses are not allowable for those purposes.

(3) In this Act references to income or profits charged or chargeable to tax include references to income or profits taxed or as the case may be taxable by deduction at source.

(4) For the purposes of any computation under this Act any necessary apportionments shall be made of any consideration or of any expenditure and the method of apportionment adopted shall, subject to the express provisions of this Act, be such method as appears to the Board or on appeal to the Appeal Commissioners or the High Court of a territory to be just and reasonable.

Exemptions and reliefs

27 (1) Subject to subsection 2 of this section a gain shall not be chargeable if it accrues to—

(a) an ecclesiastical, charitable or educational institution of a public character;

(b) any statutory or registered Friendly society:

(c) any co-operative society registered under the Co-operative Societies Act; or

(d) any trade union registered under the Trade Union Act;

in so far as the gain is not derived from any disposal of any assets acquired in connection with any trade or business carried on by the institution or society and the gain is applied purely for the purpose of the institution or society as the case may be.

(2) If any property to which subsection (1) above relates which is held on trust ceases to be subject to such trust—

(*a*) the trustees shall be treated as if they had disposed of, and immediately re-acquired, the property for a consideration equal to its market value, any gain on the disposal being treated as not accruing to the institution or society; and

(*b*) if and so far as any of that property represents, directly or indirectly, the consideration for the disposal of assets by the trustees, any gain accruing on that disposal shall be treated as not having accrued to such institution or society, and,

notwithstanding anything in this Act limiting the time for making assessments, any assessment to capital gains tax chargeable by virtue of paragraph (*b*) above may be made at any time not more than three years after the end of the year of assessments in which the property ceases to be subject to such trusts.

28 (1) There shall be exempt from capital gains tax any gains accruing to any local or native authority.

(2) Gains accruing to any of the bodies mentioned in this subsection shall be exempt from capital gains tax, that is to say—

(*a*) gains accruing to any company, being a purchasing authority established by or under any law in Nigeria, empowered to acquire any commodity in Nigeria for export from Nigeria; or

(*b*) gains accruing to any corporation established by or under any law for the purpose of fostering the economic development of any part of Nigeria in so far as the gains are not derived from the disposal of any assets acquired by the corporation in connection with any trade or business carried on by it or from the disposal of any share or other interest possessed by the corporation in a trade or business carried on by some other person or authority.

29 (1) A gain shall not be a chargeable gain—

(*a*) if accruing to a person from any disposal of investments held by him as part of any superannuation fund but so that where part only of that fund is approved under section 17 of the Income Tax Management Act 1961 the gain shall be exempt from being a chargeable gain to the same extent only as income derived from the assets would be exempt under that section;

(*b*) if accruing to a person from his disposal of investment held by him as part of any national provident fund or other retirement benefits scheme established under the provisions of any Act for employees throughout Nigeria,

and such gain shall be exempt from tax under this Act in the same manner as investment income of any of those funds is exempt under paragraph (*w*) of the Third Schedule of the Income tax Management Act 1961.

(2) No chargeable gain shall accrue to any person on the disposal of a right to, or to any part of any sum payable out of any sum payable out of any superannuation fund,

(3) In this section, 'superannuation fund' means a pension, provident or other retirement benefits fund, society or scheme approved by the Joint

Tax Board under section 17(1) (*f*) of the Income Tax Management Act 1961.

30 A gain shall not be a chargeable gain if it accrues on the disposal by any person of a decoration, awarded for valour or gallant conduct which he acquires otherwise than for consideration in money or money's worth.

31 Gains accruing to a person from a disposal by him of Nigerian government securities shall not be chargeable gains under this Act.

32 (1) If the consideration which a person carrying on a trade obtains for the disposal of, or of his interest in, assets (in this section referred to as 'the old assets') used, and used only, for the purposes of the trade throughout the period of ownership is applied by him in acquiring other assets, or an interest in other assets (in this section referred to as 'the new assets') which on the acquisition are taken into use, and used only, for the purposes of the trade and the old assets and new assets are classes of assets listed in the section, then the person carrying on the trade shall, on making a claim as respects the consideration which has been so applied, be treated for the purposes of this Act—

(*a*) as if the consideration for the disposal of, or of the interest in, the old assets were (if otherwise of a greater amount of value) of such amount as would secure that on the disposal neither a loss nor a gain accrues to him, and

(*b*) as if the amount or value of the consideration for the acquisition of, or of the interest in, the new assets were reduced by the excess of the amount or value of the actual consideration for the disposal of, or of the interest in, the old assets over the amount of the conideration which he is treated as receiving under paragraph (*a*) above,

but neither paragraph (*a*) nor paragraph (*b*) above shall affect the treatment for the purposes of this Act of the other party to the transaction involving the new assets.

(2) Subsection (1) of this section shall not apply if part only of the amount or value of the consideration for the disposal of, or of the interest in, the old assets is applied as described in that subsection but if all of the amount or value of the consideration except for a part which is less than the amount of the gain (whether all chargeable gain or not) accruing on the disposal of, or of the interest in, the old assets is so applied, then the person carrying on the trade, on making a claim as respects the consideration which has been so applied, shall be treated for the purposes of this Act—

(*a*) as if the amount of the gain so accruing were reduced to the amount of the said part (and, if not all chargeable gain, with a proportionate reduction in the amount of the chargeable gain), and

(*b*) as if the amount or value of the consideration for the acquisition of, or of the interest in, the new assets were reduced by the amount by which the gain is reduced under paragraph (*a*) of this subsection,

but neither paragraph (*a*) nor paragraph (*b*) above shall affect the treatment for the purposes of this Act of the other party to the transaction involving the old assets or of the other party to the transaction involving the new assets.

(3) This section shall only apply if the acquisition of, or of the interest in, the new assets takes place, or an unconditional contract for the acquisition is entered into, in the period beginning twelve months before and ending twelve months after the disposal of, or of the interest in, the old assets, or at such earlier or later time as the Board may by notice in writing allow:

Provided that, where an unconditional contract for the acquisition is so entered into, this section may be applied on a provisional basis without waiting to ascertain whether the new assets or the interest in the new assets, is acquired in pursuance of the contract, and, when that fact is ascertained, all necessary adjustments shall be made by making assessments or by repayment or discharge of tax, and shall be so made notwithstanding any limitation in this Act on the time within which assessments may be made.

(4) If two or more persons are carrying on a trade in partnership, this section shall not apply in relation to any one of them unless he is, under this Act, to be treated both as making disposal of a share in, or in the interest in, the old assets, and as acquiring a share in, or in the interest in, the new assets; and if those shares are different, that partner's share shall be taken for the purposes of this section to be the smaller share.

(5) This section shall not apply unless the acquisition of, or of the interest in, the new assets was made for the purpose of their use in the trade, and not wholly or partly for the purpose of realising a gain from the disposal of, or of the interest in, the new assets.

(6) The classes of assets for the purpose of this section are as follows—
Class 1. Assets within the heads A and B below.

A. Except where the trade is a trade of dealing in or developing land, or of providing services for the occupier of land in which the person carrying on the trade has an estate or interest—

(a) any building or part of a building and any permanent or semi-permanent structure in the nature of a building occupied (as well as used) only for the purposes of the trade, and

(b) any land occupied (as well as used) only for the purposes of the trade.

B. Fixed plant or machinery which does not form part of a building or of a permanent or semi-permanent structure in the nature of a building.

Ships: Class 2
Aircraft: Class 3
Goodwill: Class 4

(7) If, over the period of ownership or any substantial part of the period of ownership, part of a building or structure is, and any part is not, used for the purposes of a trade, this section shall apply as if the part so used, with any land occupied for purposes ancillary to the occupation and use of that part of the building or structure, were a separate asset, and subject to any necessary apportionments of consideration for an acquisition or disposal of, or of an interest in, the building or structure and other land.

(8) If the old assets were not used for the purposes of the trade throughout the period of ownership this section shall apply as if a part of the asset representing its use for the purposes of the trade having regard to the time and extent to which it was, and was not, used for those purposes, were a separate asset which had been wholly used for the purposes of the trade and this subsection shall apply in relation to that part subject to any necessary apportionment of consideration for an acquisition or disposal of, or of the interest in, the asset.

(9) This section shall apply in relation to a person who, either successively or at the same time, carries on two trades which are in different localities, but which are concerned with goods or services of the same kind, as if, in relation to old assets used for the purposes of the one trade and new assets used for the purposes of the other trade, the two trades were the same.

(10) This section shall apply with the necessary modifications in relation to a business, profession, vocation or employment as it applies in relation to a trade, and in this section the expressions 'trade', 'business', 'profession', 'vocation', and 'employment' have the same meanings as in the Income Tax Acts, but not so as to apply the provisions of the Income Tax Acts as to the circumstances in which, on a change in the persons carrying on a trade, a trade is to be regarded as discontinued, or as set up and commenced.

(11) The provisions of this Act fixing the amount of the consideration deemed to be given for the acquisition or disposal of assets shall be applied to this section.

(12) Without prejudice to the provisions of this Act providing generally for apportionments, where consideration is given for the acquisition or disposal of assets some or part of which are assets in relation to which a claim under subsection (1) or subsection (2) of this section applies, and some or part of which are not, the consideration shall be apportioned in such manner as is just and reasonable.

33 (1) This section has effect as respects any policy of assurance or contract for a deferred annuity on the life of any person.

(2) No chargeable gain shall accrue on the disposal of, or of an interest in, the rights under any such policy of assurance or contract except where the person making the disposal is not the original beneficial owner and acquired the rights or interests for a consideration in money or money's worth.

(3) Subject to subsection (2) above, the occasion of the payment of the sum or sums assured by a policy of assurance or of the first instalment of a deferred annuity, and the occasion of the surrender of a policy of assurance or of the rights under a contract for a deferred annuity, shall be the occasion of a disposal of the rights under the policy of assurance or contract for a deferred annuity, and the amount of the consideration for the disposal of a contract for a deferred annuity shall be the market value at that time of the right to that and further instalments of the annuity.

34 (1) The rights of the insured under any insurance effected in the course of a capital redemption business shall constitute an asset on the disposal of which a gain may accrue to the person making the disposal but subject to

that neither the rights of the insurer nor the rights of the insured under any policy of insurance whether the risks insured relate to property or not shall constitute an asset on the disposal of which a gain may accrue.

(2) Notwithstanding subsection (1) above sums received under a policy of insurance of the risk of any kind of damage to, or the loss or depreciation of assets are for the purposes of this Act and in particular for the purposes of section 6 of this Act sums derived from the assets.

(3) In this section—

(a) 'capital redemption business' means the business (not being life assurance business or industrial assurance business) of effecting and carrying out contracts of insurance, whether effected by the issue of policies, bonds or endowment certificates or otherwise, whereby, in return for one or more premiums paid to the insurer a sum or a series of sums is to become payable to the insured in the future;

(b) 'industrial assurance business' means the business of effecting and carrying out contracts of insurance in connection with any industrial assurance whereby in return for one or more premiums paid to the insurer a sum or a series of sums is to become payable to the insured in the future; and

(c) 'policy of insurance' does not include a policy of assurance on human life.

35 (1) Subject to subsection (2) below, sums obtained by way of compensation or damages for any wrong or injury suffered by an individual in his person or in his profession or vocation shall not be chargeable gains within the meaning of this Act; and the foregoing provision of this subsection shall extend to compensation or damages for personal or professional wrong or injury including wrong or injury for libel, slander or enticement.

(2) Sums obtained by way of compensation for loss of office shall not, however, be chargeable gains, except where the amount of such compensation or damages exceeds ₦10 000 in any year of assessment.

36 (1) This section applies to a gain accruing to an individual so far as attributable to the disposal of, or of an interest in –

(a) a dwelling-house or part of a dwelling-house which is, or has at any time in his period of ownership been, his only or main residence, or

(b) land which he has for his own occupation and enjoyment with that residence as its garden or grounds up to an area (inclusive of the site of the dwelling-house) of one acre or such larger area as the Board may in any particular case determine, on being satisfied that, regard being had to the size and character of the dwelling-house, the larger area is required for the reasonable enjoyment of it (or of the part in question) as a residence.

In the case where part of the land occupied with a residence is and part is not within this subsection, then (up to the permitted area) that part shall be taken to be within this subsection which, if the remainder were separately occupied, would be the most suitable for occupation and enjoyment with the residence.

(2) The gain shall not be a chargeable gain if the dwelling-house or part

of a dwelling-house has been the individual's only or main residence throughout the period of ownership, or throughout the period of ownership except for all or any part of the last twelve months of that period.

(3) So far as it is necessary for the purposes of this section to determine which of two or more residences is an individual's main residence for any period –

(a) the individual may conclude that question by notice in writing to the Board given within two years from the beginning of that period, or given by the end of the year 1967–68, if that is later, but subject to a right to vary that notice by a further notice in writing to the Board as respects any period beginning not earlier than two years before the giving of the further notice,

(b) subject to paragraph (a) above, the question shall be concluded by the determination of the Board, which may be as respects either the whole or specified parts of the period of ownership in question.

and notice of any determination of the Board under paragraph (b) above shall be given to the individual who may appeal to the Appeal Commissioners against that determination within thirty days of service of the notice.

(4) This section shall not apply in relation to a gain unless the acquisition of, or of the interest in, the dwelling-house or the part of a dwelling-house was made for the purpose of residing in it and not wholly or partly for the purpose of realising a gain from the disposal of it, and shall not apply in relation to a gain so far as attributable to any expenditure which was incurred after the beginning of the period of ownership and was incurred wholly or partly for the purpose of realising a gain from the disposal.

(5) Apportionments of consideration shall be made wherever required by this section and, in particular, where a person disposes of a dwelling-house only part of which is his only or main residence.

37 (1) Subject to this section a gain accruing on a disposal of an asset which is tangible movable property shall not be chargeable gain if the total amount or value of the consideration for the disposal does not in a year of assessment exceed ₦1000.

(2) The amount of capital gains tax chargeable in respect of a gain accruing on a disposal of an asset which is tangible movable property for a consideration the total amount or value of which exceeds ₦1000 shall not exceed half the difference between the amount of that consideration and ₦1000.

For the purposes of this subsection the capital gains tax chargeable in respect of the gain shall be the amount of tax which would not have been chargeable but for that gain.

(3) If two or more assets which have formed part of a set of articles of any description all owned at one time by one person are disposed of by that person, and –

(a) to the same person, or

(b) to persons who are acting in concert or who are, in terms of section 24 above, connected persons,

Whether on the same or different occasions, the two or more transactions shall be treated as a single transaction disposing of a single asset, but with any necessary apportionments of the reductions in tax under subsection (2) of this section, and this subsection shall also apply where the assets, or some of the assets, are disposed of on different occasions on the first of April, 1966, but not so as to make any gain accruing on that date a chargeable gain.

(4) If the disposal is of a right or interest in or over tangible movable property –

(*a*) in the first instance subsections (1) and (2) of this section shall be applied in relation to the asset as a whole, taking the consideration as including the market value of what remains undisposed of, in addition to the actual consideration;

(*b*) where the sum of the actual consideration and that market value exceeds ₦1000 the limitation and the amount of tax in subsection (2) above shall be of half the difference between that sum and ₦1000 multiplied by the fraction equal to the actual consideration divided by the said sum.

(5) The foregoing provisions of this section shall apply in relation to a gain accruing on a disposal of two or more assets (not necessarily forming part of a set of articles of any description) which are tangible movable properties in the same manner as they apply in relation to a gain accruing on a disposal of an asset, or two or more assets which formed part of a set of articles, if in a year of assessment the total amount or value of the consideration is ₦1000 or more.

(6) This section shall not apply in relation to a disposal of currency of any description.

38 A mechanically propelled road vehicle constructed or adapted for the carriage of passengers shall not be an asset for the purposes of this Act unless it is a vehicle of a type not commonly used as private vehicle and is unsuitable to be so used.

39 Subject to the provisions of this Act where a person disposes, by way of a gift, of an asset acquired by him by way of a gift or otherwise (not being an acquisition on a devolution on death), the person making the disposal shall not be chargeable to capital gains tax under this Act by reference to that disposal.

In this section, 'gift' has the same meaning as in section 7 (2) above.

40 (1) Gains shall not be chargeable gains if the gains accrue to a diplomatic body, and such gains shall be exempt from capital gains tax under this Act in the same manner as the income of a diplomatic body is exempt from income tax under paragraph (*b*) and (*i*) of the Third Schedule of the Income Tax Management Act 1961 and sections 9, 10 and 11 of the Diplomatic Immunities and Privileges Act 1962, and those provisions shall be construed accordingly.

(2) In this section 'diplomatic body' includes a diplomatic representative, a foreign envoy, a foreign consular officer and an employee of any foreign state, or any organisation the members of which are foreign

Powers to which section 11 of the Diplomatic Immunities and Privileges Act 1962 applies.

41 (1) For the purposes of giving relief on double taxation, in relation to capital gains tax and tax on chargeable gains charged under the law of any country outside Nigeria, in sections 22, 23 and 24 of the Income Tax Management Act 1961 and section 36 and 37 of the Companies Income Tax Act 1961 (double taxation relief and unilateral relief) for references to income and profits there shall be subsituted references to capital gains, and for references to income tax there shall be substituted references to capital gains tax, meaning (as the context may require) tax charged under any law in force in Nigeria or tax charged under the law of a country outside Nigeria; and the enactments mentioned as aforesaid in this subsection shall apply accordingly.

(2) Any arrangement set out in an order made under the said section 24 of the Income Tax Management Act 1961 and section 37 of the Companies Income Tax Act 1961, after the commencement of this Act shall, so far as they provide (in whatever terms) for relief from tax chargeable in Nigeria on capital gains by virtue of this section have effect in relation to capital gains tax.

(3) So far as by virtue of this section capital gains tax charged under the law of a country outside Nigeria may be brought into account under the said provisions of the Income Tax Management Act 1961 and the Companies Income Tax Act 1961 as applied by this section, that tax, whether relief is given by virtue of this section in respect of it or not, shall not be taken into account for the purposes of those provision of the Income Tax Management Act 1961 and the Companies Income Tax Act 1961 as they apply apart from this section.

(4) Section 24(3) of the Income Tax Management Act 1961 and section 37(3) of the Companies Income Tax Act 1961 (which relate to disclosure of information for purposes of double taxation) shall without prejudice to the foregoing provisions of this section apply in relation to capital gains tax as they apply in relation to income tax.

42 (1) A person charged or chargeable for any year of assessment in respect of chargeable gains accruing to him from the disposal of assets situated outside Nigeria may claim that the following provisions of this section shall apply on showing that –

(a) he was unable to transfer those gains to Nigeria, and

(b) that inability was due to the laws of the country where the income arose, or to the executive action of its government, or to the impossibility of obtaining foreign currency in that territory, and

(c) the inability was not due to any want of reasonable endeavours on his part.

(2) If he so claims then for the purposes of capital gains tax –

(a) there shall be deducted from the amounts on which he is assessed to capital gains tax for the year in which the chargeable gain accrued to the claimant the amount as respects which the conditions in paragraphs (a), (b) and (c) above are satisfied, so far as applicable, but

517

(*b*) the amount so deducted shall be assessed to capital gains tax on the claimant (or his personal representatives) as if it were an amount of chargeable gains accruing in the year of assessment in which the said conditions cease to be satisfied.

(3) No claim under this section shall be made in respect of any chargeable gain more than six years after the end of the year of assessment in which that gain accrues.

(4) The personal representatives of a deceased person may make any claim which he might have made under this section if he had not died.

Administration provisions, etc.

43 (1) Capital gains tax shall be under the care and management of the Board and the provisions of the Income Tax Acts in the Schedule of this Act shall apply in relation to capital gains tax as they apply in relation to income tax chargeable under those Acts subject to any necessary modifications.

(2) An appeal shall lie against any assessment to capital gains tax made in accordance with section 49 of the Companies Income Tax Act, 1961 or section 30 of the Personal Income Tax (Lagos) Act 1961, as the case may be under section 55 of the Companies Income Tax Act 1961.

44 (1) Without prejudice to section 40 above a notice under section 44 of the Companies Income Tax Act 1961 or section 24 of the Personal Income Tax (Lagos) Act 1961 (as applied under this Act) which relates to returns of profits and income respectively for purposes of a claim, the Board may require particulars of any assets acquired by any person on whom the notice is served (or if the notice relates to income, profits or chargeable gains of some other persons, of any assets acquired by that other person) in the period specified in the notice, being a period beginning not earlier than 1st April, 1967 but excluding any asset acquired as a trading stock.

(2) The particulars required under this section may include particulars of the person from whom the assets were acquired and of the consideration for the acquisition.

(3) Without prejudice to the provisions of the Stamp Duties Act, the Commissioner of Stamp Duties shall demand tax clearance certificates when checking documents on sale by any company of landed properties and other assets before accepting such documents for stamping.

45 (1) In this Act unless the context otherwise requires,

'the Board' means the Lagos State Inland Revenue Board.

'chargeable gains' has the meaning given in section 1 above;

'company' includes any body corporate but does not include a partnership or a corporation sole;

'connected person' has the meaning given in section 24 above;

'disposal of assets' has the meaning given in section 6(1) above:

'gift' has the meaning given in section 6(1) above:

'part disposal' has the meaning given by section 6(2) (*b*) above;

'personal representatives' means the legal personal representatives of a deceased person;

'market value' has the meaning given by section 22(1) above; and
'year of assessment' means, in relation to capital gains tax, a year beginning with 1st April and ending with 31st March in the following calendar year and '1967–1968' indicates year of assessment beginning on 1st April 1967 and ending 31st March 1968.

(2) References in this Act to any person to whom any chargeable gains accrue include –

(*a*) references to any company or other body corporate established by or under any law in force in Nigeria or elsewhere to whom such gains accrue; or

(*b*) references to a person to whom the Income Tax (Armed Forces and Other Persons) (Special Provisions) Act 1972 applies to whom the gains accrue.

(3) A hire-purchase or other transaction under which the use and enjoyment of an asset is obtained by a person for a period at the end of which the property in the asset will or may pass to that person shall be treated for the purposes of this Act, both in relation to that person and in relation to the person from whom he obtains the use and enjoyment of the asset, as if it amounted to an entire disposal of the asset to that person at the beginning of the period for which he obtains the use and enjoyment of the asset, but subject to such adjustments of tax, whether by way of repayment or discharge of tax or otherwise, as may be required where the period for which that person has the use and enjoyment of the asset terminates without the property in the asset passing to him.

(4) In the case of a disposal within section 4 of this Act the time of the disposal shall be the time when the capital sum is received as described in that section.

(5) For the purposes of section 4 above there shall be treated as received in Nigeria in respect of any gain all amounts paid, used or enjoyed in or in any manner or form transmitted or brought to Nigeria.

(6) Where two or more persons carry on a trade or business in partnership –

(*a*) tax in respect of chargeable gains accruing to them on the disposal of any partnership assets shall, in Nigeria be assessed and charged on them separately,

(*b*) any partnership dealings shall be treated as dealings by the partners and not by the firm as such, and

(*c*) subject to the provisions of this Act, the provisions of the Income Tax Management Act 1961 and the Companies Income Tax Act 1961 relating to residence of partnerships shall, in so far as the provisions are not inconsistent with the provisions of this Act, apply in relation to tax chargeable in pursuance of this Act as they apply in relation to income tax: so however that any reference to the income of a partner from a partnership shall be construed as a reference to such proportion of gains of the partnership as is attributable to the partner in the computation of capital gains accruing to that partner on the disposal of any partnership assets.

(7) Any provision of this Act introducing the assumption that assets are

sold and immediately re-acquired shall not imply that any expenditure is incurred as incidental to the sale or re-acquisition.

(8) The reference in this Act to any enactment apart from this Act is a reference to that enactment as amended, altered, subsituted or replaced by any other enactment or law relating to the subject-matter and applicable.

46 (1) This Act may be cited as the Capital Gains Tax Act.

(2) This Act shall be deemed to have come into operation on the 1st of April, 1967.

SCHEDULE   Provisions of the Income Tax Acts applied to Capital Gains Tax

Companies Income Tax Act 1961 (1961 No. 22)

Part II	(administration) except sections 4(8), 5(1), and 6 to 13.
Part VIII	(person chargeable, agents, liquidators, etc.).
Part IX	(returns).
Part X	(assessments).
Part XI	(appeals).
Part XII	(collection, recovery and repayment) except section 61(1)(*a*).
Part XIII	(offences and penalties).
Section 76	(conduct of proceedings in Magistrates Court).

(Note: The above Act has been repealed and replaced by the Companies Income Tax Act 1979. See Destination Table at page 1 for the corresponding provisions.)

Income Tax Management Act 1961 (1961 No. 21)

Sections 28 to 30   (disclosure and procurement of information, power to appoint agent and returns).

Personal Income Tax (Lagos) Act 1961 (1961 No. 23)

Section 3 and 4	(administration) except section 3(8).
Section 7	(power to amend First Schedule).
Section 9 to 11	(official secrecy, forms, service and signature of notices).
Sections 20 and 21	(deductions to be claimed and proof of claims) except section 21(2).
Part V	(persons chargeable and returns).
Part VI	(assessments) except section 29.

520

Part VII	(appeals) except section 42.
Part VIII	(collection, recovery and repayment of tax) except sections 44(1)(*a*), 47, 48, 50 and 51.
Part IX	(offences and penalties) except section 58.
Part X	(powers of Tax Collectors).

Income Tax Act 1962 (1962 No. 35)

Section 5   (collection of tax for which a deceased person was answerable). Included in section 29(3) of the Income Tax Management Act, 1961 in this handbook.

Appendix 5
Industrial Development (Income Tax Relief) Act, 1971

Pioneer conditions

1 Publication of list of pioneer industries and products and issuing of pioneer certificates.
2 Mode of application for pioneer certificate, etc. and fee payable.
3 Terms of pioneer certificate.
4 Amending of pioneer certificate by adding additional pioneer product.
5 Provisions where pioneer certificate operates retrospectively.
6 Certifying the date of production day and the amount of qualifying capital expenditure, etc.
7 Cancellation of pioneer certificates.
8 Information.
9 Publication of pioneer certificate, etc.

Income Tax relief

10 Tax relief period.
11 Provisions governing old and new trade or business.
12 Restrictions on trading prior to end of tax relief period, etc.
13 Power to direct in certain events.
14 Capital allowances and losses.
15 Returns of profits.
16 Profits exempted from income tax.
17 Exemption of certain dividends from income tax.
18 Restriction on distribution of dividends and on the granting of loans.
19 Exclusion of small companies relief.
20 Provisions for plantation industry.

Miscellaneous and general

21 False information.
22 Offences by body corporate, etc.
23 Liability under undertaking enforceable notwithstanding proceedings.
24 Repeal, savings and transitional provisions.
25 Interpretation.
26 Citation, construction, commencement and extent.

Pioneer conditions

1 (1) Where the Federal Executive Council (hereinafter in this Act referred to as 'the Council') is satisfied that –

    (a) any industry is not being carried on in Nigeria on a scale suitable to the economic requirements of Nigeria or at all, or there are favourable prospects of further development in Nigeria of any industry; or

    (b) it is expedient in the public interest to encourage the development or establishment of any industry in Nigeria by declaring the industry to be a pioneer industry and any product of the industry to be a pioneer product,

the Council may direct publication in the Gazette of a list of such industries and products (hereinafter in this Act referred to as 'the list of pioneer industries and pioneer products') and upon publication as aforesaid, but subject to subsections (5) and (6) below, application may at any time thereafter be made under this Act, for the issue of a pioneer certificate to any company in relation to any such pioneer industry or pioneer product, and the Council may, in accordance with the provisions of this Act, issue the certificate to the company in any proper case.

(2) An application may also be made under this section for any industry to be included in the list of pioneer industries and pioneer products.

(3) Any application under this section may be made by a company incorporated in Nigeria, or by a group of persons on behalf of a company which is to be so incorporated.

(4) No application for the issue of a pioneer certificate to any company shall be made under this section unless the estimated cost of qualifying capital expenditure to be incurred by the company on or before production day (if the application is approved) is an amount which –

    (a) in the case of an indigenous-controlled company, is not less than ₦50 000; or

    (b) in the case of any other company, is not less than ₦150 00.

(5) The council may from time to time, on any ground which appears to it sufficient, amend the list of pioneer industries and pioneer products.

(6) Where, in exercise of the powers conferred under subsection (5) of this section, any industry or product is deleted from the list of pioneer industries and pioneer products, then –

    (a) no application under this section shall thereafter be made by any company in relation to that industry or product; and

    (b) as respects any pending application made under subsection (1) of this section, no pioneer certificate shall be issued under this Act to any company in relation to that industry or product.

2 (1) Subject to the provisions of this Act, every application under section 1 of this Act shall be addressed to the Commissioner and shall be in such form as he may from time to time specify.

(2) Every such application shall state the grounds upon which the applicant relies and, if the application is for the issue of a pioneer certificate to any company, the applicant shall –

    (a) state whether the company is, or the proposed company, when incorporated shall be, an indigenous-controlled company;

(*b*) give particulars of the assets on which qualifying capital expenditure will be incurred by the company, including their source and estimated cost –

  (i) on or before production day, and

  (ii) during a period of three years following production day;

(*c*) specify the place in which the assets, in respect of which qualifying expenditure will be incurred by the company or proposed company, are to be situated;

(*d*) estimate and state the probable date of production day of the company or proposed company;

(*e*) specify any product and by-product (not being a pioneer product) proposed to be produced by the company or proposed company, and give a reasonable estimate of the quantities and value of such product and by-product during a period of one year from production day;

(*f*) give particulars of the loan and share capital, or the proposed loan and share capital, of the company, or proposed company, including the amount and date of each issue or proposed issue, and the source from which the capital is to be or less than raised;

(*g*) in the case of a company already incorporated, give the name, address and nationality of each director of the company and the number of shares held by him; and (*h*) in the case of a proposed company, give the name, address and nationality of each promoter of the company.

(3) Every such application shall contain a declaration signed by the applicant that all the particulars contained in the application are true and an undertaking to produce proof, if required, to the satisfaction of the Commissioner, of the truth of any such particulars and of any further particulars which, under subsection (5) below, the Commissioner may require the applicant to furnish.

(4) The application shall be accompanied by a fee of ₦100 (which sum shall not be refundable to the applicant, whether the application is approved or not) and the fee shall be credited to the Consolidated Revenue Fund of the Federation.

(5) Where an application is submitted to the Commissioner under this section he may require the applicant to furnish such further particulars as the Commissioner may consider necessary to enable the Council to consider the application.

(6) As soon as may be after the application is submitted to the Commissioner or, as the case may be, after any further particular required by the Commissioner under subsection (5) above has been furnished to him by the applicant, the Commissioner shall submit the application (together with his observations thereon) to the Council for consolidation and, subject to the provisions of this Act, the Council may approve or disapprove the application.

3 (1) Without prejudice to subsection (3) of this section, every pioneer certificate shall be in the terms of the application to which it relates:

Provided that the Council may make any variation in any such application.

(2) A pioneer certificate may specify any permissible by-product which may be produced by the pioneer company in addition to the pioneer product and, if the Council thinks fit, the pioneer certificate may limit the proportion of the permissible by-product in relation to the pioneer product, either in quantity or in value or both.

(3) Where an application for the issue of a pioneer certificate made on behalf of a proposed company is approved by the Council, it shall –

(a) specify the period within which the company must be incorporated, not being later than four months after the date of notification of the approval to the applicants;

(b) specify any other conditions to be endorsed on the pioneer certificate when it is issued.

(4) Any pioneer certificate to be issued to any company to which subsection (3) relates shall be issued only after the company has been incorporated and the certificate shall be effective from a date not earlier than the date on which the application for the pioneer certificate was submitted to the Commissioner or the date on which the company is so incorporated, whichever is the later, and the Council may require that an undertaking shall be given by the company for the purpose of ensuring the due compliance by the company with any conditions endorsed on its pioneer certificate.

(5) Notice of any condition specified by the Council under subsection (3) of this section, or of any undertaking required under subsection (4) thereof, shall be given by the Commissioner to the applicants concerned.

(6) Notwithstanding anything contained in section 10 of this Act, in any case where a pioneer company –

(a) has acquired or proposes to acquire assets from any company to which a pioneer certificate has been granted under the Aid to Pioneer Industries Act 1952, the Industrial Development (Income Tax Relief) Act or this Act; or

(b) has taken over or proposes to take over the whole assets of any other company which is not a pioneer company,

the pioneer certificate may specify the maximum tax relief period, not exceeding five years, to be enjoyed by the pioneer company.

4 (1) At any time during its tax relief period, a pioneer company may make an application in writing to the Commissioner for its pioneer certificate to be amended by the Council by adding any additional product to the pioneer product or products specified in the certificate.

(2) Every such application shall specify the additional pioneer product and the reasons for the application and, subject as aforesaid, the provisions of subsections (3), (5) and (6) of section 2 of this Act shall apply in relation to an application made under section 1 of this Act.

(3) Where an application under this section is approved by the Council, (with or without variations), it shall amend the pioneer certificate of the pioneer company in such terms and subject to such conditions as the

Council may think fit.

5 (1) Subject to the provisions of section 6 of this Act, where a pioneer certificate is to be operative from a retrospective date, then any act or thing which has been done or which has happened for the purposes of the principal Act since that date but which would not have been done or happened if the pioneer certificate had been in force at that date, shall, whenever necessary for the purposes of this Act and the principal Act, be treated as not having been done or not having happened, and if the act consists of the payment of any tax by a company certified to be a pioneer company, that tax shall, as soon as may be after the expiration of three months from the production day of that company, be repaid to the company by the Board.

6 (1) Not later than one month after the material date a pioneer company shall make an application in writing to the Director to certify the date of its production day and shall propose a date to be so certified and give reasons for proposing that date.

(2) Not later than one month after the production day of a pioneer company has been finally determined and certified under this section, or within such extended time as the Board may allow, a pioneer company shall make an application in writing to the Board to certify the amount of the qualifying capital expenditure incurred by the pioneer company prior to production day and the company shall supply full particualrs of the capital expenditure so incurred.

(3) In determining the amount of qualifying capital expenditure incurred by a pioneer company prior to its production day, any sum derived directly or indirectly by that company from any disposal (made before that day) of any asset on which qualifying capital expenditure has been incurred shall be taken into account for the purpose of reducing the amount of the qualifying capital expenditure; but where the disposal of such asset is by way of bargain not made at arm's length or is to any person who is controlled by the pioneer company or who has control over the pioneer company, the asset shall be deemed to have been disposed of for an amount which in the opinion of the Board the asset would have fetched if sold in the open market at the date of the disposal, less the amount of any expenses which the company might reasonably be expected to incur if the asset were so sold.

(4) After considering any application made under subsection (1) of this section, together with such further information as he may call for, the Director shall issue a certificate to the pioneer company certifying the date of its production day.

(5) After considering any application made under subsection (2) of his section, together with such further information as it may call for, the Board shall issue a certificate to the pioneer company certifying the amount of qualifying capital expenditure incurred by the company prior to production day.

(6) The provisions of Parts X and XI of the principal Act (which relate to objections and appeals) and of any rules made thereunder shall apply, mutatis mutandis, to any certificate issued by the Director or the Board

under this section as if such certificate were a notice of assessment given under the said provisions of the principal Act.

(7) The Director shall notify the Commissioner and the Board of the date of the production day of the pioneer company when the same has been finally determined and certified by the Director.

(8) When the amount of the qualifying capital expenditure incurred by the pioneer company prior to production day has been finally determined and certified by the Board, the Board shall notify the Commissioner of that amount.

(9) On the receipt of the notifications mentioned in subsections (7) and (8) of this section, the Commissioner shall require the pioneer company to declare within a period not exceeding thiry days in what respects the proposals and estimates made in its application for a pioneer certificate, or any conditions contained in its pioneer certificate, have not been fulfilled.

(10) Where a certificate issued by the Director under subsection (4) of this section certifies that the date of the production day of a pioneer company is more than one year later than the estimate thereof given in the company's application for a pioneer certificate, the Commissioner shall report that fact to the Council and the Council shall cancel the pioneer certificate of that company unless it is satisfied that the delay is due to causes outside the control of the company or to other good and sufficient cause.

(11) Where a certificate issued by the Board under subsection (5) of this section certifies that the pioneer company has on or before production day incurred qualifying capital expenditure of an amount which –

(*a*) in the case of an indigenous-controlled company, is less than ₦50 000; or

(*b*) in the case of any other company, is less than ₦150 000.

the Commissioner shall report that fact to the Council and the Council shall cancel the pioneer certificate of the company.

(12) For the purposes of subsection (1) of this section, 'material date' means –

(*a*) in relation to a pioneer company engaged in a pioneer industry consisting of the provision of services, the date on which the company is ready to provide such services on a commercial scale; and

(*b*) in relation to a pioneer company engaged in a manufacturing, processing, mining, agricultural or any other pioneer industry, the date on which the company begins to produce a pioneer product in marketable quantities.

7 (1) The Commissioner shall cancel a pioneer certificate upon the application of the pioneer company concerned.

(2) Subject to the provision of this section and without prejudice to section 6(10) and (11) of this Act, if the Commissioner is of the opinion that a pioneer company has contravened any provision of this Act or has failed to fulfil any estimate or proposal made in its application for a pioneer certificate or any conditions contained in its pioneer certificate, the Commissioner shall report the circumstances to the Council which

may either cancel the pioneer certificate of the company or restrict the tax relief of that company to such period as the Council may, notwithstanding the provisions of section 10 of this Act, consider appropriate.

(3) The effective date of cancellation of a pioneer certificate of a company shall be –

(*a*) where the company has been in operation as a pioneer company for a period less than one year after the pioneer date, the pioneer date, and

(*b*) where the company has been in operation as a pioneer company for a period of not less than one year after the pioneer date, the date of the last anniversary of the pioneer date,

and in this subsection 'the pioneer date' means the date from which a pioneer certificate takes effect.

(4) Where the pioneer certificate of a pioneer company is cancelled or the tax relief period of a company is restricted under subsection (2) of this section, the Commissioner shall give notice of the cancellation (specifying the effective date thereof) or of the restriction, to the pioneer company concerned.

8   When authorised to do so by the Commissioner, an officer of the Federal Ministry of Industries not below the rank of Assistant Secretary may require a pioneer company to give information in sufficient detail to his satisfaction –

(*a*) as to the local production costs and factory prices of the products of the company;

(*b*) in any appropriate case, as to the relative cost (including freight and insurance) of imported products equivalent or similar to the pioneer products produced by the company;

(*c*) as to any other matter which the Commissioner may, in the case of that company, reasonably require for the purposes of this Act.

9   (1) The Commissioner shall cause to be published in the Gazette –

(*a*) the name of any company to which a pioneer certificate has been given and the pioneer industry or pioneer product to which the certificate relates;

(*b*) the name of any company the pioneer certificate of which has been cancelled and the effective date of the cancellation;

(*c*) any restriction of the tax relief period of a pioneer company.

(2) Subject to the provisions of subsection (1) of this section, the contents of any application made, or of any pioneer certificate given, under this Act with respect to a pioneer company shall not, except at the instance of the company, be published in the Gazette or in any other manner.

Income Tax relief

10   (1) The tax relief period of a pioneer company shall commence on the date of the production day of the company, and subject to sections 3(6) and of 7(2) of this Act the tax relief period shall continue for three years.

(2) The tax relief period of pioneer company may at the end of the three years be extended by the Council –

(*a*) for a period of one year and thereafter for another period of one

528

year commencing from the end of the first period of extension; or

(b) for one period of two years.

(3) The Council shall not extend the tax relief period of a pioneer company in exercise of the power conferred under subsection (2) of this section unless the Council is satisfied as to –

(a) the rate of expansion, standard of efficiency and the level of development of the company;

(b) the implementation of any scheme –

(i) for the utilisation of local raw materials in the processes of the company;

(ii) for the training and development of Nigerian personnel in the relevant industry;

(c) the relative importance of the industry in the economy of the country;

(d) the need for the extension, having regard to the location of the industry; and

(e) such other relevant matters as may be required.

(4) A pioneer company wishing to obtain a certificate for the purposes of subsection (2) of this section shall make an application in writing to the Board not later than one month after the expiration of its initial tax relief period of three years or of any extension thereof, and such application shall contain particulars of all capital expenditure incurred by the company by the requisite date which the company claims should be accepted as qualifying capital expenditure.

(5) The Board shall, after considering any application made under subsection (4) of this section together with such information as it may call for, issue a certificate to the company certifying the amount of the qualifying capital expenditure incurred by the company by the requisite date; and section 6(3) of this Act shall apply for the purposes of determining the amount of the qualifying capital expenditure incurred by the requisite date as it applies for the purposes of determining the amount of qualifying capital expenditure incurred prior to a production day as if for the reference in that subsection to the words 'prior to its production day' there were substituted a reference to the words 'by the requisite date.' (6) Where the Board is satisfied that a pioneer company has incurred a loss in any accounting period falling within a tax relief period specified in the foregoing provisions of subsections (1) and (2) of this section, it shall issue a certificate to the company accordingly.

(7) The provisions of Parts X and XI of the principal Act (which relate to objections and appeals) and of any rule made thereunder shall apply, mutatis mutandis, to any certificate given by the Board under the provisions of this section, or any notice of refusal to give a certificate under this section, as if the certificate or the notice of refusal were a notice of assessment given under the said provisions of the principal Act.

(8) In this section 'the requisite date' means the date when a tax relief period expires.

11 Where a trade or business of a pioneer company is carried on by the company before and after the end of its tax relief period, then for the

purposes of the principal Act and this Act –

(*a*) the trade or business of that company shall be deemed to have permanently ceased at the end of the tax relief period of the pioneer company;

(*b*) in respect of that trade or business, the pioneer company shall be deemed to have set up and commenced a new trade or business, on the day next following the end of its tax relief period;

(*c*) the pioneer company shall make up accounts of its old trade or business for the following periods, that is to say –

(i) a period not exceeding one year commencing on its production day;

(ii) successive periods of one year thereafter; and

(iii) a period not exceeding one year ending at the date when its tax relief period (determined under subsections (1) and (2) of section 10 of this Act) ends;

(*d*) in making up the first accounts of its new trade or business the pioneer company shall take as the opening figure for those accounts the closing figures in respect of its assets and liabilities as shown in its last accounts in respect of its tax relief period; and its next accounts of its new trade or business shall be made up by reference to the closing figures in the said first accounts and any subsequent accounts shall be similarly made up by reference to the closing figures of the preceding accounts of its new trade or business.

12 (1) Prior to the expiration of its tax relief period, a pioneer company shall not carry on any trade or business other than a trade or business the whole of the profits of which are derived from its pioneer enterprise.

(2) Where, prior to the expiration of its tax relief period, any profit is earned by a pioneer company from any operations or activities whatsoever other than its pioneer enterprise, the profit shall be deemed, for the purposes of the principal Act, to be derived from Nigeria and shall be liable to tax under that Act.

13 (1) For the purposes of the principal Act, the Board may direct that –

(*a*) any sums payable to a pioneer company in any accounting period which, but for the provisions of this Act, might reasonably and properly have been expected to have been payable in the normal course of business after the end of that period shall be treated as not having been payable in that period but as having been payable on such date after that period as the Board thinks fit, and where such date is after the end of the tax relief period of the pioneer company, as having been so payable on that date as a sum payable in respect of its new trade or business; and

(*b*) any expense incurred by a pioneer company within one year after the end of its tax relief period which, but for the provisions of this Act, might reasonably and properly have been expected to have been incurred in the normal course of business during its tax relief period, shall be treated as not having been incurred within that year but as having been incurred for the purposes of its old trade or business and on such date during its tax relief period as the Board thinks fit.

530

(2) Where a direction has been given under this section with respect to a pioneer company and thereafter the length of the tax relief period of the pioneer company is varied under any of the provisions of this Act, the Board may amend that direction accordingly.

(3) In determining whether a loss has been made in an accounting period for the purpose of section 10(6) of this Act, and for that purpose only, the Board may in its absolute discretion exclude such sum as may be in excess of an amount appearing to the Board to be just and reasonable paid or payable by a pioneer company in respect of –

    (*a*) remuneration to directors of the company;

    (*b*) interest, service, agency or other similar charges made by a person who is a shareholder of the company or by a person controlled by such shareholder.

14 (1) The profits of a pioneer company in respect of its old trade or business falling to be ascertained in accordance with the provisions of the principal Act for any accounting period shall be so ascertained, after making any necessary adjustments in consequence of a direction under section 13 of this Act, without any regard to the provisions of sections 27 and 27A of the principal Act.

(2) Where any asset is used for the purposes of the new trade or business of a pioneer company, any capital expenditure incurred by the pioneer company in respect of that asset before the end of its tax relief period shall, for the purposes of the Third Schedule of the principal Act, be deemed to have been incurred on the day next following the end of its tax relief period.

(3) Where a pioneer company incurs a net loss during an accounting period in its old trade or business that loss shall be deemed for the purposes of computing total profits (but not profits) to have been incurred by the company on the day on which its new trade or business commences.

(4) For each accounting period the Board shall issue to the pioneer company a statement showing the amount of income ascertained under subsection (1) of this section or loss computed in accordance with subsection (3) thereof; and the provisions of Parts X and XI of the principal Act (which relate to objections and appeals) and of any rules made thereunder shall apply, mutatis mutandis, to the statement as if such statement were a notice of assessment given under the said provisions of the principal Act.

(5) For the purposes of subsection (3) of this section, 'net loss' means the aggregate of losses incurred during the tax relief period after deduction of profits, if any, made at any time during that period; and a loss shall be computed in the same manner as profits are computed under the provision of subsection (1) of this section and without regard to the provisions of section 13 (3) of this Act.

15 The provisions of Part IX of the principal Act shall apply in all respects to the profits of a pioneer company from its old trade or business as if those profits were chargeable to tax under that Act.

16 (1) Subject to the provisions of subsection (2) of this section and section

17(6) of this Act where in the application of Parts X and XI of the principal Act, a statement issued under section 14(4) of this Act has become final and conclusive, any profits shown by that statement shall not form part of the assessable profits or total profits of the pioneer company for any year of assessment and shall be exempt from tax under the principal Act,

(2) The Board may, in relation to any statement issued under section 14 (4) of this Act, declare that the whole or a specified part of the profits is not in dispute, and any such undisputed profits shall be exempt from tax under the principal Act pending the statement becoming final and conclusive,

17 (1) Wherever any amount of profits of a pioneer company is exempt from tax under section 16 of this Act, that amount shall immediately be credited by the pioneer company to an account to be kept by it for the purposes of this section.

(2) Where at the date of payment of any dividends by the pioneer company the said account is in credit, the dividends, or so much of the dividends where (after the end of its tax relief period) the amount thereof exceeds such credit as equals the amount of such credit, shall be debited to the account.

(3) So much of the amount of any dividends so debited to the account as are received by a shareholder in the pioneer company shall, if the Board is satisfied with the entries in the account, be exempt from tax in the hands of that shareholder and shall for the purposes of the principal Act and the Income Tax Management Act 1961 be deemed to be paid out of the profits on which tax is not paid or payable.

(4) Any dividends so debited to the account shall be treated as having been distributed to the shareholders or any particular class of shareholders of the pioneer company in the same proportions as those shareholders were entitled to payment of the dividends giving rise to the debit.

(5) Whenever called upon so to do by notice in writing sent by the Board to the registered office of a pioneer company, the company shall, until such time as the Board is satisfied that there is no further need for maintaining the account, deliver to the Board a copy of the account made up to a date specified by the Board in the notice.

(6) Notwithstanding the provisions of section 16 of this Act and of this section, where it appears to the relevant tax authority that any amount of exempted profits of a pioneer company, or any dividend exempted in the hands of a shareholder, ought not to have been exempted by reason of –

(a) a direction under section 13 of this Act having been made with respect to a pioneer company, after any profits of that company has been exempted under the provisions of section 16 of this Act; or

(b) the cancellation of a pioneer certificate,

the relevant tax authority may at any time within six years of the direction or cancellation make such additional assessment upon the pioneer company or shareholder as may appear to the relevant tax authority necessary in order to counteract any benefit obtained from the amount which ought not to have been exempted.

(7) For the purposes of subsection (6) of this section 'relevant tax authority' has the same meaning as in section 2 of the Income Tax Management Act 1961, and in relation to any additional assessment to be made on a company under the said subsection (6) it means the Board.

18　During its tax relief period a pioneer company shall not –

(*a*) make any distribution to its shareholders, by way of dividend or bonus, in excess of the amount by which the account, to be kept by the company under section 17 of this Act, is in credit at the date of any such distribution; or

(*b*) grant any loan without first obtaining the consent of the Commissioner, whose consent shall only be given if he is satisfied that the pioneer company is obtaining adequate security and a reasonable rate of interest for any such loan.

19　A pioneer company shall not be entitled to any relief under section 33 of the principal Act.

20　For the purposes of the principal Act and this Act, the trade of a company which operates a plantation and to which a pioneer certificate has been granted shall be deemed to have commenced on the date when planting first reaches maturity, and any expenditure incurred on the maintenance of a planted area up to that date shall be deemed to have brought into existence an asset and the expenditure shall be qualifying plantation expenditure for the purposes of the Third Schedule of the prinicipal Act.

Miscellaneous and general

21　(1) Any person who for the purpose of obtaining a pioneer certificate or of complying with any provisions of this Act –

(*a*) makes or presents any declaration or statement which is false in any material particular; or

(*b*) produces any invoice or undertaking which is false in any material particular or has not been given by the person by whom it purports to have been given or which has been in any way altered or tampered with, shall be guilty of an offence under this section unless he proves that he has taken all reasonable steps to ascertain the truth of the statement made or contained in any document so presented or produced or to satisfy himself of the genuineness of the invoice or undertaking.

(2) Any person who is guilty of an offence under this section shall be liable on conviction to a fine not exceeding ₦1000 or to imprisonment for five years or to both such fine and imprisonment.

22　Where an offence under this Act is committed by a body corporate, or firm or other association of individuals –

(*a*) every director, manager, secretary or other similar officer of the body corporate;

(*b*) every partner or officer of the firm;

(*c*) every person concerned in the management of the affairs of the association; or

(*d*) every person who was purporting to act in any such capacity as aforesaid,

shall severally be guilty of that offence and liable to be prosecuted and punished for the offence in like manner as if he had himself committed the offence, unless the act or omission constituting the offence took place without his knowledge, consent or connivance.

23 The institution of proceedings for, or imposition of, a fine or term of imprisonment under this Act shall not relieve any person from liability to payment of any sum for which he is or may be liable under any undertaking given by him under any provision of this Act.

24 (1) Subject to the provisions of this section, the Industrial Development (Income Tax Relief) Act is hereby repealed.

(2) Subject as aforesaid, and notwithstanding the provisions of section 6 of the Interpretation Act 1964 (which relates to the effect of repeals) any pioneer certificate given under the Industrial Development (Income Tax Relief) Act (hereafter in this section referred to as the 'repealed Act') by which an industry was declared to be a pioneer industry or a company was declared to be a pioneer company (being a certificate which was in force immediately before the relevant date), shall from that date have effect as if it were a pioneer certificate issued under this Act.

(3) Where any part of an initial tax relief period of two years granted to a company before the relevant date under the repealed Act has not expired at the relevant date and the qualifying capital expenditure incurred by the company concerned on or before its production day is –

(*a*) in the case of an indigenous-controlled company, not less than ₦50 000; or

(*b*) in the case of any other company, not less than ₦150 000, the initial tax relief period shall be construed as if that period were three years instead of two years; and thereafter an application may be made by the company for an extension of the tax relief period under section 10(2) of this Act.

(4) Where, in any case other than a case mentioned in subsection (3) of this section, a pioneer certificate granted under the repealed Act to any company is in force immediately before the relevant date, the company may, on or before the expiry date of its pioneer certificate or tax relief period, apply under the provisions of section 10(2) of this Act for an extension of its tax relief period; and the provisions of section 1(4) of this Act shall apply in relation to any application under this section as it applies in relation to an application under section 1 of this Act for the issue of a pioneer certificate.

(5) A further tax relief period may be granted under section 10(2) of this Act, to a pioneer company to which subsection (3) or (4) of this section applies, but nothing in this section shall have effect or be construed so as to authorise the grant, in any such case, of a tax relief period (under the repealed Act and this Act) in excess of five years from the production date of the pioneer company.

(6) Notwithstanding anything in this section the Council may amend or cancel any pioneer certificate to which subsections (2), (3), (4) or (5) of this section applies.

(7) Where an application for a pioneer certificate made under the repealed Act is pending on the relevant date, the provisions of section 2 of this Act shall apply thereto as if the application had been made under this Act, and the Commissioner may –

(a) require the applicant to furnish any particulars, or enter into any undertaking, which if the application had been made under this Act, would have been required to be included in the application or to be given in respect thereto;

(b) require the applicant to pay the fee prescribed under the said section 2, before the application is proceeded with under this Act.

(7A) Where an application for a pioneer certificate made under the repealed Act has been approved by the Federal Executive Council but no pioneer certificate had been issued in respect thereof any certificate issued thereafter shall be deemed to have been in force immediately before the relevant date and effect shall be given thereto as if it were a pioneer certificate issued under that Act.

25 (1) In this Act, except where the context otherwise requires, the following expressions have the meanings hereby assigned to them respectively, that is to say –

'accounting period' means a period for which accounts have been made up in accordance with paragraph (c) of section 11 of this Act;

'Board' means the Federal Board of Inland Revenue established under section 3 of the principal Act;

'company' means a company (other than a private company) limited by shares and incorporated and registered in Nigeria and resident in Nigeria;

'the Council' means the Federal Executive Council;

'the Commissioner' means the Federal Commissioner for Industries;

'the Director' means the director appointed pursuant to section 1(3) of the Industrial Inspectorate Act 1970;

'Gazette' means the Federal Gazette and includes the Gazette of any State in the Federation;

'new trade or business' means the trade or business of a pioneer company deemed under the provisions of section 11 of this Act to have been set up and commenced on the day following the end of its tax relief period;

'old trade or business' means the trade or business of a pioneer company carried on by it during its tax relief period in accordance with the provisions of section 11 of this Act and which either ceases within that period or is deemed, under those provisions, to cease at the end of that period;

"permissible by-product" means any goods or services so described in any certificate given under section 1 of this Act being goods or services necessarily or ordinarily produced in the course of producing a pioneer product;

'pioneer certificate' means a certificate given under this Act certifying, among other things, a company to be a pioneer company, or any such certificate as amended under this Act;

'pioneer company' means a company certified by any pioneer certificate to be a pioneer company;

'pioneer enterprise', in relation to a pioneer company, means the production and sale of its relevant pioneer product or products;

'pioneer industry' means any trade or business of the kind included in any list published under section 1 of this Act;

"pioneer product" means goods or service of the kind included in any list published under section 1 of this Act;

'principal Act' means the Companies Income Tax Act 1961;

'production day' means the day on which the trade or business of a pioneer company commences for the purposes of the principal Act;

'qualifying capital expenditure' means capital expenditure of such a nature as to rank as qualifying expenditure for the purposes of the Third Schedule of the principal Act;

'relevant pioneer product', in relation to any pioneer company, means the pioneer product or products and the permissible by-product or products specified in its pioneer certificate; and

'tax relief period' means the period specified under subsection (1) of section 10 of this Act and any extension of that period made under that section.

(2) References in this Act to an indigenous-controlled company are references to any company in which –

(a) the beneficial ownership of the whole of the equity capital of the company and of all other class of shares conferring voting rights in the company is vested in persons who are citizens of Nigeria, otherwise than by naturalization or registration; and

(b) the persons mentioned in paragraph (a) of this subsection control the composition of the board of directors of the company.

(3) Nothing in this Act shall be taken as prejudicing the effect of section 3 of the Industrial Inspectorate Act 1970 (which relates to notice of intention to incur capital expenditure) or any other provision of that Act.

26 (1) This Act may be cited as the Industrial Development (Income Tax Relief) Act 1971 and shall be read as one with the principal Act.

(2) This Act shall be deemed to have come into force on 1st April 1970 and shall apply throughout the Federation.

Supplement (1985)

The Finance (Miscellaneous Taxation Provisions) Decree 1985 otherwise known as Decree No.4 published in the *Federal Gazette* No. 16 Vol.72 of 22 March 1985 introduced new dimensions to the Nigeria tax system.

The new decree, which came into effect on 21 March 1985, seeks to serve four purposes:

(1) to enable tax to be payable on interests accruing to a foreign company or persons regardless of whichever way the interest might have accrued:

(2) to stipulate circumstances for which tax is payable to the taxing authorities in respect of interest, dividends and rents;

(3) to substitute new tables for capital allowances allowable under the 1965 Act, and

(4) to amend the Companies Income Tax Act, 1961 and to prescribe among other things, types of transactions for which tax clearance certificates are applicable and to formalise tax measures and incentives.

The current rate which allows for a personal allowances of ₦1200 for earned income of ₦6000 and below, and additional allowance of $12\frac{1}{2}$ per cent in addition to ₦1200 for earned income in excess of ₦6000 is inadequate. This feeble change in personal taxation had ignored the effect of increased disposable income in the hands of consumers, the relationship between high level of taxation on management and the innovative efforts of management personnel.

Earned income is defined to include income from trade, business, employment, profession or vocation, but does not include ordinarily such incomes as rents, dividends, interest or royalties except such incomes as are deemed to fall under business or trading profits, by a relevant tax authority.

Criticisms centred on tax deductions on interest and dividends, payment of corporate tax on profits, restrictions on capital allowances, withholding tax on investment by pensions funds, Capital Gains Tax and the Unit Trust schemes. Due to the prevalent economic downturn, the decree should have aimed at stimulating capital formation by reducing taxes on interests rather than increasing it to 15 per cent. More taxes had the tendency of dampening investment especially from the angle of the foreign entrepreneur who is subjected to bigger taxation on dividends. The result of increased taxation on dividends is the emergence of ambivalent business tycoons who shy away from direct manufacturing and would rather operate as middlemen and manufacturer's agents. These would assume strategic but unspecified tax positions that enable them to maximise profits at maximum losses to the nation.

Withholding of 15 per cent tax on dividends should become either a more flexible instrument or in the alternative, dividend restraint of 60 per cent should be eliminated to encourage investment. To encourage businessmen to go into manufacturing, it is suggested that a distinction be made between companies already in operation without pioneer status and those already in industry.

The decree made only a feeble change in personal taxation in relation to personal allowance. Under the new arrangement there is a personal income allowance for ₦1200 for persons earning up to ₦6000. After ₦6000 $12\frac{1}{2}$ per cent is chargeable on any excess income earned.

What the state governments should do is to improve their tax collection machinery to increase their tax revenue. The case of *Alhaji S.A. Adetunji v Director of Internal Revenue of Oyo State* Suit No. 1/293/84, High Court No.3 Ibadan (unreported) who was alleged to have paid ₦15, ₦25 and ₦35 tax for the years 1979–80, 1980–81 and 1981–82 during the 1984 Currency Exchange exercise which revealed that he deposited ₦236 700 (his legitimate earnings) with the Central Bank is an eye-opener. Surprisingly the 'accused' became the accuser, as it was the taxpayer who sued the Director of Internal Revenue.

The new Decree tends to give free income to some management consultants, be it company or individual, who are able to obtain the Minister's consent. Before the Decree, expenses incurred in obtaining management fees were not allowable deductions. Any management consultant takes care of his expenses in charging his fees and also has a comfortable margin of profit. Expenses incurred in obtaining management fees are not necessarily the same with the running cost of his trade, business or profession, it is allowed.

One's fear here is that the government is likely to collect less revenue, more so when those who are likely to obtain the Minister's approval are the management consultants to big projects worth millions of Naira. Let us now look at it critically. Once the agreement giving rise to such management fees has the consent of the Minister, then management expenses could be claimed. At the time, such agreement would be tendered before the Minister, the management fee would be an estimate giving (+) or (–) 5% for unforeseen circumstances. How would the Revenue Authority be able to control these expenses?

For instance a government contract is awarded to ABC Ltd (a foreign company) to construct a plant worth ₦200 million. The company employs the services of Messrs Oz & Co. Ltd. Management fee is agreed at 5% of the contract price which is ₦10 million over the period of the contract. The company incurs, over the years, ₦5 million management expenses outside Nigeria and ₦3 million within Nigeria. Apart from these expenses other allowable expenses amount to ₦1.5 million. The taxable profit would then be:

Management fees		₦10 000 000
Less management expenses:		
Outside Nigeria	₦5 000 000	
Within Nigeria	3 000 000	8 000 000
		2 000 000
Less other allowables		1 500 000
Taxable profit		500 000
Tax thereon at 45%		₦225 000

The Government would have to be extremely careful in implementing this provision of the new Decree as there could be a very high loss of revenue. What happened in the past with government contract awards still applies today when foreign companies would ensure that permission is sought to exempt them from paying local taxes. Those who do not obtain approval include the taxes to be paid as part of the contract price, and there is no way the Revenue Authority could know that the contract price is thus inflated.

It could be suggested that at the time the approval for the management fee is to be sought, expenses should be laid down such that it could be fairly estimated and the question of whether those expenses would be exclusively, wholly, reasonably and necessarily incurred in the performance of the management service has to be determined.

Before the Decree the tax collectible on the above contract would have been:

Management fees	₦10 000 000
Less allowable expenses	1 500 000
	8 500 000
Tax thereon at 45%	3 825 000

From the above, the government would be losing ₦3 600 000, on one company alone. This new provision would be subject to abuses unless there is a formula for determining expenses to be allowed as management expenses.

Deduction at source: General

Going through the amendments, it is clear that the Decree now gives the Federal Board of Inland Revenue a wide power to deduct tax at source on payments made to any company or class of companies. The rate of tax was not fixed by the Decree but the Board has the discretionary power to fix such rate by taking into account:

(a) assessable profits of the company for the year arising from any other source chargeable to Income Tax under the Act,

(b) any Income Tax or arrears of tax payable by that company for any of the six preceding years of assessment.

Such discretionary power, if not properly laid out, may cause confusion rather than solve the problem. The company or companies which may fall under this provision must be clearly defined. In the past, there was a provision of $2\frac{1}{2}$ per cent on turnover (now repealed) on construction/building industry and there was much confusion as to which class of companies fell within this classification. One hopes that regulations for operating this provision would made public very soon to assist both taxpayers and the Federal Board of Inland Revenue.

Amendment of the Capital Gains Tax legislation as incorporated in the Finance (Miscellaneous Taxation Provisions) Decree, 1985 is overdue. This is to off-set capital losses against capital gains and consequently to reduce the amount of Capital Gains Tax payable in addition to aiding the development of the securities market. The existing tax legislation causes investors who foresee that a transaction might result in capital loss to hold on to their stocks.

Tax deduction from dividends

The law on dividends is governed by sections 10, 12 and 21 of the Income Tax Management Act, 1961 as amended by sections 5 and 11 of the Finance (Miscellaneous Taxation Provisions) Decree, 1985 otherwise known as Decree No. 4. Section 10 states:

The income from a dividend paid by a Company other than a Nigerian Company, or from any other source outside Nigeria, shall be the amount of that income brought into or received in Nigeria;

Provided that –

(i) if the income arose in a country to which section 23 dealing with double taxation in foreign tax applies the amount of that income to be taken for assessment shall be the amount thereof so brought into or received in Nigeria increased by the appropriate amount of any foreign tax relative thereto;

(ii) if the income arose in a country to which section 24 dealing with double taxation or foreign tax applies, the amount of that income to be taken for assessment shall be the amount computed under subsection (5) of section 25;

The Law, under Section 11 of Finance (Miscellaneous Taxation Provision) Decree, 1985 is now as follows:

(1) where any dividend or such other distribution becomes due from or payable by a Nigerian Company to any person, the company making such payment shall, at the date when the amount is paid or created whichever first occurs, deduct therefrom tax at the rate prescribed under subsection (2) of this section and shall forthwith pay over to the relevant tax authority the amount deducted.

(2) The rate at which tax is to be deducted in this section shall be 15 per cent.

(3) In accounting for the tax so deducted to the relevant tax authority, the company shall state in writing the following particulars that is to say –

(a) the gross amount of the dividend or such other distribution;

(b) the name and address of the recipient;

(c) the accounting period or periods of the company in respect of the profits out of which the dividend or distribution is declared to be payable and the date on which payment is due; and

(d) the amount of tax so deducted.

While the government encourages companies investing in shares such as Unit Trusts, it at the same time discourages individuals from making such investments within the present Decree. For companies, the tax law now recognises dividend income as franked investment income once the 15% tax deduction has been made. This means that the income would not suffer further tax. In the past, such income would suffer 45% tax. The company is also allowed to offset tax suffered at source when such income is redistributed.

An individual, on the other hand, can pay as high as 70% tax on dividend income received although only 15% would be deducted at source. Assume an executive director of a company with a total salary of ₦40 000 and other fringe benefits worth ₦10 000 receives dividend of ₦1000 from his investment in YZ Ltd.

His total income, exclusive of his dividend income, is ₦50 000. Assuming his personal reliefs come to ₦15 000, his taxable income would be ₦35 000 and ₦5000 of this amount would be taxed at 70%. The dividend income would fall into the higher bracket. The individual would now pay 85% (i.e. ₦850) of the dividend income since dividend income is not regarded as franked investment income and there is no provision in the Act allowing the individual to off-set the tax deducted at source from his total tax liability. In this regard the new tax law is not explicit enough.

541

Foreign investors' dividends

For foreign investors, the 15 per cent tax on dividend, interest, rent or royalty is taken as final tax.

With regard to personal income tax, the 15 per cent tax is not final tax. As an illustration, X has investments in several areas, he pays the initial tax of 15 per cent at the various sources at which such investments are made. After this, he pools his income from these sources together and pays another income tax on the basis of his total income. The initial tax is to facilitate collection of tax and to minimise tax evasion.

However, this is not so with the foreign investor who gets away with just the 15 per cent as the final tax. This move will also encourage foreign investors.

Franked investments

The law now recognises franked investments. This means that if for instance a company has invested in some other companies (either by way of share purchase or otherwise), it is not expected to pay tax on income from that source provided that the company in which the investment was made, has paid the 45 per cent tax on the portion to be distributed as dividend and withholding tax. Once such payments have been made in the company or source of investments, such income is referred to as franked investment which is not subject to further tax.

This had in the past hindered the development of specialised institutions such as Unit Trusts, and investment societies, which had hitherto been facing the problem of multiple taxation.

Franked investments now pay limited liability companies but not individuals, as dividends received by one company from another company will suffer withholding tax of 15% in the hands of the paying company, while no tax will be paid by the receiving company. This is not the case in respect of individuals who have to aggregate such incomes with their global income and pay additional tax.

Where franked investment income is again distributed and tax is to be accounted for on the gross amount, the company may off-set the withholding tax which it has suffered on the same income. Failure to account for the withholding tax to the Board with attract a ₦5000 fine in addition to the deducted tax and interest at prevailing commercial rate.

Rent

Section 21c of ITMA 1961 as amended by section 11 of the 1985 Decree states:

(1) Where any rent becomes due or payable to any person, the payer of such rent shall at the date when the rent is paid or credited, whichever first occurs, deduct therefrom tax at the rate prescribed in subsection (2) of this section and shall forthwith pay over to the relevant tax authority the amount so deducted.

(2) The rate at which tax is to be deducted for the purpose of this section shall be 15 per cent of gross rent.

(3) In accounting for the tax so deducted to the relevant tax authority, the payer shall state in writing the following particulars which shall accompany the remittance, that is to say –

(a) the gross amount of the rent
(b) the amount of tax being accounted for
(c) the name and address of the recipient and the period for which the rent has been paid or credited and
(d) the address or accurate description of the location of the property concerned.

(4) For the purpose of this section, the relevant tax authority shall be determined in accordance with the provisions of section 2 of this Act.

(5) The 'payer of such rent' in subsection (1) above refers to any Company (corporate or unincorporate) including Government, Ministries and departments, parastatals, statutory bodies, institutions and other established organisations approved for the operation of Pay As You Earn system whether it is or is not liable itself to tax under any enactment or law relating to taxation of income in Nigeria or elsewhere.

The new Decree has removed the obstacle experienced by individual rentpayers previously, for in the past all individuals were expected to deduct tax at source including the payer of ₦10 per month for a single room.

The State Internal Revenue has no statutory power to collect money at source on rent from a tenant who has not been defined as 'a payer'. The Revenue has to wait till the individual landlords submit their returns, in order to assess them accordingly. One notices therefore that the Amendment Decree should have merely shifted responsibility from the tenants to the landlords as the majority of tenants are not defined as 'payer', knowing full well that the level of voluntary compliance is very low in Nigeria. Hence the removal of the statutory power would cause loss of revenue to the State Internal Revenues.

One suggestion is that the Federal Inland Revenue Department should now liaise with State Internal Revenue where a company pays rent to individuals. The Federal Inland Revenue Department may assess the company and credit the money so collected to the State Internal Revenue concerned. The administration of this type of taxes cannot be left in the hands of the payer of such rent alone for effectiveness.

Interest and royalties

Section 11 of Finance (Miscellanous Taxation Provision) Decree, 1985 amends the ITMA 1961, creating Section 21D which states as follows:

(1) Where any payment such as interest or royalty becomes due or payable to any person, the payer at the date when the payments is made or credited whichever occurs first, shall deduct therefrom tax at the rate prescribed in section (2) of this section and shall forthwith pay over to the relevant tax authority the amount so deducted.

(2) The rate at which tax is to be deducted for the purpose of this section shall be 15 per cent of gross interest or royalty.

(3) In accounting for the tax so deducted to the relevant tax authority, the payer shall state in writing the following particulars, that is to say –
(a) the gross amount of the payment;
(b) the name and address of the recipient; and
(c) the amount of tax being accounted for.

(4) For the purpose of this section the relevant tax authority shall be determined in accordance with the provisions of section 2 of this Act.

(5) The 'payer' in subsection (1) above refers to any company (corporate or unincorporate) including Government Ministries and departments, parastatals, statutory bodies, institutions and other established organisations approved for the operation of the Pay As You Earn system whether or not liable itself to tax under any enactment or law relating to taxation of Income in Nigeria or elsewhere.

(6) The provisions of this section shall not apply to any person engaged in banking business in Nigeria including any person charged with the administration of the Federal Saving Bank.

Interest on money loaned by foreign individuals

See section 11 of the Income Tax Management Act, 1961, as amended by the Finance (Miscellaneous Taxation Provisions) Decree, 1985, otherwise known as Decree No. 4 of 1985 dealing with interest on money loaned by a foreign individual states:

'The income from any interest on money lent by an individual, or an executor, or a trustee, outside Nigeria to a person in Nigeria including a person who is resident or present in Nigeria at the time of the loan shall be deemed to be derived from Nigeria if –
(1) There is a liability to payment in Nigeria of the interest regardless of what form the payment takes and whenever the payment is made.
(2) The interest accrues in Nigeria to a foreign company or person regardless of whichever way the interest may have accrued.

Withholding tax on rent, interest, dividends and royalties

Introduction

Payers of rent, interest, dividends and royalties are authorised to withhold an initial tax of 15 per cent of such payments. However, this involves only companies paying to companies, parastatals or to individuals. It does not extend from individual to individual or individual to company. The reason for the exemption is that an attempt to execute the provision in the case of individual to individual payments could lead to abuse, pandemonium and bloodshed. The rent position is already bad and the nuisance value of the new provision may be too heavy on Nigerians.

In the case of interest, no tax is payable on interest earned on savings and bank deposits – a move that will encourage the savings habit among Nigerians.

In a move to encourage lending to the export manufacturing sub-sector, the new law has exempted interest earned by banks on loans to this section from being taxed. The export manufacturing sector is one of the preferred sectors in the Central Bank of Nigeria credit guidelines for 1985.

By the new provision, while recipients of such loans enjoy favourable terms, and the lending banks are compensated by their not paying any tax on the interest accruing therefrom. Although this move is seen as an indirect subsidy and encouragement for exports, one wonders if it will not be more beneficial to exclude export manufacture from paying excise duty. Some countries wanting to boost their export trade are known to have adopted this approach.

Sections 21 c, d, e, of ITMA 1961 have been amended to ensure that a withholding tax of 15 per cent is deducted at source whenever any payments of interests, royalties, rents and dividends are made or credited to any person which ever first occurs by recognised payer. For the purposes of this exercise, a payer includes any company (corporate or unincorporate) government ministries and departments, parastatals, statutory bodies, institutions and other established organisations approved for the operation of PAYE.

In the case of interest payments, banks are expected to continue with the present practice of notifying tax authorities of the names and addresses of recipients of interest on savings and deposits over ₦30. The interests which the banks themselves earn from customers are regarded as part of the profits of the banks and need not be subjected to a withholding tax.

The tax clearance certificate

The history of the tax clearance certificate, now adopted throughout Nigeria, began with the memoranda submitted by C.S. Ola (the former Commissioner of Internal Revenue in the former Western Nigeria) to the Cabinet Committee of the former Western State of Nigeria in 1974 under the Military Governor C.O. Rotimi.

Section 13 of the Finance (Miscellaneous Taxation Provision) Decree, 1985 which creates a new section 33 to the ITMA 1961, as amended states:

Whenever a tax authority is of the opinion that tax assessed on the income of any person has been fully paid or that tax is due on such income, it shall issue within a reasonable time a tax clearance certificate to the person whenever such certificate is demanded by that person.

Any Ministry, department or agency of Government or any company with whom any person has any dealing with respect to any of the transactions mentioned in subsection (4) of this section shall demand from such person a tax clearance certificate for the three years immediately preceding the current year of assessment.

A tax clearance certificate shall disclose in respect of the last three years of assessment:

(a) chargeable income;
(b) tax payable;
(c) tax paid;
(d) tax outstanding or alternatively a statement to the effect that no tax is due.

The provisions of subsection (2) of this section shall apply in relation to the following, that is:-

(a) application for government loan for industry or business;
(b) registration of motor vehicles;
(c) application for firearms licence;
(d) application for foreign exchange or exchange control permission to remit funds outside Nigeria;
(e) application for certificate of occupancy;
(f) application for award of contracts by government, its agencies and registered companies;
(g) application for approval of building plans;
(h) application for trade licence;
(i) application for transfer of real property;
(j) application for import or export licence;
(k) application for plot of land;
(l) application for buying agent licence;
(m) application for pools or gaming licence;
(n) application for registration as a contractor;
(o) application for distributorship;
(p) confirmation of appointment by Government as Chairman or members of public board, institution, commission, company or to any other similar position made by the Government;
(q) stamping of guarantor's form for Nigerian passport;
(r) application for registration of a limited liability company or of a business name;
(s) application for allocation of market stalls.

An applicant for exchange control permission to remit funds to a non-resident recipient in respect of income accruing from rent, dividend, interest, royalty, fees or any other similar income shall be required to produce a tax clearance certificate to the effect that tax has been paid on the fund in respect of which the application is sought or that no tax is payable whichever is the case.

When a person who has deducted any tax pursuant to the provisions of the Act fails to pay the tax so deducted to the appropriate tax authority, no tax clearance certificate may be issued to that person even if he has fully discharged his own tax liability under this Act.

Penalty for failure to deduct tax

Section 11 of the 1985 Decree, creating section 21F to the ITMA Act 1961, as amended stipulates:

'Any person who being obliged to deduct any tax under section 21C, 21D, or 21F of this Act fails to deduct or having deducted fails to pay to the relevant tax authority within 30 days from the date the amount was deducted or the time the duty to deduct arose, shall be guilty of an offence and shall be liable on conviction to a fine of ₦5000 in addition to the amount of tax deducted plus interest at the prevailing commercial rate'.

Withholding tax from interest, royalty and rent (section 59)

Section 59 of the Companies Act 1979 as amended by section 32 of the 1985 Decree, reads:

(1) Where any interest or royalty becomes due from one company to another company or to any person to whom the provisions of the Income Tax (Armed Forces and other Persons) (Special Provisions) Act 1972 apply, the company making such payment shall, at the date when payment is made or credited, whichever first occurs, deduct therefrom tax at the rate prescribed in subsection (2) of this section and shall forthwith pay over to the Board the amount so deducted.

(2) The rate at which tax is to be deducted in this section shall be 15 per cent.

(3) For the purposes of this section, persons authorised to deduct tax include government departments, parastatals, statutory bodies, institutions and other establishments approved for the operation of Pay As You Earn system.

(4) The tax, when paid over to the Board, shall be the final tax due from a non-resident recipient of the payment.

(5) In accounting for the tax as deducted to the Board, the company shall state in writing the following particulars, that is to say –

  (a) the gross amount of the interest or royalty;
  (b) the name and address of the recipient; and
  (c) the amount of tax being accounted for.

Section 33 of the Decree creates new sections 59A, B and C in CITA 1979. Section 59A reads:

(1) Where any rent becomes due from or payable by one company to another company or to any person to whom the provisions of the Income Tax (Armed Forces and Other Persons) (Special Provisions) Act 1972 apply, the company paying such rent shall, at the

date when the rent is paid or credited, whichever first occurs, deduct therefrom tax at the rate prescribed under subsection (2) of this section and shall forthwith pay over to the Board the amount so deducted.

(2) The rate at which tax is to be deducted under this section shall be 15 per cent.

(3) For the purposes of this section, persons authorised to deduct tax include government departments, parastatals, statutory bodies, institutions and other establishments approved for the operation of Pay As You Earn system.

(4) The tax, when paid over to the Board, shall be the final tax due from a non-resident recipient of the payment.

(5) In accounting for the tax so deducted to the Board, the company shall state in writing the following particulars, that is to say –
   (a) the gross amount of the rent payable per annum;
   (b) the name and address of the recipient and period in respect of which such rent has been paid or credited;
   (c) the address and accurate description of the property concerned; and
   (d) the amount of tax being accounted for.

Tax on interest does not apply to those engaged in banking business in Nigeria.

Withholding tax on dividend

Section 59B of Companies Income Tax Act 1979 reads:

(1) Where any dividend or such other distribution becomes due from or payable by a Nigerian company to any other company or to any person to whom the provisions of the Income Tax (Armed Forces and Other Persons) (Special Provisions) Act 1972 apply, the company paying such dividend or making such distribution shall, at the date when the amount is paid or credited whichever first occurs, deduct therefrom tax at the rate prescribed under subsection (2) of this section and shall forthwith pay over to the Board the amount so deducted.

(2) The rate at which tax is to be deducted under this section shall be 15 per cent.

(3) Dividend received after deduction of tax prescribed in this section shall be regarded as franked investment income of the company receiving the dividend and shall not be charged to further tax as part of the profits of a recipient company. However, where such income is redistributed and tax is to be accounted for the gross amount of the distribution in accordance with subsection (1) above, the company may off-set the with-holding tax which it has itself suffered on the same income.

(4) The tax, when paid over to the Board, shall be the final tax due from a non-resident recipient of the payment.

(5) In accounting for the tax so deducted to the Board, the company shall state in writing the following particulars, that is to say –
   (a) the gross amount of the dividend or such other distribution;
   (b) the name and address of the recipient;
   (c) the accounting period or periods of the company in respect of the profits out of which the dividend or distribution is declared to be payable and the date on which payment is due; and
   (d) the amount of tax so deducted.

This provision does not extend to individuals and as it is not prudent for an individual to own large shareholdings in profitable ventures.

Deduction of tax at source

Section 59C reads:

(1) Income tax assessable on any company whether or not an assessment has been made, shall, if the Board so directs, be recoverable from any payments made by any person to such company.

(2) Any such direction may apply to any person or class of persons specified in such direction, either with respect to all companies or a company or class of companies, liable to payment of income tax;

(3) Any direction under subsection (1) shall be in writing addressed to the person or be published in the *Gazette* and shall specify the nature of payments and the rate at which tax is to be deducted.

(4) In determining the rate of tax to be applied to any payments made to a company, the Board may take into account –

    (a) any assessable profits of that company for the year arising from any other source chargeable to income tax under this Act; and

    (b) any income tax or arrears of tax payable by that company for any of the six preceding years of assessment.

(5) Income tax recovered under the provisions of this section by deduction from payments made to a company shall be set-off for the purposes of collection against tax charged on such company by any assessment, but only to the extent that the total of such deductions does not exceed the amount of the assessment.

(6) Every person required under any provisions of this Act to make any deduction from payments made to any company shall account to the Board in such manner as the Board may prescribe for the deduction so made.

(7) The Minister of Finance on the advice of the Board may make regulations for the carrying out of the provisions of this section.

Penalty for failure to deduct tax

S.59D reads:

Any person who being obliged to deduct any tax under section 59, 59A or 59C of this Act fails to deduct or having deducted fails to pay to the Board within 30 days from the date the amount was deducted or the time the duty to deduct arose, shall be guilty of an offence and shall be liable on conviction to a fine of ₦5000 in addition to the amount of tax deducted plus interest at the prevailing commercial rate.

Tax deducted at source

Further to section 33 of the Finance (Miscellaneous Taxation Provisions) Decree No. 4 of 1985, the Federal Ministry of Finance has released the rate at which tax payment for some activities are to be deducted at source from companies, government ministries and departments, parastatals, statutory bodies, institutions and other establishments approved for the operation of Pay As You Earn scheme.

The notice, which took effect from 14 May 1985, stated that any person from whom any payments are due is required to deduct the accompanying tax in respect of the following activities.

Activities	Rate at which tax is to be deducted
All aspects of building construction and related activities	$2\frac{1}{2}$ per cent
All types of contracts other than sale and purchase of goods and property	$2\frac{1}{2}$ per cent
Consultancy services	10 per cent
Management services	10 per cent
Technical services	10 per cent
Commissions	10 per cent

The notice stipulated that the deductions are not and should not be regarded as additional cost of contracts or services rendered and should therefore not be built into costs since they are deductions in lieu of tax.

Taxpayers are to be issued receipts for the amount of tax deducted by the deducting authority and the statement showing details are to be forwarded to seventeen area offices of the Board of Inland Revenue in the country.

For the purposes of final assessment, the company beneficiary of such income that had suffered deduction of tax at source shall present the original receipt issued in respect of the tax deducted at source to the Board for scrutiny wherever a claim for tax is made.

Penalty for failure to deduct or pay over such tax, after deduction to the Board within thirty days from the date the tax was deducted or the duty to deduct tax arose shall be liable on conviction to a fine of ₦500 in addition to the amount of tax deducted together with interest at the prevailing commercial rate.

Such payments may also be disallowed as deductions from income or profits for tax purposes to defaulters.

Pre-operational levy

A levy of ₦500 for each year of assessment has been imposed by section 27 of the 1985 Decree amending section 28 of the Companies Income Tax Act, 1979 on a company which is yet to commence business after six months of incorporation but before submitting accounts for the first 12 or 18 months.

Tax exemption on loan interest

Under section 18 of the 1985 Decree which amends section 9 of Companies Income Tax Act 1979 by creating a new subsection, interest on bank loans granted on or after 1 April 1980 for companies manufacturing goods for export shall be exempted on foreign loans or agricultural loans as follows:

Repayment period including moratorium	Grace period	Tax exemption
(a) Above 7 years	No less than 2 years	100%
(b) 5–7 years	No less than 18 months	70%
(c) 2–4 years	No less than 12 months	40%
(d) Below 2 years	NIL	NIL

Incentives to companies engaged in agriculture

The 1985 Decree has introduced the following incentives to boost agricultural production:
  (i) Losses for tax can be carried forward indefinitely
 (ii) Investment allowance of 10% is allowed on plant and equipment used in agricultural production in addition to normal capital allowances granted. Investment allowance is grantable on a new asset. (Section 26 of the 1985 Decree.)
 (iii) Pioneer status to exempt such companies from tax for the first 3–5 years of operation can be granted.
 (iv) Qualifying equipment qualifies for the highest rate of Annual Allowance, $33\frac{1}{3}$%.
  (v) Interest on bank loans to finance agricultural production is exempted from tax on a prescribed scale.
 (vi) The bank landing rate for agricultural purposes is less than the normal commercial rate.
(vii) Agricultural industry is a preferred sector of the economy for Federal Government and bank loans.
(viii) Non-resident shareholders can own as much as 80% of the equity of the company under the Nigerian Enterprises Promotion Act.
 (ix) Agricultural inputs are supplied at subsidised rates.

Annual Allowance

Section 36 of the 1985 Decree which amends Schedule 2 to Companies Income Tax Act, 1979, substitutes a new paragraph for paragraph 7. Annual Allowance is now claimable on qualifying asset in a basis period at the newly prescribed rates but based on a straight line method and on cost of the asset after deducting the Initial Allowance and retaining ₦10.00 in the capital allowances computations until the asset is disposed of.

In the case of an asset on which an allowance has been granted before the 1985 assessment year, Annual Allowance on the residue shall be claimed equally over the remaining number of assessment years from acquisition to equal the number of years of assessment for which allowance is to be made. But where allowances have been claimed for a number of years which are equal to or more than the specified number of years allowed, a single allowance shall be made subject to the retention of ₦10.00 until the asset is disposed of.

Initial Allowance (with effect from the 1985 year of assessment)

Plant	20% of Cost
Industrial buildings	15% of Cost
Other buildings	5% of Cost
Mining	20% of Cost
Plantation-equipment	20% of Cost
Motor vehicle	20% of Cost
Housing estate	20% of Cost
Ranching and plantation	25% of Cost

Annual Allowance (with effect from the 1985 year of assessment)

Plant 1	10% of Cost or written down value
Industrial buildings	10% of Cost or written down value
Other buildings	10% of Cost or written down value
Mining	10% of Cost or written down value
Ranching and plantation	15% of Cost or written down value
Plantation Equipment	$33\frac{1}{3}$% of Cost or written down value

| Housing estate | 10% of Cost or written down value |
| Motor vehicle | 25% of Cost or written down value |

Illustration (capital allowances)

The Profit and Loss Account of Give and Take Mortgage Company, Ltd, for the year ended 31 September 1986 was:

Directors' remuneration	₦520	Interest receivable	₦3422
Staff salaries	825	Rent receivable	1274
Rent payable	132	Insurance commission	27
Moneylender's expenses	25		
Electricity	13		
Building maintenance	177		
Insurance	30		
Interest on deposits	502		
Transport expenses	76		
Postage & telegrams	9		
Office maintenance	32		
Telephone	22		
Printing and stationery	20		
General expenses	51		
Interest on loan	21		
Bad debts written off	53		
Bank charges	32		
Legal expenses	63		
Audit fees	42		
Depreciation:			
Building ₦301			
Equipment 18	319		
Transfer to General Reserve	200		

Provision for		
Income Tax	716	
Proposed		
dividend (net)	1074	Balance b/f at
Unappropriated		1 October
profit c/f	22	1985 253
	4976	4976

The written-down values of industrial buildings and equipment at 30 September 1983 for capital allowance purposes were ₦10 784 and ₦140 respectively. The company wishes to claim in respect of the 1987 assessment. One building of four flats was acquired for ₦5000 on 10 May 1984. General expenses included ₦15 donated to a church on the occasion of its Harvest Thanksgiving, ₦9 for periodicals and newspapers and ₦27 for office entertainment. ₦80 was given to a member of the Managing Director's family. This has been charged to the Bad Debts Account.

The figure for building maintenance comprised the following items:

Replacement of wooden gate with iron gate	₦82
Labour on above	17
Night watchman's salary	36
Water rate	16
Stamp duty (Rent agreement)	6
Minor repairs	3
Agency commission	17
	177

You are required to calculate the relevant capital allowances

Answer

Give and Take Mortgage Company Ltd
capital allowance computation

	Build-ing	Equip-ment	Total Allow-ances
Written-down values at 31 December 1984	₦10 784	₦140	
Addition (10 May 1984)	5 000	–	
	15 784	140	

1985
Initial Allowance

(5%)	₦250		
Annual Allowances	1 821		16
		2 071	
Written-down values:		13 713	124
1986			
Annual Allowances		1 821	16
Written-down values:		11 892	108
Addition (Improve-			
ment – see note 1)		99	–
		11 991	108
1987			
Initial Allowance	15		
Annual Allowances	1 828	1 843	16
Total Capital			
Allowances			₦1 849
1987			
Written-down values:		10 148	92

Notes

1. Replacement of wooden gate (₦82) with related workmanship (₦17) is an improvement to a building and it is, therefore, of a capital nature.
2. Computation of capital allowance has been based on the provisions of the new decree that Annual Allowance on any qualifying asset shall be at the specified rate to be applied on straight line basis on the cost of the asset after deduction of Initial Allowance where applicable but retaining ₦10.00 in the capital allowances computations until the asset is disposed of.

   In addition, Annual Allowance on residue of an asset on which an allowance has been granted before the 1985 assessment year, shall be claimed equally over the remaining number of assessment years from acquisition to equal the number of years of assessment for which allowance is to be made. But in case of an asset on which allowances have been claimed for a number of years which is equal to or more than the specified number of years allowed, a single allowance shall be made subject to the retention of ₦10 until the asset is disposed of.

(a) 1985 assessment year: buildings

Annual Allowance on residue b/f: ₦10 784 less ₦10 = ₦10 774 to be spread over remaining 8 years since capital allowance has been claimed in 1982 & 1983

$$= \frac{10\,774}{8} = ₦1347$$

Initial capital allowance on additions: ₦5000 = 5% × 5000
$$= ₦250$$
Annual Allowance on additions = ₦5000 − 250 & 10 = ₦4740
to be spread over 10 years = ₦474 p.a.
Total Annual Allowance = ₦1347 + ₦474 = ₦1821
same calculation goes for Residue b/f on equipment (8 years).

Balancing Allowances and Charges

The following example is to initiate students into the new method of capital allowances calculation which started with the 1985 year of assessment.

Example

Titi buys a vehicle, registration number LA 2961, qualifying for Initial and Annual Allowances in the basis period for the year 1991. She has been trading for some years and makes up account to 30 September. The cost of the vehicle is ₦1000. The allowances for the years 1991, 1992 and 1993 are:

1991		
Cost	–	₦1000
Less 20% Initial Allowance	₦200	
Statutory Residual value	10	210
		790
25% Annual Allowance		197.50
Residue at 1 October 1992		592.50
1992		
25% Annual Allowance		197.50
Residue as at 1 October 1983		-395.00
1993		
25% Annual Allowance		197.50
Residue as at 1 October 1994		197.50

Disallowable expenses

Section 18 of ITMA 1961, as amended by section 6 of Finance (Miscellaneous Taxation Provisions) Decree, 1985, otherwise known as Decree No. 4, states:

No deduction shall be allowed for the purpose of ascertaining the income of any individual in respect of –

(a) domestic or private expenses;

(b) capital withdrawn from a trade, business, profession or vocation and any expenditure of a capital nature;

(c) any loss or expense recoverable under an insurance or contact of indemnity;

(d) rent or cost of repair to any premises or part of premises not incurred for the purpose of producing the income;

(e) taxes on income or profits levied in Nigeria or elsewhere except as provided in section 105F, ITMA, 1961;

(f) any payment to a pension, provident, savings or widows' and orphans' society, fund or scheme save as permitted by paragraphs (e) and (f) of section 17 of ITMA, 1961;

(g) the depreciation of any asset;

(h) any sum reserved out of profits except bad debt or as may be estimated by the relevant tax authority, to represent the amount of any expense deductible under the provisions of that section the liability for which was irrevocably incurred during the period for which the income is being ascertained;

(i) Any expense of any description incurred within or outside Nigeria for the purpose of earning management fee unless prior approval of an agreement giving rise to such management fee has been obtained from the Minister;

(j) any expense whatsoever incurred within or outside Nigeria as management fee under any agreement entered into after the commencement of this paragraph except to the extent as the Minister may allow;

(k) any expense of any description incurred outside Nigeria for and on behalf of any Company except of a nature and to the extent as the Board may consider allowable.

Allowable expenses

Section 17 of ITMA 1961, deals with this topic.

These are all expenses which are wholly, exclusively, necessarily and reasonably incurred during that period and ultimately borne by that individual in the production of the income including:

(a) interest payable upon money borrowed and employed as capital in acquiring the income and interest on loans for developing an owner-occupied residential house where the value of such property does not exceed ₦100 000.

(b) rent for that period payable in respect of land or buildings occupied for the purpose of acquiring the income, subject, in the case of residential accommodation so occupied, to a maximum of –

(i) ₦28 000 per annum for each building and ₦4000 per annum for each flat in the Lagos area, and

(ii) ₦20 000 per annum for each building and ₦5000 for each flat in any other part of Nigeria.

(c) any expense incurred for repair of premises, plant, machinery or fixtures employed in acquiring the income, or for the renewal, repair or alteration of any implement, utensil or article so employed.

(d) bad debts incurred in any trade, business, profession or vocation proved to have become bad during the period for which the income is being ascertained and doubtful debts to the extent that they are respectively estimated to have become bad during the said period.

The test for allowable expenses is that they must have been incurred, wholly exclusively, necessarily and reasonably for the production of the income. The words 'necessarily', and 'reasonably' were added to the test because of the general flair for high spending.

In Simon's *Taxes*, revised edition, it was expressed: 'In many cases it may be difficult to establish as a fact that the expenditure was given wholly and exclusively for the purposes of the trade, rather than satisfying the moral obligation felt by the trader'.

The problem is, when a businessman decides to buy two cars instead of one for his business, how does the tax official contend the reasonableness of the expenditure?

Air Travel Levy

Section 10 of the 1985 Finance (Miscellaneous Taxation Provision) Decree 1985, effective from 2 January 1985, states that any person travelling beyond Africa by air on a ticket bought in Naira shall pay a levy of ₦100. However, there are some persons exempted from this levy. Section 21A of the 1961 Act, as inserted by the Finance (Miscellaneous Taxation Provisions) (No. 2) Act, 1977 and as amended by section 10 of the 1985 Decree states –

(1) Except as otherwise provided in this section, as from 2 January 1985 any person making a journey by air on a ticket paid for or payable in Naira shall pay an air travel levy of ₦100.

(2) The provisions of subsection (1) of this section shall not apply in respect of any ticket issued for the purpose of a journey within Africa.

(3) Any person who intends to make a journey to which this section relates shall present evidence of payment of the levy in a form approved by the Minister, at the port of embarkation.

(4) The provisions of subsection (1) of this section shall not apply where the person making the journey is –
(a) the Head of the Federal Military Government;
(b) the Chief of Staff, Supreme Headquarters;
(c) the Governor of a State;
(d) a diplomatic consular or United Nations' agency personnel who under any enactment or other arrangement is ordinarily exempted from paying taxes or other charges in Nigeria;
(e) a transit passenger whose ticket was purchased in a country outside Nigeria even if such passenger is required to pay any surcharge or additional fare in Nigeria;

(f) an infant of not more than 2 years old;

(g) such other person as the Minister may by Order published in the *Gazette* from time to time exempt from the provisions of this section.

(5) The Minister may make regulations for the collection and administration of the levy imposed under subsection (1) of this section.

This air travel levy is a consumption tax on those who can afford to travel outside Africa, whether for business, official business, or for as pleasure. It is also a tax aimed at those who draw on the nation's foreign exchange earnings, since Nigerians who travel outside Africa have to look for foreign currency.

Disclosure of information (section 28)

In view of the fact that banking, institutions would not normally disclose any information in respect of their customers for tax purposes because they are not obliged to do so under the Banking Act, section 28(3) of ITMA 1961 now empowers the relevant tax authority to request from any bank any information about customers and the banks are now obliged to attend to such requests and release any information at their disposal for tax purposes, provided the request for such information is in writing and is authorised by the director of internal revenue of the relevant tax authority.

Failure to comply with such disclosure requirement attracts on conviction a fine of ₦500 in the case of an individual and ₦5000 in the case of corporate body.

(1) Where a tax authority is in possession of any information, document or record relating to any individual which in the interests of the public revenues in Nigeria should be disclosed or transfered to any other tax authority or to the Board, such information, document or record shall be so disclosed or transferred notwithstanding any provisions as to secrecy contained in any Income Tax law of a territory.

(2) A member of the Board, its Secretary, and any person employed in the offices of the Board shall not disclose any information respecting the income, tax or personal circumstances of any person which has come into his possession in the course of his duties except as may be expedient in any legal proceedings arising from this Act, or to any tax authority, or in accordance with any provision of an arrangement with respect to taxes made with any other country, and any such information disclosed to a tax authority shall thereafter be subject to the provisions of the foregoing subsection and to any secrecy provisions of the income tax law administered by that authority.

(3) Subject to the foregoing provisions of this section, for the purpose of obtaining information relative to tax, a tax authority may give notice to any person including a person engaged in banking business in Nigeria and any person charged with the administration of the Federal Savings Bank to provide within a time stipulated in the notice information including the name and address of any person specified in the notice. Provided that a person engaged in banking business in Nigeria including any person charged with the administration of the Federal Savings Bank shall not be required to disclose any further information under this section unless such disclosure is required by a notice signed by the Director of a State Internal Revenue Department.

Index

allowance, 115–32; for expenditure prior to commencement, 117–19; overlap of, 117

Bicycle Allowance, 69

Board: and Capital Gains Tax, 393; and corporate taxation, 185–91 *passim*; jurisdiction of, 187–8; *see also* State Tax Board

body of individuals, 15

bonus, 19, 39, 40, 65, 66

book debts, 262

book-keeping, *see* accounting

buildings: as qualifying expenditure, 113–14; lessors of, and capital allowances, 132–3

business, 201: capital allowances for, 119; changes in, 256–62; date of change of, 259–61; new, basis period for, 51; profits from, 18; sale of, 325–6; *see also* trade

business premises, 46–7

cable undertakings, 326

capital, 48

capital allowances, 106–11, 265–6; and lessor, 109–10, 131–3; and partnerships, 140–5 *passim*, 171; rate of, 553; for settlement/ trust/estate, 431–2; *see also* capital expenditure

capital expenditure, 80, 124, *see also* capital allowances

capital gains, computation of, 504–11

Capital Gains Tax, 198, 393–6; administration of, 397–8, 520–2; computation of, 396–406; and gains chargeable to tax, 500–504; and provisions of income tax acts, 522–3; and savings exemption, 442–5

Capital Gains Tax Act, 1967, 394, 496–523

capital investment tax credit, 374

capital receipt, 16, 17, 203–4

Capital Transfer Tax, 414–19; collection of, 420–21; computation of, 421–7; payment of, 415–16

carry-forward relief, 103–4

cars, and capital gains tax, 394

casing-head petroleum spirit, 351

casual worker, 77

cessation: of business, 54–9; of partnerships, 140–5 *passim*, 293

charge, creation/release of (Rent Act), 86–7

chargeable assets, 394–6

chargeable income: cases 44–5; computation of, 346–8; of insurance company, 332–4

chargeable oil, 351

chargeable persons, 13–14

chargeable profit: of non-life insurance company, 330; in petroleum operations, 350, (assessment of, 353–5)

chargeable tax, 350, 358–9; computation of, 360–1, 366–9

charges, 96

charitable organisations, 15, 185, 394, 511

child benefit, xxii–xxiv

Children's Allowance, 149–50

circulating capital, 16

Clothing Allowance, 69–70

collection of tax, in US, 477

commencement of partnerships, 140–5 *passim*, 293

commission, 19, 39, 65, 66

common law, 1

companies: assets of, and capital transfer tax, 418–19; and double taxation, 390

company income, *see* corporate taxation

compensation, 22; for breach of contract, 234–5; and Capital Gains Tax, 394, 507–8; for loss of beneficial contract, 233–4; *see also* revenue compensation

complex interests, 120

compulsory purchase, 503

computed income: apportionment of, 432–3; of estate/settlement/trust, 430–33; of partnership, 170–1

confidentiality, *see* secrecy

'connected person' and asset disposal, 395–6, 509–10

consumption, methodology of taxation, 446–7

Consumption Tax, 437–8

contractual restrictions, receipts from, 236

cooperative society, exempt, 185, 511–12

copyright, income from, 233

corporate taxation, 178–80; administration of, 180–2; computation of, 266–81; exemptions from, 185–93

credit relief, 380–1; *see also* double taxation
criminal transactions, 19
current-year loss relief, 99–103
current-year relief, 99–103
customary law, 1

damages, 239
data service, in US, 475–6
death of taxpayer, 16, 35
deductible expenses, 44, 241–5 *see also* capital allowances
deductions, disallowable, 253–4, 356–7
deed of partnership, 169–70
dental expenses, 68
Dependent Relative Allowance, 150–1
depreciation, 81, 254; accelerated, 136–7
depreciation allowance, 178–9; for air/shipping companies, 326–7, 328
devaluation, 205
direct taxes, 2–3
Director of Internal Revenue, 12–13
directors, and PAYE, 43
discounts, 94
discretionary payments, 45
discrimination, 60–62
disposal, 127–8; and Capital Gains Tax, 395–6; without ownership change, 131–2
distrainment, 310, 342, 416
dividends, 92–3; and double taxation relief, 378, 389–90; Nigerian, 92; State Government, 92–4; tax deduction from, 94
donations, 251–3
double taxation, 91, 377–81, 519; and Capital Gains Tax, 412–13; and companies, 390; computation of, 381–4, 385–90; and settlement/trust/estate income, 433; *see also* tax treaties, credit relief
double taxation agreements, 96, 390–1
drilling costs, 351–2

earned income, 7–8
economic development company, exempt, 190
educational bodies: exempt, 394; and Capital Gains Tax, 394, 511
election, instrument of (Rent Act), 86–8 *passim*

Ely Bernard Properties v FBIR, 344–5
employee, 77; duties of under PAYE, 75; expatriate, 20–22 *passim*; rights of under PAYE, 74–5; taxation of, 19–22
employer, 76; and PAYE, 76
employment, 19; and residence determination, 7–10
Entertainment Allowance, 68–9, 253
equity, 4
errors, 152
estates, 133–4, 428–34 *passim*
examination, of US tax returns, 476–7
excess profit, 321
exchange transaction income, 238–9
Excise Tax (US), 471
executor, 14, 428; assessments on, 430; charge of Income Tax on, 430; and determination of residence, 7–10
exempted income, FBIR notes on, 491–3
exemptions, from Capital Gains Tax, 394, 406–13, 511–20; from corporate taxation, 186–93 *passim*; exemption, of saving from Income Tax, 442–3; from VAT, 460–1
Expenditure Tax, 445–6
expenses, 68–71, 243–4, *see also* allowances; non-essential, 44
export, exempt, 512

family, assessment of, 14, 15
Federal Board of Inland Revenue, 27–35 *passim*, *see also* Board
Federal Government (US), tax as revenue of, 479
Federal Revenue Court, 339, 340
fee, for pioneer application, 526
fines, 343, 366, 415
fiscal reform, VAT as, 466–7
fixed capital, 16–17
fixtures, qualifying, 112–13
flow of receipts, 202–3;
foreign employment, 8, 64
foreign service, Nigerian, 27
frequency of transactions, 204–5
friendly society, exempt, 190, 394, 511
funeral expenses, 415

gains, 16, 46; chargeable, 500–4; non-chargeable, 512–13

337–8, 533
lump sum payments, 22, 66–7, · 245

machinery, qualifying, 111–13
management agent expenses, 255
marginal propensity to save, 438–41 *passim*
market value, 509
Married Allowance, 151
meal vouchers, 71
medical expenses, 68
messages, transmission of, 326
mileage allowance, 69
military personnel, 27, 28
mines, qualifying, 114–15
misappropriations, deductible, 245
mistakes, and relief, 152
Mitchell (Supervisor of Taxes) v Egyptian Hotels, 222–3, 225
money, unclaimed, 238
motive, and trading, 200–201
Motor Allowance, 69

National Assembly, 6
Native Authority Law, 190
natural gas, 351
'necessary' expenses, 315 *n*53
net Nigerian rate, 390
Nigerian company, 195
Nigerian dividends, 92
Nigerian employment, 8, 63–4
Nigerian Federal Savings Bank, 190
Nigerian Post Office Savings Bank, 94
Nigerian Savings Certificates, 94
non-life insurance companies, 328–31
non-residence in Nigeria, and Double Taxation Relief, 387
non-resident, trade of, 49–50

objections, 28, 32, 308
offences: under Companies Income Tax Act, 343; and corporate taxation, 311; under Petroleum Profits Tax Act, 366–7; *see also* penalties
oil-marketing companies, 352
oil-mining lease, 351
oil-prospecting licence, 351
oil-transportation companies, 352
output tax, 451; *see also* VAT
overcharging, relief for, 153
ownership, length of, and trading, 198

PAYE, 39–43 *passim*, 62–78, *see also* Tax Clearance Certificates; calculation of, 75–6; and duties of employee, 75; failure to pay, 41–3; income exempted from, 71–4; rights of employee under, 74–5; and VAT, 450
panel of Board of Appeal, variation in, 208–14 *passim*
part-exemption from VAT, 461
partnership agreement, registration of, 172
partnership income, 273
partnerships, 168–9; capital allowances in, 133–4; cessation and commencement provisions for, 140–5; and commencement/ ceasing provisions, 293; and continuity of assessment, 59; determination of residence of, 7; limitation on formation, 170; losses in, 104–5
passages, payment for, 68
patent rights, 233
pay, assessment of, 65–71
payment: of Capital Transfer Tax, 415–16; forms of, 19–20; of tax, extension of period for, 30
payments, 45, 70
payments received, after cessation, 59
penalties; appeal against, 344–5; and corporate taxation, 309, 311; and fraudulent pioneer certificate claims, 535–6; under Companies Income Tax Act, 343; under Petroleum Profits Tax Act, 366; for tax evasion, in US, 475; for unpaid tax, 342
pension contribution deductible, 151
pension fund, 22, 250–1
pension income, assessment of, 39
pension plans (US), 478
pension scheme, payment to, 255
pensions: exempted from income tax, 491; Government, and double taxation relief, 378; Nigerian 9; non-income, 94; overseas, taxation of, 28; and residence determination, 8–9, 65
Personal Allowance, 149
petroleum operations, 351
Petroleum Profits Tax, 349, 365–6
pioneer certificate, amendment to, 527; cancellation of, 529–30;

fraudulent claims for, 535–6
pioneer companies, 334–40;
Income Tax relief for, 530–35
pioneer conditions, 525–30
pioneer period, termination of,
339–40
plant, qualifying, 112–13
plantation expenditure, 179
pleading, 214–16
political payments, 245–8
premises, business, 46–7
premium, 23
proceedings, irregular, 208–14
production day, 336
profession, 49, 119
profit, 16, 45–7 *passim*; of air/
shipping companies, calculation
of, 326–8; distributed, 139–40;
reinvested, 139–40; total,
ascertainment of, 264–6;
undistributed, 146 *n*32
profit of income, 194–201
profit-making, and trade, 48, 198
property, 85; and Capital Gains
Tax Act, 499; disposal of, and
Capital Gains Tax, 515–16;
expenditure not allowed, 81;
income from, 23, 48; *see also*
Rent Act
property maintenance expenses,
248–50
property tax, 485–6
provident fund, 22, 151
purchasing authority, exempt, 190

qualifying expenditure, 111–15;
prior to commencement,
117–19; restricted, 130–1

receipts, 16, *see also* capital
receipt, revenue receipts,
windfall revenue receipts
Reconstruction Allowance, *see*
Investment Allowance
redundancy payments, 67
regions, and taxation, 3–4
Reiss & Co. (Nigeria) Ltd v FBIR,
207–32
relative, 396
relevant interest, 119
relevant period of ITMA, and
partnerships, 145
relief, 148–52; from Capital
Gains Tax, 406–13, 511–20;
against employment income,
22; for losses (example), 293–5;
for traders, 51–4; Income Tax
and pioneer company, 530–35;

see also allowances, loss relief
religious bodies, exempt, 185, 394
Remainder, 110–11
rent, 23; deductible, 248–9; tax
on, 84; *see also* letting
Rent Act, 84; method of
assessment, 86–90
rent in advance, 84–5
rent relief, 151–2
repayment of tax, time limit on,
35
residence: change in, 59;
determination of, 7–10, 63–5;
main, 517; outside Nigeria, 16;
and PAYE liability, 63–5; of
partnerships, 171–2; temporary,
22; *see also* non-resident
residue, 108, 109, 123
restrictions, contractual, receipts
from, 236
retirement benefit, *see* pensions
return of income, 23; assessment
before receipt, 25–6; not
requested, 25; requirement for,
29–30
revenue compensation, 17–18
revenue receipts, 16, 17, 203–4
royalties, 351

Sales Tax, 486–7; in the US, 471
saving, 436; encouraged, 436–41;
exempt, 442–5
savings scheme, 255
school fees, xxi
seasonal worker, 77
secrecy, 12–13
self-employment, 43–4
separate assessment, 32
service of notice, 23–5, 353
settlements, 428–34 *passim*;
capital allowances in, 133–4
severance pay, 67
sex discrimination, 60–61
shareholders outwith Nigeria, 28
shares, disposal of, 503, 504
shipping companies, 326–8;
exempt, 190
shipping profits, and double
taxation relief, 378
social security number (US),
474–5, 481–2
sporting organisations, exempt,
189
staff training, (US), 478–9
States, and corporate taxation,
183
State Government dividends, 92–4
State Government (US), tax as